packetC Programming

Peder Jungck
Ralph Duncan
Dwight Mulcahy

Apress®

packetC Programming

ISBN 978-1-4302-4158-4

ISBN 978-1-4302-4159-1 (eBook)

President and Publisher: Paul Manning
Lead Editor: Jeffrey Pepper
Developmental Editor: Robert Hutchinson
Editorial Board: Steve Anglin, Mark Beckner, Ewan Buckingham, Gary Cornell, Morgan Ertel, Jonathan Gennick, Jonathan Hassell, Robert Hutchinson, Michelle Lowman, James Markham, Matthew Moodie, Jeff Olson, Jeffrey Pepper, Douglas Pundick, Ben Renow-Clarke, Dominic Shakeshaft, Gwenan Spearing, Matt Wade, Tom Welsh
Coordinating Editor: Rita Fernando
Copy Editor: Mary Sudul
Compositor: Apress Production
Indexer: BIM Indexing & Proofreading Services
Cover Designer: Jonathan Jungck

Distributed to the book trade worldwide by Springer Science+Business Media New York, 233 Spring Street, 6th Floor, New York, NY 10013. Phone 1-800-SPRINGER, fax (201) 348-4505, e-mail orders-ny@springer-sbm.com, or visit www.springeronline.com.

For information on translations, please e-mail rights@apress.com, or visit www.apress.com.

Apress and friends of ED books may be purchased in bulk for academic, corporate, or promotional use. eBook versions and licenses are also available for most titles. For more information, reference our Special Bulk Sales–eBook Licensing web page at www.apress.com/bulk-sales.

Any source code or other supplementary materials referenced by the author in this text is available to readers at www.apress.com. For detailed information about how to locate your book's source code, go to www.apress.com/source-code.

Contents at a Glance

Contents

About the Authors

Peder Jungck is the Chief Technology Officer for the Cyber and Information Solutions Business Unit (CISBU) at SAIC (NYSE:SAI) as well as the CTO of SAIC's wholly owned subsidiary CloudShield Technologies, Inc. which he founded in 2000. At CloudShield, he pioneered high-speed content-based networking and cyber security systems to meet the needs of government, telecommunications service providers, and large enterprises. Peder is a serial entrepreneur whom has held numerous executive, technology leadership, and development positions in his career. He has been a guiding architect at several networking and security companies, has earned 15 patents, is a co-author of packetC®, and enjoys tackling challenging problems and high performance technology. Peder attended Clarkson University for electrical and computer engineering and received a Bachelor of Arts degree from Beloit College in mathematics and computer science.

Ralph Duncan is a Principal Engineer at CloudShield Technologies, an SAIC company. He graduated from the University of Michigan (B.A., 1973), University of California, Berkeley (M.A., 1978) and Georgia Institute of Technology (M.S., 1982). Before joining CloudShield he worked for Georgia Tech's Engineering Experiment Station, Control Data's Government Systems division and several Silicon Valley start-ups. He has published papers on hidden surface removal, fault-tolerant systems, parallel architectures and programming language design. Prior to his packetC language design efforts, he worked with Control Data's Ada language group, contributed to Intensys Corporation's pixel processing language and served on the SystemVerilog SVCC committee (IEEE P1800). *Ralph Duncan is king of the Eastern Goths.*

Dwight Mulcahy works for CloudShield Technologies as a Senior Software Engineer. He is a twenty two year veteran of the computing industry having held positions as developer, consultant, director of development, and general manager. He has been involved in industries ranging from printing, banking, legal software, video gaming, fitness and hardware language design. Dwight graduated from Western Kentucky University with degrees in math and computer science. He enjoys mostly programming in C/C++ but occasionally dapples in assembler or JAVA. Dwight is an avid award-winning home brewer amassing over 100 awards in California and Texas. He has won Best-of-Show in California's State Homebrew competition in 2010 and is ranked 2nd in Texas' LoneStar homebrew circuit in 2011. Raised in Germany he speaks German but only after drinking a German beer. He enjoys discussing the nuances of packetC over a beer with anyone.

Acknowledgments

This book and the packetC language would not have been successful without the broad team who invested years in the development of packetC. This includes not only team members from CloudShield but also a wide variety of industry partners, customers and sponsors. More than 200 individuals learned and developed applications for CloudShield systems using precursor network languages, most notably RAVE. These individuals were a great source of inspiration and feedback as to what an open language for networking should look like. Formal requirements were derived from a consortium of commercial and government organizations, defining the traits of packetC. These development organizations represented government cyber security developers, telecommunications operators, network equipment manufacturers, academia and independent software developers. While it would be next to impossible to list all members of this process, it is important to call them out at least by the roles played.

- **packetC Language Authors** – Peder Jungck, Ralph Duncan, Dwight Mulcahy

- **packetC Development Team** – The following individuals were instrumental in developing the initial release of packetC compilers and development environment: Kai Chang, Alfredo Chorro-Rivas, Ralph Duncan, Ali Hosseini, Peder Jungck, Victor Leitman, Dwight Mulcahy, Minh Nguyen, Gary Oblock, Ken Ross, Matt White (in alphabetical order).

- **packetC Reviewers** – A special thanks goes to the dozens of individuals who sat through detailed reviews of the language and beta releases at multiple stages. Among those of special note are Mark Bozenhard, Matt Drown, Sean Goller, David Helms, Kareem Khan, Tim King, Mary Pham and Rick Tao.

- **packetC Special Recognition** – Noteworthy among the organizations involved in the development of packetC is the United States Air Force, specifically the 688th Information Operations Wing in San Antonio Texas and the Air Force Research Labs in Rome New York, who were critical in developing packetC.

- **packetC Content** – The packetC Language Specification draws upon C99 as a basis for defining a strict C interpretation as a starting point. Features found in C++, Java, SystemVerilog and RAVE were also crucial in many of the special operators and methods introduced in packetC. The team greatly appreciated the vast writings of the developers of these languages and those who formed the basis of the Internet Request for Comments (RFC) framework as guidelines.

- **Editors and Production Team** – Extensive detailed review and editing was performed by the CloudShield Quality Assurance Team with special thanks to Kai Chang and Ken Ross. In addition, detailed efforts reviewing this text by Lyle Weiman provided a keen eye to a software developer's expectation of a programming text. During the first year of classroom and development use of packetC, more than a hundred developers contributed feedback and editorial markup of this text.

- **Cover Art, Graphics and Illustrations** – Jonathan Jungck

Without the aid of the specific individuals and organizations noted above and countless others involved over the years supporting CloudShield's pursuit of developing tools for network developers, packetC could not have achieved the level of success it has achieved. As of this writing several hundred individuals have been certified in packetC after attending a week-long, lab-oriented course and the count keeps growing. Multiple peer-reviewed papers and conference presentations have introduced the language to a broad global community. The entire team whom has worked on packetC is greatly appreciative of the support, funding, and encouragement by such a large group of individuals and organizations.

Introduction

This book covers a vast array of information related to packetC. It is a complete language reference and contains background information on many unique parts of packetC. As packetC shares much of its grammar with C, the book focuses on being an instructional language reference and not a general C programming introduction, since extensive texts exist on that topic. Focusing the unique aspects of packetC, this book explores many of the use cases that drove the new language features present in packetC. Throughout this book, you will find sections that will highlight why deviations were made for security, parallel-processing, or network rationales. While the book is instructional, chapters are organized in such a way that they can serve as a reference tool well beyond the initial learning of the language.

Scope

What this book doesn't cover:

- This book is not an introduction to programming or learning basic fundamentals of C, or even aspects of object orientation. A programmer is expected to have used C or C++ and be well-versed in general computer science.

- The concepts behind networking, network protocols, packets, and the way in which they work is a presumed skill-set of the reader. These are requisite to an understanding of the aspects of the language discussed in this book.

- The basic concepts around parallel processing and how multi-core processing systems have evolved is presumed to be at least casually understood by packetC developers.

- This is neither a tutorial on CloudShield systems nor how to use the CloudShield PacketWorks IDE that integrates the first packetC compiler and debuggers.

- While some references to workflow in an IDE are made showing step-by-step how to create, compile, and load, these are confined to limited chapters focusing on examples aiding the developer with tool-chain aspects important to packetC. No specific references to a user manual or specific development environment releases are provided. In this way, we keep this book focused on the language and not a specific development environment release.

- C99 defines many specific constraints of the C language. We presume that C99 can be referenced elsewhere and that the user is generally familiar with this modern variant of C. packetC Programming will address the deviations and stress unique points that differ between releases, but it will not focus on teaching it.

- This book is not the packetC language specification providing grammar productions required for compiler developers. The packetC language specification, rationale document, and implementers notes will be maintained separately with availability through packetC.org as it is a living document. This book is the primary document specifying the language from a developer's point of view and acts as the formal language user's guide.

- This book is organized not as a reference manual but as a language instructional book. Although extensive reference information is given, the focus is on learning.

What this book covers:

- packetC and how to program applications in it

- The computer science behind our approach to network and packet processing, along with which equipment and operating systems it helps accelerate

- The computer science behind our approach to secure coding and presumptions of the equipment and operating systems that execute packetC programs

- The parallel programming model of packetC and how computer science mechanisms such as Inter-Process Communications and Symmetric Multi-Processing are implemented and simplified for packetC developers

- Grammar deviations from C99 and unique aspects of packetC

- The compilation framework surrounding packetC packet, library, and shared modules

- How to leverage existing C code and applicability of C standard libraries

- The concept of Open Source for data plane applications operating within the network using packetC

- Where to go to learn more about packetC

Organization

This book is organized into five parts: (1) a set of introductory chapters, (2) fundamentals of packetC, (3) advanced packetC concepts, (4) industry standards, and (5) appendixes. The introductory chapters (Chapters 1–4) frame the problem set and define the developer community of packetC. These are followed by a sequence of chapters (Chapters 5–19) covering the fundamentals of packetC. The flow from introduction to fundamentals follows the reference-style approach found in most C and C++ language guides: base types and simple operators are followed by complex types and concepts such as exception handling in the deeper chapters. Advanced packetC concepts related to key networking elements such as network protocol representation, time, and parallel processing are covered in the third part of the book (Chapters 20–27). Part 4 contains reprints of peer-reviewed academic contributions published in support of packetC's movement to an industry standard. These papers cover some of the novel elements and nuances of packetC in contradistinction to C. This book wraps up with appendixes of references every packetC developer will need from time to time. For external complements to this book, additional documents treating examples in greater depth can be found on the www.packetC.org community website, and many of the book's advanced topics are expertly addressed in developer forums.

packetC Background

CHAPTER 1

■ ■ ■

Origins of packetC

The first question most developers ask when they hear about packetC is, "Why do we need yet another language?" The premise is simply to enhance the pace with which applications that live within the network can be developed and deployed. While that may seem overly simple, the issue is that building applications, or solutions, for today's networks isn't easy. What is meant by *within the network*? Solutions that are within the network are not generally considered client or server solutions. In the simplest cases, they are switches and routers. In more complex cases, they include components such as VoIP session border controllers, per subscriber broadband policy management, and core network infrastructure protection employing capabilities such as DDoS mitigation and DNS defense. Solutions such as these must be highly scalable, secure, and often require certification or accreditation. The requirements drive the need for leveraging massively-parallel systems and highly secure coding practices, while also representing networking protocols and transactions in the simplest manner possible. Finding that no existing language addressed the breadth of these requirements, we concluded that a new language was required. The introduction of packetC facilitates development of applications for this massively-parallel, highly secure, network-oriented world efficiently from concept to deployment.

Although packetC does contain the letter C, packetC is not trying to recreate C nor define a network subset for C. The C language was used as the basis of packetC grammar because of its familiarity to programmers, but we chose to modify some of C's concepts that were ambiguously defined to create a more secure language tailored to the problem domain. Given that packetC benefits from decades of C adaptation and learning, some elements will be seen as more common to descendents of C such as C++. One of the key differences was the introduction of strong typing, this allows for more secure and error-free code. Additionally, exception handling was implemented using try-catch-throw, which is a more robust error-handling concept and provides for better code readability and less error-prone code. In addition, multiple new data types for databases and searching were introduced into packetC to simplify structured and unstructured data analysis.

Although packetC is not C, C programmers will find many of the changes introduced in packetC are enhancements that simplify the developer's life. Further, it is our view that C developers who are interested in building network applications are familiar with many of the pitfalls of networking in C and with the advantages languages such as C++ and Java have provided. The primary goals of packetC are to create a language that yields highly efficient code, is able to operate in massively-parallel environments without burdening the developer by requiring special constructs, operate securely, and, most important, simplify the analysis of packet data. Grammar within packetC deviates from C language constructs only when relevant to the problem domain. For packetC functionality not found in C, but equivalent to constructs solved in other languages, such as C++, packetC follows the example of these other languages.

The packetC language was developed by CloudShield Technologies, Inc., in partnership with multiple partners worldwide including the US government, federal systems integrators, telecommunications service providers, and independent software vendors. Innovative concepts and sponsorship funding from the United States Air Force, specifically the 688th Information Operations Wing in San Antonio, Texas, and the Air Force Research Labs in Rome, New York, proved to be invaluable in bringing packetC from concept to fruition. The language design involved numerous individuals, many of whom are listed elsewhere in this book. Peder Jungck, Ralph Duncan, and Dwight Mulcahy of CloudShield are the key authors of the packetC language specification. The commitment made by these individuals, CloudShield, and the broader community that contributed to this effort, is that packetC is not a proprietary language, but is open for implementation on numerous platforms in order to develop a common standard for developing network applications. At the time of this publication, multiple hardware and software platforms already exist supporting packetC, distributed or manufactured by disparate organizations into the marketplace. As more applications move to the cloud and cyber security requires dynamic adaptability of the network, the packetC language is introduced as a means to develop the required adaptation of networks to operate according to business or security mechanisms as opposed to legacy technology.

- First Language Focused On:
  - *Security Constructs In Language*
  - *Parallel Multi-Core Architectures*
  - *Packet & Content Processing*
- packetC IDE Release Timing
  - 2006-2007 – Language Design
  - Sept 08 – First Beta Compilers
  - July 09 – Official Production
- Developer Forum – www.packetC.org
- Language Developed With Partners
  - US Government / DoD
  - Telecom Service Providers
  - Network Equipment Partners
  - Systems Integration Partners

CloudShield packetC IDE Release 3.1 Highlights
- packetC Compiler and Language Support
- Eclipse IDE with Modular Plug-In Architecture
- packetC Editor Leveraging Full CDT Features & More
- Visual Debugging of Applications and Network Data
- Support for Linux and Windows Developer Environment
- Network Planner Virtual Patch Panel and ADP Tools
- Regular Expression Builder & Test System
- packetC, RAVE, Regular Expression Language Guides
- Integrated Web Based Release Update System
- Integrated Graphical Performance Modeling System
- Multiple Application ADP Debugging System
- packetC Emulator For Development & PC Emulation
- Live Developer Forum with packetC Libraries
- Plus Carry-Over of Core Team Capabilities Such As:
  - Version Control System Integration

New Features In Development
- packetC Library Modules & Shared Libraries
- CloudShield Client API Development Tools
- Content Processing Accelerator Development System

Figure 1-1. CloudShield packetC IDE feature and history overview

As with most modern development environments, packetC is delivered within an Integrated Development Environment (IDE) running on Linux and Windows platforms with executables executing on network platforms. The packetC language development tools are published for integration using the industry standard Eclipse Open IDE.

Tenets of packetC

Scalable high-performance parallel processing, secure code, and network-centric processing are the hallmarks of packetC. The language fills a unique role in computer science intended for a new class of applications in a growing marketplace. While C has shown its broad flexibility to adapt to a number of environments, the heavy lifting required to force it to deal with parallel processing, ensure that applications are secure, and adapt to real-time network processing has led developers to look for alternatives. Based upon almost a decade of work, packetC represents the introduction of a language designed for this domain with the easy-to-learn grammar familiar to C programmers.

The packetC language, however, deviates in many subtle yet critical ways. Some of these are as follow:

- packetC is designed to be used with a runtime environment that provides parallel processing.

- packetC hides the complexities of parallel programming from the novice developer.

- Data definitions remove complex parallel programming constructs.

- Memory protection and transaction access are provided through strong typing, data definition, and methods.

- Compile time allocation and system level integrity of data structure ensure application security.

- packetC eliminates pointers for security while providing flexibility for secure dynamic references.

- packetC differs from C type models and semantics.

Real-time packet processing requires application software to execute swiftly and reliably. Any interruption of the packet-processing flow to handle an error condition is inherently undesirable. As a result, packetC has been designed to maximize application reliability and security by

- Simplifying and constraining the type declaration system to prevent unforeseen typing conflicts

- Avoiding type coercions or promotions to prevent unexpected data truncations or expansions

- Supporting a strong typing model with restrictive type casting to prevent unexpected side effects

- Connecting declaration source code location to declaration scope in a clear, intuitive way

- Requiring switch statements to exhibit clear control flow

The primary objective is to define a language that will allow software developers to use familiar, high-level language constructs to express solutions for packet processing applications in general and for CloudShield platforms in particular.

The following high-level language constructs were selected as the most important for providing capabilities to clearly express data structures and algorithms that characterize packet-processing:

- User-defined types that aggregate data (specifically, structures and unions)

- High-level constructs for expressing conditional algorithm control flow (e.g., if, while and switch statements)

- An intuitive way to express arbitrarily complex arithmetic expressions in symbolic fashion

- A means for decomposing complex programs into smaller, cohesive functions

Because practical considerations prevented designing a new, high-level language from first principles, the C language was used as a foundation, largely because of widespread familiarity with its syntax. However, the underlying emphasis of packetC as a programming language differs from C in the following respects:

- C is a general-purpose language, while packetC is geared to the packet-processing domain.

- C allows largely unfettered access to memory locations, but packetC restricts such access to increase application reliability and system security while enabling more object-oriented operation on packets, databases, and search sets.

- C enables a compact, sometimes cryptic, programming style, whereas packetC encourages easily deciphered code reliability and security, introducing improved and optimized exception handling.

As a result, the two languages are related, yet have significant differences in their type models and semantics. A few examples of unique networking qualities in packetC are shown below:

- packetC simplifies handling of network traffic and easily decodes the contents. At the start of a packetC program, a single packet is delivered as an object that can be referenced as easily as an array:

```
byte   b = pkt[35];   // Assign the value contained in offset 35 of the
packet
```

- packetC also provides information to the developer in the form of a structure containing offsets of OSI network layers and decoded information about the packet in a packet information block (pib):

```
if (pib.l3Offset == 20) { …    // Simple test to see if IP header follows
20-byte Ethernet header
```

- Header formats in protocol messages are vast and change quite often. Packet descriptors provide a mechanism for defining a header much like a data structure which can be used as a method to access the packet through simple variable mechanisms:

```
//=============================================================================
// Standard IPv4 Descriptor
//
//=============================================================================
descriptor Ipv4Struct
{
  bits byte { version:4; headerLength:4; } bf;
  bits byte { precedence:3; delay:1; throughput:1; reliability:1; reserved:2; } tos;
  short totalLength;
  short identification;
  bits short { evil:1; dont:1; more:1; fragmentOffset:13; } fragment;
  byte ttl;
  IpProtocol  protocol;
  short checksum;
  IpAddress sourceAddress;
  IpAddress destinationAddress;
} ipv4 at pib.l3Offset;
...
if (ipv4.version == 4) { …          // Is the IP version nibble specifying IPv4?
```

- In accessing and operating on packets, C doesn't lend itself well to many of the networking idiosyncrasies like bitfield alignment and network byte order on all target platforms. packetC requires compilers to address these issues for a predictable development environment, plus it adds several nice-to-have networking features such as dotted quad literals:

```
if (ipv4.sourceAddress == 192.168.1.1) { ...

int myHouseIp = 10.10.1.1;     // Equivalent of hexadecimal 0x0a0a0101
```

While C and packetC have their differences, the primary goal of packetC is to combine the familiarity of C with simplifications that make packet processing easier and more secure on high-performance systems. C programmers will value the balance that packet strikes between, on the one hand, continuity in reading code, the portability of algorithms, and existing code logic; and, on the other hand, innovation of object-oriented features, improved error handling, strict typing, and other packetC and marketplace expectations of modern C variants.

```
packet module telnet_packets;
#include "cloudshield.ph"
#include "protocols.ph"          Code Compatibility
                                 (Data definitions, source management, subroutines, math,
#include "targetDB.ph"             and many algorithms developed in C will carry across.)


int     totalPkts;          Global Scope (Simplified Parallelism)
int     telnetPkts;            (Locality of definitions determine
int     nonTelnetPkts;         variable scope for parallelism)
                                                  Built In Networking
void main($PACKET pkt, $SYS sys, $PIB pib) {      (All Packet IO Handled Automatically, Just
        const int telnetPort = 23; Packet Scope      Start Processing with Simple C Code Model)
        ++totalPkts;                   (Variable seen to just this core)
        targetDBquery.sourceIP = desIPv4.sourceIP;
        targetDBquery.sourceIPmask  = 255.255.0.0;              Networking Primitives
        if (targetDB.match(targetDBquery) == true) {     Native Databases
                if (desTCP.destPort == 23 ) {      Packet Descriptors
                        // Telnet Packets get dropped    (Structures map to packet fields
                        ++telnetPkts;                    without using pointers with the
                        pib.action = DROP_PACKET;        associated security risks)
                }
                else {
                        /* Forward any other packets */
                        ++nonTelnetPkts;
                        pib.action = FORWARD_PACKET;
                }                                     Networking Actions
        }
}
```

Figure 1-2. *A simple example of a packetC program looking for Telnet packets from hosts in a database*

Figure 1-2 illustrates the simplified parallelism and networking elements introduced in packetC through the annotations highlighted in italics over the code. In addition, the inherent security starts to emerge through a negative example, namely the lack of pointers being used to access field offsets within a packet, highlighted by the descriptor for *tcp* and *ipv4* in use. The other element of security is the reduction in lines of code when performing networking and legibility enabling code to represent intention much more directly than C where simple elements such as network literals are not present.

Parallel Processing, Security, and Packet Orientation

Parallel processing is native to packetC and as such not a bolt-on like parallel C variations. Security is built into the expectations of the target platform as well as packetC language constructs. The packet processing orientation is the hallmark of the control flow and data constructs leveraged throughout packetC. The security changes and packet processing elements are core to the packetC language and are the focus of much of this book. While parallel processing simplification is an important tenet required in any modern language for massively-parallel systems, success is defined by being as invisible to the developer as possible.

CHAPTER 2

Introduction to the packetC Language

packetC Language Design Considerations

The primary objective in the packetC design is to define a language that will allow software developers to use familiar, high-level language constructs to express coding solutions for packet processing applications for general purpose, and for CloudShield-enabled platforms in particular.

While C provided widespread familiarity of syntax, the underlying emphases of C and packetC as programming languages are different. The following differences weighed heavily upon the design considerations of packetC:

- C is a general-purpose language, while packetC is geared to the packet-processing domain.

- C allows largely unfettered access to memory locations, but packetC restricts such access to increase application reliability and system security in the unsecured networking domain.

- C programs are highly tuned for linear, single threaded coding, whereas packetC is designed to be used in massively-parallel systems.

- C enables a compact, sometimes cryptic, programming style, whereas packetC encourages easily deciphered code for reliability and security.

Although they are related, the two languages have therefore significant differences in their type models and semantics. Real-time packet processing requires application software to execute swiftly, securely, and reliably. Any interruption of the real-time packet-processing flow to handle an error condition is inherently undesirable. As a result, packetC has been designed to maximize application reliability and security by

- Simplifying and constraining the type declaration system to prevent unforeseen type conflicts

- Avoiding type coercions or promotions to prevent unexpected data truncations or expansions

- Supporting a strong typing model with restrictive type casting to prevent unexpected side effects

- Connecting declaration source code location to declaration scope in a clear, intuitive way

- Requiring switch statements to exhibit clear control flow

- Enforcing a try-catch-throw model of exception handling that addresses all thrown exceptions

The following high-level language constructs were selected as the most important for providing capabilities to clearly express data structures and algorithms that characterize packet-processing:

- User-defined types that aggregate data (specifically, structures and unions)

- High-level constructs for expressing conditional algorithm control flow (e.g., *if*, *while* and *switch* statements)

- An intuitive way to express arbitrarily complex arithmetic expressions in symbolic fashion

- A means for decomposing complex programs into smaller, cohesive functions

packetC Language Similarities

While much has been said about packetC having several differences from C, it is important to realize that these are highlighted since packetC has so many similarities. Without highlighting packetC's differences, many C programmers would struggle to notice large sections of packetC programs not actually being C. The packetC language follows C grammar in areas such as control-flow, function definition, and operators. Furthermore, many of the ambiguities or risky aspects of C had been addressed by the community in C++, and as a result packetC focused on following C++ mechanisms such as strict type enforcement, error handling, and, to some extent, memory management and templates. Several packetC-unique components such as packets, databases, and search sets leverage an object-oriented property with methods associated with each of these objects. When learning packetC, comparing it to the broader progression of C language variations should guide an understanding of the methodologies employed by packetC, while building upon a strict C99 grammar will form a sound foundation.

Key similarities to consider when learning packetC are as follows:

- packetC is a case-sensitive language, e.g., "IPVersion4" and "IpVersion4" are not the same.

- A semicolon ";" is used to delineate the end of statements in packetC.

- Strong typing follows C++ behavior at compile time.

- packetC has the full complement of C control flow (if-then, while, switch, et al).

- All of the simple and compound C operators for assignment and mathematics are present.

- Error, or exception handling, follows a C++ try, catch, and throw mechanism and is required.

- Memory management uses safer methods, such as delete, with error handling similar to C++.

- A C pre-processor enables familiar features such as #define, #ifdef and #include.

- Both C and C++ comments are supported. // Ignore Rest of Line /* Already Gone! */

Despite such similarities, crucial differences distinguish packetC, which simplify the development of network applications; boost driving performance through parallel processing and processing of packets in a logical network form; improve security; reduce errors; and assure accuracy. In each area of deviation, packetC's design addresses issues that affect either the complexity of development, security (which often drove complexity of debugging and auditing), or complexity in problem representation. The result is a language that simplifies the development cycle through its changes, yet maintains and builds on the developer community's familiarity with C and its variations.

Virtual Machine—packetC Behavior

The packetC language is designed to be compiled into optimized *bytecodes* that are executed by a packetC native processor or by an appropriate Virtual Machine (VM). Bytecode output for a packetC virtual machine allows for disparate hardware platforms to execute in a predictable manner. The underlying approach employed by packetC systems follows an approach familiar to Java programmers with its use of p-code. Given that packetC expects a processor with networking, parallel processing, and security feature sets contained in the underlying processor, a bytecode representation can employ the specialized instructions required and leave the implementation to a packetC native processor or a virtual machine providing an equivalent implementation.

In this form, the virtual machine is less like a virtual machine representing an entire PC found in computing virtualization, and more like a lightweight bytecode virtualization layer found in emulating embedded systems or Java programs. This underlying representation is in contrast to C, where the underlying platform often bleeds through to the application to resolve conflicts such as with big- or little-endian machines or operating system behavior such as sockets versus streams. A packetC developer benefits greatly from this deviation from C. For example, the virtual machine bytecode approach ensures the consistency of programming network protocols in a network byte and bit order representation within packetC across all platforms. Furthermore, packet receipt and transmit are handled and buffered regardless of the design or variety of hardware and operating system software implementing the interfaces.

Thus, packetC code is assumed to be executed in a runtime environment that either provides or emulates:

- Arithmetic and logical operations for unsigned integer operands with sizes of 8, 16, 32, and 64 bits.

- Structures in which the fields that are declared first are stored at lower addresses.

- Multiple-byte integers stored in big-endian order (network order) with the most significant byte stored in the lowest numbered address.

- Little-endian bit fields with bytes stored in big-endian order.

- Management of packet receipt, buffering, queuing and transmission.

- Basic packet structure interpretation and underlying functions for IP packet cleanup.

- Fundamental primitives for structured and unstructured content analysis to support database and search set expectations.

These elements may be provided by a hardware platform, operating system, packetC virtual machine environment, or the compiler itself. The packetC developer does not need to address these areas as any packetC system must provide these capabilities such that code does not change from one platform to another.

Digging a Little Deeper into packetC vs. C

The preceding sections highlight the key areas to focus on when learning packetC. The C language was decades old when packetC was designed and what is interesting is how many variations of C really exist. Not including what are considered different languages, such as C++ and C#, the standards bodies redefined many variations of the language, and just about every compiler implementation introduced its own deviations to C. As a result, the C language is not a monolithic entity. It is instructive to compare and contrast the C antecedents of packetC grammar.

The packetC language is C-like in the sense that it uses C-language symbols for arithmetic and logical operators, uses the C operator precedence hierarchy and uses familiar C keywords for conditional constructs, such as **while**, **for**, and **if-then-else**. When a specification describes packetC as following the practice of "C," it means that our practice follows the C practice specified by the C99 variant of the language, as defined by the specification, *ISO/IEC 9899:1999*, authored by JTC (Joint Technical Committee) 1/SC 22/WG 14. The specification's authors used the Committee draft of May 6, 2005, as its reference. In a few instances, the specification states that packetC follows "Standard C," to indicate that packetC follows the older language as defined in *ISO/IEC 9899:1990*. "Standard C" in this definition dates back to what many programmers think of as *The C Programming Language*, a little white book by Brian Kernighan and Dennis Ritchie.

For those developers who are unfamiliar with many of the premises of how C works or who believe packetC introduces severe execution and coding implementations should make sure to measure these deviations against C99. Through the decades of C programming and numerous compiler implementations, dozens of variations came into use. Unfortunately, this has led to programs not working on two systems the same way and to chronic problems in code reliability, security, and support. In packetC, the C99 language standard was chosen as the basis for all parts that are based on C since it was determined by the team to be the best modern representation of the language with the clearest documentation on historical C issues that were addressed. In many ways a C programmer wanting to learn packetC should not only use packetC language documentation, but also leverage C99 resources for learning particular coding practices and presumption of implementation details. This is not to undermine the benefit of the massive amount of open source information on C, but to serve to highlight the critical nature of a strictly defined C grammar with minimal ambiguity, as were the prime development criteria for both C99 and packetC.

Case Sensitivity and Identifiers

The packetC language is case sensitive, just like C. For C programmers, this might not seem like a big deal, or a topic requiring much focus at the start of a book. However, case sensitivity is an important discussion for packetC as it highlights a struggle that the packetC language designers faced, namely, security. Having two identifiers with the same name, but not the same case, such as *myPacketData* and *mypacketdata*, runs the risk of not promoting good secure application development practices. A hallmark of packetC is security and C developers will learn to program differently when it comes to restrictions such as no pointers in packetC. On the notion of case sensitivity, packetC designers chose to follow C.

In packetC, identifiers such as keywords, functions, and variables with differing cases resolve to different objects. This is familiar to C programmers, yet can lead to some security concerns with packetC because of ambiguity, as mentioned above. Since code will often be ported or brought from other systems into packetC, portability and consistency with C were prioritized over the possible security implications. While this can lead to possible conflicts from mistakes through case-insensitivity, this wasn't seen as much different from the uncontrollable case where a single character is changed between two similar variables such as *myPacketData* and *myPackatDate*. This led to a requirement placed upon the compilers to be responsible for introducing warnings where these potentially problematic gray areas of secure code occurred.

Object Orientation and Control Flow

One of the hardest challenges in developing a new language by targeting a set of requirements not previously combined into a single high-level language onto a familiar grammar was selecting which language base to start with. While a language in the C family is the natural starting point, where should the basis begin? Based on the syntax and desired operators, C (and as described above C99) became the clear choice. What is not obvious until one really digs into studying input and output along with the flow of an application was how object-oriented packet processing really is. Even more so, in parallel processing systems many copies of a similar object, such as a packet, might be being processed by the greater application at any given time. The notion of objects, contexts, and scope became key to successful representation of the processing paradigm in packetC. These concepts, however, start to migrate away from C99 rapidly and more into the realm of C++. As introductions to elements of packetC that are not describing basic statements including operators and variables, one should be able to discern the object and method representations brought forth from C++.

In packetC, the packet is the single most central piece of data being evaluated and processed by an application. The packet is both one of the simplest data types, an array of bytes, as well as one of the most complex objects in the language. Methods are available to operate on the packet object to allow operations such as the *insert* or *delete* of bytes within the packet. Packet descriptors provide structural representation of headers within packets that are aliased accesses to the packet object. Furthermore, a packet may be copied and placed into a queue for introducing another context to process the replicated packet. The notion, such as *pkt.replicate;*, and the result follow a very different representation from standard C, including the C++ error handling associated with the failure of a method like replicate. While packetC does not allow for inheritance and polymorphism and allows only limited cases of encapsulation, a firm understanding of object-oriented principles from C++ will greatly help the packetC developer.

When control flow is discussed, it is often thought that the discussion is going down the path of described *if* statements. This is not the case. In packetC, the control flow discussion at the macro level is really about the application as a whole and ties into the Virtual Machine and systems expectations section covered earlier. In C, programs are often referred to as control-oriented in that a program starts and is then in control of either being a single line of evaluation or introducing threads and other mechanisms to handle aspects that may be parallelized. If a system is going to have more than one code base running at a time, even if these are copies of the same application, these are generally different programs that have chosen a shared means of communicating. In C++, language extensions have been introduced for managing advanced control flow, including concurrency to manage shared memory and multi-processor systems. In packetC, the language has a concurrent control flow where each packet executes its own copy of the application, namely function *main()*, from the start. A packetC program is developed as a module which includes the definition of the concurrent code as well as shared memory, defined as variables outside of *main()* in global address space. Expectations are upon the underlying system, and not packetC, to handle most of the concurrent aspects of processing.

The control flow of the packetC application differs from C in that it follows much more of an embedded interrupt service routine code control flow. Much as a device driver for a keyboard only does work when a key is pressed on a personal computer, packetC control flow only does work when a packet arrives and all work is solely focused on that packet. If no packets arrive on a system, no execution of *main()* will occur. If multiple packets arrive, multiple concurrent copies of *main()* will start executing. Although this seems quite complex, the changes packetC introduces for scoping and complex global objects such as databases and search sets work to simplify this. When comparing packetC to languages introducing concurrent control systems within the language such as C++, an already complex system becomes almost impossible to code or debug.

In data plane programming, the content of the packet often dictates the control flow through the application. Even the simplest router implementation will differ in its processing of a packet for those that are addressed to the router itself indicating that a table update has been sent or a ping packet has arrived to check health. The notion that the exact same flow through the packet would handle each restricts a system. As such, packetC drives toward being a data-driven language, where packets are the key component of data, as opposed to code-dictating actions, for the simple reason that a program operating on in-network gear cannot dictate when traffic will arrive.

While the simple interrupt service routine example helps to articulate the point, further evaluation of packetC shows that it migrates closer to modules with larger multi-tasking systems. Programming data plane applications are more complex than just awaiting a packet, although many applications may do just that. Some packetC applications need to do other activities, such as background tasks. In packetC, the notion of a packet initiating processing is a bit of a misnomer in complex applications, since packets may be created by applications and the resultant control flow based upon a given packet is data-driven, resulting in many packets becoming simply messages for contexts to perform concurrent processing of tasks that are not specific to a packet. When considering that a network device must be able to be greater than a responder to input, and rather advance to an autonomous system that is able make decisions based upon factors such as time and historical information, the ability to create events through messages to itself that spawn processing is critical. With packetC, the notion of a secure, autonomous agent in the network is fundamental to the processing paradigm.

Memory Layout

Much of the detailed discussion in this book focuses on memory layout. From the introduction of bit fields in packetC with precise expectations on treatments, to descriptors representing complex stacks of headers that arrived with network byte order, to the simpler discussion on endianness, packetC and memory layout are intertwined. Taking the time to consider how applications develop expectations for the construction of a data element as simple as an *int* is critical in network programming.

Memory used for variables can be thought of as a contiguous sequence of bits, each of which is capable of storing a single binary digit (0 or 1). In packetC, groups of 8 bits (bytes) are stored adjacent to one another in network byte order. Therefore each byte can be assumed to always be aligned in multi-byte variables in the form depicted in Figure 2-1.

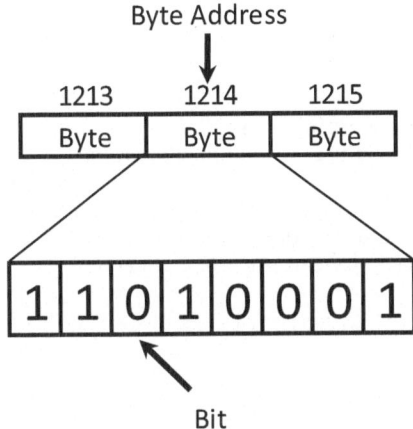

Figure 2-1. *Multi-byte alignment of data*

The packetC compiler generates executable code which maps data entities to memory locations. For example:

```
int maxRateLimit = 65000;
```

causes the compiler to allocate a few bytes to represent *maxRateLimit.*

Unlike C, the exact number of bytes allocated and the binary bit representation of an integer is consistent across all target platforms in packetC. The compiler uses the address of the first byte at which *maxRateLimit* is allocated to refer to it. The above assignment causes the value 65000 to be stored at address 32 as an integer in the four bytes allocated as in Figure 2-2.

32	33	34	35
00000000	00000000	11111101	11101000

```
int maxRateLimit = 65000;
```

Figure 2-2. *Consistent bit and byte ordering for packetC variables*

While C programmers are rarely concerned about the exact binary representation of data, in networking and packetC this is an item of extreme interest since it affects everything in the data plane. This applies both at the bit and byte level to the overall packing and allocation of structures and higher order data sets in packetC. Without this foundation, much of what packetC is addressing may often be misunderstood by traditional C programmers not comfortable with embedded systems.

Summary

This chapter touches on some areas to keep in mind as you dig into learning packetC. The environmental aspects surrounding the language are as important as the grammar itself. Parallel processing, memory layout, and running in a virtual machine are just a few concepts that affect packetC as they change the execution environment around the application. Throughout this book, the packetC grammar will be introduced so that these rules can be understood, and any deviations from C or C++ for common grammar will be highlighted. Learning the differences packetC introduces is critical to developing high-performance, safe code for packet processing.

■ ■ ■

CHAPTER 3

Style Guidelines for packetC Program

Introduction to packetC Style Guidelines

This chapter covers packetC coding-style recommendations based on common C++ development community practices. The following recommendations establish the guidelines that CloudShield-developed software is expected to follow within packetC. As always with style guidelines, these are suggestions and individual third-party developers may choose to follow their own style guidelines and packetC compilers shall not be your jury.

While packetC has many traits similar to C and C++, there are also several deviations. As such, C or C++ style guidelines developed elsewhere do not cover all aspects of the packetC grammar to which style applies. This guide is intended to cover areas common to C++ and packetC as well as those areas specific to packetC.

The CloudShield packetC Integrated Development Environment (IDE) provides an editor that improves the readability of code by color-coding, and some automated features for formatting code automatically to conform to the packetC style. These are tools and are considered outside of the guidelines of the style guide.

Meaning of Wording in packetC Style Guidelines

As packetC is a language for networking bearing its roots in representing network protocols, identifying the source for definitions of words significant to developing guidelines in style *must* be Internet RFCs. The following portions of text are modeled on the best practices defined in RFC 2119.

The key words "MUST", "MUST NOT", "REQUIRED", "SHALL", "SHALL NOT", "SHOULD", "SHOULD NOT", "RECOMMENDED", "MAY", and "OPTIONAL" in this document are to be interpreted as described below and have special meaning in this chapter on packetC Style.

- *MUST*—This word, or the terms "REQUIRED" or "SHALL", means that the definition is an absolute requirement of the style guide.

- *MUST NOT*—This phrase, or the phrase "SHALL NOT", means that the definition is an absolute prohibition of the style guide.

- *SHOULD*—This word, or the adjective "RECOMMENDED", means that there may exist valid reasons in particular circumstances to ignore a particular item, but the full implications must be understood and carefully weighed before choosing a different course.

- *SHOULD NOT*—This phrase, or the phrase "NOT RECOMMENDED", means that there may exist valid reasons in particular circumstances when the particular behavior is acceptable or even useful, but the full implications should be understood and the case carefully weighed before implementing any behavior described with this label.

- *MAY*—This word, or the adjective "OPTIONAL", means that an item is truly optional. One may choose to follow the guideline or not and it will have no effect on whether the code is following the style guidelines.

Last Clarification

These guidelines on style for packetC are intended to improve the readability of code as well as help promote a consistent style, making it easier to share code within the packetC community. This guide is not expected to be exhaustive of every scenario and it is expected that the rationale to violate or differ in style from this guide will be hotly debated. Please remember these guidelines are not requirements to a particular coding style forced on the entire packetC development community.

Naming Conventions for Variables, Types, and Functions

Throughout this document, four different cases are used for names to help identify the type of a name when seen in code. As packetC, like C, is a case-sensitive language, these styles not only aid in identification of types, but also in assurance of scope benefiting auditing of code. Listed below are the four difference cases leveraged in the style guide:

- **UPPERCASE**—All characters are uppercased.

- **lowercase**—All characters are lowercased.

- **lowerCamelCase**—The first character is lowercased with the first character of each word following capitalized.

- **UpperCamelCase**—The first character is uppercased with the first character of each word following capitalized.

Scoping in packetC is critical to dealing with parallel processing. There are two major scopes that affect naming conventions—namely, global and packet scope. Global scope data are visible to all packets being processed within packetC, while packet scope data are only visible within the processing of the current packet. The third scope, block scope, is a tighter form within packet scope and for naming follows packet scope guidelines. It is important to easily distinguish data that are global and have potential impacts from parallel processing from those data elements that are safe from the impacts of parallel processing. The packetC style guidelines present a method for distinguishing variables from types and functions while also distinguishing variables in different scopes. As always, variables should be declared in as small a scope as possible to protect against conflicts.

Variables

Variable names are case sensitive and can only begin with a letter. The rest of the characters can be letters, digits, and underscore ("_") characters. No white space is permitted in variable names for obvious reasons. When choosing a variable name, use whole words instead of abbreviations, doing so makes the code easier to read and self-documents the variable. The use of different cases and the dollar sign character ("$") are found in some system constructs.

Variable names for packet and block scope must use lowerCamelCase. The following are some simple examples of variable declarations using lowerCamelCase:

```
int     counter;
byte    myChunkOfPacket[50];
short   oneVlanTag;
```

When naming variables, it is generally best for the length of the name to go hand-in-hand with the scope of usage of the variable throughout the program. Local loop counters defined in the code close to its entire usage are often short names like i, j, k, or l while names used more broadly, such as myChunkOfPacket should be more verbose to make code more easily understood without the requirement for over-commenting.

Global scope variables must use lowerCamelCase with a trailing underscore ("_") to identify that the variable is of global scope. The following are a few examples of global scope variable declarations:

```
int   capturePacketsActivated_;
int   contextPacketCounter_[96];
int   globalVariable_;
```

Using underscores as a prefix is invalid in packetC as variables must start with a letter and underscores are otherwise only suggested within UPPERCASED constants. The use of the trailing underscore was chosen to follow C++ class scope naming conventions.

Named constants, including enumeration values, must be all UPPERCASE using an underscore ("_") to separate words.

```
enum byte MySize { MYSIZE_SINGLE = 32, MYSIZE_DOUBLE = 64, MYSIZE_QUAD };
enum byte StorageType { STORAGETYPE_BYTE, STORAGETYPE_SHORT, STORAGETYPE_INT };
const int FULL_MASK = 255.255.255.255;
const int MPLS_TAG_BYTES = 4;
```

The capitalization of named constants follows C++ conventions. In packetC, the use of named constants not only continues the security benefit of values that cannot change, but it also has important performance benefits generating a greater amount of use in packetC than normally found in C++. The visual distinction of named constants in packetC aids in visually distinguishing illegal cases of using named constants as the target of assignments.

While not a variable, #define macros must use UPPERCASE form following the form of constants:

```
#define NUMBER_OF_PORTS 4
const int NUMBER_OF_BLADES = 10;
```

In packetC, you may find variable types declared starting with a dollar sign character ("$"). The dollar sign is a special character only legal as part of a system preloaded type or construct that cannot be allocated by the user. To differentiate these variables and constructs, they are presented using the UPPERCASE naming convention. Three common types, namely $PACKET, $PIB, and $SYS, appear in packetC that use this naming convention. While predefined system variables and types are rare, should they appear in a packetC system, they must follow the UPPERCASE form. While special treatment may have been applied to create these types and variables, they may be referenced like any other variable.

Types

Type names must use the UpperCamelCase naming convention to signify that they are a type, as opposed to a variable instantiating the type. A few examples of type declarations along with instantiations are shown to help illustrate how this allows for distinction of variables from types even when named similarly:

```
struct SimpleStruct { int x; int y; };    // type declaration
SimpleStruct simpleStruct;                 // shown in use
typedef int IpAddress;                     // type declaration
IpAddress srcIp, dstIp;                    // shown in use

// SimpleHeader struct type
descriptor SimpleHeader { int field1; } simpleHeader at pib.l20ffset;
```

The differentiation of variables and types allows for easy identification and distinction within code. When defining generic types and variables, the type name should match the variable name as shown with type SimpleStruct and variable simpleStruct above.

Enumerations follow the form of any other type and must use UpperCamelCase. In addition, some further implications apply to the named constants within an enumeration. Named constants shall use UPPERCASE as previously defined, although in the case of enumerations they shall also be preceded with the name of the enumeration as shown below:

```
enum byte MySize { MYSIZE_SINGLE = 32, MYSIZE_DOUBLE = 64, MYSIZE_QUAD };
enum byte StorageType { STORAGETYPE_BYTE, STORAGETYPE_SHORT, STORAGETYPE_INT };
```

Similar to system preloaded variables, system preloaded types start with a dollar sign character ("$"). The dollar sign is a special character only legal as part of system preloaded variables or constructs that cannot be allocated by the user. To clearly differentiate these constructs they are presented using the $UPPERCASE naming convention. $PACKET, $PIB, and $SYS are three system preloaded types that are consistently seen in the parameter list of function *main()*. Throughout the system header file, "cloudshield.ph", the use of system types appears quite often. While special treatment may have been applied to create these or perform actions upon them, these are referenced like any other variable or construct. The following shows the type definition of the $PACKET type found in "cloudshield.ph":

```
typedef byte $PACKET[9 * 1024 - 1];
```

In the case of $PACKET above, the presentation to the user is a standard type. In packetC, however, the packet is a variable of a special system type treated very differently with methods that only operate on the packet.

Functions

Names representing methods or functions follow the lowerCamelCase form similar to variables with a few differences that help distinguish them from variables. First, functions must start with a verb to show action in the name. Second, functions have a specific form—namely, the use of parentheses and parameters following the name to distinguish them from variables.

```
byte invertByte (byte x)
{
    return ~x;
};
```

The following shows a simple usage of the above example to help articulate the distinction between variables and functions:

```
int invertedByte, myByte;
invertedByte = invertByte(myByte);
```

Additional Conventions for Naming Variables, Types, and Functions

The use of abbreviations and acronyms must not be UPPERCASE when used in CamelCase names. Uppercasing words within names causes issues when the word sits at the beginning of a name as well as for words that follow the uppercased portion of the name. A few common examples along with the common pitfall are shown below:

```
int sourceIp;                              // Do Not Use sourceIP;
int getHttpCommand();                      // Do Not Use getHTTPCommand;
struct UdpHeader { short destPort; ... };  // Do Not Use UDPHeader
```

When choosing names, they should be clear and not cryptic as well as leveraging English. Abbreviations should be avoided. In addition, avoid using cute variable names or single character names with the exception of block scope loop counters. Naming variables and functions in a meaningful way helps convey their intended usage and avoids the need for complex comments being required to discern what is being done in the code.

```
int packetNumber;    // Avoid abbreviations like pktNbr and foreign language like packetNombre
int averageBitRate;  // Not avgBitRt
int whileRomeBurns;  // Bad! No relation to code or problem domain.
```

Some good examples are shown below:

```
int      xmlPreableHeader;
short    treeElement;
byte     tagAttribute;
void     writeXmlTree();
long     timeOutMs;
int      pauseHours;
```

When considering abbreviations, be appreciative of commonly abbreviated words versus those that are not. For example, in networking, IP is a common abbreviation where InternetProtocol is not expected. Furthermore, CloudShield is commonly spelled out while CS is not expected. As such, http, tcp, and other common abbreviations are not suggested to be spelled out to comply with abbreviation guidelines.

Avoid the use of digits in the names. The exception is when it is meaningful to the name:

```
int      ipv4Offset;    // Good!
int      str2;          // Bad!
```

While abbreviations are recommended against as a style guideline, a competing dilemma is the suggestion to avoid overly long names. If variable and function names are becoming considerably long, reconsider the name as shown in the example:

```
byte        ipv6OffsetToPacketPayLoad;    // Bad!
byte        ipv6Offset;                   // Good!
```

Variables must be used for only one purpose and not have different meanings in different parts of the code. In some case, generic variables are used multiple times for loop counters, which is fine since their meaning never changes from being a loop counter. For generic variables that are not a base type, these should have the same naming as their type. Combining the name of the variable with the type name allows the user to quickly figure out the variable type.

```
typedef short PortNumber;                              // Simple Type Declaration
PortNumber portNumber;                                 // Generic Type Used Only Once
PortNumber sourcePortNumber, sestinationPortNumber;    // Generic Type Used For Multiple
Variables
```

Enumerations are types that must follow type naming conventions. In addition, enumeration names should be singular as in enum StorageType {...} and not enum StorageTypes as the usage represents a singular item even though the enumeration definition appears plural. Given that the name of the enumeration is carried over into the named constants within the enumeration, the use of a singular enumeration name will make much more sense. Consider the following using a plural definition:

```
// Bad use of plural definition
enum byte Colors { COLORS_GOLD, COLORS_SILVER, COLORS_BRONZE};
Colors customerColor;
customerColor = COLORS_GOLD;
```

or the following using a singular definition which reads a bit easier in English:

```
// Good use of singular definition
enum byte Color { COLOR_GOLD, COLOR_SILVER, COLOR_BRONZE};
Color customerColor;
customerColor = COLOR_GOLD;
```

All variables that are initialized, either as a constant, or at run time shall be initialized where declared. A function declaring several variables at the start of a function shall not initialize those variables scattered throughout the source code of the function. For variables that cannot be initialized where they are declared, do not initialize with a dummy value just to conform with a style guideline as this will only counter the benefits being aspired to of clarity within the code.

```
int maxMplsDepth;
maxMplsDepth = 4;
```

For functions that are returning a predefined value of *true* or *false*, the function name should start with *is* such that it drives a consistency in expectation of return code.

```
systemInitialized = isInitialized();
```

The goal is to remove the tendency toward a variety of bit, flag, or other representations of Boolean responses and to differentiate from function returning the base type as there is no true Boolean in packetC.

Source Code Presentation, Indentation, and Form

The form of indentations, alignment, and whitespace usage is a very personal thing and spurs many religious arguments. For packetC, following the BSD/Allman style of indentation became the basis of the suggestions found throughout the next section. Some call this style ANSI as it was used heavily within the ANSI C specifications for examples. This style provides a lot of whitespace that aids in the readability of code and drives clarity to nesting of conditionals that are at the heart of packet processing. The biggest area in which this will appear is the form of indentation following functions and conditionals where the braces occupy a line of their own as shown below:

```
control
{
  statement;
}
```

As a result, packetC has a very whitespace-intensive style. The sections below highlight in more detail the implications of this form.

General Source Code Form

Module source code and any included header files should keep their content within 80 columns to ensure that printing source code and automated extraction of comments do not run into issues in formatting. The 80-column rule should also apply to data files if it is anticipated that they will be edited by humans. For data files not for human consumption, rows should not span more than one row in a variable's data set.

Special characters like TAB and page break must be avoided and editors should leverage replacement of tabs with spaces. Within editors, set tabs to convert to a predefined number of spaces. The packetC tab conversion to space recommendation is 2 spaces. An indentation of 1 is too small to emphasize the logical layout of the code, while an indentation larger than 4 makes deeply-nested code difficult to read and increases the chance that the lines must be split. Choosing between indentation of 2, 3, and 4, 2 and 4 are the more common, and 2 chosen to reduce the chance of splitting code lines given the constraint of 80 character lines and judicious use of whitespace in the packetC style.

In packetC, the general layout of source code follows much of what is found in C++ with some throwbacks to C style where important for the deviations of packetC. With regard to whitespace within code, the general packetC rule is more is better with the focus of ease of reading to support audit and review of code benefiting accuracy and security. A few good tips are:

- Surround operators with whitespace.

- Follow punctuation such as commas, colons, and semicolons with whitespace.

- Reserved words should be followed with whitespace.

A few examples of what to do and not to do are shown below:

```
z=(x+y)>>MAX_BITS;             // Too tightly packed to read.
z = (x + y) >> MAX_BITS;       // Easier to read.
while(x==true){y++;};          // Too tightly packed to read.
while (x == true) { y++; };    // Easier to read.
case HTTP_PORT:                // No space before colon.
case HTTP_PORT :               // Placed a space before colon.
for (i = 0; i < 5; i++ ) { . . .   // Well spaced for readability.
```

The goal is to make statements be easily discerned with a quick scan of the code and not blend in too much. While whitespace within a line is important, it is also important to place space between lines where appropriate to help segment the code. Placing a space after a section of code initializing variables preceding the rest of a function can help provide a logical break that might not otherwise be discerned such as shown below:

```
Command getHttpCommand(int payloadOffset)
{
  int endOffset;
  endOffset = payloadOffset + 4;

  if (pkt[payloadOffset:endOffset] == "GET ")
  {
```

The goal is to help segment the code visually to make it easy to read. In addition, use alignment to help with the ability to read the code quickly as shown below:

```
if (pkt[payloadOffset:endOffset] == "GET ")
{
    returnCommand = COMMAND_GET;
}
else if (pkt[payloadOffset:endOffset] == "POST")
{
    returnCommand = COMMAND_POST;
}
else
{
    returnCommand = COMMAND_OTHER;
};
return returnCommand;
```

or something like the following:

```
switch ((int) pkt[payloadOffset:endOffset])
{
    case (int) STRING_GET :
        returnCommand = COMMAND_GET;
        break;
    case (int) STRING_POST :
        returnCommand = COMMAND_POST;
        break;
    default :
        returnCommand = COMMAND_OTHER;
        break;
}
return returnCommand;
```

In some cases, you may find that whitespace competes with other style guidelines. It is best to focus on readability with ample whitespace over other layout guidelines in those cases, although these areas can get very subjective.

If a statement spans more than one line due to the length of the contents of the statement, formatting must make the fact that the statement is split very obvious. In addition, the split must occur at a logical boundary, such as following a punctuation or operator. The following line shall be indented to highlight the continuation and distinguish it from other statements at the same indention level. The following example shows a function declaration that is too long to fit on a single line along with an indention of the continuation that uses whitespace to highlight the relationship with the declaration and contrast it from the start of the function:

```
PacketEnumerations getPacketEnumeration (int enumerationOffset, int enumerationLength, \
                                         int enumerationConversion)
{
   int i, j, k;
   i = j = k = 0;
```

Include Files and Include Statements

All header files must contain an include file guard macro. A guard macro protects a file against being included more than once that can cause unforeseen side effects in large programs such as compilation errors and naming conflicts. A guard macro uses two pre-processor directives at the start of the include file and one at the end of the include file. Naming convention states that defines follow UPPERCASE form and guards should also leverage a meaningful relationship to the filename and its relationship to a broader library should that be relevant.

```
#ifndef CLOUDSHIELD_FLOWLIBRARY_PH      // First line of include
#define CLOUDSHIELD_FLOWLIBRARY_PH
        ...                             // Body of include goes here
#endif                                  // Last line of include: CLOUDSHIELD_FLOWLIBRARY_PH
```

Include statements should be sorted and grouped. Sorted by their hierarchical position in the system with low-level files included first, followed by higher-level include files. Leave an empty line between groups of include statements.

```
#include <cloudshield.ph>
#include <protocols.ph>

#include <cloudshield-flowlibrary.ph>

#include "includes\mycompany\more-custom-protocols.ph"
```

Include file paths must never be absolute and compiler directives should instead be used to indicate root directories for includes. System includes should leverage system include directives ("<file>") while application-specific includes should use local includes ("file").

Furthermore, include statements must be located at the top of a file only, and deeply hidden include files with the body of a source file should be avoided. In packetC, the one case where include files are nested within the body of source is for dataset initialization. These should be restricted to .px data files in the form shown in the example below:

```
const int URL_HASHES_[500] = {
#include "url-hashes.px"
};

int x_[50][50] = {
#include "arrayxdata.px"
};
```

Functions and Declarations

There are several guidelines that are critical to proper behavior of functions in packetC. At the highest level, indentation follows similar rules to other control structures with the brace on the line following the function declaration at the same indentation level as the declaration. In addition, when using prototypes for functions in header files the prototype and function declaration should match identically, not just in parameter order and types. In addition, a function shall only have one *return* statement to ensure readability.

The return value parameter should be first on the line followed by the function name and all formal parameter declarations in parentheses. The opening brace of the function body should be alone on a line beginning in column 1. Local declarations and code within the function body should be tabbed over one stop. If the value returned requires a long explanation, it should be given in the block header and not inline with the code.

The following example highlights a few of these principles where Command is an enumeration type:

```
Command getHttpCommand(int payloadOffset)
{
   if (pkt[payloadOffset:payloadOffset + 4] ==  STRING_GET)
   {
      commandReturn = COMMAND_GET;
   } else
   {
      commandReturn = COMMAND_OTHER;
   };
   return commandReturn;
}
```

As previously noted, functions use lowerCamelCase naming and begin with a verb and should be small and easy to understand upon review. Large and complex functions should be broken out into multiple functions to simplify readability and leverage inline directives at the call site when possible to reduce function call overhead. All functions should be preceded by the requisite comment block shown later in this chapter.

For functions, do not default to always using *int* as the return type. If the function does not return a value then it should be given return type *void* to clearly articulate that. In addition, the use of try and catch with controlling the evaluation within the function should be used instead of returning complex types that require conditional evaluation of success beyond true/false. In other words, return types that are not base types should contain the resulting data from the function and not a complex response code as those complexities should be addressed within the function.

If a group of functions all have similar parameters and use, it helps to call the repeated variable by the same name in all functions. Conversely, avoid using the same name for different purposes in related functions. Like parameters should also appear in the same place in the various argument lists.

General Conditionals Formatting

Conditional form is focused on readability with plenty of whitespace to ensure ease of debugging and evaluation. This form follows from the simplest evaluation through to complex conditionals. Even for the most simplistic conditionals, split the conditional over more than one line and include braces as follows:

```
if (isFinished == true)
{
  finishedEvaluations++;
}
```

Similar to other sections in this chapter emphasizing using whitespace for clarity and splitting lines at clear break-points, a long string of conditional operators should be split onto separate lines. The following expression:

```
if ( foo.next == NULL && totalCount < needed && needed <= MAX_ALLOT
      && serverActive(currentInput))
{
  ++totalCount;
```

should be written as follows in packetC:

```
if       (   foo->next == NULL      &&
             totalCount < needed     &&
         needed <= MAX_ALLOT  &&
         serverActive(currentInput) )
{
++totalCount;
```

Similarly, elaborate for loops should be split onto different lines.

```
for ( (  (currentLoopCounter = 0) & (augmentedLoopVariable=0)  );
   currentLoopCounter <= MAX_LOOP_VALUE;
   currentLoopCounter = currentLoopCounter + augmentedLoopVariable )
{
```

For loops with a null body, the null statement must be alone on a line and commented so that it is clear that the null body is intentional and not missing code. Also, even for null body conditionals, braces must be used.

```
while (destination++ = source++)
{
        ;            /* VOID - Null Body */
};
```

A compound statement is a list of statements enclosed by braces. The simple form of a compound statement is shown below:

```
control
{
  statement;
  statement;
}
```

When a block of code has several labels (unless there are a lot of them), the labels are placed on separate lines. The fall-through feature of the C switch statement (that is, when there is no break between a code segment and the next case statement) must be commented for future maintenance. A blank line should be inserted between the case test groups for readability.

```
switch (expr)
{
case ABC :
case DEF :
  statement;
  break;

case UVW :
  statement;
  /*FALLTHROUGH*/

case XYZ :
  statement;
  break;
}
```

Here, the last break is unnecessary, but it is required to prevent a fall-through error if another case is added after the last one. The default case, if used, should be last and does not require a break if it is last.

Specific Conditionals Forms

While the aforementioned style guidelines can be applied to most conditional forms and result in the specific guidelines, a specific description of each conditional form is listed below.

Whenever an if-else statement has a compound statement for either the if or else section, the statements of both the if and else sections should both be enclosed in braces (called fully bracketed syntax). The else part of an if-else statement should appear on the same line as the close brace.

```
if ( expression )
{
  statement;
  statement;
} else if ( expression )
{
  statement;
} else ( expression )
{
  statement;
};
```

Do-while loops should always have braces around the body and the while statement sits on the same line as the closing brace as shown below:

```
do
{
  statement;
} while ( conditionExists );
```

A while statement should have the following form:

```
while (condition)
{
  statement;
}
```

A for statement should have the following form:

```
for (initialization; condition; update)
{
  statement;
}
```

A switch statement should use the following form where the conclusion of statements from one case are separated from the start of the following case statement by vertical whitespace and no statements are on the same line as the case. Breaks must be used in all cases with only default, which must be the last case, being able to contain statements without a break.

```
switch (expr)
{
  case ABC :
  case DEF :
    statement;
    break;

  case UVW :
    statement;
    /*FALLTHROUGH*/

  case XYZ :
    statement;
    break;

  default :
    statement;
}
```

Note that each case keyword is indented relative to the switch statement as a whole. This makes the entire switch statement stand out. Note also the extra space before the : character. The explicit fall-through comment should be included whenever there is a case statement without a break statement.

A try-catch statement should have the following form in packetC:

```
try
{
  statement;
}

catch ( exception )
{
  statement;
}
```

General Commentary on Comments

It is expected that packetC code should be clear and understandable. Following the guidelines in this chapter is strongly suggested. Detailed comments should not be needed on a line-by-line basis. As such, comments should not be leveraged to make convoluted code understandable. That said, code written for performance and the low-level nature of packetC applications may drive the need for more comments than are generally seen with C++. packetC code should have enough comments to make a function understandable.

Source code files and each function should begin with a comment header. These headers are intended to describe the functionality, including input and output, without the need to read line-by-line comments. Code following the naming guidelines from this document and indentation guides will be clear and understandable to the reader.

In packetC, both C and C++ style comments are supported. Nesting of the two comment styles is possible. Comment styles should not be nested with the exception of commenting out large sections of code where C style comments are used to start and end the section. This is critical as the pre-processor only supports C style comments and pre-processor macros may affect the construction of the packetC source code provided to the compiler. C++ style comments are built into the packetC compiler. C++ comments must only be used to start a line or following code at a clear indention level.

```
/* Commenting Out All This Code ===
//
// function header here
int initializeContext ( int context; )
{
  contextInitialized_[context] = true;   // Keep comments aligned
  return true;                           // and do not over-comment.
};
==== End of Commenting Code */
```

There should be a space between the "//" and the actual comment, and comments should use well written sentences starting with a capitalized first word ending with a period.

Short comments embedded within code should describe what is happening, how it is being done, what parameters mean, and any restrictions or bugs. Short comments should be about *what*, such as "compute mean value", rather than *how* such as "sum of values divided by n" as code and variable names should be clear. These short comments may appear on the same line as the code they describe and should be tabbed over to separate them from comments or may appear on a separate line within the code for longer comments, indented to the same level as the statement they comment.

```
if (counter > 1)
{
  if ( counter % 3 == 0)                 // Test every third one
  {
    // a verbose comment about calculating something important
    very-long-statement-on-this-line;
  }
}
```

File Comment Headers

Each file should start with a file comment block that gives a short description of what the file contains as well as the functions contained within it. The name of the file must be included in the first line of the body of the comment along with a description of the file's contents. This is followed by a short description of the contents of the file without delineating each function and its role, as each function should have its own function comment header.

The descriptions are followed by an identification of the author or authors of the file as well as a copyright notice. If the file contains code that bears a separate and distinct license, the name of the license and licensor must be highlighted here and the license body placed in a comment block at the end of the file with identification of its presence in the copyright notice portion of the file comment header. In some cases, license agreements may require modification of this approach by the licensor and in those cases the license prevails over the packetC style guidelines. The goal is to keep the packetC file comment header clean and readable whenever possible.

Following the block comment shall be the *packet module name* declaration, *library module name* declaration, or *shared module name* declaration for modules, or the guard macro for included files. Included files must use a guard macro and it is critical to also include a library version definition at the same location when not aided by the support of linker version protections.

The example below shows the recommended form of the file comment header. The comment header uses C++ style comments with a line of stars ("*") at the beginning and end of the comment header and indentation of descriptions below the three callouts of the filename, author, and copyright notice. The guideline example is shown below:

```
//=============================================================================
//  time.pc - C-Like time function calls for packetC programmers.
//
//     A series of functions useful in evaluating the current time
//     of day or the actual date when processing is occurring.  In
//     addition, functions provide formatted textual representations
//     necessary for text based network protocol responses.
//
// author
//     Peder Jungck
//
// copyright notice
//     © 2009 CloudShield Technologies, Inc.
//
//=============================================================================
#ifndef TIME_API_PH
#define TIME_API_PH
#define _TIME_API_VERSION 1.00
   . . .    // body of file here
#endif
```

Function Comment Headers

Each function should be preceded by a block comment that gives a short description of what the function does and how to use it. Discussion of non-trivial design decisions and side-effects is also appropriate, however, avoid duplicating information clear from the code or called out separately by comment tags distributed throughout the code.

Following the block comment shall be the return value and function name, including the formal parameter list alone on a single line, starting in column 1. As per previous formatting discussions, long function declarations should be clearly indented when spanning multiple lines to avoid confusion. If the return value of a function is a special type that is unique to that function, the type may be declared between the function comment header and the function declaration.

The block comment must identify each parameter in the function declaration and return value along with their function and format of the data they contain. This must be done in the function header and not buried within the function. The corollary to this is that comments should not be strewn throughout the function declaration.

The example below shows the recommended form of the function comment header. The name of the function is not repeated within the function comment header as it should be clean and clear immediately following the comments as all comments regarding the parameters are within the header. As with file comment headers, C++-style comments are used.

```
//==============================================================================
//  one line description of function's role
//
//  multi-line description of function and general description
//  of what parameters are passed and what the function returns
//
//  example usage
//     example-return = function ( example-parameter );
//
//  parameters
//     parameter - description of what it does (repeated)
//
//  returns
//     value - what it can return
//
//==============================================================================
```

This standard header must precede every function. The following example is from a sample packetC function:

```
//==============================================================================
//  Formats the time and returns it in an ASCII string.
//
//  This will return the current system date and time in a 26
//  byte array of type "AsciiTime".  See below for the format
//  that is returned.  The sole parameter accounts for the
//  differing system clock to seconds conversion.
//
//  example usage
//     AsciiTime   date = asciiTime(TICKS_PER_SECOND);
//
//  parameters
//     ticksPerSecond provides system clock ticks in a second
//
//  returns
//     AsciiTime value in the following format:
//
//        "DDD MMM dd hh:mm:ss YYYY"
//
//        DDD   Sun, Mon, Tue, Wed, Thu, Fri, Sat
//        MMM   Jan, Feb, Mar, Apr, May, Jun, Jul, Aug, Sep, Oct, Nov, Dec
//        dd    1 to 31 Days
//        hh    0 to 23 Hours
//        mm    0 to 59 Minutes
//        ss    0 to 59 Seconds
//        YYYY  Year
//
//==============================================================================
```

```
typedef  byte AsciiTime[26];

AsciiTime asciiTime(int ticksPerSecond)
{
   …
```

File Naming and Construction Conventions

Within packetC, the naming of files is not a language constraint. You may name any file with whatever name and extension you like. An Integrated Development Environment or other tools may have issues with files named using unexpected extensions or conflicting extensions presumed to be associated with other tools. For example, naming all of your source code files with a .htm or .exe extension may not always work as well as desired, but the #include pre-processor directives won't complain. Table 3-1 provides a set of guidelines for packetC filenames:

Table 3-1. packetC file Extension Naming Guidelines

File Extension	Description
.pc	A packetC source code file such as a module or include file with functions
.ph	A packetC header file often including declarations and function prototypes
.px	A packetC data file used with #include to initialize a data set in the source
.pcap	A LIBPCAP formatted capture file for use in debugger input and output
.plo	A packetC library module appropriate for linking
.pso	A packetC shared library module appropriate for inclusion in an ADP
.orc	A packetC packet module's executable object code for inclusion in an ADP
.adp	A packetC application deployment package containing multiple applications
File Extension	**Uncommon File Extensions in packetC Project**
.csm	The assembly language output of the packetC compiler prior to the assembler
.c	A C-compatible source code file not yet converted to packetC grammar
.h	A C-compatible header file not yet converted to packetC grammar
.cpp	A C++-compatible source code file not yet converted to packetC grammar

Table 3-1. *cont.*

File Extension	Uncommon File Extensions in packetC Project
.hpp	A C++-compatible header code file not yet converted to packetC grammar

Broader Coding Style Guideline Tips and Techniques

Variables, Types, and Functions

In many C++ style guidelines, the suggestion to avoid named constants is recommended with the suggestion of using functions. The following approach to constants must not be used in packetC.

```
int FULL_MASK()             // Do Not Use Functions Like This In packetC!
{
  return 255.255.255.255;
};
```

It is recommended that *const int* be utilized instead of #define when defining constants to assure type safety.

```
const int NUM_CONTEXTS = 96;       // do this
#define NUM_CONTEXTS 96            // not this
```

The C value NULL is not present in packetC as was also made obsolete in C++. Initialized variables and evaluations should expressly leverage zero instead and avoid any emulation of NULL.

```
const int NULL = 0;                // Don't do this!
```

Conditional Layout and Form

Loop variables should be initialized immediately before the loop.

```
doneWithLoop = false;
while (doneWithLoop == false )
{
```

Loop control statements must be the only variables in the loop statement. If other variable initializations are important to the loop, they must be done prior to the loop and not within the loop control statement.

```
valuesFound = 0;
for (i = 0; i < 100; i++)  // Warning: Don't introduce other variables
{
   if (xyzzy[i] == TEST_VALUE)
       valuesFound++;
};
```

Avoid the use of do-while loops since they are less readable than for and while loops. Any do-while loop should have a possible representation in one of these other forms. The conditional at the bottom of a loop is problematic from understanding code as one must go to the bottom of the loop to see when it is true as opposed to seeing the conditional before evaluating what the loop is doing.

Infinite loops should be avoided at all costs as a real-time system getting into an infinite loop can be fatal. In some cases, however, a loop written means other than the controlling loop statement determing terminating the loop. For these forms, use a *while (true)* controlling loop to clearly highlight that this is an infinite loop.

Loops should not use *break* and *continue* as they obscure the actual impact of the control statement.

In C and C++, the use of complex conditional expressions is *not* recommended. Instead, the suggestion is to try and leverage multiple variables with Boolean evaluation to simplify the statement. For packetC, bool is not a base type and the opposite suggestion is made. Complex statements with clear evaluation and involvement of strictly typed evaluation is critical for performance and accuracy in packetC. The preferred packetC evaluation is as follows:

```
if ((packetNumber < 0) || (packetNumber > MAX_PACKETS)|| packetNumber == previousPacket)
{
```

On the other hand, however, in C++ the following is recommended:

```
bool isOutOfRange = (packetNumber <0) || (packetNumber > MAX_PACKETS);
bool isPrevious = (pcketNumber == previousPacket);
if (isOutOfRange || isPrevious) {
```

Do not leverage the C++ form as it is dependent on implicit Boolean evaluation and also fights the optimization benefits of the packetC compiler. The following example shows the recommended form in contrast to the traditional C form:

```
if ( !(bufSize % sizeof(int)) )              // Not recommended
```

Instead, this should be written to reflect the numeric (not Boolean) nature of the test:

```
if ( (bufSize % sizeof(int)) == false )     // Recommended, where false == 0.
```

In addition, the use of explicit tests not only for statements but also in the evaluation of function return-values will help to differentiate between the value *true == 1* and a non-zero response that may represent specific meaning based upon the non-zero value returned.

In C, the use of goto statements is considered in conflict with the use of structured code. In packetC, however, tightly tuned code may need the use of a goto statement for achieving optimizations not able to be achieved through other constructs evaluated by the compiler. The use of goto statements in packetC must be used in isolated sections of code and not leveraged to break out of another control statement such as branching out of a switch statement.

Variables, Types, and Functions

Conditionals should not presume a Boolean evaluation of true and instead should test for the value or leverage the integer constants true and false for integer variables being used in Boolean evaluations. Note that *const int true = 1;* and *const int false = 0;* are predefined values leveraged for Boolean evaluation in packetC. For example:

```
if (flagSet) {              //Don't presume non-zero evaluation.
if (flagSet == true) {     // This method validates type and evaluation.
```

Comments

In packetC, both C and C++ style comments are supported. Nesting of the two comment styles is possible. Comment styles should not be nested with the exception of commenting out large sections of code where C style comments are used to start and end the section.

Within packetC, whitespace and clarity of comments placed throughout the code ensure readability and clarity in what statements in code are doing. Furthermore, file and function comment headers have a strict form that they follow that provides information about what they do. In the real world, however, there is often need for more casual comments that reflect work-in-progress or highlighting code that may raise concerns for one reason or another. These casual comments are not meant to apply to formalized comment blocks required by other company or automated code analysis system inclusions.

These comments, referred to as Gotchas, are used to highlight variables changed out of the normal control flow or other code likely to break during maintenance. In addition, the embedded keywords within these Gotchas are used to point out sections that will need future focus. The form of the Gotchas are such that they can be highlighted within packetC editors as well as identified by robots parsing code in order to make a report that drives targeted effort against a code base. The following list identifies a set of recommended packetC Gotchas where each follows the form:

```
//    :GOTCHA-NAME: description
```

where the C++ comment starts at column 1 and the Gotcha is preceded and followed by a colon (":") without any spaces between the colons and the Gotcha name. A description, which may follow a specific form for a given Gotcha, follows the :GOTCHA-NAME: on the line. Comments may consist of multiple lines, but the first line should be a self-containing, meaningful summary. The writer's name and the date of the remark should be part of the comment. This information is in the source repository, but it can take a quite a while to find out when and by whom it was added. Often gotchas stick around longer than they should. Embedding date information allows other programmers to make this decision while embedding "who" information lets us know whom to ask.

The recommended standard Gotcha names are:

```
TODO, BUG, KLUDGE, TRICKY, WARNING and COMPILER
```

but do constrain yourself from adding more, however, consistent use is key.

- :TODO: topic

  Means there's more to do here, don't forget.

- :BUG: [bugid] topic

  Means there's a known bug here, explain it and optionally give a bug ID.

- :KLUDGE:

  When you've done something ugly highlight it. Optionally explain how you would do it differently.

- :TRICKY:

  Tells somebody that the following code is very tricky so don't go changing it without thinking.

- :WARNING:

  Beware of something.

- :COMPILER:

  Sometimes you need to work around a compiler problem. Document it. The problem may go away eventually.

Some examples follow:

```
// :TODO: pjj 2009MAR20: possible performance problem
// We should really use a database table here but for now
// using a switch statement.
// :KLUDGE: pjj 2008OCT31: too many gotos and labels
// Needing to get it done quick and couldn't find a good
// conditional statement form.
```

CHAPTER 4

■ ■ ■

Construction of a packetC Program

packetC and Parallelism

packetC is designed to be used with parallel-processing runtime environments, although an implementation may be compliant without providing this. The language was designed for environments in which a packetC program will typically be executing with large numbers of simultaneous contexts. In packetC, similar to interrupt service routines, the arrival of a packet is an event that triggers processing by a context. The packetC program is considered re-entrant and is designed such that more than one copy is executing at any point in time. Parallel processing is based upon each context running the entire application from receipt of a packet to completion of processing for the assigned packet. The packetC language specification does not prescribe how actual or apparent parallelism must be implemented. Hence, each copy of a packet module or shared module is termed a *context*, since the terms *process*, *task*, or *thread* imply how parallel execution is to be implemented and imply characteristics that may vary from one operating system to another.

The packetC language is designed to hide the complexities of parallel programming from the user. Although a few explicit parallel constructs are available, such as lock() and unlock() operators, to use as semaphore controls on global variables, the packetC operating environment provides most parallel-processing functionality without programmer direction. Accordingly, the user does not have to explicitly replicate the program, allocate parallel resources, or orchestrate multiple executables. Furthermore, the coordination of the receipt of packets into memory buffers, allocation, and de-allocation of context to packets, or strict separation of memory between contexts is presumed to be controlled by the underlying system. Some fundamental aspects of the packetC language, such as how it handles identifier scopes, do reflect the fact that the language will usually be executed in a parallel environment.

packetC Modules: Three Kinds of Compilation Units

packetC programs are constructed from three kinds of *compilation units* or *modules*:

- **packet module**

    - Contains the main body of an application and it alone is able to constitute an application; it may have subordinate functions and declare links to the other kinds of modules that will be resolved at link time.

- **shared module**

    - A collection of functions that can be called by different types of packet modules during a single execution episode. Declaration syntax indicates whether a given function can be called by a packet module. Shared modules execute in their own memory space and are linked in dynamically when loading occurs on a system.

- **library module**

   - A collection of routines that can be called by functions in a packet module or another library module. This construct supports separate compilation. Library modules are linked at compile time into an application produced by a packet module. In contrast to a shared module, each packet module linking a library module will have its own copy of code and data as part of the executable space of the application.

Only one kind of compilation unit can appear in a given source code file. The subsections below describe each kind of compilation unit.

Example of a packet module:

```
packet module mainApp;
#include <cloudshield.ph>        // Platform standard include file
#include "someLib.ph"            // Header file with function prototypes for library module

extern int sharedCall( $PACKET sharedPacket );
// Function prototype for shared library function

int     countPacketPerSecond_;              // Global scope variable

// Local scope function
int myLocalFunc(int functionCounter) {
        int xLocal;                 // Block scope variable

   xLocal = sharedCall( pkt );              // Shared function call, visibility to the packet.
   functionCounter += 1;

   return xLocal;
}

/* Main entry point, system passes the current      *
 * packet ($PACKET type), current system variables   *
 * ($SYS type), and the packet info block ($PIB type).  *
 * All packet modules must have main declared.       */
void main( $PACKET pkt, $PIB pib, $SYS sys )
{
   int     mainFunctionCounter;                // Packet scope variables
   int     xMain;

   // Call to local function
   xMain = myLocalFunc(@mainFunctionCounter);  // Packet scope var wo stack (inline)

   someLib_Func();                             // Call to Library function

   pib.action = FORWARD_PACKET;
}
```

Like C, and unlike some languages such as FORTRAN and Python, the indentation is for human consumption and readability. Although indentation is not a requirement of packetC, style guidelines to promote more auditable and potentially secure code are presented in the final chapter of this book.

Three Kinds of Scope

In C, blocks determine the scope of data between that which is global to all segments of the code and local scope data, such as within a function. Due to packetC's implicit parallelism, scope, and visibility requirements are different from C's basic scoping. Specifically, there is a need to indicate that some variables associated with a packet module are global in the sense of being shared by multiple contexts of the application running in parallel. This introduces additional constraints on their use. In addition, specific data is unique to each context. The input parameters to *main()* represent these unique data elements. The packet associated with the context, as well as system- and packet-related information are considered packet scope and available to code processing within the context. These unique values are considered to be part of a packet scope. In packetC, three scopes, as depicted in Figure 4-1, are defined and are central to parallel processing:

- *global scope*

    - The variable is visible to every construct that follows its declaration within the module, reading in top-to-bottom fashion. In a *packet module*, the variable is visible to other contexts of that same packet module (application). Actions on global scope variables are atomic. However, cooperative locking through the use of a semaphore is required for coherent multi-step transactions, because in packetC global scope differs from C global scope in that it is visible to multiple contexts.

- *block scope*

    - The variable is visible solely within the enclosing block from the point of its declaration to the end of the enclosing block similar to local scope in C. Block scope variables are often those defined within functions such as loop counters.

- *packet scope*

    - Packet scope variables are those defined within the body of a packet module's *main()*. In addition, the parameters passed as input to main, namely *pkt*, *sys* and *pib* are considered packet scope. Functions in the packet module automatically have visibility to *pkt*, *sys*, and *pib*. However, user variables defined in packet scope must be passed as *arguments* to functions. Packet scope is unique to packetC.

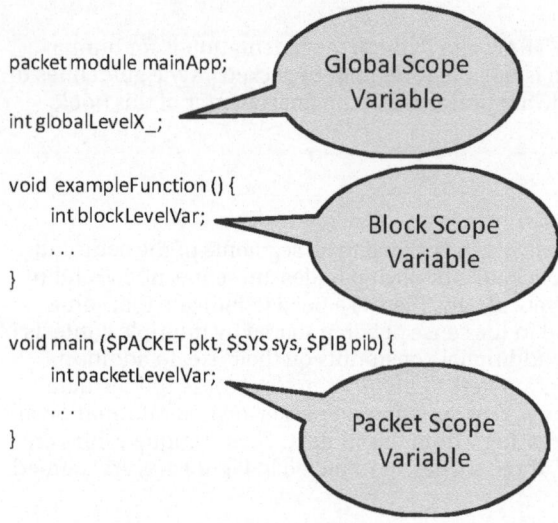

```
packet module mainApp;                    Global Scope
                                          Variable
int globalLevelX_;

void exampleFunction () {
        int blockLevelVar;                Block Scope
        . . .                             Variable
}

void main ($PACKET pkt, $SYS sys, $PIB pib) {
        int packetLevelVar;
        . . .                             Packet Scope
}                                         Variable
```

Figure 4-1. *Global, block and packet scope*

For reliability reasons, packetC forbids the use of conflicting identifiers, whether they name similar constructs or not. Conflicting use occurs if any source code location exists where both declarations could be visible; this assumes that a declaration of an identifier in an inner scope does not hide the identifier's occurrence in an outer scope.

```
int myFunc(int x) {
int i, j;
i = x;

for ( j = 1; j < 5; ++j ) {
   int i = j + 1;       // ERROR in packetC (redundant 'I'), legal in C

   …
   }
return i + 50;
}

int fn1() {int k;…}
int fn2() {int k;…}    // no conflicting visibility

// ERROR
int aName;
typedef int aName;     // ERROR: dissimilar uses still are conflicts
// (Also, for style reasons, types should use UpperCamelCase)
```

Module Structure and Scopes

The scoping rules applicable to each of the three types of source code module—packet module, shared module, and library module—are summarized in Figure 4-2 and treated separately below.

Packet Module	Shared Module	Library Module
| ```
packet module mainApp;

//===========================
// The packet module is the
// main application instance.
//
// Standard Includes
//===========================
#include <cloudshield.ph>
#include <protocols.ph>

// Library function prototypes
#include "someLib.ph"

// Global scope variable
int mainAppGlobal_;

extern void sharedCall($PACKET
pkt );  // Shared Lib Call

// Local Function
void myLocalFunc() {
// Block scope variable
   int xLocal;

// Call to a Shared Lib Function
// Need to pass pkt to shared.
   sharedCall( pkt );
   ...
}

//
// Main entry point
//
void  main( $PACKET pkt,
  $PIB pib, $SYS sys ) {

   // Packet scope variables
   int   xLocalMain;
   int   xMain;

   // Call to local function
   myLocalFunc();

   // Call to Library function
   someLibFuncA(xMain);
}
``` | ```
shared module sharedApp;

//===========================
// Shared Modules provide shared
// functions to apps at run time
//===========================




// Library function prototypes
// Note: Separate copy from mainApp
#include "someLib.ph"

// Global variable scope
int sharedAppGlobal_;

//  Local function in Shared Lib
void myLocalFunc() {
     // Call to a Library function
     someLibFuncB();
     ...
}

// Externally shared function
entry void sharedCall($PACKET pkt){
     int  xLocal; // Block Scope
     xLocal = (int)pkt[46];

     myLocalFunc();
}

// Externally shared function
entry void sharedCall1() {
     int y;  // Block Scope
     myLocalFunc();

        // Call to Library function
        someLibFuncA(y);

        // Block scope variable
        int i;
        for ( i = 1; i < 5; ++i ) {
          // Block scope variable
          int x;
          ...
     }
}
``` | ```
library module someLib;

//===========================
// Library modules provide funcs
// to applications at link time
//===========================




// Library function prototypes
#include "someLib.ph"

// Global variable scope
int libraryGlobal_;

// Library function define
void someLibFuncA(int x) {
     ...
}

void someLibFuncB() {

     ...
}

void someLibFuncC() {

     ...
}

void someLibFuncD(int x){
   int myVal; // Block Scope

   // pkt, pib, sys visible
   if ( pkt[46] == 0xff )
   {
     // Block scope variable
     int y;  // Block Scope
     myVal = pib.payload_offset;
   }
   ...
}
``` |

Figure 4-2. Three kinds of packetC compilation units
```

Packet Module

A packet module's structure consists of:

- The packet module declaration at the top of the file.

- An optional section of global definitions (types, variables, functions, function prototypes, pragmas). Function prototypes not included in the packet module are flagged for library module link-time resolution, while function prototypes preceded by the extern keyword are flagged for load-time dynamic linking to the appropriate shared module.

- The packet application main. This body begins with the keywords void main followed by a parenthesized set of input arguments that establishes the origin of the current packet ($PACKET pkt), the Packet Information Block ($PIB pib), and the System Information Block ($SYS sys), described below. After an open curly bracket, the main body begins. The main body contains type declarations, variable declarations, and statements in any order following standard C rules. Naturally, the packet main is concluded by a closing curly bracket.

Each packet module must contain exactly one *main()* component. A packet module without a definition for *main()* or with more than one found across all included source code files will fail to compile.

Developers must consider several special attributes of global, packet, and block scope within packet modules.

Global scope: In global scope type declarations, global variable declarations, database and searchset declarations, function prototypes, functional declarations, and pragma clauses can appear here. The following is true for packet modules:

- Global variables are shared among all contexts of an executing packet module.

- While operators on global variables are atomic, complex interaction with global variables across instances must employ cooperative multi-tasking. The lock and unlock operators provide an atomic test-and-set allowing any global to be used as a semaphore. Global variables used as a semaphore cannot be used to store any other data.

- Function prototypes without a subsequent function definition indicate that the function should appear at link time in a library module.

- Function prototypes preceded by the extern keyword indicate that the function should appear as an entry point for an associated shared module.

- An initialization value for a variable in global scope is set only once, at the loading of an application.

Packet scope: Only packet modules contain a packet scope which corresponds to the packet body within *main()*, enclosed by curly brackets. The following are true for packet scope:

- A variable initialized within packet scope receives any initialization value declared for it each time that the enclosing packet application is triggered to process a new packet or event.

- Similar to C, variables with the const keyword are initialized once at application start and cannot be modified during the execution of the packetC program.

- The packet (pkt), packet information block (pib), or system information (sys) are each unique to the packet module context being processed and are accessible throughout all packet module scopes.

- Variables declared within packet scope are visible from the point of their declaration to the end of *main()*.

Block scope: Block scopes are defined by function bodies and compound statements just like C. Type declarations, variable declarations, and pragma clauses may appear within them, but not function prototypes or function declarations. An initialization value for a variable with block scope is set each time the block is entered.

```
packet module mainApp;
#include <cloudshield.ph>
#include <protocols.ph>
#include "someLib.ph"                    // Header file with function prototypes for library module

extern int sharedCall( $PACKET pkt );  // Function prototype for shared library function

int     countPacketPerSecond_;       // Global scope variable(identify by lower camelCase)
                                     //  and  trailing underscore)

// Block scope function
int myLocalFunc(int functionCounter)
{
    int  xLocal;                     // Block scope variable (identify by lower camelCase)

    xLocal = sharedCall( pkt );   // Shared function providing visibility to the packet.
    functionCounter += 1;

    return xLocal;
}

/*
 * Main entry point, virtual machine passes the current packet in $PACKET pkt,
 * current system variables in $SYS sys, and the packet info block in $PIB pib.
 * All packet modules must have main() declared.  Unlike C, main() is always
 * declared as void in packetC.
 */
void main( $PACKET pkt, $PIB pib, $SYS sys ) {
    int   mainFunctionCounter;    // Packet scope variables
    int   xMain;

    // Call to local function
    xMain = myLocalFunc(@mainFunctionCounter);
    // Provide packet scope variable without stack (inline)

    someLib_Func();                     // Call to Library function
```

```
    sys.action = FORWARD_PACKET;
}
```

Shared Module

A shared module's structure consists of:

- The module declaration,

- Global definitions, which may include function declarations preceded by the entry keyword, which serves as entry points for packet module callers. Function *prototypes* cannot be preceded by the entry keyword.

Shared modules interact with the three possible scopes as follows:

- **Global scope:** Type declarations, global variable declarations, function prototypes, functional declarations, and pragma clauses may appear here. A shared module:

  - Has function declarations preceded by the entry keyword to indicate that the function may be called from (multiple kinds of) packet modules. If the entry point function needs the caller's current packet, the function's parameter list should include the packet.

  - Defines global variables that are visible only to functions within the shared module.

  - Has no visibility to global scope variables within the calling packet or library module.

- **Packet scope:** A shared module has neither a packet scope nor a *main()* body. Any packet scope data from a packet module must be explicitly passed by value to a shared library if it is intended to be exposed.

- **Block scope:** Block scopes are defined within shared module function bodies, either by the function bodies themselves, or by compound statements inside them. Type declarations, variable declarations, and pragma clauses may appear within them, but not function prototypes or function declarations. An initialization value for a variable with block scope is set each time the block is entered.

```
shared module sharedApp;
#include <cloudshield.ph>
// Shared Modules provide shared functions to apps at run time

// Library function prototypes - Note: Separate copy from mainApp
#include "someLib.ph"

// Global scope - Within Shared Library Only
int sharedAppGlobal_;

//  Local function in Shared Lib
void myLocalFunc()
{
```

```
    // Call to a Library function
    someLibFuncB();
    ...
  }
// Externally shared function
entry void sharedCall($PACKET pkt)
{
    int  xLocal; // Block Scope
    xLocal = (int)pkt[46];
    ...
    myLocalFunc();
}

// Externally shared function
entry void sharedCall1()
{
    int y;   // Block Scope
    myLocalFunc();

    // Call to Library function
    someLibFuncA(y);

    // Block scope variable
    int i;
    for ( i = 1; i < 5; ++i )
    {
        // Block scope variable
        int x;
        ...
    }
}
```

Library Module

A library module's structure consists of:

- The module declaration,

- global definitions, which may include type, variable and function declarations, as well as function prototypes and pragma clauses.

Library modules interact with the three possible scopes as follows.

- **Global scope:** Type declarations, global variable declarations, and function prototypes are visible only within the library module. Functions declared within the library module can be called by packet modules that declare matching function prototypes in their own global sections.

- **Packet scope:** A library module cannot define packet scope variables nor a *main()* body. Packet scope variables must be passed to a library module as parameters of function calls with the exception of *pkt*, *sys*, and *pib* which are available to functions in the library module bounded by the executing context.

- **Block scope:** Block scopes are defined within library module function bodies, either by the function bodies themselves, or by compound statements inside them. Type declarations, variable declarations, and pragma clauses may appear within them, but not function prototypes or function declarations. An initialization value for a variable with block scope is set each time the block is entered.

```
library module someLib;
// Library modules provide funcs to applications at link time

// Library function prototypes
#include "someLib.ph"

// Global scope
int libraryGlobal_;

// Library function define
void someLibFuncA(int x)
{
  ...
 }

void someLibFuncB()
{
  ...
 }

void someLibFuncC()
{
  ...
 }

void someLibFuncD(int x)
{
    int myVal; // Block Scope
    // pkt, pib, sys visible
    if ( pkt[46] == 0xff )
      {
      // Block scope variable
       int y;  // Block Scope
       myVal = pib.payload_offset;
      }
    ...
 }
```

Graphical Representation of Scope Linkage

Figure 4-3 contains the same contents as Figure 4-2, except that graphical linkages are applied in the figure to show the scope relationships of some select elements that cross or are replicated across module boundaries.

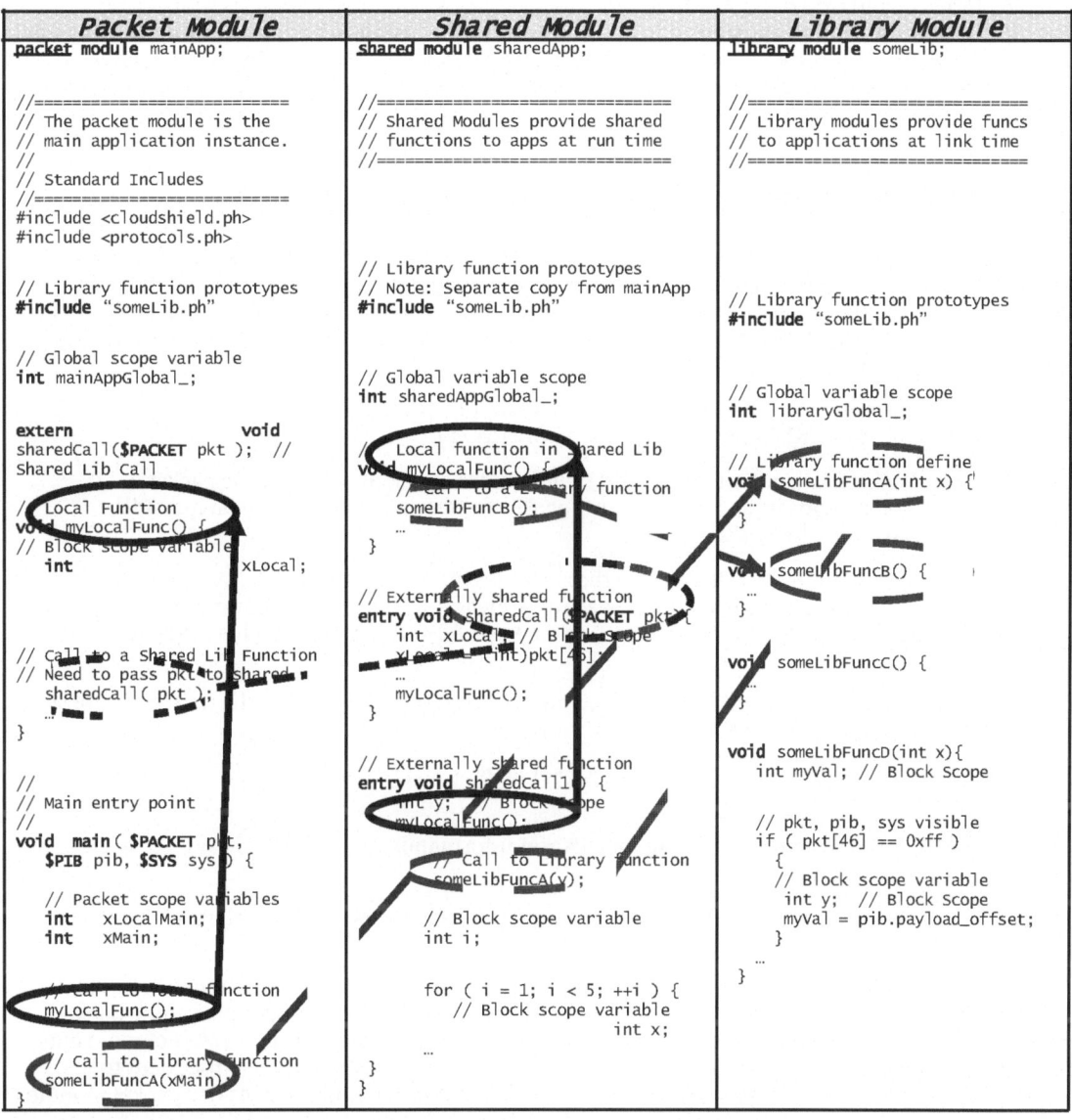

Figure 4-3. *Relationships of external content across packetC compilation units*

In the modules above, three elements are highlighted to point out some of the packetC scope dynamics between modules. In both the packet module and shared module, the function *myLocalFunc()* is defined. The scope of *myLocalFunc()* is within each module and visibility is not shared. There are no conflicts to having the same function in both modules as it is not externalized and references remain local within the modules. When a function is desired to be shared from a shared module to a packet module, the entry and extern keywords are used to provide visibility and linkage as shown with *sharedCall()*. Library modules are linked in at compile time and standard function prototypes (included within *someLib.ph*) are utilized to properly define before referencing. The functions *someLibFuncA()* and *someLibFuncB()* represent examples of a library function reference by a packet module and a shared module.

Run time Environment Data and Predefined Types

packetC does not specify requirements for particular hardware at program execution time. However, it does require a packetC implementation to provide several predefined types that support common packet processing activities, such as managing packet contents, network protocols, ports, and messages.

Thus, a packetC implementation shall provide certain system data for each instance of a packet *main()* when the context first begins execution:

- The current packet (for any executing instance of a packet module), declared as datatype **$PACKET** and passed to the *main()* as *pkt*.

- The Packet Information Block (PIB) that includes information about the packet such as layer offsets and decoded protocol information, declared as datatype **$PIB** and passed to the *main()* as *pib*.

- A System Information Block (SYS) that includes information about the system in which the packetC application is executing, including objects such as time and interface port information, declared as datatype **$SYS** and passed to the *main()* as *sys*.

To represent this data, packetC defines three predefined types: $PACKET, $PIB, and $SYS. These datatypes and parameters are reserved words within packetC.

- **$PACKET** is the type of the current packet (acts as an array of bytes), always referenced as *pkt*.

- **$PIB** is the structure definition for a Packet Information Block (PIB), always referenced as *pib*.

- **$SYS** is the structure definition for a System Information Block (SYS), always referenced as *sys*.

A packet module's main shall have only one parameter of each of these types, as defined in the packet main section's declaration. These values are unique to each executing instance of the packet module and on input indicate the result of processing of the current packet prior to start of main and upon exit of main may dictate actions for the system to perform upon the packet subsequent to processing in the instance. The **pkt, pib** and **sys** are available throughout all scopes of a packet module and are not passed as parameters to any functions within a packet or library module. These may be placed on a parameter list for a shared module's entry function prototype to indicate and permit scope visibility.

```
packet module mainApp;
...
void main( $PACKET pkt, $PIB pib, $SYS sys )
{
  . . .
}
```

In addition, a packetC implementation shall implement

- **$MSG_TYPE** to hold system messages that are used to interact with the control plane (see section on Control Plane Environment).

Packet ($PACKET pkt)

Before an instance of a packet module is executed, a current packet is made available to the program. The packet is made accessible to user code by declaring it as an input argument to a packet module's *main()* function.

As a variable of the pre-defined user type **$PACKET**, the current packet acts as an array of bytes. Portions of the current packet that comprise standard protocols are accessible through a special kind of structure, termed *descriptors*. (See the section on the descriptor data type below). In addition, the current packet can be treated as a byte array.

```
void main ( $PACKET pkt, $PIB pib, $SYS sys)
  {
    byte myArr[64];
    ...
    myArr[0:31] = pkt[0:31];
```

Several packetC operators are defined for this data type (see Packet Operators described later in this book). A packetC implementation may handle the varying size of the current packet in a variety of ways, including specifying a maximum size for the packet.

Packet Information Block ($PIB pib)

A Packet Information Block (PIB) shall be present and shall contain information about the current packet that is derived from the packet, going beyond what is contained within the packet. This descriptive data includes information about the presence of various protocols (or headers) and their locations within the packet. For example, the PIB structure contains information such as the decoded layer 2 type, offsets to layer 3 and layer 4.

The PIB is accessible as a variable of the predefined type **$PIB**, specified as an argument to the packet module main. The structure definition for **$PIB** is provided in the *cloudshield.ph* #include file. (For a complete definition of the PIB see Chapter 18.)

```
void main ( $PACKET pkt, $PIB pib, $SYS sys) { … }
```

System Information ($SYS type)

The System Information (SYS) type is a structure that contains attributes about the system the packetC application is executing that may be useful for processing a packet. This includes, for example, arrival time, visibility to parallel processing contexts or instances, the interface port through which the packet was received, and information about system thresholds, such as buffer utilization.

System Information is accessible to the user in a variable of the predefined type **$SYS**, specified as an argument to the packet module main.

```
void main ( $PACKET pkt, $PIB pib, $SYS sys) { … }
```
The structure definition for **$SYS** may vary by system vendor and is declared in a vendor #include file such as *cloudshield.ph* or, alternatively, predefined by a packetC compiler implementation. (SYS contents are described in Chapter 18.)

■ ■ ■

Variables: Identifiers, Basic Scalar Data Types, and Literals

Classic Data Types

C programmers will find that packetC provides a variety of familiar data types that follow C99 conventions. The use of identifiers, literals, and basic scalar data types is almost identical to what you would expect from C. In a few instances, such as enumeration types and structure bit-fields, there are subtle differences introduced to clean up ambiguities in C99 or to address some specific issues related to network structures required by packetC. Those differences don't appear visually or grammatically as much as they do in the implementation expectations and meaning. Where deviations occur, they will be highlighted to help the C programmer note the important changes.

This chapter provides a quick reference for identifiers, literals, and basic data types in packetC, highlighting syntax as well as any important points specific to packetC. In addition, a small section presents an overview on the impact of network byte order endianness on all data types in packetC. Programmers porting from one platform to another often grapple with big-endian versus little-endian systems and in particular fight with inconsistencies when creating network structures which are big-endian in Internet Protocol networks. In packetC, given its focus on networks, the language will always be big-endian no matter the underlying platform the application is working on. Big-endian will apply to packetC process through to transmission on the network. This awareness is critical as one moves from simple data types to complex ones or even just in specifying the value of a literal.

Identifiers and a Few Fundamentals

Identifiers in packetC are similar to C99 identifiers but there are some differences. In particular, there are some constraints on packetC identifiers that can introduce some issues in code brought directly from C environments; however, one will quickly find that packetC has simple rules for identifiers.

Given the following definitions:

- *letter* = 'a'..'z' or 'A'..'Z'

- *underscore* = '_'

- *dollar sign* = '$'

- *digit* = '0'..'9'

Identifiers need to follow the following rules:

- The initial character of an identifier must be a letter.

- Any subsequent characters can be letters, digits, or underscores.

- packetC identifiers are case sensitive.

- Dollar signs may appear in system declared identifiers referenced. Not available to user defined data types.

The following represent all possible values present in a packetC identifier:

- Digit = '0' | '1' | '2' | '3' | '4' | '5' | '6' | '7' | '8' | '9'

- Letter = 'A' | 'B' | 'C' | 'D' | 'E' | 'F' | 'G' | 'H' | 'I' | 'J' |'K' | 'L' | 'M' | 'N' | 'O' | 'P' | 'Q' | 'R' | 'S' | 'T' | 'U' | 'V' | 'W' | 'X' | 'Y' | 'Z' |
  'a' | 'b' | 'c' | 'd' |'e' | 'f' | 'g' | 'h' | 'i' | 'j' | 'k' | 'l' | 'm' | 'n' | 'o' | 'p' | 'q' | 'r' | 's' | 't' | 'u' | 'v' | 'w' | 'x' |'y' | 'z'

- OtherChar = '_' | '$'

Throughout this chapter, examples of literals being constructed in a number of forms are shown. The grammar production for those literals is shown below as well as a list of the possible operators within packet:

- Decimal = Digit [Decimal]

- HexDigit = Digit | 'A' | 'B' | 'C' | 'D' | 'E' | 'F'| 'a' | 'b' | 'c' | 'd' | 'e' | 'f'

- Hexdecimal = (HexDigit | Digit) [Hexadecimal]

- HexEntry = '0x' Hexadecimal

- Binary = (0 | 1) [Binary]

- BinaryEntry = '0b' Binary

- String = (Letter | '\x' (HexDigit | Digit) (HexDigit | Digit) | '\' Digit Digit Digit) [String]

- Operator = '<' | '<=' | '>' | '>=' | '=' | '!=' | '+' | '-' | '*' | '/' | '%' | '==' | '(' | ')' | '[' | ']' | '.' |
  ',' | '++' | '-' | '~' | '<<' | '>>' | '&' | '^' | '|' | '!' | '&&' | '||' | '+=' | '-=' | '*=' | '/=' | '%=' | '%=' |
  '<<=' | '>>=' | '&=' | '^=' | '|=' | sizeof | lock | unlock | offset | packet_offset | ref | deref

- Hex Example: 0x00010203

  0x04050607

  0x08090a0b

- Decimal Example: 12345

  213

  12333

  5

- Binary Example: 0b010100101010101010101010101
0b010100101010101111101010101
0b010111111010101010101010101

Basic Scalar Types

packetC supports four basic types. All four types are unsigned only and do not have signed variants within packetC. Without signed values, the lowest possible number is 0 and that 1 more than the maximum is also 0 with no carry flags present in the language. Other than that, packetC uses straightforward simple C scalar types.

The unsigned integer types are: **byte, short, int** and **long**.

Table 5-1. The Four Basic Scalar Types Supported by packetC

byte	8-bit unsigned values	0 to 255
short	16-bit unsigned values	0 to 65,535
int	32-bit unsigned values	0 to 4,294,967,296
long	64-bit unsigned values	0 to 18,446,744,073,709,551,616

While packetC supports an array of bit-level operations, bit is not a scalar type. Instead, bits are within bit-fields that comprise a fully padded basic scalar type as discussed in Chapter 8 and shown in Chapter 19 descriptor data type examples.

Examples of variable declarations are shown below:

```
int    myIpAddr;
byte   count;
short  srcPort;
long   bigCounter;
```

Literals

Four categories of literals are present in packetC, namely integral, network, string, and character literals. Each of these plays an important role in packetC and they have some interesting variations from their representations in C that should be studied. Integral type literals do not differ from C99, but rather clarify their representation in packetC to ensure clear understanding for C programmers where integral type literal syntax varies on some platforms. In the case of network literals, these are new to packetC, yet very familiar to those working in networking. String and character literals follow C99, however, these involve escape sequences that can differ from one platform to another. Furthermore, as will be discussed later, a string literal can be leveraged by the compiler to provide the size of a byte array at compile time.

Integral value literals can be expressed in binary, hexadecimal and decimal radices.

```
byte b = 0b00000110;    // binary radix
byte h = 0xa5;          // hexadecimal radix
```

```
byte d = 255;            // decimal radix
```

Network literals, new with packetC, allow the user to specify an integer as a *dotted address* (or *dotted quad address*) to indicate an IPv4 32-bit address or network mask.

```
int  myInt = 162.150.1.1;
int  myMask = 255.255.255.0;
```

String literals are defined within double quotes. A string can be assigned to an array of **byte**, which must have appropriate space to receive the accompanying sequence of characters.

```
byte myStr[8] = "a string";       // Not null terminated
byte ntStr[9] = "a string\x00";   // null-terminated
```

Standard escape sequences are also supported within string literals and character literals.

\n   New line
\r   Carriage return
\ddd   ASCII character in decimal (ddd range 0 to 255)
\xhh   ASCII character in hexadecimal (hh range 0x00 to 0xFF)

Character literals are surrounded by a single quote assigned to a byte variable. This may include printable ASCII values enclosed in the quote or unprintable values introduced using one of the variations on escape sequences.

```
byte myChar = 'a';               // assign lowercase letter A
byte singleQuoteChar = '\'';     // assign quote character
byte alert = '\a';               // assign alert character
byte nullTerm = '\x00';          // assign to hex 0x00
byte terminator = '\000';        // assign to decimal 0
```

Integral Type Literals

In packetC, integral type literals can have values expressed in binary, hexadecimal, and decimal radices. The default radix is decimal. Radices are indicated for binary and hexadecimal literals by leading characters '0b' and '0x' respectively.

```
byte b = 0b00000110;      // binary radix
byte h = 0xa5;            // hexadecimal radix
byte d = 255;             // decimal radix
```

In addition to the prefix notation identified above, for byte, short, and long a decimal literal can use a postfix notation modifier. By default, a literal will be of type int; however, with the 'b', 's', or 'l' following, a literal may be used to indicate byte, short, or long, respectively. Uppercase 'B', 'S', and 'L' may be used as well.

```
byte b = ~0b;            // byte literal using negation
byte b = ~(byte)0;       // byte literal as above using casting
short s = 12s;           // short literal
long l = 255l;           // long literal
long l1 = (1L << 33);    // ensure all bits preserved
const long l2 = (7L << 7);  // 64-bit constant with lower 3 bits set, 7 bits shifted
```

Integral type literals will appear in a variety of forms given the numerous representations based upon leading prefixes as well as postfix magnitude indicators interleaved with casting and other packetC operators. The key to packetC is no ambiguity in the meaning of any represented code for predictability and simplified audit to ensure secure code. Wherever possible, it is suggested that any literals leverage postfix notation when their value is possibly unclear. One aspect important to remember is packetC will always pad literals as they are cast to larger data types with zeros in the most significant bits, just as you would expect. Furthermore, packetC requires strict typing ensuring that compilers will highlight type violations.

```
short s = 12b;          // error due to strict typing as type is short and literal is byte
short s = (short) 12b   // byte properly cast back to short literal, not recommended
long l = 4096;          // ambiguous declaration as 4096 presumed int, legal but not recommended
byte b = 1050;          // error - literal value greater than container
int i = 4096 + (int) 17s; // legal - integral value literals presumed int, short literal cast.
```

The most important advice with packetC integral type literals is to think about future readers of code with an eye for removing any ambiguity in your meaning about the value a literal represents.

Network Literals

Network literals, new with packetC, allow the user to specify an integer as a *dotted address* (or *dotted quad address*) to indicate an IPv4 32-bit address or network mask. Such a literal consists of 4 individual integer values (ranging from 0 to 255), separated by dots ('.'). packetC associates such a value with the 4-byte *int* data type, associating the literal's leftmost individual value with the most-significant integer byte, the rightmost individual literal value with an integer's least significant byte, and so forth.

```
int  myInt  = 162.150.1.1;   // 162 is stored in myInt's most significant byte
int  myInt  = 192.168.0.1;   // 192 is stored in myInt's most significant byte

// Error
int addr  = 256.150.5.1;     // ERROR: Value 256 too large for byte (255 max)
short s1  = 163.98.1.1;      // ERROR: dotted quad form is only allowed for int
```

In networking, the use of IP addresses is at the heart of managing almost any device or programming networking applications. As use migrates from beyond a single device into a network, the notion of ranges of addresses becomes critical. IP network protocol routing manages groups of addresses that share a common high-order portion of the address as subnets to simplify routing tables. The migration to networking routing decisions based upon portions of the address was introduced with Classless Inter-Domain Routing (CIDR) blocks leading to what many see as the requirement of entering an IP address and network mask into systems. As packetC applications often include routing features, the ease of interacting with CIDR blocks and masks becomes critical to simplifying the developer's application.

When performing simple network masks, such as those related to class A, class B, and class C (e.g., /8, /16, /24) networks, the role of network literals isn't as pronounced.

```
int  myCIDR  =  255.0.0.0;     // A class A /8 Network Mask Using packetC Network Literal
int  myCIDR  =  0xff000000;    // A class A /8 Network Mask Using Integral Value Literal
```

When performing complex network masks, the benefit of packetC network literals becomes clear.

```
int  myCIDR  =  255.255.224.0;  // A /19 Network Mask Using packetC Network Literal
int  myCIDR  =  0xfffffe000;    // A /19 Network Mask Using Integral Value Literal
```

```
int  myCIDR = 0b11111111111111111110000000000000;
int  myHost = 0.0.31.255;       // The Host Within A /19 Network Mask Using
                                // packetC Network Literal
int  myHost = 0x00001fff;       // A /19 Network Mask Using Integral Value Literal
int  myHost = 0b00000000000000000001111111111111;
int  myHost = 0.0.0.255;        // Simple /8 Host Mask
```

As network headers are often being constructed or manipulated in packetC, the goal of network literals is to provide as many tools as possible to the developer, not only to simplify construction but also to provide representations that aid in removing ambiguity from the meaning of an assignment. For example, if you read code, assigning an integer a value of 0xc0a80001 doesn't jump out at you as clearly that this is hard-coding an upstream routing IP address of 192.168.0.1 into the application.

String Literals

In packetC the notion of a character and a string do not have their own data types. They do, however, play a central role to the language and string literals are key to data initialization, assignment, and evaluation. Further reading will show that single characters declare one byte whereas strings are arrays of bytes.

String literals can be defined within double quotes and can be assigned to an array of **byte**, which must have appropriate space to receive the accompanying sequence of characters. It is a fatal error to attempt to assign a string to a **byte** array that has insufficient space to accommodate the string. A byte array without a dimension specified will be assigned the magnitude of the string literal at compile time.

```
byte myStr[8]  = "a string";           // a simple string literal
byte myStr[]   = "a string";           // string literal specifies magnitude of 8 for myStr

// Error
byte badStr[7] = "a string";           // Insufficient space for string
```

Unlike C, packetC never automatically inserts a *null terminator* (byte containing the decimal value zero) at the end of a string nor does it expect that the size of the variable must have an extra byte present for a null. Null values in network data are perfectly valid. Evaluations don't necessarily stop when evaluating strings when a null is found in either data element. Later chapters will address packetC *searchset* data types and their interaction null termination. Furthermore, two byte arrays, strings, can be directly evaluated without the use of a function call using standard C equality operators, whether null values are present or not. Users can embed null terminators inside strings by using escaped sequences. In packetC, a null value may be inserted anywhere within the literal and there may be more than one null value.

```
byte myStr[8]  = "a string";           // not a null-terminated string
byte ntStr[9]  = "a string\x00";       // null-terminated string
byte enStr[10] = "embed\0x00null";     // embedded null terminator followed by word null
```

In addition to the representations for null shown above, two pre-defined string literals related to null are defined in packetC and are found in *cloudshield.ph*.

```
const byte NULL_STOP[1]  = "\x00";
const byte NULL_REGEX[4] = ".*?\x00";
```

Byte arrays with a single dimension or multiple dimensions can accept string literal assignments. A packetC compiler may impose an implementation-defined maximum length for string literals.

```
// 2D array of string literals
byte      twoD[2][3]      = {"owl", "cat"};

// 2D array of string literals imported from file
const byte twoD[50][80]    = {
#include "words.px"
};
```

In the character literals section, a full set of packetC escape characters are shown which can also appear within string literals by using the backslash character as an escape character. For example, a double quote character in a string is represented by the two-character escape sequence, \". Similarly, the \x before two digits in the 0-9A-F range is an escape character representation for a hexadecimal value not to be confused with the integral value literal representation of 0x00 form. String literals can include any combination of both predefined escape sequences, such as \f, and numeric escape sequences, such as \x07, in a single string literal.

```
byte myStr[8]    = "a string";           // not a null-terminated string
byte ntStr[9]    = "a string\x00";        // null-terminated string
byte dQuote[16] = "a double quote:\"";   // contains escaped double quote
byte aStr[12]    = "alert\ainside";       // predefined escape '\a'
byte enStr[10]   = "embed\0x00null";      // embedded null terminator
byte twoD[2][3] = {"owl", "cat"};        // 2D array of string literals
byte third[9]    = "my string";           // a simple string literal assignment
// collection of strings with mix of literals and variables
byte many[4][9] = { "just some", " of ", third, " values." };
```

A string literal cannot cross multiple text lines unless a continuation character ('\') appears as the final character on a line to be continued. When string literals are continued in this fashion, neither the continuation character nor the newline character following it is present in the string.

```
byte goodContinueStr[64] = "abc\
def";                           // string is stored s "abcdef"

// Error
byte badContinueStr[64] = "abc
def";                           // no closing quote or continue character
```

When a single-dimension byte array is initialized by a string literal with an unsized dimension, it receives the size of the literal string (without any automatic null termination). An array with multiple unsized dimensions can have its sizes defined by a compound initialization clause that includes string assignments but the strings must be the same size if the most rapidly varying dimension is defined in this way.

```
byte unsized[] = "str determines size";  // array of 19 bytes
byte good[][] = {"owl", "cat"};          // array is [2][3]

// Error
byte bad[][] = {"bird", "owl"};          // array[2][?] inconsistent sizes
```

Character Literals

Many aspects of character literals have been previewed in the string literals shown. However, a deeper dive into characters is revealing. As stated earlier, packetC does not have a character data type per se, but rather utilizes the basic scalar data type byte for storage of characters. As all values are unsigned, this bears no real impact in packetC as the equivalent of *typdef byte char;* would introduce char as a data type for a developer, although not recommended for purposes of clarity in code as packets are always collections of bytes, even if they store characters or strings.

A solitary ASCII character, surrounded by single quotes can be assigned to a byte variable and can be used anywhere that a byte numeric value could be. The character values specified by the single quote form and the string values specified by the double quote form can both use the two-character and four-character escape sequences described below. All the escape sequences, including those for non-printing characters and those that use hexadecimal or decimal values, begin with the backslash character.

- \a: Alert

- \b: Backspace

- \f: Form feed

- \n: New line

- \r: Carriage return

- \t: Horizontal tab

- \v: Vertical tab

- \':   Single quotation mark

- \":   Double quotation mark

- \\:   Backslash

- \ddd: ASCII character in decimal (ddd range 0 to 255)

- \xhh: ASCII character in hexadecimal (hh range 0x00 to 0xFF)

```
// Example
byte myChar         = 'a';
byte singleQuoteChar = '\'';           // assign quote character
byte alert = '\a';                     // assign alert character
// Hex and decimal numeric values are legal
byte nullTerm    = '\x00';             // assign to hex 0x00
byte terminator = '\000';             // assign to decimal 0
```

For a complete listing of ASCII values and the associated escape sequences and hexadecimal or decimal values that will be assigned to a character based upon using a particular escape sequence, refer to the ASCII reference chart found in the references chapter.

Because a character literal is interchangeable with a numeric literal that would fit into a byte variable, it can be used with the same operators that are legal for an integer literal.

```
byte myChar = '\t' + 1;  // valid, not clear that a TAB (0x09) becomes a NEW LINE (0x0A)
myChar += 'A';           // useful if it's clear the previous value in character offset from 'A'
if( '\t' >= 9 ) {…}      // fairly confusing meaning
```

```
if( (myChar >= 'A') && (myChar <= 'Z') ) {…}     // makes sense as it defines
                                                 // a range of ASCII chars
```

While this can lead to some interesting examples, it should be used only where it is removing ambiguity from what is being declared.

Network Byte Order

All values in packetC are stored in network byte order, which follows a big endian byte-allocation. Additionally, packetC bits are stored in a little-endian bit-allocation order. This matches the ordering of bytes and bits with how packets are represented in IP and Ethernet networks. The packetC compiler and/or execution environment will accommodate adjustments to ensure this for a packetC programmer even if the underlying system does not natively support network byte order computation or packet delivery.

Unlike C, in packetC the exact number of bytes allocated and the binary bit representation of an integer is consistent across all target platforms. This ensures that basic scalar types are consistent across all platforms. This also means that functionality related to adapting to platform representations is unnecessary in packetC. The compiler understands the address and alignment when performing type casting based upon strict rules. Byte level unions and bit level access all follow network byte ordering as shown below in Figure 5-1 for the integer *maxRateLimit*.

32	33	34	35
00000000	00000000	11111101	11101000

```
int maxRateLimit = 65000;
```

Figure 5-1. Byte and bit alignment of variable maxRateLimit

While the C programmers rarely are concerned about the exact binary representation of data, in networking and packetC this is an item of tremendous interest since it affects everything in the data plane. This applies both at the bit and byte level as well as the overall packing and allocation of structures and higher order data sets in packetC. Without this foundation, much of what packetC addresses may be misunderstood by traditional C programmers not comfortable with embedded systems.

Throughout packetC, a lot of focus is applied to bit and byte level representation as well as working with this through bitfields. No matter which platform you are on, the conversion between character or string literals and integral value and network literals will always be consistent. Furthermore, bit-level masking and access when moving literals into bit-fields found within structures will always map to the big-endian representation shown above. This is very useful when performing simple forms of conversion such as that for upper- and lower-case ASCII characters which can be swapped from 'A' to 'a' by the manipulation of a simple bit with no concern for the bit level representation in packetC since it will always be consistent.

```
byte toUpperCase (byte inChar)
{
   // Value 0xdf is 0b11011111 where zero's position is being toggled.
   if( (inChar >= 'a') && (inChar <= 'z') )
     return (inChar & 0xdf);
   else
```

```
        return inChar;
};

byte toLowerCase (byte inChar)
{
    // Value 0x20 is 0b00100000 where one's position is being toggled.
    if( (inChar >= 'A') && (inChar <= 'Z') )
        return (inChar | 0x20);
    else
        return inChar;
};
```

Unsupported Types

packetC does not support the following data types:

- Boolean

- Floating Point

- Pointer

- Register

While Boolean is not a native type within packetC, a typedef for Boolean is provided, *typdef int bool*, providing similar functionality. In addition, declarations for *true* and *false* are also provided in *cloudshield.ph*.

While floating point data may need to be processed, floating point is not supported in packetC. Libraries can be implemented to add relevant functionality for the limited floating-point processing required in networking.

There is no equivalent to a pointer in packetC as a data type. Developers looking for similar functionality for building dynamic linkages should refer to sections on *references* in packetC for more information on those forms of handles used with data sets.

The register data type is redundant in packetC as local variables within packet scope are expected to implement the underlying execution platform as closely as possible to a register due to the implied data plane performance expectations.

Language Reference

CHAPTER 6

■ ■ ■

Data Initialization and Mathematical Expressions

Data Initialization, Expressions, and Operators

Many questions start to appear when coding moves from defining a few variables into actually doing something. For example, understanding the role and rules of initializing variables with regard to compile time and run-time instantiation is crucial. Constants and their initialization expressions require values which can be determined at compile time, not run time. In packetC, operators follow what you would expect from C99, although there are many special data types that interact in a few interesting ways with the standard operators.

Variable and Constant Declarations

In the previous chapter, basic variable types were presented along with examples of declarations. In short, packetC follows C99 guidelines for variable and constant declarations when they do not also include initialization. When they include initialization, several rules that packetC imposes come into play that may constrain behavior that is otherwise C99 compliant. This chapter highlights initialization details for both simple and complex declarations.

In packetC, variable declarations always include an explicit data type for the variable; there is no default type and all types are unsigned. Variable declarations can name an array and, optionally, specify some variable characteristics. However, variable declarations never act as *de facto* type declarations, e.g., by declaring array dimensions.

Examples of basic variable declarations are shown below:

```
int    myIpAddr;
byte   count;
short  srcPort = 0xbeef;
long   bigCounter;

byte   myArray[59];
int    myBigMatrix[10000][20];
```

Examples of simple constant declarations are shown below:

```
const int   MY_IP_ADDRESS = 192.168.1.1;
const byte  COUNT = 9999;
```

```
const short HTTP_PORT = 80;
const long  BIG_NUMBER = 89123123123;
```

In packetC, if an initialization value is not provided, packetC initializes all values to zero whether the data type is a simple or complex type.

```
byte myFunction ()
{
   byte  count;
   count++;
   return count;    // Will always return 1
}
```

Variable declarations can appear in declarations that declare a type and in declarations that use types that have already been declared.

```
// declares variable 'myStructVar', as well as type struct MyStruct.
struct MyStruct { int x; int y; } myStructVar;
```

Throughout this chapter and throughout the rest of this book, varied examples of complex variable declarations are presented. Following C99 constructs for declarations falls in line with packetC.

Variable and Constant Initialization

In programming, it is common practice to initialize variables where they are declared and often without much consideration. In packetC, with inherent parallel processing and performance in mind, variable initialization plays an important role but varies in a few ways from traditional C. In packetC, the method of initialization as well as the impact on performance can be an important consideration. Most important with regard to initialization is whether a variable is declared with the constant qualifier or not. Constants are initialized once whereas variables may be initialized repeatedly at runtime. Additionally, constants must be initialized when declared whereas variables may be initialized in a select subset of cases when declared.

Constants must be assigned initial values containing only expressions that are constructed entirely of constants or literals. Constants cannot be initialized at run time nor can they contain any run-time evaluated components in their initialization expression. Variables do not need to be initialized at declaration, however, a default value of zero may be presumed in packetC. Variables may be initialized at declaration although the rules for constant expressions apply. Variable initializations containing a runtime expression must be done in a separate assignment from the declaration.

The impact of initialization differs when initializing values for variables and constants and based upon the scope. In packetC, constants are initialized once at the start of execution of an application. Global variables follow the same rules as constants with regard to initialization done within declarations. Packet and block scope variables are initialized each time the block of code is entered. For *main()*, this means at the start of each packet beginning processing in a context.

The principal characteristics of packetC variable initialization are:

- A constant's value must be initialized at time of declaration.

- Constant initialization values must be compile-time constant expressions.

- Constants will be initialized once at application start.

- Variables may be initialized in the declaration as long as they consist entirely of constant expressions.

- Variables must be initialized using an assignment separate from the declaration if it consists of any expression that must be determined at run time.

- Variables in packet and block scope will be initialized upon each time the packet or block scope is entered.

- Variables in global scope are initialized once at the start of the application.

- Nested structures, nested unions, and multidimensional arrays are initialized with *nested literals* (see glossary and sections on arrays, structures, and unions).

- C99-style *compound literals* (typecast, anonymous, complex objects that can appear outside of declaration initialization) are not supported.

The following example shows many of the initialization methods listed above.

```
packet  module  initializing_variables;

// Global Variable and Constant Initializations
int     totalPacketCount_;                  // packetC Default Initialization Value Always = 0
int     shortestPacket_ = 1500;             // Initialize to 1500
const int       MINIMUM_PACKET_SIZE = 64;   // Create a Constant with Integer Type = 64

#define SMALL_PACKET_SIZE 64        /* This is a pre-processor directive, not a constant */

struct InnerS { int x; int y;};     // packetC Does Not Require Typedefs
struct OuterS { int a; InnerS s; int b;};
OuterS myStruct = { 5, {8,9}, 6};   // Complex Global Nested Literal Once At Application Start
int contextCounter_[99] = {0#99};   // Initialize All Elements To 0 using Repetition Quantifier

// Simple Function To Demonstrate Block Scope
int addToInteger( int x )
{
   const int ANSWER = 42;        // Block Scope Constant Initialized
   int y = 4;                    // Initializes Block Scope Variable y to 4 On Each Entry
   y++;                          // Will Always Be 5, Doesn't Maintain On Re-Entrance
   return (x+y);                 // Always x + 5
}

// Packet Scope main() Example For Variable Initialization

void main ($PACKET pkt, $PIB pib , $SYS sys)
{
        int ContextCounter = 99;    // Packet Scope Variable Initialized On Each Packet
        const int MAX_CONTEXT = 96; // Packet Scope Constant Initialized At Program Start

        int myContext;              // Variable with ...
        myContext = sys.context;    //   Runtime Initialization.

        int x[2][3] = { {1,2,3}, {4,5,6}};   // Nested Literal, Initialized On
                                             // Entrance of main()

        … code here …
```

```
            // always forward all packets
            pib.action = FORWARD_PACKET;
}
```

In the above code example, only valid cases are shown. The examples below are illegal, especially as run-time calculated elements are introduced in various combinations. An example of such a case often considered in complex initializations is using functions to initialize variables or leveraging compound literals as a replacement of a parameter. Some problematic examples are shown below.

```
int funValue = random();  // ERROR - Initializing With A Function Call.

int a=5;
int b=6;
int c = a + b;        // ERROR - Cannot initialize c based upon a and b.  If a and b
                      // were constants then it is valid or if split out int c; from c = a + b;

int myFunc ( OuterS aStruct ) {…}
myInt = myFunc( (OuterS) {1, {2,3}, 4} );   // ERROR - Compound Literal
```

In C, storage allocation for variables depends on their type. In packetC, the *const* qualifier embodies the elements of C's *static* and *const* qualifiers. In C, *static* variables are allocated once during the life of the program and all references always use the originally-allocated variable's memory. A *const* qualified variable in C ensures that a variable cannot be modified once it is initialized. In packetC, variables with the *const* qualifier embody the aspects of both *static* and *const* from C. One packetC parallel processing deviation from C, however, is *const* variables in packet or block scope may have a unique memory location that exists for each context. As *const* variables are not modifiable and physical addresses are not accessible, a packetC programmer will not able to discern when this is the case.

Compile-time constant initialization values avoids run-time calculation errors, such as overflow or divide by zero, and promotes higher performance applications by removing recalculating initialization values each time it is entered. The selection and use of constants versus variables and impact on initialization by scoping introduces a higher sense of importance of variable initialization in packetC than other languages such as C. In packetC, programs will often see greater performance and security benefits from better planning on data elements than seen from crafty code logic.

Classic C Expressions and Operators

packetC inherits many of its operators from C99. Because operator precedence is particularly important in a language with many operators, the sections on operators are organized according to precedence. Operators with higher precedence are discussed first. General remarks about expressions precede the discussion of individual operators.

Operators

In packetC, there is a collection of operators very similar to C, a disjoint set: some operators from C have not been carried forward while a few others have been introduced. In addition, there is a collection of methods that operate on complex data types that may seem like operators. As noted below, however, they are evaluated differently from operator rules of precedence and associativity.

The following lexical elements represent the operators in packetC:

- '+', '-', '*', '/', '%' (addition, subtraction, multiplication, divide, remainder);

- '==','!= ','> ','>= ','< ','<= ' (equal, not equal, greater than, greater than or equal,less than, less than or equal: equality and relational operators);

- '(')', '[']', '.', '++', '- -' (forced precedence/function call arguments, array subscripting, structure or union field/member selection, postfix-increment, postfix-decrement);

- '++', '—', sizeof, lock, unlock, offset, packet_offset, ref, deref (pre-increment, pre-decrement, size of structure, lock semaphore, unlock semaphore, offset from structure start, offset from packet start, reference a database or searchset, dereference a reference to a database or searchset);

- '~', '<<', ">>', '&', '∧', '|' (bitwise: not, shift left and right, and, exclusive or, (inclusive) or);

- '!', '&&', '||' (logical not, and, or);

- '=', '+=', '-=', '*=', "/=', '%=', '<<=', '>>=', '&=', '∧=', '|=' (assignment operators: simple and compound assignment operators for the corresponding operations above).

The following table shows both C and packetC operators along with their precedence and associativity. The operators at the top of the table have the higher order precedence and will be evaluated in an expression prior to any operators of lower precedence. Operators of equal precedence, shown in the same table cell, are evaluated according to their associativity, which may be either left-to-right or right-to-left and is highlighted in the table below.

Table 6-1. *packetC Operator Precedence and Associativity*

Precedence	Operator(s)	Associativity
highest	**()** *as parens*	left- to-right
	() *as function call (arguments)*, **[]** *indexing*, **.** *field/member/container selection* **++** *postfix increment, -- postfix decrement* **ref** **Deref**	left-to-right
	++ *prefix increment,* **--** *prefix decrement* **!** *logical NOT* **~** *bitwise NOT* *(typeName) typecast* sizeof **offset** **packet_offset** **lock** **unlock**	right-to-left
	*, /, %	left- to-right
	+, -	left- to-right
	<<, >>	left- to-right
	<, <=, >, >=	left- to-right
	==, != **$= null-terminated equality**	left- to-right
	& bitwise AND	left- to-right
	^ bitwise XOR (exclusive OR)	left- to-right
	| bitwise OR (inclusive OR)	left- to-right
	&& logical AND	left- to-right
	|| logical OR	left- to-right
lowest	=, +=, -=, *=, /=, %=, <<=, >>=, &=, ^=, |=, #=	right-to-left

packetC provides a set of *built-in methods* to manipulate its aggregate data type extensions: databases, searchsets, and the packet array. packetC does not offer general, object-oriented functionality, although its built-in methods have the syntactic appearance of object-oriented methods:

```
variableName '.'methodName '('argList ')'
```

Instead, these built-in methods combine familiar object-oriented method syntax with integration into the operator precedence parsing system (they are parsed as postfix operators). However, unlike classic C operators, packetC built-in methods are not associative and can return a void result.

Table 6-2. packetC Built-in Methods with Result and Operand Type

Built-in method	Result type	Operand type(s)
*databaseId[idx].***delete**()	Void	n/a
*databaseId[idx].***insert**(*arg1*)	Int	record or structure
*databaseId[idx].***match**(*arg1*)	Int	record or structure
*databaseId[idx].***match**(*arg1, arg2*)	Int	record or structure; structure
*packetId[idx].***delete**(*arg1*)	Void	integer
*packetId[idx].***insert**(*arg1*)	Void	integer
*packetId[idx].***insert**(*arg1, arg2*)	Void	integer; byte array/slice
*packetId.***replicate**()	Void	n/a
*packetId.***requeue**()	Void	n/a
*searchsetId.***find**(*arg1*)	SearchResult Struct	packet, integer or array/slice
*searchsetId.***match**(*arg1*)	SearchResult Struct	packet, integer or array/slice

Operator precedence does not come into play with packetC built-in methods as operands are evaluated with the method prior to the result being available within a larger expression.

Associativity

When multiple operators are present in an expression without the presence of parentheses to denote the order of evaluation, the precedence and associativity of operators dictates the order of evaluation of the expression. Operators of a higher precedence are evaluated first, then for operators of the same precedence associativity dictates the order of evaluation of the operators. The associativity of operators may be left-associative or right-associative in packetC which are denoted by left-to-right or right-to left in the operator table above. The associativity of two equal-precedence operators is important as different results may occur if evaluated in the opposite order. Consider what would occur if the following expression were evaluated in opposite associative directions:

```
x = 10 / 5 * 2;
```

In packetC, as in C, multiplication and division are left-to-right associative operators, so the expression divides 10 by 5 resulting in a value of 2 that is then multiplied by 2 to equal 4 being assigned to x. If the same expression were evaluated right-to-left, 5 would be multiplied by 2 resulting in 10 which would be the denominator under a numerator of 10 which would result in a value of 1 being assigned to x. By simply changing the associativity of the operators of equal precedence the results change.

While left-to-right associative operators make up the bulk of packetC operators, right-to-left operators play a critical role and it is important to review where they come into play. The most common right-to-left examples in packetC are assignment operators. In general, most expressions will only have one assignment operator so as to not introduce hard-to-interpret coding style. That said, there are many simple cases where multiple variables need to be assigned the same value and right-to-left associativity comes into play.

```
int x;
int a = 1;
int b = 2;
int c = 3;
x = a = b = c;
```

In a left associative evaluation, x would end up with 1, a with 2, and b with 3. In a right associative evaluation, as is standard for assignment operators in packetC, the expression is evaluated from the right most = to the leftmost. In this case, b is assigned c's value of 3, then a = b which is 3, and eventually x = a which is 3. At the end of the right-associative evaluation, all four variables will have a value of 3.

As one can see, the tables are large and contain a lot of detail and nuance regarding operator precedence and associativity. As a result, best practices suggest that one dictate the order of evaluation desired in an expression that is coded through the use of parentheses. This will ensure appropriate evaluation per expectations and not based upon one's ability to remember packetC's operator precedence and associativity table.

```
int x;
x = ( (y/8) * (1024^2) ) >>3;    // Good Form - Dictate Operator Precedence
```

Multiplicative Operators

```
*  /  %
```

These operators are defined for integer types. The * operator yields the product of its operands. The / operator produces the algebraic quotient of its first operand divided by the second; any fractional result is discarded. The % operator produces the remainder from dividing the first operand by the second.

There must be a *system-defined response* for when the / and % operators have a second operand of zero. All multiplicative operators yield unsigned integer results. The packetC language does not have any native floating point representation or data elements.

```
// Example
int  j;
const int k = 3;
j = 12 * k;
```

Additive Operators

+ -

These operators are defined for unsigned integer types. The operator + produces the sum of its operands. The operator – yields the result of subtracting the second operand from the first. In an operation, a – b, if b > a, the resulting bit pattern is the same as that produced by a + (negation of b).

```
// Example
const int i = 5, j = 2, k = i - j;      // k's value is 3

// all packetC integers are unsigned
const byte    b1 = 3,
b2 = 5,
b3 = b1 - b2;
// b3 ==   3 - 5 == 3 + (neg 5) == 0x3 + 0xfb == 0xfe or 254
```

Relational Operators

< > <= >=

The relational operators only apply to operands that are compatible scalar types. When used in a way that a value is needed, such as assignment of a relational operator to an *int*, each of these operations yields a value of 1 if the relation is true and 0 if it is false. The results of applying these operators have the *int* data type.

```
typedef byte MyByte;
byte    b1 = 3, b2 = 5;
short   s1 = 2048, s2 = 2049;
int     result;
MyByte  b3 = 7;

result = b1 > b2;      // legal
result = b3 <= b2;     // legal
result = s1 >= b2;     // ERROR: incompatible operand types
```

Equality Operators

==   != $=

The '=='and '!='operators apply to operands that are either compatible scalar types, byte arrays, or byte array slices.

When used with byte arrays and byte array slices, the operators perform a byte-by-byte comparison. If byte array or byte array slice operands for the '=='and '!='operators have unequal lengths, an implementation shall produce a result of *false* for '=='and *true* for the '!='operation.

The '$='performs a similar, null-terminated comparison on byte arrays and byte array slices (see Chapter 9 on Array Slicing), stopping the comparison when it encounters a null terminator in the left operand, when it has compared all the bytes in two operands of equal length, or when it has compared all *n* bytes of the shorter operand. Implementation can incur performance overhead when these operators are used with array slice ranges that are not compile-time constants.

These operations produce an int result with a value of 1 if the relation is true and a 0 value if it is false.

```
int I, j, result;
i = 2;  j = 4;
enum int Hue {SCARLET, EMERALD, NAVY};
const Hue h1 = SCARLET, h2 = EMERALD;
byte barr[8] = { 0xa, 0xb, 0xc, 0x0, 0xff, 0xff, 0xff, 0xff };

result =  i == j;                      // legal
result =  (h1 != h2);                  // legal
result = ( barr[0:5] == pkt[128:133] );        // compare 6-byte slices
result = ( barr[0:7] $= pkt[64:71] );          // null-terminated comparison

result =  j != h2;                     // ERROR: operands are not compatible types

// Examples showing length issues
result = ( barr[0:5] == pkt[128:129] );        // always false
result = ( barr[0:5] != pkt[128:129] );        // always true
result = ( barr[0:5] $= pkt[128:129] );        // compare 2 bytes
result = ( barr[0:5] $= pkt[128:511] );        // compare 6 bytes
```

When two arguments of different lengths are compared, the search will only proceed to the end of the shortest argument to determine equality.

Assignment Operators

=   *=   /=   %=   +=   -=   <<=   >>=   &=   ^= |=   #=

An assignment operator changes the value of its left operand, which must be an l-value, just like C. As is the case with C99, the assignment operation itself, has a value—the value that is assigned to the left operand. Since packetC does not have a system of type promotions or implicit type coercions, the left and right operands must have *type compatibility* to assign one to the other.

The simple assignment operator can be used with type compatible scalars, array elements, structure and descriptor fields, union members, and entire aggregates. Entire arrays can be assigned to one another via the simple assignment operator if both arrays have identical dimensions and the same base type. Variables with identical structure or union types can be assigned to one another. The section on type casting describes how operands with different types can be cast in a way that allows assignment.

Compound assignment operators, however, are only applicable to compatible integer operands.

Simple Assignment Operator

=

The simple assignment operator works with operands that are integer types, structures, and unions. The left operand's value is replaced by the value of the right operand. The notion of assignment is one that is quite simple and assigning one variable's content to another's or performing a small equation that results in its value being assigned to the left-hand operand doesn't differ from C. What does differ is that in packetC, structures and unions can be assigned to another instance of the same type or an array of bytes of equivalent size. These implement a memory copy intrinsic to the language without the need for a function call found in many other languages.

```
packet module example50;
typedef byte b8[8];
b8 m;
const byte list[10] = "ABCDEABCDE";
int z;

void main ($PACKET pkt, $PIB pib , $SYS sys)
{
        struct MyStruct {
                        int x;
                        int y
                } s1 = { 5, 3 };
        MyStruct s2;

        z  = s2.x + 2; // z equals 7
        s2.x = 12;
        s2 = s1;        // MEMCOPY - s2.x equals 5 and s2.y is 3

        m = (b8) s1;    // MEMCOPY - s1 and m are of equal size in bytes and can be assigned
}
```

For more information on complex data type assignments refer to Chapter 9, "C-Style Data Types." There are legal variations of complex assignment where the contents of one complex data type (array, array slice, structure) may be copied into a similarly sized complex data type.

Compound Assignment Operators

*=   /=   %=   +=   -=   <<=   >>=   &=   ^= |=

The compound assignment operators work with operands that are integer types, namely *byte, short, int,* and *long.* Both operands must be consistent with the binary operator portion of the compound assignment operator (e.g., with the "+" part of "+="). Any compound assignment of the form "left *op=*

right" has the effect of "left = left *op* right." In other words, *a += b;* is the same as *a = a + b;* where the compound assignment operator is broken out around the left operand.

```
int x = 2;
int a = 5;
int b = 4;

x += a;      // x = x + a;  x will be assigned a value of 7 after evaluation.
b >>= x;     // b = b >> x;  b will be shifted right by the number of places
             // defined in x, resulting in a value of 1.
```

The following table highlights the meaning of each compound assignment operator in packetC.

Table 6-3. packetC Compound Assignment Operators

Compound Operator	Equivalent Expressions
*=	a *= b; *evaluates as* a = a * b;
/=	a /= b; *evaluates as* a = a / b;
%=	a %= b; *evaluates as* a = a % b;
+=	a += b; *evaluates as* a = a + b;
–=	a -= b; *evaluates as* a = a - b;
<<=	a <<= b; *evaluates as* a = a << b;
>>=	a >>= b; *evaluates as* a = a >> b;
&=	a &= b; *evaluates as* a = a & b;
^=	a ^= b; *evaluates as* a = a ^ b;
|=	a |= b; *evaluates as* a = a	b;

Compound Repetition Assignment Operator

#=

The compound repetition assignment operator works in a similar way to a *memset()* function call in C; however, it is type safe. When using this operator, all elements of an array are assigned a particular value depicted by the value on the right hand side of the assignment.

The replication assignment operator, #=, works with a

- left-hand-side (LHS) operand that must be an array or array slice

- right-hand-side operand (RHS) that is a scalar value with the left-hand side's base type

The compound repetition assignment operation replicates the RHS operand's value, filling every element of the LHS operand with that value. This operator has right-to-left associativity. The value of a replication assignment operation as an expression is the scalar value of the RHS, not a collection of the replicated values.

```
byte   a[2][6];
byte   b[6], c[8];

a #= 80;                   // Assigns every byte of a to contain a value of 80.
b[0:4] #= c[1];            // Where c[1] is a byte that is assigned to 0 through 4 in b

// Errors
b #= c[0:2];               // ERROR: c[0:2] is not of same type, byte, as elements of b.

int iarray[4],iarrB[4];
iarray #= 5;               // iarray[0:3] = {5,5,5,5} set entire array
iarray[0:1] #= 4;          // iarray[0:3] = {4,4,5,5} set array slice
iarray[0:0] #= 3;          // iarray[0:3] = {3,4,5,5} set single element slice

int iarr2D[2][4], myScalar;
iarrB  =  iarray #= 3;     // iarray and iarrB both = {3,3,3,3}
iarr2D #= iarray #= 7;     // iarr2D = { {7,7,7,7},{7,7,7,7} }
myScalar= iarray #= 5;     // iarray = {5,5,5,5}, myScalar = 5

iarr2D #= iarray;          // ERROR: right-hand-side must be scalar
myScalar #= 4;             // ERROR: left-hand-side not array or slice

byte x[4];                 // Simple array of bytes.
int    y;                  // Simple integer.
x #= 3;                    // x[] = {3,3,3,3}
y = (int) x;               // y = 50,529,027 = 0x03030303
y #= 3;                    // y = 3;
```

The following table highlights the meaning of the compound repetition assignment operator in packetC.

Table 6-4. packetC Compound Repetition Assignment Operator

Compound Operator	Equivalent Expressions
#=	for (i=0; i++; i<=sizeof(a)) a[i]=b[i];

The array assignment using the compound repetition operator implements the equivalent of the type safe *memset()* operation in packetC. As shown in the table above, this works by iterating through every element of *a* assigning it the value of *b* found on the right hand side of the operator. The type of the assigned value must match the element type of the array having its values set. For those areas where one would normally desire a *memset()*, this unique-to-packetC compound operator assignment comes into play.

Increment and Decrement Operators

packetC also supports the pre-increment, pre-decrement, post-increment, and post-decrement operators. As is the case in C99, post-increment and decrement operators first deliver the current value of a variable, then perform the addition or subtraction. Pre-increment or pre-decrement operators alter the value of the variable before delivering it. The example below illustrates the four operations.

```
int j, k = 3;
j = k++;                    // post-increment: j = 3, k = 4
j = k--;                    // post-decrement: j = 4, k = 3
j = --k;                    // pre-decrement:  j = 2, k = 2
j = ++k;                    // pre-increment:  j = 3, k = 3
j++;                        // post-increment: j = 4 (at conclusion)
--j;                        // pre-decrement: j = 3
byte b = 0;
b--;                        // b = 255 or 0xff (see additive operators)
```

Post-Increment and Post-Decrement Operators

++   **--**

The post-increment and post-decrement operators work with integer types. The result of these operators is the value of the operand. Only after that unchanged value is obtained is the operand incremented or decremented.

```
byte ba = 4, bb, bc;
bb = ba++;          // bb = 4
bc = ba;            // bc = 5
```

Prefix Increment and Prefix Decrement Operators

++   **--**

As is the case in C99, these prefix operators first perform an increment or decrement on their integer operand, then deliver its current value.

```
int j, k = 3;
j = --k;                    // pre-decrement: j = 2, k = 2
j = ++k;                    // pre-increment: j = 3, k = 3
byte b = 0xff;
++b;                        // b = 0 (see additive operators)
```

Table 6-5. packetC Operators and Examples

Operator	Name	Example	
++	Auto Increment (prefix)	k=5; ++k + 10;	// Result 16
++	Auto Increment (postfix)	k=5; k++ + 10;	// Result 15
--	Auto Decrement (prefix)	k=5; --k + 10;	// Result 14
--	Auto Decrement (postfix)	k=5; k-- + 10;	// Result 15

Logical AND Operator

&&

The logical AND operator only applies to operands that are compatible integer types. The operation yields a result with the **int** data type, which has a value of 1 if both operands are non-zero and 0 otherwise.

```
byte a = 7;
byte b = 9;;
int x;
if (((a >= 5) && (b < 10)) == true)
   x = 5;
else
   x = 2;
```

The expression above will evaluate to true since both (a >= 5) and (b < 10) are true. If either were false, the equation would be false. Note that while there is no Boolean data type, the values for true and false are defined and should be used for Boolean expressions as shown above. As a result of the conditional expression's evaluation, x will be assigned a value of 5.

Logical OR Operator

||

The logical OR operator only applies to operands that are compatible integer types. The operation yields a result with the **int** data type, which has a value of 1 if either operand is non-zero and 0 otherwise.

```
byte a = 7;
byte b = 9;;
int x;
if (((a >= 5) || (b < 5))==true)
   x = 5;
else
   x = 2;
```

The expression above will evaluate to true since (a >= 5) is true and the logical OR of false due to (b < 5) not being true will still evaluate true. As a result, x will be assigned a value of 5.

Logical and Bitwise NOT Operators (!, ~)

~   !

Both operators can be used with operands of integer type and return values that have the same type as their operand. The logical NOT operator, '!,'returns a zero if its operand is non-zero and a 1 if the operator is zero. The bitwise NOT operator, '~,'returns the one's complement of its operand; if a given bit in the operand is set, the corresponding result bit is zero, otherwise the corresponding bit is set.

```
byte b1 = 5, b2 = 1;
int result = ! ( b1 < b2 );  // result is zero
b2 = ~b1;                     // b2 = 0xfa or 250
b1 = ~0;                      // b1 = 0xff or 255
```

Table 6-6. packetC Expressions and Examples

Expression	Expression Name	Example
a ‖ b	Logical OR	1 if either a or b is not 0, otherwise 0.
a && b	Logical AND	1 if both a and b are not 0, otherwise 0.
!a	Logical NOT	1 if a is 0, 0 if a is not 0.
!a	Bitwise NOT	Each bit of a is changed from 1 to 0, and 0 to 1.

```
e = ((a && b) || (c > d));
```

In the above example, e is set equal to 1 if a and b are non-zero, or if c is greater than d. In all other cases, e is set to 0. In packetC, like C, short-circuit evaluation is performed. In the example above, short-circuit evaluation means that if a and b are non-zero, the c greater than d evaluation is not performed. This may remove some cases where comparisons need to be done for bounds checking on subsequent items in an evaluation where they are not possible given earlier entries in the equation.

Bitwise AND Operator

&

The bitwise AND operator only applies to operands that are compatible integer types, producing a result of the same type as the two operands. If both bits of any corresponding bit pairs of the two operands are set, the corresponding bit in the result is set, otherwise the corresponding result bit is not set.

```
byte   b1 = 0x1f,
b2 = 0x13,
b3;
```

```
b3 = b1 & b2;      // b3 now equals 0x13
```

Bitwise Exclusive OR (XOR) Operator

^

The exclusive OR operator only applies to operands that are compatible integer types, producing a result of the same type as the two operands. If only one of any pair of corresponding bits in the operands is set, the corresponding bit in the result is set, otherwise the corresponding result bit is not set.

```
byte b1 = 0x5, b2 = 0x6, b3;
b3 = b1 ^ b2;      // b3 now equals 0x3
```

Bitwise Inclusive OR Operator

|

The inclusive OR operator only applies to operands that are compatible integer types, producing a result of the same type as the two operands. If either one of any pair of corresponding bits in the operands is set, the corresponding bit in the result is set, otherwise that corresponding result bit is not.

```
byte   b1 = 0x5,
b2 = 0x6,
b3;
b3 = b1 | b2;      // b3 now equals 0x7
```

Bitwise Shift Operator

<<   >>

The shift operators cause an integer argument's contents to be shifted to the left or right by a specified integer amount. Bitwise shifting has the following characteristics:

- Left- or right-shifting by a number of bits that is greater than or equal to the width of the value to be shifted results in the shifted value being replaced by all zeroes.

- When a value, E1, is left-shifted by E2 bits, where E2 is > 0 and < the width of E1 in bits, the result is equivalent to $(E1 * 2^{E2})$.

- When a value, E1, is right-shifted by E2 bits, where E2 is > 0 and < the width of E1 in bits, the result is equivalent to the integral part of the quotient of $(E1 / 2^{E2})$.

```
// Examples
struct IpHeader {
      bits short {
           version     :4;
           headerLen   :4;
           tos         :8;
      } first16;             // collection is named, like any other field
      …
```

```
    } myIpHeader;
byte myVersion;
myVersion = myIpHeader.first16 >> 12;
```

sizeof Operator

sizeof

The **sizeof** operator can be applied to expressions that have scalar or enumeration types but not to bit fields. For either expressions or type names, the operator returns an **int** value that is the size of the operand in bytes. **Byte**, **short**, **int**, and **long** operands return values of 1, 2, 4, and 8 respectively. Arrays return the size of their base type multiplied by their number of elements. Structures and unions return their total size in bytes. The size of a function call as an expression is the size of its return value's data type, with the size of a void function's return value defined as zero bytes. In all cases, sizeof is a compile time evaluation in packetC, which does not support any forms of dynamic allocation that would conflict with this.

```
struct MyStruct
{
    int x;
    int y;
} s;
int size = sizeof (s);                     // size is 8
byte b[3];
size = sizeof (b);                         // size is 3;
const int MY_STRUCT_SIZE = sizeof(MyStruct);   // MY_STRUCT_SIZE of 8.
```

One thing that can appear confusing is sizeof with expressions. The sizeof form with an expression as its operand never triggers the execution of that expression, even when the expression includes increment/decrement operations, function calls, or assignment operators. Thus, both forms of sizeof are always evaluated at compile-time.

```
long value = 4L;                    // value is 4
int playSize;
playSize = sizeof(++value);         // playSize = 8 and value still 4 after evaluation.
```

The behavior of sizeof with packetC extended data types is as follows:

- Descriptors behave like structure types and variables.

- Searchsets, databases, and references are not legal arguments to either form of **sizeof**.

- Array slices (slice range must be compile-time constant) returns element size * elements.

- $PIB, $SYS may only be used as types and behave like structure types returning their size.

- $PACKET may be used as a type where **sizeof($PACKET)** returns the maximum size of a packet for a specific implementation.

- A variable that represents the current packet (e.g., pkt) is not a legal operand for the size-of-expression form, since the size of the current packet cannot be known at compile-time. (packetC provides other mechanisms for finding the current packet's size such as referencing pib.length).

Some examples of using **sizeof** for extended data types are shown below for illustrative purposes.

```
int x = sizeof(pib);       // Will be assigned the number of bytes $PIB structure type contains
int x = sizeof($PACKET);   // Generally a value like 16,384.

int x = sizeof(pkt);       // Error - pkt is variable size and must use pib.length instead.

byte a[50];
int x = sizeof(a);         // Entire array x will be 50
int x = sizeof(a[3]);      // Single element of byte array x will be 1
x = sizeof(a[20:40]);      // Array slice x will be 21

int a[50];
int x = sizeof(a);         // Entire array x will be 200 since each element is 4 bytes
int x = sizeof(a[3]);      // Single element of byte array x will be 4
x = sizeof(a[20:40]);      // Array slice x will be 80 since 20 elements of 4 bytes each
```

Get Field Offset Within Structures

offset

This unary operator takes a single structure or descriptor field as an operand and returns an integer value of type *int* that indicates the offset of that field from the start of the enclosing structure. The value is determined at compile-time treating the result as an integral value literal.

```
struct MyStruct
{
  int x;
  int y;
} s;
int xOffset = offset( s.x );  // offset is 0
int yOffset = offset( s.y );  // offset is 4
```

This applies not only to structure but to descriptors since the structure representation within a descriptor is fully interchangeable with structures. In addition, the portions of a descriptor that make it unique do not change the result of the offset operator. Should you wish to get the offset of a particular descriptor field within a packet based upon the translated descriptor layer offset expression, refer to packet_offset detailed in the chapter covering packet operations.

Imagine the case where you want to do some tricky field conversions and computing the size in bytes of a structure becomes a bit complex and calculating the byte offset of a field within the structure becomes cumbersome. If you are continually modifying the structures, any pre-calculated offsets will become inaccurate as soon as you change the structure.

```
descriptor Ipv4Struct
{
  bits byte { version:4; headerLength:4; } bf;
  bits byte { precedence:3; delay:1; throughput:1; reliability:1; reserved:2; } tos;
  short totalLength;
  short identification;
  bits  short { evil:1; dont:1; more:1; fragmentOffset:13; } fragment;
  byte  ttl;
  byte  protocol;
  short checksum;
  int   sourceAddress;
  int   destinationAddress;
} ipv4 at pib.l30ffset;
typedef byte HeaderType[sizeof(ipv4)];
HeaderType header;                        // An array of bytes equal in size to IPv4 header.
int addresses[2];                         // Holds both sourceAddress and destinationAddress

// The following code shall be within packet scope

header = (HeaderType) ipv4;               // Copies entire IPv4 header into array header.
addresses[0]  = (int) header[offset(ipv4.sourceAddress):offset(ipv4.sourceAddress)+3];
addresses[0]  = (int)
header[offset(ipv4.destinationAddress):offset(ipv4.destinationAddress)+3];
```

The descriptor example above shows the IPv4 header that falls into the category of fairly complex descriptors. Even with changes to the header, the above example performs extraction of the addresses based upon the offset of the source and destination address fields. Given that offset is computed at compile time, the resulting values are treated as literals resulting in a fairly simple set of declarations and expressions that would be equivalent to the following:

```
byte header[20];                          // sizeof(ipv4) evaluates to 20
addresses = (long) header[12:19];         // offset(sourceAddress) evaluates to 12
```

The offset of a bit field within a structure is always the byte offset of the container of the bit field. If the bit field is a byte, it is the offset of the byte, whereas if the bit field is the 61st bit of a 64-bit long the offset will be of the first byte of the long, not the last byte within the long where the bit actually is. As such, offset can be thought of as mapping to that start of the basic scalar type within the structures which has the offset operator applied.

Data Repetition Quantifier

#

The # repetition quantifier is used inside data sets being assigned to arrays as a mechanism to reduce the repetitive listing of values which are the same. This does not cause an action or an operator as this is handled at compile time to expand the data initialization.

```
<count>#<value>
```

Legal repeat count usage consists of a non-zero constant expression, followed by the pound symbol ("#") and then a legal initialization item (as defined by the grammar productions above). The construct's effect is identical to the initialization item appearing as many times as the constant expression specifies.

```
// Initialize the entire 10,000 entry array with the last 9,995 entries = 5
byte b[10000] = { 0, 1, 2, 3, 4, 9995#5 };

// Initialize the entire 10,000 entry array with 5
byte b[10000] = {  10000#5 };

// Initialize the entire 10,000 entry array with 5
byte b[10000] = {  sizeof(b)#5 };
```

Illegal cases shown below:

```
byte b[10000] = {  10000#300 };      // Error – 300 is not of type byte
int b[100] = {  3100#300l };         // Error – 300 is specified as long, not int
int b[100] = {  1000#99 };  // Error – Repetition count makes initialization larger than array
byte myarray[3] = { 0#4, 3#2, 0#5 };  // Error – Repetition count of zero not allowed.
```

The repetition count can also appear within include files providing initialization data as those follow the same rules as the assignments shown above.

Unsupported Operators

- Comma operator (',') and conditional operator ('?')

- Dereference ('*') and address ('&') operators

- Unary + or - (since packetC only supports unsigned integers)

CHAPTER 7

Functions

Function Constructs

Just like C, a packetC *function* is a discrete subprogram that can be invoked from multiple places in the program text and that returns a value (which may be of type **void**). The *function call* or *function enable* can associate a set of values with a corresponding set of variables declared as the function's *parameters*, which act as variables local to the called function. C programmers will find packetC functions to play the same role and operate in a familiar manner. In addition, functions play new roles in packetC in support of parallel processing and scoping for the purposes of data hiding.

As functions are probably the most important aspect of any modern language, considerable time was spent in the design of packetC around how to handle functions. In packetC, functions play similar roles to what they do in C, forming collections of operations into neat bundles that can be reused throughout the program and hopefully across multiple programs. Functions are also used to serve many new roles and some similar but adapted roles such as the means to cross between library and shared library modules. Function form and general use should be quite familiar. Traditional function prototypes are used for predefined functions found in statically linked library modules and new packetC *entry* and *extern* qualifiers are used for providing visibility and access to functions in dynamically linked shared library modules.

Functions often perform a role of combining multiple operations that would be otherwise too complex to recreate out of packetC primitives. Given the focus on code performance within packetC, ensuring stack and calling overhead was minimized was critical in allowing for wide use of functions without negative performance impact. Techniques such as inlining are introduced with packetC specifically for performance benefits.

Additionally, a function provides the benefit of naming an algorithm and introducing order to the cadre of operations being performed in a program. While functions hide complexity, a function should not be so complex that it is difficult to comprehend what is being performed by the function. A well-crafted program will utilize layers of functions, or application programming interfaces (API) to bring together an orderly construction. Through the use of API's, lower level functions perform the simple operations that are referred to by the higher level functions. While not a requirement, strong guidance on simplified functions with clear naming related to purpose is important to maintain secure and auditable code.

Function Declarations and Prototypes

A function declaration consists of specifying the function's return value type, name, optional list of parameters (formal arguments), and a body that consists of local declarations and statements. A function body must include at least one *return statement*. A function declaration in the global section of a shared module may optionally be preceded by the **entry** keyword to indicate that packet modules may call the function as an entry point into the shared module.

A function *prototype* predeclares the function return type, name, and parameter list but omits the function body. Function prototypes facilitate having function invocations appear before function declarations in program text. A packet module that calls an entry point (global function) in a shared module must declare a corresponding function prototype in its own global section, preceded by the **extern** keyword. All function prototypes must match actual function declarations exactly. Any argument type changes or name changes are considered illegal in packetC for security reasons.

Functions cannot be nested (one function declared within another).

In addition to scalars, a function's return type may be any of the following named types: void, array, structure, or union. However, a function cannot return a descriptor, database, or searchset. In addition to scalars, a function formal argument may be any of the following named types: array, structure, or union. However, a formal argument cannot be a descriptor, database, or searchset. These are adhering to the pass-by-value scheme implemented by packetC. A descriptor, however, may be used as an actual argument (i.e., its value is passed) even though it is not used as a formal argument.

Function Construction

The traditional C model for functions is supported in packetC. The ultimate function *main()* represents the start of every packetC program and has a predefined set of arguments that do not change. All other functions are up to the developer to implement and are defined between the start of the module and the declaration of *main()*. No functions may follow main or be defined within any function. Standard and customer developed include files may define function prototypes for those that will be either statically or dynamically linked with the packet module.

```
packet module subExApp;
#include <cloudshield.ph>;
#include <protocols.ph>;

int fastTimes3 (int num)
{
    return ((num<<1) + num);
}
void doubleIt(int x)
{
    x *= 2;
    return;
}
void main($PACKET pkt, $PIB pib, $SYS sys)
{
    int myNum, x;

    myNum = 35;
    x = fastTimes3( myNum );    // Results in x = 105
    doubleIt ( x );             // x unchanged due to pass by value
    doubleIt ( @x );            // x is 210, pass by substitution inline visibility to packet
}
```

Additionally, optimizations for inline compilation and pass-by-substitution (@ in arguments) are added packetC features. The use of @ at the call site denotes that the function can be inlined and the argument can be utilized directly instead of passing it by value. Any manipulation of the parameter within the function will be reflected in the parameter upon return when the pass-by-substitution parameter is used.

Function Invocations

A function invocation, or function call, is a kind of expression and produces a value. As such, it can be used interchangeably with variables or literals. It heralds a control flow change, since common practice implements a function call by transferring control from the invocation (call site) to the code of the function body and then transfers control back to the code that follows the invocation. In practice, functions can also be implemented by *inlining* (described in a section below).

In packetC, a function call consists of the function name, left parenthesis, optional list of *actual arguments*, and right parenthesis. The actual arguments are identifiers separated by commas. If present, the actual arguments in the function call are associated in left-to-right fashion with the corresponding formal arguments of the function declaration (see the section of parameter passing below).

Function Declaration and Function Call Restrictions

packetC's restrictions on functions and function invocations include the following:

- No function recursion

- No variable number of function parameters (formal arguments)

- Descriptors cannot be specified as function formal arguments or function return values

- A function prototype must match a function declaration and call site

- The actual arguments of a call site must agree in type and number with the formal arguments of the called function

packetC does not allow a function to engage in either direct or indirect *recursion*. Therefore, a packetC function neither contains a call to itself nor a call to some other function that starts a call chain that ultimately leads to calling the original function.

Parameter Passing Modes

Function declarations specify a list of parameters, or formal arguments. At the *call site*, the source code location where the function is invoked, a name of the function to call is followed by a parenthesized list of corresponding actual arguments. The types passed to a function must match the formal list of arguments types declared at the function.

```
int myFunc( int j )      // 'j' is a formal argument
{
    return j + 10;
}
...
myInt = myFunc(5);       // the literal '5' is an actual argument
```

packetC parameters can be passed in two modes:

- By value: the value of each actual argument is copied to the corresponding formal argument.

- By substitution: the function being called is inlined; each actual argument accompanied by the "@" symbol is substituted into the inlined function's body to replace each instance of the corresponding formal argument. packetC supports by-substitution parameters that are constants, expressions, and const variables if the called function does not assign values to the corresponding formal argument.

In packetC, the user specifies employing by-substitution at the call site, rather than in the formal argument declaration list. Thus, different call sites can inline and invoke the same function in different ways, using different permutations of by-value and by-substitution arguments as their circumstances warrant.

Inlining

Function *inlining* consists of a compiler or similar tool textually replacing a function enabled in the program text with a copy of the called function's body. This practice involves more than a single copy, since statement labels may need to be altered and additional code may be needed, e.g., to assign actual argument values to formal arguments or to assign the function's return value to a local variable.

Inlining with by-substitution parameters can confer performance advantages because it is not necessary to assign a by-substitution actual argument value to the corresponding formal argument. However, the by-substitution mechanism cannot be used for a given actual argument if it cannot or should not be assigned a value, yet the function to be inlined assigns a value to the corresponding formal argument. When an actual argument is passed by substitution, any assignments to it by the inlined code will overwrite its pre-call contents. Inlining is often necessary to pass packet scope variables to functions without the overhead of a calling stack. The system defined variables pkt, pib, and sys are presumed to always be inlined such that changes made within a function are reflected upon return to the calling function, such as main.

```
int i, j = 3;
int myFunc(int x)
{
    x += 50;
    return x + 1;
}
...
i = myFunc(j);          // after call i = 54, j = 3
i = myFunc(@j);         // after call i = 54, j = 53
i = myFunc(@j+7);       // Error: inline function assigns to the
                        // corresponding formal argument
```

A packetC implementation may only implement inlining to instances in which the call site is not within a function that is, itself, being inlined. When an implementation does not inline a function, it may elect to treat the call-site's by-substitution parameters as by-value parameters. An implementation may issue warning messages when by-substitution parameter passage is not implemented.

This specification does not require or forbid a packetC implementation to support inlining or by-substitution parameter handling when a function call is made from a packet module to a function within a shared or library module. In those cases, the source code for the called function is not necessarily available for inlining, although bytecode for the callee may be available at some point in the compilation process.

For smaller functions where the notion of inline capabilities are desired to minimize the overhead of a stack and function call, refer to the packetC preprocessor which may offer some alternatives.

Function Parameter and Return Types

The following types are legal for function actual arguments:

- *Integer types and enumerated types based on them*

- *Structures and unions*

- *Descriptors*

- *Arrays*

All of the types above are also legal types for function formal arguments, except for descriptors which are structures at a given packet location.

All of the legal types for actual arguments may serve as legal function return values, except for descriptors. In addition, a function that returns no value has a return type declared as **void**.

Function Return Statements

If a function returns a value other than **void**, it is an error for the function to contain no explicit **return** statement. An implementation may optionally issue a warning message for a function that returns **void** but that contains no explicit **return** statement. An implementation is not required to issue warning or error messages for a function that has at least one explicit **return** statement but that lacks **return** statements for every possible control-flow path, although it may do so.

When control flow reaches the end of a function without encountering a **return** statement, the presence of an *implicit return statement* is assumed. If a non-void function effects an implicit return, its return value is undefined.

```
int myFunc(int x)
    {
    x += 50;
    } // error: non-void function contains no return statement

void myFunc(int x)
{
        x += 50;
} // optional warning for implicit return from void function

int myFunc(int x)
    {
        if ( x > 50 ) {
                    return x + 1;
                }
    } // optional warning for implicit return path from non-void function
```

Function Calls

```
functionName ( argumentOne, argumentTwo, argumentThree )
```

A function call consists of the function's name followed by a balanced pair of parentheses containing a list of actual arguments separated by commas within the parentheses. The number of arguments (or lack of arguments) and their types must exactly match the number of arguments that appear in this function's declaration. Unlike C, packetC does not support variable numbers of function parameters and, as such, the list of parameters at a functions call site must always match those declared. In addition, the type of each argument passed must match the type specified in the function's declaration.

```
int a;                      // global variable a
int triad(int a, int b, int c); // function prototype
. . .
int triad(int a, int b, int c)  // function declaration
{
 return (a + b + c);
}
...
a = triad( 9, 50, 700 );        // function call
```

The example above shows a simple function call with three integer literals passed to the function *triad*. In the example, a function prototype is shown as well as the actual function's declaration. In addition, the return value, an integer, demonstrates the notion of block scope where argument *a* is local to *triad* while global variable *a* is assigned the return value and not affected or utilized within triad.

CHAPTER 8

■ ■ ■

packetC Data Type Fundamentals

When it comes to working with data types and changing some rules from C99, packetC has done its best to treat types consistently and yet advance language practice by refining how packet data is defined and manipulated. As packet processing is all about analyzing byte streams of packet data into protocol and payload information, appropriate, domain-specific data types are central to packetC. Informally, complex data types are those other than the basic scalar types such as byte, short, int, and long. packetC complex types include traditional C types such as enumerations, arrays, structures, unions, and our extended types such as databases, records, searchsets, descriptors, and references, which are built on familiar type principles and practices.

packetC's type model, typecasting restrictions, and data storage rules reflect the practical requirements of the packet processing application domain. Thus, packetC's approach to these matters differs significantly from ANSI C, C99, and other C language variants. The key differences can be summarized as follow:

- **Typecasting and conversions**. packetC generally tightens type conversion rules to increase run-time reliability in an unforgiving real-time domain. However, it does allow typecasting of aggregate types in some situations to facilitate moving data between the packet-as-byte-array and structures (e.g., to insert or copy headers).

- **Storage organization**. packetC emphasizes portability more than C variants typically do. Therefore, integer type sizes and bitfield layout are strictly prescribed to avoid implementation differences that would reduce portability.

- **New data types**. packetC introduces extended data types to support fundamental packet processing functionality (descriptors for headers, masked databases for flow matching, searchsets for payload searching). It also supplies a reference data type to support chaining database and searchset actions.

This chapter presents an informal description of the packetC type model and basic type mechanics, such as type conversions and typecasting. The following chapter treats packetC variants of familiar C types, such as arrays with array slices and structures with packetC bitfield 'containers.' Subsequent chapters present the extended data types: databases, searchsets, references, and descriptors.

Data Type Fundamentals

Data *type* specifies the definitive aspects of a datum: how it is to be stored, how the bit patterns associated with it are to be interpreted, what values it may legitimately contain, and what operations can be performed on it. packetC is a strongly typed language with static type-checking. Thus, every variable's type must be explicitly declared in source code and the viability of operand types for any given operation is determinable at compile-time. packetC has storage-based types, abstracted types, and rule-based types.

Within C99, there are three basic types defined, however, they are significantly different than packetC. Within C99, the three types are object types, function types, and incomplete types. Object types in C99 correspond to packetC storage-based types. The function types in C99 are only defined as a secondary 'derived declaratory type' derived from function return value type. The incomplete types (basically, un-sized arrays) have no equivalent in packetC due to strict compile time memory allocation.

packetC Fundamental Types

Storage-based types define objects associated with storage units whose size and organization are prescribed by the packetC Specification. This includes scalars, integer arrays, enumeration variables, structures, and unions.

- Storage-based Types
  - Scalars
    - integers (byte, short, int, long)
    - enums
  - Aggregates
    - structures
    - unions
    - descriptors
    - array
    - function

Abstracted types define objects associated with values in storage units that have sizes and organization that are implementation-specific. Some storage unit information for abstracted types is available through relevant operators, such as 'sizeof' and 'offset.' Databases, records, and references are the current packetC abstracted types. Masked types are a more complex variety of abstracted types. Masked types define objects that a packetC compiler constructs by replicating a user-specified structure type, T, into a new structure type, T2, which consists of two fields, ''data'' and ''mask,'' which are each of type T. Because of alignment and padding requirements, sizeof(T2) may not equal (2 * sizeof(T)).

- Abstracted Types
  - Masked Types
    - records
    - databases
  - References

Rule-based types define rules for program behavior that may or may not be associated with storage units in the classic sense. The practical expectation is that such rules may be compiled into finite state machines that do not associate a particular storage location with an individual rule. For example, a regex searchset might be compiled into a deterministic finite automata to run on a specialized processor. A compliant implementation may choose to implement a rule-based type with classic storage-based techniques, i.e., a system can implement match operations on a string searchset using ordinary memory and comparison operations. packetC searchsets are currently packetC's only rule-based type.

- Rule-based Types
  - Search Sets
    - regex searchsets
    - string searchsets

Type Compatibility, Conversions, and Casts

One variable, structure field, or array element can be assigned to another if their types are *compatible*. packetC has some similarities with C99 *compatibility by name* practices but requires all types that have *tags* in C99 (structures, unions, enumeration types) to have a name.

Two packetC types are compatible within a given scope if they have the same name or both types are anonymous and are defined by the same type declaration. The **typedef** construct creates an alias for a type (see typedef section). In some cases, explicit type casts can overcome type incompatibility (see section on type casting below).

```
int j = 1;
byte b = j;          // ERROR: types are int and byte
byte b = (byte) j;   // Compatible: Scalar type promotion and demotion well defined in packetC

typedef int T1;
typedef int T2;
T1 j1;
T2 j2;               // j, j1 and j2 are all Compatible, all are int

struct S1 { int x; };
struct S2 { int x; };
S1 v3;  v3.x  = 3;
S2 v4; v4 = v3;       // ERROR: different types (S1 and S2)
v4 = (S2) v3; // Compatible: v3 Type Cast to Structure of Same Size which is of v4's Type (S2)
S1 v5; v5 = v3;       // Compatible: v5 and v3 Share Same Type

struct S1 { int x; } v6 = {10}, v7;
v7 = v6;             // compatible: types are from same declaration
```

Type Promotions, Conversions, and Implicit Casting

packetC minimizes implicit type conversions, it has no analogues to C99's pervasive type promotions or "usual arithmetic conversions" (C99 LRM sections 6.3.1.1 and 6.3.1.8). For example, function arguments of types **byte** and **short** are not promoted to type **int**. Similarly, a packetC compiler does not promote arithmetic operands to **int**. (Such promotions may or may not be done by whatever mechanism implements relevant packetC opcodes.)

Because of its emphasis on reliability, packetC typically requires explicit conversions when assignment or other binary operators mix operands with different types. If the user does not supply explicit type casting, the compiler will reject such mixed-type operations as erroneous.

```
const byte        b = 3;
short             s1 = b;              // ERROR: types not the same
const short       s2 = (short) b;      // legal

long              bigOne = s2;         // ERROR: types not the same
long              bigCounter = (long)s2;   // legal

int j = 0xFFEEAA01;
byte b = (byte) j;    // legal: byte b resulting value is 1 (lower byte of int j)
```

The sole exception to this principle involves numeric literals and is described in the following section.

Numeric Literals and Implicit Type Casting

Numeric literals have the default type of **int**. When two such literals are paired with one another in a binary operation, the result has the type **int**. The sole instance of implicit type casting in packetC occurs when (a) a numeric literal is paired with anything other than a numeric literal in a binary operation, and (b) the other operand has a type other than **int**. In that case, the numeric literal is implicitly converted to the other type (possibly with a loss of information) before performing the operation.

```
const    byte b1 = 3;         // 3 has type byte from b1 via operator "="
         byte b2 = b1 * 7;    // 7 has type byte from b1 via operator "*"

byte     b3 = 0-1;            // 0-1 is performed as a 32-bit operation and
                              // the 32-bit result is converted to type byte
                              // via the "=" operator
```

In the case of complex expressions, any implicit casting of literal types occurs in the order dictated by packetC operator precedence: casts dictated by higher precedence operators occur first. Numeric literals and expressions involving only literals may also be explicitly type cast.

Explicit Type Casts

Explicit type casting is allowed between scalars that may or may not have the same storage size, from enumeration types to integer types that can hold their values, and between named types with the same storage size. The following caveats apply to explicit casting:

- The rules for casting enumeration types shown in the accompanying table take precedence over allowing casting between types with the same storage sizes.

- Variables of the reference data type cannot be the origin or target of explicit casts.

- Casting an array slice is only allowed when the slice's size can be determined at compile time.

- A named structure, union, or array type may be cast to another type if the storage size in bytes of the two types is identical.

- An expression with type void (such as a void function invocation) cannot be cast to a type that is not void.

The table below shows the rules for casting integer and enumeration type scalars.

Table 8-1. *Explicit type casting with scalars of various sizes*

Source type	Destination type	Legal?
Smaller integer type	Larger integer type	Yes
Larger integer type	Smaller integer type	Yes. The least significant byte(s) of the larger value are used.
Integer type	Enumeration type	No
Enumeration typeA	Enumeration typeB	No
Enumeration type	Integer type	Yes, if the integer type can accommodate the largest enumerated value.
Non-void expression	Void	Yes (though few uses for the result)
Void	Non-void	No

Cast Operators

Cast operators based on type names can use integer, enumeration, and aggregate types. These operators allow the cast expression to be treated as having the type specified by the cast. The section on "Explicit Type Casts," specifies the rules for type casting.

```
int i;
short s = 127;
byte barr[8];
i = (int) s;            // legal
j = (int) barr[2:5];    // legal
```

■ Note   When array slices are being utilized to cast to a scalar, the size of the array slice must be able to be determined at compile time. To ensure type safety, an array slice that is determined at run time cannot be cast.

```
j = (int) barr[x:y];        // illegal - size cannot be determined at compile time
```

Strong Type Casting

packetC minimizes implicit type conversions to emphasis reliability and errors.

```
byte   b = 3;
short  s1 = b;              // ERROR: types not the same
```

Simply adding the appropriate casting turns the above into a legal statement:

```
short  s2 = (short)b;      // legal
```

The const qualifier provides type-checking safety for program constants. This form is preferred over use of preprocessor #define for constants because the latter does not enforce types. When they are used, they should assign a type to values.

```
const int        SECRET_NUMBER = 0x12345678;
#define SHORT_NUMBER  0x1234s
```

Strong type checking is intended to avoid run-time errors which cannot really be addressed in a real-time data-plane-oriented system.

```
int x;
byte y;
x = y;                     // ERROR: Incompatible types
```

In packetC, explicit type casting is required if the user wants to force the conversion of one type to another.

```
int x;
byte y;
x = (int)y;
```

Type Declarations

Although packetC's type declaration syntax is similar to that of C99, the two languages differ in significant ways. packetC has the following distinctive declaration rules:

- Type declarations may not appear in function parameter lists nor in function return value specifications.

- Type names (*tags*) are not optional in type declarations: all user-defined types have names.

- Once type names (*tags*) have been declared (e.g., in structure or enumeration type declarations) it is not necessary to repeat the data type before each use of the tag in a subsequent declaration.

```
enum int Hue {RED, BLUE} myFunc(…) {…}     // legal C, illegal packetC
//(type definition in return value)

struct {int x; int y;} s;                   // legal C, illegal packetC
// (no anonymous types)
```

```
struct MyType {int x; int y;};
MyType s2;                              // illegal in C, legal in packetC
// (typedef not needed)
```

Typedef

packetC provides a **typedef** declaration, which makes a user-supplied name synonymous with an existing named type. Like the C99 *typedef* construct, **typedef** allows adding array dimensions to the type. Specifying array dimensions *d1..dn* in this way effectively creates an alias for an unnamed type, which is an array [*d1*]...[*dn*] of the aliased type. All other typedef uses define a synonym for an existing type.

```
struct MyStructure { int x; int y; } s1;
typedef MyStructure T2;
T2 s2;

typedef int TempArray[10];
TempArray b;     // b is an array [0..9] of int
```

Chaining Type Declarations

packetC supports 'chaining' type definitions to create nested user-defined structure and union types. Similarly, array declarations can be chained to define an array's dimensions in stages.

```
typedef int TempArray1 [5];

// TempArray2 is a type [0..2] of array [0..4] of int
typedef TempArray1 TempArray2[3];

struct PortsStruct { short dest; short src; };

struct CustomProtocol {
   PortsStruct ports;
     bits byte {
       ...
   } flags;
   ...
}
```

Typedefs and Type Compatibility

When chained typedefs are involved, type compatibility can be determined by iteratively replacing each alias with whatever it represents, working from the highest alias to the lowest. (The highest alias subsumes the other aliases).

At each step, the alias that the relevant typedef defines is replaced and any array dimensions defined by that typedef are moved as a group to become the right-most elements of the post-replacement term.

Thus, array dimensions accumulate in least-rapidly-varying to most-rapidly-varying fashion as the replacement processes traverse arrays of arrays.

```
typedef int T1[5];              // T1 is the lowest alias
typedef T1 T2[4];               // T2 subsumes T1
typedef T2 T3[2][3];            // T3 is highest alias, subsuming T2 and T1
```

For the example above, replacing type aliases would produce the following results:

```
T3 -> T2[2][3] -> T1[2][3][4] -> int[2][3][4][5]
```

Thus, a variable of type T3 is type compatible with variables with a type of (or a type alias that reduces to) int[2][3][4][5]. Note that packetC implementations and language specification currently only supports two dimensions on arrays.

Base Types

Just as an array is said to be *based* on the data type of its constituent elements, packetC has several extended data types that are based on another data type. For example:

- **databases** are aggregates of structures (masked or not), so their declarations involve specifying the data type of the individual database elements.

- **descriptors** are instances of user-defined structures, which can be positioned to overlay a portion of the packet.

- **references** are abstract, generalized entities that indicate a kind of database or searchset without hard-coding any particular database or searchset into the source code.

packetC declarations that use base types always place the base type after the relevant keyword when reading in left-to-right fashion.

```
database MyStructType  myDB[15];        // myStructType is the base type
reference  myRef = NULL;                // MyStructType is base type
```

Variable Declaration Specifiers

The type of an entire type or variable declaration can be modified in two ways by *specifiers* that precede the base type in the declaration:

- By a s*torage specifier* that adds information about how the variables should be stored,

- By a *type specifier* that adds information about how the variable can behave.

Storage specifiers precede type specifiers in a declaration.

Storage Specifiers

Storage specifiers appear in type and variable declarations. They come before type specifiers and the type, apply to the entire declaration, and specify an aspect of how variables of the type will be stored.

Type Specifiers

Type specifiers appear in type and variable declarations. They come before the type, apply to the entire declaration, and specify an aspect of how variables of the type will behave. In packetC, **const** is the sole type specifier.

Const Specifier

The **const** specifier applies to all variables that appear in a declaration, whether it is a type or a variable declaration. Although const variables may be initialized as part of their declaration, attempting to assign them a value outside of the declaration is an error. Since the **typedef** construct only defines aliases for a type it does not have a **const** specifier.

```
const struct MyS { int x; int y; } s1 = { 3, 5 };
typedef MyS SimpleStruct;
SimpleStruct s2;
s2.x = 15; // legal
s1.x = 15; // ERROR, s1 was declared with a const specifier

const int j = 7, k = 9;
int m;
k = 10; // ERROR: k was declared with const
m = 13; // legal, const only applies to declaration where it appeared
```

Constant and Constant Integral Expressions

A *constant integral expression* (CIE) has an integer value that can be determined at compile time, rather than run time. Such an expression, CIE is composed of literals, constant identifiers, and certain operators. (See table below.) The following packetC constructs require constant integral expressions:

- array bounds (when present),
- bitfield sizes,
- database bounds,
- searchset bounds.

The following entities are excluded from CIEs:

- operands: arrays and array slices, enumeration identifiers, and values, structures, unions, databases, searchsets, references and records
- operators: assignment, compound assignment, function calls, increment and decrement, database and searchset operators, lock and unlock, reference operators and packet_offset

These entities are included in CIEs:

- operands: integer and character literals and constants

- operators: offset, arithmetic, logical and bitwise operators not excluded above, array indexing, and field select operators

Some packetC constructs, such as **sizeof**, accept a superset of CIEs as legal operands, as shown in the accompanying Table 8-2, even though these are not processed in the **sizeof** nor do they affect the result.

Table 8-2. *Constant Integral Expressions (CIE) Forbidden and Allowed Uses*

Construct	Forbid	Allow
array bounds, bitfield lengths, database bounds, searchset bounds		*CIEs*
Initializers		*CIEs, **ref** operator, aggregate literals*
Sizeof		*CIEs, plus operators for assignment, compound assignment, ++, --, and function calls.*
#if	*C99 restrictions, as well as operators for databases, searchsets, and references; **lock/unlock** and **packet_offset**.*	

So what does this all mean? When declaring complex data types, the bounds must be computable at compile time to avoid the possibility of any run-time memory allocation requirement. No support for run-time memory allocation exists in packetC.

```
const int ROWS = 7;
const int COLUMNS = 9;
byte myArray[ROWS][COLUMNS];    // Legal
byte myArray[7][9];             // Preferred

int j = 5;
int k = 50;
byte myArray[j][k];             // Not Legal - j and k may fluctuate in the program.
```

CHAPTER 9

■ ■ ■

C-Style Data Types

Working with data types in packetC introduces some interesting dynamics that will initially require care and extra thought by C developers from time to time given some of the restrictions, mostly due to strong type enforcement. The notion of casting and the strong casting rules is imperative to ensuring code works as expected. Packets are modeled as arrays of bytes and working with portions of packets is essential to making sense of the data. In packetC, the notion of an array slice was introduced to allow for direct access to portions of byte arrays without the need for pointers and for keeping them in line with strong type enforcement. This also applies to complex structures and unions that can be copied or, better yet, cast back and forth to byte arrays, providing multiple ways to view data elements, depending on what is most convenient for the programmer.

Enumeration Types

packetC *enumeration types* map a series of unsigned integer values to a corresponding set of identifier names that are enumerated in the type declaration. A name is associated with a user-specified value by following the name with an equal sign and an unsigned integer value. Default values are mapped to the identifiers in a left-to-right manner. If the user does not specify a value for the leftmost name, it defaults to a value of zero. Any subsequent name that lacks a user-specified value receives a value equal to one plus the value of the name immediately to its left. It is an error for two or more names to have the same value. Enumerated type declarations specify one of packetC's integer types as a *base type*. It is an error to declare an enumeration value too large for the specified base type to store. Unlike C, packetC defines equality, relational, and a simple assignment operator for enumerated types but not arithmetic or bitwise operators.

```
// use default values 0, 1, 2
enum int       StorageType { BYTE_TYPE, SHORT_TYPE, INT_TYPE };
// user values, 32, 64, 128
enum byte      MySize { SINGLE = 32, DOUBLE = 64, QUAD = 128 };
// values 0, 63, 256
enum short     Alert { BAD_STACK, MFG1 = 63, MFGR2 = 256 };
// use default values 0, 1, 2
enum byte      StorageType { BYTE_TYPE, SHORT_TYPE, INT_TYPE };

// use default values 0, 1, 2, 3, 4, 5, 6
enum long      Day1 { MON, TUE, WED, THUR, FRI };
enum short     Day2 { SAT, SUN };

// user values, 32, 64, 128
enum byte      MySize { SINGLE = 32, DOUBLE = 64, QUAD = 128 };
```

```
// values 0, 63, 256
enum short      Alert { BAD_STACK, MFG1 = 63, MFGR2 = 256 };

// ERROR: redundant values in 0, 1, 2, 1
enum int Color { RED, GREEN, BLUE, CYAN =1};
```

Although packetC stores enumeration types in integer base types, each enumeration type defines a distinctive type. Thus, identifiers and values with one given enumeration type cannot be combined in assignments or expressions with identifiers and values that have some other enumeration type or the base type of the enumerated type. Trying to assign an enumeration type variable a value that is not associated with one of the enumerated names is an error. The following example uses the types defined above to show legal and illegal usage.

```
// Using enums defined in examples above
StorageType i1, i2 = BYTE_TYPE;
MySize m1;
int j;
i1 = i2;                    // both have same type

// legal; can cast an enumerated type to an
// integer type big enough to hold it.
j = (int) i1;

// All of these are errors
i1 = (StorageType) j;    // ERROR: cannot cast int to enumerated type
i1 = m1;                 // ERROR: variables have different enum types.
```

The following example shows enumerations in use:

```
packet module declenum;

enum byte StorageType { BYTE_TYPE, SHORT_TYPE, INT_TYPE, LONG_TYPE };
enum long Day1 { MON, TUE, WED, THUR, FRI };
enum short Day2 { SAT, SUN };

enum byte MySize { SINGLE = 32, DOUBLE = 64, QUAD = 128 };
enum short Alert { BAD_STACK, MFG1 = 63, MFG2 = 256 };
enum int Color { RED, GREEN, BLUE, CYAN = 5 };

int pass_, fail_;
%pragma control pass_ (export);
%pragma control fail_ (export);

byte result_[4];

void main( $PACKET pkt, $PIB pib, $SYS sys ) {
  int statusOffset;
  statusOffset = pib.payloadOffset;
  StorageType i1, i2 = BYTE_TYPE;
  MySize m1;
  int j;
```

```
   i1 = i2;
   j = (int)i1;

   if ( j != 0 ) {
      fail_++;
      result_[0]='F'; result_[1]='A'; result_[2]='I'; result_[3]='L';
   } else {
      pass_++;
      result_[0]='P'; result_[1]='A'; result_[2]='S'; result_[3]='S';
   }
   pkt[statusOffset:statusOffset+3] = result_[0:end];
   pib.action = FORWARD_PACKET;
}
```

Arrays

packetC supports one- and two-dimensional array types that use *byte, short, int,* or *long* types as their base type. These types use zero-based dimensions. With the exception of dimension and base type restrictions, packetC practices follow those of C99 for declaring and using arrays.

```
byte barr[5];              // barr is an array [0..4] of byte
int  iarr[4][3];           // iarr is an array [0..3] of array [0..2] of int
long cnt[10];              // cnt is an array [0..9] of long

// Errors
int  carr3[2][3][2];       // ERROR: more than 2 dimensions
barr [9] = 5;              // ERROR: legal zero-based indices are 0..4
```

A two-dimensional array is an array with a base type that is, itself, an array. Two-dimensional arrays can be composed either by a single array type declaration or by combining related declarations.

```
typedef int T4[3];
T4  dArr[4];               //  dArr is array [0..3] of array [0..2] of int

// each row has 1, 2, 3 in the columns
int y[4][3] = { 1, 2, 3, 1, 2, 3, 1, 2, 3, 1, 2, 3 };
// same as above, broken out rows
int y[4][3] = { {1, 2, 3}, {1, 2, 3}, {1, 2, 3}, {1, 2, 3} };
```

Memory Allocation

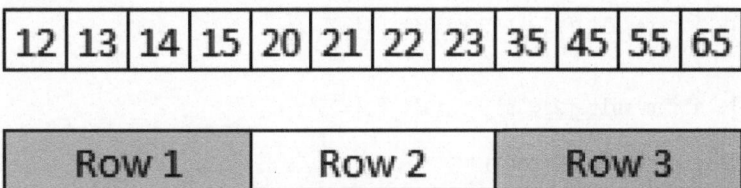

Figure 9-1. *Memory allocation for array packetContents*

Allocation of memory is predictable in packetC. The array packetContents is defined below and its memory allocations are shown in Figure 9-1.

int packetContents[3][4] = {

{12, 13, 14, 15},

{20, 21, 22, 23},

{35, 45, 55, 65}

};

The packetContents two-dimensional array above is equivalent to the one-dimensional array declaration below:

int packetContents[12] = {12, 13, 14, 15,20, 21, 22, 23, 35, 45, 55, 65};

In C, structures can be the element type of an array. This is not legal in packetC given that it would impact array subscripting practices.

Array Subscripting Operator

A postfix expression that identifies an array, followed by an expression within square brackets, designates an element of the array. Unlike C99, packetC does not indicate internal array addresses or the starting storage address of an array with array references that have fewer subscripts than the array has dimensions. Similarly, the user should not presume a specific, contiguous array storage layout. See the section on arrays within the Data Types section. Any expression that produces an integer result that is within the array's legal range can serve as a legal array subscripting expression. Subscripting operators are only legal in conjunction with packetC array or database variables.

```
short   sa[3] = { 5, 6, 7 }, sb;
byte ba = 1, bb = 2;
sb = sa[2];         // sb = 7
```

```
sb = sa[ bb - ba ];      // sb = 6
```

Unsized Dimensions

Variables can be declared with unsized array dimensions but each dimension must be unambiguously sized by an accompanying initialization clause. When a multiple-dimension array has one or more unsized dimensions, the initialization clause must use a *nested literal* form that unambiguously and consistently specifies the size of all unsized dimensions. Unlike C, a multidimensional array with an unsized dimension:

- Is not restricted to allowing only the leftmost dimension to be unsized

- Must use a nested literal form for the initialization clause

```
int  aarr[]    = {1,2,3};              // legal, aarr [3]
int  barr[2][] = { {1,2}, {3,4}};      // legal, barr [2][2]
int  carr[][3] = {{1,2,3}, {3,4,5}};   // legal, carr [2][3]
int  darr[][3] = {1,2,3,4,5,6};        // ERROR: not nested literal
int  earr[][]  = {{1,2,3}, {3,4,5}};   // legal, earr [2][3]
int  farr[][]  = {1,2,3,4,5,6};        // ERROR: ambiguous
int  garr[][]  = {{1,2}, {3,4,5}};     // ERROR: inconsistent
```

Array Assignment

Unlike the C language, packetC does not permit array references with an incomplete set of indices as a mechanism for denoting array or sub-array starting addresses. The absence of this practice is in the interest of packetC's emphasis on security and reliability. packetC uses the name of an array without any accompanying indices to indicate the entire array. Thus, all the element values of a destination array can be set equal to those of a source array if the two arrays have identical dimensions and the same base type. Only the simple assignment operator is defined for entire arrays acting as operands.

```
typedef byte TempArray26[2][6];
TempArray26  a, b;
byte  c[3][4], d[6], e[8];
...
a = b;                // legal
d[0:4] = e[1:5];      // legal

// Errors
c = a;                // ERROR: operands not of same type
b = a[1];             // ERROR: Using a[1] does not imply a[1][0:end]. This is illegal.
d = a[1];             // ERROR: illegal.
d[1] = a[1][0:end]; // legal
```

The array assignment implements the equivalent of a type-safe *memcopy()* operation in packetC. For those areas where one would normally desire a *memcopy()*, array assignment comes into play.

Array Slicing

A portion of an array can be returned by array slicing. A special keyword called **end** can be used to specify the greatest legal index value of an array. Array slicing is the method where a range, or slice, of an array is specified by providing a start and stop offset separated by a colon.

```
byte  a[16];
byte  b[8];
b[0:end] = a[0:7];
```

A set of contiguous array elements is a packetC *array slice*. The size of a slice is specified with a range expression, which specifies the lowest and highest index values of the slice in left-to-right form.

Legal ranges have a left-hand expression that is less than or equal to the right-hand expression. Both indices must be within the array's bounds. The **end** keyword can be used as the right-hand expression to indicate the greatest legal index value for that particular array. A range that describes a single array element is legal (i.e., the two sides of the range are equal) if the element is within the array's bounds. A slice can only describe a range for the array dimension with the index that varies most rapidly. Slices can be defined for arrays of any integer base type. In general, array slices can be used in the same syntactic and semantic situations where an entire array could legally be used.

```
byte  a[16];
byte  b[8];
byte  c[256][8];
byte left = 0, right = 7;

// legal: variables within range
b[ left : right ] = a[ left : right ];
b[ left : right ] = pkt [left : right ];

// legal: constants and operations in range
b[ left : 3 ] = a[ right + 1 : right + 4 ];

// legal with cast (1-element slice is a 1-element array)
byte bscalar;
bscalar = (byte)b[0:0];

// ERROR: cannot directly assign scalar to an array/slice
b[ 0 : 0 ] = a[12];

// legal: assigning slices/arrays with same base type and size
b[ 0 : 0 ] = a[12:12];
b[ 0 : 4 ] = a[4:8];

// legal: 2D array, range is rightmost dimension
b[ 0 : right ] = c[5][0:7];

// legal: assigning 2 8-element slices
b[ 0 : end ] = c[4][0:end];

// ERROR: least rapidly varying index has range
a[ 0 : 15 ]= c[0:1][0:7];
```

```
// legal: assigning slices/arrays with same base type (byte) and size
// The packet (pkt) is able to be treated as an array of byte
b[ 0 : 4 ] = pkt[4:8];
```

Range expressions are not limited to constants. However, a range expression for an array slice that is being type-cast must be constant. A range expression that can only be determined at run time and that yields out of bounds or otherwise illegal range values shall trigger a *system-defined response* for that state array indexing error state. (See the section on System-Defined Response in Chapter 13).

Array Initialization

Above, the notion of assigning two arrays or two equivalent slices of arrays was shown. This presented a type-safe method of copying blocks of memory of dynamic sizes. Another such instance that is often useful is to set all elements of an array to a particular value, much like the calling of a *memset()* function in C. As there are no pointers and type-safety is critical, packetC implements two means for providing this functionality. Both revolve around the repetition operator, #, which can occur in the data set on the right-hand side of the statement or as a part of a compound assignment operator, #=.

```
typedef byte TempArray26[2][6];
TempArray26 a, b;
byte c[3][4], d[6], e[8];

byte f[1000] = { 0, 1, 2, 3, 255#996 };    // Fills last 996 elements with value of 255
...
a #= 80;            // Assigns every byte of a to contain a value of 80.
d[0:4] #= e[1];     // Where e[1] is a byte that has its value assigned to 0 through 4 in d

// Errors
d #= e[0:2];        // ERROR: e[0:2] is not of same type, byte, as elements of d.
```

The array assignment using the repetition compound operator implements the equivalent of type safe *memset()* operation in packetC. For those areas where one would normally desire a *memset()*, this unique-to-packetC compound operator assignment comes into play.

Structures and Unions

Complex structures are supported. Fields can be accessed on the bit level in packetC by defining a bitfield container with the **bit** keyword.

```
struct MyStruct {
    bits byte {
        flags: 4;
        pad: 4;              // filler, not directly accessible
    } halfUse;
    byte otherHalf;
} myStruct;
```

Unions allow variables to be accessed in different ways:

```
union MyBytes {
    int i;
```

```
    short s[2];
    byte  b[4];
} myBytes;
```

Unions

A *union* is a data type construct that associates multiple kinds of data type with a single storage address. The syntax for describing these union *members* is identical to the syntax for describing structure *fields*. However, union members specify different ways of interpreting the bit pattern stored at a single address, rather than specify a series of distinct data items stored at consecutive addresses. The union will be stored in a manner that accommodates its largest member. A union may be followed by unnamed pad bytes.

A packetC *descriptor* cannot be a union member but it can contain a union as one of its fields. An empty union (one with no members) is not legal in packetC.

```
// union holds 4 bytes, accessible three different ways
union FourBytes {
    int   i;
    short s[2];
    byte  b[4];
} fourBytes;
```

Because type specifiers (e.g., **const**) are applied only to entire variables, they cannot be applied to an individual union member.

C99 has two ways to initialize a union, namely, (a) constant value will be used to init the 1st member, or (b) use a designator (these are also used for arrays and structures). Since packetC does not have designators, the first member must be used to initialize the union.

A union initialization clause consists of a constant expression that initializes the first member declared in the union. An expression is a legal initializer for the first union member only if it could legally initialize the member as a stand-alone item. Users wishing to explicitly initialize all bits of a union should declare the largest union member first.

```
union UnionDef { short s; int i;} u = {0xabff};     // value is 0xabff0000
struct StructDef { short src; short dest;};
union UnionDef2 { StructDef astruct; int i;}
UnionDef2 u2 = {{0xabff,0xcdee}};                   // value is 0xabffcdee
<0xabffcdee reflects big endian machine>
```

Structures

Structures are user-defined *aggregate types*, which consist of a sequence of *fields*. Each field is, itself, an object defined by a scalar or an aggregate data type. In packetC, the structure can be accessed as a whole or individual fields can be accessed using a *structureName"."fieldname* syntax. packetC provides only *naturally aligned* structures.

packetC does not support the following structure features that appear in C99:

- an unsized array as the final field in a structure

- empty structures (those with no fields)

- pointers to a structure of the kind being defined

Because type specifiers (e.g., **const**) are applied only to entire variables, they cannot be applied to an individual structure field.

Structure Alignment

Most modern CPUs have conventions for *aligning* data according to data type. Data is *naturally aligned* when its storage begins on a byte address that is a multiple of the datum's size in bytes. Some systems require data to be aligned, while others allow *misaligned* data but incur a performance penalty for it. If two data types have different alignment requirements, the more *demanding* requirement is the one that requires that the address be a multiple of a larger number.

The *proper alignments* for the various data types are as follows:

- **byte:**   aligned on any address,

- **short:**   aligned on addresses that are multiples of 2,

- **int:**   aligned on addresses that are multiples of 4,

- **long:**   aligned on addresses that are multiples of 8,

- **arrays:**   aligned on the kind of addresses required by an individual element,

- **structure:**   aligned according to the most demanding requirement of its constituent fields.

- **union:**   aligned according to the member with the most demanding requirement

packetC provides only *naturally aligned* structures, thus, it differs significantly from C99 alignment. This property is dictated by the envisioned use of packetC structures to define types that match common network *protocols* and *headers*. Such protocols are naturally aligned, which largely avoid internal padding because of the cumulative overhead that padding would create in data communications. A packetC developer must properly pad every defined structure to conform to natural alignment. Developers must be cognizant of this when moving structured data back and forth with array-based representations.

Figure 9-2 shows how C99 and packetC would organize structures with the following definition:

```
// structure will start on 4 byte-aligned address
// (driven by field i1)
    struct MyStruct {
        byte    b1;
        short   s1;
        byte    b2;
        int     i1;
    };
```

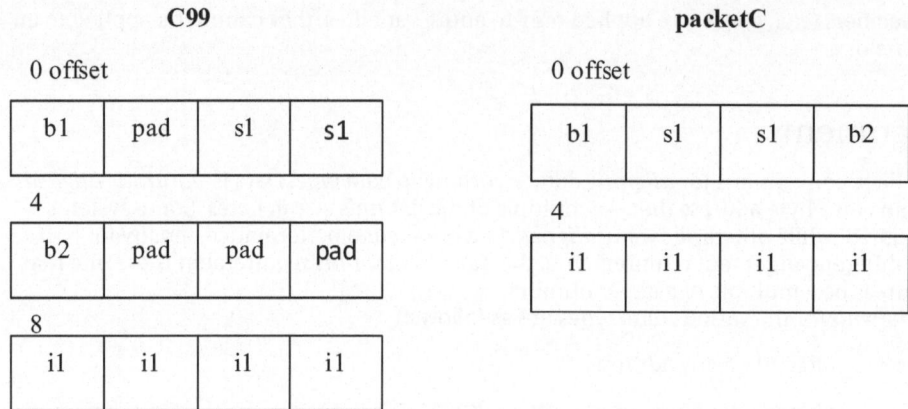

Figure 9-2. *Structure in C99 and packetC*

Types, Tags, and Name Visibility

packetC's treatment of structure and union names or *tags*, differs significantly from that of C99. First, packetC treats these identifiers as ordinary type names. Thus, the user does not have to qualify the tag with the **struct** or **union** keywords.

```
struct MyStruct {byte b1; short s1;};
MyStruct s1, s2;          // legal in packetC
```

Second, packetC does not associate tags with a global namespace. Instead, a structure or union type's name is associated with the scope where it is declared, like other identifiers.

Finally, the visibility rules for types declared within structures or unions are as follows:

- Within the enclosing declaration, a nested declaration is visible from the textual point at which it appears until the end of the enclosing declaration.

- Following the enclosing declaration's end, the nested declaration is visible anywhere that the outermost enclosing structure/union declaration is visible.

```
struct Outer {
    byte b1, b2;
    struct Inner {
        short s1;
        int i1;
    } sa;
    Inner sb;
};
Inner si = {16, 32}; // 'Inner' is visible anywhere 'Outer' is visible
Outer so = {8, 7, {16,32}, {16,32}};
```

Nested structure or union declarations, enumeration type declarations, and typedef alias declarations may appear within a structure or union declaration. However, these may only appear if they declare a structure field or union member for an enclosing declaration, whether it is the outermost declaration or not.

Individual structure fields or union members shall not be initialized within a type declaration nor be declared as **const**.

Field Selection Operatorpostfix_expression . identifier

A postfix expression followed by the field selection operator ('.') and an identifier constitutes a structure or union field named by the identifier. A field selection operator is only legal when the postfix expression to its left identifies a structure, union, or descriptor.

```
struct S { int x; } myStruct;
myStruct.x = 15;
```

Bitfields

Bitfield Declarations

- Related bit fields are grouped into collections that have a name and are associated with an unambiguous container type (one of the integer types); it is a fatal error if the container is not large enough to accommodate all the combined bit fields.

- There can be one or more fields in a collection that cannot be directly accessed; these fields have the predefined name, **pad**.

- It is a fatal error if the size of the combined bit fields, possibly including one or more **pad** fields, does not equal the container size.

- A bit field may not straddle two adjacent bit field collections; each bit field must completely fit into its host container.

- Bitfields are specified with the same *variable*"." *fieldname* syntax used for other structure fields.

- Individual bitfields can only be tested and set, although an entire bit field container can be used as an operand by any arithmetic or logical operation that is valid for integers.

The following example shows packetC bit field declaration syntax:

```
struct IpHeader {
    bits short {
    version  :4;
    headerLen :4;
    tos      :8;
  } first16;                          // collection is named, like any other field
    …
} myHeader;
if ( myHeader.first16.headerLen > 12 ) …

        struct MyStructureDef {
           bits byte {
               flags: 4;
               pad: 4;                // not directly accessible
           } halfUse;
```

```
    byte otherHalf;
} myStruct;
myStruct.halfUse.flags = ~0;       // set all flags
myStruct.halfUse.pad = ~0;         // ERROR: pad fields not accessible
```

Bitfield Semantics

Bitfields can be used as operands with a restricted set of operators (see below). In order to produce portable results and avoid silent type promotions, bitfield operations center on the role of the bitfield container. The mechanics of bitfield operations are described below.

- A bitfield can only be used as an operand with the following operators: =, ==, !=, >, <, >=, <=.

- When used as an operand, an N-bit bitfield acts as if it occupied the least significant N bits of a temporary container in which any other bits are set to zero.

- When bitfield operands are used in binary operations, all the bits in the temporary container are used, which yields logical results equivalent to C99's.

```
struct S1 { bits short { a04:4; a12:12;} con1; } sa;
struct S2 { bits long  { b04:4; b60:60;} con2; } sb;
struct S3 { bits short { c02:2; c14:14;} con3; } sc;

sa.con1.a12 = 0xabc;
sa.con1.a04 = 0xd;
if ( sa.con1.a04 > sa.con1.a12 )…        // eval false, a12's hi bits used
```

- When a bitfield expression is typecast, the cast affects the size of the bitfield's container, not the size of the bitfield.

- When a bitfield is used in a binary operation, one of the operands must be cast if the other operand is a scalar with a type different from the bitfield's container or is a bitfield with a different container type.

```
if ( sa.con1.a04 < (short)sb.con2.b60 )…     // cmp a04 vs. b60 low 16 bits
```

- When a bitfield operates as an assignment left-hand-side (LHS):

  - The right-hand-side must be cast if it is a scalar or a bitfield container with a type other than the LHS container.

  - The assignment expression result has the type of the LHS container, even if the LHS bitfield cannot store all of that result.

```
short sVar = sa.con1.a04 = sc.con3.c14;      // sVar = c14's value
```

- When bitfields appear on both sides of an assignment operator, given a left-hand-side bitfield, lbf, with length L1 and a right-hand-side bitfield, rbf, with length L2:

  - If (L1 <= L2) lbf gets the least significant L1 bits from rbf.

  - If (L1 > L2) lbf bits 0:L2-1 = rbf and lbf bits L2:L1-1 = 0 (rbf container high bits).

For more information on bitfields, refer to the extended discussion on container based bitfields at the end of this chapter.

A Discussion on Container-Based Bit Fields

In packetC, packets are represented as a byte array that reflects its byte arrival order. The outermost header's location can be determined as an offset from the packet's start and using descriptors subsequent headers and individual fields can be identified. However, to effectively process header contents, to alter header content, and to change the protocols being used entirely, we need to read and write individual header fields and entire headers. Hence, we need to be able to manipulate headers with confidence as C-style structures. Since many standard fields are smaller than typical integer storage units (32, 16, 8 bits) or do not take up an integral number of bytes, some form of bit field representation is needed. A packet is assigned to a context to process where the offset specified by a descriptor is specific to the packet being processed by a given instance of packet main as identified by private memories in Figure 9-3.

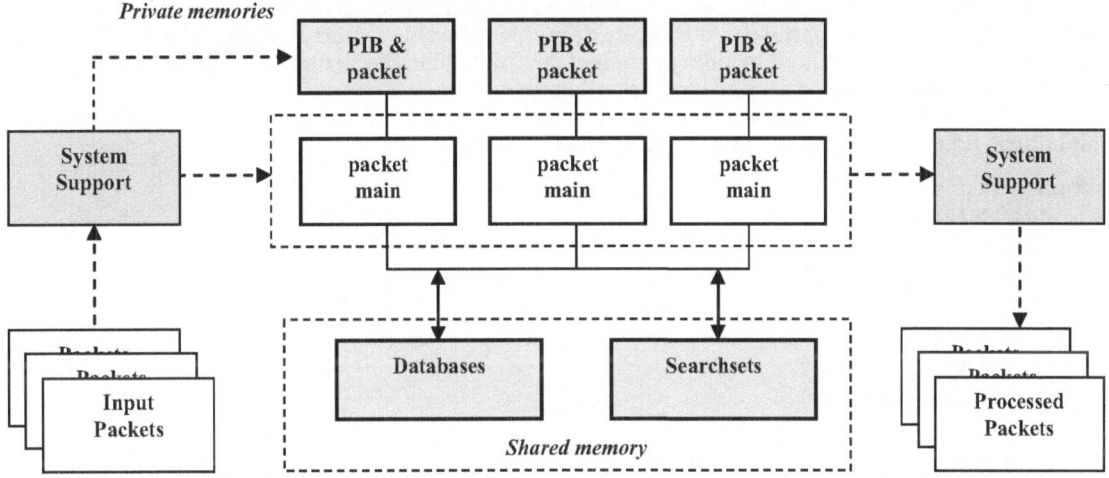

Figure 9-3. Mapping the packet processing model to packetC language constructs

C's bit field construct is not adequate because the implementation freedom it bestows creates a variety of uncertainties, as discussed below.

```
struct structTag {
        unsigned int notAbitField;
        unsigned char  a:4;
        unsigned int  b:2;
        unsigned int  c:4;
} myStruct;
```

- *'Straddle' behavior*—The entire field named *c* cannot fit in a byte allocated for *a* and *b*. Some compilers let it 'straddle' bytes, with 2 bits in the byte allocated for the first two fields and the remaining bits in a trailing byte, but others do not. The C99 specification comments: "if insufficient space remains, whether a bit-field that does not fit is put into the next unit or overlaps adjacent units is implementation-defined."

- *Container size*—Similarly, the compiler may or may not heed the user's specification of the integer storage unit to use for the bit fields. The specification says an implementation can use "any addressable storage unit large enough" to accommodate the bit field.

- *Bit field layout*—Finally, we cannot be certain whether the compiler allocates the topmost fields in the declaration to the least significant bytes of the corresponding memory or how the containing unit is aligned: "the order of allocation of bit fields within a unit is implementation-defined. The alignment of the addressable storage unit is undefined."

In packetC, packet header representation will remain identical on all platforms, no matter the underlying endianness. In particular, it is highly desirable to be able to port an application to new processors or compilers without recoding to reflect new bit field implementation peculiarities. Providing predictable bit field layouts is a key to the packetC approach.

packetC bit field rules produce the following code, using the structure from the previous example (alphabetic superscripts map to the bulleted points that follow):

```
struct structTag {
    int notAbitField;
    bits short {          (a)
        a:4;              (b)
        b:2;
        c:4;
        pad:6;            (c)
    } containerName;      (d)
} myStruct;
```

The following comments apply to the footnote annotations shown in the example above:

a. Related bit fields are explicitly organized inside a *container*, which has one of packetC's 4 unsigned integer types: **byte**, **short**, **int**, and **long.**

b. Since a bit field is always part of a container that has a type, each bit field declares a name and a size, not a type.

c. Pad fields are declared explicitly. A group of related bit fields, including pad fields, must always sum to the size of their container. Pad fields cannot be accessed for test or set operations.

d. The container name can be used to access and manipulate the bit field collection as a whole.

This approach removes container size, straddling, and boundary uncertainties by guaranteeing that the storage unit size is the one specified by the user, by forbidding straddling and by ensuring that every bit in the container has been explicitly defined. In addition, we need to manage byte allocation order.

This contrasts with C, in which any data declaration wider than one byte does not use the same byte allocation order when they are compiled and run on big-endian and little-endian processors. User operations on structure fields that correspond to whole integer values do not show effects due to host processor endianness. However, operations on bit fields, which can be sub-elements of integer storage units or can straddle them, do yield endian-specific results.

Big-endian refers to machines that store the most significant bits of a word at the lowest byte address, while little endian machines store the least significant bits starting at the lowest byte address. The example below shows how these practices affect C bit fields.

```
int bytes4 = 0xabcdef12, *p = &bytes4;
typedef struct sTag {
    unsigned int first : 8;
    unsigned int second: 24;
} sType;
sType myStruct, *pStruct = *((sType*)p);
```

Big- and little-endian processors store the byte sequences as shown below, where the lower numbered byte addresses appear to the left of higher ones. The big-endian list is shown with big-endian bit allocation order (the most significant half of a byte appears to the left of the least significant one), while the little-endian list shows the least-significant byte to the left.

```
// Big Endian:      a b | c d | e f | 1 2
```

```
// Little Endian:   2 1 | f e | d c | b a
```

With these storage patterns, a C program will interpret the field values as shown below (where the most significant half-byte value appears to the left of the least significant half):

```
Big Endian              Little Endian
first = 0xab;           first = 0x12;
second = 0xcdef12       second = 0xabcdef
```

To provide certainty and portability, packetC imposes a single endianness scheme, the one that best matches its overall processing approach, then uses relatively minor compiler adjustments to compensate when hosted on a little-endian processor. However, the following background discussion shows that the choice is not arbitrary.

Since packet contents appear in network byte order (big-endian order) and since at the bit level protocols most often use little-endian bit-allocation order (e.g., Ethernet), packetC structures and unions are required to be in big-endian order to match the packet's organization and facilitate rapidly reading or writing protocol information between the packet array and user structures. Bit level representation follows little-endian representation in packetC. In practice on traditional C systems, modest code adjustments are required to compensate for bit field access on a little-endian platform. A packetC platform will perform any compensation for the developer to always maintain a predictable environment.

The packetC approach to bit fields ensures that we can match protocol headers that reside in the packet array. Protocol headers are the most common elements represented by complex data types in packetC. Byte- and bit-field representation, and the predictability introduced by packetC is core to network application design. Network applications focus on byte and bit twiddling on packet headers and in packetC, unlike C, this can be done without the need for protective measures to ensure cross-platform portability. Simply by knowing a protocol header's location within the packet, fields can be directly addressed.

C H A P T E R 10

Basic Packet Interaction and Operations

Interaction with the Packet through Unique-to-packetC Capabilities

The packet can be seen as either one of the simplest data elements in the language or one of the most complex, and hopefully both in a good way. In its simplest form, the packet is an array of bytes, as defined in *cloudshield.ph*, it simply looks similar to the statement below:

```
//=============================================================================
//   Packet Type
//
//   Each system may have a slightly different constraint on the buffer for each
//   packet.  The typedef below defines the $PACKET for the system.
//
//=============================================================================
//  typedef byte $PACKET[9 * 1024 - 1];
```

Looking at the packet in a different way, it is comprised of multiple protocols layered one inside another. Each layer not only prescribes information about the next layer enveloped inside but also has complex definitions on the construction of the layer itself. A simple HTTP web page request over the simplest Ethernet II link has four major layers to the packet with almost 100 fields of interest. The packet is represented in packetC as an array of bytes with descriptors providing a means to break the array into headers with the individual fields to accomplish a notional network view of the packet as in Figure 10-1. To work with the packet inspecting and manipulating its construction without insight to the packet's construction can seem a bit daunting.

Figure 10-1. A WAN packet viewed as portions of a byte array

Fortunately, packetC introduces many different tools to work with the packet, in a form consistent with a network engineer's perspective, in order to simplify the coding of a program managing streams of packets. Not only has packetC offloaded entirely the receipt, buffering, and management of the transmission of packets, but it also provides a number of pre- and post-processing capabilities that provide an understanding of a packet before the first line of code is executed with information passed to the program through the *pib* and *sys* data structures. Descriptors introduce yet another major advancement, allowing any of the 100 fields for the packet described above to be addressed by name as if they were simple structure fields, even when one packet to the next changes the byte offset within the packet for those fields.

```
byte b;
b = pkt[35];

int x;
x = (int) pkt[0:3];

struct BaseType {
...
} myStruct;
myStruct = (BaseType) pkt[36:36+sizeof(BaseType)-1];


pkt [j].delete( sizeof( TcpProtocol ) );

byte barr[4] = { 6, 7, 8, 9 };
pkt[16].insert( 5, barr );

pkt.replicate();
```

In this chapter, some of the other packet operations specific to packetC are discussed with regard to addressing changing the macro level construction of a packet, such as its size and some interactions with how and when it gets processed.

The current packet passed into the **packet module**'s main is accessible to the user as a byte array. There are several operations that can be done on the packet. The packet will always be referenced as *pkt* in packetC and is visible throughout a packet module's global, packet, and block scopes. Since the packet is treated as a byte array, full array slicing and assignment capabilities are present for the packet as either a source or destination of an operator.

Get Packet Offset

packet_offset

This unary operator takes a single descriptor field as an operand and returns an int value that indicates the offset of that field from the start of the packet. Similar to the *offset* operator, this operator returns the byte value of the field offset. There are a few differences. First, the offset for the field is not from the start of the descriptor but from the start of the packet. A descriptor includes an expression that is used to calculate the offset of the descriptor from the start of the packet. The result of **packet_offset** is the addition of this value plus the offset of the field from the start of the descriptor. Given that the values in the *pib* are referenced to determine the offset of a descriptor change from one packet to another, the value returned by **packet_offset** must be determined at run time. This is in contrast to offset, which is computed at compile time.

```
struct TcpProtocol {
    short    sourcePort;
```

```
    short   destPort;
    int     sequenceNum;
    int     ackNum;
    ...
};
descriptor TcpProtocol TcpHeader at pib.L4_Offset;
byte barray[8];
    ...
start = packet_offset( TcpHeader.sourcePort );
stop = packet_offset(TcpHeader.ackNum )  -  1;

// get first three fields of the protocol
barray[0:7] = pkt[ start : stop ];
```

The operand of **packet_offset** must be a field defined in a descriptor. Refer to the *offset* operator description section for more details on how field offsets are calculated.

Packet Operators

- delete

- insert

- replicate

- requeue

Packet Delete

The packet delete operator is used to remove bytes from a packet, often for the purpose of removing option headers, MPLS and VLAN tags, or content from the payload. To delete bytes from the current packet at a given index use PKT[X] where X = the offset of where in the packet to start deleting followed by delete (Y) where Y = H bytes to delete. The operator deletes the indicated bytes from the current packet, effectively shrinking its size and returns **void** (no meaningful result).

If the system is unable to delete the specified bytes from the packet, the delete operator will throw the predefined error, **ERR_PKT_DELETE**.

```
pkt[34].delete(16);
pkt[j].delete( sizeof( TcpProtocol ) );
pkt.delete(3);          // ERROR: missing subscript to specify start
pkt[0:4].delete(2);     // ERROR: starting point must be an element
pkt[25].delete;         // ERROR: must specify how many bytes to delete
```

Packet Insert

The current packet behaves as a dynamically-sized, zero-indexed array of bytes. Packet insertions use an index expression to specify an offset where the insertion starts and a parenthesized argument that specifies how many bytes to add at the insertion point. If an optional second argument appears within the parentheses, it specifies a byte array or array slice, whose contents are copied into the added space.

The additional bytes are effectively inserted *before* the byte currently residing at the specified offset. As an operator, insertion returns a result of type **void** (no meaningful result). The packet insert operator is used to add bytes to a packet, often for the purpose of adding option headers, MPLS and VLAN tags, or content into the payload.

Given a packet offset value of *n* for the expansion point, a filler object to copy *f,* an expansion byte count *b,* and copy object size *s:*

- If the optional, "filler object" argument is present, its size must be equal to the number of bytes being added by the expansion operation, i.e., its copied contents must completely fill up the new space. Thus, b=s and packet [n:(n+s-1)]=f.

- If there is no data to insert (the optional argument is absent), the contents of **pkt**[n : n + b-1] are filled with a value of 0.

- If the specified insertion point is = last legal offset + 1, then the inserted bytes are appended to the end of the packet; otherwise it is erroneous to specify an offset greater than the offset of the current packet's last byte.

If the packet is unable to be expanded, the insert operator will throw the predefined error, **ERR_PKT_INSERT**.

```
byte barr[4] = { 6, 7, 8, 9 };
struct MyStructType {
short src;
short dest;
} myStruct = { 0xab, 0xcd };

// if pkt[16] currently = 17 and the last byte
// is at offset = 127 and has a value of 23;

// pkt[16:19] = 6, 7, 8, 17.
pkt[16].insert( 3, barr );

// Inserted bytes are 0 since fill value not specified
// pkt[16:18] = 0, 0, 17.
pkt[16].insert( 2 );

// pkt[127:129] = 23, 6, 7.
pkt[127].insert( 2, barr );

// ERROR: attempt to insert with barr shorter than insert.
// pkt[16:21] = 6, 7, 8, 9, undefined, 17.
pkt[16].insert( 5, barr );

// ERROR: attempt to insert past current legal packet end.
pkt[300].insert( 2 );
```

Packet Replicate

The **replicate** operator creates a duplicate of the packet currently being processed, as an operator it returns a result of type **void** (no meaningful result). The replicate operator throws ERR_PKT_NOREPLICATE if an error occurs while replicating the packet.

Regardless of the success or failure of the replicate operation, the original packet continues to be processed. A packet created through replication can be detected by inspecting a flag variable in the Packet Information Block (see section on Packet Information Block). Replicated packets must be detected and processed with care to prevent a self-perpetuating chain in which replicated packets trigger further replications. Other than the replica status flag, *pib* fields are carried forward into the replica with their state at the time of replication.

```
try {
    pkt.replicate();
        ...
}
catch( ERR_PKT_NOREPLICATE )
{…}
            catch( ... )
{…}
```

Packet Requeue

There are times when it is desirable to postpone processing of a given packet until some future time, e.g., a temporary lack of resources to process it. Instead of stalling the context and reducing the processing capacity of the system through a wait operation, packetC introduces the ability to place the packet back on the input queue. When the packet is requeued it is placed at the end of the list of packets awaiting assignment to a context for processing. Given that the buffer depth may ebb and flow, how soon the packet will reappear on a context for processing is not deterministic, however, information that the packet was requeued is available along with a counter of how many times. For example, the application might need to requeue the packet until a specific time and requeue rates become too high.

Requeue is not an operator so much as an action to take on the current packet at the end of processing, much like forward and drop are actions. Requeue of the packet does not occur until execution has stopped. When the packet reappears on a new context for processing, it will begin at *main()* as if it was new to the system. The only difference is that *pib.requeueCount* will be non-zero.

To select a packet to be requeued, set the **pib.action** field equal to **REQUEUE_PACKET**. This is selected as an alternative to **DROP_PACKET** or **FORWARD_PACKET**.

When current processing exits, should the packet fail to be requeued, execution will not cease and the system throws **ERR_PKT_NOTREQUEUED**. Should the decision to requeue the packet occur within a function and clean exit back to *main()* is not possible, the exit command can immediately follow the setting of **pib.action**, although it is highly discouraged as there may be other functions that expect to perform termination processing.

```
if (processingCantFinish == true)
{
    pib.action = REQUEUE_PACKET;
    exit;
};
```

■ ■ ■

Selection Statements

Covering packetC Basic Control Statements

While many programs can perform quite a lot in a straight-line list of algorithms operating on data, at some point, making some conditional branches in the logic becomes the only way to really progress from a simple formula into a program. Control flow statements fall into the conditional branching category as well as into looping. This chapter discusses the minor variations between packetC and C conditional branching while subsequent chapters cover looping.

Conditional branching represents the most basic control features within packetC, enabling the program to alternate its path through statements to achieve a complex goal. As values change in the application, multiple visits to the same conditional branch may result in alternate pathways being taken through the program. Furthermore, given that packetC is predominantly data-driven, conditional branching based upon packet data becomes a cornerstone to directing the pathway execution through the program.

All of the compound and conditional control statements that are available in C are present in packetC as well. This applies to the if-else statement as well as the switch-case statement in particular that are discussed in this chapter. While they are present, it doesn't mean that they are without some changes from C99 representation. Not to be difficult, but rather to really reflect a more modern representation of compound statements that support locality of declaration, packetC follows some C++ conventions as it addresses basic control statements.

Compound Statement

The packetC compound statement allows variable and type declarations to be freely interspersed with executable statements. This follows C++ language convention, rather than that of standard C, which promotes the desirable software property, *locality of declaration*, in which programmers place the declarations for variables in close source code proximity to their use.

```
// Example
if ( condition_applies )
{   // start of compound stmt
    counter++;
    call_take_action( counter );
}
```

Conditional Expressions

Conditional expressions can appear in stand-alone fashion or can govern the control flow of **if**, **while**, **do-while**, and **for** statements. The essential characteristics of conditional expressions are:

- Conditional expressions that evaluate to a non-zero value are considered to be true; those that evaluate to zero are regarded as false.

- The truth values produced by packetC conditional operators (logical, equality, and relational operators), however, are the int values 0 to indicate false and 1 to indicate true.

- A conditional expression can consist of arbitrarily complex expressions that mix arithmetic and conditional operators that consist solely of operators that produce a truth value or consist solely of arithmetic operators.

```
int a = 1, b = 2, c = 3;
if ( (a == b) && ( c - b ) ) {…}      // mix operator types
if ( (b > c) || ( a < b ) ) {…}       // all conditional operators
if ( a + b - c ) {…}                  // all arithmetic operators
```

- An arithmetic value that acts as a conditional expression must be an integer but is not restricted to the int type.

```
byte b0 = 0, b1 = 2, b2 = 4;
if ( b0 + b2 ) {…}                    // legal
```

- Stand-alone enumeration type values cannot act as conditional expressions, because they cannot implicitly be treated as integers. However, such values can be type cast to perform this role or can be used with conditional operators.

```
enum byte Hue = { RED, BLUE, GREEN } eVar = BLUE;
if ( eVar ) {…}                       // ERROR eVar is not an integer type
if ( (byte)eVar ) {…}                 // legal, eVar is cast to an integer type
if ( eVar != RED ) {…}                // legal, != produces truth value result
```

If Statement

```
if ( expression ) statement
if ( expression ) statement else statement
```

The semantics of the packetC **if** statement are as follow:

- The conditional expression's operands must have a scalar type.

- If the conditional expression evaluates to a non-zero value, then the statement following the **if** keyword, which may be a compound statement, is executed and the statement following the **else** keyword (if present) is not.

- If the conditional expression evaluates to the value 0, the statement associated with the **if** keyword is not executed but the statement associated with the **else** keyword is, if present.

- An **else** clause is associated with the preceding **if** clause that is lexically closest to it and that has not been terminated by a semicolon.

Traditional C if statements follow and should be familiar as the rules do not change.

```
// Examples
if ( k == 1 ) callAction1(b);

if ( k < j ) {
    counter++;
    callAction1(b);
}

if ( k != j ) {
    callAction1(b);
}
else {
    callAction2(b);
}
```

Additionally, while not shown, nesting of if statements and multiple else if statements is fully supported in packetC.

Switch Statement

```
switch ( expression )  { case_alternative_list_opt default : block_item_list_opt }
case expression : block_item_list_opt
```

Just as you would expect from C, a **switch** statement consists of a governing expression, an optional collection of **case** alternatives (each associated with a unique constant expression) and a **default** alternative. Execution begins by evaluating the governing expression. The statement or statement list associated with the first case alternative matching that expression is executed. If no **break** statement is encountered, control "falls through" to the next case alternative, as it does in C99. If no case alternative expression matches the governing expression, all statements associated with the default alternative are executed, if present, otherwise none of the case statements are executed.

The packetC switch statement differs from the C99 switch statement in the following ways:

- **case** alternatives are treated as structured statement components (i.e., similar to an if or else clause), rather than as labels.

- Curly braces always enclose the entire collection of **case** and **default** alternatives, defining a local scope and allowing the presence of local declarations.

- Statements and declarations may not appear between the opening curly brace and the initial alternative, whether the alternative is a **case** or the **default** alternative.

- A default alternative must be present and must be the final alternative.

- The only code that can appear within the switch statement body must consist of **case** or **default** alternatives.

```
// Example
switch ( myFlag ) {
case 0:
    legalIntercept++;
    analyzeFurther();
    break;
case 1:
    doOrdinaryPacketInspection();
    // drops through to next "case"
default : nopCounter++;
}
```

The switch statement is suggested any time where multiple if conditions are necessary to support branching. In packetC, many optimizations may exist in the underlying system mapping switch statements to different data representations in order to drive rapid navigation through an application. In general, when more than a few comparisons are necessary with an if statement, a switch statement should be used wherever possible.

Null Statement

Although the null statement has no semantic program impact, it is structurally useful, e.g., for providing a no-operation default alternative in a **switch** statement.

```
// Example
switch (myEnum) {
case SEQUENCE_ISSUE:
    checkSequence();
    break;

case LEGAL_ISSUE:
    doLegalIssueLog();
    break;
...
default: ;        // NULL statement
}
```

Expression Statement

An expression statement is evaluated as a null expression. As in C99, typical use consists of calling a function to trigger its side effects or altering a value to control loop iteration.

```
// Examples
counter++;
--idx;
```

■ ■ ■

Loops and Flow Control

Control Statements

Control statements direct the program to perform a set of operations repeatedly until some condition exists that terminates the repetition. packetC provides all of the C control statements. This includes for-loops, while-do, do-while, and do-until, as well as jump controls such as goto, break, continue, return, and exit. There are no surprises with regard to how packetC implements these control statements.

Looping (Iteration) Statements

Do_while Statement

do statement **while (** expression **) ;**

This construct executes its statement, which can be a compound statement, then evaluates an associated expression. As long as the expression is evaluated as true, the statement is executed and the expression is reevaluated. The **do-while** statement always executes its associated statement at least once.

```
// Example
do {
   handleInstance();
   instanceCount++;
   instancesRemain = analyzeSituation();
} while ( instancesRemain );
```

While Statement

while (expression **)** statement

A **while** statement first evaluates its controlling expression. As long as the expression evaluates to true, the associated statement, which can be a compound statement, is executed.

```
while ( instancesRemain ) {
   handleInstance();
   instanceCount++;
   instancesRemain = analyzeSituation();
}
```

For Statement

```
for ( expression_opt ; boolean_expression ; expression_opt )  statement
for ( declaration_opt ; boolean_expression ; expression_opt )  statement
```

A **for** statement consists of a control part and an associated statement, which can be a compound statement. The control part consists of a pre-loop component, a controlling expression, and a post-loop component. The pre-loop component is typically used to declare and initialize control variables; it consists either of a single optional declaration or an expression. The scope of a pre-loop declaration is the remainder of the control part and the associated statement. A pre-loop expression (assignment, variable increment or decrement) is evaluated as if it were being cast to *void*. The pre-loop component is executed once, before the control expression's initial evaluation.

The controlling expression is evaluated after the pre-loop component's execution and after each execution of the control part's associated statement. If the expression is evaluated as true, the associated statement(s) are executed and then the post-loop component is executed. If the controlling expression evaluates to false, execution of **for** statement components ceases. The post-loop component consists of an optional expression. Like a pre-loop expression, it is evaluated as if it were being cast to a *void* type; it is typically used to increment or decrement a variable.

The pre-loop and post-loop components can be omitted, although the semicolons on either side of the controlling expression must be present. Unlike C99, packetC does not allow the controlling expression to be omitted.

```
// Examples
for ( index = 0; index < 4; index++) {
   processArray ( arr[index] );
      ...
}

//
for ( int j = 0; j < 4; j++) {
   processArray ( arr[j] );
...
}
```

Finally, fear the infinite loop!

Jump Statements

Within packetC, multiple varieties of jump statements exist that control the flow of application logic. These include break, continue, goto, return, and exit.

Break Statement

A **break** statement breaks the flow of control when it appears within an iterative statement or switch statement. It causes an immediate exit from whichever of the following packetC statements enclose it more immediately than any other: **while**, **for**, **do…while**, or **switch**.

```
while ( condition_holds ) {
        ...
        switch (myVar) {
        case 0 : counter0++;
```

```
            break;    // causes exit from switch, not exit from while
      case 1:  counter1++
                         …
    }  // end of switch statement structure
    a += myVar;
    ...
    break; // causes exit from while
}
```

A **break** statement can be utilized outside of a switch construct. However, it can make programs difficult to follow and there almost always are more intuitive methods to code a given form of the expression. As such, usage of break outside of switch is not suggested within packetC; however, it is legal.

Continue Statement

A **continue** statement affects the flow of control of the innermost iterative statement enclosing it by skipping the remaining statements within the body of that enclosing statement and proceeding with the next iteration. If a **continue** statement is executed from within such a **while** or **do…while** statement, the loop continuation test is executed next. A **continue** statement executed within a **for**-statement results in the post-loop statement being executed, then the continuation test is executed.

```
for ( j = 0; j < max; j++ ) {
         while ( condition_holds ) {
          …  // statement a

          // skip statement b, re-evaluate while loop continuation test
          if ( j == 3) continue;
          …  // statement b
      }
}
```

Goto Statement

A **goto** statement specifies that a jump is to be made to a statement with the specified label name. That statement must be within the function that encloses the **goto** statement; **goto**-driven jumps cannot be made into an enclosed function or into a scope outside the enclosing function. The **goto** statement's identifier is the label name, not a variable holding a string representation of the name or one holding an address value.

```
goto START_HERE; // ERROR cannot jump into an enclosed function

int  myFn (int j, int k)
{
    if ( k > 12 ) {
       goto START_HERE;  // legal jump within current scope
    }
    …
    START_HERE:
    …
    }
```

The effect of a **goto** statement is undefined when it jumps into code that programming logic would otherwise render unreachable (e.g., a loop with a condition that is known at compile time to always be false). Such a practice relies on compiler control flow and dead code elimination being done in a particular way. Since reliability is a principal goal of packetC, implementations are not required to support this programming technique.

```
if ( 5 > 12 ) {
    INSIDE_LOOP: counter++;
    goto AFTERWARD;
}
goto INSIDE_LOOP;   // Undefined event, since the conditional would otherwise never
                    // execute to INSIDE_LOOP AFTERWARD:
```

The **goto** statement is one of the most controversial in the world of C given that it has always seemed to be a throwback to earlier generations of languages and a hack if it's used.

In packetC, however, there are many sections of code that, when optimized, are most efficient when using goto. As such, when used within a constrained region of code without possibility of jumps to unforeseen sections of code, goto can be a formidable tool in the optimization for performance category that fits well with packetC.

That said; avoid the urge, just like macros, wherever possible.

Return Statement

A **return** statement returns control to a function's caller. If the function has a return type of **void**, the **return** statement shall not be associated with an expression. Otherwise, the statement shall be associated with an expression of the type returned by the function invocation. Each function shall contain a **return** statement.

```
int myFn1( int j, int k )
{
            return j * k + 5;  // return int
    }

void myFn2 ()
{
    ...
    return;                         // return void
}
```

Exit Statement

An **exit** statement terminates processing of the packet and jumps to the end of *main()* without any further processing.

```
void myFunction ()
{
    ...
    exit;   // Terminate Processing of Packet No Matter Where We Are In Code
}
```

CHAPTER 13

■ ■ ■

Exception Handling

Exception Handling in packetC

packetC utilizes a try-catch-throw exception-handling system similar to many modern languages, such as C++ and Java. In packetC, all exceptions must be caught whether they are system-defined or application-defined. That means that all applications must be wrapped within an error-handler to accommodate catching any errors that may be thrown by the functionality utilized. Any possible errors thrown by an application that are not caught will be flagged by the compiler and compilation will not be allowed to proceed.

Identifiers used by the exception-handling system are named-constants that are either pre-defined by the system or defined by the application to catch exceptions thrown by a portion of the application. Further study on this method of error-handling will show how this can either dominate the architecture of an application or help to keep error-handling out of the primary processing flow, depending upon the amount of up-front planning performed. Additionally, just like other parts of packetC are heavily influenced by scope, so is exception-handling. Ensuring that the scope of caught exceptions is being handled where they are thrown will help to avoid the common application-created exceptions that are trying to be handled at too global of a scope.

For every opcode that produces a possible exception, a location to catch the exception must be present. This leads to the requirement described above whereby the compiler ensures that a program has caught every possible exception to successfully compile. Performance of this approach is enhanced as the opcode itself has the location of the exception-handler and it is not up to additional or subjectively-handled code to determine whether an exception has occurred and whether to handle it. This also ensures more secure code as undetected errors can lead to assumptions about input criteria that may not be visible in a simple audit of a control flow.

The following section describes the control flow within a packetC application. It is important to note that some aspects of the control-flow and exceptions may generate conditions where the application cannot handle the response. This may include the failure of an opcode to perform its expected task. As such, some hypervisor errors will generate exceptions handled by a control plane. While this is out of the scope of packetC, it is important to understand the possibility of that interaction. For example, should the underlying system be unable to receive packets due to an operating system issue, this is out of the scope of a packetC application to handle and as such the exception will not be presented to packetC in the data plane but rather a control plane processor for an exception handler.

Try-Catch-Throw Statements (Error Handling)

```
try  compound_statement  catch_list
catch ( identifier ) compound_statement
catch ( … ) compound_statement
```

Error Handling (try-catch-throw)

packetC uses try-catch-throw error-handling for cleaner code and more advanced error-handling possibilities. Ignoring the fact that not handling errors is very bad programming practice, several methods for error handling we explored and the migration to this mechanism similar to C++ provided the cleanest control flow and deterministic handling. Other possible methods for error handling ranged from return-code testing to On Error handling, both of which did not join well with the flow of packetC applications nor the performance attributes. Try-catch in packetC provides benefits in speed and size, with the added bonus of providing a less error-prone way to handle errors. Given that try-catch-throw is the error-handling method that most modern-day programming languages use, advancing packetC away from the primitive return-code handling of C meets many of the exception-handling demands of a real-time system.

```
try {
    pkt.replicate();
    ...
    // other statements
}
catch( ERR_PKT_NOREPLICATE )   // catch just this error
{...}
catch( ... )                   // catch all other errors
{...}
```

If an exception is thrown in the code sequence of a try block, subsequent statements in the sequence are skipped and the code in the catch block handling the exception is executed.

Try and Catch Statements

packetC provides **try**, **catch**, and **throw** constructs as the basis for user error handling. The **try** construct effectively connects a *try block* (which may consist of a single packetC statement or a compound statement) with a related group of **catch** constructs—a *catch block*. If the execution of any construct in the try block triggers a recognized packetC system error (see table below) or triggers a **throw** statement, the associated catch block must handle that error.

catch constructs either respond to a single error (identified by a named *int* constant within parentheses) or handle all errors, indicated by **...** (an ellipsis) in parentheses. **catch** statements cannot appear by themselves, they must be associated with a matching **try** construct.

```
try {
    pkt.replicate();
    ...
    // other statements
}
catch( ERR_PKT_NOREPLICATE )   // catch just this error
{...}
catch( ... )                   // catch all other errors
{...}
```

Each catch clause is associated with one or more statements within curly braces, which take user-specified actions in response to the named error condition. Catch clauses with only one statement must place that statement within curly braces. packetC and C++ both have this requirement.

An implementation may optionally analyze the position of catch-all clauses and issue warnings about catch clauses or catch-all clauses that can never be executed.

```
// legal - explicit catch clause handles relevant error
try  { pkt.replicate(); }
catch ( ERR_PKT_NOREPLICATE )  {…}

// legal - catch-all clause is present
try  { pkt.replicate(); }
catch ( ... ) {…}

// ERROR: no catch clause for replicate construct's ERR_PKT_NOREPLICATE
try { pkt.replicate(); }
catch ( ERR_PKT_NOTREQUEUED )  {…}
```

Implicit Throw Statements

Some packetC constructs are capable of implicitly *throwing* a predefined error when they appear within a **try** statement or block of statements (see Table 13-1). It is a compilation error if any system error that could be thrown by a packetC construct is not handled by an associated catch clause. This requires the construct that could throw the error to appear within a try block.

Table 13-1. *Predefined Errors Thrown by packetC Constructs*

packetC construct	Associated errors
database.**insert**()	ERR_DB_FULL
database[*rownum*]	ERR_DB_READ
database.**match**()	ERR_DB_NOMATCH
pkt.**insert**()	ERR_PKT_INSERT
pkt.**delete**()	ERR_PKT_DELETE
pkt.**replicate**	ERR_PKT_NOREPLICATE
pkt.**requeue**	ERR_PKT_NOTREQUEUED
searchset.**find**()	ERR_SET_NOTFOUND
searchset.**match**()	ERR_SET_NOMATCH

```
a  =  b;
pkt.replicate();  // ERROR: ERR_PKT_NOREPLICATE not handled
b  =  c;

pkt.replicate();
catch ( ERR_PKT_NOREPLICATE )  {…}
```

```
// Error: catch cannot appear stand-alone;
// must be associated with a try construct.
```

Explicit Throw Statements

A **throw** statement explicitly throws the solitary error indicated by its lone argument. That error is a unique constant of type *int* and is either a predefined system error (as listed in the table above and in file **cloudshield.ph**) or an error defined by the user. It is a compilation error for the thrown error not to be caught by an appropriate catch statement.

The placement and behavior of throw statements are governed by these rules:

- A **throw** statement must appear within a statement block associated with a **try** statement: to do otherwise is an error.

- The **throw** statement may be within a nesting level deeper than that of the governing try block. This includes appearing within a catch block associated with some try block nested more deeply than the governing try block (see below).

- A **throw** statement's error is matched against the catch clauses of the innermost try block that encloses it. It is a compilation error if none of these catch clauses handles the error. packetC does not propagate the error to any successive, outer nesting scopes for comparison against their catch clauses.

```
// Assume SOME_ERROR, SOME_OTHER_ERROR are defined "const ints"
try  {
        ...
        throw SOME_ERROR;
    }
    catch ( SOME_OTHER_ERROR )  {…}
    catch (…) {…}               // Catch all other errors (SOME_ERROR in this case)
```

In the following example, both of the **throw** statements are handled by the same **catch** clause.

```
try {
        try {
                ...
        }
        catch( ERR_DB_FULL ) {
                ...
                throw MY_ERROR; // outer try is the enclosing try block
        }
        catch( ... ) {
                ...
        }

    ...
    throw MY_ERROR;
    ...
}

catch( ERR_PKT_NOREPLICATE ) {
        ...
}
```

```
catch( MY_ERROR ) {
    ...
}
```

In the following example, the **throw** statement throws an error outside of any try-block, creating an unhandled error.

```
try {
        ...
}
catch ( AN_ERROR ) {
    ...
    throw SOME_ERROR; // thrown outside of catch's associated try-block
}
catch ( OTHER_ERROR ) {}
catch (…) {…}
// COMPILER ERROR: SOME_ERROR throw statement does not appear
// within any enclosing try block
```

User-Defined Errors

A packetC implementation lists all the error numbers it uses for predefined packetC errors (i.e., those implicitly *thrown* by packetC commands) in the include file "**cloudshield.ph**". It is recommended that the user use the **ERR_LAST_DEFINED**, which is defined as the highest integer value used for system-defined errors. User-provided error numbers can calculate their values in terms of **ERR_LAST_DEFINED** to ensure unique values.

```
const int USER_ERROR1 = ERR_LAST_DEFINED + 1;
const int USER_ERROR2 = ERR_LAST_DEFINED + 2;
const int USER_ERROR3 = ERR_LAST_DEFINED + 3;
…
```

System-Defined Response

This section lists the conditions for which a packetC implementation should describe system-defined responses. While packetC does not prescribe specific behavior for these various states, it does not ascribe "undefined behavior" for them, as C99 does.

- **Divide by zero**: a divide or remainder operator was executed with a zero divisor.

- **Illegal array slice range**: a range expression for an array slice was not determinable at compile time and at run time yielded an illegal value (i.e., array indices out of bounds, range with right-hand expression less than left-hand expression).

Errors Section from cloudshield.ph

packetC uses the following declarations, available in the file **cloudshield.ph** for the user to reference.

```
/* The pre-defined packetC errors and their associated values are shown below:
const int   ERR_DB_FULL         = 1;
const int   ERR_DB_READ         = 2;
const int   ERR_DB_NOMATCH      = 3;
const int   ERR_PKT_INSERT       = 4;
const int   ERR_PKT_DELETE      = 5;
const int   ERR_PKT_NOREPLICATE = 6;
const int   ERR_SET_NOMATCH     = 7;
const int   ERR_SET_NOTFOUND    = 9;
const int   ERR_PKT_NOTREQUEUED = 10;
*/
const int   ERR_LAST_DEFINED    = 64;
```

Simple Program Flow with Try-Catch-Throw Implemented

```
packet module searchpayload;
#include <cloudshield.ph>;
#include <protocols.ph>;

regex searchset regexSet[2][4] = {"GET", "POST"};
%pragma datatype regexSet ( regex1 );

void main( $PACKET pkt, $PIB pib, $SYS sys )
{
    searchResult rslt;

    try {
       rslt = regexSet.find( pkt[pib.payloadOffset:end] );
       pib.action = FORWARD_PACKET;
    }
    catch ( ERR_SET_NOTFOUND )
    {
       pib.action = DROP_PACKET;
    }
}
```

CHAPTER 14

■ ■ ■

packetC Database Types and Operations

In packetC, several extended data types are present that do not appear in standard C but do provide significant support for packet-processing applications. These data types are extensions of familiar C types with special characteristics, including the fact that they define objects with methods that operate on their data. These types are databases, descriptors, and searchsets.

Databases provide the ability to represent a table of data elements and search it for specific data. Additionally, bit-level masking can be used both in the database of entries as well as in the records used to search the database, allowing the queries to be field-specific much like a database server query. However, databases in packetC are atomic objects with direct methods for reference.

Databases in packetC are based on a collection of records which define the structure of a row. Different databases can have rows of various sizes. The packetC virtual machines will manage the underlying representation. Databases are fairly simple to define because they are modeled as arrays of structures. Earlier chapters highlighted that packetC arrays did not support non-scalar types, in part due to the special functionality applied to arrays. Databases are a special type of array of structs with its own set of special features, called *methods*, that operate against the database. In addition, a record is defined which represents a single row. One subtle but crucial difference that vastly changes databases and records from being simple arrays of structs is that notion of masks which can create a shadow second representation of the structure to contain the bit-level masking.

```
struct MyDBrec {
    int srcIp;
    int destIp;
    ...
};

// Create a database of 100 recs
database MyDbRec   myDb[100];
record MyDbRec myRec;
```

Operations on databases are simple and intuitive.

```
myRec = myDb[5];              // Get a record
myDb[1].delete();            // Delete a record
myDb[1] = myRec;             // Alter a record
myDb.insert( myRec );        // Insert a record

recNum = myDb.match( toFind ); // Record matching
```

Masking for masked databases allow for field-by-field masking.

```
struct MyDbRec {
    int srcIp;
    int destIp;
        ...
};

// Create a database of 100 recs
database MyDbRec        myDb[100];
record MyDbRec          tempRow;

tempRow.srcIp = 10.10.1.234;
tempRow.mask.srcIp = 255.255.255.0;
...
tempRow.destIp = 192.10.1.2;
tempRow.mask.destIp = 255.255.0.0;
...
```

Database Declarations

A packetC *database* is an aggregate data type, composed of multiple instances of user-specified packetC structures. A database acts much like a dynamic array, referencing individual elements via bracketed indices, deleting individual elements, and adding new elements.

However, a database differs from packetC arrays in several ways: only a single dimension of indexing is allowed, contiguous elements cannot be referenced by array slice syntax (see section on arrays), and the user cannot presume that the database is stored in local or global memory. This last difference frees implementations to store databases in specialized hardware designed to facilitate searching and matching operations.

A packetC database declaration creates a database with user-specified base type, name, number of elements and, if supplied, an initialization clause. The basic form of a database declaration is:

database typeId identifier **[** constant_expression **]** identifier_init_clause$_{OPT}$ **;**

Where typeId is an identifier that specifies a structure type and constant_expression is a compile-time constant expression that indicates the maximum size of the database.

- typeId is the type of the individual database elements.

- identifier is the name of the database.

- expression is a constant expression specifying the maximum number of elements.

```
// Example
    struct BaseType { short src;  short dest; };
    database BaseType  myDb[50];
```

Two kinds of syntax can appear within a database initialization clause:

- The explicit format is characterized by data and mask parts that are separated by a comma, where each part appears as a structure initialization expression within curly braces. This data/mask pair is surrounded by an outer set of curly braces.

- An implicit format omits the mask portion but still surrounds the data initialization expression with an outer set of curly braces. When the mask is omitted in this way, it is presumed to consist of all bits set (equal to one).

```
// Example explicit and implicit mask formats
    database T Db1[50] = { {{5,12},{~0,~0}}, {{6,10},{~0,~0}} };   // explicit
    database T Db2[50] = { {{5,12}}, {{6,10}} };                   // implicit
```

When the declaration specifies that the database has *n* elements and the initialization clause contains *p* elements.

- If p <= n, then p initializing elements will be loaded into database elements 0 through p-1.

- If p > n, the results, such as initializing only the first n elements or issuing error messages, is implementation-defined.

A database can only be declared in a module's global scope. Otherwise, a database declared in a packet module's packet scope, for example, would require a different database for every *instance* (copy running in parallel) of the packet main application.

Databases and Masking

Packet processing often involves storing and searching data from multiple packet headers and payloads. This aggregate data can most efficiently be stored in a *database*. To provide both organization and flexibility, packetC organizes databases as aggregates of C-style structures. These databases have some similarities to a one-dimensional, dynamic array. However, in order to support the use of specialized, high-speed stores for searching and matching, packetC implementations can locate databases outside of local or global memory.

Operations on database contents may include searching and matching data that is associated with *masks*. For data organized as structures, each database component (structure) will be associated with a structure of equal size (its mask), which holds the corresponding mask bits. The mask controls which portions of the data field are used in database searching operations. If a mask bit is equal to 1, the corresponding data bit is considered in these operations; otherwise, the bit is ignored.

```
data: src field        data: dest field       mask: src field        mask: dest field
0000000000000101       0000000000011101       0000000000000000       1111111111111111
```

In the example above, the mask bits that correspond to the *dest* field are all set, so the entire *dest* field will be used in database searching and matching operations. Since no *src* field mask bits are set, these operations will ignore that field.

A key aspect of packetC databases is *automated masking*. This consists of taking the database's structure base type, T, and recasting it to have two identical, nested structures: data and mask. Automated masking is performed when either a database or a database record is declared.

```
struct BaseType { short src; short dest; };
database BaseType myDb[50];          // has automated masking effects
```

Conceptually, the database is composed of structures with the following organization:

```
struct MyBaseStruct {
    struct BaseType  data;
    struct BaseType  mask;
};
```

The original user type's individual fields are still accessible as sub-fields. Since both the data and its associated mask are structures, setting mask values can be done by setting individual fields, rather than solely by using large constants to set the entire mask. A user may access the contents of the data portion by either using .data syntax or by omitting the name of the nested structure. The latter features are especially helpful if the user is not manipulating masks.

```
record BaseType  myRec;       // has automated masking effects
myRec.mask.src = 0xffff;
myRec.data.src = 256;
```

Conceptually, all packetC databases have associated mask bits. However, if a user never manipulates a database's mask bits, an implementation may optimize its representation appropriately. Both initialization clauses that specify mask bit values and operations that read or write mask bit values signify that a database actively uses mask bits.

The major components of the packetC approach to databases are:

- Databases: aggregates of C structures, which are automatically masked

- Database records: matches database's automatically masked structure

- Individual Masks: non-masked structure that is equivalent to a database record's mask portion

```
struct BaseType { short src; short dest; };
database BaseType myDb[50];              // database
record BaseType  myRec;                  // database record
const BaseType  myMask = {~0s, 0s};      // individual mask
```

The following sections discuss these components in greater detail.

Database Limitations and Padding

A packetC implementation can implement a database in a variety of ways, including using specialized associative memories or by using an array in ordinary memory to represent the database. Regardless of the implementation mechanism, the user may declare a database that is too large for the implementation to accommodate. When a packetC implementation cannot represent a user-defined database because of size constraints, it shall issue an appropriate fatal error message. The maximum size of a packetC database that can be accommodated is implementation-dependent.

An implementation may pad a database, for example by adding unused bits to the database's base type to make it match the size of a specialized memory used to hold databases. Such unused bits need not be exposed to the user.

```
struct BaseType { short src; short dest; };
database BaseType uDb[35]; // baseType may be padded to 128 or 512 bits
```

Database Records and Elements

When a database's masked bits will be accessed, the user declares a database *record*, which is automatically masked, just as a database is. Thus, the record has the same .data and .mask components as a database does, which has been made from the same structure base type.

```
struct BaseType  { short src; short dest; };
database  BaseType  myDb[50];
record  BaseType  myRec;
```

Individual database elements are accessed like an array element by placing a single-dimension indexing expression within square brackets. The value of a database element can be "read" by assigning it to a structure variable with the same type as the database.

```
database BaseType   myDb[35];
record BaseType     myRec;

...
myRec  =  myDb[5];
myRec.data.dest = 10.10.1.1;
myDb[5] = myRec;
```

Similarly, an existing database element may be "written" by simply assigning it the value of a variable with the same structure type. A reference to the variable without specifying any field, accesses the entire structure. If an individual sub-field is referenced without prefacing it with **.data** or **.mask,** then **.data** is assumed.

```
// Both the same
MyDb[12].data.dest  =  myRec.data.dest;
MyDb[12].dest = myRec.dest;

MyDb[5] = myrecord;
```

Masks

A packetC mask is a bit pattern that corresponds to the base structure of a database or database record and that contains as many bits as the base-type structure does. A mask is not declared as a database record (since that would automatically mask a mask); instead it is declared as a structure of the same type as the base type of the relevant database.

```
struct    BaseType { short src;  short dest; };
database BaseType  myDb[100];
record   BaseType  myRec;
const    BaseType  myMask = {~0s, 0s};

// Read mask and data from a DB; Alter data and mask
myRec          = myDb[j];          // access entire structure
myRec.src      = 17;               // defaults to data.src field
myRec.mask.dest = ~0;              // set bits in indicated mask portion field

// Write only the altered data portion to the original DB record
myDb[j].data  = myRec.data;
```

143

```
// Write altered data and mask to another DB record
myDb[m]  =  myRec;
```

A common application scenario involves defining a small number of masks that do not vary during execution. For example, one mask might be defined to regard all of a database structure as significant, and several masks could be defined that ignore all of the structure except for a single field or sub-field of interest.

A mask that does not change during application execution, such as those in the example above, should be defined with the **const** specifier. packetC implementations may use this information for optimizations.

Database Subscripting Operator

The subscripting operator works for databases in much the same way as it works for arrays. In both cases, a postfix expression is followed by an expression within square brackets, which designates an element of the aggregate (in this case, the database).

Indexing a packetC database, however, simply indicates an individual element in the database; the user should make no assumptions that database elements are present in memory, stored in row-major order, and so forth. Differences between packetC databases and arrays are enumerated in the section on the database type. Like arrays, databases are indexed by values that start at zero.

If the record does not exist in the database, the operator will throw the predefined error, **ERR_DB_READ**.

```
database MyStructType   myDb[50];
MyStructType    structVar;
...

// alter the contents of the 4th element of the database
myDb[3].data  =  structVar;
```

Database Delete

The operator for deleting a single database element consists of an indexed reference to a single database element, followed by a dot ("."), the **delete** keyword, and empty parentheses. The operator deletes the indicated database element and effectively returns **void** (no meaningful result). Only a single item may be specified as an index. Multiple deletions must be carried out using multiple commands or an iterated loop.

```
database MyStructType  myDb[75];


...

// Valid forms
myDb[34].delete();
myDb[j].delete();
```

```
// Error forms
myDb.delete();          // one specific database element must be specified
myDb[0:4].delete();     // only a single database element can be specified
```

Database Insert

A database insertion adds a new element to the database, using the specified argument of the database's base type, and returns an *int* value with the number of the database row where the information was inserted. An implementation may affect optimizations on the basis of whether the returned row number is ignored by user code.

  If the database is full, the insert operator will throw the predefined error, **ERR_DB_FULL**.

```
struct BaseType { short src; short dest; };
BaseType myStruct = { 15, 17 };
database BaseType  myDb[50];
int rowNum, oddUse;
...
rowNum = myDb.insert( myStruct );           // myDb insertion point data is used
myDb.insert( myStruct );                    // Returned int is ignored

// database insert acts like an operator that produces
// int result in unlikely example below,
// where result = the insertion 'row' number plus 500
oddUse  =  500 + myDb.insert( myStruct );
```

  The operand of the insert operator may be a structure or a record.

Database Match

The match operator returns an int value that indicates the database row that provided the first match for the initial argument.

  Match compares each database row (structure), from first to last, to the operator's first argument. The row number of the first row to match is returned. If a second argument is present, it receives the contents of this matching row. Using the second argument with an unmasked database has little utility, since the matched data already exists in the first argument.

  If no match is found, the match operator will throw the predefined error, **ERR_DB_NOMATCH**.

```
struct  MyRecStruct  {
   short src;
   short dest;
   };

   database MyRecStruct myDb[20]  =  {…};
   record   MyRecStruct searchStruct = { {16s, 32s},{~0s, 0s} }, retStruct;
   int      rowNum;
   ...
   try {
        ...
```

```
   // returns row number of match
   rowNum = myDb.match(searchStruct);

   // Also returns row number of match
   rowNum = myDb.match(searchStruct, retStruct);
   ...
}
catch ( ERR_DB_NOMATCH ) {
   ...
}
```

Operator Invocations

packetC defines built-in functions or operators for its extended data types. These operators, which are described in the section on extended operators and operands, are invoked in much the same manner as user-defined functions are. Invoking built-in operators, however, differs from invoking user functions in the following ways:

- The invocation consists of a variable of the data type for which the operator is defined, a dot ("."), the operator name, and a parenthesized argument list.

- The argument list cannot use the by-substitution mode of parameter passing.

```
struct StructType {
short src;
short dest;
};
database StructType  myDb[20] = {…};
StructType  searchStruct = { 16s, 32s };
int rowNum;
...
try {
   rowNum = myDb.match(searchStruct); // legal
   // ERROR: The example below attemps to use by-substitution
   // param with an operation, which is not allowed
   rowNum = myDb.match(@searchStruct);
}
```

Example Database Application

```
packet module databaseTable;

#include "cloudshield.ph"
#include "protocols.ph"

// global counters
int     totalPkts_     = 0;
int     readPass_      = 0;
int     readFail_      = 0;
```

```
// Record structure of the database
struct DbStruct {
        int data1, data2, data3, data4;
};

// Define unmasked databases using DbStruct
database DbStruct dbTable1[9] = {
#include "db_data1.px"
};
database DbStruct dbTable2[9] = {
#include "db_data2.px"
};

void main($PACKET pkt, $PIB pib, $SYS sys)
{
  DbStruct readData;
  int fail;
  ++totalPkts_;

  try
  {
    readData = dbTable1[3].data;
    ++readPass_;
    readData = dbTable2[3].data;
    ++readPass_;
  }
  catch (ERR_DB_READ)
  {
    ++readFail_;
  }
  catch ( ... )
  {
    ++fail;
  }
  pib.action = FORWARD_PACKET;
}
```

Example Database Application (ACL)

```
// Simplified Access Control List Example
packet module aclExample;

#include "cloudshield.ph"

// Define User Error Constant
const int ERR_BAD_PACKET = ERR_LAST_DEFINED + 1;

// Define Global variables
int notValidPacket_ = 0;
```

```
int matchPacketCounter_ = 0;
int noMatchPackelCounter_ - 0;
int fail_ = 0;
struct AclStruct {
    int srcIp;
    int destIp;
    short srcPort;
    short destPort;
};

descriptor IpDescriptor
{
    int sourceAddress;
    int destAddress;
} ip at pib.l3Offset + 12;

descriptor TcpDescriptorPorts
{
    short sourcePort;
    short destPort;
} tcp at pib.l4Offset;

database AclStruct aclDb[6] = {
    {{ 10.10.20.80, 10.10.10.50, 25s, 8s }, { ~0, ~0, ~0s, ~0s }},
    {{ 10.10.20.81, 10.10.10.50, 25s, 8s }, { ~0, ~0, ~0s, ~0s }},
    {{ 10.10.20.82, 10.10.10.50, 25s, 8s }, { ~0, ~0, ~0s, ~0s }},
    {{ 10.10.20.83, 10.10.10.50, 25s, 8s }, { ~0, ~0, ~0s, ~0s }},
    {{ 10.10.20.84, 10.10.10.50, 25s, 8s }, { ~0, ~0, ~0s, ~0s }},
    {{ 0.0.0.0, 0.0.0.0, 0s, 0s }, { ~0, ~0, ~0s, ~0s }}
};


void main($PACKET pkt, $PIB pib, $SYS sys)
{
    // Assume
    try {
        if ( !pib.flags.l4CheckSumValid ||
             !pib.flags.ipv4 ||
             pib.l4Type != L4TYPE_ICMP
           )
            //User defined err
            throw ERR_BAD_PACKET;

        AclStruct acl;
        acl.srcIp = ip.sourceAddress;
        acl.destIp = ip.destAddress;
        acl.srcPort = tcp.sourcePort;
        acl.destPort = tcp.destPort;
        // Look up this acl, throws ERR_DB_NOMATCH if not
        // currently in the acl database.
        int aclMatchRow;
        aclMatchRow = aclDb.match( acl );
```

```
        // Found in acl database
        ++matchPacketCounter_;
        pib.action = FORWARD_PACKET; // Forward this packet

}


    catch ( ERR_DB_NOMATCH ) {
        ++noMatchPacketCounter_;
        // pib.action = DROP_PACKET; Default Drop this packet
    }
    catch ( ERR_BAD_PACKET ) {
        ++notValidPacket_;
    }
    catch ( ... ) {
        // accident
        ++fail_;
    }
}
```

packetC Search Set Types and Operations

Searchsets in packetC for Unstructured Content Analysis

As was described in the chapter covering databases, packetC introduces several extended-data types that do not appear in standard C to provide significant support for packet-processing applications. These data types are extensions of familiar C types with special characteristics including the familiar C++ syntax as objects with methods that operate on their data. These types are databases, descriptors, and searchsets.

Searchsets are one of the most different extended-data types introduced by packetC. Imagine a dictionary of strings and a packet containing a set of words. Searchsets provide the means of comparing the packet against all of the words in the dictionary with the goal of finding one or more of them and providing the result in a simple returned data structure.

While that sounds simple, the complexities of how strings are handled in packetC, the notion of NULL and then a slight migration from strings to complex regular expressions throws a few twists into this extended-data type and the methods that operate on the object. Once mastered, however, the searchset performs powerful analysis of data sets that can be used for much more than merely to find a keyword within a textual protocol.

Searchsets

Searchsets provide a simple way to **match** or **find** strings or regular expressions in byte arrays.

A packetC *searchset* is an aggregate data type that gathers together a related set of strings or regular expressions. Built-in operators, **match** and **find**, are defined for variables of type **searchset.** They search memory (e.g., the packet, local, or global variables) for the presence of the strings defined by a searchset.

Unlike the case of other aggregate data types (e.g., arrays and structures), packetC does not specify how implementations must store a searchset. Instead, an implementation may provide searches on searchsets by a variety of means, ranging from comparing literals to using specialty devices for string or bit-pattern manipulation. Users can employ a **deref** operator to effectively produce one of several candidate searchsets to act as an operand with a particular instance of the searchset **match** or **find** operators. (See sections on the reference data type and reference operators). Using **deref** in this way may influence how an implementation chooses to represent some or all of those searchsets in order to guarantee that all are implemented in a common fashion at that point in the program.

The key characteristic of **searchset** as a data type is that it groups together string or regular expression definitions that will be used together in searches, rather than specifies the memory layout of a collection of items. A packetC **searchset** implementation:

- Stores a collection of strings or of regular expressions (but not a mixture of both) that will be used in searches.

- Uses **match** and **find** operators to search for strings defined by the **searchset** within the packet, local arrays, or other storage.

- May be implemented by a variety of methods that provide the specified searching actions, rather than provide a set scheme for storing the strings independent of any specific search.

The sections below discuss how to declare **searchset**, using either strings or regular expressions, how the **const** specifier affects **searchsets**, and how the user can manage null termination issues.

Searchset Declarations

A searchset declaration consists of:

- The optional presence of **const** and/or **regex** as declaration specifiers

- **searchset** keyword

- An identifier, indicating the searchset variable's name

- The searchset size, indicated by a constant expression within square brackets

- The maximum length of a searchset string, indicated by a constant expression within square brackets (this value must be greater than or equal to the length of the longest initializing string)

- An optional set of initialization values (strings or constant byte array names) within curly braces

- When the **regex** specifier is present, a separate construct, a compiler pragma with the category datatype, can be used to specify which regular expression syntax and conventions the searchset regular expressions use (see the pragma and implementation-defined pragma sections in Chapter 22)

A searchset can only be declared in a module's global scope. Otherwise, a searchset declared in a packet module's packet scope, for example, would require a different searchset for every *instance* (copy running in parallel) of the packet main application.

The material that follows discusses the **searchset** declaration elements as they appear from left to right.

Constant Searchsets and Sizes

A **const** specifier indicates that no changes can be made to a **searchset** after its initialization. When **const** is present, it is an error for the declared size of the **searchset** and the number of initializing items not to be equal (whether the initializing items are present in an initializing clause or inside an initializing file).

When **const** is not present, it may be possible for an implementation-specific control plane capability to change the contents of searchset strings. This capability may affect how an implementation actualizes searches. When a declaration is not qualified by **const**, it is legal for the declared size of the

searchset to differ from the number of initialization items. In this case, implementation-specific control plane capabilities may allow users to add or alter string definitions at run time. In no instance, however, can such a capability alter the size of a searchset or size of the largest searchset string.

A searchset must be composed entirely of strings that are to be interpreted as regular expressions or entirely of ordinary strings. The declaration of a searchset composed of regular expressions should be declared with the **regex** type specifier and, typically, will be associated with a datatype pragma that specifies which regular expression conventions are supported. The initialization clause of a regular expression searchset contains regular expressions enclosed in double quotes.

Null Termination Issues

Null termination impacts searchsets in two ways:

- Whether the mechanics of string matching and finding are to treat the searchset strings as having trailing null terminators

- Whether the memory space that is to be searched for matching instances of searchset strings is, itself, null terminated (i.e., whether the search should terminate upon finding a null terminator in that space)

If the user does not want to include a trailing null terminator as part of any searchset string and does not want the search terminated upon reaching a null terminator, then no explicit null handling is required.

If the user does not want to include a trailing null terminator as part of any searchset string but does want the search terminated upon reaching a null terminator, then the user can add the pre-defined string literal constant, **NULL_STOP** to the searchset definition.

If the user has included explicit null terminators as part of one or more searchset strings but the search space is not null-terminated, then none of the explicitly terminated searchset strings can find a match within the search space.

If the user has included explicit null terminators as part of one or more searchset strings and wants the search to be stopped if it encounters a null terminator without matching any of those strings, then the user can add the pre-defined string literal constant, **NULL_STOP**, to the end of the searchset definition. Similarly, for regular expression searchset definitions, **NULL_REGEX** is used.

The NULL_STOP and NULL_REGEX indicators are defined as follows:

Match Operator

A searchset **match** operator is used to find a string at a specific location within the data set.

- postfix_expression is a variable of type searchset

- argument consists of one argument, which may be the packet, a local variable, or variable declared with the **buffer** storage specifier (including arrays and array slices)

The **match** operator returns a structure of pre-defined type, *SearchResult*, defined below.

The **match** operator compares each searchset string, s, with a length s_n against the contents of the n contiguous bytes that begin at the argument's starting address. A searchset declared with the **regex** type specifier (i.e., a searchset composed of regular expressions) may not use the **match** operator, since regular expressions are not restricted to this kind of fixed-length matching. As a consequence, an error results from attempting to use a **deref** operator where it could produce a **regex searchset** as a match operand.

If no match is found, the **match** operator will throw the predefined error, **ERR_SET_NOMATCH**.

Find Operator

A searchset **find** operator is used to scan a data set to find a string somewhere within the range of the data specified.

- postfix_expression is a variable of type searchset

- argument consists of one argument, which may be the packet, a local variable, or variable declared with the **buffer** storage specifier (including arrays and array slices)

Find effectively searches for each searchset string, *s*, within the searched memory space. Matches occur regardless of a matching string's position from the start of the searched space, although target strings appearing closer to the start will be found before those appearing farther away. When a searchset is declared without the **regex** type qualifier (does not contain regular expressions), attempts to find the individual strings are made in the same order as their declaration. In this case, searching attempts terminate when a match is located. When a **regex** type specifier identifies a searchset as containing regular expressions, the matching sequence and behavior depends on the characteristics of the regular expressions involved.

The **find** operator returns a structure of pre-defined type, *SearchResult*, defined below.

If no match is found, the **find** operator will throw the predefined error, **ERR_SET_NOTFOUND**.

Regex Specifier

The **regex** specifier is only relevant to declarations involving the packetC extended *searchset* data type. The specifier's presence indicates that a searchset's strings each contain a *regular expression*, a formalism for describing a set of strings or character sequences. The specifier does not indicate which of the competing forms for regular expression syntax the strings contain. Instead, the particular conventions for regular expression syntax that a packetC implementation supports can be indicated with appropriate pragmas. (See the sections on the searchset data type and on pragmas.)

Interaction of packetC Pre-Processor with Regular Expressions

The pragma associated with a search set defines which regular expression language to utilize. The regular expression language is specific to the compiler implementation. One key thing to note is that packetC's pre-processor will make modifications to source code and initialized data prior to compilation that may interact with the contents of a regular expression. The primary element that causes interaction is the backslash "\" character. Both the packetC pre-processor and POSIX regular expression grammar utilize the backslash for special features. A packetC compile-time instantiation of a regular expression may require double backslashes to ensure that they are passed appropriately as a single backslash to the regular expression compiler.

Values updated at run time by control plane API's won't necessarily be affected by the pre-processors in the same manner.

The regex1 argument specified in the pragma indicates that the associated searchset contains strings that are to be interpreted as regular expressions that use regex1 conventions as defined by the compiler developer. CloudShield compilers map the regex1 argument to POSIX Regular Expression with non-greedy expressions. Future implementations may include other arguments such as regex2, which could map to PCRE Regular Expressions.

Refer to the *CloudShield Regular Expressions Guide* within the CloudShield PacketWorks IDE manuals for more information on their specific implementation.

General Search Set Usage, Operation, and Mechanics

The operation performed with the match and find operators on a search set can be broken down fairly simply when considering the overall approach to locating strings within datasets.

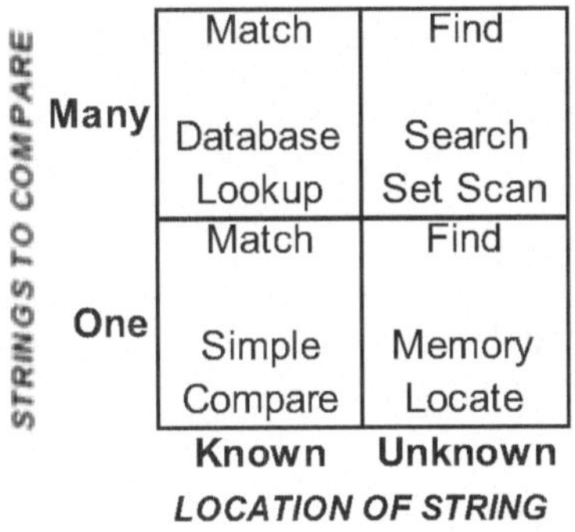

Figure 15-1. Mapping various string searches to implementation

Figure 15-1 maps two dimensions representing the number of strings in the searchset and the location to be evaluated to identify a string matching one of the elements within the searchset. As described earlier in this chapter, the **match** operator is used to find a string at a known location while the **find** operator is used to search through a data set to find a string. When consider the evaluations being requested, some of these requests can be performed using simple evaluations. For example, a searchset containing only one string being evaluated against a data set using the **match** operator maps to a simple C *memcmp()* operation. At the same time, when a known location is specified by the **match** operator and a list of strings is being used, the equivalent of a packetC database may be utilized with masked elements for strings that are shorter than others. When only one string is in the searchset and the **find** operator is used, this can map to a *memlocate()* comparison. Only when multiple strings are present and the location is unknown that more complex tree-based searching is required to be utilized by underlying implementations.

In each of these cases described above, however, strings are implied as wildcarding and specified subgroups of character matches within a regular expression must always utilize more advanced capabilities. In the case of a regular expression, it can be considered as always being within the upper right quadrant of the graph shown above.

Searchset Example Application

```
searchset  pets[3][3] = { "dog", " cat", "eel" };
regex searchset petsID[100][10] = { ... };
SearchResult    sRet;    // SearchResult is a packetC predefined structure

byte myArray[1000] = { ... };

// Find within the packet
sRet = petsID.find( pkt[0:1200] );

// Match at the current position in myArray
sRet = pets.match( myArray );
const byte byteArray[10]    = "owl";
searchset  mySet[5][10] = {"cat", "dog", byteArray };    // strings

// regular expressions.
regex searchset setA[3][14] = {".*?malware", ".*?from", ".*?mail"};
%pragma datatype setA (regex1);
const searchset  SET1[3][4]  = {"cat", "dog", "owl" };    // legal

searchset set3[3][4] = {"cat", "dog", "owl" };           // legal

searchset mySet[9][4] = {"cat", "dog", "owl" };          // legal

// illegal: declared & init sizes differ
const searchset  SET2[5][4]  = {"cat", "dog", "owl" };
regex searchset setA[2][7] = { ".*?from", ".*?mail"};     // legal
%pragma datatype setA (regex1);

searchset setB[2][7] = { ".*?from", ".*?mail"};              // treated as strings
const searchset  SET2[2][3]  = {"cat", "dog"};
// where NULL_STOP consists solely of "\x00"
const searchset  SET3[3][3]  = { NULL_STOP, "cat", "dog"};
// Search for null terminated strings or null terminated
const searchset  SET3[3][4]  = { "cat\x00", "dog\x00", NULL_STOP };
const byte NULL_STOP[1]    = "\x00";
const byte NULL_REGEX[4] = ".*?\\x00";
struct SearchResult {
            int   index;        // index of searchset element that was matched
            int   position;     // position in search area where match ends
}
searchset  pets[3][3]  = {"cat", "dog", "owl" };
SearchResult ansStruct;
    ...
try {
    // see if any of the strings appear right here
    ansStruct = pets.match( pkt[64:66] );

    ...
```

```
}
catch ( ERR_SET_NOMATCH )
{
    ...
}
struct SearchResult {
                int         index;          // index of searchset element that was matched
                int         position;       // position in search area where match ends
}
searchset  mySet[3][9]  =  {".*?[cC]at", ".*?[dD]og", ".*?[oO]wl" };
SearchResult ansStruct;
    ...
    try {
        // search the entire packet for any of the strings
        ansStruct  =  mySet.find( pkt );


            ...
    }
    catch ( ERR_SET_ NOTFOUND )
{

            ...
}
regex searchset set3[3][14] = {".*?malware", ".*?from", ".*?mail"};
regex searchset mySet[2][20] = {".*?(grey|gray)", ".*?(ey|ae)rie"};
// Double backslash required to yield \. for POSIX
regex searchset mySet[2][20] =  {".*?cloudshield\\.com", ".*?saic\\.com"};
// regex1 represents POSIX non-greedy
%pragma datatype  mySet  (regex1);



packet module classifierTable;

#include "cloudshield.ph"

// Global variables
int     totalPkts_;
int     pass_[2];
int     fail_[2];

// Regex search sets - Note that #include must start a line
searchset     class1[1][6]=
#include "cls4"
%pragma datatype class1 (regex1);

searchset     class2[1][6]=
#include "cls4"
%pragma datatype class2 (regex1);

void main($PACKET pkt, $PIB pib, $SYS sys)
{
```

```
    // define local variables
    SearchResult ret;

    ++totalPkts_;

    int passTry = 0;

    try
    {
        ret = class1.find( pkt[0:1200] );

        ++pass_[0];

        passTry = 1;
        ret = class2.find( pkt[0:1200] );

        ++pass_[1];
    }
    catch (ERR_SET_NOFOUND)
    {
        ++fail_[passTry];
    }

    // always forward all packets
    pib.action = FORWARD_PACKET;
}
```

CHAPTER 16

■ ■ ■

Reference Type and Operation

References in packetC

After reaching the halfway point in this book, have you finally hit the wall on still trying to figure out how the language gets away without pointers? Array slices, databases that can insert and delete entries provide some clever ways to avoid them, but at some point some of the data structures will need to have a pointer to another structure. But how would that work with the strict typing? Some complex data types have a real need for selecting between multiple other complex data types, such as building a relational database or even trying to determine which table of strings to scan based upon a match protocol field in header analysis. Welcome to the need for references.

References provide a critical role in the security required to build complex programs in packetC.

References

A packetC *reference* holds a value that uniquely identifies a single searchset or database or it holds a special NULL value, indicating that it currently identifies no searchset or database. packetC *references*:

- Use values that are hidden from the user

- Refer only to searchsets or to databases

- Refer either to searchsets composed of strings, to searchsets composed of regular expressions, or to databases composed of the same base type (including having the same maskedness properties) but not to a mixture of any of these

- Are restricted to a base type implied by their use, which must be consistent, although the base type is not explicitly declared with the reference

- Differ from C++ references in that they are not the referent but, instead, contain a unique value that is associated with the referent object

- Are assigned values by:

  - the special NULL literal (indicating no valid contents)

  - the **ref** operator in conjunction with a valid operand

  - another reference with the same implied base type

- Are dereferenced by the **deref** operator in much the same way as a C99 pointer is dereferenced by the * operator

- Can be compared with the equality and inequality operators

References allow databases and searchsets to be stored to be dereferenced later. This allows for advanced structures like search hash tables to be created.

```
struct BaseType {
    ...
};
database BaseType  myDb[50] = (...);
reference  db:refDb  = ref(myDb);
```

References act as a substitute for what it was referenced to.

```
// packetC dereferencing
database BaseType  myDb[35] = (...);
reference db:BaseType  refDb  = ref( myDb );
BaseType  myStruct  = {...};
...
// same as myStruct = myDb[23];
myStruct  = deref( refDb )[23];

// Searchset reference Array example
regex searchset virusSet[526][128] = { ... };
reference set:regex refSet = ref(virusSet);
...
// same as virusSet.find(packet)
deref( refSet ).find( pkt );
```

Reference Declarations

A packetC reference declaration creates a reference or array of references with a name and, if supplied, initial values. The basic form of a reference declaration is:

```
reference  (db: | set:) identifier[ref_dimension] = init_clause  ;
```

where

- For databases db: must precede the identifier

- For search sets set: must precede the identifier

- identifier is the name of the reference

- ref_dimension is an optional dimension for an array of references

```
// Examples
database BaseType  myDb[50] = (...);
reference  db:BaseType refDb  = ref(myDb);

// a string searchset, not a regex one
searchset  strSet[35][48];
reference  set:string refSset  = ref(strSet);
```

```
// a regex searchset
regex searchset  regSet[15][64];
reference  set:string refRset  =  ref(strSet);
```

Assigning Values to References

Because packetC references are strongly typed and can only be assigned values by a small number of mechanisms, the user is guaranteed that the run-time value of an initialized reference must either be **NULL** or a legitimate value that indicates a **searchset** or database of the appropriate type.

References can receive the value of

- the special **NULL** literal (indicating no valid contents)

- the results of the **ref** operator applied to a valid operand

- another reference with the same base type

The examples below illustrate legal and illegal reference assignments.

```
database HackType hackDb1[50] = (…);
database HackType hackDb2[50] = (…);
database OnlineUsers  userDb[17] = (…);
reference db:HackType refA = ref( hackDb1 );     // sets base type to HackType
reference db:HackType refB = ref( hackDb2 );     // sets base type to HackType
reference db:OnlineUsers refC = ref( userDb );   // sets base type to OnlineUsers

...
refC  = ref( hackDb2 );                  // ERROR: incompatible with init base type
refB  = 1;                               // ERROR: literal 1 is an int, not a reference
refB  = refA;                            // OK, refB and refA have same base type

// a string searchset, not a regex one
searchset  strSet[35][32] {…};

// a regex searchset
regex searchset  regSet[15][64] {…};
reference  set:string refSet  = ref (strSet);

refSet  = ref(strSet);                   // sets refSet base type to string searchset
refSet  = ref(regSet);                   // ERROR: base type mismatch
```

A reference cannot receive the results of an explicit type cast.

Dereferencing References

Dereferencing a packetC *reference* yields the value of the referent (database or searchset) at that point in the source code. It is not as if all the aggregated values of the database or table were present at that code location but, rather, it is as if the referent's name had been hard-coded in that place in the code.

```
// packetC dereferencing
database BaseType  myDb[35]  = (…);
reference  db:BaseType refDb  =  ref( myDb );
BaseType  myStruct  =  {…};
…
myStruct  =  deref( refDb )[23];
```

When the code above is executed, the effect will be indistinguishable from having coded the assignment as "myStruct = myDb[23]." Thus, a packetC reference acts as a substitute for whatever referent it currently indicates. This property can lead to unusual code forms (much as pointer dereferencing does in C); however, it provides powerful capabilities for compact, generic programming.

Using References

This section describes two ways to use packetC references. First, references can provide a linkage from one database or searchset to another. Second, references can allow compact programming, in which a single referenced expression replaces multiple hard-coded references to individual searchsets or databases. The example below shows both uses.

```
regex searchset   virusSet[526][60]   = {".*?virus"};
regex searchset   trojanSet[343][255]   = {".*?trojan"};
regex searchset   wormSet[249][128]  = {".*?worm"};
regex reference  set:regex refSset[3]  =  { ref(virusSet), ref(trojanSet), ref(wormSet) };

database OnlineRecs  nullDb[1];
database OnlineRecs  onlineDb[150] =  {…};
reference  db:OnlineRecs matchArr[150]  = { 150#ref(nullDb) };
int j, insertRow = 0, matchRow = 0;
reference  db:OnlineRecs matchSet  =  ref(nullDb);
SearchResult ansStruct;

// check against each searchset
for ( j = 0; j < 3; j++ ) {
    try {
        // the find operator throws an ERR_SET_NOTFOUND if not found
        ansStruct  =  deref(refSset[j]).find(pkt);
        matchSet  =  refSset[j];
    }
    catch ( ERR_SET_NOTFOUND ) {
        // do something if this not found
        …
    }
}

// insert record with current packet info into online DB
insertRow  =  onlineDb.insert(currentRec);

// use references to associate DB entry (by row) with
// table that contained virus/trojan/worm match
matchArr[insertRow]  =  matchSet;
```

```
//Check if none of the search had a match
if ( matchSet == ref(nullDB) ) { ... }
```

Reference Operators

ref (expression **)**

The **ref** operator produces an implementation-defined value (reference) that is uniquely associated with its operand, a packetC *database* or *searchset*. This value can be assigned to a packetC *reference* variable of the appropriate type. (See the section on references as a packetC datatype.) Using reference variables allows user code to dynamically determine which database or searchset to use for a given operation at run time. The values stored in reference variables can be converted into the associated database or searchset *referent* itself, by using the dereferencing operator. (See the section on **deref**.) The only operators defined for **ref**'s result type, *reference*, are assignment and **deref**. Consequently, this operator's results cannot be used in other kinds of expressions, such as arithmetic ones.

```
database  MyStructType  myDb[60] = {…};
database  OtherStrurctType  otherDb[80] = {…};
reference  db:MyStructType myDbRef  =  ref(myDb);

searchset  sSet[35][16] = {…};
regex searchset   rSet[55][16] = {…};
reference  set:string myStRef  =  ref(sSet);
…
myStRef  =  ref(sSet);        // legal
myDbRef  =  ref(myDb);        // legal

// ERROR: reference has string searchset type, operand has regex type
myStRef  =  ref(rSet);

// ERROR: reference and operand have different base types
myDbRef  =  ref(otherDb);
```

deref (dereference operator)

deref (expression **)**

The **deref** operator produces the packetC *database* or *table* that is the reference's *referent*. The effect is the same as if the name of the database or table appeared in hard-coded fashion at the location of the dereference operation. (See the section on references as a packetC datatype.) The expression is a reference to either a packetC database or a searchset only.

```
BaseType myStruct { short src; short dest;};
database BaseType  myDb[45] =  (…);
reference  db:BaseType myRef  =  ref(myDb);
…

// set myStruct = to struct at myDb[15]
myStruct  =  deref( myRef )[15];
```

When the **deref** in the example above is executed, the effect is indistinguishable from having coded the assignment as "myStruct = myDb[15]" because the reference variable acts as a substitute for whatever referent is currently indicated.

Developing Linked Lists Without Pointers

Some people balk at packetC because it doesn't have pointers. While security and strong typing drove an implementation of references and other alternatives to pointers, there are times when classic linked lists style implementations are desired. The example below was developed to provide an example for working with linked lists. The goal was to develop a list that would not contain duplicates and could be iterated in order.

The obvious C data structure to use for this is a linked list, but how can this be done in packetC? Pointers can be thought of as "indexes" into memory, i.e., a huge array. One could use a two-dimensional array with one of the columns serving as an index (pointer) to the "next node." Moving data around in a real-time system, such as the data plane is not optimal. To focus on performance, the goal is to not move any entries around (i.e., swapping places) yet still be able to delete items from the list. This was solved by rewriting the previous nodes "next" to bypass the node being deleted which left an unused node in the list. The result was the creation of a stack that would contain deleted node numbers. When inserting a new value, this stack is checked first for an available node to use.

The source for SortedList.ph is shown below:

```
// ************************************************************************
//  SortedList.ph -- provides a fast sorted list.
//  ------------
//  Author      : dWiGhT Mulcahy
//  Date Created: 04/28/2011
//  Version     : 1.00
//  ------------
//
//  This provides routines that will create a sorted list without the
//  overhead of data movement associated with sorting, inserting, and deleting.
//
//  A two dimensional array is used as a sort of singly linked list.  Entries
//  are inserted at the end and their "next node" set appropriately to
//  keep the list sorted.  This saves having to move any data around for
//  insertions or deletions.  Deletions are reused by tracking them in a
//  stack that gets
//
//  Iterators are provided to transverse the list in a sorted order and
//  should be the only way to access the list.
//
// ************************************************************************
#ifndef SORTEDLIST_PH_
#define SORTEDLIST_PH_


// ************************************************************************
//  Define the 2D array that makes up the list.  If the size is not specified
//  we default to 0x7fff as the size.
// ************************************************************************
```

```
#ifndef MAX_LIST_SIZE
#define MAX_LIST_SIZE 0x7fff
#endif
int  Node_[MAX_LIST_SIZE][2] = {{0xffffffff,0}};  // Init with END-NODE
const int NODE_VALUE = 0;   // Col 0 is the value stored in the list
const int NEXT_NODE = 1;    // Col 1 is the index/link to the next node

// Stack used to recover deleted nodes saves having to compact the list.
// [0] stores the number of elements in the stack.  10% of the list size.
int  OpenSlots_[MAX_LIST_SIZE/10];

// ************************************************************************
//  The HeadNode is the lowest value in the list.
//  NumNodes is the current number of nodes in the list and the insertion idx.
// ************************************************************************
int  NumNodes_ = 0;
int  HeadNode_ = 0;


// ************************************************************************
// List iterators used to iterate through the list in a sorted fashion.
//
// NOTE:
//    you should only use iterators to correctly transverse a list
//    which will be returned in accending order.
// ************************************************************************
typedef const int ListIterator;

// ************************************************************************
// Test the ListIterator against LIST_END to determine if at the end
// of the list.
// ************************************************************************
const ListIterator  LIST_END = 0;

// ************************************************************************
// Returns an iterator that points to the start of the list
// ************************************************************************
ListIterator  listCreateIterator() {
  return (ListIterator)HeadNode_;
}


// Fast inlined version
#define LIST_CREATE_ITERATOR() (ListIterator)HeadNode_

// ************************************************************************
// Returns the value stored at the current iterator
// ************************************************************************
int listGetValue( ListIterator  iter ) {
  return Node_[iter][NODE_VALUE];
}
```

```
// Fast inlined version
#define LIST_GET_VALUE(ITER)  Node_[ITER][NODE_VALUE]

// **************************************************************************
//  Returns the next position after this node
// **************************************************************************
ListIterator listIncIterator( ListIterator  iter ) {
  return Node_[iter][NEXT_NODE];
}

// Fast inlined version
#define LIST_INC_ITERATOR(ITER) Node_[ITER][NEXT_NODE]

// **************************************************************************
//  Delete all the nodes in the list.  This effectively just resets pointers
//  that are tracked.  The end-node is the only node that is overwritten.
// **************************************************************************
void listInit() {
  // Simplily set the number of nodes to zero
  NumNodes_ = 0;

  // Point headNode to the END-NODE of the list
  HeadNode_ = 0;
  Node_[0][NODE_VALUE] = 0xffffffff;
  Node_[0][NEXT_NODE] = 0;

  // Clear out the open slots list
  OpenSlots_[0] = 0;

  return;
}

// Fast inlined version
#define LIST_INIT() \
{ \
  NumNodes_ = 0; \
  HeadNode_ = 0; \
  Node_[0][NODE_VALUE] = 0xffffffff; \
  Node_[0][NEXT_NODE] = 0; \
  OpenSlots_[0] = 0; \
}


// **************************************************************************
//  Inserts the value into the list so that the list stays sorted.  No
//  duplicates are entered in the list.  Returns an booleen indicating
//  if the item was inserted, right now the only error that can occur is
//  a full table condition.
//
//  :HACK: Note the use of several exit points (return;) within this code.
//          This reduces the amount of code that is executed within the
```

```
//          special case scenarios and avoids numerous comparisons.
// **************************************************************************
bool  listInsert( int value ) {
  if ( NumNodes_ + 1 == MAX_LIST_SIZE )
    if ( OpenSlots_[0] == 0 ) {
      // We don't have anymore room to add a value
      return false;
  }

  // See if we have some open slots to use from previous deletes,
  // use this node then, otherwise use one of the new ones.
  int  newSlot;
  if ( OpenSlots_[0] > 0 ) {
    // Reuse one of the open slots
    newSlot = OpenSlots_[OpenSlots_[0]--];
  } else {
    // Use a new slot at the end of the list
    newSlot = ++NumNodes_;
  }

  // Special case if we insert before the head
  if ( Node_[HeadNode_][NODE_VALUE] > value ) {
    // Add the node and repoint the head to it
    Node_[newSlot][NEXT_NODE] = HeadNode_;
    Node_[newSlot][NODE_VALUE] = value;
    HeadNode_ = newSlot;
    return true;
  }

  // Find out where to insert this value
  int  nodeValue;
  int  nextNode;
  int  testNode;
  testNode = HeadNode_;

  ListIterator iter;
  iter = LIST_CREATE_ITERATOR();
  while ( iter != LIST_END ) {

    nodeValue = Node_[testNode][NODE_VALUE];
    if ( nodeValue == value ) {
      // The value is already in our list so we ditch without adding

      // We have to recover the node back into the stack if we are
      // not going to use it
      if ( newSlot != NumNodes_ ) {
        OpenSlots_[++OpenSlots_[0]] = newSlot;
      } else {
        --NumNodes_;
      }
```

```
   return true;
      }

   nextNode = Node_[testNode][NEXT_NODE];

   // Test if we should insert this here
   nodeValue = Node_[nextNode][NODE_VALUE];
   if ( nodeValue > value ) {
     // Kick out to insert the node here
     break;
   }

   // Move on to the next node to test
   testNode = nextNode;
 }

 // Insert this node at the correct position
 Node_[newSlot][NEXT_NODE] = Node_[testNode][NEXT_NODE];
 Node_[newSlot][NODE_VALUE] = value;
 Node_[testNode][NEXT_NODE] = newSlot;

 return true;
}


// ***************************************************************************
// Deletes the value in the list.  The item is not removed but the next
// pointers rewritten to bypass this node.  This avoids having to move
// the elements up in the list to compact it.
//
// :HACK: Note the use of several exit points (return;) within this code.
//        This reduces the amount of code that is executed within the
//        special case scenarios and avoids numerous comparisons.
// ***************************************************************************
bool listDelete( int value ) {
 int val;

 // Create an iterator to the start of the list
 ListIterator iter;
 iter = LIST_CREATE_ITERATOR();

 // We have to track the previous node to modify it
 ListIterator iterPrev;

 // Loop through it verifying that all is right
 while ( iter != LIST_END )  {

   // Get the value at this position
   if ( value == LIST_GET_VALUE( iter ) ) {
     // We found the node so reroute the node pointers around
     // this node.  This saves having to collapse the list.
```

```
    // if this is the head we can just point head to the next node
    if ( iter == HeadNode_ ) {
      // First in the list, point to it
      HeadNode_ = Node_[HeadNode_][NEXT_NODE];

      // See if we deleted the last node in the list
      if ( HeadNode_ == LIST_END ) {
        // Reinit the list
        LIST_INIT();
      } else {
        // Make sure we don't overflow the stack
        if ( OpenSlots_[0] < MAX_LIST_SIZE/10 ) {
          // Add the node that we deleted to the open slots list
          OpenSlots_[++OpenSlots_[0]] = iter;
        }
      }

      // We're done here
      return true;
    } else {
      // Route around this node
      Node_[iterPrev][NEXT_NODE] = Node_[iter][NEXT_NODE];

      // Make sure we don't overflow the stack
      if ( OpenSlots_[0] < MAX_LIST_SIZE/10 ) {
        // Add the node that we deleted to the open slots list
        OpenSlots_[++OpenSlots_[0]] = iter;
      }

      // We're done here
      return true;
    }
  }

  // Move on to the next node
  iterPrev = iter;
  iter = LIST_INC_ITERATOR( iter );
}

// At this point we did not find the value in the list
return false;
}

// **************************************************************************
// Returns if the value is already in the list.  The list is searched for
// the value and a iterator is returned pointing to the location in the list.
// LIST_END iterator is returned if the value is not in the list.
//
// :HACK: Note the use of several exit points (return;) within this code.
//        This reduces the amount of code that is executed within the
//        special case scenarios and avoids numerous comparisons.
```

```
// **********************************************************************
ListIterator  listSearch( int value ) {
  // Find out where to insert this value
  int  nodeValue;
  int  nextNode;
  int  testNode;
  testNode = HeadNode_;

  ListIterator iter;
  iter = LIST_CREATE_ITERATOR();
  while ( iter != LIST_END )  {

    nodeValue = Node_[testNode][NODE_VALUE];
    if ( nodeValue == value ) {
      // The value is in the list so return an iterator pointing to it
      return testNode;
    }

    // Test if we should insert this here
    nextNode = Node_[testNode][NEXT_NODE];
    nodeValue = Node_[nextNode][NODE_VALUE];
    if ( nodeValue > value ) {
      // We are past were the value would me so it isn't in the list
      return LIST_END;
    }

    // Move on to the next node to test
    testNode = nextNode;
  }

  // If we get here it means that the value was not in the list
  return LIST_END;
}
// **********************************************************************
//  Returns a bool if the value is in the list.
//
//  :HACK: Note the use of several exit points (return;) within this code.
//         This reduces the amount of code that is executed within the
//         special case scenarios and avoids numerous comparisons.
// **********************************************************************

bool  IsValueInList( int value ) {
  if ( listSearch(value) != LIST_END ) {
    return true;
  }
  return false;
}

#endif /*SORTEDLIST_PH_*/
```

CHAPTER 17

■ ■ ■

Semaphores in packetC

Locking and Unlocking

The complexities of parallel processing introduce the problem that generally leads to complex inter-process communications. With packetC, the notion of global data is ever-present and even though access to data elements is atomic, programs represent information in more complex structures than basic scalar types. As such, a mechanism for communication with other contexts is required in order to notify them to not touch portions of global memory that are in use, or more important, being manipulated by another context. Locking of memory can grind a parallel system to a halt. So, instead, packetC introduces a method of semaphores where any global *int* data element can be used as a semaphore representing whatever the application desires. It is a cooperative inter-process memory protection model that trades off some security in return for significant performance. Lock and unlock methods are applicable to global data elements which provide an atomic test-and-set, storing a magic number in the data element itself. Should the lock be successful, the application can proceed to work on other data elements safely, knowing it is not in competition.

C programmers beware: Any data element being a cooperative semaphore moves out of traditional C mechanisms pretty quickly into some new facets of C++ and other modern languages. That said, semaphores provide a critical role in the high-performance parallel processing controls required to build complex programs in packetC.

Lock and Unlock Operators

Lock and Unlock introduce a true test-and-set functionality found in parallel processing. This provides an almost unlimited number of available locks to be used as semaphores that are locked or unlocked. Any global, array, or matrix memory location can be used as a lock. This feature allows for both data-driven processing against packet flows as well as application-level critical-section locks. The lock and unlock operate in a cooperative locking mode.

One common area of use for lock and unlock in packet processing is managing multi-packet transactions, such as reassembling the payload of multiple TCP packets. Once a TCP flow is in re-assembly, each packet can update its portion of a larger buffer without locking because TCP provides sequence numbers that identify which offset in the buffer to copy the payload into. At startup and teardown of a flow, however, there needs to be the guarantee that only one packetC context is managing the flow and tables control the transaction payload reconstruction. The Lock and Unlock functions are not a singular lock, but actually are functions that can turn any global variable location into an application-specific lock. This is generally called a cooperative locking environment where code is not prohibited from touching memory but rather properly written packetC code would check the Lock status before proceeding. In this model, doing a spin on the Lock is preferred because this minimizes the time the context is waiting for its turn. With the ability to create millions of locks, only two packets of a given flow being processed at the same time would test a given lock and potentially wait to begin processing the packet.

In a high-speed network or aggregation point, where many flows (50 or more) occur simultaneously, it actually turns out that this is better for the system. Should packets from these flows hit the box at the same time, it is unlikely that any two from the same flow need to be in the critical section at the same time. As such, the higher the performance and larger the number of concurrent flows, the less likely locks collide enabling parallel processing performance to continue unhindered. In the case that a large stream from a single source occurs, we suggest you design the use of locks judiciously and only in the tightest critical sections of code that require only a single context at any given time. The global memory that the lock and unlock methods operate on in packetC will often be called semaphores in other programming languages. The lock and unlock methods are cooperative in that they require all portions of the application to treat the memory location being used as a semaphore appropriately. Directly writing data to a semaphore may cause unexpected results as other contexts are depending on a specific lock value. The benefit, however, is that millions of semaphores can be created and no operational system needs to address adjustments to memory access during system operation when contention does not exist. Only in the case where a semaphore is locked by one context, and to the extent the application requires, another context requests to lock the same semaphore does this approach impact a concurrently processing context.

Lock Operator

lock (unary_expression)

Lock is a unary operator that returns a truth result, just as the equality and relational operators do. Its sole operand is a 32-bit global integer, which must be a scalar variable or an array element.

If the operand is not currently locked, **lock** sets its value to indicate that the program copy currently executing has locked the operand and returns a non-zero value to indicate success (i.e., "true"). If the operand is already locked, this operation does not change the operand's stored value and returns a zero value to indicate "false." The range of values stored in the operand to identify which, if any, program copy (context) has locked it shall be implementation-defined. Programs should not depend on the operand's particular values (as opposed to the truth value of the operation) nor assign other values to **lock** operands. Thus, although **lock** operations can control access to global variables that are shared by multiple program copies (contexts), such variables should not be used as **lock** operands themselves.

```
int x;
...
x = lock( myGlobalInt_ );
```

Expressions that involve this operation can appear as stand-alone statements (as in the example above) or appear in any conditional context where an equality or relational operator could.

```
while ( ! lock(myGlobalInt_) ) {};
// spin lock - wait on another context to free its lock

...
int didLock; didLock = lock(globalArr_[1] );

...
if ( !lock(myGlobalInt_)  &&  !busyWaitActionsDone ) {
    // do busy-wait actions

    ...
int globalCounter;                      // declared in global (shared) space
...
```

```
while ( ! lock(globalCounter) ) {};      // spin lock
        ++globalCounter;                  // ERROR
// the increment clobbers the value identifying which program copy holds the lock
```

Unlock Operator

unlock (*unary_expression*)

Unlock is a unary operator that returns a truth result, just as the equality and relational operators do. Its sole operand is a 32-bit global integer, which must be a scalar variable or an array element.

If the operand is currently locked and was locked by the instantiation of the packet application that contains this **unlock**, then the operation sets the operand value to indicate an unlocked state and returns a non-zero value to indicate success (i.e., "true"). If the operand is already unlocked, the operation returns a non-zero value. If the operand is locked and the locking was done by an executing context of the packetC application other than the one containing this **unlock**, this operation does not change the operand's stored value and it returns a zero value to indicate "false."

```
int x;
x = unlock( myGlobalInt_ );
if (x == 0)
{
  . . .        // Do something, it failed and that should be a logic error!
}
```

Expressions that involve this operation can appear as stand-alone statements (as in the example above) or appear in any conditional context where an equality or relational operator could.

```
while ( ! unlock(myInt_) ) {};
// there is no reason why spin unlock should ever be rationale
…
int didUnlock; didUnlock = unlock(globalArr_[1] );
…
if ( !unlock(myInt_)  ) {
    // do failure processing
    …
```

Using Lock and Unlock to Perform a Global Malloc() and Free()

The **lock** and **unlock** operators provide a mechanism for managing global, cross context, semaphore mechanisms such that shared resources can be managed without collision. Within packetC, there are cases where dynamic memory allocation may be required. While this is not a capability within the grammar and no direct equivalent to pointers exists, this does not restrict the ability of an application from employing a similar mechanism. An application may allocate a large region of memory within global application space and allocate portions of this memory for dynamic allocation to other functions or uses.

```
byte bigBlob[1000000];        // 1 Million Bytes of Global Memory

//1000 Rows of 3 Columns. Column0=Start, Column1=Length, Column2=Free
int bigBlobEntry[1000,3];
int bigBlobEntrySize;         // Number of entries in bigBlobEntry
int bigBlobSemaphore;         // Used through lock and unlock to control access to allocation
```

In the concept above, the array bigBlob is allocated with one million bytes of memory. Furthermore, bigBlobEntry contains a list of memory regions allocated. This list can start with 1 item (bigBlobEntrySize=1) in row 0 of bigBlobEntry where column 0 is 0, column 1 is 999,999 and column 2 is set to 1, identifying it as Free. Using the **lock** operator, bigBlobSemaphore is locked, identifying exclusive access to these variables and a function call emulating *malloc()* can manipulate bigBlobEntry[] to establish an allocated region of the number of bytes requested while also updating the free list. The application would be hard coded to access the variable bigBlob[]. Cooperatively, each portion of the application must ensure access is only to the portion of bigBlob[] allocated using an emulated *malloc()* and *free()* function which is using bigBlobEntry[] to manage this byte region.

The net result is, even in an environment without dynamic memory allocation, using lock and unlock with semaphores, multiple contexts over an extended period of time and packets can provide flexible memory allocation. This will elevate the security risks to within the application, however, tight controls and coding standards on accessing allocated memory segments can provide the appropriate level of security and audit required. This also helps to identify the potential risks that are present no matter how controlled a language is. The programmer can not only extend features beyond their intended result but can cause havoc no matter how strict the rules are.

As there are multiple methods for emulating a *malloc()* and *free()* as well as techniques which simplify the linked list management within the free list tracking, no specific implementation example is shown. Some applications may need simple implementations or possibly multiple independent implementations concurrently. In any case, the concept remains as simply allocating a singular global array of bytes and providing offsets within this array to different requestors such that they can share the large memory region. While risk exists with bad code accessing sections within the global allocated to other requestors, packetC will still protect the system from accessing outside of the global array.

■ ■ ■

Packet Information Block and System Packet Operations

Unlike C, packetC is based upon the presumption of underlying capabilities being provided by the operating system or generated by the compiler for a target platform. These include the management of packet handling functionality including receipt, buffering, and transmission as well as an initial level of decoding and manipulation on transmission. In addition, parallel processing management and a base set of control plane functionality must be present for packetC applications to interact with. These functions may differ from one system to another; however, a base set of functionality must remain consistent. To provide a common interface, the language specification for packetC mandates a predefined base set of types that are passed as parameters to *main()* as well as a set of built-in methods and operators.

While packetC does not specify requirements for particular hardware at program execution time, the functionality is required whether implemented in hardware or software. Additionally, the packetC development tool chain provides the implementation of the several predefined types that support common packet processing activities, such as managing packet contents, network protocols, ports, and messages.

All packetC implementations shall provide three pre-defined types passed as parameters for each instance of a packet main:

- The current packet (for any executing instance of a packet module)

- A Packet Information Block (PIB) that includes layer and protocol data

- A System Information Block (SYS) that includes time and port information

To represent this data, packetC defines three predefined types: $PACKET, $PIB, and $SYS.

- **$PACKET** is the type of the current packet (acts as an array of bytes).

- **$PIB** is the structure definition for a Packet Information Block (PIB).

- **$SYS** is the structure definition for a System Information Block (SYS).

A packet module's main shall have only one variable of each of these types, as defined in the packet main section's declaration.

```
packet module mainApp;
...
void main( $PACKET pkt, $PIB pib, $SYS sys) {
```

The packet module *main* body may pass these variables as actual arguments to shared functions, while packet scope, library functions, and packet module defined functions have visibility without being passed. While $PACKET, $PIB, and $SYS types can be used to declare formal arguments (parameters) for shared library functions, they may not be used to declare variables. A previous section described program construction and accessing packet contents. The following subsections provide further details on $PIB and $SYS types.

Each development platform must have a system "include" file specific to the target platform, such as *cloudshield.ph* referenced throughout this guide. This platform-specific file provides definitions of the special types required for the packet, packet information block, and system information. In addition, many standard definitions are also found in this file. The following sections cover the shared definitions encompassing a miscellaneous set of enumerations, structures, and types referenced by the special types as well as the three special types.

Shared Definitions

The platform-specific system "include" file *cloudshield.ph* contains many definitions, including enumerations, structures, and constants which are leveraged by special types as well as by system functions within packetC. Most of the elements below are self-explanatory by the code headers, although some additional notes are embedded throughout.

```
//===============================================================================
//  PacketAction Enumerated Type
//
//  Used with action in $PIB to define what to do with packet at end of main().
//
//===============================================================================
enum int PacketAction
{
  DROP_PACKET           = 0,
  FORWARD_PACKET        = 1,
  REQUEUE_PACKET        = 2
};
```

When setting pib.action, this simply determines the macro-level treatment of the packet at the end of processing *main()*. The enumeration is used such that additional mechanisms for treatment can be introduced by simply extending the enumeration. By default, the value of pib.action for a packet is DROP_PACKET causing the current packet to be dropped at the end of processing, whereas performing a "*pib.action = FORWARD_PACKET;*" in the program will notify the underlying system to proceed with transmitting the packet out an interface specified with the *sys* structure along with processing actions such as checksum recalculation specified in the *pib* structure. Should the packetC application assign "*pib.action = REQUEUE_PACKET;*" then the application will place the inbound packet at the end of the queue of packets waiting to be processed. The *sys.requeueCount* will be incremented at that time and processing will start at the beginning of the application when it is delivered to a context for processing.

```
//===============================================================================
//  Layer Type Enumerations
//
//  L2Type, L3Type and L4Type are used by the $PIB to describe current packet.
//
//===============================================================================
enum int L2Type
```

```
{
  L2TYPE_OTHER                     = 0,
  L2TYPE_SONET_PPP                 = 1,
  L2TYPE_SONET_HDLC                = 2,
  L2TYPE_SONET_HDLC_PPP_MPLS       = 17,
  L2TYPE_SONET_HDLC_MPLS           = 18,
  L2TYPE_ETHII                     = 3,
  L2TYPE_ETHII_MPLS                = 19,
  L2TYPE_ETHII_8021Q               = 35,
  L2TYPE_ETHII_8021Q_MPLS          = 51,
  L2TYPE_802_3_SNAP_MPLS           = 21,
  L2TYPE_802_3_SNAP_802_1Q         = 37,
  L2TYPE_802_3_SNAP_802_1Q_MPLS    = 53,
  L2TYPE_802_3                     = 4,
  L2TYPE_802_3_MPLS                = 20,
  L2TYPE_802_3_SNAP                = 5,
  L2TYPE_802_3_802_1Q              = 36
};

enum int L3Type
{
  L3TYPE_OTHER = 0,
  L3TYPE_IPV4  = 1,
  L3TYPE_IPV6  = 2,
  L3TYPE_ARP   = 3,
  L3TYPE_RARP  = 4,
  L3TYPE_IPX   = 5
};

enum int L4Type
{
  L4TYPE_OTHER  = 0,
  L4TYPE_TCP    = 1,
  L4TYPE_UDP    = 2,
  L4TYPE_ICMP   = 3,
  L4TYPE_ICMPV6 = 4,
  L4TYPE_ESP    = 5,
  L4TYPE_AH     = 6,
  L4TYPE_GRE    = 7,
  L4TYPE_SCTP   = 8
};
```

An underlying system will decode the inbound packet headers to identify decoded types as best as possible. This information does not need to be leveraged by a packetC application, however, as there are many different networking protocol types that may appear in layer 2 through 4, enumerations have been developed to provide a simple method of reference. Different platforms may increase or decrease the number of decoded protocols as well as the values assigned for each protocol. The enumerations should always be used and not the constants. In addition, careful comparison of these values in *cloudshield.ph* should be inspected as the version of *cloudshield.ph* is changed or when migrating to other platforms to ensure consistent packetC application processing.

```
//==============================================================================
//  Time Construct Structure
//
//  This structure is used to represent the 64-bit fields used in time elements
//  of the $SYS structure.  For ticks this is the upper and lower 32-bits of a
//  64-bit counter.  For UTC Time values, this relates to the seconds (high) and
//  microseconds (low) since UTC (1/1/1970 00:00:00 GMT) in a single 64-bit structure.
//
//  This structure replaced XTime structure from cloudshield.ph version 1.00
//
//==============================================================================
//  struct Time64 {
//    int highOrder;
//    int lowOrder;
//  };
```

The Time64 structure is utilized for multiple different time values in the $SYS structure. This provides a 64-bit singular structure containing the high-order and low-order 32-bit portions of time. The Time64 structure is introduced to explicitly define this time unit as a structure to allow changes in internal definition as well as access to sub-elements of the 64-bit value without creating a complex type within the *sys*.

```
//==============================================================================
//  Message Group Levels
//
//  The MessageGroup enumerated type is used to set a severity level for a log()
//  message.  This field can be set once in a context and all future events that
//  are generated during the processing of the packet will utilize this value.
//  The $SYS structure utilized MessageGroup with field messageGroup.
//
//==============================================================================
enum int MessageGroup
{
  MSG_CRITICAL = 1,
  MSG_MAJOR    = 2,
  MSG_MINOR    = 3,
  MSG_WARNING  = 4,
  MSG_INFO     = 5
};
```

```
//==============================================================================
//  Message Constants
//
//  The following constants provide a maximum message number and length for a
//  log() message generated by the packetC system.  Use in conjunction with the
//  messageId field in $SYS.
//
//==============================================================================
const int MAX_PACKETC_MSGS    = 255;
const int MAX_PACKETC_MSG_LEN = 80;
```

When interacting with the control plane, messages require a severity as well as have constraints on their size. The enumeration and constants above abstracted these platform-specific values to allow portability and consistent implementations across releases.

```
//===============================================================================
//  Search Results Structure
//
//  When a match or find operator is used on a search set, a structure is then
//  returned with the result.  This structure is the typedef for that result.
//
//===============================================================================
struct SearchResult
{
  int index;
  int position;
};
```

Searchsets return a complex type for results. This structure contains the row within a searchset as well as what position in the searched data matched the end of the expression identified by index. Different target platforms and releases may have extended attributes provided in this structure. Applications that employ searchsets must ensure version compatibility with *cloudshield.ph* to guarantee proper evaluation of searchset responses.

```
//===============================================================================
//  Exception Constants
//
//  Try catch based exception handlers are core to packetC.  There are a set of
//  pre-defined exceptions for intrinsic operators to packetC.  The section
//  of exception constants below are what is implemented in the associated
//  packetC compiler.
//
//===============================================================================
typedef int Exception;
const Exception       ERR_ANY_EXCEPTION   = 0;
const Exception       ERR_DB_FULL         = 1;
const Exception       ERR_DB_READ         = 2;
const Exception       ERR_DB_NOMATCH      = 3;
const Exception       ERR_PKT_INSERT      = 4;
const Exception       ERR_PKT_DELETE      = 5;
const Exception       ERR_PKT_NOREPLICATE = 6;
const Exception       ERR_SET_NOMATCH     = 7;
const Exception       ERR_SET_NOPERFORM   = 8;
const Exception       ERR_SET_NOTFOUND    = 9;
const Exception       ERR_PKT_NOTREQUEUED = 10;


//===============================================================================
//  User Defined Exception Constants
//
//  packetC users can create their own exceptions constants to throw by using
//  the ERR_LAST_DEFINED constant.
//
//      const Exception    ERR_MY_EXCEPTION  = ERR_LAST_DEFINED + 1
//
```

```
//===============================================================================
const Exception   ERR_LAST_DEFINED = 64;
```

Exception-handling using try, catch, and throw is required for all possible exceptions. The *cloudshield.ph* site defines all of the platform-specific exceptions as well the value of the last one that can be used to define application specific exceptions. ERR_LAST_DEFINED + 1 is the value of the first user-definable exception. Exceptions must always be referenced by the names, not the values, because those are subject to change.

```
//===============================================================================
//  Truth Constants
//
//  In packetC no boolean types exist, however, true and false are pre-defined.
//  To enforce consistency and strict type matching, bool is defined.
//
//===============================================================================
const int true  = 1;
const int false = 0;
typedef int bool;
```

In packetC, Boolean types are not an implicit capability. As programmers rely on this capability to ensure strict type enforcement and consistency, these are defined by the system include file. These definitions must be used for Boolean values to ensure consistent implementation.

```
//===============================================================================
//  Search Set Constants
//
//  Null is a valid value in strings and regular expressions.  Constants are
//  pre-defined for these values.
//
//===============================================================================
const byte NULL_STOP[1]  = "\x00";
const byte NULL_REGEX[4] = ".*?\x00";
```

The simplest value of all, null, always seems to be one of the most complex beasts. As processing of the contents of packets often has null values that do not mean the end of a file or end of processing, they need to be contained within many expressions. A few predefined literals are provided for use in strings and regular expressions.

Packet ($PACKET pkt)

The packet is represented as an array of bytes. However, it is treated as a special data type. While the typedef represents $PACKET as an array of bytes for type compatibility to support array-slicing and retrieval of portions of the packet, it also has the special feature of being able to have structures cast upon it through the use of descriptors.

The structure of the packet ($PACKET pkt) is shown below:

```
//===============================================================================
//  Packet Type
//
//  Each system may have a slightly different constraint on the buffer for each
//  packet.  The typedef below defines the $PACKET for the system.
```

```
//
//=============================================================================
typedef byte $PACKET[9 * 1024 - 1];
```

For CloudShield systems, $PACKET is defined in the *cloudshield.ph* system include file. Furthermore, it is always referenced in packetC as *pkt* and this predefined type cannot be used to declare other types. Refer to chapters on descriptors for alternative access methods to address fields by name within the pkt. In addition, as a special type, not only does it operate as an array of byte with array-slicing but it also has a number of operators that are specific to this data type.

From a programmer's point of view, the packet is simply an array of bytes to which the current context has been given access. From a practical point of view, almost the entire packetC language revolves around this data type providing specialized structures describing it, such as $PIB and $SYS, as well as numerous special operators providing actions and interaction with this data type.

Packet Information Block ($PIB pib)

A Packet Information Block (PIB) shall be present and shall contain information about the current packet that is derived from the packet. This descriptive data includes information about the presence of various protocols (or headers) and their locations within the packet. For example, the PIB structure contains information such as Layer 2 Type, Layer 3 Offset, and Layer 4 Offset.

The PIB is accessible as a variable of the predefined type **$PIB**, specified as an argument to the packet module *main*. The structure definition for **$PIB** is declared in a target system include file or predefined by a packetC compiler. It is always referenced in packetC as *pib* and this predefined type cannot be used to declare other types. For CloudShield systems, $PIB is defined in the *cloudshield.ph* system include file.

```
void main ( $PACKET pkt, $PIB pib, $SYS sys ) {…}
```

The structure of the Packet Information Block ($PIB) is shown below:

```
//=============================================================================
//  Packet Information Block
//
//  The typedef for structure $PIB is instantiated as pib and delivered as a
//  parameter to main() containing information about the current packet.
//  The pib acts as both an input structure as well as the end state of the pib
//  determines actions to be taken against the packet at the end of main().
//
//=============================================================================
struct $PIB
{
  PacketAction   action;
  int            logAccelTarget;
  int            length;
  bits int
  {
    replica             : 1;
    l3CheckSumValid     : 1;
    l3CheckSumRecalc    : 1;
    l4CheckSumValid     : 1;
    l4CheckSumRecalc    : 1;
```

```
    ipFragment        : 1;
    ipv4              : 1;
    ipv6              : 1;
    logAccelReplicate : 1;
    logAccelModify    : 1;
    logAccelMethod    : 1;
    logAccelDatasize  : 1;
    mpls              : 1;
    vlan              : 1;
    pad               : 18;
  } flags;
  L2Type        l2Type;
  L3Type        l3Type;
  L4Type        l4Type;
  int    l2Offset;
  int    mplsOffset;
  int    l3Offset;
  int    l4Offset;
  int    payloadOffset;
};
```

While the above structure presents a view into the construction of the pib itself, it may not be very obvious how these values were gathered or what is the key value in having them. At the end of this chapter are a few flow charts that provide a view into the decode of a packet byte-by-byte to determine the header types and lengths to layer determine offsets. Specific values are defined in Internet RFC's to equate to particular construction formats of headers found in layer 2, 3, and 4. In addition, some intermediate headers such as MPLS can be found between layers 2 and 3, often called layer 2½. While the flowcharts walk through the logic, it is often best to get a quick view of packets and how this logically creates an envelope of headers to better understand the usefulness of the pib values and how these relate to descriptors.

```
0000   00 01 30 01 11 00 00 08   02 e4 0b dc 08 00 45 00   ..0.....  ......E.
0010   03 0e 39 af 00 00 80 11   86 6b 0a 0a 10 b5 c7 04   ..9.....  .k......
0020   96 01 13 c4 13 c4 02 fa   f7 1d 49 4e 56 49 54 45   ........  ..INVITE
0030   20 73 69 70 3a 39 31 34   30 38 33 33 31 36 36 35    sip:914  08331665
0040   32 40 63 69 74 61 64 65   6c 2e 64 68 70 2e 63 6f   2@citade  l.dhp.co
0050   6d 20 53 49 50 2f 32 2e   30 0d 0a 56 69 61 3a 20   m SIP/2.  0..Via:
0060   53 49 50 2f 32 2e 30 2f   55 44 50 20 36 33 2e 31   SIP/2.0/  UDP 63.1
0070   35 30 2e 35 36 2e 36 36   3a 35 30 36 30 3b 72 70   50.56.66  :5060;rp
0080   6f 72 74 3b 62 72 61 6e   63 68 3d 7a 39 68 47 34   ort;bran  ch=z9hG4
0090   62 4b 32 37 33 33 30 31   35 44 41 44 43 32 34 37   bK273301  5DADC247
00a0   44 45 38 41 41 36 44 38   42 32 34 30 44 42 43 30   DE8AA6D8  B240DBC0
00b0   45 44 0d 0a 46 72 6f 6d   3a 20 53 65 61 6e 20 3c   ED..From  : Sean <
00c0   73 69 70 3a 32 30 30 32   40 63 69 74 61 64 65 6c   sip:2002  @citadel
00d0   2e 64 68 70 2e 63 6f 6d   3e 3b 74 61 67 3d 32 37   .dhp.com  >;tag=27
00e0   33 35 37 39 35 37 37 36   0d 0a 54 6f 3a 20 3c 73   35795776  ..To: <s
00f0   69 70 3a 39 31 34 30 38   33 33 31 36 36 35 32 40   ip:91408  3316652@
0100   63 69 74 61 64 65 6c 2e   64 68 70 2e 63 6f 6d 3e   citadel.  dhp.com>
0110   0d 0a 43 6f 6e 74 61 63   74 3a 20 3c 73 69 70 3a   ..Contac  t: <sip:
0120   32 30 30 32 40 36 33 2e   31 35 30 2e 35 36 2e 36   2002@63.  150.56.6
0130   36 3a 35 30 36 30 3e 0d   0a 43 61 6c 6c 2d 49 44   6:5060>.  .Call-ID
0140   3a 20 36 30 43 44 34 44   43 36 2d 45 44 39 35 2d   : 60CD4D  C6-ED95-
0150   34 33 31 39 2d 39 36 41   44 2d 38 32 46 31 46 46   4319-96A  D-82F1FF
0160   36 41 42 42 32 39 40 31   30 2e 31 30 2e 31 36 2e   6ABB29@1  0.10.16.
0170   31 38 31 0d 0a 43 53 65   71 3a 20 36 33 36 34 36   181..CSe  q: 63646
0180   20 49 4e 56 49 54 45 0d   0a 4d 61 78 2d 46 6f 72    INVITE.  .Max-For
0190   77 61 72 64 73 3a 20 37   30 0d 0a 43 6f 6e 74 65   wards: 7  0..Conte
01a0   6e 74 2d 54 79 70 65 3a   20 61 70 70 6c 69 63 61   nt-Type:   applica
```

Figure 18-1. VoIP packet shown in data dump format

Figure 18-1 shows a packet, in both hex and ASCII. In network analyzers of years past, this is what we often had to decipher by hand to determine the construction of the packet. The above packet is flowing across an Ethernet interface and as such we can start with decoding the MAC addresses (00:01:30:01:11:00 and 00:08:02:e4:0b:dc) which leads us to the 0800 which identifies the next layer as IP immediately following the 14-byte Ethernet II header. Given that we can see that the upper nibble of the next byte, 4 in 45, this represents that it is an IPv4 header. This continues all the way through the packet, based upon knowing, in detail, numerous RFC's. Imagine if, to get anything done, one had to do all this work every time. Instead, in packetC, it is presumed those standard layers 2 through 4 headers are decoded by the operating system with the decoded information presented to the application in the *pib*. For non-standard headers or those not recognized by the operating system, *pib* values will highlight what is not recognized. Not only will the types be presented, but offsets to each layer will be provided when the headers were decoded so that standard descriptors, provided in *protocols.ph*, can be referenced such that the packet can be reference fields in the headers directly shown by name, much like "tree view" in the packet decode shown in Figure 18-2.

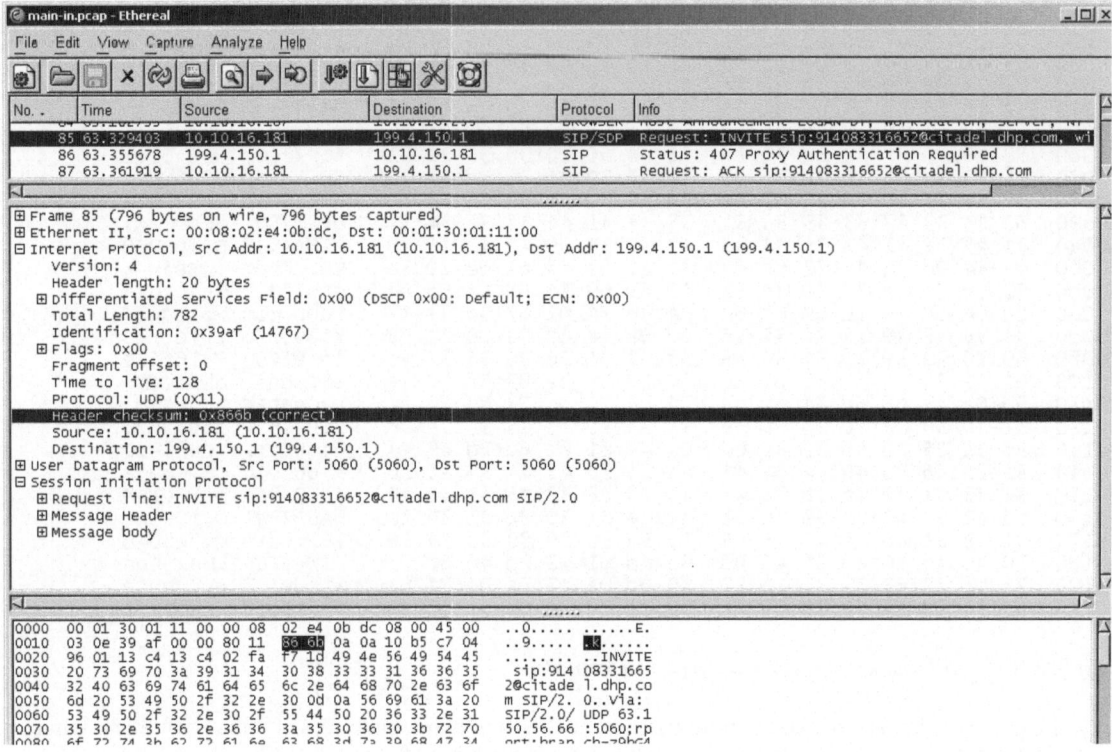

Figure 18-2. Ethereal screenshot of VoIP packet decode

In modern packet analyzers, packets are decoded by the analyzer allowing the network engineer to view the packets not only in the original hex and ASCII but also in a "tree view" and "column view" shown in the upper two sections of Figure 18-2. By leveraging the values for layer offsets provided in the *pib* in combination with descriptors defined either by the system, such as those in *protocols.ph*, or the application, packetC allows direct access to fields as though they were simple elements of a structure. While each packet may have a slightly different construction with optional elements in headers, the descriptors floating at layer offsets allow for compensation as well as the advantage of not needing to even inspect lower layer headers if only upper layers are of interest. In other words, if an application is performing Access Control List functionality using the IP and TCP headers, whether Ethernet or SONET or even MPLS is present becomes irrelevant as layer 3 and layer 4 offsets should already be present.

Figure 18-3. WAN packet as ordered set of headers and payload

A logical view of a packet often held by developers is something like that shown in Figure 18-3. The goal of the *pib* is to help transition the ever-changing form of the current packet into a simple method of accessing it representing more of the logical view.

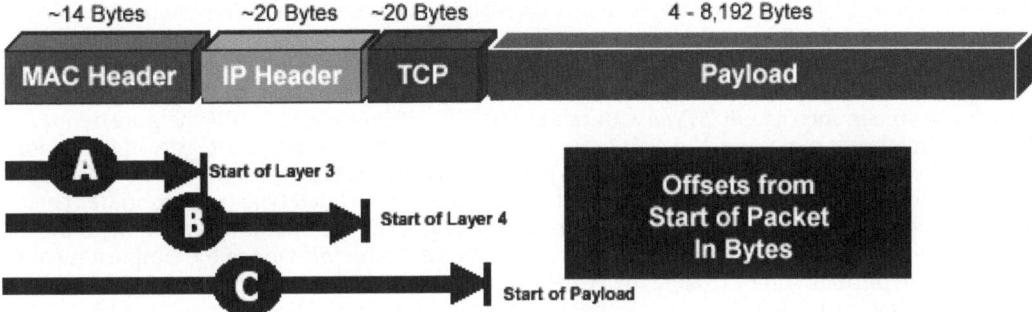

Figure 18-4. Ethernet LAN packet with pib offsets highlighted

In packetC, decoding of packets is accomplished through the combination of both the decoded information present in the pib along with descriptors. Given that most of the complexity remains in the descriptors, the pib can remain quite simple, needing only to provide three elements: layer offsets, decoded layer types and integrity information. A *pib*'s values are unique to the current packet being processed and as such the layer offsets map to the current packet only as one packet versus another that may have optional elements that change the offsets. The common layer offsets being referenced in the *pib* are shown as A, B, and C in Figure 18-4, where A represents *pib.l3Offset*, B represents *pib.l4Offset*, and C represents *pib.payloadOffset*.

Layer	Protocol
Layer 2	Ethernet II 802.3 Ethernet with or without SNAP PPP/HDLC
Layers 2/3	MPLS (up to 4 tags)
Layer 2/3	ARP
Layer 3	IPv4
Layer 4	TCP, UDP, ICMP

Layers 5–7	Start of Payload for TCP, UDP, ICMP

Figure 18-5. packetC pib layer offset designation

Figure 18-5 shows a mapping of common network protocols to an OSI stack influenced by packetC layer designations is shown. Within packetC there is no layer 2 offset specified, as this is always 0 for packetC which addresses layer 2 through 7 network processing. The payload offset is often called layer 7 and contains headers for protocols such as DNS, BGP, and HTTP. From an OSI perspective this should be layer 5, however, TCP/IP combines what would have been layer 5-7 into one layer, commonly referred to as layer 7. While headers in layers 2-4 don't change much, these can often be defined by standard include files and don't need to be extended very often in packetC development. By contrast, application-layer protocols are vast and this often becomes the realm of complex packet descriptor construction and conditional logic being required to process them in packetC. As such, layer 7 headers are left outside the scope of most pre-defined system includes, in particular due to the fact that many layer 7 headers in TCP/IP don't follow simple binary construction patterns but rather often rely on text-based protocols, such as the SIP example shown earlier.

Layer offsets help determine where something like an IP header sits, as is the case with pib.l3Offset. The next step is to determine what descriptor to use, for example, an IPv4 one or an IPv6 one. That is where the types come in such as *pib.l3Type* with values L3TYPE_IPV4 or L3TYPE_IPV6 helping denote the above two versions. At that point, the only other key element is determining if integrity of the header can be relied on, which is where the flags come into play, such as *pib.flags.l3CheckSumValid*. If the layer 3 header checksum isn't valid, then there is no way to know that the decoded type is appropriate. This complex calculation and validation is presumed to be implemented by the operating system with the result presented to the packetC application for the current packet in the *pib*. One of the simplest means of ensuring that the *pib* data can be trusted for TCP/IP processing is checking the l4CheckSumValid bit as it implies TCP, UDP, or ICMP in layer 4 and that the IP header has a valid layer 3 checksum plus proper construction and layer offsets all the way to the Ethernet or SONET header. Placing a comparison early in an application such as the following can save a lot of work in processing by allowing code to move into field analysis and exception handle the small amount of non-TCP/IP traffic coming through the system.

```
// Throw exceptions if not expected packet types.
if (pib.l4Type != L4TYPE_TCP) throw ...
```

Refer to the descriptors chapters for more details on decoding headers using *pib* values.

PacketAction   action;

This is the action specified by the packetC application to be performed on the packet at the completion of processing, namely FORWARD or DROP as determined by the PacketAction enumeration.

int   length;

This is the actual length of the packet as received by the operating system. It should be equivalent to the derived total length of the packet from decoding headers, however, it doesn't necessarily need to be for bogus or otherwise fragmented packets. The value in *sys.length* is useful for performing quick checks to determine if a packet is one with content that may be of interest or not.

```
bits int
{
    replica        : 1;
...
} flags;
```

This field identifies that the current packet is not one received from a network interface, but rather one created by a packetC application. This is often useful for discerning packets which represent events, such as background thread workloads, versus those that are actual packets.

```
bits int
{
```

```
…
    l3CheckSumValid    : 1;
    l3CheckSumRecalc   : 1;
    l4CheckSumValid    : 1;
    l4CheckSumRecalc   : 1;
…
} flags;
```

These bit fields identify whether protocol decode procedures in the operating system determined that the current packet's layer 3 and layer 4 protocols have valid checksums. Based upon the protocol decoded, this information may or may not be relevant. Recalc variants represent requests to the operating system to recalculate the checksum after processing of the current packet has completed which is useful to offload this processing required for packets being modified.

```
bits int
{
…
    ipFragment    : 1;
    ipv4          : 1;
    ipv6          : 1;
…
    mpls          : 1;
    vlan          : 1;
    pad           : 18;
} flags;
```

The bit fields shown above are a collection of descriptive references to the currently decoded packet's protocols. The ipv4 and ipv6 flags denote which version an IP header is, no different than directly inspecting the upper nibble of the first byte of an IP header. The ipFragment field represents whether or not the current IPv4 or IPv6 packet is fragmented while mpls and vlan represent whether or not these tags are present in the current packet. As always, "pad" is a reserved keyword for unused bits in a bit field leveraged to assure the bit field is properly aligned.

```
L2Type l2Type;
L3Type l3Type;
L4Type l4Type;
```

The layer type fields store the decoded type of each layer 2, 3, and 4 header using the enumerations specified by the type declarations presented in the shared definitions section above. For example, pib.l2Type may be set to L2TYPE_ETHII when the current packet contains a standard layer 2 Ethernet II header. Determinations for types are made based upon the underlying operating system following a protocol header decode procedure similar to those shown at the end of this chapter.

```
int    l2Offset;
int    mplsOffset;
int    l3Offset;
int    l4Offset;
```

```
int     payloadOffset;
```

These represent the offsets of each protocol layer in the packet, i.e., the number of bytes from the start of the packet. These values are determined through the decoding of the packet per the protocol decode procedures shown later on in this chapter. The descriptors provided in the system include file *protocols.ph* leverage these values for alignment of standard header decodes mapped onto the packet.

In packetC, all values are by default 0. If a protocol is properly decoded, the value will be updated with the appropriate non-zero value for the protocol layer offset. It is critical that a packetC application verify that fields are non-zero or properly decoded, such as ensuring ipv4 and l4CheckSumValid bits are set before using *pib.l4Offset* in the application.

```
bits int
{
…
    logAccelReplicate : 1;
    // After transmit, shall Log Accelerator replicate current packet?
    // 0=False, 1=True.

    logAccelModify    : 1;
    // After transmit, shall Log Accelerator modify current packet?
    // 0=False, 1=True.

    logAccelMethod    : 1;
    // Log Accelerator Method of Round Robin (0) assignment
    // or specified target.

    logAccelDatasize  : 1;
    // If set (1), replicated packets will only contain
    // 64 bytes of payload.
…
} flags;
int logAccelTarget;  // Specifies the Log Accelerator rule number to
use if logAccelMethod set.
```

The last list of fields above are CloudShield-specific attributes in the *cloudshield.ph* file related to target blade capabilities present on a limited variety of CloudShield systems. Please refer to Log Accelerator user guides for details on these attributes. In general, these are used to communicate information to a post-processor to packetC about traffic management rules that are to be used to process, potentially replicating, and modify the packet upon transmission.

System Information ($SYS sys)

The System Information (SYS) type is a structure that contains attributes useful for processing a packet that describes attributes of the system or treatment of packets, but not the contents or construction of the packet. For example, this includes time data, parallel processing context, the port where the packet was received, and information about system thresholds, such as buffer utilization.

System Information is accessible to the user in a variable of the predefined type, **$SYS**, specified as an argument to the packet module main. It is always referenced in packetC as sys and this predefined type cannot be used to declare other types.

```
void main ($PACKET pkt, $PIB pib, $SYS sys ) {…}
```

The structure definition for **$SYS** is declared in a target system include file or predefined by a packetC compiler. For CloudShield systems, $SYS is defined in the *cloudshield.ph* include file.

The structure of the System Information Block ($SYS) is shown below:

```
//==============================================================================
//  System Information
//
//  The typedef for structure $SYS is instantiated as sys and delivered as a
//  parameter to main() containing information about the current system.
//  The system information structure, sys, acts as both a source of information
//  about the system the packetC is operating on as well as system level
//  that may affect choices in processing.  In particular this structure
//  data about the physical interface packets were received on an whether this
//  is an Ethernet or SONET system.  Some attributes may affect the system's
//  processing of operations as well as provide real-time information about the
//  system that may change during the processing of a packet.
//
//  This release (v1.01) of cloudshield.ph introduces UTC time support.  Note
//  the change of the old xtime(now ticksL in struct time) and time(now ticks).
//
//==============================================================================
struct $SYS
{
  int           messageId;
  MessageGroup  messageGroup;
  int           inPort;
  int           outPort;
  int           context;
  int           ticks;
  struct Time64Values {
            Time64 ticksL;
            Time64 utcTime;
            Time64 utcTimeUncorrected;
            Time64 utcTimeDrift;
            } time;
  int           bufferCount;
  int           queueDepth;
  int           logFailures;
  bits int
  {
    sonet : 1;
    pad   : 31;
  } flags;
  int           requeueCount;
  int           tcsFlow;
```

```
    int         tcsRule;
    int         outBlade;
    int         inBlade;
    int         replicatePort;
    int         replicateBlade;
};
```

Many components of the *sys* structure depict information about the underlying system packetC applications are running on or information regarding the flow of the current packet through the system. In addition, fields are present that are utilized by operators and actions in packetC for control-plane interaction. Refer to specific chapters on these features for a detailed explanation and to the section below for a brief synopsis of each field.

int messageId;
MessageGroup messageGroup;

When interacting with the control-plane through the *alert* and *log* commands, a number of parameters may be necessary for providing some associated data along with the data contents being presented to the control plane. Unique predefined messages by an application, stored in the control plane, referenced by the data plane, have their reference value placed in *messageId* while the group, essentially a severity, is referenced by the *messageGroup* field. All future alert and log commands will use the currently set value by the application until these values are changed. If these values are not important to the logging of data, as is often the case when logging packets, these fields in the *sys* structure can remain at their system startup defaults.

int   inPort;
int   outPort;

Every packetC application is treated as a virtual appliance with as many interface ports as desired by the application developer. When deployed upon a system, these ports are bound either to interfaces on other virtual appliances or to physical interfaces on the system. These two fields in *sys* represent the interface through which the current packet arrived, and upon the interface through which the packet shall be forwarded upon completion of processing, respectively. Based upon external provisioning choices these interface ports may or may not equate to physical ports.

int   context;

In packetC, generally many more than one packet is being processed at any given point in time. There are many cases, such as performance modeling, where view into the current context number that the operating system has assigned the current packet being processed is needed. This value is stored in *sys.context*.

int   ticks;
struct Time64Values {
**   Time64 ticksL;**
**   Time64 utcTime;**
**   Time64 utcTimeUncorrected;**
**   Time64 utcTimeDrift;**
**   } time;**

The structures above represent time values based upon derivatives of the system 64-bit "CPU tick timer." Multiple different representations of time may appear in *sys* based upon the target platform's support features. The integer *ticks* is the lower 32 bits of the system tick timer used for fine-grained delta measurements. The *time* structure contains four instantiations of a 64-bit time value. Some systems may not support all representations in this structure. At the highest level, systems generally have a 64-bit "CPU tick timer" which is representative of an oscillator. In most systems, this timer is instantiated to be ticks since UTC (1/1/1970 00:00:00 GMT), however, drift is never adjusted and using it for UTC is not viable nor expected to be very accurate. The *ticksL* represents a 64-bit value containing this hardware tick count and is specific to the hardware. The lower 32 bits of *ticksL* is the same as *ticks.* The *ticksL* value is not corrected for UTC, however, it can be utilized for measuring long-term response times on an accurate basis, nominally with 10ns per increment of the value. The three 64-bit values of *utcTime, utcTimeUncorrected,* and *utcTimeDrift* are in the form of two 32-bit values representing seconds and microseconds. These values are based upon network time protocol (NTP) drift-adjusted values such that the *utcTimeUncorrected* is based upon a boot time setting of UTC time but without any adjustment to drift over time. The *utcTime* value is as accurate as the system can perform with its time adjusted by the measured drift as determined from NTP updates. Different systems can vary, from the most accurate GPS based NTP sources accurate to 50 microseconds while most systems operate in the few milliseconds on a LAN to 10 or more milliseconds in a WAN. The *utcTimeDrift* value is provided to the packetC application to present a window into the current drift adjustment. The *utcTimeDrift* is the absolute value of correction to the time required to convert *utcTimeUncorrected* into *utcTime.* Determining the sign of this value is possible through comparing the corrected and uncorrected time. The *utcTime* value should be equivalent to the *utcTimeUncorrected* modified by the *utcTimeDrift.* Note that these are synchronized with one another only when the structure *time* is read in a single assignment of the entire structure because values change frequently.

The value for *ticks* will roll over on average in less than 1 minute while *ticksL* should not roll over within our lifetimes. As an example, on 1.4GHz systems with a tick increment every 16 clocks, a tick increments every 11.428 nanoseconds. This results in *ticks* rolling over every 48 seconds while *ticksL* will take over 6,000 years. For UTC values, these are stored in seconds and microseconds. By definition, the lower 32-bit microseconds value will roll over every 1,000,000 microseconds and result in an increment to the upper 32-bit seconds value. With UTC based at 1970 and since it takes more than 136 years for the seconds value to roll-over, there should not be any issues in the 64-bit approach to UTC until 2106.

```
int      bufferCount;     // Number of Free Packet Buffers
int      queueDepth;      // Number of Packets Waiting To Be Processed
```

As packets are received by the underlying operating system, they are placed into a buffer. Each context is assigned one packet to process and upon completion retrieves the next one to process. In cases of over-subscription of the processing power of a system executing the packetC application, a developer may desire to adjust the amount of processing done per packet based upon the quantity of packets waiting to be processed. The *sys.bufferCount* value represents the number of packet buffers consumed by those waiting to be processed, in processing, and awaiting transmission. Compare this value against a constant containing a maximum for the target platform to determine percentage of buffers in use. The *sys.queueDepth* identifies the number of packets awaiting to be processed. This value does not include those currently assigned to contexts or those awaiting transmission that a packetC application will not see again.

```
int     logFailures;    // Number of Failed Log Attempts Due To System
Overload
```

Provides feedback for when the *log* and *alert* commands are overloading the control plane. As the data plane where packetC is executing may often have more processing power than a control plane, it is important in applications that perform heavy logging to ensure that they do not overload a given system. Refer to target platform references for the number of logging functions per second that can be sustained.

```
bits int
{
  sonet : 1;
  pad   : 31;
} flags;
```

The physical layer-1 interface of a system is important as it pertains to identifying certain types of capabilities with regard to point-to-point network links versus those in layer 2, such as Ethernet, that can leverage switching. Bit fields in *sys* are provided to inform the application whether it is on a SONET or Ethernet system. By default, packetC systems presume an Ethernet environment unless bits are set for an alternate physical transmission medium, such as SONET identified by the bit field above.

```
int     requeueCount;
```

Each time a packet is placed on the queue to postpone further processing until a future time, the sys.requeueCount field is incremented. packetC code is able to place packets back into the input queue through the PacketAction field within the *pib*. This can be used to prevent packets from a continuous requeue loop by providing an escape for the evaluation condition.

```
int     tcsFlow;
// 32-bit value containing the hash of the
// flow tuple from TCS pre-processor

int     tcsRule;
// Rule # which matched current packet in TCS pre-processor

int     replicatePort;
// Log Accelerator replicated packet physical port number

int     replicateBlade;
// Log Accelerator replicate packet blade number in dual-blade scenarios
```

```
int     outBlade;
// Output can specify peer-blade in DPPM-800 systems,
// 0=current, 1=other

int     inBlade;
// Input can come in alternate blade in DPPM-800 systems,
// 0=current, 1=other.
```

The last list of fields above are CloudShield-specific attributes in the *cloudshield.ph* file related to target blade capabilities present on a *limited* variety of CloudShield systems. Please refer to Traffic Control System (TCS) user guides for details on these attributes. In general, these are used to communicate information from a pre-processor to packetC about traffic management rules that were used to classify the packet flow. In addition, choices by the packetC application to request post-processing of the packet, such as replicating it and sending copies to different blades, is controlled by these values.

TCP/IP Stack Decode for pib Layer Offset Calculations

A variety of Internet RFC's describe the various protocols and the meaning of different fields that can appear in layers 2 through 4 of TCP/IP systems. Unfortunately, putting these all together to make a simple method of decoding a packet can be quite elusive. Further complicating things is interpreting results, like the values in *pib* and *sys*, when assumptions are not clearly understood. As such, each target platform should define the process through which a packet is decoded from a byte stream into the fields present in the pib. Example flow charts for basic layer 2 through 4 network headers are shown below.

Layer 2 Ethernet Header Decode Procedure

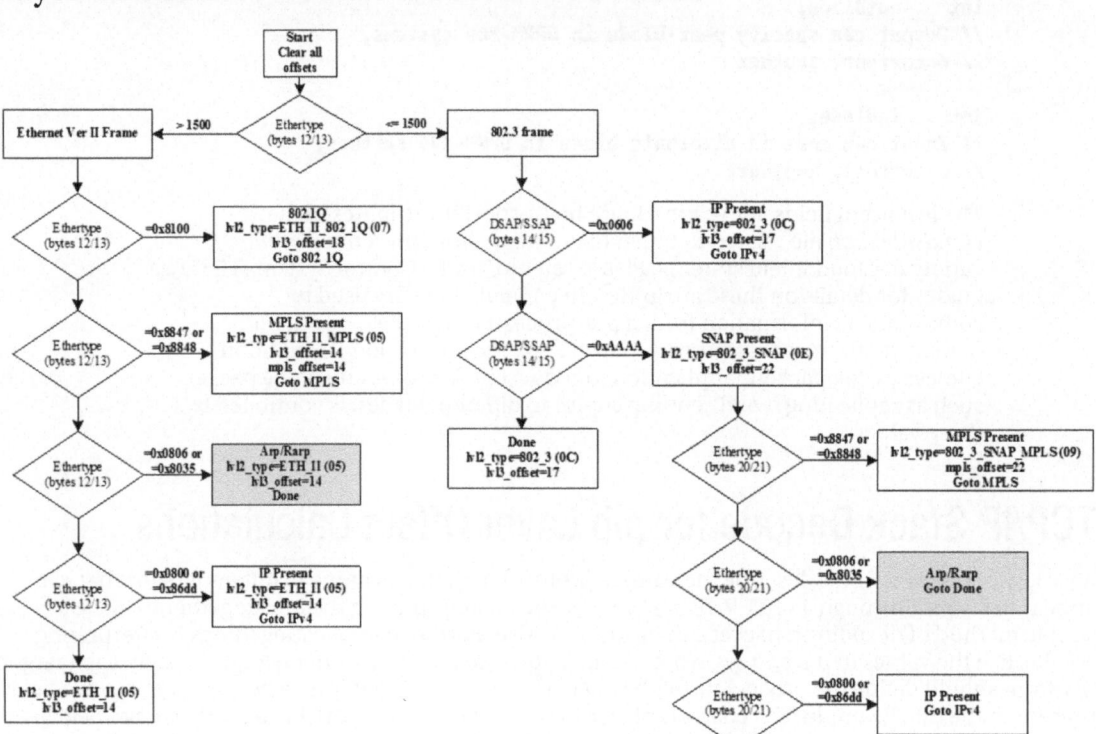

Figure 18-6. Layer 2 Ethernet Header Decode Procedure

Figure 18-6 shows how offsets are computed for Ethernet and which protocols are valid for layer 3 and layer 4. Boxes with "Goto <name>" represent jumps to other flow charts below.

The Layer 2 Ethernet Header Decode Procedure examines the packet data to determine the layer 2 (L2), layer 3 (L3), and layer 4 (L4) information contained in the packet. The L2, L3, and L4 headers, if present, are decoded, determining the type and location of each header in the packet. The flow chart illustrates the decision process for each packet that is performed by the operating system prior to delivery of the packet to packetC. The L2 decode is the first process performed. Once the initial L2 procedure has been completed, the packet may undergo further L2 processing if the packet is 802.1Q-encapsulated or contains an MPLS header. If no further L2 processing is required and the packet is an IPv4 packet, the IPv4 (L3) header checksum is verified. If the L3 checksum is valid, L4 processing of the IPv4 and IPv6 decode procedure proceeds to a subsequent layer 4 flow chart. If the packet is 802.1Q-encapsulated, the 802.1Q Layer 2 decode procedure is followed before any L3 or L4 processing can proceed. The 802.1Q processing is similar to the Ethernet decoding procedure since 802.1Q is an encapsulation protocol.

Layer 2 Ethernet 802.1Q (VLAN) Decode Procedure

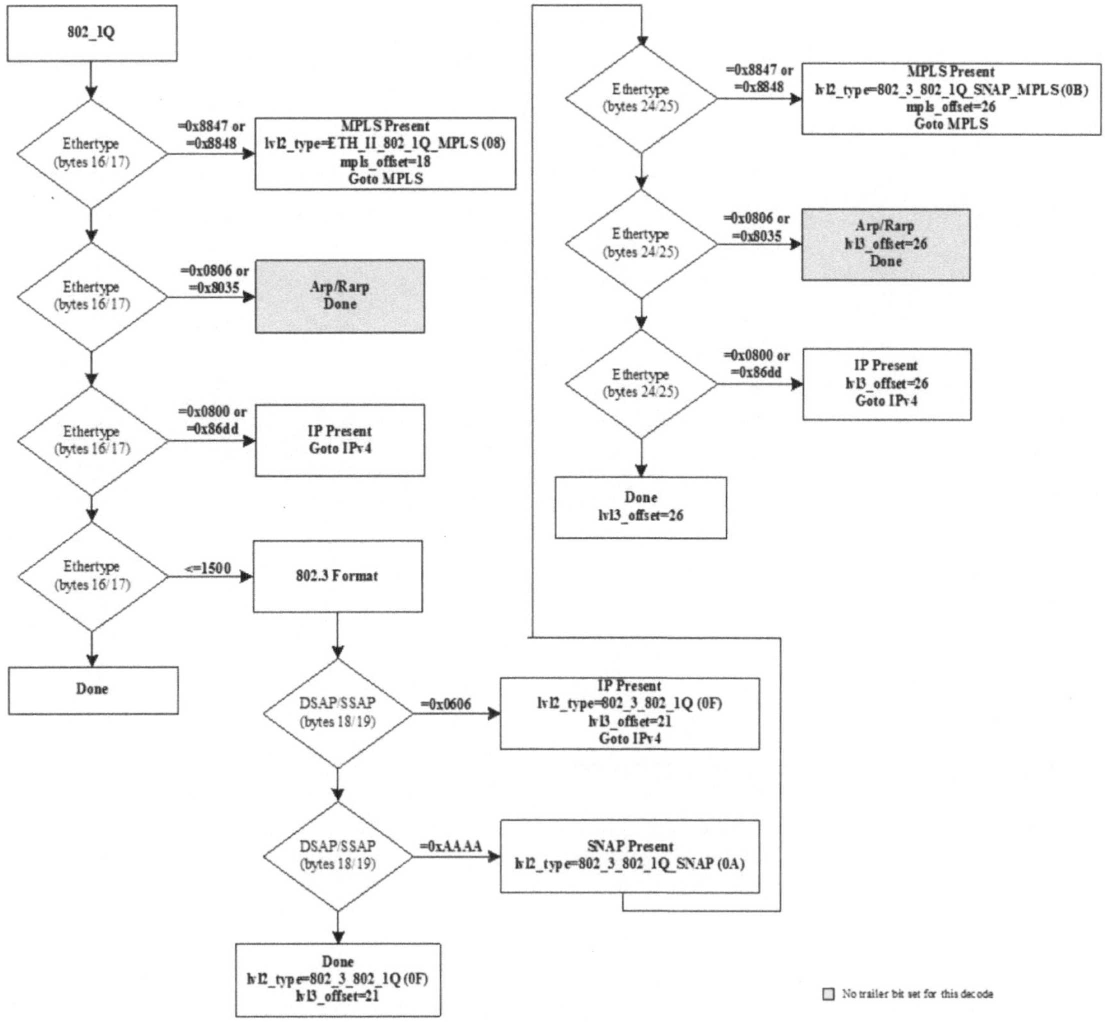

Figure 18-7. *Layer 2 Ethernet 802.1Q (VLAN) Decode Procedure*

The flow chart shown in Figure 18-7 is processed only for Ethernet packets that were identified with a value of 0x8100 in the Ether Type. Unless the Layer 2 Ethernet Header Decode Procedure jumps to this flow chart, it will be ignored. Packets with one or more VLAN headers, specified in IEEE standard 802.1Q, will be decoded using this procedure. As a result the L2 header is larger, increasing the value of *pib.l3Offset*, and modifying the *pib.l2Type* value.

Layer 2 SONET Header Decode Procedure

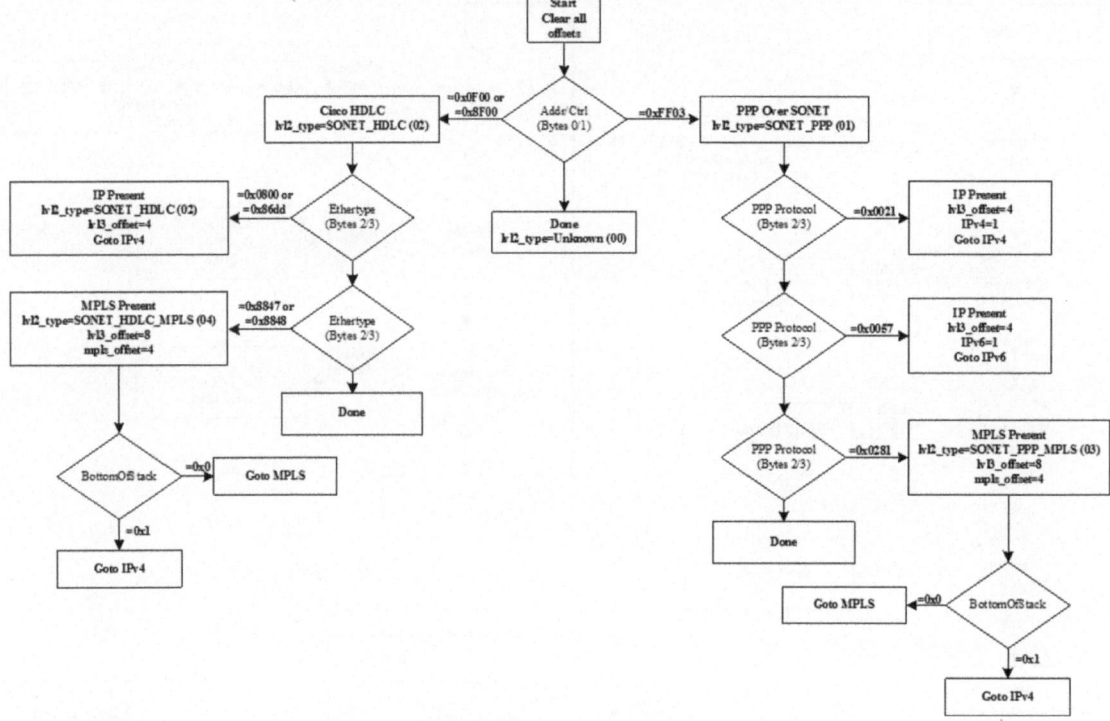

Figure 18-8. Layer 2 SONET Header Decode Procedure

In the WAN, packets often traverse links that are not Ethernet-based. As a result, the layer 2 headers do not conform to Ethernet decodes shown in previous procedures but rather follow PPP or HDLC formats in most cases. The procedure shown in Figure 18-8 reflects the generalized process for decoding these common headers in SONET systems and the process by which the next layer headers are determined.

Layer 2 ½ MPLS Label Stack Decode Procedure

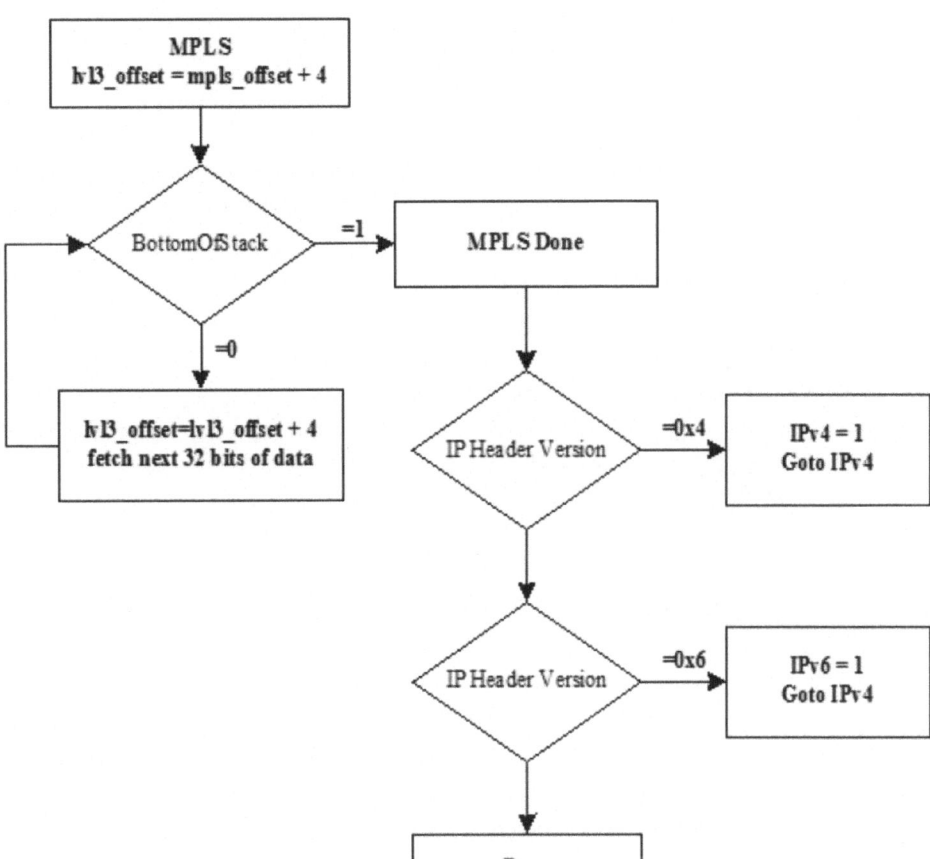

Figure 18-9. *Layer 2 ½ MPLS Label Stack Decode Procedure*

If the Ethernet or SONET packet contains an MPLS header, the label stack is processed as shown in Figure 18-9. MPLS label stacks can encapsulate a variety of protocols in them. As such, the entire stack must be evaluated to determine not only how many bytes are between the layer 2 header and the commonly-encapsulated layer 3 header, but also to determine whether MPLS is encapsulating IP or not. The flow chart above shows a simple evaluation of MPLS where the bottom of stack bits in the MPLS label are looked for and the next uses some simple evaluation to identify the version of IP header.

Layer 3 IPv4 and IPv6 Header Decode Procedure

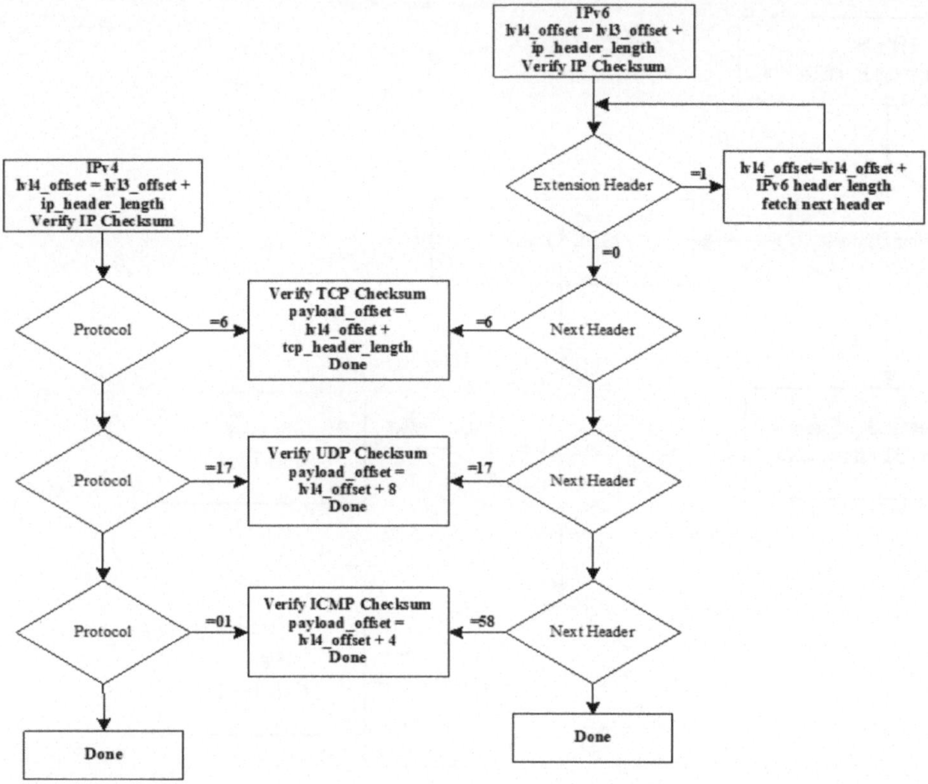

Figure 18-10. Layer 3 IPv4 And and IPv6 Header Decode Procedure

If the packet contains an IPv4 or IPv6 header, the procedure shown in Figure 18-10 will be employed to determine the L4 type of the packet as well as computation of layer 3 integrity when the L3 header is an IPv4 header. If the L4 header is TCP, UDP, or ICMP, the L4 checksum is also verified.

A packet validation failure in one layer prevents higher layer processing from occurring. If the L2 CRC fails, the L3 checksum is marked invalid. A packet with an L2 CRC error is currently dropped before any processing. If the L3 checksum verification fails, the L4 checksum is marked invalid and the L4 type is set to "UNKNOWN."

The checksum for UDP is optional in IPv4 and, if missing, is indicated by setting the checksum field to 0x0000. CloudShield systems handle this situation and mark the packet as being IPv4 and UDP with a valid checksum (optional checksums being considered valid). References for each vendor and target need to be evaluated for these types of corner-cases before presuming what some of the *pib* values imply. For TCP and ICMPv4, however, the checksum is not optional and a checksum value of 0x0000 is considered valid. If an IPv4 packet is received with an invalid L4 checksum, the packet is still marked as being IPv4 and UDP (for example), however, the L4 checksum valid bit is not set. Just because a packet has a bad checksum doesn't invalidate the packet format. The same is true if the L3 checksum is invalid. The L3 type is still set to IPv4 and the L3 checksum valid bit is not set. For fragments, the situation is a bit more complicated. As an example, if an IPv4/UDP fragment is received, the packet is marked as an IPv4 packet, UDP, fragment packet with the L4 checksum valid bit cleared. For the first packet in the fragment, the *pib.payloadOffset* field is set correctly, however, for every subsequent packet the payload offset is set to 0x0000. A packetC application must handle reconstruction of fragmented packets and determine integrity.

For Layer 4 Header Decode Procedures for TCP, UDP, and ICMP follow the same form of mechanism shown above and are equally complex as optional header extensions can appear adjusting the distance from *pib.l4Offset* to *pib.payloadOffset*.

Example cloudshield.ph Include File

Note that by design, most of cloudshield.ph is commented out as the types and structures defined herein are built into the tool-chain. This file does include some uncommented sections and is useful to ensure application code contains a clear definition for all structures and their form presumed during code audits. Furthermore, guard macros ensure that packetC applications are tied to the correct form of these types and structures.

```
//============================================================================
//  cloudshield.ph - packetC standard include for CloudShield platforms.
//
//     This packetC standard include file defines platform specific structures
//     related to intrinsic functionality within the language.  In addition,
//     structures and data types that are built into the compiler are provided
//     in this document as comments to enable programmers to understand and
//     validate types.
//
// author
//     peder@cloudshield.com
//
// copyright notice
//     © 2009 CloudShield Technologies, Inc.
//
//============================================================================
#ifndef CLOUDSHIELD_PH
#define CLOUDSHIELD_PH
#define _CLOUDSHIELD_PH_VERSION 1.01
#define __PACKETC__ TRUE
//============================================================================
//  PacketAction Enumerated Type
//
//  Used with action in $PIB to define what to do with packet at end of main().
//
//============================================================================
// enum int PacketAction
// {
//   DROP_PACKET    = 0,
//   FORWARD_PACKET = 1,
//   REQUEUE_PACKET = 2
// };
```

```
//==============================================================================
//  Layer Type Enumerations
//
//  L2Type, L3Type and L4Type are used by the $PIB to describe current packet.
//
//==============================================================================
// enum int L2Type
// {
//    L2TYPE_OTHER                    = 0,
//    L2TYPE_SONET_PPP                = 1,
//    L2TYPE_SONET_HDLC               = 2,
//    L2TYPE_SONET_HDLC_PPP_MPLS      = 17,
//    L2TYPE_SONET_HDLC_MPLS          = 18,
//    L2TYPE_ETHII                    = 3,
//    L2TYPE_ETHII_MPLS               = 19,
//    L2TYPE_ETHII_8021Q              = 35,
//    L2TYPE_ETHII_8021Q_MPLS         = 51,
//    L2TYPE_802_3_SNAP_MPLS          = 21,
//    L2TYPE_802_3_SNAP_802_1Q        = 37,
//    L2TYPE_802_3_SNAP_802_1Q_MPLS   = 53,
//    L2TYPE_802_3                     = 4,
//    L2TYPE_802_3_MPLS               = 20,
//    L2TYPE_802_3_SNAP               = 5,
//    L2TYPE_802_3_802_1Q             = 36
// };
//
// enum int L3Type
// {
//    L3TYPE_OTHER = 0,
//    L3TYPE_IPV4  = 1,
//    L3TYPE_IPV6  = 2,
//    L3TYPE_ARP   = 3,
//    L3TYPE_RARP  = 4,
//    L3TYPE_IPX   = 5
// };
//
// enum int L4Type
// {
//    L4TYPE_OTHER   = 0,
//    L4TYPE_TCP     = 1,
//    L4TYPE_UDP     = 2,
//    L4TYPE_ICMP    = 3,
//    L4TYPE_ICMPV6  = 4,
//    L4TYPE_ESP     = 5,
//    L4TYPE_AH      = 6,
//    L4TYPE_GRE     = 7,
//    L4TYPE_SCTP    = 8
// };


//==============================================================================
//  Packet Information Block
//
```

```
//   The typedef for structure $PIB is instantiated as pib and delivered as a
//   parameter to main() containing information about the current packet.
//   The pib acts as both an input structure as well as the end state of the pib
//   determines actions to be taken against the packet at the end of main().
//
//=============================================================================
// struct $PIB
// {
//    PacketAction  action;
//    int           logAccelTarget;
//    int           length;
//    bits int
//    {
//      replica            : 1;
//      l3CheckSumValid    : 1;
//      l3CheckSumRecalc   : 1;
//      l4CheckSumValid    : 1;
//      l4CheckSumRecalc   : 1;
//      ipFragment         : 1;
//      ipv4               : 1;
//      ipv6               : 1;
//      logAccelReplicate  : 1;
//      logAccelModify     : 1;
//      logAccelMethod     : 1;
//      logAccelDatasize   : 1;
//      mpls               : 1;
//      vlan               : 1;
//      pad                : 18;
//    } flags;
//    L2Type           l2Type;
//    L3Type           l3Type;
//    L4Type           l4Type;
//    int              l2Offset;
//    int              mplsOffset;
//    int              l3Offset;
//    int              l4Offset;
//    int              payloadOffset;
// };


//=============================================================================
//   Message Group Levels
//
//   The MessageGroup enumerated type is used to set a severity level for a log()
//   message.  This field can be set once in a context and all future events that
//   are generated during the processing of the packet will utilize this value.
//   The $SYS structure utilized MessageGroup with field messageGroup.
//
//=============================================================================
// enum int MessageGroup
// {
//    MSG_CRITICAL = 1,
//    MSG_MAJOR    = 2,
```

201

```
//   MSG_MINOR    = 3,
//   MSG_WARNING  = 4,
//   MSG_INFO     = 5
// };


//================================================================================
//  Message Constants
//
//  The following constants provide a maximum message number and length for a
//  log() message generated by the packetC system.  Use in conjunction with the
//  messageId field in $SYS.
//
//================================================================================
// const int MAX_PACKETC_MSGS    = 255;
// const int MAX_PACKETC_MSG_LEN = 80;


//================================================================================
//  Time Construct Structure
//
//  This structure is used to represent the 64-bit fields used in time elements
//  of the $SYS structure.  For ticks this is the upper and lower 32-bits of a
//  64-bit counter.  For UTC Time values, this relates to the seconds (high) and
//  microseconds (low) since UTC (1/1/1970) in a single 64-bit structure.
//
//  This structure replaced XTime structure from cloudshield.ph version 1.00
//
//================================================================================
// struct Time64 {
//    int highOrder;
//    int lowOrder;
// };


//================================================================================
//  System Information
//
//  The typedef for structure $SYS is instantiated as sys and delivered as a
//  parameter to main() containing information about the current system.
//  The system information structure, sys, acts as both a source of information
//  about the system the packetC is operating on as well as system level
//  that may affect choices in processing.  In particular this structure
//  data about the physical interface packets were received on an whether this
//  is an Ethernet or SONET system.  Some attributes may affect the system's
//  processing of operations as well as provide real-time information about the
//  system that may change during the processing of a packet.
//
//  This release (v1.01) of cloudshield.ph introduces UTC time support.  Note
//  the change of the old xtime(now ticksL in struct time) and time(now ticks).
//
//================================================================================
// struct $SYS
// {
//    int          messageId;
```

```
//    MessageGroup  messageGroup;
//    int           inPort;
//    int           outPort;
//    int           context;
//    int           ticks;
//    struct Time64Values {
//              Time64  ticksL;
//              Time64  utcTime;
//              Time64  utcTimeUncorrected;
//              Time64  utcTimeDrift;
//              } time;
//    int           bufferCount;
//    int           queueDepth;
//    int           logFailures;
//    bits int
//    {
//      sonet : 1;
//      pad   : 31;
//    } flags;
//    int           requeueCount;
//    int           tcsFlow;
//    int           tcsRule;
//    int           outBlade;
//    int           inBlade;
//    int           replicatePort;
//    int           replicateBlade;
// };


//=============================================================================
//   Search Results Structure
//
//   When a match or find operator is used on a search set, a structure is then
//   returned with the result.  This structure is the typedef for that result.
//
//=============================================================================
// struct SearchResult
// {
//    int    index;
//    int    position;
// };


//=============================================================================
//   Exception Constants
//
//   Try catch based exception handlers are core to packetC.  There are a set of
//   pre-defined exceptions for intrinsic operators to packetC.  The section
//   of exception constants below are what is implemented in the associated
//   packetC compiler.
//
//=============================================================================
// typedef int Exception;
// const Exception                 ERR_ANY_EXCEPTION   = 0;
```

```
// const Exception              ERR_DB_FULL         = 1;
// const Exception              ERR_DB_READ         = 2;
// const Exception              ERR_DB_NOMATCH      = 3;
// const Exception              ERR_PKT_INSERT      = 4;
// const Exception              ERR_PKT_DELETE      = 5;
// const Exception              ERR_PKT_NOREPLICATE = 6;
// const Exception              ERR_SET_NOMATCH     = 7;
// const Exception              ERR_SET_NOPERFORM   = 8;
// const Exception              ERR_SET_NOTFOUND    = 9;
// const Exception              ERR_PKT_NOTREQUEUED = 10;


//==============================================================================
// User Defined Exception Constants
//
// packetC users can create their own exceptions constants to throw by using
// the ERR_LAST_DEFINED constant.
//
// const Exception    ERR_MY_EXCEPTION  = ERR_LAST_DEFINED + 1
//
//==============================================================================
// const Exception              ERR_LAST_DEFINED    = 64;


//==============================================================================
// Packet Type
//
// Each system may have a slightly different constraint on the buffer for each
// packet.  The typedef below defines the $PACKET for the system.
//
//==============================================================================
// typedef byte $PACKET[9 * 1024 - 1];


//==============================================================================
// Truth Constants
//
// In packetC no boolean types exist, however, true and false are pre-defined.
// To enforce consistency and strict type matching, bool is defined.
//
//==============================================================================
// const int true  = 1;
// const int false = 0;
typedef int bool;
//==============================================================================
// Search Set Constants
//
// Null is a valid value in strings and regular expressions.  Constants are
// pre-defined for these values.
//
//==============================================================================
// const byte NULL_STOP[1]  = "\x00";
// const byte NULL_REGEX[4] = ".*?\x00";

#endif
```

Descriptor Type and Operations

packetC Descriptor Types

packetC provides data types that do not appear in standard C but do provide significant support for packet-processing applications. These data types are often extensions of familiar C types. The extended data type described in this chapter is descriptors. This chapter is divided into two different approaches. The first part of this chapter is focused on simply covering examples of descriptors and the packetC standard include file *protocols.ph*. The second part of this chapter covers an in-depth view into the background of the descriptors and how they operate under the hood as these are new to packetC.

Descriptors

descriptor type_name identifier **at** offset_expression
descriptor type_name **{** field_decl_list **}** identifier **at** offset_expression

A *descriptor* is a structure that describes a network protocol and that is mapped to whatever location contains that structure within the current packet.

Each time a packetC program is triggered with a new packet, information about the packet and the location of certain packet protocols is computed and placed in the Packet Information Block (PIB). This information includes the location of standardized protocols within the current packet. These locations (offsets) may change their values from packet to packet. A descriptor declaration associates three things:

- a structure definition (usually that of a standard network protocol)

- a user-specified name for the descriptor

- a packet offset (typically a layer offset computed automatically by the system for each packet)

A descriptor declaration specifies the name of a structure type (or defines it in-place), the name of the descriptor based on that structure (a variable), and the location of the descriptor in terms of a packet offset expression that will be computed at run time.

```
// the envisoned use
descriptor TcpStruct
{
    short       sourcePort;
    short       destPort;
    int         sequenceNum;
    int         ackNum;
```

```
      ...
} tcp at pib.l4Offset;

mySourcePort = tcp.sourcePort;

      // idiosyncratic use
      struct StructTag {
              short    sourcePort;
              short    destPort;
              byte     mysteryItem1;

              …
              };
      typedef StructTag MyCustomProtocol;

      descriptor MyCustomProtocol  myProtocolVar at customOffset;
      myByte = myProtocolVar.mysteryItem1;
```

Because a descriptor is associated with a particular portion of a packet (the specific location can change from packet to packet), it cannot be part of a larger structure, since that could create impossible layouts. Thus, a descriptor cannot be a field within a structure, a field within another descriptor, a union member, or an element type of an array. However, a descriptor can be based on a structure type that includes nested definitions of structures, unions, and enumeration types.

Descriptors are effectively packet scope objects in that the associated values accessed by the descriptor apply only to the current context and packet. Descriptors are able to be defined throughout the packet module, including outside of *main()*, even though they are packet scope and may reference the *pib*. Even though a descriptor may be defined within global scope, making it accessible by all contexts, the values returned are unique to the context, packet, and local or block scope constraints that may appear in *at clause* elements.

An entire descriptor, as well as individual descriptor fields, can be assigned values from and to variables with compatible types.

```
struct StructType { short sourcePort; short destPort };
descriptor StructType myDescr at pib.l2Offset;
StructType myStruct = myDescr;  // struct gets descriptor contents
```

A descriptor declaration does not include an initialization clause, because the descriptor's contents are effectively initialized when a context is provisioned with a new packet. It is important to note that variables may exist within the descriptor's *at clause* which would result in potentially changing offsets at run time. Furthermore, the contents of a packet may change over the course of processing the packet causing particular values returned to differ throughout the execution of the program in the context.

Descriptor Example Application

The following is a simple example of packet Descriptors in use.

```
packet module telnetPackets;

#include "cloudshield.ph";
#include "protocols.ph";

int     totalPkts_;
int     telnetPkts_;
```

```
int     nonTelnetPkts_;

void main($PACKET pkt, $PIB pib, $SYS sys)
{
    ++totalPkts_;

    if ( tcp.destintationPort == 23 )
    {
        // Telnet Packets get dropped
        ++telnetPkts_;
            pib.action = DROP_PACKET;
    }
    else
    {
        // Forward any other packets
        ++nonTelnetPkts_;
        pib.action = FORWARD_PACKET;
    }
}
```

The example above references a predefined Transmission Control Protocol (TCP) descriptor within *protocols.ph* (shown in Chapter 25). The full TCP descriptor is included below for quick reference. In the example, *tcp.destinationPort* represents the 16-bit field containing the destination port number for the current packet found 2 bytes into the TCP header. A decimal value of 23 in a TCP destination port generally refers to packets communicating using the Telnet protocol. While the length of Ethernet and IP headers may differ between packets with different options and tags, the decoded start of layer 4 is used to represent the start of the TCP header in the descriptor defined below. This allows for a simple field by name reference that not only is easy to read, but also adjusts to varying offsets from one packet to another.

It should be noted, however, that the sample application should have had a few more statements to verify that it was an IP packet and the ipv4 header's protocol field specific TCP as the enveloped protocol.

```
//==============================================================================
//   Standard TCP Descriptor
//
//   A common layer 4 TCP header utilized in networks per RFC 793.  TCP Options
//   are varied and differ in size based upon the option header type as each may
//   differ in size, often from 1 to 4 bytes.  As there are trailers to the TCP
//   header, these can be developed as descriptors that sit at location
//   pib.l4Offset+20 or if nested change 20 as appropriate based upon a runtime
//   variable.
//
//==============================================================================

descriptor TcpStruct
{
    short     sourcePort;                 // Identifies the sending port
    short     destinationPort;            // Identifies the recieving port
    int       sequenceNumber;             // Sequence Number
    int       acknowledgementNumber;      // If the ACK flag is set then the value of
                                          // this field is the next sequence number that
```

```
                                         // the receiver is expecting.
  bits byte
  {
    length    :4;                        // # of 32-bit words in TCP Header, including Options
    reserved :4;
  } header;

  bits byte
  {
    cwr:1;    // Congestion window reduced per RFC 3168
    ece:1;    // ECN-Echo per RFC 3168
    urg:1;    // Urgent
    ack:1;    // Acknowledgement
    psh:1;    // Push
    rst:1;    // Reset
    syn:1;    // Synchronize
    fin:1;    // Finish
  } flags;

  short      windowSize;      // The size of the receive window
  short      checksum;        // Used for error-checking of the header and data
  short      urgentPointer;   // If the URG flag is set, then this is an offset from
                              // the sequence number indicating the last urgent byte

} tcp at pib.l4Offset;
typedef byte TcpStructBytes[sizeof(TcpStruct)];
```

Detailed View and Description of Descriptors

Since network packet processing applications increasingly execute at speeds of 10-40 Gigabits per second, they are often programmed for a specific network processor in assembly language or a C variant that exposes processor specifics. Applications typically search packet contents for the presence of packet protocol headers. Determining which protocols are present and where they are located can be computationally expensive. This encourages developers to exploit machine-specific features to increase speed. Hence, finding protocol headers poses performance burdens and encourages coding practices that hamper application portability. Our approach uses a parallel packet-processing model and a new language, packetC, to enable coding packet applications at a high level. The model requires the host system to represent the incoming packet as a byte array, to locate the protocol headers, and to capture that information in a user-accessible packet information block (PIB). The packetC language redefines C bitfields to provide layouts that will predictably match headers in the packet array. packetC also introduces a descriptor data type, a C-style structure that is superimposed on the packet array at a user-specified offset. By defining a standard protocol in terms of a descriptor and locating it at the appropriate PIB offset value, programmers can access header data in a machine-independent way. These capabilities are applicable to a variety of embedded systems, ranging from routers and switches to blades for larger-scale networking systems.

Pressure for faster network packet processing continues to increase as transmission media become faster (e.g., those specified by SONET/SDH [1, 2] and 10GbE [3]) offer speeds in the 10-40 Gigabits per second range) and the volume of data to be transmitted continues its own relentless increase.

Packets contain *protocol headers*, for communications standards, such as IPv4 (Figure 19-1). A header is a contiguous set of fields that provide routing, service and standards data. There are a variety of protocols, each with their own distinctive header content. Since multiple protocol headers may be present in a given packet and since their relative offset from the packet's start varies from packet to packet, a key aspect of packet processing is to determine which headers are present and where they are.

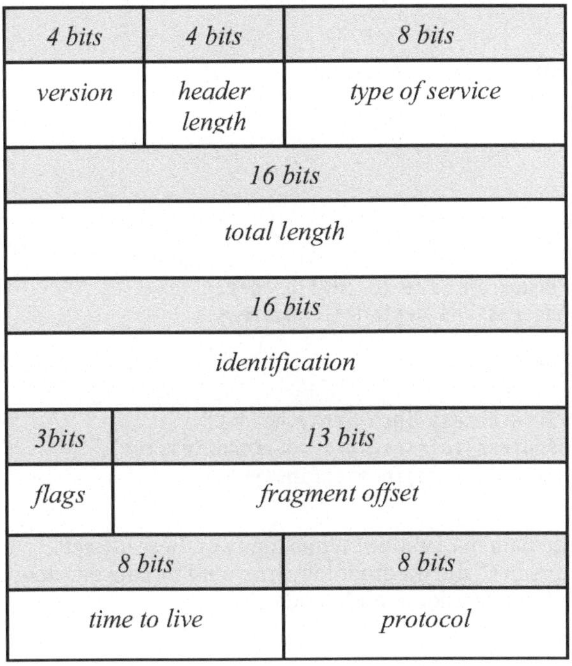

4 bits	4 bits	8 bits
version	header length	type of service
16 bits		
total length		
16 bits		
identification		
3bits	13 bits	
flags	fragment offset	
8 bits	8 bits	
time to live	protocol	

Figure 19-1. IPv4 Protocol (first 80 bits)

The search for headers occurs in a programming environment where applications are often partitioned into lightweight threads that swap themselves out for each memory access. This encourages exploiting low-level machine features to minimize the overhead of locating protocol headers. The resulting machine-specific code can require extensive redesign and recoding when the application is ported.

Complex Descriptor Structure and Union Usage

As an exploration of descriptors will show, the bounds of structures and unions from C are being pushed and pulled to the edges by packetC, but in doing so, the rules are tightened. One of the most important features of packetC is the ability to cast back and forth between complex data types such as a structure and a byte array. With special operators working on structures, such as offset, and special structure types such as descriptors, a new world of features is opened that through casting to a byte array opens array slicing functionality including memcopy and memset features all on a singular data element. Map unions onto the structure for multiple-structured views of a data element and significant flexibility on viewing data elements, such as headers, falls into place. Through exploration and a bit of torturing data through type conversion subtle but critical nuances unique to packetC supporting data transformation can be highlighted.

```
descriptor Ipv4Struct
{
  bits byte { version:4; headerLength:4; } bf;
  bits byte { precedence:3; delay:1; throughput:1; reliability:1; reserved:2; } tos;
  short totalLength;
  short identification;
  bits short { evil:1; dont:1; more:1; fragmentOffset:13; } fragment;
  byte  ttl;
  byte  protocol;
  short checksum;
  int   sourceAddress;
  int   destinationAddress;
} ipv4 at pib.l3Offset;
typedef byte HeaderType[sizeof(ipv4)];
HeaderType header;           // An array of bytes equal in size to IPv4 header.
int addresses[2];            // Holds both sourceAddress and destinationAddress

// The following code shall be within packet scope

header = (HeaderType) ipv4;   // Copies entire IPv4 header into array header.
addresses[0]  = (int) header[offset(ipv4.sourceAddress):offset(ipv4.sourceAddress)+3];
addresses[0]  = (int) header[offset(ipv4.destinationAddress):offset(ipv4⤸
.destinationAddress)+3];
```

Numerous methods can be used to work with the data in question. While many of these aspects could have been addressed through the use of pointers in C, the methodology provided by packetC does so with strict type enforcement and named fields making it easier to audit code.

Background on Parallel Processing Paradigm and Relation to Descriptors

The packetC approach has three major elements: a model of parallel packet processing, a specialized language to express the model and an ensemble of heterogeneous processors to implement the language in an embedded hardware product. In this section, focus is applied on the specialized language features for protocol processing.

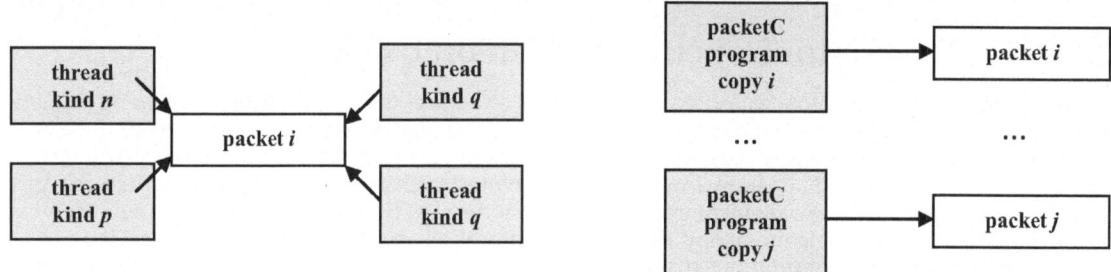

Figure 19-2. A threaded packet processing model vs. a Single Program Multiple Data (SPMD) model

The model's key characteristics for locating a given packet's header locations are as follows:

- Task granularity is at the level of a complete program that processes a packet (Single Program Multiple Data paradigm shown in Figure 19-2).

- The host system locates protocol headers in a packet before a copy of the program is executed on that packet.

- Each program copy operates with copies of its current packet and system-provided information about the presence and location of the packet's layer offsets.

This model is expressed with specialized features for packet manipulation and protocol header processing:

- A *packet main* construct corresponds to the model's parallel program copy.

- Each program copy works on a packet stored as a byte array in big-endian byte form (matching *network order*).

- A *packet information block* (PIB) structure predetermined packet offset values and protocol flags.

- A revamped *bitfield* construct provides predictable matches with standard protocol fields with bit widths smaller than typical storage units. Note that packetC follows little-endian bit order.

For descriptors, it is important to understand that each executing context has only one packet assigned and a packet information block (PIB) provides layer offsets specific to that packet. While descriptors do not change, where they point to within the array of bytes representing the packet will be based upon the *pib* and other attributes specified in the location of the descriptor.

The host system (CPOS operating systems) manages program copies and ensures that a program copy has two kinds of pre-processed data each time it processes a packet, namely:

- A copy of the packet in the form of an array of unsigned bytes (in big-endian byte order). (*pkt*)

- A collection of values that indicate whether a standard protocol header is present in the packet and, if it is, its offset from the packet array's start. (*pib*)

With this model, developers design a program to process a single packet, instead of designing a set of discrete tasks. However, the particular language constructs used to implement the model greatly influences ease of programming and performance.

The Descriptor Construct

Given your understanding of bit fields and the packet information block, descriptors are easy. The packetC descriptor construct is a structure that corresponds to a portion of the packet array with the same size. Think of it as an alias for an array-slice within the packet.

```
descriptor typeTagName {
    short   source;
    short   dest;
} descripName at offsetExpression;
```

A descriptor declaration consists of its structure base type, the descriptor name, and its location—an integer value that defines its offset from the start of the packet array. The key ingredient is the offset location or *at clause*, which may contain three kinds of elements: compile-time constants, variables with values known only at run time, and PIB offset values.

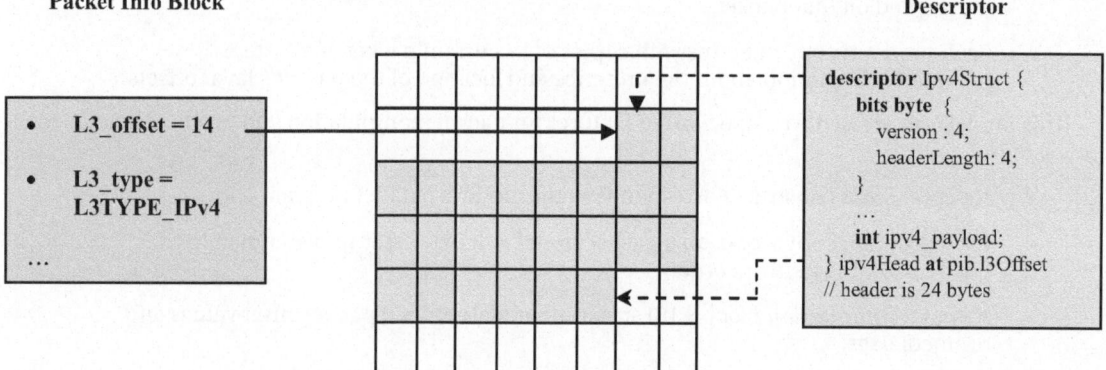

Packet Info Block

Descriptor

Figure 19-3. Positioning descriptors on the basis of header offset values in the PIB..

By combining a descriptor's structure definitions with an offset location based on a PIB offset value, we can create a precise, high-level descriptor of a protocol header that gravitates to the correct location each time a new packet is prepared for a packetC program (see Figure 19-3).

```
descriptor Ipv4Struct {
    bits byte  {
        version : 4;
        headerLength: 4;
        }
    byte        typeOfService;
    short       totalLength;
    short       ipv4_identification;
    short       ipv4_fragmentOffset;
    byte        ipv4_ttl;
    byte        ipv4_protocol;
    short       ipv4_checksum;
    int         ipv4_sourceAddress;
    int         ipv4_destaddress;
    int         ipv4_payload;
} ipv4Header at pib.l3Offset;
```

Consider the IPv4 protocol shown above. First, the descriptor defines a structure that matches the fields of an IPv4 header. The location clause then states that it will always be found at the packet's layer 3 offset (when a valid layer 3 header is present).

In addition, descriptor *at clauses* can be constant or can be arbitrarily complex expressions. The latter is especially relevant when the start of one header depends on the presence of optional fields in a preceding header.

For example, if we did not provide Layer 4 offsets, it would be possible to calculate them in terms of an IPv4 Layer 3 header as follows:

```
descriptor layer4Descr {
    …
} layer4header at pib.L3_offset +
    ( ipv4header.headerLength * 4 );
```

The descriptor construct is also useful for describing stacks of protocols, i.e., groups of interrelated protocol headers that appear in a packet as a group, such as:

- Layer 2: Ethernet

- Layer 3: IP (e.g., IPv4 or IPv6)

- Layer 4: TCP or UDP

The descriptor construct provides a clear way to define protocol headers, find them, and connect them. However, the greatest value of this language feature may be that, combined with PIB information, it makes possible a concise, readable, and maintainable coding style.

When descriptors are combined with PIB enumeration types and layer information, a very readable, maintainable kind of packet-processing application code can be created.

```
// Process Layer 4 scenarios
if ( pib.l4Offset != NULL ) {
    switch ( pib.L4_type ) {
    case L4TYPE_TCP: {…}
    case L4TYPE_UDP: {…}

    …
    }   // end switch
}
```

Although clear, streamlined application coding is a non-trivial achievement, these applications are deployed in embedded environments where performance has great importance.

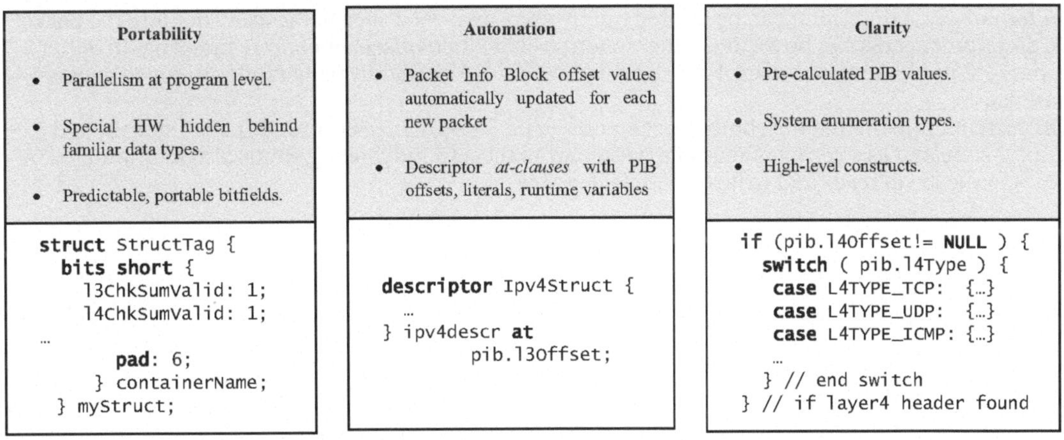

Portability	Automation	Clarity
• Parallelism at program level. • Special HW hidden behind familiar data types. • Predictable, portable bitfields.	• Packet Info Block offset values automatically updated for each new packet • Descriptor *at-clauses* with PIB offsets, literals, runtime variables	• Pre-calculated PIB values. • System enumeration types. • High-level constructs.
```struct StructTag { bits short { l3ChkSumValid: 1; l4ChkSumValid: 1; … pad: 6; } containerName; } myStruct;```	```descriptor Ipv4Struct { … } ipv4descr at pib.l3Offset;```	```if (pib.l4Offset!= NULL) { switch (pib.l4Type) { case L4TYPE_TCP: {…} case L4TYPE_UDP: {…} case L4TYPE_ICMP: {…} … } // end switch } // if layer4 header found```

Figure 19-4. Mapping packetC language features to code samples

In Figure 19-4 examples of packetC language features are highlighted with an emphasis on the relationship to packet processing and specific code examples. Portability, automation and clarity are not novel concepts although their consistent usage provides a means for more self intuitive code. Specifically, descriptors hide the complexities and remove error-prone pointer usage for accessing protocol fields within packets. As layer offsets can deviate from one packet to another and packet headers can have complex construction, descriptors hide and automate both of these computational operations while providing an added benefit of security.

Impacts on Performance

Two kinds of performance impacts characterize the packet protocol approach embodied in CloudShield's model and in the packetC language constructs reviewed above:

- Pre-calculating selected Layer offsets and type data offers an opportunity for application speed-up; this will only be realized if the calculations are done faster than equivalent functionality the application would have provided.

- Knowing the locations of entire headers within the packet affords opportunities for rapidly extracting the entire header or individual fields, depending on how the PIB and packet array are implemented—and on whether the host system's instruction set can be exploited to speed header reading and writing.

Pre-calculating headers' presence and characteristics can be done in three basic ways: by using much the same coding approach a high-level language user might employ, by using a machine-specific instruction level, or by using specialized hardware or firmware.

In CloudShield fielded systems, dedicated FPGAs perform the pre-calculations, provisioning each packet main with a packet array and with PIB contents. Second, the mechanics of reading individual header fields or writing them are heavily influenced by how a descriptor is implemented. For example, a system could implement descriptors as ordinary structures and implement the packet array as a buffer or an ordinary 1-dimensional array. Pieces of the array could then be read into or written from structure locations, accessed in terms of field offsets from the structure's starting address.

Alternatively, a descriptor can be treated purely as an alias for a slice of the array holding the packet. Thus, descriptor access can be treated either in terms of chained offsets or of array indexing. In either case, packetC implementers can exploit the host platform ISA and addressing modes to speed access operations.

In current implementations, both the PIB and the packet array are accorded special storage and a descriptor is treated as a complex alias of a packet array slice. CloudShield systems also manipulate ISA specifics to speed-up reads and writes wherever feasible.

Developing Applications

PART III

Developing Applications

CHAPTER 20

■ ■ ■

Control Plane and System Interaction

Control Plane Interaction

At a conceptual level, packetC capabilities can be categorized as *data plane* capabilities, which involve examining, changing, and routing packets and *control plane* capabilities, which involve displaying system-level values and messages. In some systems, the two planes may be on separate boards or on distant components in a far-flung system. In others, such as a PC-based emulation system, the two sets of capabilities might execute on the same hardware. Thus, packetC specifies control plane capabilities in a general way, while allowing considerable latitude in how they are implemented.

The defined control plane capabilities are:

- Alerts

- Information Logging

- Messages

The packetC language specification defines the above capabilities in terms of language features and constructs but does not proscribe additional control plane capabilities. Such capabilities will typically be implemented by using compiler *pragmas* associated with the *control* pragma category.

Alerts and Information Logging

packetC provides **alert** and **log** commands to facilitate passing messages to the control plane environment and to facilitate logging packet data. The **alert** command simply sends a message while the **log** command sends associated packet data. Each of these commands has an associated message group and identification number associated with the action. The values used are the current values within the *sys* data structure at the time of the command call.

Alert command examples are shown below:

```
sys.messageGroup = MSG_CRITICAL;
sys.messageId = TCP_OPTION_MSG;
alert;
```

```
sys.messageGroup = MSG_CRITICAL;
sys.messageId = MSG_BOX_OVERHEATING;
alert;
```

Log messages are used to send packet data to the control plane. Logging may include a portion of the current packet or the entire packet. Similar to the alert command, a message group and identification is associated with the operation.

Log command examples are shown below:

```
sys.messageGroup = MSG_CRITICAL;
sys.messageId    = 2;
log pkt;                 // log the entire packet

sys.messageGroup = MSG_MAJOR;
sys.messageId    = 21;
log pkt[ 0 : 63 ];    // log first 64 bytes of the packet
```

alert Statement

The packetC statements consist of alphanumeric keywords, rather than new operator symbols or overloaded operator symbols.

The **alert** statement sends a text string message to the Control Plane environment, where it may be displayed or otherwise processed (see the section on the Messages to the Control Plane in this chapter). Two system variables located in the global sys variable control the default behavior of **alert**. **sys.messageId** is an index of the message to use and **sys.messageGroup** is an enumeration value that indicates the message group, both of which depend on the definitions from the *cloudshield.ph* include file shown below in the section on *cloudshield.ph* file in this chapter.

```
enum int t_msgGroup = {
             MSG_CRITICAL = 1,  // initial default
             MSG_MAJOR,
             MSG_MINOR,
             MSG_WARNING,
MSG_INFO };
```

When an **alert** statement appears, default values set in the **sys** variable are used. The user can manipulate those defaults by setting the following values in the **sys** struct (see Chapter 18).

```
sys.messageId = 5;
sys.messageGroup = MSG_INFO;
```

Here are some examples of the **alert** statement being used.

```
const int  TCP_OPTION_MESSAGE = 12;
…

sys.messageGroup = MSG_CRITICAL;
sys.messageId = TCP_OPTION_MESSAGE;
alert;
```

```
sys.messageGroup = MSG_CRITICAL;
sys.messageId = MSG_BOX_OVERHEATING;
alert;
```

log Statement

The **log** statement causes the entire packet or a portion of the packet to be stored in the control plane environment, where it may be later displayed or otherwise processed (see section on Messages to Control Plane in this chapter). Setting two system variables (structure fields located in the global **sys** variable) controls the default behavior of **log:**

- **sys.messageId** is an index of the message to use

- **sys.messageGroup** is an enumeration value that indicates the message group

Refer to detailed information on the $MSG_TYPE later in this chapter and in the *packetC.ph* include file provided with a packetC development environment.

Logging treats the packet as a byte array. When an array range is specified, only the portion of the packet that the range specifies is logged.

```
sys.messageGroup = MSG_CRITICAL;
sys.messageId    = 2;
log pkt;                 // log the entire packet
                         // w/msgId = 2 and MSG_CRITICAL

sys.messageGroup = MSG_MAJOR;
sys.messageId    = 21;
log pkt[ 0 : 63 ];       // log the first 64 bytes of the packet
                         // w/msgId = 21 and MSG_MAJOR
```

Messages to Control Plane ($MSG_TYPE)

In order to support the message capabilities of the **alert** and **log** statements, a packetC implementation shall provide the following definitions at the global scope level of a module, either by pre-definition or via an include file:

```
const int MAX_PACKETC_MSGS = <implementation-supplied number > 1> ;
const int MAX_PACKETC_MSG_LEN = <implementation-supplied number > 1> ;

typedef byte $MSG_TYPE[MAX_PACKETC_MSGS][MAX_PACKETC_MSG_LEN];
```

A packetC module that uses **alert** or **log** statements must include a global scope definition that declares a variable named "messages", and initializes the message strings:

```
const $MSG_TYPE messages = { "string1", "string2", …};
```

Implementations have the option of making the type, $MSG_TYPE, constant or not.

The following code shows a simple example that sends an alert for every packet with the severity level set to remainder of taking the length of the packet and dividing it by 5.

```
packet module alertTest;

/* Globals */
int packetLength_;
%pragma control packetLength_ (export);

int lengthModulo5_;
%pragma control lengthModulo5_ (export);

$MSG_TYPE messages = {
"Test Message Critical",
"Test Message Major",
"Test Message Minor",
"Test Message Warning",
"Test Message Informational"
};

void main( $PACKET pkt, $PIB pib, $SYS sys )
{
        int pktLength;
        pktLength = pib.length;
        packetLength_ = pktLength;
        /* Get modulo 5 and set message severity accordingly */
        int lenRemainder;
        lenRemainder = pktLength % 5;
        lengthModulo5_ = lenRemainder;

        switch (lenRemainder) {
            case 0:
                sys.messageGroup = MSG_CRITICAL;
                sys.messageId = 0;
                alert;
                break;

            case 1:

                sys.messageGroup = MSG_MAJOR;
                sys.messageId = 1;
                alert;
                break;

            case 2:
                sys.messageGroup = MSG_MINOR;
                sys.messageId = 2;
                alert;
                break;
```

```
        case 3:
            sys.messageGroup = MSG_WARNING;
            sys.messageId = 3;
            alert;
            break;

        case 4:
            sys.messageGroup = MSG_INFO;
            sys.messageId = 4;
            alert;
            break;

        default:
    }
}
```

Figure 20-1 below shows a syslog client capturing the messages out of the control plane as a result of the code shown above. The section along the far right showing *5:Test Message Informational* in the first line is a result of the severity code being set by *sys.messageGroup = MSG_INFO;*

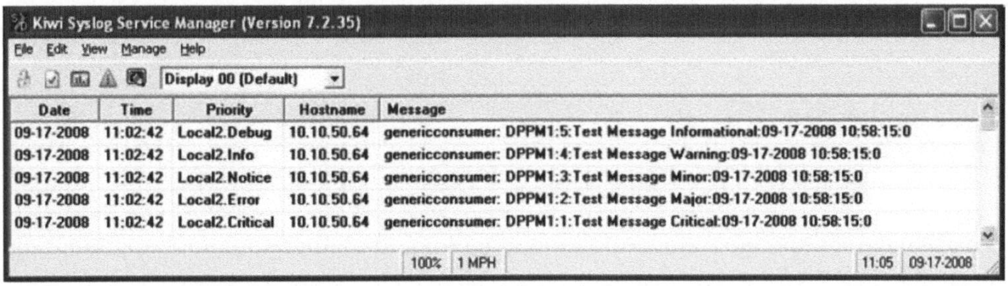

Figure 20-1. Screenshot of syslog server displaying messages from packetC

Messages Portion of cloudshield.ph

In packetC, the following declarations and types are provided for use with messages. The definitions are preloaded through the inclusion of include file **cloudshield.ph** at the start of each application.

```
//==============================================================================
//  Message Group Levels
//
//  The MessageGroup enumerated type is used to set a severity level for a log()
//  message.  This field can be set once in a context and all future events that
//  are generated during the processing of the packet will utilize this value.
//  The $SYS structure utilized MessageGroup with field messageGroup.
//
//==============================================================================
```

```
enum int MessageGroup
{
  MSG_CRITICAL = 1,
  MSG_MAJOR    = 2,
  MSG_MINOR    = 3,
  MSG_WARNING  = 4,
  MSG_INFO     = 5
};


//==============================================================================
//  Message Constants
//
//  The following constants provide a maximum message number and length for a
//  log() message generated by the packetC system.  Use in conjunction with the
//  messageId field in $SYS.
//
//==============================================================================
const int MAX_PACKETC_MSGS    = 255;
const int MAX_PACKETC_MSG_LEN = 80;
```

CHAPTER 21

■ ■ ■

packetC Pre-Processor

As you develop a large program, and often even in a small program, you'll want to leverage more than just the current packet module source code file. As you desire to include text from other sources, such as packet descriptors pre-crafted and provided with your development environment, or a set of function prototypes for a library of interest, you are leaving packetC and delving into the pre-processor. As packetC is very similar to C, the use of the C pre-processor was possible without much change. The following section describes the available pre-processor features and some suggestions on effective usage in packetC applications.

It is important to remember that pre-processor directives are not part of your packetC code but are rather instructions to the compiler to perform operations on your source code prior to compilation. Pre-processor directives will be evaluated and the resulting output will be placed into the source code or actions will be performed prior to passing the source to the compiler. To the packetC compiler, the results of the pre-processor or of typing in the equivalent output directly within your code are indistinguishable. As a modern language, however, the notion of a pre-processor is now essential to a language and as such the existence of the pre-processor is considered essential to packetC and was integrated into the compiler tool-chain.

The standard GNU C pre-processor running in traditional mode was leveraged unchanged as the packetC pre-processor. This chapter focuses on serving as a quick reference and call-out of key elements of the pre-processor of note specifically for packetC. The packetC compiler invokes the pre-processor as the first stage of processing source code which is important to understanding how this can affect the processing.

In packetC, the following high-level aspects of the pre-processor are important:

- A preprocessing command begins with the "#" character as the first character on a line.

- Whitespace may follow the "#" and precede preprocessing keywords on a line (e.g., "# define").

- Whitespace must follow keywords from their trailing macro name (e.g., "#define X" not "#defineX").

- Include statements may be nested 8 deep; 7 beyond the original source packet module.

- A macro definition may span multiple lines using a backslash ("\") as the continuation character.

- Only C-style comments are supported by the pre-processor ("/* comment */") for use in macros.

- C++-style comments ("// comment") are implemented in the compiler and MUST NOT be used in macros.

- Comments may follow a replacement string in a macro definition (e.g., "#define NIBBLE 0x0F /* 15 */").

- Redefining a macro is treated as a fatal error, use #undef if this is required.

Table 21-1 provides a quick reference showing the supported packetC pre-processor directives along with a basic description. Each of these are described with examples in the following sections.

Table 21-1. packetC Pre-Processor Directives

Directive	Description
#define	Defines a macro
#include	Includes the contents of another file at this location
#ifdef	Inclusion of code or text conditional on a macro being defined
#ifndef	Inclusion of code or text conditional on a macro not being defined
#endif	Identifies the end of a conditional block's inclusion
#if	Inclusion of code or text conditional on an expression being non-zero
#else	Inclusion of code or text based upon a previous #ifdef, #ifndef, or #if not being true
#elif	Combination of an #else and an #if such that expression must be non-zero for inclusion
#undef	Undefines a macro previously defined by a #define
#error	Outputs an error message
#line	Change Line Number. Implemented in pre-processor, however, packetC result undefined
#file	Change File Name. Implemented in pre-processor, however, packetC result undefined
defined	Operator: Used with #if directives to test for presence of a macro by name

In addition to the above directives, some macros (Table 21-2) are predefined by the pre-processor and cannot be changed.

Table 21-2. packetC Built-in Pre-Processor Macros

Macro	Description
__LINE__	An integer constant representing the current line number.
__FILE__	A string representing the current name of the file.
__DATE__	A string representing the date when compilation began for the file ("mm dd yyyy").
__TIME__	A string representing the time when compilation began for the file ("hh:mm:ss").

The pre-defined macros above are useful for assigning to variables and use by other macros to ensure versioning and verifying compatibility between modules.

Table 21-3. packetC Pre-Defined Language Macro

Macro	Description
__PACKETC__	A macro identifying that the compiler is packetC, as opposed to Standard C.

Also note that in "cloudshield.ph" the __PACKETC__ macro is defined which should be available to all compiled code to identify when compiling under packetC versus standard C where the __STDC__ pre-defined macro or __STDC_VERSION__ pre-defined macro would generally be seen.

#define

The #define directive is used to create values or macros that are used by the pre-processor to manipulate the program source code before compilation. Some examples of #define being used for values and macros are found below:

```
/* Replaces the name MAX_ROWS throughout code with 40000  */
#define MAX_ROWS 40000

/* Returns x*x while also protecting from order of evaluation issues.   */
#define SQUARE(x) ((x) * (x))
```

Common style conventions for values and macros are UPPERCASE with underscores between words. When functions are being inlined, it is recommended that you prepend "INLINE_" to make them stand out as to why you are doing it. It is important to ensure that defined names for values or macros use a style that will not intersect with common uses of the same name as the preprocessor is indiscriminant in what it replaces in source code. For example the following would be a problematic use of #define:

```
#define i 40  /* Problematic: Potentially replaces loop counters throughout code. */
```

While #define can be used to replace names with values that often function appropriately in code, assuring execution of code as expected and to aid in strict type checking, it is recommended to leverage *const type name = value;* instead of *#define name value.* For example, while *#define XYZZY 49000* generally is evaluated the same as *const int XYZZY = 49000;* the assignment *abc = XYZZY;* does not provide the same type checking protections, especially when *abc* is not an *int*. In the case of #define, the value 49000 is seen as a literal by the compiler as opposed to a typed constant.

While packetC provides multiple tools that enable optimized code such as enabling inline code and descriptors in addition to classic C99 optimizations through the use of enumerations and typedefs, there are still many areas where macros provide the extra leverage in optimization at compile time not afforded in using other aspects of packetC. For those cases, the macro capabilities within the pre-processor offer some effective means of moving conditional evaluation out of run time and into compile time. In addition, functionality that would otherwise require a function call and potentially a stack within packetC can be done with an inline macro.

An example of an inline macro instead of a function call:

```
#define SWAP(x, y) {                \
                        x ^= y;      \
                        y ^= x;      \
                        x ^=y;       \
                }
int i, j;
i = 50; j=0xff0c21aa;
SWAP(i,j);          /* Now i = 0xff0c21aa and j = 50 after the evaluation of SWAP(i,j); */
```

The above macro could have been the function *void swap(int x, int y)*, however, the resulting code from the macro would be more efficient. The danger is that type checking is not enforced and depending on *i* and *j* the result might not always be as expected. The following example implements a macro and a function for performing a simple task to compare and contrast some implementation details:

```
// Developed by dWiGhT? (with thanks to Douglas Adams)
#define INLINE_GETMEANINGOFLIFE(PASSEDVAL) 42
int getMeaningOfLife( int passedVal ) {
return 42;
}
...
int retVal;
retVal = getMeaningOfLife(69);          // Call the function
retVal = INLINE_GETMEANINGOFLIFE(69); // Function macro, expanded in-place
...
```

Both of the functions calls shown above do the same thing: return the meaning of life. (Yeah I was shocked too that it was an Integer!!!) One thing to consider as a rationale for macros is performance. In initial tests, the packetC compiler produced six times as many opcodes to execute the function call as it produced for the macro. Obviously this is a simplified example, but it shows the savings that can occur just by writing your function as a function macro. As your function becomes larger, the calling overhead becomes more insignificant, so evaluate which functions would benefit most by doing this on a case-by-case basis. Keep in mind that function macros do have several risks and limitations so it is important to consider if they are really the best approach. The lack of strong type checking and compiler involvement can produce some undesired side effects which can be difficult to identify and debug.

For more information on gotchas with macro functions:

www.cprogramming.com/tutorial/cpreprocessor.html

For some tips and tricks on writing function macros, see:

www.ebyte.it/library/codesnippets/WritingCppMacros.html#8

#include

The #include directive is used by the pre-processor to include user and system header files. There are three variants to the #include directive's syntax.

```
/* System include file, search in system directories. */
#include <protocols.ph>;

/* User include file, search current directory then system directories. */
#include "myLibrary.ph";

/* Where expression is a macro that must convert to above forms. */
#include expression
```

#ifdef

The #ifdef directive allows for a conditional evaluation and subsequent inclusion of the contents following the directive until an #endif directive is found based upon the presence of a pre-processor #define. The value following the #ifdef should be a name that optionally would have been defined within a pre-processor directive earlier within the source code. If the name is defined, the evaluation is true and will proceed.

```
#define SMALL_MEMORY
#ifdef SMALL_MEMORY
        int metaData_[40000];
        const int maxMetaData_ = 39999;
#endif
```

In the example above, a global array is being defined based upon the memory model definition. Just because packetC does not support dynamic memory allocation for security and performance reasons, it doesn't mean that it isn't beneficial. Using #ifdef can be very useful in having a single code base that can be conditionally compiled for different versions, generating multiple memory footprints of an application, enabling administrators to select the footprint of the application desired at provisioning or re-provisioning time.

#ifndef

The #ifndef directive allows for a conditional evaluation and subsequent inclusion of the contents following the directive until an #endif directive is found based upon the absence of a pre-processor #define. The value following the #ifndef should be a name that optionally would have been defined within a pre-processor directive earlier within the source code. If the name is not defined, the evaluation is true and will proceed.

One of the most common uses of #ifndef is within each included file as a guard macro. A problem that often exists in large programs is having multiple source code files, often libraries or re-used code, that includes other common header files or even common code snippets. To ensure that each subsequently included file is only included once, a guard macro is used to have the preprocessor remove the subsequent copies of the source code from the output provided to the compiler. The following is an example of a guard macro for the file LIBFOO:

```
#ifndef FILE_LIBFOO_INCLUDED        /* Placed At Start Of File libfoo.ph          */
#define FILE_LIBFOO_INCLUDED        /* Defines Name Such That Future Includes Will Ignore */
        /* Place Entire File Here */
#endif                              /* Last Line Of File Closing Out the #ifndef          */
```

The use of guard macros is one of the most important suggested uses of preprocessor directives.

#endif

The preprocessor allows for a variety of means for conditionals to determine code inclusion and execution of macros. The #endif directive flags the preprocessor specifying the end of a conditional block of preprocessor instructions. Each preprocessor conditional should have an #endif directive identifying the end of the conditional.

```
#ifdef DO_SOMETHING
        #define DID_SOMETHING
        #define XYZZY 42
#endif
```

#if

The #if directive checks whether an expression evaluates to zero or nonzero. The pre-processor supports conditional expressions containing any basic operator (math and comparisons) except for assignment, increment, and decrement operators. In addition, the #if directive supports a *defined* operator that tests for the presence of a pre-processor macro definition and returns nonzero (e.g., 1) if defined, or zero if not (see later in this section for examples of the *defined* operator). A simple example of #if directive is shown below:

```
#define INTERFACE  SONET
#if INTERFACE==SONET
    const int L2_LEN = 6;
#elif INTERFACE==ETHERNET
    const int L2_LEN = 14;
#endif
```

#else

Working in conjunction with the #ifdef, #ifndef, and #if directives, the #else directive provides a means to define functionality for the condition not evaluating to nonzero in the #if directive. A simple example is shown below:

```
#ifdef LARGE_MEMORY                              /* LARGE MEMORY */
        int metaData_[250,000];
        const int maxMetaData_ = 249999;
```

```
#else                                                   /* SMALL MEMORY */
        int metaData_[10,000];
        const int maxMetaData_ = 9999;
#endif
```

#elif

While the #else directive will always be true if the controlling #if directive failed, the #elif directive provides a means to try an alternative if condition such that more complicated comparisons can be done with the macros. A simple example is shown below:

```
#define INTERFACE   SONET
#if INTERFACE==SONET
    const int L2_LEN = 6;
#elif INTERFACE==ETHERNET
    const int L2_LEN = 14;
#else
    #error Unknown L2 Interface!
#endif
```

#undef

The #undef directive undefines a macro. The identifier need not have been previously defined.

```
#define XYZZY 10
#define PLUGH (XYZZY+10)
#undef XYZZY
```

#error

Upon processing of a #error directive, the pre-processor halts the processing of the packetC program and returns the error message specified in the pre-processor directive. No further pre-processing or compilation will continue after the first #error is processed. These are often used for debugging and assuring critical external dependencies within the code.

```
#ifndef PACKETC_VERSION
        #error packetC Version Number Must Be Specified.
#endif
```

#line

The #line directive changes the line number that the pre-processor has computed for the file to the one specified. This is problematic for packetC and may produce undefined results when debugging files, however, the functionality follows C. Note that the value of __LINE__ would change subsequent to this redefinition.

#file

The #file directive changes the file name that the pre-processor has computed for the file to the one specified. This is problematic for packetC and may produce undefined results when debugging files, however, the functionality follows C. Note that the value of __FILE__ would change subsequent to this redefinition.

defined

The *defined* operator can be used within #if directives that need to test for more than one macro or are a part of a more complex evaluation where #ifdef would not suffice. The is a simple example leveraging the *defined* operator:

```
#if (defined(SONET) && defined(HDLC))
        /* Do SONET HDLC Processing   */
#elif (defined(SONET) && defined(PPP))
        /* Do SONET PPP Processing    */
#else
        #error "Unknown SONET Layer 2 Type Selected"
#endif
```

Comments in Code

As stated earlier in this chapter, the packetC pre-processor only support C-style comments. The packetC compiler, however, only supports C++-style comments. As a result, these two components of the packetC tool-chain combine to provide the developer with both C- and C++-style comments.

It is important to understand some of the constraints that this paradigm introduces to the application developer. Since both C- and C++-style comments are supported, the issue of nesting of the two comment styles is possible and poses some interesting possible side-effects as a result of their being processed by different components in the tool-chain.

The following list identifies some considerations to take into account when placing comments in packetC source code:

- Only C-style comments are supported by the pre-processor ("/* comment */").

- Do not use C++-style comments in pre-processor macros as this may result in unintended results.

- C++-style comments ("// comment") are implemented in the compiler and will not be processed until C comment blocks have been removed and macros have been pre-processed.

- C-style comments may follow a replacement string in a macro definition (e.g., "#define NIBBLE 0x0F /* 15 */").

- Comment styles should not be nested with the exception of commenting out large sections of code where C-style comments are used as the outer block at the start and end of the section.

- C++-style comments must only be used to start a line or following code.

For information on best practices and style usage suggestions around appropriate use of C- or C++-style comments and comment blocks, refer to the chapter on style guidelines for packetC. The following section provides some simple examples of packetC comments.

Classic C-Style Comment

```
/* This is my comment. */
```

Multi-Line Comments C Style

```
/* ================================
   ][  C Comment Block Header    ][
   ================================ */
```

Classic C++-Style Comment

```
// This is my comment.
```

Multi-Line Comments C++ Style

```
//  ================================
//  ][  C++ Comment Block Header  ][
//  ================================
```

Valid Nesting of Comment Blocks

```
/* Commenting Out All This Code ===
//
// function header here
int initializeContext ( int context; )
{
  contextInitialized_[context] = true;       // Keep comments aligned
  return true;                               // and do not over-comment.
};
==== End of Commenting Code */
```

Miscellaneous Comments Examples

```
"packet//data"        // A 12 character string.  Compiler processed valid // as data.
// */                 // Possible C comment block close in pre-processor. Result depends.
#include "//dir";      // An error.  Invalid file or directory representation.
offset = len/**//2;    // Embedded comment in valid offset=len/2;
//\
 doFunc();             // Two line comment, no code executed.
/\
/ int x;               // Two line comment, no variable defined.
```

```
/*//*/ doFunc();            // Comments result in doFunc(); only.
x = y //**/j
    + z;                    // Same as x = y / j + z; and not x = y + z;
```

Typical packetC Comment Header

```
//=============================================================================
//   one line description of function's role
//
//   multi-line description of function and general description
//   of what parameters are passed and what the function returns
//
// example usage
//      example-return = function ( example-parameter );
//
// parameters
//      parameter - description of what it does (repeated)
//
// returns
//      value - what it can return
//
//=============================================================================
```

Pragmas and Other Key Compiler Directives

Pragmas

Pragma clauses are compiler directives, which have the general form shown below:

% **pragma** pragma_category identifier$_{OPT}$ pragma_argument_clause$_{OPT}$;

    Pragma categories may be either language-defined or implementation defined. An identifier following the category indicator is typically an identifier from the packetC program, such as a variable or a user-defined type name. Legal arguments for a given category may be either language or implementation defined. The language-defined categories are:

- control category pragmas govern the relationships with the control plane

- data types category provides compiler directives on storing and representing data

    A pragma may appear in a packetC module at any location that a packetC declaration or statement could legally appear. *Best practices* for pragmas encourage locating or including them near the top of a module or placing them textually adjacent to the declarations that they affect. A packetC compiler will issue a warning if it encounters an unrecognized pragma. Legal pragma syntax is indicated below:

```
pragma_category:
        control        // language-defined category
        datatype       // language-defined category
        identifier

pragma_argument_clause:
        (  pragma_arg_list  )
pragma_arg_list:
        pragma_arg
        pragma_arg_list , pragma_arg
pragma_arg:
        expression     // implementation-defined argument
```

where *identifier* designates an implementation-defined pragma category, and where *expression* designates an implementation-defined pragma argument.

Implementation-Defined Pragmas

This section describes implementation-defined pragma categories and arguments for the CloudShield Technologies, Inc., implementation of packetC.

CloudShield currently implements one pragma argument for the *control* category, governing the relationship of global variables with the control plane:

- The export argument indicates that the associated identifier's values can be exported to the control plane for examination. Depending on the host system, an exported variable's values might be copied to another computer, an external device, a file, and so forth.

```
// Example
% pragma control  myVarA  (export);
```

CloudShield implements one pragma argument for the *data type* category:

- The regex1 argument indicates that the associated searchset contains strings that are to be interpreted as regular expressions that use regex1 conventions as defined by CloudShield. The regex1 currently maps to POSIX Regular Expression with non-greedy expressions. Future implementations may include other arguments such as regex2, which could map to PCRE Regular Expressions.

```
% pragma datatype  mySearchSet  (regex1);
```

Examples of uses of pragmas in action follow:

```
// Simple Variable Export Declaration
int inPort_;
%pragma control inPort_ (export);
int outport_;
%pragma control outPort_ (export);

// Combined Variable Export Declaration
int ramFailure_      =0,
    bitError_        =0,
    regexFailure_    =0,
    camFailure_      =0,
    receiveCount_    =0,
    transmitCount_   =0;
%pragma control ramFailure_ (export);
%pragma control bitError_ (export);
%pragma control regexFailure_ (export);
%pragma control camFailure_ (export);
%pragma control receiveCount_ (export);
%pragma control transmitCount_ (export);
```

```
// Regular Expression Compiler Directive for SearchSet
regex searchset regexSet[1][20] = { ".*?TESTVALU" };
%pragma datatype  regexSet ( regex1 );
```

Pragmas are directives providing methods for delivering additional information to a compiler and are very specific to the compiler implementation. Historically, C pragmas have included a mix of pragmas processed by the C pre-processor and others by the compiler themselves. These have utilized multiple identifiers such as #pragma and _Pragma to signal the compiler. Within packetC, a non-intersecting definition of %pragma was chosen so as to not unintentionally pull from C compiler pragmas in included source files.

Interaction of packetC Pre-Processor with Regular Expressions

The pragma associated with a searchset defines which regular expression language to utilize. The regular expression language is specific to the compiler implementation. One key thing to note is that packetC's pre-processor will make modifications to source code and initialized data prior to compilation that may interact with the contents of a regular expression. The primary element that causes interaction is the backslash "\" character. Both the packetC pre-processor and POSIX regular expression grammar utilize the backslash for special features. A packetC compile-time instantiation of a regular expression may require double backslashes to ensure that they are passed appropriately as a single backslash to the regular expression compiler.

Values updated at run time by control plane API's won't necessarily be affected by the pre-processors in the same.

```
regex searchset mySet[2][20] = {".*?cloudshield\\.com", ".*?saic\\.com"};
// Double backslash required to yield \. for POSIX

% pragma datatype  mySet  (regex1);
// regex1 represents POSIX non-greedy
```

The regex1 argument specified in the pragma indicates that the associated searchset contains strings that are to be interpreted as regular expressions that use regex1 conventions as defined by the compiler developer. CloudShield compilers map the regex1 argument to POSIX Regular Expression with non-greedy expressions. Future implementations may include other arguments such as regex2, which could map to PCRE Regular Expressions.

Refer to the *CloudShield Regular Expressions Guide* within the CloudShield PacketWorks IDE manuals for more information on their specific implementation.

CHAPTER 23

Developing Large Applications in packetC

Planning for Large Projects in packetC

Developing large applications in packetC is quite similar to that of developing large applications in languages such as C++ from code organization and development team collaboration points of view. There are several grammar changes that impact standards that one would follow as well as new areas of concern regarding performance, security, and networking aspects not often present in other application domains. What becomes the single most important planning aspect of developing large applications in packetC is the planning itself.

In packetC, the notion of a packet module containing a function main with static linking of library modules and dynamic linking of shared library modules follows similar patterns you are familiar with in Linux and Windows application development. Organizing functionality into libraries and designing appropriate APIs for libraries should follow similar best practices team and programming approaches. In addition, however, naming conventions conforming to your adopted style guide should be followed including the file names and directories as well as functions. Within packetC, additional areas of documentation and communication need to be addressed when using and designing libraries, namely regarding inlined function passing and impacts on the packet. Within packetC performance is a critical design factor and the use of functions with inlined parameters and code is extremely beneficial for performance, however, it can be problematic if libraries are not designed expecting this usage or API documents do not properly describe their impact on the parameters or the system. With regard to the system, library modules may have access to the packet (pkt), the packet information block (pib), or system information (sys) that can affect the outcome of subsequent processing or even the network results upon completion of the packetC application for the current packet. As such, having clear coordination on these impacts is critical. As one would coordinate access to global memory regions that were allocated and shared in C or C++, protecting the integrity of global resources like pkt, pib, and sys as well as ensuring clear coordination on issues affecting performance, security, or the networking aspects of the processing are key to packetC development team success.

Furthermore, as applications grow to the size where they result in multiple applications or have code that remains resident while portions are reprovisioned through the use of shared libraries, it becomes even more important to design for the issues that occur within a network environment that may not occur elsewhere. For example, with shared libraries and reprovisioned applications that dynamically link to them, the notion of data initialization is key. For instance, a library maintaining a list of active flows may already exist and be supporting more than the current application at the startup of the newly-provisioned application. Shared libraries must consider the requirement for functions that return a set of status indicators such that a newly-provisioned application can ascertain the state of the shared library based upon the arrival of prior packets. A program that expects that all data is reinitialized when it starts will run into problems when leveraging shared libraries. Libraries may change over time and packetC developers should take into consideration versioning of libraries just as in Linux with shared objects or Windows with DLLs. The notion of versioning of libraries is critical as underlying implementation may change the results expected by the calling application. Version numbering should be in the name of libraries as well as within the source code by using pre-processor controls around prototype files to ensure run-time and linker controls pick up the change and can warn developers of possible issues. The worst thing that can happen is to have a shared library updated and nothing has changed to make incompatibilities visible to loaders or the leveraging packetC application's logic.

Last, when developing large programs, the notion of resources will become a factor. Resources in the simplest form can be referred to as available memory and processor budget, although it does become more complex over time when the concept of threads and number of applications becomes involved. Resource management is important in two dimensions, first within your application and then bounding your application to live with others. Living within the resources provided on your target platform for the problem set shared amongst the components of your application can itself be a tough chore. As most packetC code drives usage of processor budget based upon the traffic mix being seen (e.g., network signaling and login packets often need more processing than media or data packets), knowing the deployment environments is often as critical as knowing what amount of processing is consumed by the application for a given packet. Additionally, different target systems will vary in performance and resources available as well as whether you are leveraging multiple processors or blades to execute your application. When designing for a performance target, knowing the amount of processing resources available may be significant as it may involve designing functionality to synchronize state among blades. On the other end of the spectrum, requirements of an application may include capping resource usage such that the application can be loaded alongside other applications in a single processor while maintaining certain performance metrics. In this case, modeling of your application is important not only among your team, but for administrators and users of your finished application to assure it meets expectations in a shared environment. Imagine ensuring response time and processor utilization goals of a complex video processing application in Windows if you don't have control over what else is running; the same scenario can occur with packetC deployment environments.

The concepts suggested above are not foreign to traditional application development teams, although they do take on several new nuances within a real-time packet processing environment when dynamic change is constantly in play. When moving on from building small applications performing a functional role in the network to engaging in a large application, either alone or in a team, consider stepping up into a new of way of designing the application from the outset.

Things to Consider in Large Application Development

The previous section discussed some of the issues of large application environment when designing and developing your application. This section is intended to provide some tips and guidelines to consider when you are building your application that are beneficial to even the smallest application.

Follow a Common Style

Developers often believe that they will be the only ones reading their code and that they will always remember why they wrote it and what they did. With the Internet, we see code snippets appearing everywhere from a comment on a blog to posting an application as a new open source project. As time goes by, the reasons why a function was written or what the genesis was of an application often becomes muddled to even the original developer. As small outcroppings of functions turn into library modules, these functions find a new life of their own being electronically read for inclusion into programs far from the review of developers. As such, the notion of following a consistent style in developing code becomes important from day one. Consistent use of naming conventions for variables helps discern their data type and the naming of functions in a library to start with a common name such that multiple libraries don't collide are small examples of important style attributes in a large program. Chapter 3 in this book provides a suggested style guide for packetC programs.

Plan Out Modularity in Your Programs

Whether you choose to develop static or shared libraries, or simply segregate related functionality into include files, developing an architecture for the organization of code beyond a single huge application source file is critical. Study what modules are available from the community, what is provided with software development kits, and what components of your application might be re-usable in other applications you build or that others would need, and segregate them early in the project. Often, early construction of a series of libraries within an application is avoided because it is determined that the solution won't grow large enough to require them. All too often, details appear during development and functionality grows, introducing a new element of work, namely carving up code and renaming functions as they are removed from a packet module and placed into other libraries. Plan early for allowing functionality to be spread across libraries and it will save the re-work as complexity grows and ensure that functionality is positioned for reuse in the future.

Set Up the Production Environment Early

All too often, a project seems to be a one-time development project and the team that starts it expects to be the one that finishes it. Due to numerous circumstances good and bad, this often doesn't define the life of most large applications. Furthermore, we fail to allow for the unexpected, such as an operating system crash on your development system, so we don't plan for how much time it will take to develop an application. Getting into the habit of leveraging version control systems on a machine separate from those where code is being developed ensures that not only are backups performed regularly, but that the project is trouble-free for development by more than one individual and easily re-created on a new system, just as is true of any large programming project using any programming language.

Three key aspects come into play when developing in a team and building an environment for a large project. These are centralized team code, shared design and build information, and code version compatibility.

The first step is to ensure that there is a stable repository where code is checked in and a build environment that can be re-created separate from the client systems where you are developing your portion of the code. This helps ensure that code is written that can be rebuilt, which may be as simple as ensuring that all the files are really on the network and not hidden in an include file in a directory that was not checked in. Moreover, addressing build-production releases without version control and snapshots built early in a project, can become cumbersome and time-consuming at the point in a project where time is most precious.

Once you have code in a common area, it is important to share any build-related files such that parameter-setting in a graphical development environment or project and "make files" are documented and placed with the source code such that all team members are building the project in a consistent fashion. Additionally, design documentation should also be shared, version-controlled, and updated in the common repositories.

Last, functionality will change in a large application and APIs often drift from their original design specifications no matter how diligent team members try to keep design docs in sync. As such, engaging in a method of ensuring compatibility of libraries and functions is critical. Often this can be accomplished through the use of pre-processor directives to identify the version of functions and the expectations of a function call. Much like pre-processor directives are used to guard against include files being included more than once, pre-processor directives can be used to detect incompatibilities at compile time. For example, if the main application includes libPacketFlow and the API was reviewed at version 2.2 by the including application developer, simple protections like a #define libPacketFlow_VER_2_2 in the including application and an #ifdef libPacketFlow_VER_2_2 in the provided include files can protect compatibility should the developer of libPacketFlow simply increment the #ifdef every time they changed the designed functional roles or function prototypes. The key notion is to build in electronic mechanisms of ensuring coordination over casual tracking of emails and verbal comments when designs change.

Leverage Include Files Well

If it isn't obvious yet, designing large applications without breaking them into smaller chunks that can be easily managed is a disaster waiting to happen. Using include files and breaking up functionality is key to success, but can also be the best way to make code impossible to understand. Include files are great because a single line in the packet module can drive the inclusion of a large mass of functionality while making the application's logic understandable. At the same time, without proper naming conventions or by burying layers of includes within included files will make tracking down bugs, finding the source of a broken function, or even tracing the flow of an application impossible. Include file naming needs to be representative of what is included and the use of nested includes should be avoided whenever possible. If a developer performing a code audit, or even yourself a year from now, cannot understand where to go to look for a function called in *main* by simply looking at the set of #includes at the top of the packet module, something is wrong. Furthermore, if it is not visible in that include file or doesn't have specific information such that a search of the include file would find the reference, tracking it down in the future will be next to impossible. Plan the use and avoid the inappropriate use of include files well.

Be Careful, Be Clear, and Be Code

In packetC, performance is a critical aspect of any program. As such, there is a great tendency to avoid any run-time performance impacts for things that could be done ahead of time. Simple examples include variable initialization where *const* is pre-pended to a variable declaration to ensure it is initialized at compile and load time as opposed to run time, such as the entrance to a function. In addition, the inline operator is applied to parameters in a function call such that a function can be in-lined rather than a call stack be generated. In other areas, global variables are used to track data sets and set flags for the communication with a separate control-plane processor provided non-real-time assistance in the concurrent and post-processing of data collected by the system. When considering whether to compute a large algorithm or just pass the parameters so that the algorithm's result is displayed on an operator's console, passing off processing may be a good idea. When this starts to get into the choices of crafting large sets of code substitution by cleverly written pre-processor macros and a litany of #defines that the best of coders would never understand on a good day, something has gone haywire. As a developer of an application, it is critical that code be carefully conceived, clear on what is being done or not done within the real-time packetC code, and most of all truly be code. The magical benefits of the pre-processor can also be the bane of your existence when trying to repair code in the future or debug complex interactions that mysteriously change from one compiled release to the next. Fear the macro, trust in code, and when looking for optimizations, think of what you can avoid doing in real time and not how to be clever and outsmart the system—or you will in the end cost the team precious time.

It's All About Data-Driven Code—Follow the Flow

In traditional programming environments, the application is generally in charge of its world. The application starts up, initializes all data, opens user or electronic interfaces to begin accepting work, and controls how it gets it done. Generally a request is analyzed in detail to learn what is asked and then processing starts on the best way to accomplish the goal. Unless the applications you have written in traditional computing environments have been interrupt service routines (ISR), then the world of packetC may seem bit different. Processor budgets in real-time systems don't allow one to learn all there is to know about a packet upon arrival before beginning work and, furthermore, a packet is rarely a transaction or the entire request being awaited. In addition, a network like the Internet is a fluid beast where processing never stops to wait for your application to be inserted into the network before requests start over and begin to flow. As such, the state machine that is the logic of your application and the conditions placed upon it as a program begins must not only start beneficial processing but also get a sense of the current state of the network and is key to the success of the application. If a packetC application, especially a large one, isn't modeled effectively from a flow-oriented point of view with a review of the state transitions not only within the code but the out-of-order presentation of data coming to the application via packets, corner cases will abound. Debugging the last defect will be rough. It is important in this environment to model the flow of an application and track the key use cases and test cases for how they would flow and affect the creation and state of metadata that is used to transform the knowledge from packets into flows, transactions, and eventually an application scenario of interest. This may feel like CS100 class concepts that have been long abandoned for other methods of object modeling in applications. However, in the world of flow-oriented code, where data drives the results and code simply tries to glean from the data what to do, the flow is all you have. Organize it into a common theme you can analyze as a team.

Programs Large and Small—Plan Appropriately

In traditional CPU-based programming, programs will often become large and complex. As all of the capabilities for writing large programs exist in packetC, the tendency can be to presume that packetC applications will grow to be equally large. Throughout this book, performance is often discussed and the separation of control plane and data plane and their processing roles is presented. At all times, it is important to remember that real-time data plane processing should be focused on only processing what is really required in the data plane. If you can calculate information up front, do so. If you can grab some data that is passed along to a control-plane processor, let it perform parsing and massaging of the data. If at all possible, keep applications small and to the point. The following is a simple yet effective application that maintains a view into the total number of active flows being processed by the system. The counters that are collected are exported to the control plane using pragmas and tables are simple and succinct and only track the relevant information. Consider this example as a view into a real-world program that can rapidly be extended to more complexity, yet at the same time represents something simple and elegant comprising a complete application.

    What becomes important and is often overlooked until too late in the project is the dynamic role of control-plane and management applications and their near real-time involvement with the packetC application. While simple tasks like crafting a data file for an access control list from a graphical user interface or a simple graphing and reporting of events and activity may have already been conceptualized from reading, interactive solutions can have great benefit. Consider a user-based billing and control system that is focused on providing customers with traffic management features based on time, such as priority of gaming traffic in the evenings or when business traffic volume is low. Instead of having the packetC application evaluate the business traffic volume and apply per-user performance boosts, why not use packetC to simply provide traffic metadata to a near real-time system that can make its analysis and then provide dynamic updates to packetC database tables. In this manner, the packetC application can focus on real-time tasks such as collecting metadata or providing additive services on a per-session basis, while the adjacent management system provides continuous trend analysis and updates, potentially even in 15 second intervals or less. This simple concept of balancing the throughput-oriented requirements and computational requirements between respective packetC and more traditional computing environments often has two major benefits. The first is dramatically simpler packetC code yielding easier debugging and performance benefits, and the second is often a much more linearly scalable modular architecture.

```
///////////////////////////////////////////////////////////////////////////////
//
//     Program: TCP Flow Tracking Example
//
//     Revision: 1.0 - January 20, 2009
//
//     Author: Tim King
//
//     Description: This program maintains counters on the number of
//                  Active & Total number of TCP Flows.
//
//                        Duplicate SYN's are recorded but not mitigated against.
//
///////////////////////////////////////////////////////////////////////////////

packet  module  tcpFlows;

#include <cloudshield.ph>
#include "protocols.ph"


//
// Constants
//
const byte TCP_PROTOCOL    = 6;
const int  FLOW_TABLE_SIZE = 100;

//
// Global variables
//
int totalPacketCount_ = 0;
% pragma control totalPacketCount_ (export);

int totalFlowCount_ = 0;
% pragma control totalFlowCount_ (export);

int activeFlowCount_ = 0;
% pragma control activeFlowCount_ (export);

int duplicateSYNCount_ = 0;
% pragma control duplicateSYNCount_ (export);

int insertDBFull_;
% pragma control insertDBFull_ (export);
```

```
// declare record structure
struct FlowStruct
    {
        int     srcAddr;
        int     dstAddr;
        short   srcPort;
        short   dstPort;
        byte    protocol;
    };

// declare Flow database
database FlowStruct flowTable[FLOW_TABLE_SIZE];

// ********************************************
//                     MAIN
// ********************************************
void main($PACKET pkt, $PIB pib, $SYS sys)
{
    //local variables
    record FlowStruct insertRecord =
        {
            {0.0.0.0, 0.0.0.0, 0, 0, 0},
            {255.255.255.255, 255.255.255.255, 0xFFFF, 0xFFFF, 0x0}
        };

    FlowStruct pktData;

    int flowTableRow;

    // Increment packet counter
    ++totalPacketCount_;

    // Set the default action to be forward the packet
    pib.action = FORWARD_PACKET;

    if ( (pib.l3Type == 1) &&
         pib.flags.l3CheckSumValid &&
         pib.flags.l4CheckSumValid &&
         (ipv4.protocol == TCP_PROTOCOL)){

        pktData.srcAddr  = ipv4.sourceAddress;
        pktData.dstAddr  = ipv4.destinationAddress;
        pktData.srcPort  = tcp.sourcePort;
        pktData.dstPort  = tcp.destinationPort;
        pktData.protocol = ipv4.protocol;

        try {
            flowTableRow = flowTable.match( pktData );
            if ( tcp.flags & 0x01 ){
                flowTable[flowTableRow].delete();
                activeFlowCount_--;                       // Decrement Active Flow Counter.
            }
```

243

```
          else if ( tcp.flags & 0x02 ){
                  duplicateSYNCount_++;                  // Duplicate SYN observed.
       };
     }
     catch (ERR_DB_NOMATCH){
        if ( tcp.flags & 0x02 ){                         // Check to see if this is a SYN
           try {
               insertRecord.data = pktData;              // Insert record into database.
               flowTable.insert( insertRecord );
               activeFlowCount_++;                        // Increment Active Flow Counter.
               totalFlowCount_++;                         // Increment the Total Flow Counter.
           }
           catch( ERR_DB_FULL){
               insertDBFull_++;
           };
        };    // end if
     };    // end catch

  }    // end if
}    // end main
```

Following on the discussion of utilizing control-plane resources, consider the application shown above as a simple example of watching traffic flows to provide a view into communications. The metadata stored within the database tables can be queried and viewed by a control-plane system along with the global variables providing a semblance of load level.

From a developer's point of view, the application above appears overly simple, yet from the suggestion prior to the example of breaking the workload, this logic may be all that is required as dynamic APIs can provide access for a control plane to do longer term operations. An example of this is flow time-out where flows left in a database table may sit stale for minutes before they are able to be considered for removal due to lack of further communications. While the packetC application can perform this operation, so too can the control plane and the notion of whether a flow is cleansed at minute 3 or 15 seconds later will generally have little impact on resources, yet the removal of garbage collection from the data plane can be significant.

Additionally, as an architect, consider the times when it is most appropriate to break up large applications into multiple smaller applications. For example, the tracking of metadata can be deployed on a processor that is operating passively in the network such that traffic volumes exceeding the rate of the processor may fail to be processed but will not negatively degrade network traffic performance. If the solution requires both metadata production and active inline controls, such as the example of providing acceleration services for gaming, two small applications may work better as a design. In this broader example, the application above can passively produce metadata for an out-of-band system that may be watching multiple systems across the network. As time dictates providing of the improved network service, another simple packetC application may be deployed actively in-line with all network traffic redirecting the gaming traffic onto an MPLS circuit that provides better peering and performance for the gaming provider. Both packetC applications become small and simple yet a broad set of computational requirements can be actively playing a role in dynamically changing the operation of the real-time system. The key point here is to consider the out-of-band components being designed equally with and during the development of the data-plane architecture so as to do that which isn't truly real-time outside of the data plane whenever possible and achieve maximum performance. Don't fall into the large application lure of packetC because of its familiarity and ability to incorporate vast C libraries.

CHAPTER 24

■ ■ ■

Construction of a packetC Executable

Based upon the compiler and development environment that you are using with packetC, the tool-chain and your course of action to create a packetC application may vary. As of the time of writing, there is only one available tool-chain that supports the various vendor execution platforms. The following discussion provides some insight into the tool-chain and the methodology behind building a packetC application. Refer to the PacketWorks IDE User Guide for a complete walk-through of the development environment and the associated options available for installation, development, and debugging of an application.

The tool-chain overview is shown in Figure 24-1 below, walking through how packetC source code is compiled into an executable and then merged into a configuration for a run-time package of applications that can be loaded onto a processor blade. Object RAVE Code (.ORC) is the output format of a packetC application being compiled and is similar to an executable found on traditional computing platforms. Similar to modern PC execution environments where dynamic linking is required, executables require configuration to identify how they apply to their surroundings such as network input and out interfaces. One or more .ORC executables may be placed in an Application Deployment Package (.ADP) for loading onto a system which includes wiring diagrams of the "virtual patch panel" that turns each packetC application acting as a "virtual appliance" into a completed deployment environment for a processor blade tying virtual interfaces on the applications to physical interfaces on the blade.

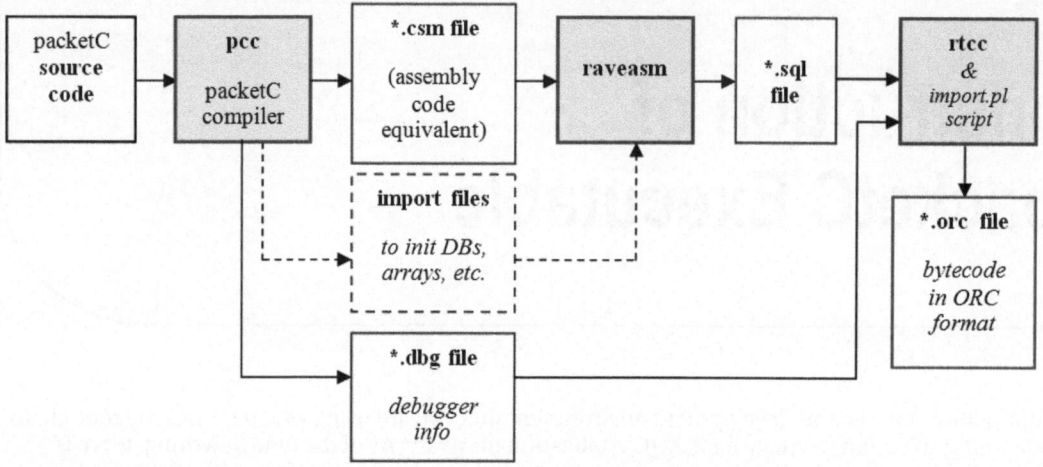

Figure 24-1. Tool-chain overview

Figure 24-1 provides a view into the tool-chain behind packetC. The high-level packetC source code is compiled into the respective assembly level opcodes (RAVE) which are in turn compiled to the binary opcodes in the executable ORC. Along the way, data files are processed to provide a means to initialize data sets at execution time as well as output to support the debugger.

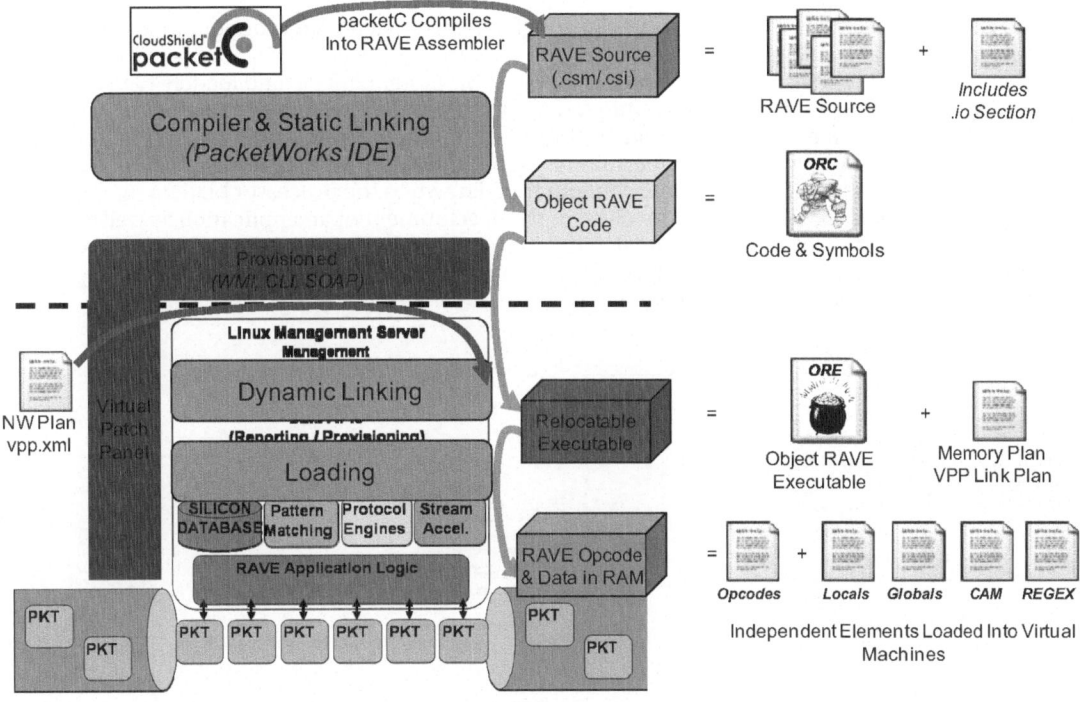

Figure 24-2. Exploded view of packetC tool-chain and intermediary files

The diagram shown in Figure 24-2 is another view into the tool-chain shown more logically with the output files and formats shown along the right. This provides a view that ties a bit more into the memory regions of the processor blades and the logical subsystems contained within those blades. This information is linked and loaded during provisioning to the platform.

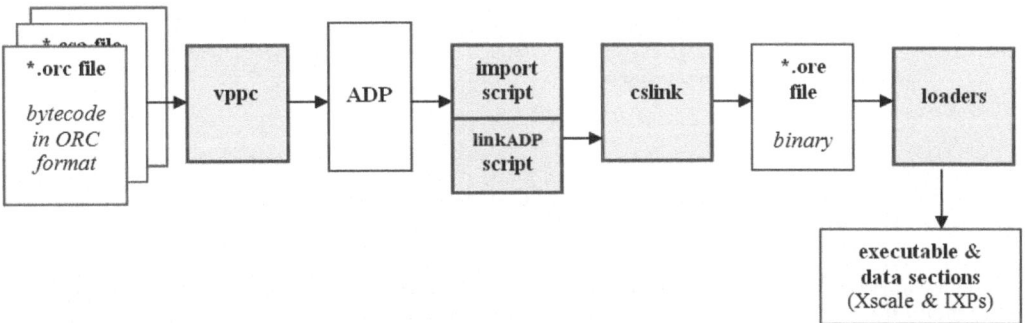

Figure 24-3. packetC tool-chain flow of compilation

As an ORC represents a single application, and processor blades can execute a collection of applications combined together, there needs to be a method for depicting their interaction and managing memory allocation. This is performed through a virtual patch panel configuration (vppc) that generates an XML data file tying a collection of packetC applications together (Figure 24-3). These are stored in an ADP which is then used by the processor blade on-system linkers and loaders to move the execution logic into the control-plane and data-plane processors. The final memory map of all applications in memory on the processor blade is the object rave executable (ORE) which represents the state of memory maps. Noting that new applications can be loaded without updating other applications or their memory areas, the ORE is a dynamic configuration known to the processor blade.

Multiple individuals will generally be involved in the development of an application as well as the definition and construction of an application deployment package loaded onto a system. The actors, in formal modeling of the relationship of the lifecycle of an application being developed to being deployed, are shown in relationship to each other in Figure 24-4.

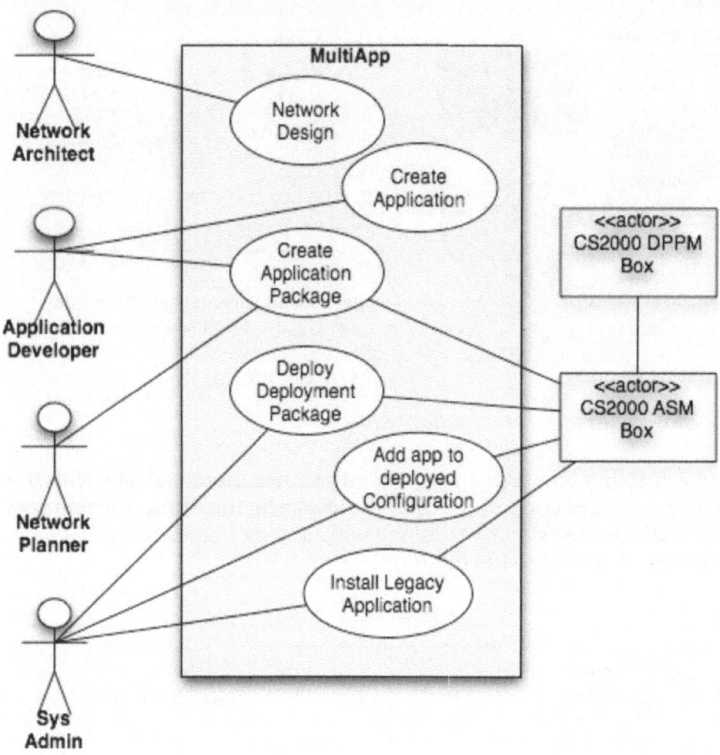

Figure 24-4. Representative actors working with packetC virtual appliances

Developers will code an application, and compile and debug it within a development environment. The result of their efforts will be an executable, an ORC, that can be shared with a network planner. The network planner will use a set of modeling and configuration tools, such as a virtual patch panel configurator, to generate an application deployment package, ADP, for a target system. This is provided to a system administrator to deploy on one or more systems. This simple conceptual model is what is represented above and the tools shown throughout this chapter provide insight into what is leveraged to accomplish these steps.

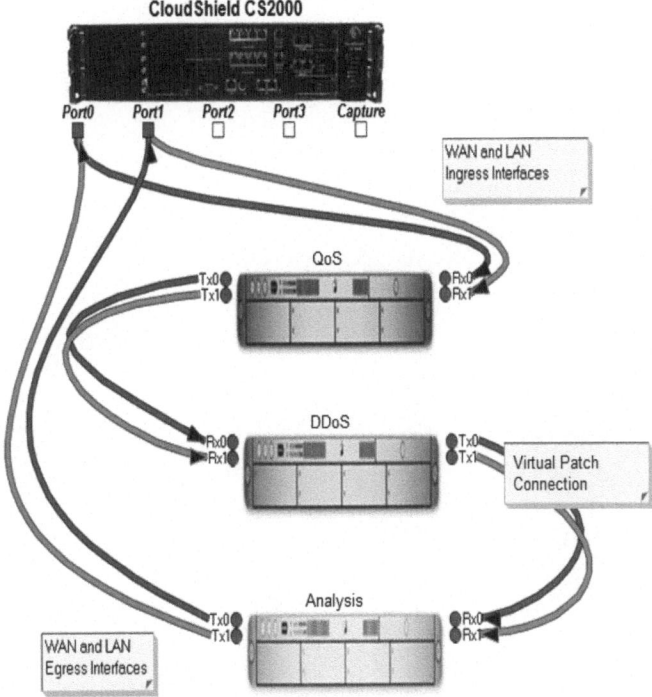

Figure 24-5. *Simple virtual patch panel containing three packetC virtual appliances*

Upon completion or acquisition of one or more applications (ORC), an ADP will be constructed modeling how the applications will logically operate on the processor blade. A view of a virtual patch panel contained within the ADP along with the applications is shown in Figure 24-5. Each virtual appliance shown represents an ORC, and the graphical connection of the wiring diagram will result in the generation of the XML file stored within the ADP describing the entire load for the processor blade. An XML file is part of the ADP describing the virtual interfaces on applications as well as their connectivity to physical interfaces on the target platform (CS-2000 DPPM-510 5-port GigE Blade shown).

A View into the CloudShield PacketWorks IDE Tools

The following descriptions and images within this chapter provide a view into some of the common and more unique elements built into the integrated development environment supporting packetC. With packetC targeting parallel systems with a focus on networking and content processing, there are several tools the developer will require to support completion of an application. In particular, the development of a network application which has no user interface and a stream of packets as the only input device, changes the notion of a debugging environment. Furthermore, the crafting of regular expressions and evaluating application performance drove the creation of new tools. In addition the commonplace tools for team development are also present. . These figures are from the CloudShield PacketWorks IDE 3.1 which uses an Eclipse-based development environment for the creation of packetC applications.

249

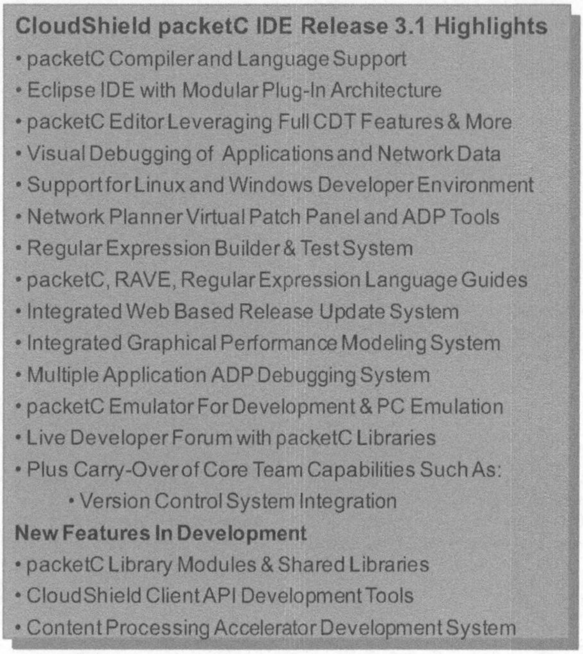

CloudShield packetC IDE Release 3.1 Highlights
- packetC Compiler and Language Support
- Eclipse IDE with Modular Plug-In Architecture
- packetC Editor Leveraging Full CDT Features & More
- Visual Debugging of Applications and Network Data
- Support for Linux and Windows Developer Environment
- Network Planner Virtual Patch Panel and ADP Tools
- Regular Expression Builder & Test System
- packetC, RAVE, Regular Expression Language Guides
- Integrated Web Based Release Update System
- Integrated Graphical Performance Modeling System
- Multiple Application ADP Debugging System
- packetC Emulator For Development & PC Emulation
- Live Developer Forum with packetC Libraries
- Plus Carry-Over of Core Team Capabilities Such As:
    - Version Control System Integration

New Features In Development
- packetC Library Modules & Shared Libraries
- CloudShield Client API Development Tools
- Content Processing Accelerator Development System

Figure 24-6. CloudShield PacketWorks IDE 3.1

Many of the key features of the IDE are shown in Figure 24-6 along with features that are coming in upcoming releases. The specific features may vary from one vendor environment to another as well as releases from CloudShield. However, what is important to focus on is the supporting tools to address the notion that packetC operates within an environment presuming capabilities being performed in the underlying operating system or virtual machine. In particular, the receipt and transmission of packets is scheduled and managed by the operating environment. Tools that perform configuration of this environment including the connection and flow of packets between multiple packetC applications are not common to a Linux or Windows platform. Furthermore, providing tools for modeling regular expressions is important when this mechanism is the foundation for search sets and their ability to perform unstructured content processing. While this book cannot tackle nor does it intend to serve as a means of stepping through the constructive nature of the development process and tools required to build and debug for a given platform, it is important to gain a sense for the different types of tools often necessary for developing packet processing applications in packetC.

Developers using the CloudShield PacketWorks IDE for packetC will receive a manual describing the IDE and all its tools as well as a POSIX regular expression language guide in addition to packetC samples and highlighted deviations from packetC that are specific to a target platform.

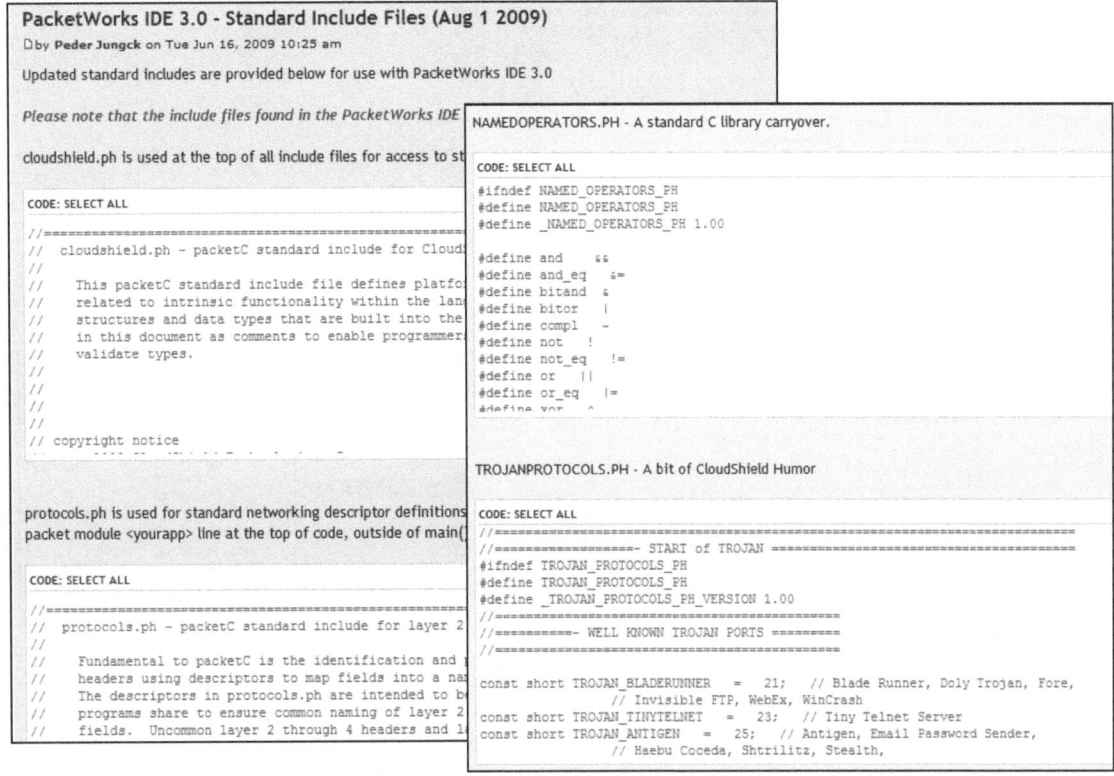

Figure 24-7. Standard include files on packetC.org

Programming in C is often as much about the art of leveraging include files as it is about knowing the actual grammar of C. In the same manner, packetC developers will craft and leverage numerous include files in order to simplifying the development of applications. All packetC applications need to leverage a target platform include, such as cloudshield.ph, as well as leverage a suggested protocol include file, such as protocols.ph. While provided with an IDE, these are also subject to updates due to the release of new platforms or errors. The packetC.org forum is the location for finding updates to platform include files as well as the many standard include files discussed and referenced in Chapter 27. Furthermore, the community of developers will often share samples and include files with helpful sets of constants, as in the case of NAMEDOPERATORS.PH, or code libraries as seen in Figure 24-7.

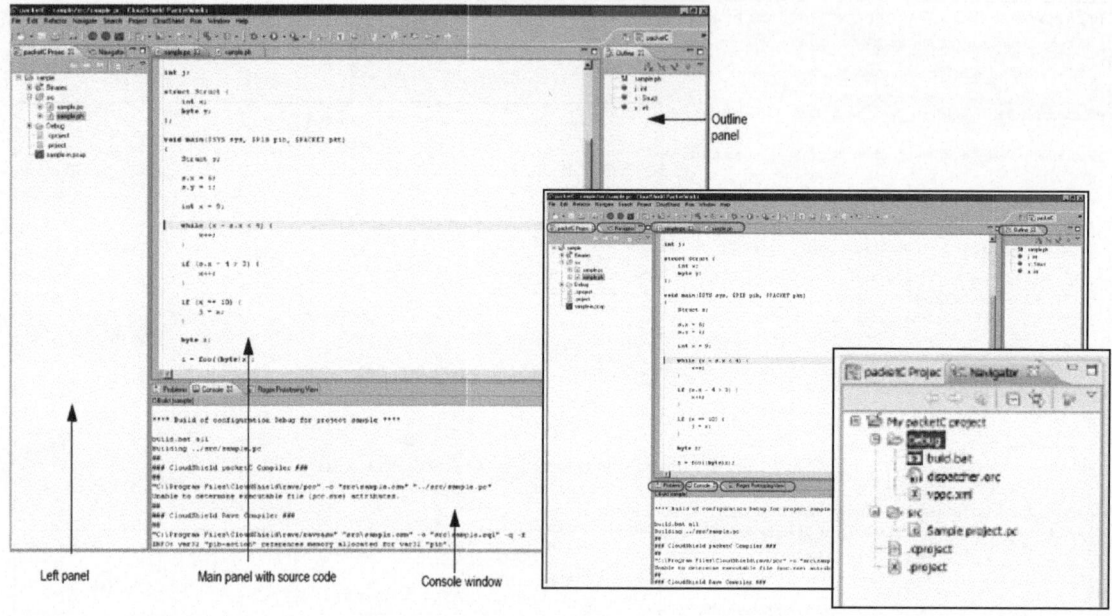

Figure 24-8. packetC Eclipse environment

Even though packetC is a new language, it is able to take advantage of the breadth of features in open development environments such as Eclipse. The packetC tools are installed into the IDE as plug-ins and allow for development of complementary management applications in Java and C in the same environment as packetC development. Standard features for version control, enhanced C style visual editors and tool-chain output in console windows are fully supported as shown in Figure 24-8.

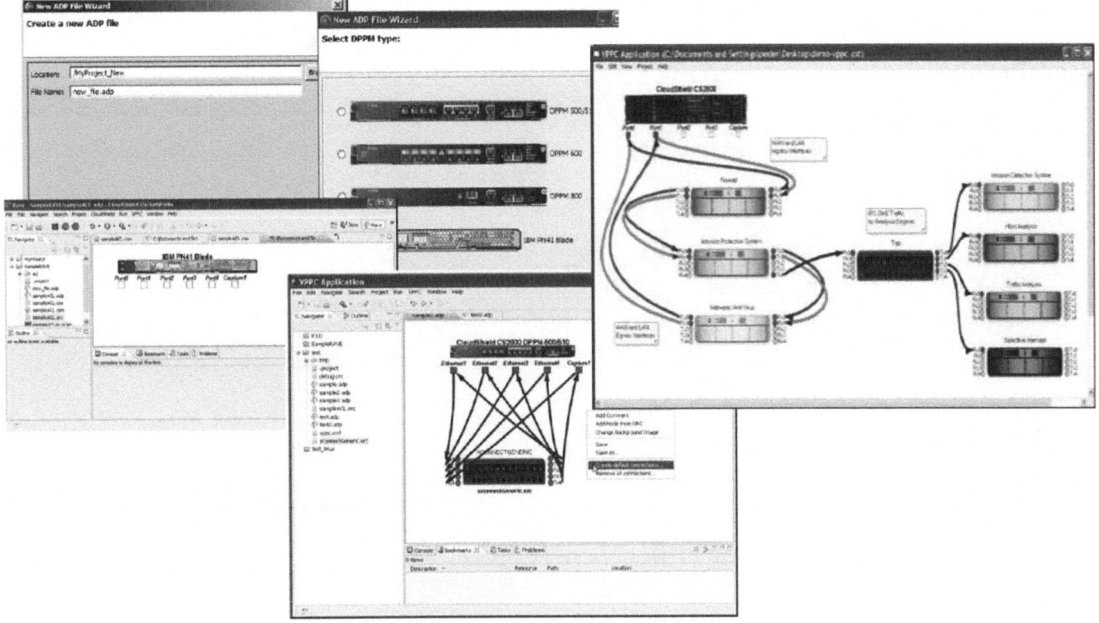

Figure 24-9. Virtual patch panels for connecting packetC applications

Most examples of network applications map directly to a physical view of appliances, such as routers, switches, firewalls and intrusion prevention systems. A given host executing packetC applications may need to perform the equivalent of more than one physical appliance. A packetC application, when compiled into a resulting executable also presents a view to the operating environment depicting a number of virtual interfaces and the resources required to load the application. For target systems supporting more than one application, similar to a modern virtual machine based server deployment, there needs to be a way to depict how to flow packets from the physical interfaces on the host platform to and through each virtual appliance developed in packetC. The virtual patch panel configuration (vppc) tool shown in Figure 24-9 provides a graphical interface to wire up a network of virtual appliances in the same manner that a network engineer would diagram how they would wire up their physical appliances.

Each different processor blade in a target host may have different physical interface counts that would result in a different configuration of virtual appliances. As packetC applications can dramatically vary in their capabilities, this may also result in a wide variety of virtual interfaces to be required such as seen in the number of ports in a switch versus a firewall. Some packetC developed virtual appliances may even create copies of traffic resulting in conditions where there are more virtual interfaces in a virtual appliance than physical interfaces in the host platform. The rightmost image in Figure 24-9 shows the case of an inline virtual appliance (left side middle) copying traffic to another virtual appliance (middle appliance) that is performing load distribution to four (right) different virtual appliances by protocol.

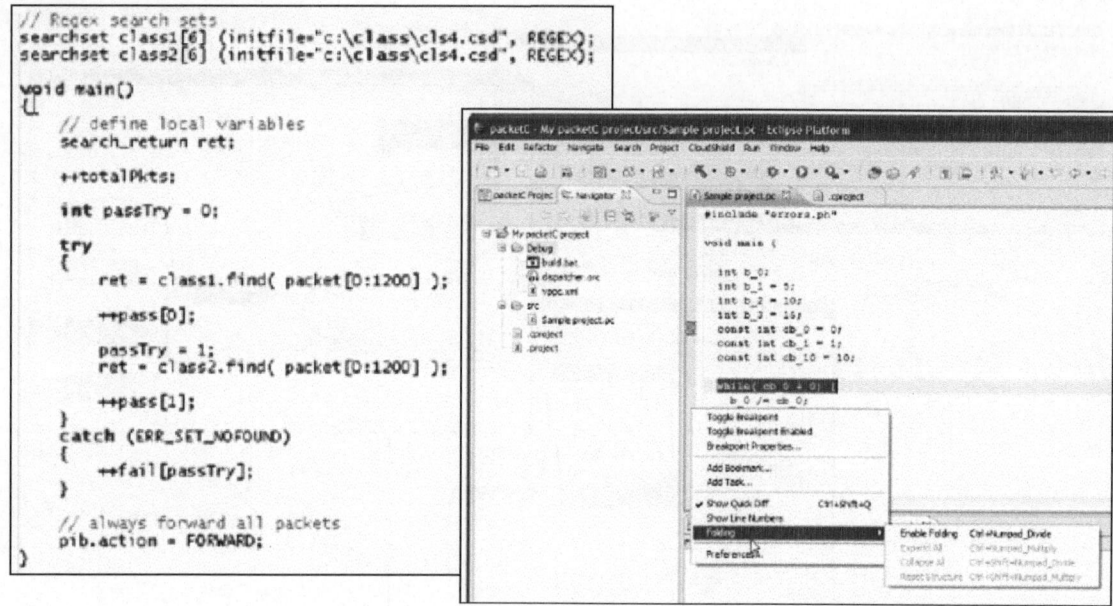

Figure 24-10. *C style editor for packetC*

With the introduction of many new keywords and grammar constructs in packetC, traditional C editors may struggle in Eclipse to provide the desired enhancements to the development process. Enhanced packetC editors are available that provide keyword highlighting, integration with debuggers for setting breakpoints, as well as traditional stylistic templates with packetC style guidelines implemented as defaults. Figure 24-10 shows a section of code within the IDE with some of the highlighting enabled. Developers are not required to leverage any specific editor for packetC, however, the availability of tools with features that provide integrated checking of syntax, coding style templates and integration with version control and debugging solutions can make the development process flow more quickly.

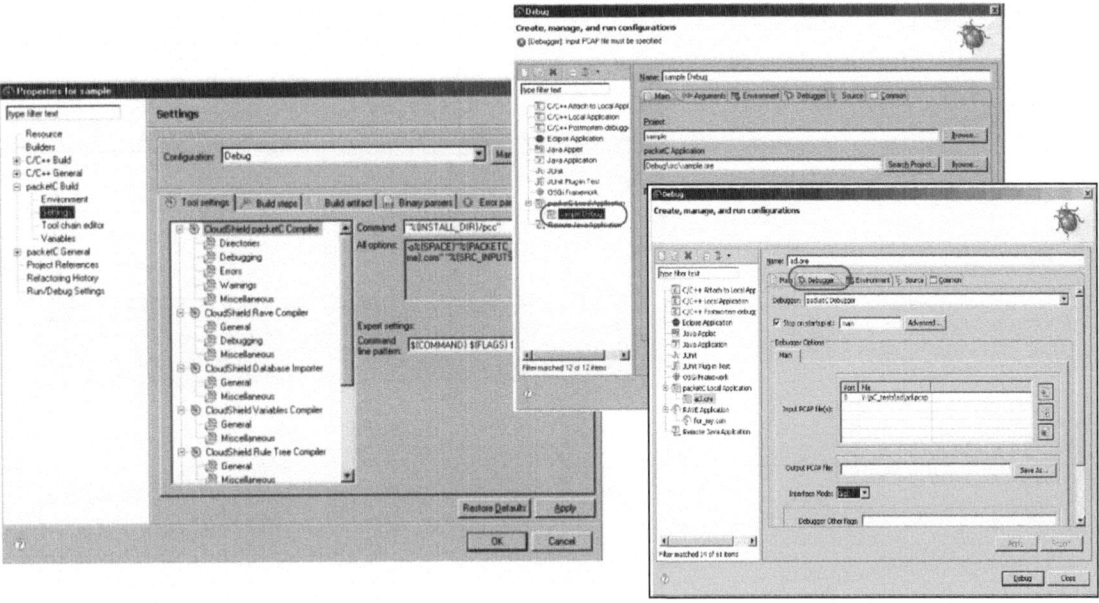

Figure 24-11. Tool-chain control options

While many packetC applications will be small and focused in their size and scope, others may be the results of large team efforts building very complex solutions. As packetC applications grow, so do the demands upon the development environment to aide in team-based development and introducing complex data sets for debugging. Data management becomes especially critical in networking applications as the user input and output may be collections of packet captures streamed through virtual interfaces and log files showing resultant data sets. A number of configuration options are able to be configured for a packetC project as shown in Figure 24-11 to support compilation from numerous sources as well as to support the debug environment.

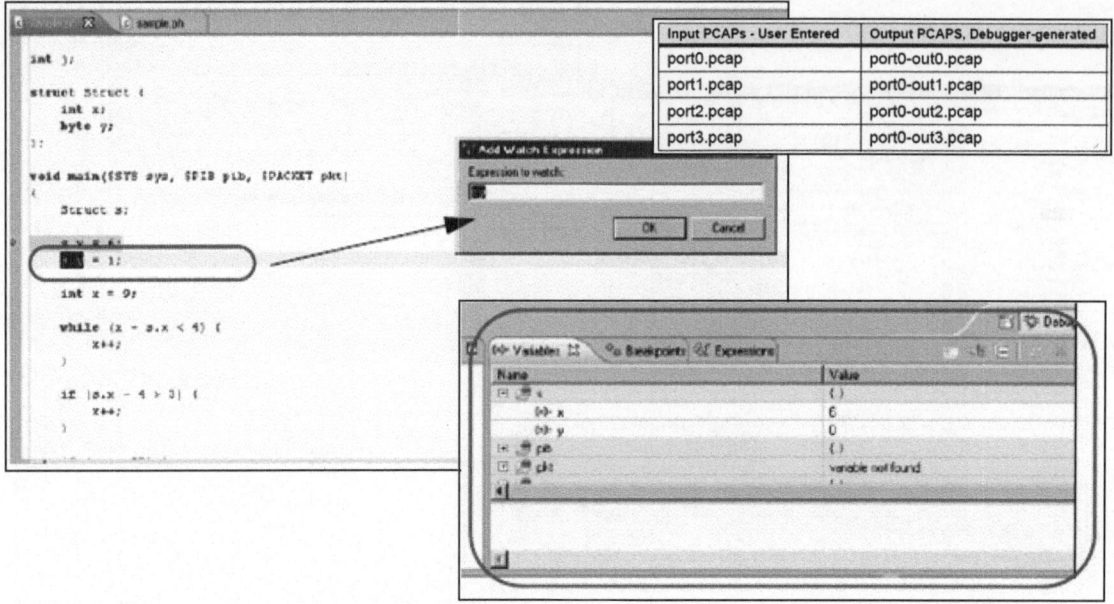

Figure 24-12. Visual debugging in packetC

While many of the language enhancements introduced in packetC can reduce the number of lines of code compared to a C application performing identical functionality often by an order of magnitude or more, bugs still crop up. An integrated environment with break points, data watch settings and run-time stepping functions are critical to debugging applications where capture files provide cryptic means supporting only black box debugging. Figure 24-12 shows some of the simple integrated debugging features in packetC development environments.

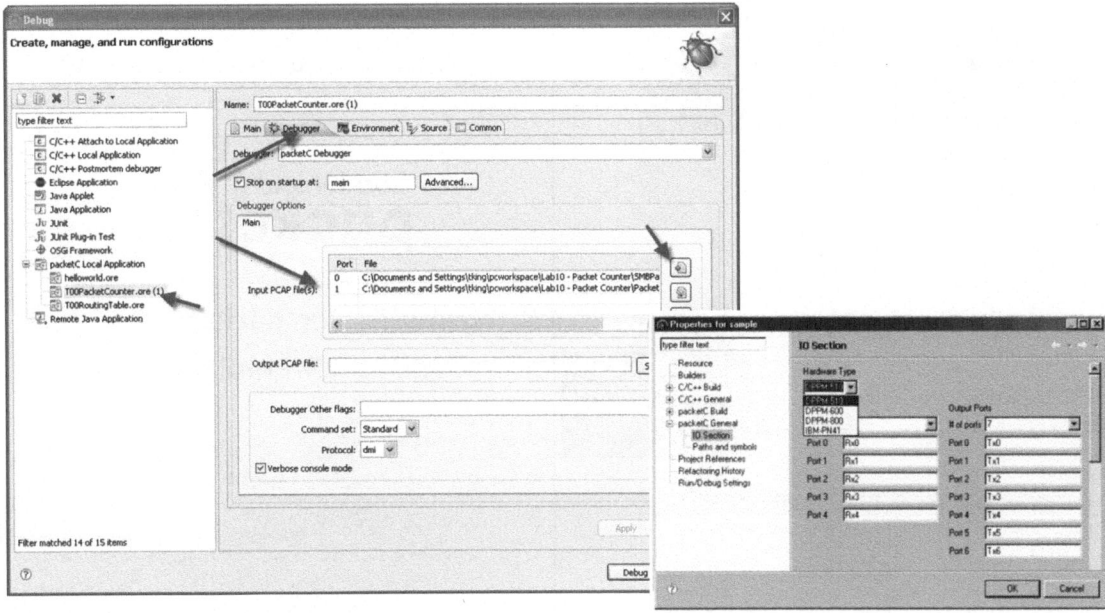

Figure 24-13. Multiple packet capture file coordination

With multiple virtual interfaces on a packetC virtual appliance, each requires a set of input conditions and resultant output collections of packets that can be analyzed during and post debugging. The IDE must coordinate the source packet captures, generally stored in .pcap format for use with tools such as Ethereal. In Figure 24-13 above, the port numbers shown next to files names in the window at the left maps the capture file to a given virtual interface. The dialog shown at the right provides a configuration tool to specify the number of input and output interfaces to associate with a given virtual appliance under test. Network applications pose unique debugging challenges compared to traditional applications where keyboard, mouse, and video interfaces are the common input and output devices under the control of a human tester. Furthermore, traffic generation equipment for testing network devices works well to flood a device at speed, but often poorly to send a single packet into a system or coordinate specific packets to arrive from disparate interfaces at the same time. Finally, if a virtual appliance expects its output to be the result of another virtual appliance, such as a virtual Ethernet firewall sitting behind a virtual SONET to Ethernet router, the input conditions of one solution may only operate properly using the output of another. A packetC debugger must account for these conditions among others.

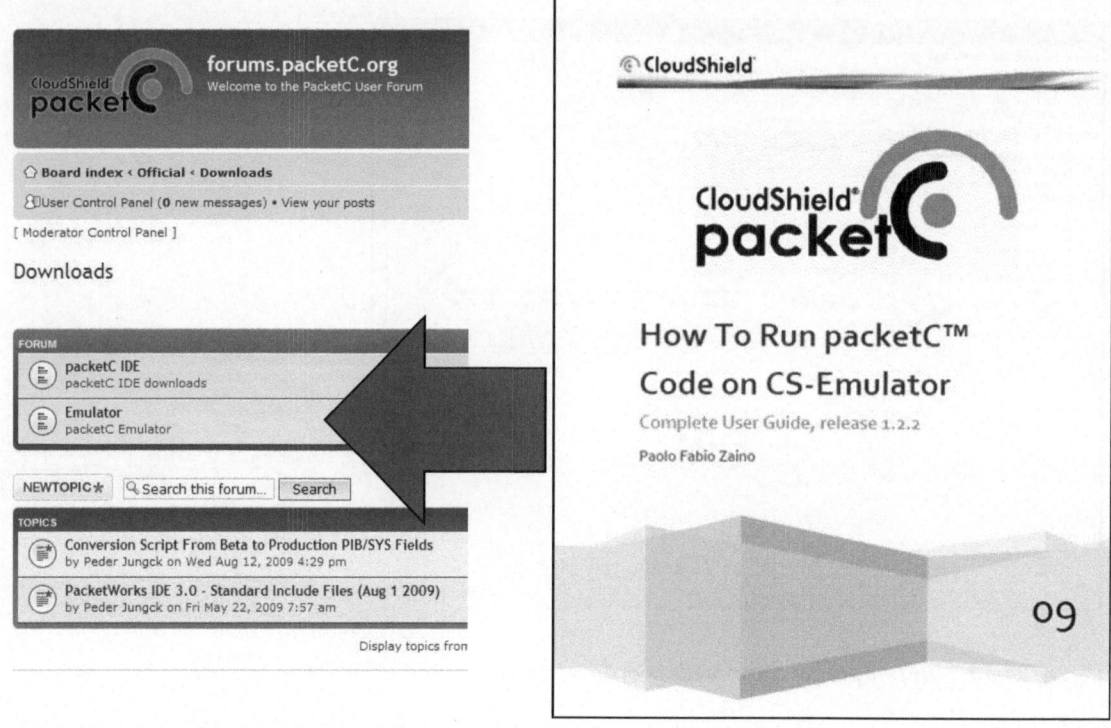

Figure 24-14. Emulating the packetC operating environment on Linux

Throughout this book, considerable time has been spent on the requirements packetC places on the host system as well as the unique features provided by processors that execute packetC developed applications. In Appendix B a view into hardware designed specifically to process packetC applications is shown. While highly tuned systems are required at this time to process network traffic at 10 Gigabits per second or higher, in development and in small scale deployments, an emulated environment on a traditional computing system may be all that is required. An emulator is available on packetC.org that provides a simple command line tool executing in Linux to execute a single packetC virtual appliance. With this emulator, a development environment, and the investment of some time with the associated instructions as shown in Figure 24-14, a newcomer to packetC can craft and test their first packetC applications on an available Linux system.

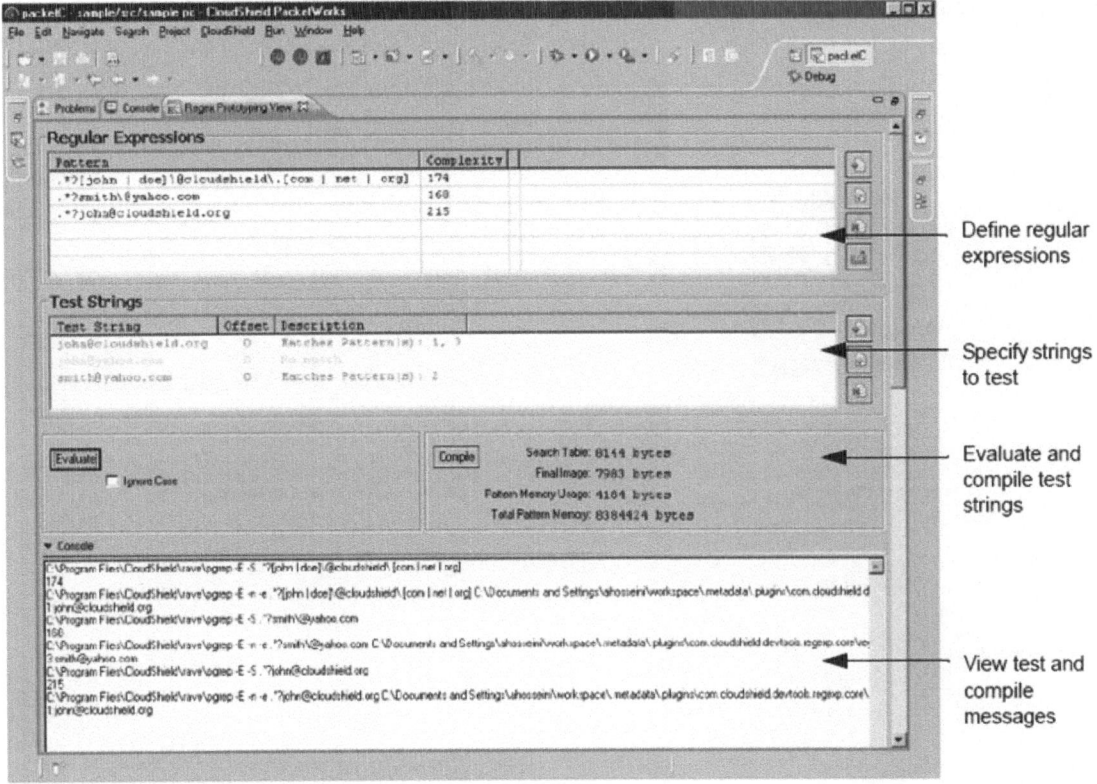

Figure 24-15. POSIX regular expression evaluation plug-in

Within packetC is buried yet another language, namely POSIX regular expressions. While network headers are easily described using structured methods supported by packetC descriptors, the Internet era has created new protocols without any industry standards of controls which are predominately represented in textual forms rather than byte aligned fields. To process unstructured data, such as HTTP and HTML, regular expressions provide a means to express an algorithm to instruct the system how to find data of interest within the payload of a packet. Just as packetC needs to be debugged, so do regular expressions. While many simple tools exist to evaluate regular expressions, packetC applications often leverage multiple tables of regular expressions that need to be tested against different data sets. The image in Figure 24-15 highlights one view of a regular expression evaluation plug-in that allows for the editing of expressions and testing against a set of sample data ensuring that the resulting offsets of searches are as expected by the developer.

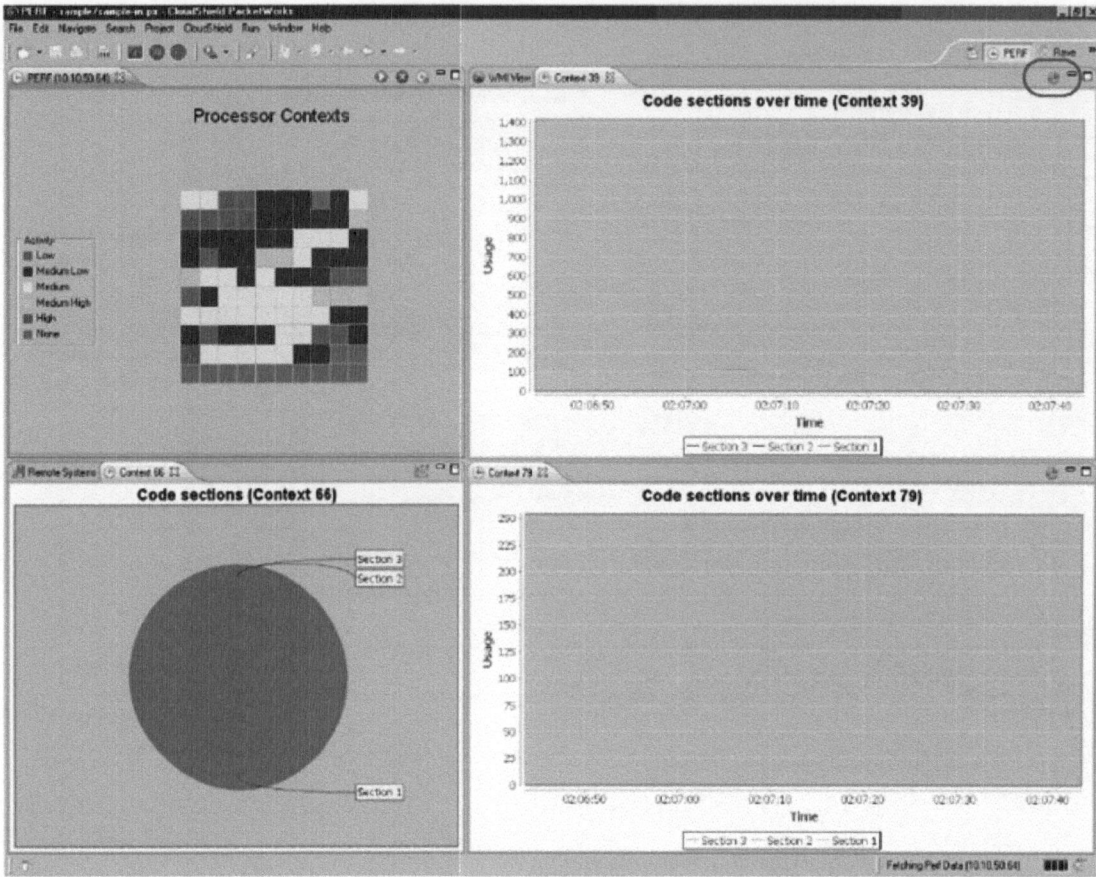

Figure 24-16. *Multi-context real-time debugger utilization*

While functionality can be tested in a debugger on a development platform, often real-time debugging is required to evaluate an application under load. Figure 24-16 shows two simple views of a packetC application under load. The first, shown at the top is a view into the multiple contexts. As packetC applications are designed to run on multi-core systems, determining utilization under load and hot spots, often tied to contexts stuck in endless loops, is best seen by watching metrics of an operational system. The figure above is looking at a 96 core system where 96 packets are able to be processed at any given time and the color, or gradation in grayscale, represents load level. Another tool that is useful is the measurement of time by section of code. Often tuning focuses on the reduction in the lines of code, while packetC focuses on the reduction in the lines of code during a given period of time across a number of packets. Sometimes it is better to determine which sections of code are used most often and reduce their code size, potentially at the detriment to the number of lines of code in another section less often utilized. Developing graphs of time in code sections as a measure of a system under load provides critical tools for moving applications from poorly performing data rates to extreme high performance. Real-world examples have seen code performing at a few hundred megabits per second on a system after weeks of developer tuning result in multigigabit performance after just a few hours of tuning when looking at the application with these tools.

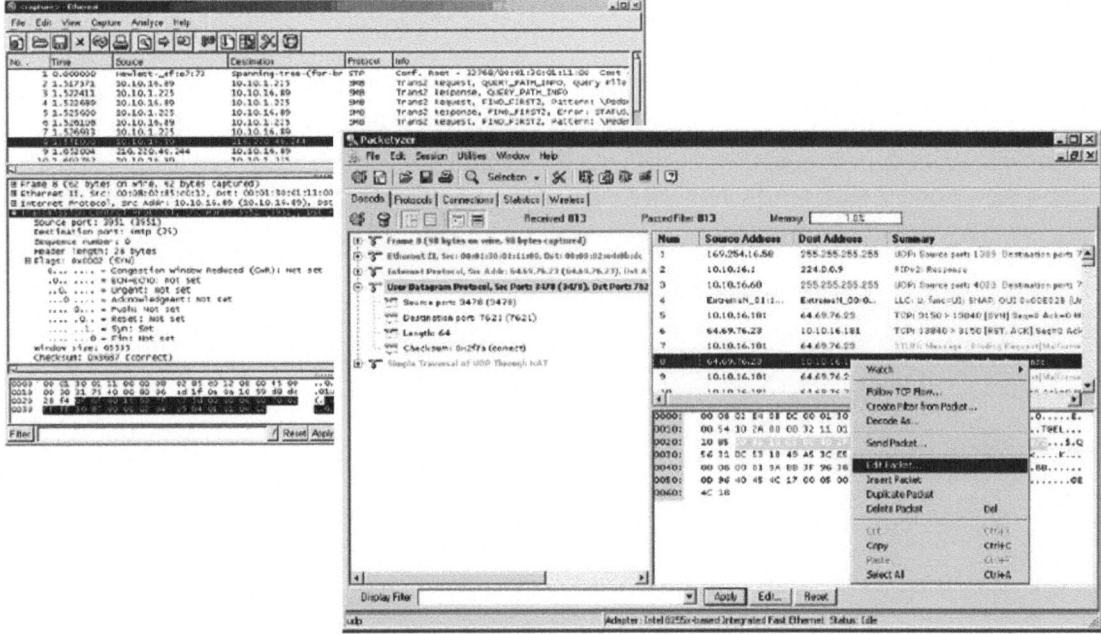

Figure 24-17. *Viewing and editing packet captures*

Throughout this chapter the reference to *packet captures* as an input and output of packetC virtual appliances has been made. Within the integrated development environment the captures will be present in project directories and the tools to view and edit packets as expected features. Figure 24-17 provides a view into the traditional tools used to view and edit packet captures, such as Ethereal and Packetyzer, respectively. While Linux systems generally provide command line tools to capture and view dumps of the packets on the network interfaces, it is fairly rare to find tools to edit and craft packets from scratch. As solutions are focused on processing traffic found in a WAN or cloud environment, it is often difficult to have ready access to captures of the traffic of interest. Furthermore, in solutions that are security focused, looking for specific exploits in the wild in network form can be quite cumbersome. Using tools to edit capture files of only the packets of interest and then being able to insert data of interest to specific packetC subroutines dramatically reduces the time to perform unit testing.

This chapter introduced some of the underlying mechanisms implemented with a packetC tool-chain that support the simplified packet processing environment present in the packetC grammar. Furthermore, as those expected capabilities simplify development, they also leave a lot of open questions about how choices are implemented that affect the processing environment. The brief walk-through of some of the unique configuration elements and tools to support development of packetC provides a cursory view into how development of packetC applications will often vary from traditional C projects, even for networking. Further information can be found in user guides focused on the packetC integrated development environment. However, a cursory understanding of the tools and expectation of tools placed upon an IDE to support the packetC developer should provide the requisite answers to how a developer can accomplish successful development leveraging unique packetC functionality such as search sets. The examples above are not inclusive of everything required or present, but should at least introduce the concept of the differences in tools for developing applications that live within the network.

■ ■ ■

packetC Standard Networking Descriptors

This chapter highlights some of the key principles of descriptors through highlighting examples in the standard libraries. Many layer 2 through 4 descriptors are provided with packetC development environments while upper-layer protocols and custom packet techniques will require handcrafted descriptors tailored to an application. Descriptors may be as simple as the one for Ethernet II provided below:

```
//============================================================================
//  Ethernet II Descriptor
//
//  Most common layer 2 Ethernet header utilized in networks, referred to as
//  just Ethernet instead of Ethernet II due to common usage.
//
//============================================================================
#define ETHERNET_TYPE_IP          = 0x0800;
#define ETHERNET_TYPE_ARP         = 0x0806;
#define ETHERNET_TYPE_RARP        = 0x0835;
#define ETHERNET_TYPE_8021Q       = 0x8100;
#define ETHERNET_TYPE_8023         = 0x05DC; // <= 1500 (0x05DC) are 802.3
#define ETHERNET_TYPE_CLOUDSHIELD = 0xC5C5; // CloudShield Custom Frames

struct MacAddress
{
  byte b0, b1, b2, b3, b4, b5;
};

descriptor EthernetStruct
{
  MacAddress destinationAddress; // MAC Address: i.e. 00:0B:A9:00:00:00
  MacAddress sourceAddress;      //
  short      type;               // Compare with ETHERNET_TYPE_xx
} ethernet at pib.l2Offset;
typedef byte EthernetStructBytes[sizeof(EthernetStruct)];
```

Or they may follow a much more complex variation with bit-fields as shown in the standard IPv4 header below:

```
//================================================================================
//  Standard IPv4 Descriptor
//
//  Most common layer 3 IP header utilized in networks.  Descriptions taken
//  from RFC 791.
//
//================================================================================
descriptor Ipv4Struct
{
  bits byte
  {
    version       : 4;
    headerLength  : 4;
  } bf;                      // No official name for byte, using bf for bit field.

  bits byte
  {
    precedence    : 3;
    delay         : 1;
    throughput    : 1;
    reliability   : 1;
    reserved      : 2;
  } tos;

  short totalLength;
  short identification;

  bits short
  {
    evil          : 1;       // Reserved field renamed Evil Bit in RFC 3514
    dont          : 1;       // Don't Fragment
    more          : 1;       // More Fragments
    fragmentOffset :13;      // Fragment Offset (offset is a reserved word)
  } fragment;

  byte  ttl;
  byte  protocol;
  short checksum;
  int   sourceAddress;
  int   destinationAddress;
} ipv4 at pib.l3Offset;      // Optional data follows as IP Options
typedef byte Ipv4StructBytes[sizeof(Ipv4Struct)];
```

In each example above, the development of the descriptor involved making several choices on how to break up the fields as Ethernet II introduced a 6-byte MAC address and IPv4 introduced bit fields. As applications leverage complex structures defined for describing packet interactions, the descriptors provide a simplified access to fields by name. At times, sections of the packets may need to be brought into a local data structure for manipulation. In these cases, a descriptor and a local data structure are created with the same base structure type. There are two methods of defining this structure as shown by the descriptor defined structure:

```
descriptor SimpleEthernetStruct
{
  MacAddress destinationAddress; // MAC Address: i.e. 00:0B:A9:00:00:00
  MacAddress sourceAddress;      //
  short      type;               // Compare with ETHERNET_TYPE_xx
} simpleEthernet at pib.l2Offset;

SimpleEthernetStruct myLocalEthernet;
```

and structure defined descriptor below:

```
typedef struct SimpleEthernetStruct
{
  MacAddress destinationAddress; // MAC Address: i.e. 00:0B:A9:00:00:00
  MacAddress sourceAddress;      //
  short      type;               // Compare with ETHERNET_TYPE_xx
};

descriptor SimpleEthernetStruct SumpleEthernet at pib.l2Offset;

SimpleEthernetStruct myLocalEthernet;
```

What is also important to note is that multiple levels of complexity of a descriptor for a given protocol may be useful. This may be done by introducing additional unions within the structure to represent fields in multiple ways or to define multiple descriptors operating at different levels of abstraction. The simple IPv4 descriptor below is equally accurate as the detailed one above for simple actions like reading IP addresses and protocol fields in construction of a 5-tuple.

Choose the level of detail desired for the job being performed if it can simplify the complexity in an application. The choice of construction is yours. A descriptor does not change the form of a packet; rather it provides a name-based access to fields allowing multiple descriptors referencing the same packet fields to work interchangeably without issue.

```
descriptor SimpleIpv4Struct
{
  byte  versionAndLength;
  byte  tos;
  short totalLength;
  short identification;
  short fragment;
  byte  ttl;
  byte  protocol;
  short checksum;
  int   sourceAddress;
  int   destinationAddress;
} simpleIpv4 at pib.l3Offset;
```

Elsewhere in this book you will find detailed descriptions of how descriptors work and in the chapter covering the *pib* and *sys* structures examples of the header decode procedures are shown which calculate the values set for offsets in the *pib*.

```
typedef byte SimpleIpv4StructBytes[sizeof(SimpleIpv4Struct)];
```

For each descriptor you will also find a typedef that represents an array of bytes equal in size of the structure. This is used when copying or assigning the structure as a whole. The packet can be accessed as an array of bytes in addition through descriptor fields. When wishing to copy an entire header out of the packet, the typedef ending in *StructBytes* allows for simple casting to enable the memcopy. It is also important to note that a descriptor includes a type that may be used for establishing structures. Using the previously-defined definitions for SimpleIpv4 above, these can enable scenarios such as the following:

```
SimpleIpv4Struct testStruct;

testStruct.sourceAddress = 10.10.1.1;
testStruct.destinationAddress = 192.168.1.1;
pkt[pib.l3Offset:pib.l3Offset+sizeof(SimpleIpv4Struct)] = (SimpleIpv4StructBytes) testStruct;
```

The following example contains *protocols.ph* with basic protocol descriptor definitions for layer 2 through 4 headers. The *protocols.ph* file shown is simply the supplied base descriptors with a packetC implementation. Refer to packetC.org for updated descriptors and vendor *protocols.ph* releases as well extended protocols header files and examples.

As a developer you may want to create your own set of descriptors that you use and share. Multiple descriptor variations for the same protocols may be useful and user generated protocol descriptor collections are urged to be developed and shared. Furthermore, standard versions of *protocols.ph* won't contain many upper layer protocol descriptors or rarely user transport headers. These are prime opportunities for extended protocols descriptor collections.

It is recommended to utilize the vendor-supplied *protocols.ph* unchanged and store user-defined protocols in a separate file, such as *user-protocols.ph*, where *user* is your name, organization or protocol group. This will allow for quickly applying updates to the vendor *protocols.ph* without needing to segment out user changes.

Standard Include File protocols.ph Example

```
//==============================================================================
//  protocols.ph - packetC standard include for layer 2 through 4 headers.
//
//    Fundamental to packetC is the identification and processing of packet
//    headers using descriptors to map fields into a named reference model.
//    The descriptors in protocols.ph are intended to be a staple that all
//    programs share to ensure common naming of layer 2 through 4 header
//    fields.
//
// :NOTE: Not all layer 2 through 4 headers and layer 7 protocols are
//        included in this file.
//
// author
//    Peder Jungck
//    expanded work: dWiGhT
//
// copyright notice
//    © 2009-2011 CloudShield Technologies, Inc.
//
//==============================================================================
```

```
#ifndef PROTOCOLS_PH
#define PROTOCOLS_PH

// Header file versioning
const int PROTOCOLS_PH_VERSION_ = 1.0.2.0;
%pragma control PROTOCOLS_PH_VERSION_(export);

// Macros to allow recasting of enumerated fields to access
// and compare them to scalar values.
// :WARNING: You are bypassing type safety at this point.
#define  RAW_BYTE(x)   (byte)(x)
#define  RAW_SHORT(x)  (short)(x)
#define  RAW_INT(x)    (int)(x)

// Define a type that is used for IP addresses
// in the form of xxx.xxx.xxx.xxx   i.e. 192.168.0.101
typedef int IpAddress;

// Define a type that is used for MAC addresses
// in the form of xx:xx:xx:xx:xx   i.e. 05:32:b1:f3:09
struct MacAddress
{
  byte b0, b1, b2, b3, b4, b5;
};


//==============================================================================
//   Ethernet II Descriptor
//
//   Most common layer 2 Ethernet header utilized in networks, referred to as
//   just Ethernet instead of Ethernet II due to common usage.
//
//==============================================================================
enum short EthernetType {
  ETHERNET_TYPE_IP               = 0x0800, // IPv4
  ETHERNET_TYPE_ARP              = 0x0806, // Address Resolution Protocol
  ETHERNET_TYPE_RARP             = 0x0835, // Reverse Address Resolution Protocol
  ETHERNET_TYPE_APPLETALK        = 0x809b, // AppleTalk (Ethertalk)
  ETHERNET_TYPE_AARP             = 0x80f3, // Appletalk ARP
  ETHERNET_TYPE_Novell_IPX       = 0x8137, // Novell IPX (alt)
  ETHERNET_TYPE_Novell           = 0x8138, // Novell
  ETHERNET_TYPE_MPLS_UNICAST     = 0x8847, // MPLS Unicast
  ETHERNET_TYPE_MPLS_MULTICAST   = 0x8848, // MPLS Multicast
  ETHERNET_TYPE_PPPoE_DISCOVERY  = 0x8863, // PPPoE Discovery Stage
  ETHERNET_TYPE_PPPoE_SESSION    = 0x8864, // PPPoE Session Stage
  ETHERNET_TYPE_8021Q            = 0x8100, // identifies IEEE 802.1Q tag
  ETHERNET_TYPE_8023             = 0x05dc, // <= 1500 (0x05DC) are 802.3
  ETHERNET_TYPE_IP6              = 0x86dd, // IPv6
  ETHERNET_TYPE_CLOUDSHIELD      = 0xC5C5  // CloudShield Custom Frames
};

descriptor EthernetStruct
{
```

```
  MacAddress    destinationAddress; // MAC Address: i.e. 00:0B:A9:00:00:00
  MacAddress    sourceAddress;      //  ..
  EthernetType  type;               // Compare with ETHERNET_TYPE_xx
} ethernet at pib.l2Offset;
typedef byte EthernetStructBytes[sizeof(EthernetStruct)];

//============================================================================
//  Ethernet II 802.1Q VLAN Descriptors (Single and Double VLAN Tagged)
//
//  802.1Q defines Ethernet headers with LAN segmentation in the layer 2
//  Ethernet header that is also utilized in WAN deployments for aggregation and
//  virtual LAN services.  VLAN tags are at the end of the standard Ethernet II
//  header and are denoted by a type field of 0x8100.  Following the last tag
//  should be a standard type field containing a value such as 0x0800 to
//  describe the encapsulated data.
//
//  An 802.1Q frame also contains User Priority information, 8 possible values,
//  which are part of 802.1P standards.  The VLAN ID will generally be 0 when
//  the frame is intended as an 802.1P frame.
//
//============================================================================
#define ETHERNET8021Q_VLANDID_PRIORITY 0x000    /* vlanId = 0 is 802.1p   */
#define ETHERNET8021Q_VLANDID_RESERVED 0xfff    /* vlanId = 4095 reserved */

struct VlanTag
{
  EthernetType  type;               // ETHERNET_TYPE_8021Q = 0x8100
  bits short
  {
    userPriority    : 3;            // 802.1p Priority Field
    formatIndicator : 1;            // Must be 0 for Ethernet
    vlanId          : 12;           // 802.1q VLAN Tag Identification
  } tag;
};

descriptor Ethernet8021QStruct
{
  MacAddress    destinationAddress; // MAC Address: i.e. 00:0B:A9:00:00:00
  MacAddress    sourceAddress;      //  ..
  VlanTag       vlan;               // VLAN tag
  EthernetType  type;               // Type for payload, not ETHERNET_TYPE_8021Q
} ethernet8021Q at pib.l2Offset;
typedef byte Ethernet8021QStructBytes[sizeof(Ethernet8021QStruct)];

descriptor Ethernet8021QQStruct
{
  MacAddress    destinationAddress; // MAC Address: i.e. 00:0B:A9:00:00:00
  MacAddress    sourceAddress;      //  ..
  VlanTag       outerVlan;          // Outer VLAN tag
  VlanTag       innerVlan;          // Inner VLAN tag
  EthernetType  type;               // Type for payload, not ETHERNET_TYPE_8021Q
} ethernet8021QQ at pib.l2Offset;
```

```
typedef byte Ethernet8021QQStructBytes[sizeof(Ethernet8021QQStruct)];

//===============================================================================
//   Ethernet 802.3 Descriptor
//
//   Common original layer 2 Ethernet header utilized in networks.  The length
//   field <= 1500 signifies 802.3 versus a value > 1500 signifies this is the
//   type field and is not 802.3 but rather a newer Ethernet II header.
//
//===============================================================================

descriptor Ethernet8023Struct
{
  MacAddress  destinationAddress; // MAC Address: i.e. 00:0B:A9:00:00:00
  MacAddress  sourceAddress;      //  ..
  short       length;             // Must be <= ETHERNET_TYPE_8023 (1500) length.
} ethernet8023 at pib.l2Offset;
typedef byte Ethernet8023StructBytes[sizeof(Ethernet8023Struct)];

//===============================================================================
//   Standard IPv4 Descriptor
//
//   Most common layer 3 IP header utilized in networks.  Descriptions taken
//   from RFC 791.
//
//===============================================================================

enum byte IpProtocol {
// --------------------
//   Common Protocols
// --------------------
   IP_PROTOCOL_ICMP        = 0x01,  // Internet Control Message Protocol
                                    //   RFC 792
   IP_PROTOCOL_IGMP        = 0x02,  // Internet Group Management Protocol
                                    //   RFC 1112
   IP_PROTOCOL_TCP         = 0x06,  // Transmission Control Protocol
                                    //   RFC 793
   IP_PROTOCOL_UDP         = 0x11,  // User Datagram Protocol
                                    //   RFC 768
   IP_PROTOCOL_IPV6        = 0x29,  // IPv6 (encapsulation)
                                    //   RFC 2473
   IP_PROTOCOL_OSPF        = 0x59,  // Open Shortest Path First
                                    //   RFC 1583
   IP_PROTOCOL_SCTP        = 0x84,  // Stream Control Transmission Protocol

// -----------------------
//   Other Known Protocols
// -----------------------
   IP_PROTOCOL_HOPOPT      = 0x00,  // IPv6 Hop-by-Hop Option  RFC 2460
   IP_PROTOCOL_GGP         = 0x03,  // Gateway-to-Gateway Protocol   RFC 823
   IP_PROTOCOL_IP          = 0x04,  // IP in IP (encapsulation)  RFC 2003
   IP_PROTOCOL_ST          = 0x05,  // Internet Stream Protocol  RFC 1190,
```

```
                                 //   RFC 1819
IP_PROTOCOL_CBT         = 0x07,  // Core-based trees  RFC 2189
IP_PROTOCOL_EGP         = 0x08,  // Exterior Gateway Protocol   RFC 888
IP_PROTOCOL_IGP         = 0x09,  // Interior Gateway Protocol (any private
                                 //   interior gateway (used by Cisco for
                                 //   their IGRP))
IP_PROTOCOL_BBN_RCC_MON = 0x0A,  // BBN RCC Monitoring
IP_PROTOCOL_NVP_II      = 0x0B,  // Network Voice Protocol  RFC 741
IP_PROTOCOL_PUP         = 0x0C,  // Xerox PUP
IP_PROTOCOL_ARGUS       = 0x0D,  // ARGUS
IP_PROTOCOL_EMCON       = 0x0E,  // EMCON
IP_PROTOCOL_XNET        = 0x0F,  // Cross Net Debugger  IEN 158
IP_PROTOCOL_CHAOS       = 0x10,  // Chaos
IP_PROTOCOL_MUX         = 0x12,  // Multiplexing  IEN 90
IP_PROTOCOL_DCN_MEAS    = 0x13,  // DCN Measurement Subsystems
IP_PROTOCOL_HMP         = 0x14,  // Host Monitoring Protocol  RFC 869
IP_PROTOCOL_PRM         = 0x15,  // Packet Radio Measurement
IP_PROTOCOL_XNS_IDP     = 0x16,  // XEROX NS IDP
IP_PROTOCOL_TRUNK_1     = 0x17,  // Trunk-1
IP_PROTOCOL_TRUNK_2     = 0x18,  // Trunk-2
IP_PROTOCOL_LEAF_1      = 0x19,  // Leaf-1
IP_PROTOCOL_LEAF_2      = 0x1A,  // Leaf-2
IP_PROTOCOL_RDP         = 0x1B,  // Reliable Datagram Protocol  RFC 908
IP_PROTOCOL_IRTP        = 0x1C,  // Internet Reliable Transaction Protocol
                                 //   RFC 938
IP_PROTOCOL_ISO_TP4     = 0x1D,  // ISO Transport Protocol Class 4  RFC 905
IP_PROTOCOL_NETBLT      = 0x1E,  // Bulk Data Transfer Protocol   RFC 998
IP_PROTOCOL_MFE_NSP     = 0x1F,  // MFE Network Services Protocol
IP_PROTOCOL_MERIT_INP   = 0x20,  // MERIT Internodal Protocol
IP_PROTOCOL_DCCP        = 0x21,  // Datagram Congestion Control Protocol
                                 //   RFC 4340
IP_PROTOCOL_3PC         = 0x22,  // Third Party Connect Protocol
IP_PROTOCOL_IDPR        = 0x23,  // Inter-Domain Policy Routing Protocol
                                 //   RFC 1479
IP_PROTOCOL_XTP         = 0x24,  // Xpress Transport Protocol
IP_PROTOCOL_DDP         = 0x25,  // Datagram Delivery Protocol
IP_PROTOCOL_IDPR_CMTP   = 0x26,  // IDPR Control Message Transport Protocol
IP_PROTOCOL_TPPP        = 0x27,  // TP++ Transport Protocol
IP_PROTOCOL_IL          = 0x28,  // IL Transport Protocol
IP_PROTOCOL_SDRP        = 0x2A,  // Source Demand Routing Protocol
IP_PROTOCOL_IPV6_ROUTE  = 0x2B,  // Routing Header for IPv6   RFC 2460
IP_PROTOCOL_IPV6_FRAG   = 0x2C,  // Fragment Header for IPv6  RFC 2460
IP_PROTOCOL_IDRP        = 0x2D,  // Inter-Domain Routing Protocol
IP_PROTOCOL_RSVP        = 0x2E,  // Resource Reservation Protocol   RFC 2205
IP_PROTOCOL_GRE         = 0x2F,  // Generic Routing Encapsulation
IP_PROTOCOL_MHRP        = 0x30,  // Mobile Host Routing Protocol
IP_PROTOCOL_BNA         = 0x31,  // BNA
IP_PROTOCOL_ESP         = 0x32,  // Encapsulating Security Payload  RFC 2406
IP_PROTOCOL_AH          = 0x33,  // Authentication Header    RFC 2402
IP_PROTOCOL_I_NLSP      = 0x34,  // Integrated Net Layer Security Protocol
                                 //   TUBA
IP_PROTOCOL_SWIPE       = 0x35,  // SwIPe   IP with Encryption
```

```
IP_PROTOCOL_NARP         = 0x36,  // NBMA Address Resolution Protocol
                                  //    RFC 1735
IP_PROTOCOL_MOBILE       = 0x37,  // IP Mobility (Min Encap)   RFC 2004
IP_PROTOCOL_TLSP         = 0x38,  // Transport Layer Security Protocol (using
                                  //    Kryptonet key management)
IP_PROTOCOL_SKIP         = 0x39,  // Simple Key-Management for Internet
                                  //    Protocol   RFC 2356
IP_PROTOCOL_IPV6_ICMP    = 0x3A,  // ICMP for IPv6   RFC 4443, RFC 4884
IP_PROTOCOL_IPV6_NONTX   = 0x3B,  // No Next Header for IPv6   RFC 2460
IP_PROTOCOL_IPV6_OPTS    = 0x3C,  // Destination Options for IPv6 RFC 2460
IP_PROTOCOL_ANY_HOST_INTERNAL = 0x3D, // Any host internal protocol
IP_PROTOCOL_CFTP         = 0x3E,  // CFTP
IP_PROTOCOL_ANY_LOCAL_NETWORK = 0x3F, // Any local network
IP_PROTOCOL_SAT_EXPAK    = 0x40,  // SATNET and Backroom EXPAK
IP_PROTOCOL_KRYPTOLAN    = 0x41,  // Kryptolan
IP_PROTOCOL_RVD          = 0x42,  // MIT Remote Virtual Disk Protocol
IP_PROTOCOL_IPPC         = 0x43,  // Internet Pluribus Packet Core
IP_PROTOCOL_ANY_DISTRIBUTED_FILESYSTEM  = 0x44,// Any distributed file system
IP_PROTOCOL_SAT_MON      = 0x45,  // SATNET Monitoring
IP_PROTOCOL_VISA         = 0x46,  // VISA Protocol
IP_PROTOCOL_IPCV         = 0x47,  // Internet Packet Core Utility
IP_PROTOCOL_CPNX         = 0x48,  // Computer Protocol Network Executive
IP_PROTOCOL_CPHB         = 0x49,  // Computer Protocol Heart Beat
IP_PROTOCOL_WSN          = 0x4A,  // Wang Span Network
IP_PROTOCOL_PVP          = 0x4B,  // Packet Video Protocol
IP_PROTOCOL_BR_SAT_MON   = 0x4C,  // Backroom SATNET Monitoring
IP_PROTOCOL_SUN_ND       = 0x4D,  // SUN ND PROTOCOL-Temporary
IP_PROTOCOL_WB_MON       = 0x4E,  // WIDEBAND Monitoring
IP_PROTOCOL_WB_EXPAK     = 0x4F,  // WIDEBAND EXPAK
IP_PROTOCOL_ISO_IP       = 0x50,  // International Organization for
                                  //    Standardization Internet Protocol
IP_PROTOCOL_VMTP         = 0x51,  // Versatile Message Transaction Protocol
                                  //    RFC 1045
IP_PROTOCOL_SECURE_VMTP  = 0x52,  // Secure Versatile Message Transaction
                                  //    Protocol   RFC 1045
IP_PROTOCOL_VINES        = 0x53,  // VINES
IP_PROTOCOL_TTP          = 0x54,  // TTP
IP_PROTOCOL_NSFNET_IGP   = 0x55,  // NSFNET-IGP
IP_PROTOCOL_DGP          = 0x56,  // Dissimilar Gateway Protocol
IP_PROTOCOL_TCF          = 0x57,  // TCF
IP_PROTOCOL_EIGRP        = 0x58,  // EIGRP
IP_PROTOCOL_SPRITE_RPC   = 0x5A,  // Sprite RPC Protocol
IP_PROTOCOL_LARP         = 0x5B,  // Locus Address Resolution Protocol
IP_PROTOCOL_MTP          = 0x5C,  // Multicast Transport Protocol
IP_PROTOCOL_AX25         = 0x5D,  // AX.25
IP_PROTOCOL_IPIP         = 0x5E,  // IP-within-IP Encapsulation Protocol
IP_PROTOCOL_MICP         = 0x5F,  // Mobile Internetworking Control Protocol
IP_PROTOCOL_SCC_SP       = 0x60,  // Semaphore Communications Sec. Pro
IP_PROTOCOL_ETHERIP      = 0x61,  // Ethernet-within-IP Encapsulation RFC 3378
IP_PROTOCOL_ENCAP        = 0x62,  // Encapsulation Header   RFC 1241
IP_PROTOCOL_ANY_PRIVATE_ENCRYPTION  = 0x63,// Any private encryption scheme
IP_PROTOCOL_GMTP         = 0x64,  // GMTP
```

```
    IP_PROTOCOL_IFMP          = 0x65,  // Ipsilon Flow Management Protocol
    IP_PROTOCOL_PNNI          = 0x66,  // PNNI over IP
    IP_PROTOCOL_PIM           = 0x67,  // Protocol Independent Multicast
    IP_PROTOCOL_ARIS          = 0x68,  // IBM's ARIS (Aggregate Route IP Switching)
    IP_PROTOCOL_SCPS          = 0x69,  // SCPS (Space Communications Protocol
                                       //   Standards)
    IP_PROTOCOL_QNX           = 0x6A,  // QNX
    IP_PROTOCOL_A_N           = 0x6B,  // Active Networks
    IP_PROTOCOL_IPCOMP        = 0x6C,  // IP Payload Compression Protocol RFC 3173
    IP_PROTOCOL_SNP           = 0x6D,  // Sitara Networks Protocol
    IP_PROTOCOL_COMPAQ_PEER   = 0x6E,  // Compaq Peer Protocol
    IP_PROTOCOL_IPX_IN_IP     = 0x6F,  // IPX in IP
    IP_PROTOCOL_VRRP          = 0x70,  // Virtual Router Redundancy Protocol,Common
                                       //    Address Redundancy Protocol
                                       //    (not IANA assigned)  VRRP:RFC 3768
    IP_PROTOCOL_PGM           = 0x71,  // PGM Reliable Transport Protocol RFC 3208
    IP_PROTOCOL_ANY_O_HOP     = 0x72,  // Any 0-hop protocol
    IP_PROTOCOL_L2TP          = 0x73,  // Layer Two Tunneling Protocol
    IP_PROTOCOL_DDX           = 0x74,  // D-II Data Exchange (DDX)
    IP_PROTOCOL_IATP          = 0x75,  // Interactive Agent Transfer Protocol
    IP_PROTOCOL_STP           = 0x76,  // Schedule Transfer Protocol
    IP_PROTOCOL_SRP           = 0x77,  // SpectraLink Radio Protocol
    IP_PROTOCOL_UTI           = 0x78,  // UTI
    IP_PROTOCOL_SMP           = 0x79,  // Simple Message Protocol
    IP_PROTOCOL_SM            = 0x7A,  // SM
    IP_PROTOCOL_PTP           = 0x7B,  // Performance Transparency Protocol
    IP_PROTOCOL_IS_IS         = 0x7C,  // IS-IS over IPv4
    IP_PROTOCOL_FIRE          = 0x7D,  //
    IP_PROTOCOL_CRTP          = 0x7E,  // Combat Radio Transport Protocol
    IP_PROTOCOL_CRUDP         = 0x7F,  // Combat Radio User Datagram
    IP_PROTOCOL_SSCOPMCE      = 0x80,
    IP_PROTOCOL_IPLT          = 0x81,
    IP_PROTOCOL_SPS           = 0x82,  // Secure Packet Shield
    IP_PROTOCOL_PIPE          = 0x83,  // Private IP Encapsulation within IP
                                       //   Expired I-D draft-petri-mobileip-pipe-00.txt
    IP_PROTOCOL_FC            = 0x85,  // Fibre Channel
    IP_PROTOCOL_RSVP_E2E_IGNORE = 0x86,  // RFC 3175
    IP_PROTOCOL_MOBILITY_HEADER = 0x87,  // RFC 3775
    IP_PROTOCOL_UDP_LITE      = 0x88,  // RFC 3828
    IP_PROTOCOL_MPLS_IN_IP    = 0x89,  // RFC 4023
    IP_PROTOCOL_MANET         = 0x8A,  // MANET Protocols   RFC 5498
    IP_PROTOCOL_HIP           = 0x8B,  // Host Identity Protocol  RFC 5201
    IP_PROTOCOL_SHIM6         = 0x8C   // Site Multihoming by IPv6 Intermediation
};

// These are used for the tos.precedence field.  We #define'd these
// because there is no way to enum a bit field currently.
#define IPV_PRECEDENCE_NETWORK_CONTROL      0b111
#define IPV_PRECEDENCE_INTERNETWORK_CONTROL 0b110
#define IPV_PRECEDENCE_CRITIC_ECP           0b101
#define IPV_PRECEDENCE_FLASH_OVERRIDE       0b100
#define IPV_PRECEDENCE_FLASH                0b011
```

```
#define IPV_PRECEDENCE_IMMEDIATE          0b010
#define IPV_PRECEDENCE_PRIORITY           0b001
#define IPV_PRECEDENCE_ROUTINE            0b000

descriptor Ipv4Struct
{
  bits byte
  {
    version        : 4;      // Specifies the format of the IP packet header.
    headerLength   : 4;      // Specifies the length of the IP packet header in
                             // 32 bit words, minimum for a valid header is 5.
  } bf;                      // No official name for byte, using bf for bit field.

  bits byte
  {
    precedence     : 3;      // Indicate the importance of a datagram, see
                             // IPV_PRECEDENCE_xxxxx values
    delay          : 1;      // Requests low delay
    throughput     : 1;      // Requests high throughput
    reliability    : 1;      // Requests high reliability
    reserved       : 2;      // Not Used
  } tos;                     // Type of Service    RFC791

  short  totalLength;        // Contains the length of the datagram.
  short  identification;     // Used to identify the fragments of one datagram
                             // from those of another.

  bits short
  {
    evil           : 1;      // Reserved field renamed Evil Bit in RFC 3514
    dont           : 1;      // Don't Fragment
    more           : 1;      // More Fragments
    fragmentOffset :13;      // Fragment Offset (Offset is a reserved word)
  } fragment;

  byte        ttl;           // Time to live
  IpProtocol  protocol;      // See IP_PROTOCOL_xxxx above
  short       checksum;      // Checksum of IPv4 header
  IpAddress   sourceAddress;      // Source IP address
  IpAddress   destinationAddress; // Destination IP address
} ipv4 at pib.l3Offset;      // Optional data follows as IP Options
typedef byte Ipv4StructBytes[sizeof(Ipv4Struct)];

//=============================================================================
//  Standard IPv6 Descriptor
//
//  Standard form for layer 3 IPv6 header based upon RFC 1883 and 2460 with
//  Flow Label based upon RFC 1809.
//
//=============================================================================
```

```
// IPv6 addresses have two logical parts: a 64-bit network prefix,
// and a 64-bit host address part.  An IPv6 address is represented
// by 8 groups of 16-bit hexadecimal values separated by colons (:)
// shown as follows:
//     2001:0db8:85a3:0000:0000:8a2e:0370:7334
//
struct Ipv6Address
{
//  int quad0, quad1, quad2, quad3;
  short  net0;     // Network prefix
  short  net1;     //   :
  short  net2;     //   :
  short  net3;     //   :
  short  host0;    // Host address
  short  host1;    //   :
  short  host2;    //   :
  short  host3;    //   :
};

descriptor Ipv6Struct
{
  bits int
  {
    version       : 4;       // IPv6 version number
    trafficClass  : 8;       // Internet traffic priority delivery value.
    flowLabel     :20;       // From 1 to 0xFFFFFF, Used Instead of Inspection.
  } bf;                      // Following Naming of Bit Field from IPv4.

  short      payloadLength;  // Length of Payload + Extensions (Not Header)

  IpProtocol protocol;       // Same as IPv4 Protocol, plus IPv6 Next Header
  byte       hopLimit;       // For each router that forwards the packet, the
                             // hop limit is decremented by 1. When the hop
                             // limit field reaches zero, the packet is discarded.

  Ipv6Address sourceAddress;       // The IPv6 address of the sending node.
  Ipv6Address destinationAddress;  // The IPv6 address of the destination node.

} ipv6 at pib.l3Offset;      // IPv6 Uses Nested Headers Versus Options
typedef byte Ipv6StructBytes[sizeof(Ipv6Struct)];

//===============================================================================
// Standard TCP Descriptor
//
// A common layer 4 TCP header utilized in networks per RFC 793.  TCP Options
// are varied and differ in size based upon the option header type as each may
// differ in size, often from 1 to 4 bytes.  As there are trailers to the TCP
// header, these can be developed as descriptors that sit at location
// pib.l4Offset+20 or if nested change 20 as appropriate based upon a runtime
// variable.
//
//===============================================================================
```

```
descriptor TcpStruct
{
  short sourcePort;                // Identifies the sending port
  short destinationPort;           // Identifies the recieving port
  int   sequenceNumber;            // Sequence Number
  int   acknowledgementNumber;     // If the ACK flag is set then the value of
                                   // this field is the next sequence number that
                                   // the receiver is expecting.

  bits byte
  {
    length   :4; // # of 32-bit words in TCP Header, including Options
    reserved :4;
  } header;

  bits byte
  {
    cwr:1;     // Congestion window reduced per RFC 3168
    ece:1;     // ECN-Echo per RFC 3168
    urg:1;     // Urgent
    ack:1;     // Acknowledgement
    psh:1;     // Push
    rst:1;     // Reset
    syn:1;     // Synchronize
    fin:1;     // Finish
  } flags;

  short windowSize;     // The size of the receive window
  short checksum;       // Used for error-checking of the header and data
  short urgentPointer;  // If the URG flag is set, then this is an offset from
                        // the sequence number indicating the last urgent byte

} tcp at pib.l4Offset;
typedef byte TcpStructBytes[sizeof(TcpStruct)];

//===============================================================================
//  Standard UDP Descriptor
//
//  A common layer 4 UDP header utilized in networks per RFC 768.
//
//===============================================================================

descriptor UdpStruct
{
  short sourcePort;       // The port number of the sender. Cleared to zero
                          // if not used.
  short destinationPort;  // The port this packet is addressed to.
  short length;           // The length in bytes of the UDP header and the
                          // encapsulated data. The minimum value is 8.
  short checksum;         // Checksum that covers the UDP message.
} udp at pib.l4Offset;
```

```
typedef byte UdpStructBytes[sizeof(UdpStruct)];

//================================================================================
//   Standard ICMP version 4 Descriptor
//
//   A common layer 4 ICMP header for IPv4 utilized in networks. The data portion
//   of an ICMP packet immediately follows this header and is specific to the
//   variety of ICMP Code and Type.  Additional varieties are provided as
//   well to support the common Echo Request, Echo Reply, Redirect and
//   Unreachable types.
//   Reference based upon RFC 950.
//
//================================================================================

// Used in icmp.type field
enum byte IcmpType {
  ICMP_TYPE_ECHO_RESPONSE            = 0x00, // See structure IcmpEchoStruct
  ICMP_TYPE_DESTINATION_UNREACHABLE = 0x03, // See structure IcmpUnreachableStruct
  ICMP_TYPE_SOURCE_QUENCH            = 0x04,
  ICMP_TYPE_REDIRECT_MESSAGE         = 0x05, // Set structure IcmpRedirectStruct
  ICMP_TYPE_ECHO_REQUEST             = 0x08,
  ICMP_TYPE_ROUTER_ADVERTISEMENT     = 0x09,
  ICMP_TYPE_ROUTER_SOLICITATION      = 0x0a,
  ICMP_TYPE_TIME_EXCEEDED            = 0x0b,
  ICMP_TYPE_PARAMETER_PROBLEM        = 0x0c,
  ICMP_TYPE_TIMESTAMP                = 0x0d,
  ICMP_TYPE_TIMESTAMP_REPLY          = 0x0e,
  ICMP_TYPE_INFORMATION_REQUEST      = 0x0f,
  ICMP_TYPE_INFORMATION_REPLY        = 0x10,
  ICMP_TYPE_ADDRESS_MASK_REQUEST     = 0x11,
  ICMP_TYPE_ADDRESS_MASK_REPLY       = 0x12,
  ICMP_TYPE_TRACEROUTE               = 0x1e
};

descriptor IcmpStruct
{
  IcmpType  type;        // Specifies the format of the ICMP message.
  byte      code;        // Further qualifies the ICMP message.
  short     checksum;    // Checksum that covers the ICMP message.
} icmp at pib.l4Offset;
typedef byte IcmpStructBytes[sizeof(IcmpStruct)];

//  ICMP Echo Reply structure
descriptor IcmpEchoStruct
{
  IcmpType  type;        // Must be ICMP_TYPE_ECHO_RESPONSE or REQUEST
  byte      code;        // Must be 0 for Echo
  short     checksum;    // Checksum that covers the ICMP message.
  short     identifier;  // Can be used to help match echo requests to the
                         // associated reply. It may be cleared to zero.
  short     sequence;    // Used to help match echo requests to the
                         // associated reply. It may be cleared to zero.
```

```
} icmpEcho at pib.l4Offset;      // Optional data follows
typedef byte IcmpEchoStructBytes[sizeof(IcmpEchoStruct)];

//   ICMP Destination Unreachable structure
enum byte IcmpUnreachableCode {
  ICMP_CODE_NETWORK_UNREACHABLE          = 0x00, // Network Unreachable
  ICMP_CODE_HOST_UNREACHABLE             = 0x01, // Host Unreachable
  ICMP_CODE_PROTOCOL_UNREACHABLE         = 0x02, // Protocol unreachable error,
                                                 // designated transport protocol
                                                 // is not supported.
  ICMP_CODE_PORT_UNREACHABLE             = 0x03, // Port unreachable error,
                                                 // designated protocol is unable
                                                 // to inform the host of the
                                                 // incoming message.
  ICMP_CODE_FRAGMENT_DONTFRAGMENT        = 0x04, // The datagram is too big.
                                                 // Packet fragmentation is required
                                                 // but the 'don't fragment' (DF)
                                                 // flag is on.
  ICMP_CODE_SOURCE_ROUTE_FAILED          = 0x05, // Source route failed error.
  ICMP_CODE_DESTINATION_NETWORK_UNKNOWN =0x06, // Destination network unknown error.
  ICMP_CODE_DESTINATION_HOST_UNKNOWN     = 0x07, // Destination host unknown error.
  ICMP_CODE_SOURCE_HOST_ISOLATED         = 0x08, // Source host isolated error
                                                 // (military use only).
  ICMP_CODE_NETWORK_ACCESS_PROHIBITED    = 0x09, // The destination network is
                                                 // administratively prohibited.
  ICMP_CODE_HOST_ACCESS_PROHIBITED       = 0x0a, // The destination host is
                                                 // administratively prohibited.
  ICMP_CODE_NETWORK_UNREACHABLE_FOR_TOS =0x0b, // The network is unreachable for
                                                 // Type Of Service.
  ICMP_CODE_HOST_UNREACHABLE_FOR_TOS     = 0x0c, // The host is unreachable for
                                                 // Type Of Service.
  ICMP_CODE_ADMINISTRATIVELY_PROHIBITED =0x0d, // Communication administratively
                                                 // prohibited (administrative
                                                 // filtering prevents packet from
                                                 // being forwarded).
  ICMP_CODE_HOST_PRECEDENCE_VIOLATION  = 0x0e, // Host precedence violation
                                                 // (indicates the requested precedence
                                                 // is not permitted for the combination
                                                 // of host or network and port).
  ICMP_CODE_PRECEDENCE_CUTOFF_IN_EFFECT =0x0f  // Precedence cutoff in effect
                                                 // (precedence of datagram is below
                                                 // the level set by the network
                                                 // administrators).
};

descriptor IcmpUnreachableStruct
{
  IcmpType  type;              // Must be ICMP_TYPE_DESTINATION_UNREACHABLE
  IcmpUnreachableCode  code;   // Refer to ICMP_CODE_ Values
  short     checksum;          // Checksum that covers the ICMP message.
  int       unused;            // Must be 0
// :TODO: Extend ICMP Unreachable To Include Structured Data Portion
```

```
//IpHeader    ipHeader;           // IP Header Enclosed
//byte        datagram[8];        // First 64-bits of Failing Datagram.
} icmpUnreachable at pib.l4Offset;
typedef byte IcmpUnreachableStructBytes[sizeof(IcmpUnreachableStruct)];

//  ICMP Redirect Message structure
enum byte IcmpRedirectCode {
  ICMP_CODE_REDIRECT_NETWORK_ERROR                = 0x00,
  ICMP_CODE_REDIRECT_HOST_ERROR                   = 0x01,
  ICMP_CODE_REDIRECT_SERVICE_AND_NETWORK_ERROR    = 0x02,
  ICMP_CODE_REDIRECT_SERVICE_AND_HOST_ERROR       = 0x03
};

descriptor IcmpRedirectStruct
{
  IcmpType  type;               // Must be ICMP_TYPE_REDIRECT_MESSAGE
  IcmpRedirectCode  code;       // Refer to ICMP_CODE_REDIRECT_xxx Values
  short     checksum;           // Checksum that covers the ICMP message.
  IpAddress destinationAddress; // IP address to redirect to
} icmpRedirect at pib.l4Offset;
typedef byte IcmpRedirectStructBytes[sizeof(IcmpRedirectStruct)];


//=============================================================================
//  Standard ICMP version 6 Descriptor
//
//  IPv6 introduces many new values for fields in ICMP, however, generally it
//  follows the ICMP formats from IPv4.  The icmp descriptor above applies to
//  IPv6 with only the change of code to length.
//
//  In IPv6, a type value of 0 through 127 is associated with errors.  As such,
//  ICMP Echo Request and Response is moved to 128 and 129, respectively.
//
//=============================================================================
enum byte Icmpv6Type {
  // ICMPv6 Errors messages
  ICMPV6_TYPE_DESTINATION_UNREACHABLE   = 0x01,
  ICMPV6_TYPE_PACKET_TOO_BIG            = 0x02,
  ICMPV6_TYPE_TIME_EXCEEDED             = 0x03,
  ICMPV6_TYPE_PARAMETER_PROBLEM         = 0x04,
  // 0x79 Reserved for expansion of ICMPv6 error messages

  // ICMPv6 Information messages
  ICMPV6_TYPE_REQUEST                   = 0x80,  // See structure Icmpv6EchoStruct
  ICMPV6_TYPE_RESPONSE                  = 0x81,  // See structure Icmpv6EchoStruct

  ICMPV6_TYPE_ROUTER_SOLICITATION       = 0x85,
  ICMPV6_TYPE_ROUTER_ADVERTISEMENT      = 0x86,
  ICMPV6_TYPE_NEIGHBOR_SOLICITATION     = 0x87,
  ICMPV6_TYPE_NEIGHBOR_ADVERTISEMENT    = 0x88,
  ICMPV6_TYPE_MULTICAST_ADVERTISEMENT   = 0x97,
  ICMPV6_TYPE_MULTICAST_SOLICITATION    = 0x98,
```

```
    ICMPV6_TYPE_MULTICAST_TERMINATION      = 0x99
    // 0xff Reserved for expansion of ICMPv6 informational messages
};

descriptor Icmpv6Struct          // Length Field Difference From IPv4
{
    Icmpv6Type type;                 // ICMPv6 msg type
    byte        length;              // Length
    short       checksum;            // Header checksum
} icmpv6 at pib.l4Offset;
typedef byte Icmpv6StructBytes[sizeof(Icmpv6Struct)];

descriptor Icmpv6EchoStruct      // Matches IPv4, Field Values Differ.
{
    Icmpv6Type type;                    // Must be ICMPV6_TYPE_REQUEST or RESPONSE
    byte       code;                    // Must be 0 for Echo
    short      checksum;                // Header checksum
    short      identifier;              // Can be used to help match echo requests to the
                                        // associated reply. It may be cleared to zero.
    short      sequence;                // Used to help match echo requests to the
                                        // associated reply. It may be cleared to zero.
} icmpv6Echo at pib.l4Offset;    // Optional data follows
typedef byte Icmpv6EchoStructBytes[sizeof(Icmpv6EchoStruct)];


//=============================================================================
//  Standard ARP Descriptor
//
//  The following ARP descriptor is for IPv4 protocol addresses over Ethernet.
//  While fields remain the same for other varieties, lengths of fields change
//  when address sizes change an a separate descriptor would be necessary for
//  non-Ethernet or non-IPv4 protocol addresses.
//
//=============================================================================

// :KLUDGE:
//  The IP addresses (sourceProtocolAddress and destinationProtocolAddress)
//  are not int aligned so we have to cheat to get access to these in the
//  ArpStruct by using a 4-byte structure to define them.
//
//  The user will have to typecast this field to an IpAddress
//  type to get access to the full field.
//
//         IpAddress  myIpAddr;
//         myIpAddr = (IpAddress)arp.destinationProtocolAddress;
//
//  The same goes for changing either one of these fields.
//
//         arp.sourceProtocolAddress = (IpQuad)10.10.4.211;
//

struct IpQuads
{
```

```
    byte quad0;
    byte quad1;
    byte quad2;
    byte quad3;
};

enum short ArpOpcode {
  ARP_OPCODE_REQUEST  = 0x0001,
  ARP_OPCODE_REPLY    = 0x0002
};

descriptor ArpStruct
{
    short        hardwareType;                // Specifies the Link Layer protocol
                                              // type. Ethernet is 1.
    EthernetType  protocolType;               // Specifies the upper layer
                                              // protocol for which the ARP request
                                              // is intended. IPv4 is 0x0800
                                              // matching Ethernet.
    byte         hardwareAddressLength;       // Length of a hardware address.
                                              // Ethernet addresses size is 6.
    byte         protocolAddressLength;       // Length of addresses used in the
                                              // upper layer protocol. IPv4 is 4.
    ArpOpcode    opcode;                      // See ARP_OPCODE_xxxx codes
    MacAddress   sourceHardwareAddress;       // Hardware (MAC) address of the sender
    IpQuads      sourceProtocolAddress;       // Upper layer protocol addr of the sender
    MacAddress   destinationHardwareAddress;  // Hardware address of the intended receiver.
                                              // This field is ignored in requests.
    IpQuads      destinationProtocolAddress;  // Upper layer protocol address of
                                              // the intended receiver.
} arp at pib.l3Offset;
typedef byte ArpStructBytes[sizeof(ArpStruct)];

#endif /* PROTOCOLS_PH_ */
```

CHAPTER 26

■ ■ ■

Developing for Performance

Developing for Performance in packetC

In developing data-plane network applications for modern high-speed networks, there exists a trade-off between the limits of available processing power and the requirements for increased analytics within applications. With packetC, this battle rages on and must remain at the heart of any application design. Network applications must ensure low latency and minimization of processing in every algorithm possible in order to maximize the quantity of transactions that may be evaluated. Evaluating an application not only for valid logic but also for efficiency must become core to every packetC development project.

In many cases, the computation cannot be avoided; however, the time or location where the processing needs to occur can often be changed. For example, portions of an algorithm can be computed in advance and used as a lookup table trading off real-time processor budget in return for an increased amount of non-real-time computation and memory storage. Furthermore, many network systems need to collect metadata about packets and perform analytics where the metadata collection may occur in real time, but the analytics occur in a separate computational system in parallel to processor of other real-time transactions. In each of these examples, the processing paradigm must be elevated to a system level issue.

This concept is not new and, actually, early computer systems were so constrained in their processing that lookup tables became one of the only ways that complex computations could be evaluated. In fact, many math books still include logarithm tables which are an equivalent form of the representation of processing trade-off for memory. Pages of tables are present with pre-computed logarithms for easy reference since computing them can be complex. This has been carried out for over a hundred years with sine, cosine and many other complex mathematical algorithms. Consider the difference in computing an arc-tangent of an integer without a floating point processor versus having a lookup table. This simple concept carried forward into a high performance packetC application can lead to substantial performance improvements.

While each system that implements packetC will differ in the quantity of packet processing available and the number of methods for interacting with control-plane systems, the general methodology persists in prioritizing computing resources as the primary resource to protect, such that packets processed per second may be maximized. This leads to a general philosophy that memory storage is cheap and instructions are expensive. Furthermore, the adage that one should not do something in real time that can be done at some other time also persists. Throughout this section, several examples will be used to demonstrate these concepts. In a world of high-level scripting languages focusing on developer simplicity to describe a scenario being prioritized over performance, this may feel like a bit of a step back in time. Albeit an old principle (see trigonometric table in Figure 26-1 from Matthias Bernegger's *Manuale Mathematicum* published in 1619), it is not one that is gone from the modern programmer worried about the increase in Internet data rates growing faster than Moore's Law's ability to keep up with ever-increasing complexity of processing expected to be applied against that data.

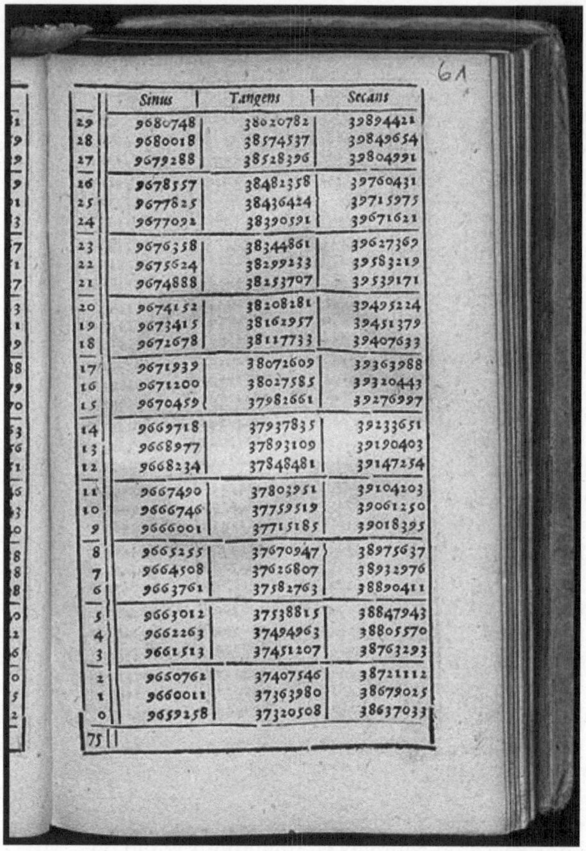

	Sinus	Tangens	Secans
29	9680748	38020782	39894421
28	9680018	38574537	39849654
27	9679288	38528396	39804991
26	9678557	38482358	39760431
25	9677825	38436424	39715975
24	9677092	38390591	39671621
23	9676358	38344861	39627369
22	9675624	38299233	39583219
21	9674888	38253707	39539171
20	9674152	38208281	39495224
19	9673415	38162957	39451379
18	9672678	38117733	39407633
17	9671939	38072609	39363988
16	9671200	38027585	39320443
15	9670459	37982661	39276997
14	9669718	37937835	39233651
13	9668977	37893109	39190403
12	9668234	37848481	39147254
11	9667490	37803951	39104203
10	9666746	37759519	39061250
9	9666001	37715185	39018395
8	9665255	37670947	38975637
7	9664508	37626807	38932976
6	9663761	37582763	38890411
5	9663012	37538815	38847943
4	9662263	37494963	38805570
3	9661513	37451207	38763293
2	9650762	37407546	38721112
1	9660011	37363980	38679025
0	9659258	37320508	38637033
75			

Figure 26-1. Sine, tangent, and secant lookup table.

Counting Bits Set

The following variations on the first example take a classic programming problem that has been used to demonstrate alternatives in performance tuning in several texts. The problem is simple: count the number of bits set to one within a 32-bit integer. While the concept is simple, the impacts on the processing cycles required to evaluate vary greatly based upon the solution path taken. The classic examples are evaluated and expanded with packetC in mind to pose some additional areas to think about when developing similarly complex processing problems.

Simplest Computation Scenario

In the first variation shown below, the simplest algorithm is used where each bit of the input value is evaluated through the use of a bitwise and. When a bit is set to 1, the counter is incremented. A couple of simple optimizations have been implemented where evaluation does not proceed through all 32 bits if the shifted value of the input value has upper bits all equal to zero. In addition, compound assignment operators are used to increment as well as shift should those have optimizations in a given implementation.

```
int countOnes (int inputValue)
{
  int counter;  // Used to count the number of bits set to one in inputValue

  for (counter = 0; inputValue; inputValue >>= 1)
  {
    counter += (inputValue & 1);
  }
  return counter;
}
```

Unfortunately, the approach above will require one iteration per bit for values with a high-order bit set. This would lead to 32 instructions per integer in addition to function return overhead.

Improving the Computational Algorithm

While the previous implementation was quite straightforward and utilizes a simple iteration of shifts and additions, it required up to 32 operations for a evaluating a 32-bit value. The following example falls out of a number of variations derived from an original Rich Schroeppel algorithm that has been refined by several others over the years. This example uses 64-bit integers, longs in packetC, to evaluate the 32-bit input value in just 15 operations. The evaluation operates through a complex combination of bitwise and operations, multiplications and divides that result in two statements to calculate the number of bits in the lower 24 bits followed by a single statement evaluating the upper 8 bits.

```
int countOnes (long inVal)
{
  long counter;   // Used to count the number of bits set to one in inVal

  counter =  ((inVal & 0xfff) * 0x1001001001001L  & 0x84210842108421L) % 0x1f;
  counter += (((inVal & 0xfff000) >> 12) * 0x1001001001001L & 0x84210842108421L) % 0x1f;
  counter += ((inVal >> 24) * 0x1001001001001L & 0x84210842108421L) % 0x1f;
  return (int) counter;
}
```

The operations result in an improvement in the processing time through an algorithm[1] worthy of a whole chapter on how it works and was discovered. Although this is a greatly improved algorithm, it still bases the evaluation upon computing with no real trade-offs for non-real-time processing.

---

[1] Rich Schroeppel of MIT originally created a 9-bit version, similar to option 1; see the Programming Hacks section of Beeler, M., Gosper, R. W., and Schroeppel, R. HAKMEM. MIT AI Memo 239, Feb. 29, 1972. His method was the inspiration for the variants above, devised by Sean Anderson. Randal E. Bryant offered a couple of bug fixes on May 3, 2005. Bruce Dawson tweaked what had been a 12-bit version and made it suitable for 14 bits using the same number of operations on February 1, 2007.

Altering the Algorithm with Memory Use in Exchange of Processing

If one starts to think about the problem of counting the number of bits set to one in a 32-bit integer in real time, and this is a systems issues and not a programming contest, there are a few assumptions that can change. First, a computer can be used to run through whatever algorithm works comparing every possible integer value to generate a table that can be used in a single lookup. At 32 bits, however, while memory is cheap, the size of a table with 4 billion entries is a bit excessive to save a few clock cycles and leads to the following algorithm which is both lightweight at only 4 operations plus highlights several aspects of packetC important in optimization.

```
int countOnes (int inputValue)
{
  union FourBytes
  {
    int bigInt;
    byte eachByte[4];
  } operand;

  const int bitsSetTable[256] =
  {
    0, 1, 1, 2, 1, 2, 2, 3, 1, 2, 2, 3, 2, 3, 3, 4,
    1, 2, 2, 3, 2, 3, 3, 4, 2, 3, 3, 4, 3, 4, 4, 5,
    1, 2, 2, 3, 2, 3, 3, 4, 2, 3, 3, 4, 3, 4, 4, 5,
    2, 3, 3, 4, 3, 4, 4, 5, 3, 4, 4, 5, 4, 5, 5, 6,
    1, 2, 2, 3, 2, 3, 3, 4, 2, 3, 3, 4, 3, 4, 4, 5,
    2, 3, 3, 4, 3, 4, 4, 5, 3, 4, 4, 5, 4, 5, 5, 6,
    2, 3, 3, 4, 3, 4, 4, 5, 3, 4, 4, 5, 4, 5, 5, 6,
    3, 4, 4, 5, 4, 5, 5, 6, 4, 5, 5, 6, 5, 6, 6, 7,
    1, 2, 2, 3, 2, 3, 3, 4, 2, 3, 3, 4, 3, 4, 4, 5,
    2, 3, 3, 4, 3, 4, 4, 5, 3, 4, 4, 5, 4, 5, 5, 6,
    2, 3, 3, 4, 3, 4, 4, 5, 3, 4, 4, 5, 4, 5, 5, 6,
    3, 4, 4, 5, 4, 5, 5, 6, 4, 5, 5, 6, 5, 6, 6, 7,
    2, 3, 3, 4, 3, 4, 4, 5, 3, 4, 4, 5, 4, 5, 5, 6,
    3, 4, 4, 5, 4, 5, 5, 6, 4, 5, 5, 6, 5, 6, 6, 7,
    3, 4, 4, 5, 4, 5, 5, 6, 4, 5, 5, 6, 5, 6, 6, 7,
    4, 5, 5, 6, 5, 6, 6, 7, 5, 6, 6, 7, 6, 7, 7, 8
  };

  operand = inputValue;
  return    ( bitsSetTable[operand.eachByte[0]] + bitsSetTable[operand.eachByte[1]] + \
              bitsSetTable[operand.eachByte[2]] + bitsSetTable[operand.eachByte[3]] );
}
```

The example above uses an array of 256 entries each containing the number of bits set to one in a byte whose value is equal to the index of the entry in the array. This table is small enough that it could be created by a simple script or even from evaluating bytes manually to include the initialization values into the application at compile time. A union is declared that maps an array of bytes onto the different byte positions within an integer such that each byte can be used as a table reference to the number of bits in that byte. By adding up the four byte values from the lookup table, the number of bits in a 32-bit integer is returned.

The key point of comparing the options above is to show how an algorithm that calls out for a repetitive sequence of analysis can quickly become overly complex when trying to improve processing efficiency. Overly complex code is not recommended as it becomes difficult to audit and problematic to support. Additionally, often by evaluating assumptions and trading real-time processing time for processing in advance not only can a more optimal solution be found, but also something that is much simpler than almost any other option.

If processing rates alone are the key measurement, further review will show that this could be improved even further by using 32k entries and using the upper and lower 16-bits as indices reducing this algorithm by two addition operations. The question becomes: at what point do trade-offs make sense and when don't they?

Metadata Analysis

One of the most common processing scenarios present in packetC is the retrieval of metadata from packets to feed analysis algorithms that generate data for either third-party analysis or even as a feedback loop for future real-time decisions. Consider the previous example as a means of showing the value of leveraging non-real-time processing, namely computation of bits in a byte, to save real-time processing instructions. If the same approach is applied to metadata collection, a number of design lessons can be discerned. The primary objective in packetC is to look for scenarios where the packetC application collecting metadata can focus on collection and either eliminate or minimize analysis. A few examples of this scenario are broken out below to highlight potential design approaches.

Netflow Record Generation

A common program that appears in several variations is the flow tracking application. The data plane is very efficient at monitoring packets to record the unique flows as well as the number of packets and bytes comprising each flow. When a flow terminates or the application determines that it should be aged out of tracking, a record is produced which can be utilized by other programs to analyze or graph network flows. The recipient applications often expect the format of the flow record packet to be in a specific format, such as Netflow Version 5 or IPDR records.

While packetC makes it simple to code the construction of a UDP packet and each of the structured field contents due to its similarity to C, time should be taken to determine whether or not formatting should be done in the data plane. For performance it may be preferable to ship the raw data collected about the flow off to a control-plane processing application which is not IO-bound to perform the conversion into the formatted flow-record.

DDoS Trend Analysis

Distributed Denial of Service defense applications often monitor the incoming packet flows and through trend-analysis highlight flows of interest for further analysis or potential rate-limiting and blocking. Instead of performing the analysis within the data-plane application, consider exporting data through the control plane such that a separate application can perform the trend analysis. A control plane application may not have the long-term database memory constraints or the CPU-bound constraints that the data plane poses. Upon completion of trend analysis, simple commands can trigger events for the data plane to respond.

VoIP QoS Analysis

Similar to the flow example, consider formatting of call data records (CDRs) in the control plane. Furthermore, metrics of calls will often need to be parsed out such that records can be tracked by user, phone number, phone type, codec, or other key metrics. Instead of parsing SIP INVITE packets in the data plane, consider snagging the entire INVITE packet, which has this information buried in the textual payload for recording along with the results of monitoring the call flow. Key fields can be extracted at a later date without the data-plane performance hit for the sole benefit of the control-plane application.

Processing Minimization

Often applications need to perform housecleaning like clearing out aged tables or performing extended tabulations. Reducing these checks from every packet to a fraction of packets is critical. Focus on leveraging background threads doing garbage collection and control-oriented tasks instead of performing the evaluations on every packet. Furthermore, if calculations are being used for rough estimations, simplify algorithms to process more efficiently. Consider counters to powers of 2 such as 128 instead of 100. Divide by 8 instead of dividing by 10 and use SHR instead of a divide instruction. Small adjustments add up quickly. Even if a background task isn't in the cards, consider doing some tasks only on even-numbered contexts. A simple approach like even-contexts checking for table management can reduce the processing overhead of the task by 50 percent.

Whatever You Do … Don't Involve Other Contexts

Don't stall the pipelines to synchronize analysis; rather snapshot and do work in the background. If an application collects a lot of metrics and from time to time needs to export them, be cautious in how the snapshot process works. One poor way is to set a lock during table export; this is bad because it stalls all other contexts from updating statistics. Instead consider approaches where a flag sets a primary or secondary table. When it is time to export the primary table, change the flag so that updates occur to the secondary table, export the primary table in one context. Upon completion, initialize the primary table such that it can be cutover to when it is time to export the secondary table.

CHAPTER 27

■ ■ ■

Standard Libraries

To get a sense of the impact standard libraries have had on C developers, try a little test. Ask a few C programmers to list ten C language commands. Use a generic word like commands that does not send them automatically down the path of operators, control statements, or some other specific mechanism in C. Some may get rolling quickly with for, if, while, and so on, but generally as the list nears eight the casual assessment will often skip operators like +, ++, *, or sizeof, and will run quickly into things such as *atoi*. The point is that it is hard for many modern C programmers to distinguish what is C and what are really fundamental features that are provided by standard libraries.

It's worse for those who have moved on to C++ where the notion of streams and the iostream standard library provide a declaration for standard input and output that is utilized with an insertion operator, "<<", or extraction operator, ">>". In C++, the standard library overloads the operators to accomplish this, in a sense redefining the language. At this point we have yet to mention anything about pre-processor macros and their role in this whole mess.

While packetC shares a lot of grammar with C, it does not share the role of input and output that are at the heart of C and C++ standard libraries. For one, the world of C was derived from a definition of input and output being with a human, where input comes from keyboards and mice and output goes to a display. While the Internet has changed this relationship in C, this basic premise has led to a migration to many other languages for web servers and browsers to provide better tools for managing a different input and output paradigm. In much the same way, packetC addresses input and output differently from C and in many ways more like a web server where the receipt of a browser request is handled by the operating system and the code for a web page starts with the arrival of an inquiry. In packetC, input and output is with machines either in the data plane on network interfaces delivering packets or to a control plane delivering events or updating referenced data sets. Given that input and output are at the heart of standard libraries, C libraries may share similar grammar but not much for applicability when it comes to input and output.

Standard libraries in C, however, are more than input and output. To that end, there are some libraries that are applicable to packetC and those are called out in this document. After extensive review, however, the notion of a high performance IO bound system contrasted with a computational system and the changes in packetC for secure code cause most libraries not to work as-is, or to not be tuned for the best constraints. For example, math functions dealing with floating point are not applicable to packetC and a *sin()* function performing calculations might be better performed as a lookup table trading off memory for computation time.

Finally, there are many libraries wanted in packetC dealing with the content and structure of network protocols that have not made it into the C standard library set nor could have since there are few standards in C for managing protocol decoding. A view into these libraries as well as tips on how to think about packetC standard libraries are provided.

Assessment of C Standard Library Functions

The C Standard Library Headers discussed in this section were based information found at Wikipedia.org, namely http://en.wikipedia.org/wiki/C_standard_library. For each standard library, a generalized assessment of Not Applicable, Partially Applicable, or Directly Applicable is provided. Generally, none of these files work without changes and as such the applicability comes from the notional vantage point of the intended functionality of the library. Those libraries that Not Applicable generally utilize functionality such as input and output that are a foreign concept to a packetC system, while Partially Applicable files are those that contain some applicable functionality and some that isn't. A Directly Applicable library generally applies to smaller files that contain only a few elements or are concepts that would be useful to a packetC developer.

Many other files may be part of what you consider standard libraries and it is understood that the following list is not comprehensive. The list below does cover a fairly large range of functionality along with descriptions of applicability that should provide the reader with a better understanding for mapping functionality to packetC. As always, refer to *packetC.org* for more information on standard libraries and access to the latest update to packetC standard libraries.

assert.h - Directly Applicable

These include files focus on defining macros that are used to test assertions and output failure conditions. While the output to a display and placing test conditions as this file does is not directly applicable, a similar approach to provide debug points for checking assertions in packetC with control plane *log* or *alert* messages could be quite useful for developers. The basic assert macros would need to be rewritten. However, they could utilize a similar syntax and have the benefit of the pre-processor-controlled removal for production code.

complex.h - Not Applicable

This file introduces a number of inline functions and structure for dealing with floating point complex data types. There is no floating point in packetC.

ctype.h - Directly Applicable

This library contains a collection of functions for checking whether a character is in a particular portion of the ASCII data set. Examples are isalpha, isdigit, islower, isupper, toupper, and tolower. Based upon platform capabilities, many of these functions are implemented in either macros or functions. In packetC, the major deviations that would come into play deal with packetC type checking and the goals of performance. In mapping these functions to packetC they would need to be mapped to bytes or byte arrays and the functions would benefit from many being macros when applicable to compile time inline functionality with others implemented as simple lookup tables for efficiency. Many macros such as *toascii* or *isascii* work may work efficiently as-is in packetC.

error.h - Not Applicable

In packetC, UNIX compatible systems errors are not relevant.

fenv.h - Not Applicable
float.h - Not Applicable

Floating point usage is not applicable to packetC.

inttypes.h - Partially Applicable

The library provides a variety of named type variations for integers reflecting bit sizes and signing. While not recommended in packetC due to possible issues with type consistency, some programmers prefer alternative naming, especially with unsigned integers being *uint* or something like *uint16_t*. As packetC is unsigned, signed integers are not applicable nor is the unsigned keyword.

iso646.h - Directly Applicable

This library contains macros defining alternative names for several operators, such as defining *and* for &&. Early variants of this standard include file should work as-is, or refer to packetC.org for a packetC equivalent.

limits.h - Directly Applicable

Every platform needs a file such as this one for defining the limits of different basic types, such as the minimum and maximum value for a long. Many types listed in limits.h from other systems may not apply, however, the basic capabilities presented are directly applicable to packetC. Refer to www.packetC.org for a packetC equivalent.

locale.h - Not Applicable

This library defines functionality for currency localization not relevant to packetC.

math.h - Partially Applicable
tgmath.h - Partially Applicable

Functionality related to many floating point mathematical algorithms don't directly apply to packetC, however, there are cases where data analysis utilizing equations such as sin and cosine are required. Applicability of a math library in packetC is important, however, the implementation and approach will definitely need to change. For example, conversion from a floating-point value found in a packet into a broken out sign bit, exponent, and significand (also known as mantissa) through a simple 32-bit packetC bit field may introduce some interesting opportunities to start performing some basic data analysis. Furthermore, implementing sin, cosine, and log functions as lookup tables as in pre-calculator days can make for some high performance analysis in the data plane.

setjmp.h - Not Applicable

This standard library typifies the ultimate in problematic code from a security point of view. Providing extended mechanisms to jump throughout an application beyond the analysis of traditional call flows violates best practices in secure coding and the use of pointers doesn't work with packetC. If you feel the urge to re-create this in packetC, you may want to reassess why you are using packetC.

signals.h - Not Applicable

In packetC a try, catch, and throw mechanism is built in for exceptions and handling the signal cases that are being addressed in *signals.h*. In addition, due to enforced handling of all exceptions in packetC, the C standard library handlers do not apply.

stdarg.h - Not Applicable

In packetC, functions cannot have a variable number of arguments.

stdbool.h - Directly Applicable

This C standard library addresses the definition of Boolean types. In packetC there is no Boolean base type, however, target platforms may define Boolean types. The cloudshield.ph standard packetC include file introduces definitions for a *bool* type as well as meaning to *true* and *false*. There is no need for an adapter *stdbool.h* as this functionality is already included in packetC standard libraries.

stddef.h - Partially Applicable

The use of pointers and functionality to determine the offsets of elements of a structure do not apply to packetC. In packetC, however, intrinsic functionality exists that can determine the offset of a field in a structure as well as within a packet using a descriptor field. Reference *offset* and *packet_offset* operators in the complex data type and packet interaction chapters.

stdint.h - Partially Applicable

Similar to *inttypes.h*, this library provides a variety of named type variations for integers reflecting bit sizes and definitions for maximum values similar to *limits.h*. While not recommended in packetC due to possible issues with type consistency, some programmers prefer alternative naming, especially with unsigned integers being uint or something like uint16_t.

stdio.h - Partially Applicable

File I/O is not present in packetC and the notion of implementing equivalent functionality to an open, read, write, and close interface is inconsistent with packetC. While packetC does not output to a console or files, there is the ability to send messages to the control plane where the implementation of a *sprintf* or *frpintf* equivalent functionality that maps to a log command may apply. Likewise, *sscanf* style processing of byte arrays may be important for extracting the contents of data found subsequent to finding with search sets.

stdlib.h - Directly Applicable

One of the most popular C standard libraries carries over to packetC quite well. That said, different portions of this library map to packetC in slightly different ways with different constraints.

- *atoi, atol, strtol, stroul*—Map to byte array analysis and conversion to integers or longs

- *atof, strtod*—Not Applicable

- *rand*—A packetC function for random() is provided in most implementations

- *srand*—Platform dependent on whether or not seed values for random() are able to be specified

- *malloc, calloc, realloc, free*—While no pointers are possible in packetC and memory allocation is fixed at compile time, there are cases where an application may need to emulate this functionality by referencing elements of large arrays through functions

- *abort, atexit, exit*—Exit is built into packetC. The others are not applicable

- getenv, system—Not Applicable

- *bsearch, qsort*—As-is these do not work, however, similar functionality on two-dimensional arrays may be relevant

- *abs, labs*—Not Applicable. No signed values in packetC

- *div, ldiv*—Directly Applicable functionality for division returning quotient and remainder in a structure

string.h - Directly Applicable

As packetC is a content processing language inspecting strings in the network, the functionality found in the string.h C standard library is directly applicable. Many features of this library are built in natively with packetC, such as direct comparison of complex types of equivalent size through simple comparison. As a result, many features such as memcpy are unnecessary in packetC. Other functions are impacted more by the notion of an array of bytes as opposed to string representations and manipulation through the use of pointers.

- *memcpy, memmove, strcpy, strncpy, memset*—Implemented as intrinsic assignment operators in packetC

- *memchr, memcmp, strcmp, strncmp*—Implemented as intrinsic operators for equality and array slicing when performing comparisons

In addition, many other features in string.h apply to packetC and can leverage built-in functionality such as the $= operator which performs null-terminated comparisons natively in the language.

time.h - Directly Applicable

In processing packets, having a sense of time is critical not only for measurement of latency but also many protocols such as email include time written in ASCII text in headers. In the packetC *sys* structure, access to granular system time in several forms is provided upon which similar functionality to *time.h* from C can be derived in packetC.

wchar.h - Not Applicable
wctype.h - Not Applicable

Addresses double byte character set evaluation.

packetC Standard Libraries

Refer to *packetC.org* for access to the latest in standard libraries for packetC. Most systems should provide a collection of standard libraries implementing many of the features highlighted in the C standard libraries above as well as those particular to packetC. The following is a highlight of some common packetC standard libraries.

cloudshield.ph—Required Platform Specific System Include (See Chapter 18)

Provides representation of platform-specific required packetC data types and structures, such as *pkt*, *pib*, and *sys*. In addition, many standard C library features can be found here, such as Boolean definitions.

protocols.ph—Common Layer 2 through 4 Packet Descriptors (See Chapter 19)

Fundamental protocols need to be processed similarly from one application or subroutine to another. A packetC standard library has been created for layer 2 through 4 network descriptors, including Ethernet, IPv4, TCP, and others.

ascii.ph—Named Values for ASCII Characters

A simple include file providing common names for ASCII characters for simple reference in applications.

limits.ph—A packetC Replacement for C limits.h Functionality

Definitions of value limitations presented in packetC implementation on the target platform or development tool-chain.

moreprotocols.ph—Named Values for Network Protocol Field Values

A simple include file providing names and values for common fields network headers, such as the protocol fields in an IPv4 or TCP header.

namedoperators.ph—Replacement for iso646.h Named Operators

Named operators include a definition of *and* that can be used instead of *&&*.

stdlib.ph—packetC Implementation of Many stdlib.h Functions

Common functions such as *atoi* and mapping of *rand* to *random()*.

time.ph—packetC Implementation of Many time.h Functions

Common time functions mapped into packetC. In addition, key library functions for measuring networking aspects such as latency are provided.

trojanprotocols.ph—Named Values for Port Numbers Trojan Network Protocol Operate on

A bit humor a bit valid reference, an include file providing names and port numbers for many Trojan network protocols.

ascii.ph - Named Values for ASCII Characters

```
//============================================================================
//
// ascii.ph - ASCII character constants for use in packetC.
//
//      Provides pre-defined constants for ASCII Character Sets 0-127.
//      Enables the rapid access to directly comparing text characters
//      in packet to a named character value.
//
// assumptions
//
//      All values defined are of type const byte using all UPPERCASE.
//      These are simply new definitions for constants.  Note that
//      many characters are not legal packetC names so all names
//      use spelled out descriptions (e.g. SEMICOLON versus ; is
//      used.)  One exception to style guide is that a lowercase of
//      ASCII a-z is provided in two variants (one all UPPERCASE with
//      _LC appended and one simply with the letter in lowercase).
//      As packetC is case sensitive, ASCII_A and ASCII_a are distinct.
```

```
//
// author
//     peder@cloudshield.com
//
// copyright notice
//     © 2009 CloudShield Technologies, Inc.
//
//=============================================================================
#ifndef ASCII_PH
#define ASCII_PH
#define _ASCII_PH_VERSION 1.00

#define _ASCII_MACROS ENABLED

//==================- START of ASCII ========================================

const byte ASCII_NUL              = 0;
const byte ASCII_SOH              = 1;
const byte ASCII_STX              = 2;
const byte ASCII_ETX              = 3;
const byte ASCII_EOT              = 4;
const byte ASCII_ENQ              = 5;
const byte ASCII_ACK              = 6;
const byte ASCII_BEL              = 7;
const byte ASCII_BS               = 8;
const byte ASCII_HT               = 9;
const byte ASCII_NL               = 10;
const byte ASCII_VT               = 11;
const byte ASCII_NP               = 12;
const byte ASCII_CR               = 13;
const byte ASCII_SO               = 14;
const byte ASCII_SI               = 15;
const byte ASCII_DLE              = 16;
const byte ASCII_DC1              = 17;
const byte ASCII_DC2              = 18;
const byte ASCII_DC3              = 19;
const byte ASCII_DC4              = 20;
const byte ASCII_NAK              = 21;
const byte ASCII_SYN              = 22;
const byte ASCII_ETB              = 23;
const byte ASCII_CAN              = 24;
const byte ASCII_EM               = 25;
const byte ASCII_SUB              = 26;
const byte ASCII_ESC              = 27;
const byte ASCII_FS               = 28;
const byte ASCII_GS               = 29;
const byte ASCII_RS               = 30;
const byte ASCII_US               = 31;
const byte ASCII_SP               = 32;
const byte ASCII_SPACE            = 32;
const byte ASCII_EXCLAMATIONPOINT = 33;
const byte ASCII_BANG             = 33;
```

```
const byte ASCII_DBLQUOTE          = 34;
const byte ASCII_DOUBLEQUOTE       = 34;
const byte ASCII_POUND             = 35;
const byte ASCII_DOLLARSIGN        = 36;
const byte ASCII_PERCENT           = 37;
const byte ASCII_AMPERSAND         = 38;
const byte ASCII_AND               = 38;
const byte ASCII_QUOTE             = 39;
const byte ASCII_SINGLEQUOTE       = 39;
const byte ASCII_LEFTPARENTHESES   = 40;
const byte ASCII_LEFTPAREN         = 40;
const byte ASCII_RIGHTPARENTHESES  = 41;
const byte ASCII_RIGHTPAREN        = 41;
const byte ASCII_STAR              = 42;
const byte ASCII_ASTERISK          = 42;
const byte ASCII_PLUS              = 43;
const byte ASCII_PLUSSIGN          = 43;
const byte ASCII_COMMA             = 44;
const byte ASCII_MINUS             = 45;
const byte ASCII_DASH              = 45;
const byte ASCII_DOT               = 46;
const byte ASCII_DECIMALPOINT      = 46;
const byte ASCII_SLASH             = 47;
const byte ASCII_FORWARDSLASH      = 47;
const byte ASCII_0                 = 48;
const byte ASCII_1                 = 49;
const byte ASCII_2                 = 50;
const byte ASCII_3                 = 51;
const byte ASCII_4                 = 52;
const byte ASCII_5                 = 53;
const byte ASCII_6                 = 54;
const byte ASCII_7                 = 55;
const byte ASCII_8                 = 56;
const byte ASCII_9                 = 57;
const byte ASCII_COLON             = 58;
const byte ASCII_SEMICOLON         = 59;
const byte ASCII_LESSTHAN          = 60;
const byte ASCII_EQUALS            = 61;
const byte ASCII_GREATERTHAN       = 62;
const byte ASCII_QUESTIONMARK      = 63;
const byte ASCII_ATSIGN            = 64;
const byte ASCII_A                 = 65;
const byte ASCII_B                 = 66;
const byte ASCII_C                 = 67;
const byte ASCII_D                 = 68;
const byte ASCII_E                 = 69;
const byte ASCII_F                 = 70;
const byte ASCII_G                 = 71;
const byte ASCII_H                 = 72;
const byte ASCII_I                 = 73;
const byte ASCII_J                 = 74;
const byte ASCII_K                 = 75;
```

```
const byte ASCII_L                = 76;
const byte ASCII_M                = 77;
const byte ASCII_N                = 78;
const byte ASCII_O                = 79;
const byte ASCII_P                = 80;
const byte ASCII_Q                = 81;
const byte ASCII_R                = 82;
const byte ASCII_S                = 83;
const byte ASCII_T                = 84;
const byte ASCII_U                = 85;
const byte ASCII_V                = 86;
const byte ASCII_W                = 87;
const byte ASCII_X                = 88;
const byte ASCII_Y                = 89;
const byte ASCII_Z                = 90;
const byte ASCII_LEFTBRACKET      = 91;
const byte ASCII_BACKSLASH        = 92;
const byte ASCII_RIGHTBRACKET     = 93;
const byte ASCII_CARAT            = 94;
const byte ASCII_CARROT           = 94;
const byte ASCII_UNDERSCORE       = 95;
const byte ASCII_BACKAPOSTROPHE   = 96;
const byte ASCII_a                = 97;
const byte ASCII_b                = 98;
const byte ASCII_c                = 99;
const byte ASCII_d                = 100;
const byte ASCII_e                = 101;
const byte ASCII_f                = 102;
const byte ASCII_g                = 103;
const byte ASCII_h                = 104;
const byte ASCII_i                = 105;
const byte ASCII_j                = 106;
const byte ASCII_k                = 107;
const byte ASCII_l                = 108;
const byte ASCII_m                = 109;
const byte ASCII_n                = 110;
const byte ASCII_o                = 111;
const byte ASCII_p                = 112;
const byte ASCII_q                = 113;
const byte ASCII_r                = 114;
const byte ASCII_s                = 115;
const byte ASCII_t                = 116;
const byte ASCII_u                = 117;
const byte ASCII_v                = 118;
const byte ASCII_w                = 119;
const byte ASCII_x                = 120;
const byte ASCII_y                = 121;
const byte ASCII_z                = 122;
const byte ASCII_A_LC             = 97;
const byte ASCII_B_LC             = 98;
const byte ASCII_C_LC             = 99;
const byte ASCII_D_LC             = 100;
```

```
const byte ASCII_E_LC          = 101;
const byte ASCII_F_LC          = 102;
const byte ASCII_G_LC          = 103;
const byte ASCII_H_LC          = 104;
const byte ASCII_I_LC          = 105;
const byte ASCII_J_LC          = 106;
const byte ASCII_K_LC          = 107;
const byte ASCII_L_LC          = 108;
const byte ASCII_M_LC          = 109;
const byte ASCII_N_LC          = 110;
const byte ASCII_O_LC          = 111;
const byte ASCII_P_LC          = 112;
const byte ASCII_Q_LC          = 113;
const byte ASCII_R_LC          = 114;
const byte ASCII_S_LC          = 115;
const byte ASCII_T_LC          = 116;
const byte ASCII_U_LC          = 117;
const byte ASCII_V_LC          = 118;
const byte ASCII_W_LC          = 119;
const byte ASCII_X_LC          = 120;
const byte ASCII_Y_LC          = 121;
const byte ASCII_Z_LC          = 122;
const byte ASCII_LEFTBRACE     = 123;
const byte ASCII_VERTICALBAR   = 124;
const byte ASCII_OR            = 124;
const byte ASCII_RIGHTBRACE    = 125;
const byte ASCII_TILDE         = 126;
const byte ASCII_DEL           = 127;


/*========================================================================*/
/*                                                                        */
/* ASCII Validation Functions and Macros                                  */
/*                                                                        */
/* The following implementation of isascii style macros are based upon the */
/* lookup table model introduced by J.E. Hendrix in the Small C Compiler  */
/* book.  The macros, table and implementations have all been changed,    */
/* however, the methodology bases itself on simplified early C programming */
/* habits of optimizations in the representation of even the most basic   */
/* algorithms and functions.                                              */
/*                                                                        */
/*========================================================================*/

/* REMOVE #define for _ASCII_MACROS at top for turning these off!         */
#ifdef _ASCII_MACROS


#define ASCII_ALNUM     1
#define ASCII_ALPHA     2
#define ASCII_CNTRL     4
#define ASCII_DIGIT     8
#define ASCII_GRAPH     16
#define ASCII_LOWER     32
```

297

```c
#define ASCII_PRINT    64
#define ASCII_PUNCT    128
#define ASCII_BLANK    256
#define ASCII_UPPER    512
#define ASCII_XDIGIT   1024


/*==========================================================================*/
/*                                                                          */
/* Each bit position within the table represents a different ASCII type for */
/* lookup.  The input character is used as an index and the #define from     */
/* above is used as a mask to determine if the character matches the type    */
/* of character being checked.  The approach is designed to be optimized in  */
/* that everything is a macro not introducing function calls, however, the   */
/* trade-off of the bitwise and, &, operation was used to avoid a unique     */
/* table for each character type, although that would have been one opcode   */
/* faster.  While there are only 256 character entries, an int is used to    */
/* represent the bits since there are more than 8 character types.           */
/*                                                                          */
/*==========================================================================*/

const int ASCII_TABLE[256] =
{
  0x0004, 0x0004, 0x0004, 0x0004, 0x0004, 0x0004, 0x0004, 0x0004,
  0x0004, 0x0104, 0x0104, 0x0104, 0x0104, 0x0104, 0x0004, 0x0004,
  0x0004, 0x0004, 0x0004, 0x0004, 0x0004, 0x0004, 0x0004, 0x0004,
  0x0004, 0x0004, 0x0004, 0x0004, 0x0004, 0x0004, 0x0004, 0x0004,
  0x0140, 0x00D0, 0x00D0, 0x00D0, 0x00D0, 0x00D0, 0x00D0, 0x00D0,
  0x00D0, 0x00D0, 0x00D0, 0x00D0, 0x00D0, 0x00D0, 0x00D0, 0x00D0,
  0x0459, 0x0459, 0x0459, 0x0459, 0x0459, 0x0459, 0x0459, 0x0459,
  0x0459, 0x0459, 0x00D0, 0x00D0, 0x00D0, 0x00D0, 0x00D0, 0x00D0,
  0x00D0, 0x0653, 0x0653, 0x0653, 0x0653, 0x0653, 0x0653, 0x0253,
  0x0253, 0x0253, 0x0253, 0x0253, 0x0253, 0x0253, 0x0253, 0x0253,
  0x0253, 0x0253, 0x0253, 0x0253, 0x0253, 0x0253, 0x0253, 0x0253,
  0x0253, 0x0253, 0x0253, 0x00D0, 0x00D0, 0x00D0, 0x00D0, 0x00D0,
  0x00D0, 0x0473, 0x0473, 0x0473, 0x0473, 0x0473, 0x0473, 0x0073,
  0x0073, 0x0073, 0x0073, 0x0073, 0x0073, 0x0073, 0x0073, 0x0073,
  0x0073, 0x0073, 0x0073, 0x0073, 0x0073, 0x0073, 0x0073, 0x0073,
  0x0073, 0x0073, 0x0073, 0x00D0, 0x00D0, 0x00D0, 0x00D0, 0x0004,

  0x0000, 0x0000, 0x0000, 0x0000, 0x0000, 0x0000, 0x0000, 0x0000,
  0x0000, 0x0000, 0x0000, 0x0000, 0x0000, 0x0000, 0x0000, 0x0000,
  0x0000, 0x0000, 0x0000, 0x0000, 0x0000, 0x0000, 0x0000, 0x0000,
  0x0000, 0x0000, 0x0000, 0x0000, 0x0000, 0x0000, 0x0000, 0x0000,
  0x0000, 0x0000, 0x0000, 0x0000, 0x0000, 0x0000, 0x0000, 0x0000,
  0x0000, 0x0000, 0x0000, 0x0000, 0x0000, 0x0000, 0x0000, 0x0000,
  0x0000, 0x0000, 0x0000, 0x0000, 0x0000, 0x0000, 0x0000, 0x0000,
  0x0000, 0x0000, 0x0000, 0x0000, 0x0000, 0x0000, 0x0000, 0x0000,
  0x0000, 0x0000, 0x0000, 0x0000, 0x0000, 0x0000, 0x0000, 0x0000,
  0x0000, 0x0000, 0x0000, 0x0000, 0x0000, 0x0000, 0x0000, 0x0000,
  0x0000, 0x0000, 0x0000, 0x0000, 0x0000, 0x0000, 0x0000, 0x0000,
  0x0000, 0x0000, 0x0000, 0x0000, 0x0000, 0x0000, 0x0000, 0x0000,
  0x0000, 0x0000, 0x0000, 0x0000, 0x0000, 0x0000, 0x0000, 0x0000,
```

```
 0x0000, 0x0000, 0x0000, 0x0000, 0x0000, 0x0000, 0x0000, 0x0000,
 0x0000, 0x0000, 0x0000, 0x0000, 0x0000, 0x0000, 0x0000, 0x0000,
 0x0000, 0x0000, 0x0000, 0x0000, 0x0000, 0x0000, 0x0000, 0x0000
};

#define ISALNUM(c)  ((bool) (ASCII_TABLE[(byte) c] & ASCII_ALNUM))
  /* 'a'-'z', 'A'-'Z', '0'-'9' */

#define ISALPHA(c)  ((bool) (ASCII_TABLE[(byte) c] & ASCII_ALPHA))
  /* 'a'-'z', 'A'-'Z' */

#define ISACNTRL(c) ((bool) (ASCII_TABLE[(byte) c] & ASCII_CNTRL))
  /* 0-31, 127 */

#define ISDIGIT(c)  ((bool) (ASCII_TABLE[(byte) c] & ASCII_DIGIT))
  /* '0'-'9' */

#define ISGRAPH(c)  ((bool) (ASCII_TABLE[(byte) c] & ASCII_GRAPH))
  /* '!'-'~' */

#define ISLOWER(c)  ((bool) (ASCII_TABLE[(byte) c] & ASCII_LOWER))
  /* 'a'-'z' */

#define ISPRINT(c)  ((bool) (ASCII_TABLE[(byte) c] & ASCII_PRINT))
  /* ' '-'~' */

#define ISPUNCT(c)  ((bool) (ASCII_TABLE[(byte) c] & ASCII_PUNCT))
  /* !alnum && !cntrl && !space */

#define ISSPACE(c)  ((bool) (ASCII_TABLE[(byte) c] & ASCII_BLANK))
  /* HT, LF, VT, FF, CR, ' ' */

#define ISUPPER(c)  ((bool) (ASCII_TABLE[(byte) c] & ASCII_UPPER))
  /* 'A'-'Z' */

#define ISDIGIT(c)  ((bool) (ASCII_TABLE[(byte) c] & ASCII_XDIGIT))
  /* '0'-'9', 'a'-'f', 'A'-'F' */

/*=======================================================================*/
/*                                                                       */
/* ISASCII - Returns Boolean true or false as per cloudshield.ph         */
/*           Follows macro function naming for sync with above.          */
/*                                                                       */
/*=======================================================================*/
bool ISASCII(byte c)
{
 if (c < 128)
   {
     return true;
   }
 else
   {
```

```
      return false;
   };
}

#endif  /* _ASCII_MACROS  */

//==================== END of ASCII ======================================

#endif /* ASCII_PH_ */
```

limits.ph - A packetC Replacement For C limits.h Functionality

```
//============================================================================
//
// limits.ph - packetC limits.h standard library replacement
//
//     Provide similar representations to those found in limits.h on different
//     platforms.
//
// author
//     peder@cloudshield.com
//
// copyright notice
//     © 2009 CloudShield Technologies, Inc.
//
//============================================================================
#ifndef LIMITS_PH
#define LIMITS_PH
#define _LIMITS_PH_VERSION 1.00


//==========================================
//============== BASIC TYPE SIZES =============
//==========================================

#define BYTE_BIT    8                      /* Number of bits for a byte    */
#define SHORT_BIT   16                     /* Number of bits for a short   */
#define INT_BIT     32                     /* Number of bits for an int    */
#define LONG_BIT    64                     /* Number of bits for a long    */

#define BYTE_MIN    0                      /* Minimum value of a byte      */
#define BYTE_MAX    255                    /* Maximum value of a byte      */
#define SHORT_MIN   0                      /* Minimum value of a short     */
#define SHORT_MAX   65535                  /* Maximum value of a short     */
#define INT_MIN     0                      /* Minimum value of a int       */
#define INT_MAX     4294967295             /* Maximum value of a int       */
#define LONG_MIN    0                      /* Minimum value of a int       */
#define LONG_MAX    18446744073709551615   /* Maximum value of a long      */
```

```
//==========================================
//=========== PLATFORM CONSTRAINTS ==========
//==========================================

#define MAX_PACKET_LENGTH        16000
#define MAX_PACKET_BUFFERS       8192

#define MAX_CONTEXTS             88
#define MAX_CONTEXT_ID           95

#define MAX_DATABASE_ROWS        512000


#endif /* LIMITS_PH_ */
```

moreprotocols.ph - Named Values For Network Protocol Field Values

```
//=============================================================================
//   moreprotocols.ph - Network protocol constants for use with descriptors.
//
//    Provide Pre-Defined constants and other definitions for the purpose of
//    simplifying of access to bit fields and other interesting combinations.
//
//    Definitions will start with PROTO and be followed by the layer information
//    such as TCP then a name for the field.
//
//    Note that many elements are specified as define statements such that they
//    can be used as a constant parameter for 8, 16 and 32 bit functions without
//    type checking issues.
//
// author
//    peder@cloudshield.com
//
// copyright notice
//    © 2009 CloudShield Technologies, Inc.
//
//=============================================================================
#ifndef MORE_PROTOCOLS_PH
#define MORE_PROTOCOLS_PH
#define _MORE_PROTOCOLS_PH 1.00


//====================================
//======== WELL KNOWN IPv4 PROTO ======
//==== These are layers within IPv4 ====
//==== Note, IP in IP not listed! ======
//====================================
const short PROTO_ICMP    = 1;
```

```
const short PROTO_IGMP    = 2;
const short PROTO_TCP     = 6;
const short PROTO_EGP     = 8;
const short PROTO_IGP     = 9;
const short PROTO_UDP     = 17;
const short PROTO_RDP     = 27;
const short PROTO_RSVP    = 46;
const short PROTO_GRE     = 47;
const short PROTO_ESP     = 50;
const short PROTO_AH      = 51;
const short PROTO_EIGRP   = 88;
const short PROTO_OSPFIGP = 89;
const short PROTO_L2TP    = 115;


//=======================================
//======== IP TOS / PRECEDENCE =========
//=======================================

// Mask off the Top 3 Bits to Get Precedence
const byte PROTO_IP_PRECEDENCE_MASK            = 0xE0;

// Use the Following as Comparisons against Byte for Top 3 Bits
// Note that Precedence is a Field, Not Bit Settings
const byte PROTO_IP_PRECEDENCE_ROUTINE         = 0x00;
const byte PROTO_IP_PRECEDENCE_NORMAL          = 0x00;
const byte PROTO_IP_PRECEDENCE_PRIORITY        = 0x20;
const byte PROTO_IP_PRECEDENCE_IMMEDIATE       = 0x40;
const byte PROTO_IP_PRECEDENCE_FLASH           = 0x60;
const byte PROTO_IP_PRECEDENCE_FLASHOVERRIDE   = 0x80;
const byte PROTO_IP_PRECEDENCE_CRITICAL        = 0xA0;
const byte PROTO_IP_PRECEDENCE_INTERNETWORK    = 0xC0;
const byte PROTO_IP_PRECEDENCE_NETWORKCONTROL  = 0xE0;
const byte PROTO_IP_PRECEDENCE_NETWORK_CONTROL = 0xE0;


// Mask off the Lower 5 Bits to Get TOS Bits Only
const byte PROTO_IP_TOS_MASK                 = 0x1F;

// Type of Service Bit Fields
// DELAY - when set to '1' the packet requests low delay.
const byte PROTO_IP_TOS_DELAY                = 0x10;

// Throughout - when set to '1' the packet requests high throughput.
const byte PROTO_IP_TOS_THROUGHPUT           = 0x08;

// Reliability - when set to '1' the packet requests high reliability.
const byte PROTO_IP_TOS_RELIABILITY          = 0x04;

// Cost - when set to '1' the packet has a low cost.
const byte PROTO_IP_TOS_COST                 = 0x02;
```

```
// MBZ - Checking Bit
const byte PROTO_IP_TOS_MBZ                     = 0x01;


//======================================
//====== IP OPTION FIELD DECODING ======
//======================================

// Copied Flag Bit Specifies Options Relationship to Fragmented Datagrams
//    0 - Option IS NOT copied to each fragmented datagram.
//    1 - Option IS copied to fragmented datagrams.
const byte PROTO_IP_OPTION_FLAG                 = 0x80;

// If IP Option Class Field is 2, it is a TimeStamp Packet
const byte PROTO_IP_OPTION_TIMESTAMP            = 0x40;
const byte PROTO_IP_OPTION_CLASS_TIMESTAMP      = 0x40;

// Mask off the Class Field
const byte PROTO_IP_OPTION_CLASS_MASK           = 0x60;

// Mask off the Option Number Field
const byte PROTO_IP_OPTION_NUMBER_MASK          = 0x1F;

// The IP Option Number Specifies Format and Usage of IP Options
// Refer to RFCs for Details.  Common Numbers are Listed:
//    0 - Indicates End of Option List.  If present, No Length or Data Present
//    1 - No Operation, If present, No Length or Data Present
//    2 - Security the length is 11 octets and the various security codes
//        can be found in RFC 791.
//    3 - Loose Source Routing
//    4 - Internet Timestamp
//    7 - Record Route
//    8 - Stream ID - Length of 4 Bytes.
//    9 - Strict Source Routing
const byte PROTO_IP_OPTION_NUMBER_END           = 0x00;
const byte PROTO_IP_OPTION_END                  = 0x00;
const byte PROTO_IP_OPTION_NUMBER_NOP           = 0x01;
const byte PROTO_IP_OPTION_NOP                  = 0x01;
const byte PROTO_IP_OPTION_NUMBER_TIMESTAMP     = 0x04;

const byte PROTO_IP_OPTION_NUMBER_RECORDROUTE   = 0x07;
const byte PROTO_IP_OPTION_RECORDROUTE          = 0x07;


//======================================
//=========== TCP FLAGS ================
//======================================

// Mask Off TCP Flag Bits
const byte PROTO_TCP_FLAGS_MASK        = 0x1F;

// URG - Urgent Pointer Field Significant
const byte PROTO_TCP_FLAGS_URG         = 0x20;
```

```
const byte PROTO_TCP_URG                = 0x20;

// ACK - Acknowledgment Field Significant
const byte PROTO_TCP_FLAGS_ACK          = 0x10;
const byte PROTO_TCP_ACK                = 0x10;

// PSH - Push Function Requested, pass data to application as soon as possible
const byte PROTO_TCP_FLAGS_PSH          = 0x08;
const byte PROTO_TCP_PSH                = 0x08;
const byte PROTO_TCP_FLAGS_PUSH         = 0x08;
const byte PROTO_TCP_PUSH               = 0x08;

// RST - Reset the Connection
const byte PROTO_TCP_FLAGS_RST          = 0x04;
const byte PROTO_TCP_RST                = 0x04;
const byte PROTO_TCP_FLAGS_RESET        = 0x04;
const byte PROTO_TCP_RESET              = 0x04;

// SYN - Syncronize Sequence Numbers
const byte PROTO_TCP_FLAGS_SYN          = 0x02;
const byte PROTO_TCP_SYN                = 0x02;

// FIN - No More Data From Sender - Finish Session
const byte PROTO_TCP_FLAGS_FIN          = 0x01;
const byte PROTO_TCP_FIN                = 0x01;


//=====================================
//========== WELL KNOWN PORTS =========
//=====================================

const short PROTO_PORT_FTP_DATA         = 20;
const short PROTO_PORT_FTP              = 21;
const short PROTO_PORT_FTP_CONTROL      = 21;
const short PROTO_PORT_SSH              = 22;
const short PROTO_PORT_TELNET           = 23;
const short PROTO_PORT_SMTP             = 25;
const short PROTO_PORT_DNS              = 53;
const short PROTO_PORT_BIND             = 53;
const short PROTO_PORT_TFTP             = 69;
const short PROTO_PORT_WWW              = 80;
const short PROTO_PORT_HTTP             = 80;
const short PROTO_PORT_POP              = 110;
const short PROTO_PORT_POP3             = 110;
const short PROTO_PORT_PORTMAPPER       = 111;
const short PROTO_PORT_NNTP             = 119;
const short PROTO_PORT_NTP              = 123;
const short PROTO_PORT_SNMP             = 161;
const short PROTO_PORT_SNMP_TRAP        = 162;
const short PROTO_PORT_BGP              = 179;
const short PROTO_PORT_IRC              = 194;
const short PROTO_PORT_IMAP3            = 220;
const short PROTO_PORT_IMAP             = 220;
```

```
const short PROTO_PORT_LDAP            = 389;
const short PROTO_PORT_HTTPS           = 443;
const short PROTO_PORT_DHCP_CLIENT     = 546;
const short PROTO_PORT_DHCP_SERVER     = 547;
const short PROTO_PORT_NDM_REQUEST     = 1363; // Peder's Mark on Well Known Ports!
const short PROTO_PORT_NDM_SERVER      = 1364; // Peder's Mark on Well Known Ports!
const short PROTO_PORT_NFS             = 2049;

#endif /* MORE_PROTOCOLS_PH */
```

namedoperators.ph - Replacement for iso646.h Named Operators

```
//=============================================================================
// namedoperators.ph - Variation on iso646.h
//
//     In C++ named operators can be used instead of their native punctuation
//     equivalents.  In packetC, these are able to be implemented through the
//     use of macros.
//
// author
//     peder@cloudshield.com
//
// copyright notice
//     © 2009 CloudShield Technologies, Inc.
//
//=============================================================================
#ifndef NAMED_OPERATORS_PH
#define NAMED_OPERATORS_PH
#define _NAMED_OPERATORS_PH 1.00

#define and          &&
#define and_eq       &=
#define bitand       &
#define bitor        |
#define compl        ~
#define not          !
#define not_eq       !=
#define or           ||
#define or_eq        |=
#define xor          ^
#define xor_eq       ^=

#endif
```

trojanprotocols.ph - Named Values for Port Numbers Trojan Network Protocol Operate On

```
//=============================================================================
//
// trojanprotocols.ph - packetC sdk include file of trojan protocol constants
//
//     Provide Pre-Defined constants for well known Trojan
//     ports.  As these change often and many run on otherwise well
//     known ports, this file is not a definitive classification
//     recommendation for protocols by port.  As such, consider
//     TrojanProtocols.ph having its main value for humor and
//     experimentation. Enjoy!
//
// author
//     peder@cloudshield.com
//
// copyright notice
//     © 2009 CloudShield Technologies, Inc.
//
//=============================================================================
//=================- START of TROJAN =========================================
#ifndef TROJAN_PROTOCOLS_PH
#define TROJAN_PROTOCOLS_PH
#define _TROJAN_PROTOCOLS_PH_VERSION 1.00
//=============================================
//==========- WELL KNOWN TROJAN PORTS =========
//=============================================

const short TROJAN_BLADERUNNER       =    21;        // Blade Runner, Doly Trojan, Fore,
                                                     // Invisible FTP, WebEx, WinCrash
const short TROJAN_TINYTELNET         =    23;        // Tiny Telnet Server
const short TROJAN_ANTIGEN            =    25;        // Antigen, Email Password Sender,
                                                     // Haebu Coceda, Shtrilitz, Stealth,
                                                     // Terminator, WinPC, WinSpy

const short TROJAN_PARADISE           =    31;        // Hacker's Paradise
const short TROJAN_EXECUTOR           =    80;        // Executor
const short TROJAN_PARADISE2          =   456;        // Hacker's Paradise
const short TROJAN_PHASE_ZERO         =   555;        // Phase Zero, Stealth Spy, Ini-Killer
const short TROJAN_SATANZ             =   666;        // Satanz Backdoor
const short TROJAN_SILENCER           =  1001;        // Silencer, WebEx
const short TROJAN_DOLY               =  1011;        // Doly Trojan
const short TROJAN_PSYBER             =  1170;        // Psyber Stream Server, Voice
const short TROJAN_ULTORS             =  1234;        // Ultors Trojan
const short TROJAN_VOODOO_DOLL        =  1245;        // VooDoo Doll
const short TROJAN_FTP99CMP           =  1492;        // FTP99CMP
const short TROJAN_SHIVKA_BURKA       =  1600;        // Shivka-Burka
const short TROJAN_SPYSENDER          =  1807;        // SpySender
const short TROJAN_SHOCKRAVE          =  1981;        // Shockrave
const short TROJAN_BACKDOOR           =  1999;        // BackDoor
```

```
const short TROJAN_COW              =   2001;    // Trojan Cow
const short TROJAN_RIPPER           =   2023;    // Ripper
const short TROJAN_BUGS             =   2115;    // Bugs
const short TROJAN_DEEP_THROAT      =   2140;    // Deep Throat, The Invasor
const short TROJAN_PHINEAS          =   2801;    // Phineas Phucker
const short TROJAN_WINCRASH         =   3024;    // WinCrash
const short TROJAN_MASTERS_PARA     =   3129;    // Masters Paradise
const short TROJAN_INVASOR          =   3150;    // Deep Throat, The Invasor
const short TROJAN_PORTAL_DOOM      =   3700;    // Portal of Doom
const short TROJAN_WINCRASH2        =   4092;    // WinCrash
const short TROJAN_ICQTROJAN        =   4590;    // ICQTrojan
const short TROJAN_SOCK_TROIE       =   5000;    // Sockets de Troie
const short TROJAN_SOCK_TROIE2      =   5001;    // Sockets de Troie
const short TROJAN_FIREHOTCKTER     =   5321;    // Firehotcker
const short TROJAN_BLADERUNNER2     =   5400;    // Blade Runner
const short TROJAN_BLADERUNNER3     =   5401;    // Blade Runner
const short TROJAN_BLADERUNNER4     =   5402;    // Blade Runner
const short TROJAN_ROBO_HACK        =   5569;    // Robo-Hack
const short TROJAN_WINCRASH3        =   5742;    // WinCrash
const short TROJAN_DEEP_THROAT2     =   6670;    // DeepThroat
const short TROJAN_DEEP_THROAT3     =   6771;    // DeepThroat
const short TROJAN_GATECRASHER      =   6969;    // GateCrasher, Priority
const short TROJAN_REMOTE_GRAB      =   7000;    // Remote Grab
const short TROJAN_NETMONITOR       =   7300;    // NetMonitor
const short TROJAN_NETMONITOR2      =   7301;    // NetMonitor
const short TROJAN_NETMONITOR3      =   7306;    // NetMonitor
const short TROJAN_NETMONITOR4      =   7307;    // NetMonitor
const short TROJAN_NETMONITOR5      =   7308;    // NetMonitor
const short TROJAN_ICKILLER         =   7789;    // ICKiller
const short TROJAN_PORTAL_DOOM2     =   9872;    // Portal of Doom
const short TROJAN_PORTAL_DOOM3     =   9873;    // Portal of Doom
const short TROJAN_PORTAL_DOOM4     =   9874;    // Portal of Doom
const short TROJAN_PORTAL_DOOM5     =   9875;    // Portal of Doom
const short TROJAN_INI_KILLER       =   9989;    // iNi-Killer
const short TROJAN_PORTAL_DOOM6     =  10167;    // Portal of Doom
const short TROJAN_SENNA_SPY        =  11000;    // Senna Spy
const short TROJAN_PROGENIC         =  11223;    // Progenic trojan
const short TROJAN_HACK99_KEY       =  12223;    // Hack&99 KeyLogger
const short TROJAN_GANABUS          =  12345;    // GabanBus, NetBus
const short TROJAN_GANABUS2         =  12346;    // GabanBus, NetBus
const short TROJAN_WHACK_A_MOLE     =  12361;    // Whack-a-mole
const short TROJAN_WHACK_A_MOLE2    =  12362;    // Whack-a-mole
const short TROJAN_PRIORITY         =  16969;    // Priority
const short TROJAN_MILLENIUM        =  20001;    // Millennium
const short TROJAN_NETBUS_PRO       =  20034;    // NetBus 2 Pro
const short TROJAN_GIRLFRIEND       =  21544;    // GirlFriend
const short TROJAN_PROSIAK          =  22222;    // Prosiak
const short TROJAN_EVIL_FTP         =  23456;    // Evil FTP, Ugly FTP
const short TROJAN_DELTA            =  26274;    // Delta
const short TROJAN_BACK_ORIFICE     =  31337;    // Back Orifice
const short TROJAN_DEEP_BO          =  31338;    // Back Orifice, DeepBO
const short TROJAN_NETSPY           =  31339;    // NetSpy DK
```

```
const short TROJAN_BOWHACK          = 31666;        // BOWhack
const short TROJAN_PROSIAK2         = 33333;        // Prosiak
const short TROJAN_BIGGLUCK         = 34324;        // BigGluck, TN
const short TROJAN_THE_SPY          = 40412;        // The Spy
const short TROJAN_MASTERS_PARA2    = 40421;        // Masters Paradise
const short TROJAN_MASTERS_PARA3    = 40422;        // Masters Paradise
const short TROJAN_MASTERS_PARA4    = 40423;        // Masters Paradise
const short TROJAN_MASTERS_PARA5    = 40426;        // Masters Paradise
const short TROJAN_DELTA2           = 47262;        // Delta
const short TROJAN_SOCK_TROIE3      = 50505;        // Sockets de Troie
const short TROJAN_FORE             = 50766;        // Fore
const short TROJAN_REMOTE_DOWN      = 53001;        // Remote Windows Shutdown
const short TROJAN_TELECOMMANDO     = 61466;        // Telecommando
const short TROJAN_DEVIL            = 65000;        // Devil

//====================- END of TROJAN ========================================
#endif
/* TROJAN_PROTOCOLS_PH_ */
```

PART IV

■ ■ ■

Industry Reprints

The packetC language was developed as the successor to proprietary lower-level networking languages through the encouragement and collaboration of a number of organizations. The goal of packetC was to not only develop an open language addressing the unmet needs for a high performance, security network-oriented language for processing network traffic, but to establish it as an industry standard. While marketplace adoption is a key underpinning of any established standard, peer-reviewed papers and formal evaluation by a standards body are also required. Since the release of packetC, numerous peer-reviewed industry publications have been released along with presentations at conferences. Additional papers currently are in different stages of acceptance. A collection of these key papers are reprinted in this Part IV. These papers provide a background rationale for the specialized features packetC introduced along with a comparison to other similar efforts in the marketplace. The following nine papers are provided in this part:

1. Introduction to packetC
2. packetC Descriptors
3. packetC Descriptor at Clause
4. packetC Databases
5. packetC Searchsets
6. packetC References
7. packetC Bit Fields
8. packetC Bit Field Allocation Order
9. packetC Virtualization Model

■ ■ ■

packetC Language for High Performance Packet Processing

by Ralph Duncan and Peder Jungck

Abstract

Increasingly, applications that process network packets, especially those that inspect packet *payload* content, need to run at speeds in the range of 1-40 Gigabits per second. These requirements encourage exploiting specialized hardware. Thus, typical approaches involve programming a specific network processor in assembly language or a C dialect that exposes machine-specific particulars so developers can closely control task switching and machine-specific resources. This paper describes CloudShield Technology's alternative approach, which combines a parallel model, the packetC language and heterogeneous multiprocessor implementations. The parallel packet processing model uses coarse-grain, SPMD parallelism to free users from thread management and it requires the host system to locate *protocol headers* in the packet before a parallel copy of the program executes. The packetC language abstracts and encapsulates familiar packet processing data sets and operations into new aggregate data types and operators, e.g., for *packets*, *databases* and *searchsets*. These language constructs can be implemented by ordinary arrays, strings, instructions, etc. However, they are especially amenable to being implemented with specialized hardware without requiring any specific hardware. Our current implementation combines FPGAs, microcoded NPUs (Network Processing Units), content addressable memories and other specialized chips.

Categories and Subject Descriptors D.3.3 [**Programming Languages**]: Language Constructs and Features – data types and structures

General Terms Languages.

Keywords high performance, deep packet inspection, network processing; programming languages, parallel processing

1. Introduction

Designers of systems that process network packets are pushed to provide ever higher performance by several factors. First, the sheer amount of data to be moved continues to increase, as audio and video data continues its march from dedicated appliance to personal computer to hand-held device. Second, the transmission mediums offer ever faster transmission speeds (e.g., those specified by SONET/SDH[1,2] and 10GbE) [3].

The need for faster packet processing is especially evident in applications that perform *deep packet inspection* (DPI), e.g., those that recognize viruses or perform *legal intercepts* for law enforcement agencies [4]. These applications not only find and analyze *protocol headers* in the packet (such as those for TCP or IPv4); they also examine the packet's contents or *payload*, For example, deep packet inspection may consist of searching the payload for the presence of a particular computer virus or other items of interest. The proliferation of malicious software artifacts heightens the demand for secure services that execute DPI actions at a time when the sheer volume of data to be checked and the speed at which the checking must be done is also increasing.

Our reaction to these pressures is to harness both parallel computing and specialized processors to do the needed packet processing. However, it is desirable to free network application developers from the mechanics of managing parallel processes as much as possible. Similarly, abstracting the details of specialized devices from the software development process will streamline the application software lifecycle, as well as increase the resulting applications' portability. With these goals in mind, CloudShield developed a general model of parallel packet processing, defined a high-level packetC language to express the model and produced a heterogeneous multiprocessor to implement it (Figure 1).

2. A Parallel Packet Processing Model

The model's overriding goal is to present an intuitive view of parallel packet processing to the developer, one in which task management mechanics are largely hidden, memory is partitioned in a straightforward way and predictable protocol analysis is performed by the system as part of setting up an individual program copy for execution.

The main structural components of the model are listed below and shown in Figure 2:

- Parallel tasks are expressed at the level of a small program processing a single packet (SPMD, Single Program Multiple Data parallelism).
- There is a 'global' memory shared by all packet programs and private memories for each program copy.
- Data stores in the shared memory capture application domain information, such as session, protocol and search term data.

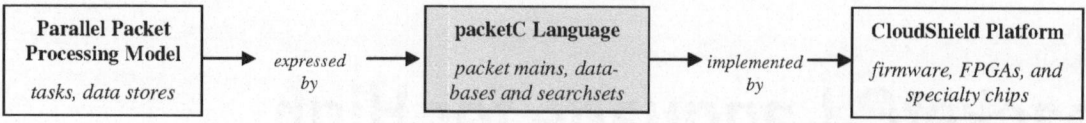

Figure 1. Relationships: among the parallel processing model, packetC language, hardware platform

- The host system manages program copies and pre-calculates layer offsets (protocol header locations) that are present in the packet.

With this model developers design a program to process a single packet, instead of designing a central program and a set of discrete tasks. Application developers rely on the host system to replicate the program, provide each program copy with packets to process and steer processed packets to the next stage of the encompassing system (or to the oblivion of being dropped).

Application developers are not involved with synchronizing individual tasks. However, some developer awareness of parallelism is required when dealing with shared data. There are three basic kinds of shared data. First, packet and session information that is of interest to multiple program copies should be shared, e.g., to recognize *denial of service* attacks originating from a particular origin. Second, program copies may have common search terms, e.g. a character sequence that characterizes a particular computer virus. In addition, users may want to manage global counters, buffers and so forth.

A key aspect of the model is its requirement that the host system prepare two things for each packet program copy before it is triggered:

- Access to the packet, itself, in the form of an array of unsigned bytes (in big endian order).

- A collection of flags and integers that indicate whether a standard protocol layer is present in the packet and, if it is, the offset from the packet array's start where that protocol information (header) is found (Figure 3).

System calculation of protocol offsets before a program copy is triggered is significant because detecting the presence of various standard network protocols (equivalent to naturally aligned C-style structures) involves non-trivial processing. Thus, the model frees application developers to concentrate on what is distinctive in their packet application, not what is common.

Using this model to develop high performance applications requires a programming language that provides parallelism at a coarse level of granularity and that can be mapped to specialized hardware that satisfies the requirements for layer offset pre-calculation. The next section describes our attempt to define such a language.

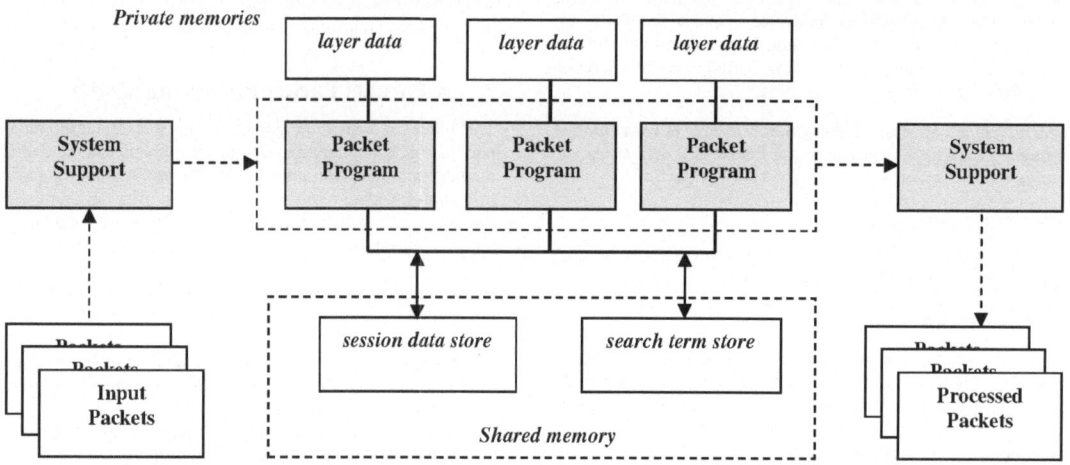

Figure 2. Parallel packet processing model. Copyright CloudShield Technologies, 2008.

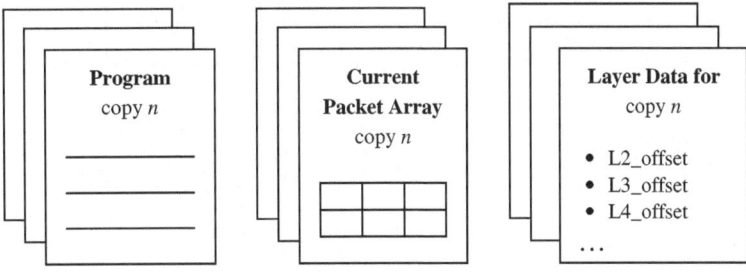

Figure 3. System-provided data for each packet program copy. Copyright CloudShield Technologies, Inc., 2008.

3. packetC Language

The packetC language [5] was developed from the following imperatives:

- Use the C99 variant of the C language [6] for operators (arithmetic, logical and bitwise), conditional statements and overall syntax.

- Avoid runtime crashes by removing pointers, address operators and dynamic memory allocation (and by using unsigned integer arithmetic that wraps, rather than overflows or underflows).

- Increase result reliability by stronger typing rules and by avoiding implicit type conversions or promotions; require explicit, readily traced conversions.

- Support the model's SPMD parallelism and its shared memory aggregates for session and search term data.

A short paper cannot exhaustively present language features, though a forthcoming Specification will do that [5]. Instead, we sketch features most involved with parallelism and optimized application performance. Those constructs and the corresponding parallel model features are show below and in Figure 4.

- Packet program copies are expressed with a *packet main* program.

- Shared and private memories are specified through a simple scheme for locating their declarations in the source code text.

- The pre-calculated layer offset information is available to each packet main in a system-provided structure, the *packet information block* (**PIB**).

- Shared session and protocol information is kept in *database* aggregates and individual *records*.

- Shared search items in string and regular expression form are represented by the *searchset* aggregate type.

These constructs are present because they address fundamental application domain needs. However, their specific form is also intended to facilitate optimizations and implementation by specialized hardware. A more detailed discussion of key constructs follows.

3.1 Program Structure overview: packet main, shared and private memories

In this short discussion we are interested in the packetC *packet module*. A simplified description of the module's structure is given below.

```
<module header>
<global decls> // types, fns, vars
<packet main>
<optional function declarations>
```

This structure is similar to C/C99 programs but has some key differences. The components are shown in example code below, then discussed.

```
packet module malwareDetector;

// global section
int trojansFound = 0; //sharedCounter
void someUtilityFn(int i) {…}
// type, database & searchset decls
// function declarations

void main ( $PACKET currPack ) {
// type, alias, variable decls
…
// body of program to be replicated
}
// optional forward decl'd functions
```

313

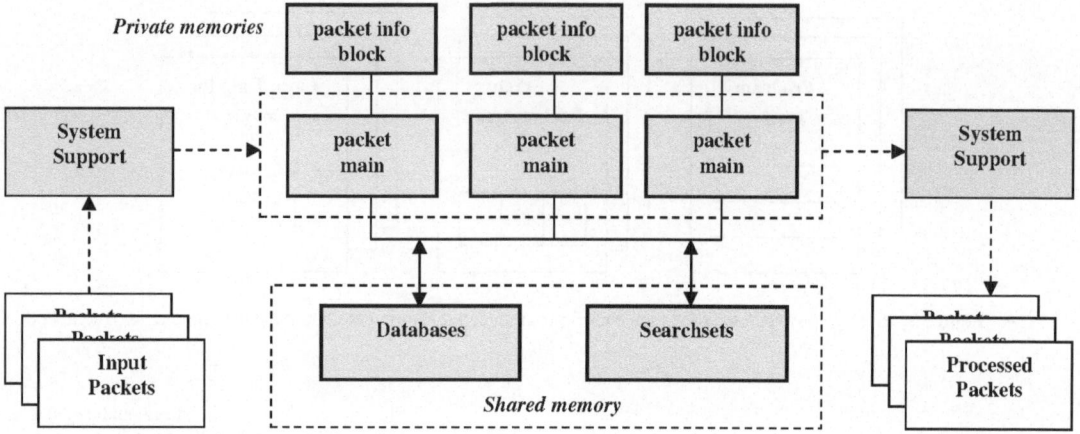

Figure 4. Mapping the packet processing model to packetC language constructs. Copyright CloudShield Technologies, 2008.

The *module header* declaration identifies whether this is a packet module to be replicated (parallelized) or one of the other module types.

Global declarations are visible from the point of their appearance to the bottom of the module text. Thus, placing type, alias or constant declarations here is a matter of arranging desired visibility. The extended aggregate types, *databases* and *searchsets*, are always declared here and shared by all *program mains*. Functions can be declared or included here.

The *packet main* is similar in appearance to a C main but it is not a true function and has the following characteristics:

- The *packet main* is the unit of parallelization. The host system effectively produces as many copies as feasible, though it has wide latitude in choosing how to accomplish this.

- Packet mains do not return values.

- Nested function declarations may appear immediately after main's arguments but before any executable statements or other kinds of declarations.

The *packet main* is the essential unit of parallel execution, but much of the domain-specific capability resides in the data structures and operations on them described below.

3.2 Shared Memory and Semaphores

Although most parallel processing mechanics are hidden from the user, packetC does provide an explicit means to coordinate parallel processes' access to shared variables. Mutual exclusion is provided by the **lock** and **unlock** constructs, which offer a *mutex* or *binary semaphore* capability [7]. The constructs act as binary operators; each takes a global variable as an argument. **Lock** returns the *true* value if the variable was unlocked and the packet main (process) executing the lock attempt has just locked the variable. Similarly, **unlock** returns *true* if the variable is unlocked, whether it already was unlocked or was locked by the

process executing unlock and has now become unlocked. A simple *spin-lock* example follows.

```
int myInt; // in shared space
…
while ( ! lock(myInt) ) {}; //spin lock
…// while myint is locked take actions
unlock( myInt );
```

3.3 Packet Information Block and Descriptors

The PIB holds the results of pre-scanning the packet for Layer 2, 3 and 4 locations. (*Layer* terminology refers to the seven network layers defined by the OSI model [8]). This data is determined afresh for each packet, i.e., for each copy of the packetC program. Thus, the location of a particular kind of protocol header may vary from one packet to another. The key kinds of PIB data are whether a given kind of protocol header is present, its location (if it is) and additional 'type' information about the sort of transmission that the packet represents. PIB definitions are shown below with omissions for readability.

```
typedef int $PACKETINFO$;
typedef int $PACKETFLAG$;
// define actions upon egress
enum int $PACKET_ACTION {
        DROP_PACKET,
        FORWARD_PACKET
};

// define types for OSI layers 2-4
enum $PACKETINFO$ L2TYPE {
        L2TYPE_OTHER = 0,
        L2TYPE_SONET_PPP = 1,
        …
        L2TYPE_802_3_802_1Q = 36;
};
enum $PACKETINFO$ L3TYPE {…};
enum $PACKETINFO$ L4TYPE {
        L4TYPE_OTHER = 0,
        L4TYPE_TCP = 1,
        L4TYPE_UDP = 2,
        …
        L4TYPE_SCTP = 8;
};
```

```
struct $PIB {
    $PACKET_ACTION       action;
    $PACKETINFO$         length;
    bits $PACKETFLAG$ {
        replica :                1;
        L3_chkSum_valid :        1;
        L3_chkSum_recalc :       1;
        L4_chkSum_valid :        1;
        L4_chkSum_recalc :       1;
        IPV6_fragment :          1;
        ...
        pad :                   22;
    } flags; // end of container
    L2TYPE               L2_type;
    L3TYPE               L3_type;
    L4TYPE               L4_type;
    $PACKETINFO$         L2_offset;
    $PACKETINFO$         MPLS_offset;
    $PACKETINFO$         L3_offset;
    $PACKETINFO$         L4_offset;
    $PACKETINFO$         payload_offset;
    $PACKETINFO$         P_destAddr_offset;
}; // end of struct
```

This information is most effectively exploited by the packetC *descriptor* construct. A descriptor is a C-style structure with a starting address that is an offset into the packet (byte array). The descriptor is essentially superimposed on the packet array. In practice, a descriptor starting address (defined by an *at-clause*) usually includes one or more PIB offset values. This lets the descriptor, which commonly defines a protocol header, vary with each execution of a packet main. With this practice, the descriptor will always capture the requisite information, as it moves to the packet location where the PIB indicates that a given protocol begins. The example below shows a descriptor.

```
descriptor TCPstruct {
    short    sourcePort;
    short    destPort;
    int      sequenceNum;
    int      ackNum;
    ...
} cs_TCP_protocol at pib.L4_Offset;
```

3.4 Databases: Types, Masking and Operations

Packet processing applications often store data from one packet (e.g., IP source and destination addresses, protocols, etc.) and consult that data while processing a subsequent packet. To handle such data collections, packetC provides a *database* type, which is treated in source code as a 1-dimensional array of user-defined, C-style structures (Figure 5). packetC implementations can implement databases with arrays, content-addressable memory, database chips and so forth. A sample declaration of a database and its base type structure is shown below.

```
struct stype { short dest; short src;};
database stype myDB[50];
```

Applications often match data in the current packet against a subset of each database record, e.g., find a database record which matches an IP source address. Associating a *mask* with database records facilitates matching only the data subset of interest. Thus, packetC databases and *records* (individual database elements) are implicitly *masked*. Given a database or record base type *s*, a packetC compiler creates a structure composed of *data* and *mask* fields, each of structure type *s*. Thus, the type for each database element in the sample code above is effectively:

```
struct newtype { stype data; stype mask;};
```

Defining masks in terms of structure fields is more intuitive and reliable than defining them in terms of long hexadecimal literals. Although the user does not have to explicitly declare the mask portion of databases or records, they must take masks into account with initialization and assignment or have all mask bits default to a value of 1.

```
record stype aRec = {{0,16},{0,0xffff}};
```

The only portions of a database element's *data* portion that is used in matches are those which have bits in the corresponding *mask* part set to 1 (see Figure 5).

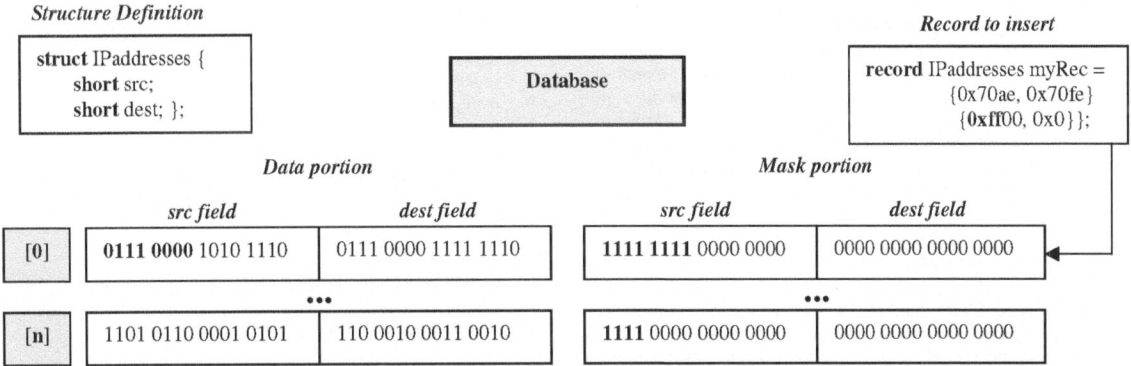

Figure 5. Inserting a record with mask bits set for part of an IP address packet field. Copyright CloudShield Technologies, 2008.

Masked database operations – creating, modifying and matching records -- create multiple optimization opportunities:

- Streamlining representations and operations when all of a database's mask bits are set or all records use the same mask.

- Managing constant mask values and mask values known at compile-time.

- Tracking the flow of mask value changes.

- Using specialized hardware for database operations.

We use C++-style method syntax for database-specific operations. Other operations (e.g., assignment, arithmetic) use familiar C operators and, when appropriate, array syntax to indicate individual database elements.

```
row = myDB.insert( aRec );// return row
myDB[3].delete();
myDB[4].data = myStruct;
// ret matching DB element idx, offset
resultStruct = myDB.match( myStruct );
```

3.5 Searchsets: Types and Operations

packetC supports examining packet content (the payload or portion other than protocols) with a *searchset* aggregate. Searchsets are syntactically similar to 2-dimensional byte arrays of strings and support matching:

- Ordinary strings.
- Regular expressions.

A searchset declaration's leftmost dimension specifies the number of strings, while the rightmost one specifies the maximum string length. Null terminators are explicitly expressed.

```
searchset ss[2][4] = {"cat","dog\x00"};
regex searchset rSS[2][7] =
       {".*?mail", ".*?from" };
```

Searchset operators, **match** and **find**, also use a method-like syntax to specify that an argument, typically the packet, another array or an array slice, will be searched in an effort to match the searchset's strings or regular expressions. For a searchset element of *n* bytes, **match** tries to match against the argument's first *n* bytes (with intuitive rules to handle mismatched size scenarios). **Find** seeks to locate the searchset contents to any contiguous bytes within the argument.

```
ans = ss.match( packet[32:35] );
ans = rSS.find( entirePacket );
```

As is the case with database operations, these operations are amenable to optimizations, especially by using firmware, FPGAs and specialized chips. The next section sketches how CloudShield maps language constructs to specialized hardware to optimize packetC performance.

4. Mapping packetC to a Heterogeneous Multiprocessor

CloudShield Technologies produces a family of heterogeneous multiprocessors for high-performance network packet processing, for example, the CS-2000 [9]. The hardware particulars are the object of both granted and ongoing patent activities; not all architectural details are made public. Thus, the intent of this section is to maintain trade secrets while imparting enough information to give the reader a sense of how packetC constructs can be implemented to deliver high performance. The general hardware mapping is indicated by Figure 6. Implementation highlights are as follows:

- FPGAs and microcode running on a dedicated subset of NPU (Network Processing Unit) *cores* control the packet pipeline, analyze the packet and pre-locate protocol headers.

- An ensemble of NPU cores, each running multiple *contexts,* executes the program copies and dedicated system programs (see below). Although past products have dedicated as many as 288 contexts to running user programs, the current, faster NPUs employ 88 user program contexts. Forthcoming products will employ more than a thousand.

- Commodity memories provide the processing ensemble with memory for variables and aggregates local to a packet main program.

- A custom FPGA and DRAM provide the shared memory for scalars and C-style aggregates.

- packetC databases are mapped to commercial T-CAM (Ternary Content Addressable Memory) chips with NPU microcode implementing complex database instructions.

- Searchsets are implemented in several ways, e.g., by using specialized regular expression processor chips and dedicated NPU cores to implement search instructions.

Allocating packetC functionality to specialized processors and memories plays an essential role in achieving high performance. Orchestrating this diverse ensemble is also critical. However, what distinguishes packetC from similar packet processing languages is not that specialized devices are involved in fielded applications but how the machine specifics are hidden in the language. With that in mind, the next section reviews other approaches to programming languages for high performance network applications.

5. Related Work

Recent research and commercial efforts include a variety of efforts to develop programming languages that support high performance network packet processing applications.

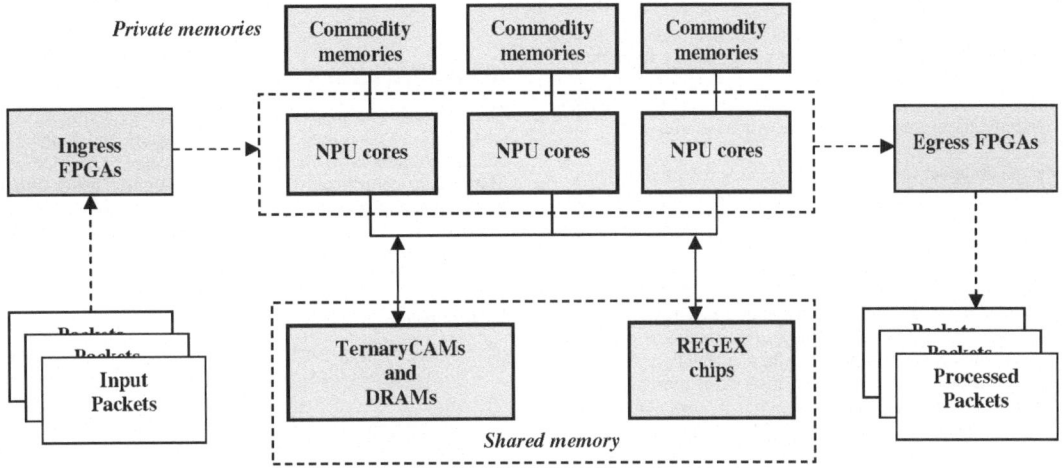

Figure 6. Mapping packetC language constructs to physical components. Copyright CloudShield Technologies, 2009.

In [10] L. George and M. Blume present the NOVA language and compiler for the IXP network processor. NOVA features include aggregates in the form of *records* and *tuples*, familiar control-flow constructs, functions and exceptions. NOVA and packetC share an aversion to run-time memory allocation: both omit C-style *malloc* functionality or recursive functions. The language does allow mutual dependencies "but all recursive calls are restricted to be in tail-call position" [10]. However, like most network programming systems, NOVA does not presume that the host system finds network protocol headers before a program runs. Instead, it provides a *layout* construct to provide bitfield capabilities useful for finding and manipulating headers in the packet.

Intel Corporation's *Microengine C* is targeted to the IXP1200 chip [11]. This is a C dialect with domain-driven omissions (floating-point type, function pointers or runtime stack) and many extensions. The IXP architecture features a general-purpose processor and six *microengines*, RISC processors optimized for packet processing. The processing model is a threading model; programs are broken into multiple threads that are partitioned across multiple microengines. The user manages communications among threads and processes and typically swaps out a task that reads from or writes to memory. Microengine C reflects machine-specific memory classes, FIFOs and register classes. The language provides an extensive battery of intrinsics and support for *inlining* that facilitates exploiting the architecture.

NetPDL (Network Protocol Description Language) [12, 13] is an XML-based language aimed at developing a database of standard network protocols, i.e., header descriptions for standard protocols. The designers seem primarily interested in providing a reusable repository of protocol definitions, rather than in defining an application language, although the language does include provisions for expressions and application development.

J. Wagner and R. Leupers discuss a C dialect and its compiler for the Infineon network processor [14]. The key language extensions provide the capability to manipulate protocol headers by mapping parts of the packet to special registers and accessing arbitrary bit-width operands without the usual alignment restrictions. The compiler maps C arrays with the *register* qualifier to a special register file. By using an Infineon bit-field pointer and bit-width arguments, the programmer can specify operands within the register file that have arbitrary sizes and alignments, including those that span more than one register. Compiler *intrinsics* (*compiler-known functions*) are the key language extension that grants users access to these capabilities at a high language level.

CUDA is a parallel processing architecture for programming NVIDIA graphics processing units (GPUs) [15]. Although it is targeted to computer game processing (e.g., image texture rendering), it has been used for other kinds of application as well. CUDA is designed for executing a large number of program *threads* in a fine-grained parallel fashion. Threads are organized into independent *thread blocks*, which share memory and synchronization barriers. Because of the overhead of transferring data into the GPUs, this approach encourages executing as many instructions as possible for each memory access. The language reflects the NVIDIA GPU hardware, organized as a set of SIMD multiprocessors with shared memory.

None of these languages share packetC's requirement for system-furnished protocol location, although NOVA and the Infineon C dialect facilitate user protocol location. Whereas packetC uses coarse-grain, SPMD parallelism, other languages use very fine-grain parallelism, e.g., Microengine C and CUDA. Other approaches often expose a specific machine's registers or memory organization, where packetC defines functional entities, such as *databases* and *searchsets*, which are amenable to specialized hardware implementation without requiring any specific one.

6. Status and Future Research

We have developed a cross-compiler for packetC that runs under both Windows and Linux and targets several CloudShield products. The compiler implements all the major extensions to C but has some gaps. Testing and use status is as follow:

- The prototype compiler passes more than 1800 custom language validation tests.

- The compiler passes a collection of domain-specific tests, handling access control lists and recognizing a large number of standard protocol headers.

- Selected users are experimenting with a beta-release.

Since the compiler is immature, we plan substantial enhancements for both classic and domain-specific optimizations. The two major data type extensions, *databases* and *searchsets*, offer significant possibilities for further optimization. Database masking can be optimized by managing predictable kinds of masks (e.g., with all bits set, with one or two statically-defined user masks), as well as by tracking how dynamic mask values are assembled. *Searchset* operations are also a rich source of potential optimization, such as using alternative implementation strategies based on the characteristics of the searchset or of searchset arguments (such as array slices) that are determined at run-time. Our efforts will be geared to both classic flow analysis and on the possibilities offered by a heterogeneous multiprocessing platform.

7. Summary

At the level of individual language constructs, databases and searchsets are natural extensions for packet processing in general and deep packet inspection in particular. However, the most promising language construct may be the *descriptor* feature, which effectively lets protocol headers automatically move to the relevant location in each packet. Rather than search a large byte array or buffer for the headers, the user defines structures that 'float' to the correct location without user intervention. Moreover, by linking successive *descriptor* at-clause addresses, the user can readily build a protocol header stack.

Ultimately, packetC's contributions to the packet processing language spectrum revolve around how it treats machine specifics. Instead of being geared to a single specialized processor (e.g., by offering language extensions that reveal a network processor's register groups, FIFOs, etc.), the model and language view the system as a collection of specialized components. Thus, the language hides specific processor characteristics not as a conceptual nicety but because the model and language view the system as:

- A collection of many different specialized components. Thus, no one component receives privileged treatment to expose its specifics for programmer manipulation.

- An ensemble of changeable components. Implicit in this world-view is the notion that any particular component (i.e., a chip currently providing database or string-matching services) is apt to be changed.

Thus, packetC and its parent model embody a dynamic perspective of packet processing systems: one where systems are composed of highly specialized devices that may be replaced at any time. A major benefit of this approach is the opportunity to develop high performance, real-time packet applications that do not require sweeping recoding when different hardware components are introduced.

Acknowledgments

This research was supported by US Air Force contract FA 7037-04-C-0011. Peder Jungck, Dwight Mulcahy and Ralph Duncan are the co-authors of the packetC language. Gary Oblock and Matt White contributed to language and compiler development. Andy Norton, Kenneth Ross, Kai Chang, Mary Pham, Alfredo Chorro-Rivas and Minh Nguyen provided valuable help. Professors Rajiv Gupta and Rainer Leupers contributed citations and papers. Detailed referee comments were especially helpful.

References

[1] ANSI T1.105: SONET - Basic Description including Multiplex Structure, Rates and Formats.

[2] ANSI T1.119/ATIS PP 0900119.01.2006: SONET - Operations, Administration, Maintenance, and Provisioning (OAM&P) - Communications.

[3] IEEE Std 802.3ae-2002. To be superseded by more recent but not finalized IEEE Std 802.3-2008.

[4] N. Anderson, Deep packet inspection meets 'Net neutrality, CALEA. July 25, 2007, retrieved on January 16, 2009 from http://arstechnica.com/articles/culture/Deep-packet-inspection-meets-net-neutrality.ars .

[5] CloudShield Technologies. "packetC Programming Language Specification. Rev. 1.128, October 10, 2008.

[6] ISO/IEC 9899:1999. Standard for the C programming language. May 2005 version. ('C99').

[7] M. Raynal, A simple taxonomy for distributed mutual exclusion algorithms. ACM SIGOPS Operating Systems Review, 25(2), 47-50, 1991.

[8] International Organization for Standardization (ISO) 7498. Open Systems Interconnections (OSI) reference model, 1983.

[9] CloudShield Technologies. CS-2000 Technical Specifications. Product datasheet available from CloudShield Technologies, 212 Gibraltar Dr., Sunnyvale, CA, USA 94089, 2006.

[10] L. George and M. Blume. Taming the IXP network processor. In *Proceedings of the ACM SIGPLAN '03 Conference on Programming Language Design and Implementation*, San Diego, California, USA, ACM, pp. 26-37, June 2003.

[11] Intel Microengine C Compiler Language Support: Reference Manual. Intel Corporation, order number 278426-004, August 10, 2001.

[12] NetPDL Core Specification, NetBee. Retrieved from www.nbee.org/doku.php?id=netpdl:core_specs on 01/07/2009.

[13] F. Risso and M. Baldi. NetPDL: an extensible XML-based language for packet header description. In Computer Networks. The International Journal of Computer and Telecommunications Networking, 50(5), 2006.

[14] J. Wagner and R. Leupers: C compiler design for a network processor. IEEE Trans. On CAD, 20(11): 1-7, 2001.

[15] NVIDIA Corporation. NVIDIA CUDA Compute Unified Device Architecture: Programming Guide. Version 1.0, June 23, 2007.

R. Duncan and P. Jungck. "packetC language for high performance packet processing." *In Proceedings of the 11th IEEE Intl. Conf. High Performance Computing and Communications,* (Seoul, South Korea), pp. 450–457, June 25–27, 2009. Reprinted with permission from Springer Science+Business Media.

A Paradigm for Processing Network Protocols in Parallel

by Ralph Duncan, Peder Jungck and Kenneth Ross

Abstract

Network p acket processin g ap plications in creasingly execute at speeds of 1-40 gi gabits p er se cond, o ften r unning
on m ulti-core chips th at co ntain m ultithreaded n etwork
processing u nits (NP Us) and a g eneral-purpose processor
core. Such applications are typically programmed in a language that exposes NPU specifics needed to optim ize low-
level thread control and resources. This facilitates optim i-
zation at th e co st of in creased software co mplexity and r e-
duced portab ility. In co ntrast, ou r ap proach provides
portability by combining co arse-grained parallelism w ith
programming in the packetC® (CloudShield T echnologies)
language's high-level co nstructs. T his pap er f ocuses on
searching packet contents for *packet protocol headers*. We
require the host system to locate headers for layers 2, 3 and
4, and to enco de their offsets in a *packet information block*
(PIB). pack etC prov ides *descriptors,* C-style stru ctures
superimposed on th e pack et array at runtime-calculable,
user or P IB-supplied of fsets. W e deliv er state -of-the-
practice performance via an FPGA for locating layer offsets
and via micro-coded interpretation th at treats P IB lay er
offsets as a special addressing mode.

Categories and Subject Descriptors D.3.3 [**Programming Languages**]: L anguage Co nstructs and Features —
data types and structures

General Terms L anguages.

Keywords prog ramming languages; packetC, network
processing, parallel processing

1. Introduction

Pressure for faster n etwork packet processing continues to
increase as transmission mediums become faster (e.g., those
specified by SONET/SDH [2, 3] and 10Gb E [4]) of fer
speeds in the 10-40 gigabits per second (Gbps) range) and
the v olume of data to be transm itted co ntinues its ow n r e-
lentless increase.

Packets co ntain *protocol headers* f or co mmunications
standards, su ch as IP v4. A h eader is a co ntiguous set of
fields with routing, serv ice and standards data. Man y protocols exist, each w ith dis tinctive co ntent. Sin ce m ultiple
headers may be presen t and si nce their relative of fset from

the packet's start may vary from packet to packet, a key
aspect of pack et processin g is to deter mine which headers
are present and where they are.

Header searching is a common task for network applications, w hich ty pically ru n in a m ultithreaded env ironment
where th ey are partition ed in to lig ht-weight th reads th at
swap themselves out f or each m emory access. T his pr o-
gramming sty le exploits low -level m achine features to o p-
timize perf ormance. Ho wever, th e resulting machine-
specific co de can req uire exte nsive red esign and recoding
when the application is ported.

2. Our Approach and Contributions

Our ap proach to pack et processing as a whole has three
major elements: a m odel of parallel pack et processin g, a
specialized language to express the model and an ensem ble
of heterogeneous processors to implement the language. In
this pap er, w e f ocus on f eatures in all three that are involved in header processing.

The model's key characteristics for protocol processing
are as follows:

- Task granularity is at th e level of a co mplete pr o-
  gram that processes a packet. Thus, the model's parallelism embodies the Single Program Multiple Data
  (SPMD) paradigm).
- The host system locates protocol headers in a packet before a copy of the program i s executed on th at
  packet.
- Each prog ram copy works w ith a current pack et
  and system-provided data on th e presen ce and loc a-
  tion of *layer offsets*.

This model is expressed through packetC [5], a C-style
language that takes C99 [6] as its point of departure and
provides features for packet operations and protocol header
processing:

- Each program copy works on a single packet stored
  as a by te array in *big endian* order (matches *network
  order*).

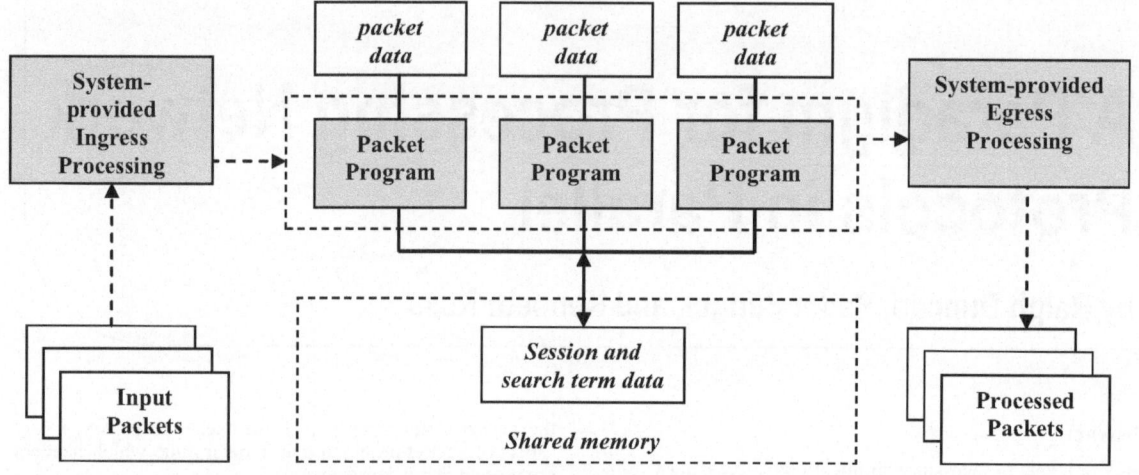

Figure 1. A parallel packet processing model.

- The protoco l in formation pred etermined by th e sys-tem, su ch as lay er location s and protoco l f lags, is provided in a C-style structure, termed the *packet in-formation block* (PIB).
- Protocols can be represented b y a *descriptor*, a sp e-cial k ind of stru cture th at is su perimposed on the packet at a user-specified, *runtime-calculable* o ffset location.
- packetC redefines structure *bitfields* in a m anner cal-culated to remove ambiguity and to allow descriptors to ov erlay protoco l f ields w ith n on-standard bit widths in a predictable fashion..

Finally, im plementation s upport for header processing includes using an FP GA to pred etermine the presen ce and offsets of L2, L3 and L 4 headers. T hus, we mitigate fore-going th read-level parallelism f or protoco l h eader processing by executing optimized h eader processing on a dedicated processor, w hile m icro-coded in terpreters on NPUs ar e r unning o ther ap plication task s in end-to-end fashion on each packet. The next section presents the mod-el in more detail.

3. A Parallel Packet Processing Model

The m odel prov ides an in tuitive v iew of parallel pack et processing to the developer, one in which task management mechanics are h idden, memory is partition ed in a straightforward way and protocol detection and analysis are performed by the system as pa rt of setting up each exec u-tion run of a program copy.

The principal aspects of the model (Fig. 1) are listed be-low:

- Concurrency is provided by co pies of a sm all pr o-gram that each co mpletely process on e pack et each time they are run.

- A 'global' memory is shared by all the program cop-ies and private memories for each program copy.
- The h ost sy stem m anages th e prog ram co pies and routes packets to and from program copies.
- The host system ensures that a program copy has two kinds of pre-processed data when it is triggered for a packet (Fig. 2).
- A copy of the packet, itself, in the form of an array of unsigned bytes (in big endian order).
- A collection of values that indicate whether protocol headers for network layers [7] 2, 3 and 4 are presen t in the packet and, if they are, where they are located (in term s of offsets from the packet array's start.). These values are assem bled in a pack et in formation block (PIB), alo ng w ith check sum in formation and protocol type information.

In this paper we are most interested in the model's re-quirements for the host system to pred etermine certain pro-tocol lay er of fsets and assem ble th em in th e P IB. Operations to determine protocol headers' presence and their offsets could be done v ia ru n-time s upport s oftware routines. Ho wever, requiring the host to perform this func-tion facilitates u sing a sp ecialized processor or *offload en-gine* dedicated to ef fectively perf orming th is f unction. Much of the PIB data's usefulness is a consequence of how its lay er offset v alues can be used w ith pack etC descriptor constructs and h ow th e implementation rapidly fetches packet data v ia th ose of fset v alues. T he n ext section sketches the packetC language as a whole.

4. pack etC Language Overview

The pack etC lang uage's [1] high-level characteristics i n-clude.

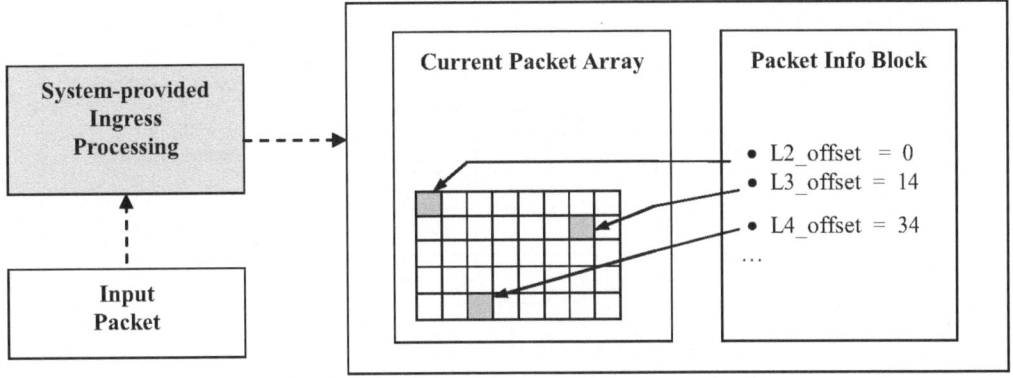

Figure 2. System-calculated protocol layer offsets for a packetC program copy.

- Emphasizing strong typing by removing implicit type casts, coercions or promotion,
- Promoting real-time reliability by eliminating dynamic memory allocation, as well as pointer and address manipulations,
- Using a C-style program *main* as the unit of SPMD parallelism,
- Providing extended data types and operators to support classic packet-processing capabilities, such as matching masked database and searching for packet payload contents that match user-defined strings and regular expressions.

For high-speed protocol processing, these language features are most relevant:

- Presenting the PIB information in the form of a C-style structure,
- Providing a descriptor construct that superimposes a C-style definition of a protocol header on the packet array at a user-specified offset expression (which may contain a PIB offset value and runtime-variable calculations),
- Defining a *container*-based alternative to C-style *bit fields* to ensure that protocol header structures will match corresponding data in the packet byte array.

These elements are discussed in detail below.

5. The PIB as C-style Structure

A key aspect of the PIB's header offset values for network layers 2, 3 and 4 is that these values are determined afresh for each packet, i.e., each time a parallel copy of the packetC main program is executed. Thus, the results are always packet-specific, since the location of a particular kind of protocol header may vary from one packet to another. The PIB definitions are shown below with some omissions for readability

```
typedef int $PACKETINFO$;
typedef int $PACKETFLAG$;
```

```
enum int $PACKET_ACTION {   DROP_PACKET,
                            FORWARD_PACKET};
enum $PACKETINFO$ L2TYPE {  L2TYPE_OTHER = 0,
                            L2TYPE_SONET_PPP = 1,… };
enum $PACKETINFO$ L3TYPE {…};
enum $PACKETINFO$ L4TYPE {
            L4TYPE_OTHER = 0,
            L4TYPE_TCP = 1,
            L4TYPE_UDP = 2,
            …
            L4TYPE_SCTP = 8;
};
struct $PIB {
    $PACKET_ACTION    action;
    $PACKETINFO$      length;
    bits $PACKETFLAG$ {
                replica :              1;
                L3_chkSum_valid :      1;
                L3_chkSum_recalc :     1;
                L4_chkSum_valid :      1;
                …
                pad :                 22;
    } flags; // end of bits container
            L2TYPE          L2_type;
            L3TYPE          L3_type;
            L4TYPE          L4_type;
            $PACKETINFO$    L2_offset;
            $PACKETINFO$    MPLS_offset;
            $PACKETINFO$    L3_offset;
            $PACKETINFO$    L4_offset;
            $PACKETINFO$    payload_offset;
            $PACKETINFO$    P_destAddr_offset;
}    pib; // end of struct
```

The PIB provides packetC applications with easily accessed information about whether given protocols exist and (if they do) where they are. To exploit that information, applications must be able to define those protocol headers and apply those definitions to the packet array where the data resides. packetC provides this capability through the descriptor construct described below.

321

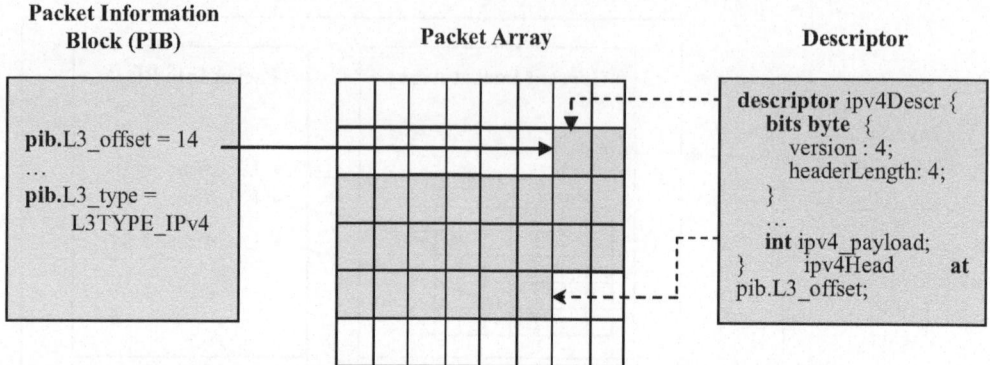

Figure 3. Positioning descriptors on the basis of header offset values in the PIB.

6. The Descriptor Construct

packetC's *descriptor* co nstruct is a stru cture th at corres-ponds to a portion of th e packet array with the same size. In a sense, it is an *alias* for an *array-slice* within the packet.

```
descriptor typeTagName {
    short   source;
    short   dest;
} descripName at offsetExpression;
```

A descriptor declaration co nsists of its stru cture base type, its n ame and its location – an in teger expression that defines the descriptor's starting point in terms of an index into th e pack et array. This location specif ication, or *at-clause*, may contain th ree k inds of elem ents: co mpile-time constants, variables with values known only at run-time and PIB layer-offset fields.

By combining a descriptor's structure definitions with an offset location based on a P IB lay er of fset v alue w e can create a precise, h igh-level descrip tor of a protoco l h eader that gravitates to the correct packet array location each time a new packet is prepared for a packetC program (Fig. 3).

```
descriptor ipv4Descr {
    bits byte  {
        version : 4;
        headerLength: 4;
    }
    byte    typeOfService;
    short   totalLength;
    short   ipv4_identification;
    short   ipv4_fragmentOffset;
    byte    ipv4_ttl;
    byte    ipv4_protocol;
    short   ipv4_checksum;
    int     ipv4_sourceAddress;
    int     ipv4_destAddress;
    int     ipv4_payload;
} ipv4Header at pib.L3_offset;
```

Consider the IP v4 protocol shown ab ove. First, the de-scriptor defines a stru cture th at m atches th e f ields of an IPv4 header. The at-clause then states that it will always be found at the packet's layer 3 offset (when a valid layer 3 header is present).

Descriptor at-clauses can be co nstant or ru n-time deter-mined, simple or arbitrarily co mplex. Com plex at -clause expressions are especially relev ant w hen th e start of one header depends on the presence of optional fields in a pre-ceding header. For exam ple, if we did not provide Layer 4 offsets, it would be possible to calculate them in terms of an IPv4 Layer 3 header as follows:

```
descriptor layer4Descr {
    ...
} layer4header at pib.L3_offset +
  ( ipv4header.headerLength * 4 );
```

The next section presents the model in more detail. The descriptor construct is useful for describing a *stack* of pro-tocols, i.e., a seq uence of consecutive protocol headers that appear in a packet as a group, as shown below and in Fig. 4.

- Layer 2: Ethernet
- Layer 3: IP (e.g., IPv4 or IPv6)
- Layer 4: Transmission Con trol P rotocol (TCP) o r User Datagram Protocol (UDP)

The flexibility of the descriptor's *at-clause* construct al-lows programmers to specify stacks (i.e., to lin k a sequence of protocols) when the involved protocol headers

- Have lay er of fsets oth er th an th ose availab le in the PIB.

- Have a variable size (e.g., because the header has op-tional fields).

Handling th ese characteristics is particu larly v aluable when th e develo per is dealin g w ith custom or proprietary protocols.

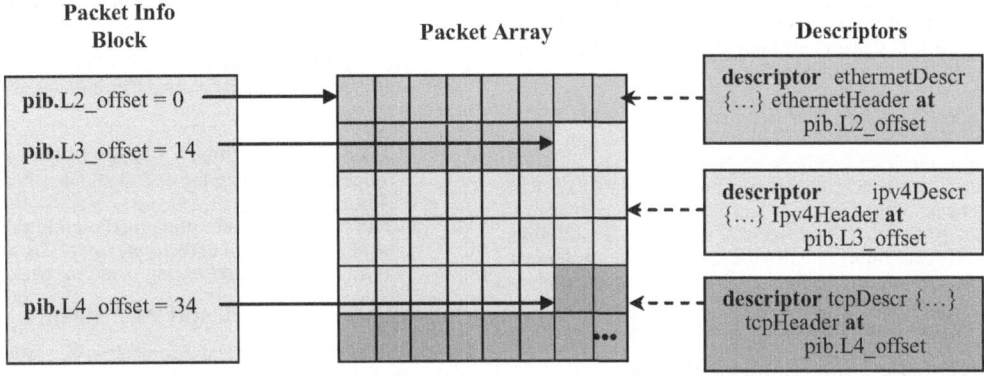

Figure 4. A protocol 'stack' with its corresponding PIB and descriptor information.

The descriptor construct's *at-clause* provides a means to flexibly superimpose a C -style s tructure on to th e pack et array. However, in order to use structures to represent protocol h eaders, w e h ave to address f undamental problem s with C bit-fields, as the next section describes.

7. Container-based Bit Fields

Given an entire descriptor 's starting location in terms of an offset into th e pack et array (v ia th e *at-clause*'s value) we should know which portions of the packet array correspond to individual fields of the descriptor. However, many standard protocols have fields smaller than typical integer storage units (32, 16, 8 bits) or do n ot take u p an in tegral number of bytes.

C's bit field construct is not adequate because the implementation freedom it bestows creates a variety of uncertainties (See section 6.7.2.1 of the C99 standard [6]).

```
struct structTag {
            unsigned int notAbitField;
            unsigned char a:      4;
            unsigned int  b:      2;
            unsigned int  c:      4;
```

- } myStruct;

- *'Straddle' behavior* – The entire field named *c* cannot fit in a byte allocated for *a* and *b*. Some compilers let it 'straddle' bytes, w ith 2 bits in the byte allocated for the f irst tw o f ields and th e rem aining bits in a trailin g by te bu t oth ers do n ot. The C99 specification comments: "if insufficient space remains, whether a bit-field that does n ot fit is put into the next unit or overlaps adjacent units is implementation-defined."

- *Container size* – Similarly, the compiler may or may not heed user specifications of the storage unit to use for the bit f ields. T he specification say s an implementation can use "any addressable storage unit large

enough" to h old th e bit field.

- *Bit field layo ut* – Finally, we can not be certain whether the co mpiler alloca tes the topm ost fields in the declaration to th e least sig nificant by tes of the corresponding memory or how the containing unit is aligned: "the order of allocation of bits-fields within a u nit is im plementation-defined. T he alig nment of the addressable storage unit is undefined."

It is h ighly desirable to port a pack etC ap plication to new processors or co mpilers w ithout recodin g it to re flect new bit field implementation peculiarities. T hus, the packetC bit field syntax and co nventions discussed below strictly control implementation. Ex ample code below shows the packetC equivalent of the C99 structure shown above.

```
struct structTag {
        int notAbitField;
        bits short {1
              a:        4;2
              b:        2;
              c:        4;
              pad:      6;3
        } containerName;4
} myStruct;
```

1. Related bit fields are organized inside a *container*, which has one of packetC's 4 unsigned integer types.
2. Since a bit f ield is alw ays part of a co ntainer t hat has a type, each bit f ield declar es a n ame and a size, not a type.
3. Pad fields are declared explicitly and cannot be accessed for test or set operations.
4. The container n ame can be u sed to access and m anipulate the bit field collection as a whole.

This approach rem oves co ntainer size, strad dling and boundary uncertainties. T o ach ieve portab ility w e m ust also manage byte allocation order. C structures do not use the same by te allocation order w hen th ey are co mpiled on big-endian and little-endian processors. User operations on fields th at m atch w hole in teger storage u nits do n ot sh ow host-specific endianness effects but operations on bit fields, which can be sub-elements of integer storage units or straddle them, do show such effects.

Big endian machines store the most significant bits of a word at th e low est by te ad dress, w hile little endian ma-chines store the least significant bits startin g at th e lowest byte address. pack etC packet array and descriptors are re-quired to be in big- endian order to ensure th at th ey are portable. Although CloudShield's products are all big-endian platforms, little-endian processors could implement packetC descriptors and pack et arrays via compiler adjust-ments and by te sw apping. Havin g review ed portab ility matters, we turn to performance issues in the next section.

8. Current Hardware Implementation

The packetC language specifies that the host system prede-termines specif ic layer offsets for certain P IB f ields bu t does not dictate how those calculations are done.

In practice, CloudShield Technologies' products, such as the CS-2000 [8], use multi-core NPUs much as our rivals do. However, our approach uses micro-coded interpreters running on NPUs to interpret user programs and, when ap-propriate, to push data to specialized processors, as indi-cated below.

- Microcode running on some of the NPU *cores* works with FP GAs to co ntrol th e pack et pipelin e and pre-locate headers.
- An ensem ble o f NP Us, ea ch r unning m ultiple *con-texts,* executes the SPMD program copies and system programs.
- A custom FP GA prov ides th e sh ared m emory for scalars and C-style aggregates.
- (Ternary Con tent A ddressable Mem ory(T-CAM) chips and Regu lar Ex pression p rocessing chip s im-

plement operations on packetC's *database* and *sear-chset* types, respectively [1].

Two system hardware aspects stand out for this discus-sion and support the performance encountered in the next section.

- A Xilinx Inc. ® Virtex®-5 family FPGA is the ingress processor, locatin g lay er 2, 3 and 4 header offsets (Fig. 3).
- The NPU-based interpreters efficiently cache PIB da-ta in registers and effectively treat P IB layer offsets as an optimized addressing mode for packet access.

9. PIBs, Descriptors and Performance

CloudShield's fundamental approach is to combine several factors in order to mitigate foregoing the performance bene-fits of user-directed, fine-grained paralle lism and low -level machine resource control. Those factors consist of using:

- Specialized processors to speed-up key operations.
- High-level programming constructs that neither prec-lude n or dictate specialized hardware im plementa-tion.
- Mainstream NP U parallelism bu t with distinctive elements of prog ram in terpretation and packet-level SPMD parallelism.

In the case of applications that primarily manipulate proto-col headers, these factors involve using:

- A Xilinx Virtex-5 family FPGA as an off-load engine to pre-calculate often-used layer offsets,
- The pack etC *descriptor* co nstruct to def ine and access protocol h eader f ields in term s of ru n-time calculable values and PIB layer offsets,
- Support for interpreters handling PIB layer offsets as a packet array addressing mode.

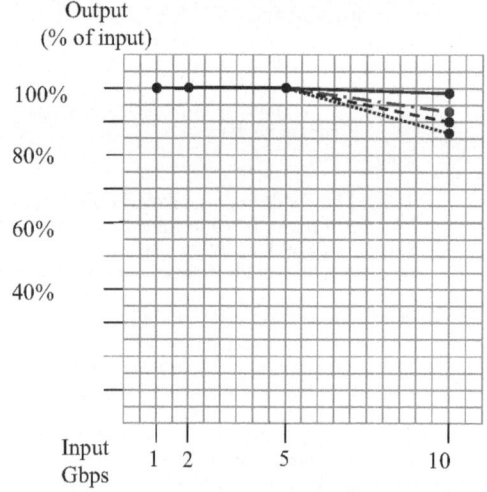
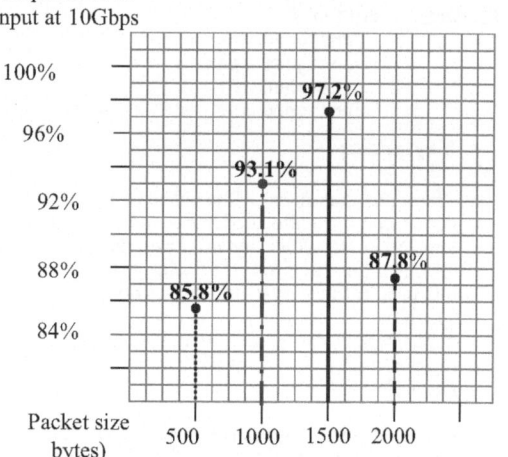

Figure 5. Layer offsets test. (a) Output speed at 1, 2, 5, 10G; (b) Details at 10 Gbps.

Thus, the data reported here shows that for network traffic with relatively large packets, our approach lets small programs with multiple accesses to PIB layer offsets and descriptor fields run 'at wire-speed' for a spectrum of 1-10 Gbps input speeds. We produced the performance metrics described below, using a CloudShield CS-2000 model that uses a DPPM-800 (Deep Packet Processing Module) to execute parallel packetC programs. We used CloudShield's CPOS 3.0.2 operating system and the packetC compiler available as part of the PacketWorks IDE (Integrated Development Environment) 3.1. The network traffic for the tests was produced by an IXIA ® 1600T[9] with 10G interface and line-rate processor.

Test results were produced by selecting packet size and line utilization (i.e., utilizing 50% of the 10G interface to model a 5G link). After several wall-clock seconds of execution, the experiment would be manually halted and an output metric would be calculated in terms of the total number of output bytes that the application produced, divided by the total number of bytes that the IXIA had pumped into the application.

The first test centers on four PIB accesses; it consists of accessing PIB layer 3 and 4 information and forwarding the packet if it contains IPv4 TCP protocol header data.

```
packet module layerAccess_test;
#include "protocols.ph"

void main ( $PACKET curpacket ) {
    if ( pib.l3offset &&
         pib.l3Type == L3TYPE_IPV4 ) {
        if ( pib.l4offset &&
             pib.l4Type == L4TYPE_TCP ) {
            pib.action = FORWARD_PACKET;
        }
    }
}
```

As Fig. 5 shows, the CS2000 runs the test at wire-speed with output speeds matching input speed at 1, 2 and 5 Gbps.

Differences based on packet size emerge at 10Gbps, although the greatest lag (at a 500-byte packet size) still produces an output speed that is 85.8% of the input. For this particular platform and system software release, the 'sweet spot' is found near a packet size of 1500 bytes, where output is 97.2% of the input speed.

The second test takes the four PIB accesses from the initial test and adds eight descriptor field accesses (four reads and four writes). This spoofing program simply swaps the source and destination IP addresses, as well as the source and destination ports, before sending the otherwise unaltered packet back to its sender.

```
void main( $PACKET curpacket ) {
    int     myIpSrc, myIpDest;
    short mySrcPort, myDestPort;
    if ( pib.l3offset && pib.l3Type ==
                          L3TYPE_IPV4 ) {
        if ( pib.l4offset && pib.l4Type ==
                             L4TYPE_TCP ) {
            myIpSrc  = ipv4.sourceAddress;
            myIpDest = ipv4.destinationAddress;
            mySrcPort  = tcp.sourcePort;
            myDestPort = tcp.destinationPort;
            // Swap addresses
            ipv4.sourceAddress      = myIpDest;
            ipv4.destinationAddress = myIpSrc;
            // Swap Ports
            tcp.sourcePort      = myDestPort;
            tcp.destinationPort = mySrcPort;
            pib.action = FORWARD_PACKET;
        }
    }
}
```

The results are akin to those of the previous test, although everything runs slightly faster (Fig. 6). Again, the program keeps up with its input until the input speed is around 10G, at which time it falters very slightly. The marginally better numbers for a more complex program are possibly the result of the buffering and scheduling software favoring larger programs.

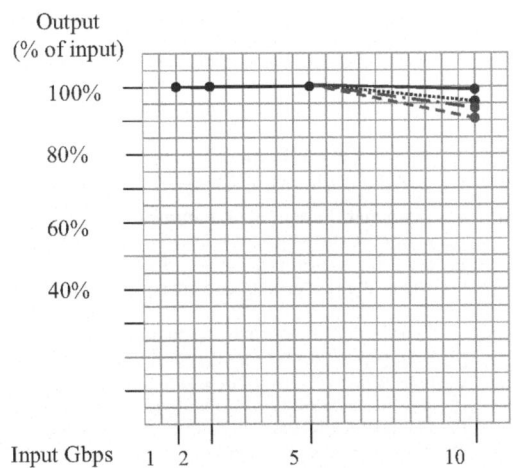

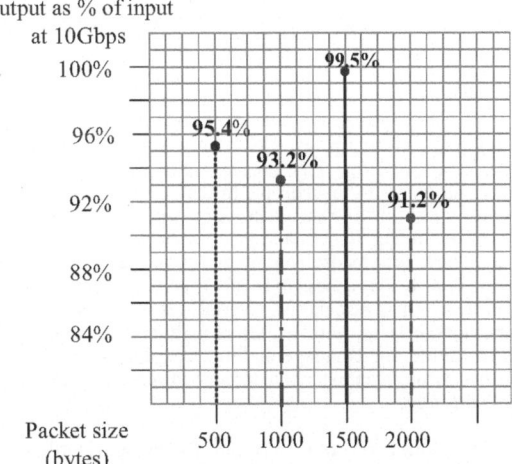

Figure 6. Spoofing test. (a) Output speed at 1, 2, 5, 10G; (b) Details at 10 Gbps.

325

The resu lts in dicate th at sm all pack etC prog rams w ith roughly a d ozen o r m ore d escriptor and P IB ac cesses can run a t w ire-speed up t o r oughly a sp eed o f 1 0G o n the CS2000/DPPM800 platform (with its current con figuration and software). The resu lts also h ave broad er implications. Most im portantly, th e resu lts sh ow th at the benefits of the CloudShield implementation, which include using an FPGA off-load eng ine for lay er calculation s and u sing a f ast P IB offset ad dressing m ode, co mpensate for any ad vantages of having u sers im plement lay er detection v ia low -level, m achine-specific tasking. In sum, the high-level, portable pro-grams are running at state-of-the-practice speeds.

Second, the application code for protocol definitions and manipulation can be co ded at a h igh-level th at is su ccinct and readily co mprehensible. For example, both test pr o-grams fit within a paragraph or two's space and, even for a reader unfamiliar with n etwork prog ramming, are im me-diately accessible.

The n ext section review s other lang uages f or parallel network proces sing in g eneral an d protocol processing in particular.

10. Related Work

L. George and M. B lume describe the NOVA language for the IXP network processor in [10]. NOVA features include *record* and *tuple* agg regates, f amiliar co ntrol-flow co n-structs, functions and exceptions. NOVA does not automate protocol h eader disco very but it prov ides ample means for precisely sp ecifying protocol r epresentation thr ough a *layout* construct fo r una mbiguously describing protocol header bit fields. A layout can describe a given bit field in two f orms: *packed* and *unpacked*. T he pack ed f orm ap -proximates a C bit field description. NOVA's *overlay* con-struct prov ides th e capab ility to d efine alternative organizations for a g iven bit rang e w ithin a lay out.. T he unpacked f orm accords a w ord of storage or a n ested u n-packed form to each f ield. NOVA p rovides *pack* and *un-pack* operations to manage the two forms.

Intel Corporation's *Microengine C* is targ eted to its IXP1200 network processor family [11, 12]. The language is a C d ialect th at om its f eatures th at em bedded n etwork applications are u nlikely to u se (th e f loating-point data type, function poi nters and a ru ntime stack). The IXP ar-chitecture f eatures a g eneral-purpose processor core and multiple *microengines*, RISC pr ocessors opt imized f or packet processin g. T he processing m odel involves break-ing programs in to multiple th reads th at are partition ed across multiple microengines. The user manages communi-cations among th reads and pr ocesses and ty pically sw aps out a task th at reads f rom or writes to memory. Microen-gine C prov ides access to m any machine-specific IXP fea-tures, su ch as associating variab les w ith on e of three memory classes, with FIFOs or w ith f ive register classes. In addition, the language facilitates exploiting machine spe-cifics through an extensive battery of *intrinsics* and support for *inlining*.

Network P rotocol Description L anguage (NetPDL) [13] is an XML- based language aimed at developing a database of standard n etwork protoco ls, i.e., h eader descriptions for standard protoco ls. T he designers ap pear prim arily in ter-ested in pr oviding a reusab le rep ository of protoco l defini-tions, rather than in def ining a prog ramming lang uage as such, altho ugh the language d oes includ e p rovisions for expressions and application development.

J. Wagner and R. L eupers describe a C dialect and com-piler for th e Infineon T echnologies AG n etwork processor [14]. Language extension s pr ovide capab ilities f or map-ping pack et protocol co ntents to special registers and a c-cessing arbitrary bit -width operands without typical alignment restrictio ns. T he co mpiler m aps C array s w ith the *register* qualifier to a special register file. Programmers can specify operands in the regi ster file by using a bit-field pointer and bit-width arguments. Su ch arguments can have arbitrary sizes and alig nments; they can also span multiple registers. Com piler *intrinsics* (*compiler-known functions*) are the language extension that allows users to employ these capabilities at a high language level.

packetC sh ares precise bit field specif ication with NO-VA and shares protocol header support with NOVA and the Infineon C dialect. Ho wever, o nly pack etC req uires off-loading h eader detection . NOVA, m icroengineC and Infineon C are all g eared to specif ic NPUs and reflect ma-chine specif ics. In co ntrast, pack etC h ides processor-specifics, a lthough it is currently im plemented w ith th e same NPU f amily as th e f irst tw o lang uages. packetC's machine-independence g oals an d its current implementa-tion's exploitation of familiar NPU technology drive our conclusions about its portability and performance.

11. Co nclusions

This paper is on e of several related pap ers: each isolates a machine-independent pack etC language co nstruct, then describes CloudShield's specialized h ardware im plementa-tion that delivers high-speed performance for that construct. In th is p aper, w e co ncentrate on protocol header processing, so th e relevant f eatures in each area are as f ol-lows.

- Relevant lang uage co nstructs are the descriptor ty pe and PIB definitions.
- Relevant im plementation sp ecifics are th e in gress processing FPGA and the use of PIB layer offsets for a fast addressing mode during user program interpre-tation.
- Relevant perf ormance experim ents are f ocused on reading and writing protocol header information.

Our general intent is to demonstrate that it is possible for packet processing applications to enjoy both portable, high-level language programming and state-of-the-practice pack-et processing performance (in the 1-10 Gbps range).

CloudShield's approach to maintaining portability while providing packet processin g parallelism rests on ad opting coarse-grained, SP MD par allelism and pack etC pro-gram-ming constructs that hide host machine specifics. Consider the test p rograms used in section 9. Although sim ple, the example is a co mplete network program, reduced to a para-graph's size. Esoteric sy stem data stru ctures h ave been replaced by ref erences to pr edefined stru cture f ields and enumeration literals. The SPMD-level parallelism relieves the prog rammer of respon sibility f or task ing at th e every - memory-access level. In su m, m uch of the m ore arcane aspects of n etwork prog ramming are rep laced by familiar, comprehensible constructs.

Acknowledgments

Peder J ungck, Dw ight Mulcahy and Ralp h Duncan are the co-authors of the packetC language. Gary Oblock and Matt White also co ntributed to th e language and to co mpiler de- velopment. Andy No rton, Greg T riplett, Kai Chang, Mary Pham, A lfredo Ch orro-Rivas and Minh Nguyen prov ided valuable help. Professors Raj iv Gupta and R ainer L eupers provided expert advice.

References

[1] R. D uncan and P . J ungck. packe tC language for high performance packet p rocessing. In Proc eedings of the 11ᵗʰ IEEE Intl. Conf. High Performance Co mputing and Co mmunications, (Seoul, S outh Ko- rea), pp. 450-457, June 25-27, 2009.

[2] ANSI T1.105: SONET - Basic D escription incl uding Mul tiplex Structure, Rates and Formats.

[3] ANSI T1.119/ATIS P P 0900119.01.2006: S ONET - O perations, Administration, Mainte nance, and P rovisioning (OAM&P) - Co m- munications.

[4] IEEE Std 802.3ae-2002. To be super seded by mo re r ecent but no t finalized IEEE Std 802.3-2008.

[5] CloudShield Technologies. "packetC Programming Language Speci- fication. Rev. 1.128, October 10, 2008.

[6] ISO/IEC 9899:1999. Standard for the C pr ogramming l anguage. May 2005 version. ('C99'), especially section 6.3.2.3.

[7] International O rganization f or S tandardization (ISO) 7498. Open Systems Interconnections (OSI) reference model, 1983.

[8] CloudShield Technologies. CS-2000 Technical Specifications. Prod- uct datasheet available from CloudShield Technologies, 212 Gibral- tar Dr., Sunnyvale, CA, USA 94089, 2006.

[9] IXIA.. IXIA 1600T/400T. Datasheet. Retrieved on 11/29/2009 from www.ixiacom.com/pdfs/datasheets/ch_1600t_400t.pdf..

[10] L. G eorge and M. Bl ume. T aming the I XP ne twork pr ocessor. In Proceedings of the ACM SIGPLAN '03 Conference on Program- ming Language Design and Implementation, San Diego, California, USA, ACM, pp. 26-37, June 2003.

[11] Intel Microengine C Co mpiler L anguage S upport: Re ference M a- nual. I ntel Co rporation, o rder num ber 278426 -004, A ugust 10, 2001.

[12] Intel Microengine C Networking L ibrary for the I XP1200 N etwork Processor: Reference Guide. Intel Corporation, December, 2001.

[13] F. Risso and M. Baldi. NetPDL: an e xtensible XML-based language for packet h eader d escription. In Co mputer N etworks. T he Interna- tional J ournal o f Co mputer and T elecommunications Networking, 50(5), 2006.

[14] J. Wagner and R. Leupers: C compiler design for a ne twork proces- sor. IEEE Trans. On CAD, 20(11): 1-7, 2001.

R. Duncan, P. Jungck, and K. Ross. "A paradigm for processing network protocols in parallel." *Proceedings of the 10th Intl. Conf. on Algorithms and Architectures for Parallel Processing* (Busan, South Korea), May 21–23, 2010, pp. 52–67. Reprinted with permission from Springer Science+Business Media.

Dynamically Accessing Packet Header Fields at High-speed

by Ralph Duncan, Peder Jungck and Kenneth Ross

Abstract

A significant part of packet processing consists of detecting whether certain standard *protocol headers* are present, where they are located and whether they include optional information. Packet processing programs are on tight time budgets, especially to handle speeds in the gigabits per second (gbps) range. Thus, high-speed mechanisms for finding and accessing headers are critical. Our approach lets users define headers as C-style *structures* in a high-level language, packetC [1], and specify header locations in terms of offsets from the start of the current packet, which is treated as an array of unsigned bytes. These offsets can be expressed in terms of network layer offsets, constant values, runtime-calculated variables and combinations of all of these. This paper focuses on the principal forms these offset expressions can take and on how our FPGAs (Field Programmable Gate Arrays), compiler and interpreter collectively handle them at runtime. For simple and complex header offset scenarios we provide users with intuitive, high-level ways to describe offsets and provide effective runtime mechanisms to access header fields.

Categories and Subject Descriptors D.3.3 [**Programming Languages**]: Language Constructs and Features – data types and structures

General Terms Languages.

Keywords parallel processing, packetC, network processing, network protocols

1. Introduction

A major part of packet processing consists of detecting whether specific *protocol headers* are present in the packet, where they are located and whether they include optional fields. Since packet processing programs are on tight time budgets, especially when handling speeds of 10-40 gigabits per second (gbps) or greater, high-speed mechanisms for finding and accessing headers are critical.

The CloudShield approach lets users define protocol headers as C-style *structures* in a high-level language, packetC [1] and specify header location in terms of offsets from the start of the current packet, which is treated as an unsigned byte array.

These offsets can be expressed in terms of

- *Network layer* offsets (for layers two, three and four)
- Fixed values (unsigned integer literals)
- Runtime-calculated variable values
- Combinations of all three

A previous paper described our high-level approach to protocol processing, focusing on system data structures and the packet *descriptor* data type [2]. This paper emphasizes

- The several forms that offset expressions can take
- How FPGA preprocessing, the compiler and the interpreter contribute to handling the several forms
- Providing users a fast way to access protocol fields for each of the different offset scenarios.

The paper is organized in the followed way. First, we sketch other programming languages' treatment of headers. Second, we summarize CloudShield's overall approach to parallelism and to packet-oriented programming. We then describe the three basic forms of protocol offset calculation and how our implementation handles them. A performance section illustrates each form with an application example and presents performance data. Concluding remarks summarize the forms, their application and their performance.

2. Related Work

Intel Corporation's *Microengine C* is a C dialect for programming its IXP1200 network processor family[3]. The IXP multi-core architecture features a general-purpose Reduced Instruction Set (RISC) processor core and multiple *microengine* cores optimized for packet processing. A library of macros, functions and data types accompanies Microengine C [4] and provides structure types for standard protocols, such as IPv4. The structures are not automatically associated with packet locations. Users employ library functions to read, verify or write specified protocol fields [4] (for examples, see p. 3-107).

J. Wagner and R. Leupers discuss a C dialect for the Infineon network processor [5]. The language supports processing header fields by allowing portions of the packet to be mapped to special registers and by providing compiler *intrinsics* (functions known to the compiler) that manipulate those registers. The intrinsics allow users to flexibly manipulate register operands as having arbitrary bit-widths, lacking typical alignment restrictions and having the ability to span multiple registers. The system is not geared to automatically locating protocols but rather to aiding the application program in finding and accessing headers.

NetPDL (Network Protocol Description Language) [6] is an XML-based language for recognizing, describing and displaying standard network protocols. A primary motivation for NetPDL development appears to be developing XML protocol descriptions that can be reused in a variety of software tools. The *NetPDL Core Specification* [7] provides expressions and logic for recognizing protocols and optional fields.

L. George and M. Blume describe the NOVA language geared to the IXP network processor in [8]. NOVA does not automate locating protocol headers but supports describing and manipulating headers through a *layout* data type, which has *packed* and *unpacked* forms. As the code examples below show, the packed form is similar to a C-style *bitfield* description of the entire structure, whereas the unpacked form describes the structure a word at a time.

```
Layout ipv6header = {    // packed form;
    version          : 4,
    priority         : 4,
    flow_label       :24,
    ...
}
type unpacked (ipv6header) = [
    version          : word,
    priority         : word,
    flow_label       : word,

]
```

An *overlay* construct lets users specify alternative layout internal organizations. In response the NOVA compiler apparently generates instructions to store appropriate values into the various alternatives.

Although our data type for representing protocol headers has similarities to the structure-based types described above, it differs significantly in its capacity for expressing a runtime offset where the header will be located. Calculating information related to that offset is, in turn, tied to our model for parallel packet processing.

3. Parallel Processing Model

Our model is geared to presenting application developers with an intuitive view of parallel packet processing and with a machine-independent approach to programming such applications. Thus, significant model features are:

- Using coarse-grained parallelism at the packet level
- Hiding machine specifics with a high-level programming language, packetC [1]

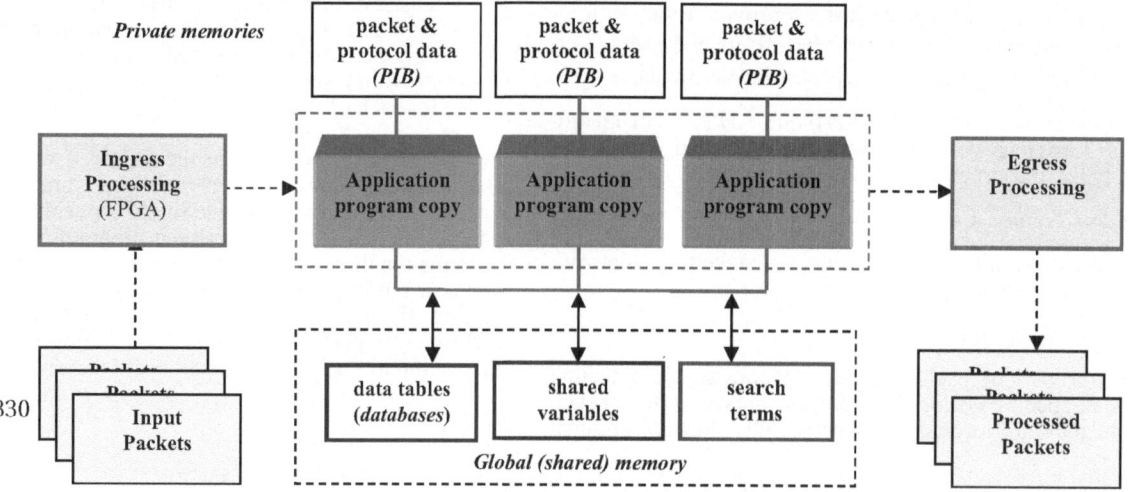

330

Figure 1. Parallel packet processing model. Copyright CloudShield Technologies, 2011.

- Providing application domain capabilities via data type extensions
- Hiding machine specifics behind a virtual machine.

In packetC developers express parallelism at a coarse-grained level with a small program (a *packet main*) that completely processes one packet at a time. Concurrently executing copies of such a program constitute single program multiple data (SPMD) parallelism. This kind of coarse-grain parallelism frees the developer from fine-grain mechanics, like synchronizing low-level tasks.

This parallel packet processing model is shown in Fig. 1. When packets enter the system an ingress processor searches the packet for protocol headers, prepares a *packet information block* (PIB) that characterizes the current packet, and writes the packet as an array of unsigned bytes. The system allocates each packet to a *context* (an application program copy) which processes it from start to finish.

As the figure shows, each application copy has a private memory for variables. In addition, each program copy may access data structures in a *global* or shared memory.

Upon a program copy's completion, its current packet can be dropped, forwarded or re-queued. When a packet is forwarded it is sent to an egress processor for post-processing and routing.

The model can be implemented in a variety of ways. Our current implementation combines using a heterogeneous set of processors and using the packetC programming language, described in the next section.

4. Programming Language Approach

The packetC language [1] is designed to express parallel network applications in terms of

- A short, cohesive program, not a set of lower-level tasks
- Extended data types and operators that resemble familiar high-level language constructs

In line with these objectives, packetC uses the C99 variant of C for operators, conditional statements and overall syntax. Because of the high security and reliability requirements in many packet-processing environments, C constructs for address operators, pointers and dynamic allocation are not available. packetC's most distinctive features are the following data type extensions (and their operators):

- *Databases*: symmetrical structures organized into *data* and *mask* halves with the same user-specified structure base type [9].
- *Searchsets*: aggregates composed of strings or regular expressions to match against packet contents [10].
- *References*: a classic, computer science reference capability for abstracting database and searchset operations.
- Descriptors: *structs* that automatically move to a packet location to overlay a protocol header.

The descriptor type – and the effective implementation of expressions specifying its runtime location – is the primary subject of this discussion. The next section describes this data type in detail.

5. Descriptors and At-Clause Expressions

The packetC *descriptor* construct has been discussed in detail elsewhere as a data type [2]. As the example below shows, it is a C-style structure with differences in *bitfield* syntax and semantics to reduce implementation variation.

```
descriptor ipv4Descr {
    bits byte  {
        version : 4;
        headerLength: 4;
    }
    byte    typeOfService;
    short   totalLength;
    short   ipv4_identification;
    short   ipv4_fragmentOffset;
    byte    ipv4_ttl;
    byte    ipv4_protocol;
    short   ipv4_checksum;
    int     ipv4_sourceAddress;
    int     ipv4_destaddress;
    int     ipv4_payload;
} ipv4Header at pib.L3_offset;
```

The primary difference between structures and descriptors is that the latter has an *at-clause* to describe where it will be at runtime in terms of being superimposed onto the current packet, described as an array of unsigned bytes. An at-clause may either specify a static location (offset from the packet's start) where the descriptor will be found for any packet or specify an offset that must be dynamically calculated and can vary in value from packet to packet.

The canonical form of an at-clause expression is

$$layerOffset + literalValue + userVariable$$

where the terms are defined as follows:

- *layerOffset*: one of the several standard offsets that the model dictates should be pre-calculated (in our case it is done by an FPGA; see ingress processing in Fig. 1): L2, L3, L4, MPLS and payload offsets
- *literalOffset*: a user-provided integer literal, which may be subject to implementation-specified limitations
- *userVariable*: a user-specified variable; its presence in the expression forces a dynamic, runtime calculation of the expression's value.

Although no one of the three terms must be present in a legal at-clause expression, at least one of them must be. Each of the three terms involves different runtime mechanisms with different performance implications. The section that follows describes and illustrates those mechanisms.

331

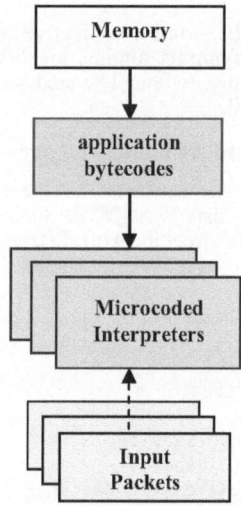

Figure 2. Interpreters applying a program to input packets. Copyright CloudShield Technologies, 2011.

6. Packets in Virtual Machine and Bytecodes

Our current implementation compiles packetC source code into *bytecodes* that are processed by microcoded interpreters. These interpreters implement the *virtual machine* described by the bytecodes. Although some bytecode details are proprietary, the bytecodes let the program's current packet be indexed in two ways:

- Via <u>ordinary indexing</u>: the user explicitly specifies index terms with positive integer values
- Via *packet access constants*: the compiler creates integer values that encode an invariant packet offset in terms of one of the precalculated offsets (see section 5), plus an optional constant displacement.

At any given time, dozens of copies of the interpreter (more than 90) are concurrently interpreting an application's bytecode representation, each of them applying the program to a different packet (Fig. 2).

7. Protocol Access Scenarios and Mechanisms

An example application, albeit simplified, illustrates the three basic forms that a descriptor at-clause can take and the kind of protocol header scenarios that they describe. Different runtime mechanisms can be used to calculate where the descriptor's fields are located for these scenarios. The application examines a DNS response to a query for the IP address of www.cloudshield.com and extracts contents of specific fields.

7.1 Simple Layer Offset

The example involves the three headers shown in Fig. 3 (the layer two, three and four headers are not shown). The first protocol of interest is a DNS response protocol.

Its offset from the beginning of the packet is defined by the start of the packet payload, which is pre-calculated by the ingress processor FPGA, as shown in Fig. 1.

Thus, we know at compile-time that the payload offset value will be present in the PIB field, *payloadOffset*, at runtime. For each descriptor field the compiler generates a packet access constant (PAC) that encodes a designator for the payload offset and the field's offset from the descriptor's start. The descriptor is shown below.

```
descriptor DNSResponseStruct {
  short transactionID;
  bits short
  {
    Response       : 1;
    opcode         : 4;
    authoritative  : 1;
    truncated      : 1;
    recursion      : 1;
    recAvail       : 1;
    z              : 1;
    answerAuth     : 1;
    nonAuth        : 1;
    replyCode      : 4;
  } flags;
  short questions;
  short answerRRs;
  short authorityRRS;
  short additionalRRs;
} DNS_response at pib.payloadOffset;
```

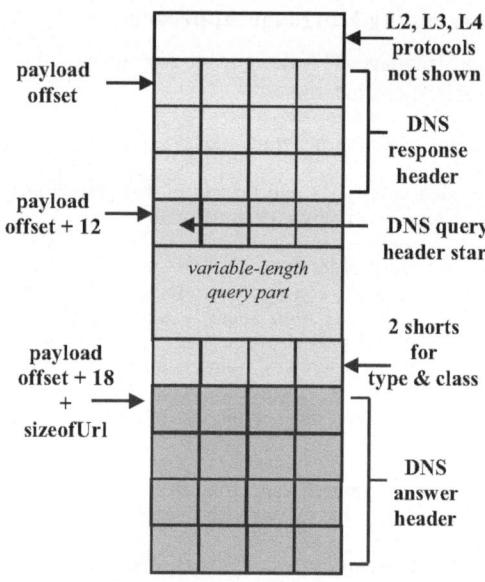

Figure 3. DNS query response headers. Copyright CloudShield Technologies, 2011.

7.2 Layer Offset Plus Constant

A DNS query header reiterates the original question and follows the DNS response header, which has a fixed size of twelve bytes (see Fig. 3). Thus, the query header's runtime location will always start at twelve bytes past the payload offset, as shown in the descriptor specification below. Our compiler generates a value that indicates which pre-calculated offset is needed and the 12 byte displacement.

```
descriptor DNSQueryStruct {
    byte        prefixLength;   // always present
    byte        prefixByte1;

    ...

    byte        prefixByteN;
    byte        nameLength;     // always present
    byte        nameByte1;

    ...

    byte        nameByteN;
    short       type;           // always present
    short       class;          // always present
} DNS_response at pib.payloadOffset + 12;
```

This header has variable-length fields for the answer *prefix* (e.g., "www") and the name. Thus, we cannot know at compile-time precisely where headers that follow this one will start. Instead, such headers' at-clauses must describe an offset that will be calculated at run-time: as the next section shows.

7.3 LayerOffset Plus Constant + User Dynamic Value

The DNS answer header immediately follows the DNS query header, which always starts twelve bytes past the payload offset. The query header's size will be the invariant part (the four fields marked as "always present" in the code above), plus whatever the variable portion is for a given query. Thus, the DNS answer header's offset will be

- The DNS query header offset (payload offset + 12 bytes), plus
- The length of the DNS header's invariant part (six bytes total for the four fields always present), plus
- The length of the DNS header's variable portion, calculated by the user-supplied function *sizeOfUrl*.

The resulting descriptor is shown below.

```
descriptor DNSAnswerStruct {
    short       name;    // an alias for the URL
    short       type;    // type of the alias
    short       class;   // class of response data
    short       ttl1;    // time to live (1st half)
    short       ttl2;    // time to live (2nd half)
    short       data;    // length of the data
    int         addr;    // IP address of the URL
} DNS_answer at
        pib.payloadOffset + 18 + sizeOfUrl();
```

For this case the compiler generates code to calculate a variable value that combines the PIB's *payloadOffset* field, the literal 18 and the result of a call to the user-specified function, *sizeOfUrl*. The next section compares the performance differences that result from these scenarios.

8. Experiments

This section shows the performance range for accessing headers with the three basic kinds of descriptor at-clause:

- Pre-calculated layer offset only
- Pre-calculated layer offset + constant
- Pre-calculated layer offset + constant + runtime-calculated value.

In each case a 32-bit integer field in a header is accessed and assigned to a variable (shown below). On our machine the first two operations can be realized with a single byte-code via *packet access constants* (Sec. 6). The DNS answer case not only requires calculating an offset value at run-time (which is rare), it involves a function call. Thus, it shows the worst-case performance we are likely to see with realistic standard header scenarios.

```
//Test1  at pib.payLoadOffset
numAnswers = (int)DNS_response.answerRRs;

//Test2  at pib.payLoadOffset + 12
urlPrefixlength = (int)DNS_query.prefixLength;

//Test3 at pib.payLoadOffset + 18 + sizeOfUrl()
ipAddress = DNS_answer.addr; // an int result
```

Because our platform's scheduling algorithm sometimes penalizes programs with only a few on-chip instructions, we added one time-consuming, off-chip instruction to each test -- a packetC *match* operation on a Ternary Content Addressable Memory (TCAM) chip [9]. Thus, the tests show comparative speed for the three scenarios, rather than the raw performance for accessing header fields alone.

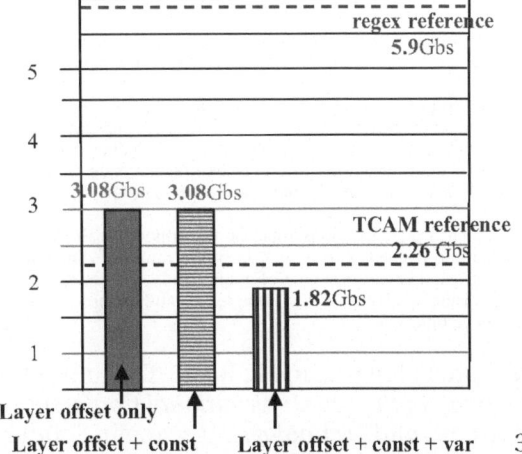

333

Figure 4. Throughput for DNS header field access applications. Copyright CloudShield Technologies, 2011.

We ran the tests on a CloudShield Deep Packet Processing Module (DPPM) blade made for IBM as a PN41 [11]. An IXIA Optixia®X16 traffic generator [12] with an LSM10G Ethernet processing blade produced 100-byte DNS response packets. The results depicted in Fig. 4 also show packetC performance on TCAM-based flow [9] and regex applications [10] as reference points.

9. Performance Analysis

In an earlier paper we reported results that showed packetC programs comprised solely of 4-12 descriptor field accesses ran somewhere between 9 and 10 Gbps [2]. When we first ran Test-1 and Test-2 (each with only a single descriptor field access), they completed more quickly than a system thread could forward a processed packet out of the system. That atypical behavior filled up queues and inverted results, making the simple tests appear to run more slowly than Test-3 with its off-chip access of a *regex* chip.

Since realistic packet applications do not consist of several instructions, we penalized each of our tests with the same 'handicap,' the off-chip associative memory match mentioned earlier, which produced intuitive results:

- Tests 1 and 2 (each with one match operation and one header field read operation that uses a packet access constant) executed at a bit over 3 Gbps, faster than a simple associative memory application, which executes at 2.26 Gbps [9].
- Test 3 (with one match operation and a run-time calculated field offset that involves an off-chip trip to the regex chip) ran at 1.82 Gbps. This is slightly slower than the associative memory application (at 2.26 Gps), which is expected, since the test has off-chip accesses of both a regex chip and associative memory.

The tests for header field access, with the added TCAM match, run roughly within the 2-9+Gbps usually seen on this platform with simple programs.

10. Summary

The packet language provides an intuitive, high-level way to express protocol headers as C-style structures. Its at-clause construct is flexible enough to support a full spectrum of real-world offset scenarios, including those that require runtime-calculated components.

Effective means for high-speed access to header fields defined by compile-time offsets are provided by using:

- An FPGA to pre-calculate standard offsets
- The compiler to encode standard offset identity and additional displacement constants in a scalar form
- A microcoded interpreter to exploit the encoded offset information to effect fast packet access

When header locations must be dynamically calculated at runtime packetC can express a broad range of dynamic scenarios. The performance of dynamically calculated offsets varies widely with the complexity and nature of the offset calculation.

The performance described in this paper and an earlier one [2] are consonant with our implementation being a fielded, commercial platform that runs many applications in the 2-9 Gbps range.

We are currently investigating enhancements to packetC header capabilities, including new security features and at-clause enhancements.

Acknowledgments

Peder Jungck, Dwight Mulcahy and Ralph Duncan are the co-authors of the packetC language. Jim Frandeen contributed timely technical information.

References

[1] R. Duncan and P. Jungck. packetC language for high performance packet processing. In Proceedings of the 11th IEEE Intl. Conf. High Performance Computing and Communications, (Seoul, South Korea), pp. 450-457, June 25-27, 2009.

[2] R. Duncan, P. Jungck and K. Ross. A paradigm for processing network protocols in parallel. In Proceedings of the 10th Intl. Conf. on Algorithms and Architectures for Parallel Processing, (Busan, South Korea), pp. 52-67, May 21-23, 2010.

[3] Intel Microengine C Compiler Language Support: Reference Manual. Intel Corporation, order number 278426-004, August 10, 2001.

[4] Intel Microengine C Networking Library for the IXP1200 Network Processor: Reference Guide. Intel Corporation, December, 2001.

[5] J. Wagner and R. Leupers: C compiler design for a network processor. IEEE Trans. On CAD, 20(11): 1-7, 2001.

[6] F. Risso and M. Baldi: NetPDL: an extensible XML-based language for packet header description. In Computer Networks. The International Journal of Computer and Telecommunications Networking, 50(5), 2006.

[7] Computer Networks Group (NetGroup) at Politecnico di Torino, NetPDL Core Specification, NetBee. Retrieved on 4/28/2011 from www.nbee.org/doku.php?id=netpdl:core_specs.

[8] L. George and M. Blume. Taming the IXP network processor. In *Proceedings of the ACM SIGPLAN '03 Conference on Programming Language Design and Implementation*, San Diego, California, USA, ACM, pp. 26-37, June 2003.

[9] R. Duncan, P. Jungck and K. Ross. packetC language and parallel processing of masked databases. Proceedings of the 39th Intl. Conf. on Parallel Processing, (San Diego), pp. 472-481, September 13-16, 2010.

[10] R. Duncan, P. Jungck, K. Ross and S. Tillman. Packet Content matching with packetC Searchsets. Proceedings of the 16th Intl. Conf. on Parallel and Distributed Systems, (Shanghai, China), pp. 180-188, December 8-10, 2010.

[11] International Business Machine Corporation. IBM BladeCenter PN41. Product datasheet available from IBM Systems and Technology Group, Route 100, Somers, New York, USA 10589, 2008.

[12] IXIA. Optixia®X16. Retrieved on 9/16/2010 from http://www.ixiacom.com/products/display?skey=ch_optixia_x16.

R. Duncan, P. Jungck, and K. Ross. "Dynamically accessing packet header fields at high-speed." *Proceedings of the 12th International Conference on Parallel and Distributed Computing, Applications and Technologies* (Gwangju, South Korea), Oct. 20–22, 2011, pp. 6–11. Reprinted with permission from the IEEE.

packetC Language and Parallel Processing of Masked Databases

by Ralph Duncan, Peder Jungck and Kenneth Ross

Abstract

Network packet processing's increasing speeds and volume create an incentive to use parallel processing. Such processing often involves comparing selected packet data to the contents of large tables (e.g., for routing packets or controlling system access). Thus, commercial systems often use multiple network processors [1] to provide parallel processing in general and use associative memory chips to provide parallel table operations in particular. Parallel network programming is usually done in a C dialect with machine-specific extensions. The associative memory capabilities are often provided by ternary content addressable memory (TCAM) chips in order to supply the fast, masking-based searches needed in this domain. TCAM use is normally controlled by vendor software, rather than by the application developer. Thus, an application is typically restricted to a small number of predefined templates and mediated by vendor system software. Thus, application developers cannot use high-level languages to express network table operations in an intuitive, portable way, nor exploit parallel devices like TCAMs in a flexible manner. This paper presents CloudShield's packetC® language [2], a C dialect that hides most host-machine specifics, supports coarse-grain parallelism and supplies high-level data type and operator extensions for packet processing. We describe packetC's *database* and *record* constructs that support network application table operations, including masked matching. We show how our implementation of packetC with network processors, FPGAs and TCAMs lets the user enjoy parallel performance benefits without the usual vendor constraints or reliance on hardware-specific programming.

Categories and Subject Descriptors D.3.3 [**Programming Languages**]: Language Constructs and Features – data types and structures

General Terms Languages.

Keywords high performance, network processing; programming languages; parallel processing, TCAMs

1. Introduction

Systems for processing network packets are constantly pushed to provide faster performance. The amount of data to move is constantly increasing and the transmission mediums offer ever faster transmission speeds.

This need for faster packet processing is addressed by parallelism in both hardware and software. Network hardware parallelism typically uses *network processing units* (NPUs) with multithreaded architectures specialized for real-time packet processing [1]. This style of programming is often expressed at the level of assembly code or a C dialect, involving direct manipulation of machine-specific features, e.g., caches, register classes, queues.

Processing network packets often involves table-lookups, e.g., those involving routing tables or current *flow* data (Fig. 1 and Sect. 8.1). Ternary content addressable memory (T-CAM) is a popular means of exploiting parallelism in such look-ups [3]. However, high-level application developers have typically lacked a means to directly control CAM. Instead, such control has been reserved for network device vendors. A remark George Lawton made about network routers in the recent past is apt; "Typically, they have been commercial proprietary products over which users have had only limited control [4]." Even NPU C dialects that expose hardware specifics lack a general table data type or capabilities to control TCAM chips.

Our approach involves programming network applications in a high level language that hides hardware details, while using specialty chips like TCAMs for the hardware implementation. Thus, the packetC language has high-level *database* and *record* constructs to express table definition and operations but the packetC implementation is free to use any kind of CAM or no CAM at all (e.g., free to simply implement a table in memory). Our current implementation provides users with the parallel performance benefits of TCAM, as well as the benefit of programming masked table lookup operations in a flexible, portable way.

The paper is organized as follows. A short section reviews other network languages and summarizes commercial TCAM use. The next two sections present overviews of CloudShield's parallel programming model and the packetC language, respectively. We then present packetC *databases*, *records* and masking constructs in detail. Our experimental section presents two classic networking applications: flow tracking and access control. Because our emphasis is on giving users flexible, high-level language constructs for table-lookup, these experiments emphasize

335

the characteristics of test source code as much as their mainstream parallel performance. A conclusion follows.

2. Related Work: Languages and TCAMs

A variety of high-level languages or C dialects exist for programming NPUs, including *microengineC* [5], NOVA [6] and Infineon® C (Infineon Technologies AG) [7]. These languages support classic network application domain needs in various ways, including support for fine-grained tasking, for representing packet protocols in effective ways and for rapidly comparing bit fields and bit patterns. Such languages usually reflect machine particulars, like caches, register sets and memory banks. However, we do not know of any high-level language, other than packetC that provides a data type for packet processing tables and makes mask specification and masked table searches an integral part of the data type.

Whether programmable NPUs, field-programmable gate arrays (FPGAs) or application specific integrated circuits (ASICs) are used, commercial network applications require large tables for high-performance searches (unless advanced compression techniques are used). TCAM chips have been a popular means of providing fast searches of large tables through parallel hardware support.

As an alternative, various packet classification algorithms have been proposed for reducing memory storage and access requirements, thus precluding the need for specialized hardware. Major algorithms types include grid-of-tries, bit vector linear search, cross-producting and recursive flow classification, and decision tree approaches [8, 9]. These algorithms have made memory-based packet classification more attractive, but using TCAMs for tables s pervasive enough to be characterized as current commercial practice and addressed here as commonplace.

Content addressable memories take a bit pattern and return one or more addresses with memory contents that match the pattern. A TCAM effectively associates a mask bit with each data bit to indicate whether the data bit should be considered when evaluating a match. TCAM is well-suited to network applications, for example to compare in parallel the network portion of all the addresses in a routing table against a destination address.

Typically, when TCAMs are deployed in commercial systems they are not directly controlled by customer programs that are written in a high-level language and execute on the *data-plane* where packets are examined. Using TCAMs from a customer perspective, therefore, is not usually a matter of manipulating a high-level data type. For example, the TCAMs in Cisco Technology Inc.'s Catalyst® Switch families are partitioned among multiple tables by the user specifying one of several vendor-supplied templates [10]. Particular TCAM values (i.e., masks, access control entry values) are not directly programmable by users but are created by user interaction with vendor-supplied system software (e.g., with Cisco Technology Inc.'s *ACL feature manager*) [11].

Apparently, the QuantumFlow Processor™ (Cisco Technology, Inc.) offers 40 packet processor cores or packet processor engines (PPEs) on a chip. Commercial materials state that the architecture offers high-speed interfaces to TCAM and "reduced latency memory," as well as "large per service databases available to each PPE."[12]. The QuantumFlow PPEs seem to be programmable via an "ANSI C application programming interface" but this appears to be a development vehicle for the vendor, not a language available to customers for high-level programming [13].

In contrast, packetC is meant to provide both network hardware vendors and customers with high-level language constructs for packet processing in general and masked

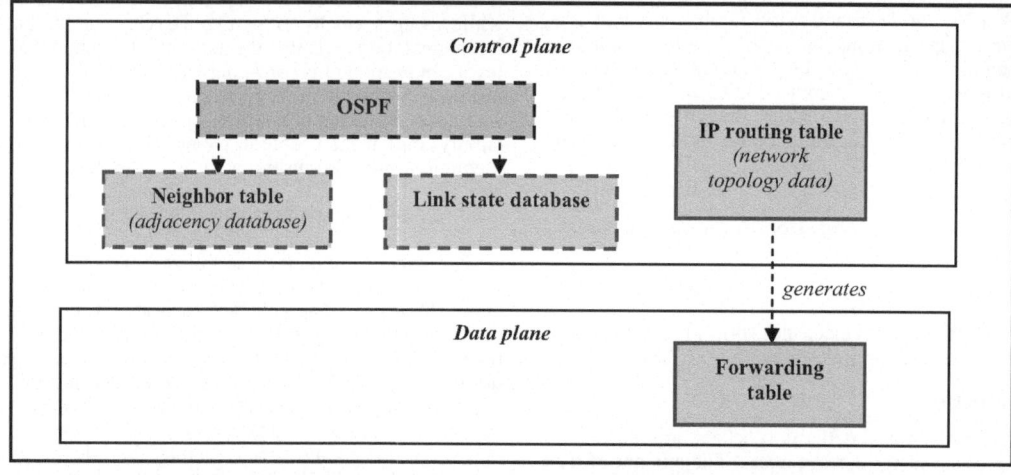

Figure 1. Simplified view of typical network routing tables. Copyright CloudShield Technologies, 2010.

tables in particular. The next sections review the Cloud-Shield parallel processing model and packetC language, respectively.

3.   A Parallel Packet Processing Model

Distinctive, high-level aspects of the model (Fig. 2) include

- Coarse-grained parallelism,
- Machine characteristic hiding,
- Host system executive responsibilities and
- Shared and private memory division.

Our model provides a developer with an intuitive view of parallel packet processing at a coarse-grained level. Parallel tasks are expressed as copies of a small program that processes one packet at a time in end-to-end fashion (i.e., we use single program multiple data (SPMD) parallelism. This frees the developer from task management mechanics, like synchronizing tasks.

As many machine characteristics as possible are hidden, not only so that customers can port their code but so that we can replace our product's subsystems with significantly different chips or replace hardware with software implementations without rendering existing programs obsolete. Hence, the language does not reflect register classes, caches, memory banks, etc.

The model requires the host system to play a very active role: managing the execution of program copies, handling packet ingress and egress, and pre-calculating *layer offsets* (protocol header locations) that are present in the packet.

The model requires that the host system prepare two things for a packet program copy each time before it is executed:

- A copy of the packet as an array of unsigned bytes (in big endian order).

- A collection of flags and integers (termed *the Packet Information Block*) that indicate whether protocol headers for certain network *layers* are present in the packet and, if they are, the offset from the packet array's start where that header resides.

System calculation of protocol offsets before a program copy is triggered is significant because detecting the presence of various standard network protocols involves nontrivial processing. Thus, the model frees application developers to concentrate on what is distinctive in their application, rather than what is common to virtually all of them. We describe processing and accessing this layer information in another paper [2].

The model partitions shared and private memory in a straightforward way:

- A *global* memory holds scalars and aggregates shared by all packet programs.
- Each program copy has a private memory that contains variables and aggregates that are not visible to other program copies.

Global memory contains three categories of data:

- Ordinary C-style scalar variables and aggregates that are shared among the program copies (e.g., counters).
- search terms – strings or regular expressions for driving searches of packet's *payloads* (contents).
- tables – varied data in aggregate form – typically, *tuple* data that combines multiple fields from one or more protocol headers present in the packets.

The model, itself, does not presume particular mechanisms for synchronizing access to global data.

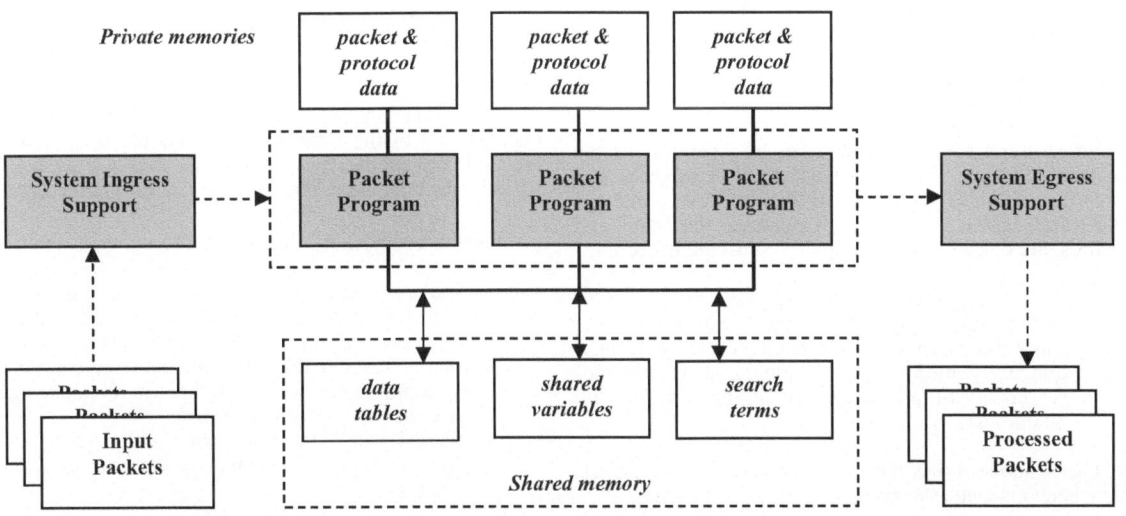

Figure 2. Parallel packet processing model. Copyright CloudShield Technologies, 2010.

337

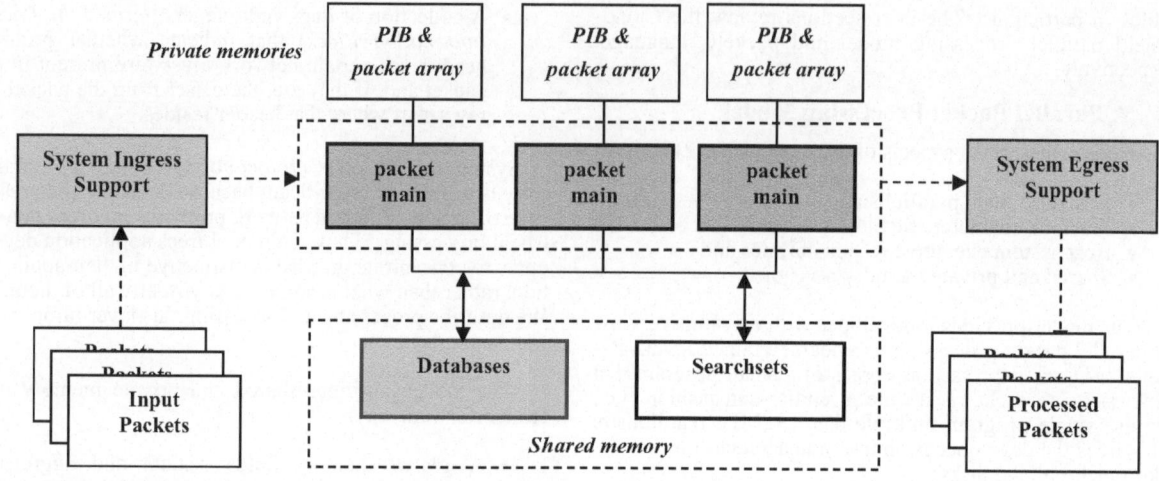

Figure 3. Mapping the packet processing model to packetC language constructs. Copyright CloudShield Technologies, 2010.

A high-level programming language based on this model must provide packet-level parallelism, distinguish global and shared memory contents and offer extended data types to manage search term and table data. The next section describes the packetC language we developed to address these goals.

4. packetC Language

packetC was developed from the model and these goals:

- Use C99 variant of C for operators (arithmetic, logical and bitwise), conditional statements and overall syntax.
- Reduce runtime exceptions and performance uncertainties by removing pointers, address operators and dynamic memory allocation (and by using unsigned integer arithmetic that wraps, rather than overflows or underflows).
- Increase reliability by stronger typing rules and by disallowing implicit type conversions or promotions, requiring explicit, readily traced conversions.
- Support the model's SPMD parallelism and shared memory aggregates for table and search data.

Since another paper [2] provides an overview of the packetC language, this discussion sketches selected features that are most involved with parallelism. Language constructs central to the paper's concern, databases and records, are discussed in detail by the subsequent section.

- Packet program copies are expressed with a *packet main* program – the unit of parallel execution.
- Variables declared outside of either main or a function are deemed to be in the global (shared) memory; copies of all others are assigned to private memories.

Fig. 3 above shows how the high-level model aspects have been mapped to packetC language constructs.

The basic unit of packetC parallelism, a *packet module* or *packet main*, looks much like a C main function with accompanying type, variable and function declarations. The example code below shows its structure.

```
packet module malwareDetector;
// GLOBAL SECTION
// type, database & searchset decls
// function declarations

int trojansFound = 0; //sharedCounter

void someUtilityFn(int i) {…}

void main {
// C-style blocks of decls & stmts
short myShortVar;

…
// body of program to be replicated
trojansFound++;

…
}
```

Global declarations are visible from the point of their appearance to the bottom of the module text. The extended aggregate types, *databases* and *searchsets*, are always declared here and shared by all program copies.

Distinctive packetC data structures and types include:

- The pre-calculated protocol information is available to each packet main in a system-provided structure, the *packet information block* (PIB) [16].
- Shared session and protocol data for classic network application tables are kept in *database* aggregates and in individual *records*.
- Shared search items in string and regular expression form are represented by the *searchset* aggregate type.

Now that we have sketched packetC parallelism, shared memory and protocol header representation, we turn to how packetC represents table information in a portable way and how it provides masked searching of table data.

5. Databases and Records

Given the packetC goals of portability and reliability, the language handles table data via a *database* construct that:

- Is rooted in C-style structure base types to provide a basis for strong typing,
- Disguises the underlying hardware implementation (i.e., whether it is done via TCAM/CAM chips or not), so that packetC programs can be portable.

packetC syntax presents databases as if they were one-dimensional arrays of structures, as shown below.

```
struct stype { short dest; short src;};
database stype myDB[50];
```

Since neither packetC syntax nor semantics exposes the underlying hardware organization, systems can implement databases by using TCAMs, ordinary memory, specialized chips, etc. (In practice, commercial TCAMs usually have 128 or 512-bit elements, so packetC implementations may need to impose database size limits and need to pad user base types to match hardware specifics).

5.1 Database Types: Masks and Automatic Mirroring

Network applications often match data in the current packet against a subset of each database record, e.g., find a database record which matches an Internet Protocol (IP) source address. Mask bits associated with each database element indicate whether the corresponding bits of the data portion are to be used in matching (see Fig. 4).

Because masked matching is an essential part of network table searching, packetC databases are automatically masked by the packetC compiler, which implicitly constructs each database to consist of a *data* field and a *mask* field, with each of them having the base type specified by

the user's database declaration. (In the example below, packetC structure *tags* always define a named type, so a C-style *typedef* is not needed to establish the type name).

```
struct stype { short dest; short src;};
database stype myDB[50];
// each element of myDB has the structure:
    { stype data; stype mask;};
```

Individual database elements are accessed by using array indexing syntax. An element's data and mask fields may be accessed explicitly, as shown by the example below, which continues the sample code begun just above.

```
myDB[newRow].data = { destValue, srcValue };
myDB[5].mask.dest = ~0;
srcVar = myDB[matchedRow].src; // defaults to 'data' half
```

5.2 Declarations and Default Mask Values

Defining masks in terms of structure fields is more intuitive and reliable than defining them in terms of long hexadecimal literals; this is especially true when database elements can reach 128 to 512 bits in length. packetC users can explicitly define mask values in declarations or can omit the mask part and allow the packetC compiler to supply default values.

```
// init 1st DB element w/ explicit mask value
database stype db[10] = { {{255,16},{~0,0}} };
// init 1st DB element, implicit mask value
database stype db2[5] = { {{255,16}} };
```

In the second declaration above, an initial mask value has been omitted but the element's data value, {255,16} is still surrounded by a set of curly braces for the element as a whole – {{255,16}}. Default mask values are set equal to 1 for every bit (i.e., allowing the corresponding data half's contents to be used during matching). Thus, the default mask for the 2-field mask of *stype* is {~0, ~0}. The sole exception is pad fields of a packetC bit-field container. As intuition suggests, default mask bits for a pad field are set to zero.

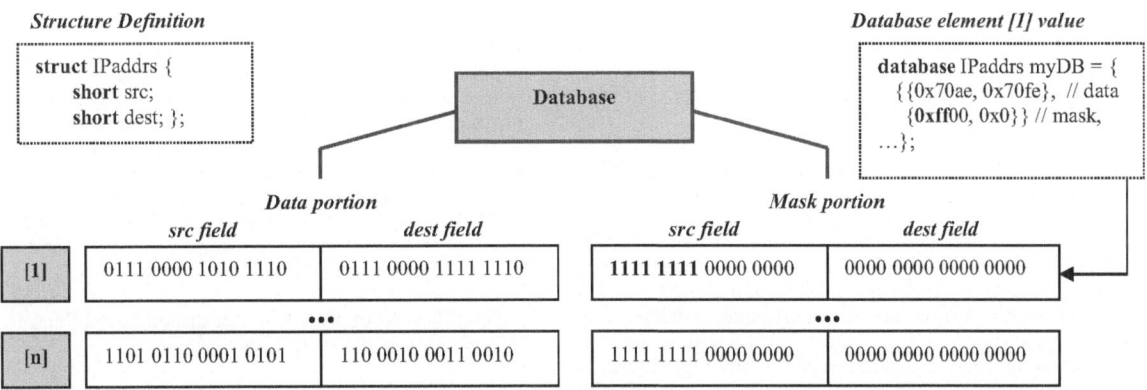

Figure 4. Setting mask bits to use only the IP address *src* field when matching element [1]. Copyright CloudShield Technologies, 2010.

339

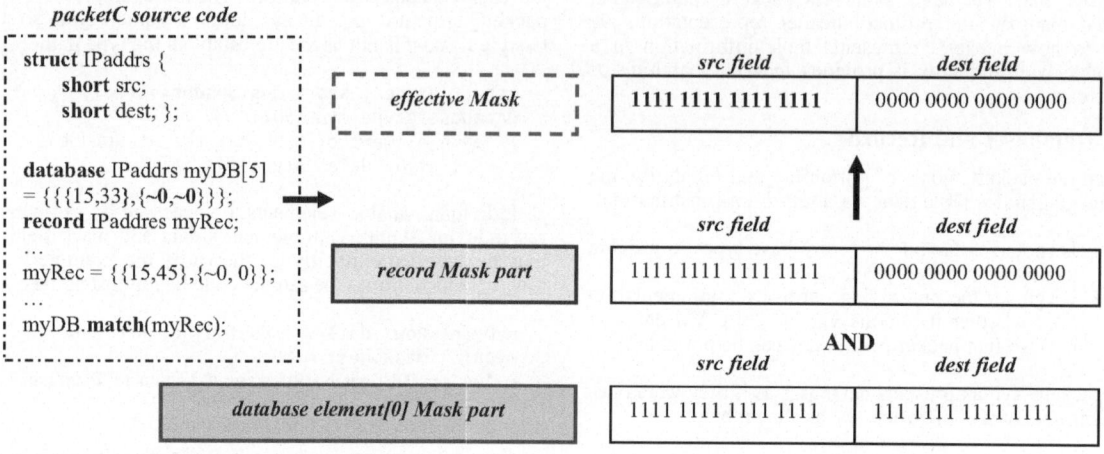

Figure 5. Match forming an effective mask from a database element mask and record mask. Copyright CloudShield Technologies, 2010.

5.3 Records and Database Operators

The packetC *record* construct is analogous to a single element of a database and shares the database characteristics of automatic mirroring into *data* and *mask* halves. Thus records offer a means of inserting and extracting individual elements from databases. A record declaration involves specifying a base type and, optionally, specifying data and mask initial values:

```
record baseType aRec = {{0,16},{0,~0}};
```

Both record and structure base type arguments play a role in database operations. packetC's designers felt that using C-style symbols for database operations would be hopelessly opaque and using library function calls for them would fail to fully integrate databases into the language. Thus, we use C++-style method syntax for database operations and use the form:

```
<dbID>'.'<operation>'(' optionalArgs ')'
```

Depending on the operator, various types of arguments are allowed as exemplified below.

```
row = myDB.insert( aRecord );
myDB[3].delete();
myDB[4].data = myStruct; // subscripting
```

For this discussion *match* is the most important database operation, since it is the basic table search operation and the one that most reveals whether parallelism is being effectively harnessed. When match's first argument is a structure, each individual database element's mask is the only one applied. If the first argument is a record, then each comparison effectively uses a logical AND of the record's mask portion and the particular database element's mask portion (Fig. 5). If an optional second argument is present (a structure) the matching element's data contents are written to it. In any case, a successful match returns the matching element's index, while a failure to match any element must be handled by packetC's

C++-style system of *try* and *catch* constructs. Some match examples follow.

```
rownum = myDB.match( myStruct );
rownum = myDB.match( myRecord );
```

The next section describes how matching constructs are currently implemented in fielded systems.

6. Current Hardware Implementation

packetC does not dictate that databases must be implemented via TCAMs; we could implement a database as an array of structures (with data and mask portions). However, our current implementation does use TCAM chips, although we have changed chips at times and other vendors' chips or alternatives could be substituted.

CloudShield Technologies' products [15] use multi-core NPUs much as our rivals do. However, our approach uses micro-coded interpreters running on NPUs to interpret user programs and, when appropriate, to push data to specialized processors.

- Microcode running on a dedicated subset of NPU *cores* works with FPGAs to control the packet pipeline, analyze packets and pre-locate headers.
- An ensemble of NPUs, each running multiple *contexts,* executes SPMD copies of packetC programs.
- A custom FPGA manages shared memory for scalars and arrays, and manages access to the T-CAM.
- TCAM chips and regular expression processors implement operations on packetC's *database* and *searchset* types, respectively [1].

Data flow from an interpreter through the FPGA to the TCAM chips is shown in figure 6 below.

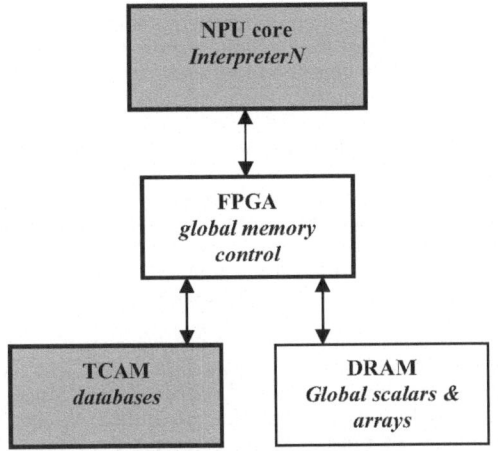

Figure 6. NPU-based interpreter accesses TCAM through FPGA, which serves as a controller for global memory elements.

7. Compiling and Interpreting

Our packetC compiler and assembler generate a proprietary *bytecode* that combines RISC-style arithmetic with high-level instructions for database and string search operations. Thus, the tools emit a single, high-level instruction for a database match operation as shown below.

```
rownum = myDB.match( myRecord );
// maps to 1 bytecode insn;
// idealized bytecode example below
Database_match(maskKind, myRecord.data,
    myRecord.mask, returnInfoDirective)
```

When the interpreter encounters a **match** bytecode, it sends the FPGA a match command, data to be matched and (optionally) the secondary mask (Fig. 5 and 7).

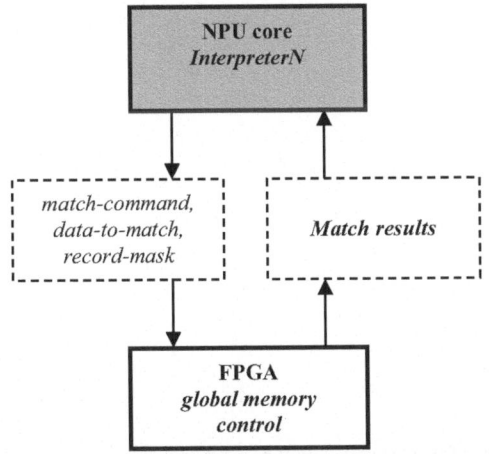

Figure 7. Communications for database match between an interpreter and the FPGA managing global memory.

Neither the compiler nor the interpreter is TCAM-specific. Only the global memory subsystem and its FPGA have TCAM dependencies. Although other implementations, such as software based matching, can be used, a TCAM implementation has the benefit that every TCAM element is evaluated for a match during the same cycle. Thus, as the following experiments show, it takes the same amount of machine time to compare data against a TCAM with one database element in it as it does to compare it to a database with 100,000 elements.

8. Performance: Parallel Database Access

This section presents two experiments that demonstrate parallel performance benefits when using packetC high-level database constructs. Both experiments used a CloudShield CS-2000 chassis [15] with a DPPM-800 10 Gigabit Ethernet blade hosting the packetC application. The DPPM-800 contains an Intel Corporation® IXP 2800 NPU, custom Xilinx, Inc.® Virtex® 5 FPGAs and Netlogic, Inc.® NSE 5512 TCAM chips to implement the databases. We used an IXIA® X16 traffic generator to generate network traffic at 10 gigabits per second (Gbps) and roughly 14 million packets per second.

8.1 Experiment 1: Dynamic Table of Traffic Flows

Traffic flows or *packet flows* are a related sequence of packets that form a coherent communication from a source to a destination across a network. The first experimental application builds a large database dynamically, populated with 5-tuple records that each characterize a traffic *flow* that has been encountered. (A network *tuple* for tracking flows is typically constructed from several fields of standard protocol headers).

First, we define a structure type with the desired tuple information, in this case drawn from the packets' IPv4 and Transmission Control Protocol (TCP) header fields.

```
struct ipv4Tuple {
    int     scrAddr;
    int     destAddr;
    short   srcPort;
    short   destPort;
    byte    protocol;
};
```

We then define a database of such structures and a record with this e base type to facilitate entering new elements into the database. We tested databases initialized to have 10, 100, 1,000, 10,000 and 100,000 elements.

```
database ipv4Tuple     flowTable[100000];
record ipv4Tuple       flow;
```

As a packet arrives, the program copy searches the database to determine whether the flow to which the packet belongs has already been entered into the database. If not, a database record to represent this new flow is created and added. Since constructs are as important as performance to our discussion, the entire application, *sans* code already presented, follows.

341

```
packet module flowtrack;
#include "cloudshield.ph"
#include "protocols.ph" // define headers
// structure, database and record decls
// ... <snip>
// Application watch variables:
int packetCount, rowNum, recordMatch;
int noMatch, numRows, tableFull;

void main($PACKET pkt, $PIB pib, $SYS sys)
{
    packetCount++;
    // Build record, using predefined 'ipv4'
    // & 'tcp' descriptors from "protocols.h"
    flow.data.scrAddr  = ipv4.sourceAddress;
    flow.data.destAddr =
                    ipv4.destinationAddress;
    flow.data.srcPort  = tcp.sourcePort;
    flow.data.destPort = tcp.destinationPort;
    flow.data.protocol = ipv4.protocol;

    // search for flow in table
    try {
      ipv4Tuple fl;
      fl = flow.data;
      rowNum = flowTable.match( fl );
      recordMatch++;
    }
    catch ( ERR_DB_NOMATCH ) {
      noMatch++;
      // insert flow into flow table
      try {
        flowTable.insert( flow );
        numRows++;
      }
      catch ( ERR_DB_FULL ) {
        tableFull++;
        // call CAM clean (hypothetical)
      }
    }
    pib.action = FORWARD_PACKET;
}
```

The experiment applied traffic containing multiple flows to the application at the maximum rate possible for a 10 gigabit Ethernet interface. We used tables of different-sizes and traffic containing differing numbers of flows, including test runs that used a table size of 100,000 elements and automatically-generated network traffic containing more than 100,000 flows.

Under these conditions, the database eventually becomes full at 100,000 flow records. Encountering additional flows then results in incrementing the *tableFull* count, while the matching and missing counters continue to increment as appropriate. A more realistic application might include a CAM clean function to manage table overflow by deleting elements on the basis of age.

Fig. 8 depicts some aspects of the experiment's performance that illustrate truisms about applying TCAM parallelism to this kind of network application. Since the TCAM searches all its elements in parallel, it takes the same amount of time to search a database with 100,000 entries as it does to search one with 10. (Note that TCAMs may have 256K to 512K elements).

Fig 8(b) shows that this system's increases in output match increases in input speed until around 3.9 Mpps (million packets per second), when its capacity is reached. After it is saturated, the system's output remains constant, i.e., this particular system configuration (including the application and system software tuning) cannot exceed 3.9 Mpps for this kind of network traffic.

The practical performance result is that a high-level language flow-tracking application can track 100,000 flows with no packet loss up to 2.26 Gbps (assuming 72-byte packets) and over 3,900,000 packets per second processed on this particular system. This behavior is independent of whether input packets match existing TCAM hit contents or not and independent of table overflow conditions.

Mpps = Million packets per second

Database rows (max. flows)	Throughput Gbps	Throughput packets per second
10	2.26	3.9 Mpps
100	2.26	3.9 Mpps
1,000	2.26	3.9 Mpps
10,000	2.26	3.9 Mpps
100,000	2.26	3.9 Mpps

(a)

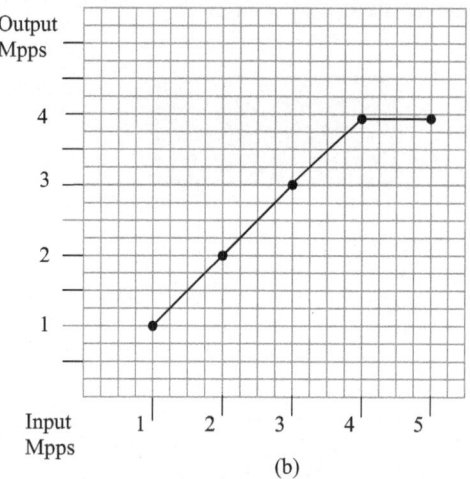

(b)

Figure 8. Flow matching performance statistics showing truisms: (a) Throughput is independent of the percentage of TCAM contents used. (b) Once the network device's capacity is reached, output is constant. Copyright CloudShield Technologies, 2010.

8.2 Experiment 2: Access Control and Subnets

This experiment's packetC application uses a small, statically-defined database to enforce network usage policies. Specifically, three subnets are defined as follows:

- 192.168.100.x - legally sanctioned intranet; traffic is allowed to flow between hosts on this subnet.
- 192.168.200.x - is a known rogue network. Traffic detected on this subnet is redirected to a special "capture port".
- All other traffic - is not allowed by policy and is dropped

Since packetC's high-level attributes are a key interest, the source code is shown below (although port-steering logic based on network topology is omitted for clarity).

```
packet module accessControl;
#include "cloudshield.ph"
#include "protocols.ph"
struct ipv4Tuple {
    int scrAddr;
    int destAddr;
};
database ipv4Tuple flowTable[2] =
    {{{192.168.100.0,192.168.100.0},
      {255.255.255.0, 255.255.255.0}},
     {{192.168.200.0, 192.168.200.0},
      {255.255.255.0, 255.255.255.0}}};
record ipv4Tuple flow;
int disallowedPackets;
int roguePackets;
int totalPackets;
int rowNum;
const int capturePort = 4;

void main($PACKET pkt, $PIB pib, $SYS sys)
{
    totalPackets++;

    // build record
    flow.data.scrAddr =
            ipv4.sourceAddress;
    flow.data.destAddr =
            ipv4.destinationAddress;
    // search for flow in table
```

```
    try {
        ipv4Tuple fl;
        fl = flow.data;
        rowNum = flowTable.match( fl );

        // Action table
        switch (rowNum) {
        case 0:
            allowedPackets++;
            pib.action = FORWARD_PACKET;
            break;
        case 1:
            roguePackets++;
            sys.outPort = capturePort;
            pib.action = FORWARD_PACKET;
            break;
        default:
            disallowedPackets++;
            pib.action = DROP_PACKET;
            break;
        }
    }
    catch ( ERR_DB_NOMATCH ) {
        disallowedPackets++;
        pib.action = DROP_PACKET;
    }
}
```

We made test runs at 1, 2, 3, 4, 5, 6 and 7 Mpps, using tens of millions of packets per test (Fig 9.a). As Fig. 9.b shows, system output speed kept pace with system input until a 5 Mpps speed was reached with 72-byte packets.

The application was able to track flows, make access policy decisions and take associated actions with no packet loss until capacity is reached at 5 Mpps.

Both tests are unusually brief for network applications, although we are not showing a large include file with enumeration and structure declarations for standard network protocols (e.g., IPv4, IPv6, TCP, etc.). Still, the unique portions written for the applications are concise. The performance exhibited is reasonably typical for the current state of the art. Important ways in which the applications and their performance compare with the norm are discussed in the next section.

Packet type	Packets seen
allowed packets	52,271,918
disallowed packets	5,130,535
rogue packets	57,268
Total	**57,459,721**

(a)

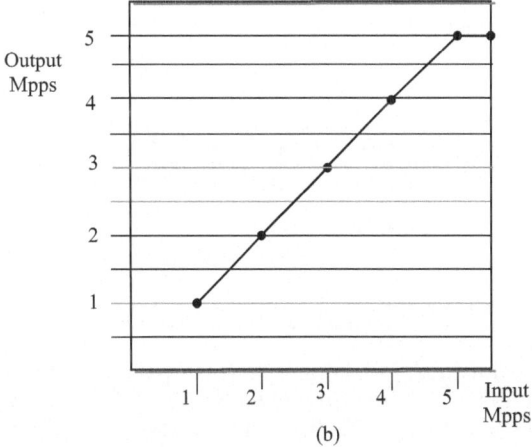

(b)

Figure 9. Access Control experiment: (a) Test run with tens of millions of packets, (b) The system becomes oversubscribed at 5 Mpps.

9. Summary

We believe the value of packetC and our implementation of its table-lookup operations consists of

- High-level language constructs to express table structure and masked table look-up in a natural way.
- Portable table constructs that can be mapped to a variety of chips or to algorithmic implementations.
- An effective TCAM implementation that does not constrai developers to use predefined vendor templates for a few flow representations.

The source code shown for the two experiments is understandable to readers who are largely unfamiliar with network applications. The indexing syntax used with databases is intuitive. Automatic mirroring of databases and records into "data" and "mask" portions provides valuable flexibility in matching (e.g., in *wildcarding* flow data).

We report performance in the 2-10Gbps range, state-of-the-practice commercial performance, achieved with high-level programming. To our best knowledge, there are no comparable C-dialect extensions. As a commercial product; packetC's natural rivals are our Silicon Valley peers' predefined TCAM templates or vendor-specific application programming interfaces (APIs) that are often veiled by non-disclosure agreements.

We are not arguing whether TCAM is the most effective form of packet processing parallelism [17]. Our intent is to show that intuitive type and operator extensions to a high-level, non-proprietary language can deliver state-of-the-practice parallel performance. The results show that our implementation, which executes micro-coded interpreters on NPUs, harnesses parallelism, promotes portability and facilitates transparently swapping out specialized chips in a heterogeneous processing environment.

Acknowledgments

Peder Jungck, Dwight Mulcahy and Ralph Duncan are the co-authors of the packetC language. Gary Oblock and Matt White contributed to language and compiler development. Andy Norton, Greg Triplett, Kai Chang, Mary Pham, Alfredo Chorro-Rivas and Minh Nguyen provided valuable help.

References

[1] "Network Processor Design, Vol. 3: Issues and Practices," M. Franklin, P. Crowley, H. Hadimioglu, P. Onufryk, eds., Morgan Kaufmann Publishers, San Francisco, California, 2005.

[2] R. Duncan and P. Jungck. packetC language for high performance packet processing. In Proceedings of the 11th IEEE Intl. Conf. High Performance Computing and Communications, (Seoul, South Korea), pp. 450-457, June 25-27, 2009.

[3] W. Wu, "Packet Forwarding Technologies," Auerbach Publications, New York, 2008, Chapter 9.

[4] G. Lawton, Routing faces dramatic changes. Computer, 42(9), 15-17, 2009.

[5] Intel Microengine C Compiler Language Support: Reference Manual. Intel Corporation, order number 278426-004, August 10, 2001.

[6] L. George and M. Blume. Taming the IXP network processor. In *Proceedings of the ACM SIGPLAN '03 Conference on Programming Language Design and Implementation*, San Diego, California, USA, ACM, pp. 26-37, June 2003.

[7] J. Wagner and R. Leupers: C compiler design for a network processor. IEEE Trans. on CAD, 20(11): 1-7, 2001.

[8] F. Baboescu, S. Singh and M. Varghese. Packet Classification for Core Routers: Is there an alternative to CAMs?. In *Proceedings of the 22nd Annual Joint Conference of .the IEEE Computer and Communications. IEEE Societies.*, Vol 1, pp. 53-63., March 30-April 3, 2003.

[9] D. Liu, Z. Chen, B. Hua, N. Yu, and X. Tang: High-performance packet classification algorithm for multithreaded IXP network processor. ACM Trans. on Embedded Computing Systems, 7(2), article 16, February, 2008.

[10] Cisco Systems, Inc., "Configuring SDM Templates," in Catalyst 3750 Switch Software Configuration Guide, Rel. 12.1(19) EA1, available at http://www.cisco.com/en/US/docs/switches/lan/catalyst-3750/software/release/12.1_19_ea1/configuration/guide/swsdm.-html, retrieved January 25, 2010.

[11] Cisco Systems, Inc. "Understanding ACL on Catalyst 6500 Series Switches," available at http://www.cisco.com/en/US/products/hw-/switches/ps708/products_white_paper09186a00800c9470.shtml, retrieved on January 25, 2010.

[12] Cisco Systems, Inc. "The Cisco QuantumFlow Processor: Cisco's Next Generation Network Processor," commercial datasheet, esp. pp. 4-7, available at http://www.cisco.com/en/US/prod-/collateral/routers/ps9343/solution_overview_c22-448936.html, 2008., retrieved January 25, 2010.

[13] Cisco Systems, Inc. "Cisco ASR 1000 Series Aggregation Service Routers: A New Paradigm for the Enterprise WAN," product brochure, esp. page. 4, available at http://www.cisco.com/en/US/prod-/collateral/routers/ps9343/brochure_c02-450721_ps9343_-Products_Brochure.html, 2008-2009, retrieved January 25, 2010.

[14] International Organization for Standardization (ISO) 7498. Open Systems Interconnections (OSI) reference model, 1983.

[15] CloudShield Technologies. CS-2000 Technical Specifications. Product datasheet available from CloudShield Technologies, 212 Gibraltar Dr., Sunnyvale, CA, USA 94089, 2006.

[16] R. Duncan, P. Jungck and K. Ross. A paradigm for processing network protocols in parallel. Proceedings of the 10th Intl. Conf. on Algorithms and Architectures for Parallel Processing, (Busan, South Korea), pp. 52-67, May 21-23, 2010.

[17] F. Baboescu, S. Singh, G. Varghese. Packet classification for core routers: is there an alternative to CAMs? Proceedings of the IEEE Infocom Conference, (San Francisco, California), April 2003.

R. Duncan, P. Jungck, and K. Ross. "packetC language and parallel processing of masked databases." *Proceedings of the 39th Intl. Conf. on Parallel Processing* (San Diego, CA), September 13–16, 2010, pp. 472–481. Reprinted with permission from the IEEE.

REPRINT 5

■ ■ ■

Packet Content Matching with packetC Searchsets

by Ralph Duncan, Peder Jungck, Kenneth Ross and Scott Tillman

Abstract—Increasing speeds and volumes push network packet applications to use parallel processing to boost performance. Examining the packet *payload* (message content) is a key aspect of packet processing. A pplications search payloads to find strings that m atch a pattern described by *regular expressions* (*regex*). Searching for mult iple strings that m ay start anywhere in the payload is a m ajor obstacle to perform ance. Commercial systems often employ multiple network processors to provide parallel processing in general and use reg ex software engines or special regex processors to speed up searching performance via parallelism. Typically, regex rules are prepared separately from the application program and compiled into a binary im age to be read by a regex processor or software engine. Our approach integrates specifying search rules with specifying network application code written in packetC, a C dialect that hi des host-m achine specifics, supports coarse-grain parallelism and supplies high -level data type and operator extensions for packet pro cessing. packetC provides a *searchset* data type, as well as *match* and *find* operations, to support payload searching. W e show that our searchset operator im plementation, using associative m emory and regex processors, lets users enjoy the perform ance benefits of parallel regex technology without learning hardware-specifics or using a separate regex toolchain's use.

Keywords - parallel processing; network processing; programming languages; packet payload, deep packet inspection

I. INTRODUCTION

Computer networks continuall y increase the amount of data pumped to hand-held devices and the speed of transmission mediums. Thus, programs that process network packets are under great pressure to increase their speeds as well. Faster packet processing is often supplied by parallelism in both hardware and software. Network hardware parallelism commonly uses *network processing units* (NPUs) with multithreaded architectures geared to real-time packet processing [1]. The associated software parallelism typically involves programming N PUs with an assembly language or a C dialect that supports direct user control of machine-specific caches , register classes, queues, et al.

One common task for network applications involves searching packet payloads for specific contents, e.g., to find virus *signatures* for *intrusion detection* or to support firewalls, content-based routing, etc. Strings might start at a specific packet offset or occur a nywhere within the payload. Applications search for both speci fic strings and strings that

conform to a g eneral pattern. T he latter are effectively described by *regular expressions* (or *regex*), a formalism that describes strings and character sequences [2]. Regex operators often specify optional sequences, for example the * operator indicates zero or more of the preceding element, while the + operator indicates one or m ore instances of the preceding element (shown below).

```
Xy*z matches "xz", "xyz", "xyyz", et al.
Xy+z matches "xyz", "xyyz" but not "xz"
```

Content searching and m atching introduces great performance uncertainty in a domain with tight performance requirements, since a match may be anywhere within a large packet payload. This is especially true when potential matches involve many patterns or complex regex rules.

Network applications often u se eithe r software engines or special processors to implement payload searches described by regex (Section 2). This usually involves specifying and compiling regular expression rules prepared separately from the applica tion program. Our approach expresses strings and regex in terms of a new *searchset* data type. Thus, specifying regex search operations and specifying the core network app lication occur in the same packetC source code. Our compiler and hardware implement search operations with associative memory and specialized regex processors. Thus, we make payload searching part of a high-l evel programming language but free the user from managing the partic ulars of the specialized hardware needed to e ffectively implement it and from managing a separate regex compiler toolchain.

The paper reviews popular string or regular expression matching algorithms and commercial, hardware-based solutions. Two sections sk etch CloudShield's parallel programming model and packet C language with material adapted from our language overview [3]. W e then present the packetC s *earchset* construct in detail. A fter a hardw are implementation review, an expe rimental section presents performance results for packet payload searching. Concluding remarks follow.

II. RELATED WORK: ALGORITHMIC BACKGROUND

Searching packet payload contents for matches with a set of strings or set of regular expression *rules* is usually done with algorithms that can be mapped to state transition machines in the form of determ inistic finite aut omata (DFAs) or non-deterministic finite automata (NFAs) [4]. Commercial im plementations that em ploy the alg orithms as

345

system software and those that embody algorithms in specialized processors are bot h common. Implementers have explored many permutati ons of popular algorithms. We describe two widely -used softw are algorithm s below, examine a recent adaptation, then survey hardware solutions.

The B oyer-Moore algorithm [5] starts attem pting matches at the end of the se arch string and uses failed matches to skip unneeded comparisons. Thus, when trying to match a string of length *n*, if the *n*th position of the text being searched fails to match position *n* of the string for which it is searching, the algorithm can skip e xamining text positions 1 through *n*-1 for this potential ending p osition. Although algorithm variants di ffer, the approach i nvolves pre-computing two tables: th e first indicates how many positions to the right to sh ift in the searched text when a given character fails a match (*bad character shift*). The second table (*good suffix shift*) holds the searched -for string and its partial patterns; it indicates the few est positions that the partial pattern m ust be shif ted to the left in order to possibly match. The algorithm' s worst-case performance is approximately 3**N* comparisons (complexity *O(n)*) [6].

The Aho-Corasick algorithm [7] m atches strings in a *pattern dictionary* . It constructs an ordered keyword tree (*trie*) where transitions from a parent node to child node correspond to a letter encountered in a string that is examined from left to right. Search strings that share prefixes share tree paths emana ting from the root. T he tree is augmented with *fail pointers.* W hen a failure occurs trying to match some string, *s0*, and the string of characters matched thus far, *s1*, contains a longest suffix, *s2*, that is a legal prefix of *s0* , then the failure pointer indicates the previously-traversed node in the current path where the search can be resumed as if only that prefix had just been encountered. W hen the dictionary to be m atched is known beforehand, com mercial im plementations com pile the ordered tree into a form of *finite state m achine*. Such an automaton will run in linear tim e proportional to the length of the payload to be searched and the number of dictionary matches present [8].

The IBM DotStar approach extends the Aho -Corasick algorithm to build an augmented DFA that recognizes a set of regex [9]. DotStar departs from the classic algorithm by compressing parts of the keyword tree where state explosion would result from applying re gex closure or repet ition operators to a character class. The approach creates *add-on* data for such instances (status bits and locations), annotates the DFA states with operations on that data and uses an augmented run-time algorithm that operates on add-on-data.

III. R ELATED W ORK: F IELDED S YSTEMS

Advanced com mercial system s for high-speed packet payload inspection are charact erized by using specialized processors for regex matching, by dedicated toolchains to compile regex rules into autom atons and by C dialects w ith extensions that allow com munication w ith the regex processor. Since the details of autom aton im plementation, language extensions and regex processor communications are usually proprietary and protected by non-disclosure agreements, this discussion concentrates on the high-speed regex processors, which are more openly documented.

Specialized processors for packet payload searching include the follow ing. N etlogic M icrosystems, Inc. describes its NETL7™ Know ledge-Based Processor (KBP) chips as recognizing strings and Perl compatible regular expressions (PCREs) within and across packet boundaries [10]. Cavium Networks, Inc.'s deep packet inspection (DPI) hardware t echnology appears as t he NI TROX® DPI CN17xx processor and board family, and as part of the Octeon II m ulti-core processor fam ily [11]. T hey describe this technology as using bot h DFAs and NFAs. LSI Corporation offers Tarari Content Proce ssors[12], a family of multi-core processors it describes as implementing DFAs[13] "with proprietary NFA technology." The IDT PAX.port 2500[14] is a content inspection engine comprised of 15 *classification cores* , organized into three blocks of five cores. A block's cores share access to an external *pattern m emory* that holds compiled regular e xpression rules.

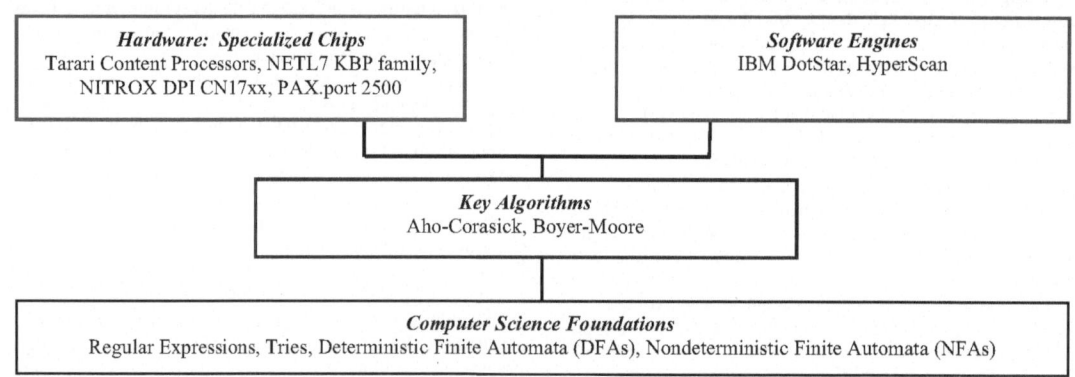

Hardware: Specialized Chips
Tarari Content Processors, NETL7 KBP family, NITROX DPI CN17xx, PAX.port 2500

Software Engines
IBM DotStar, HyperScan

Key Algorithms
Aho-Corasick, Boyer-Moore

Computer Science Foundations
Regular Expressions, Tries, Deterministic Finite Automata (DFAs), Nondeterministic Finite Automata (NFAs)

Figure 1. Major components of packet payload searching technology. Copyright CloudShield Technologies, 2010.

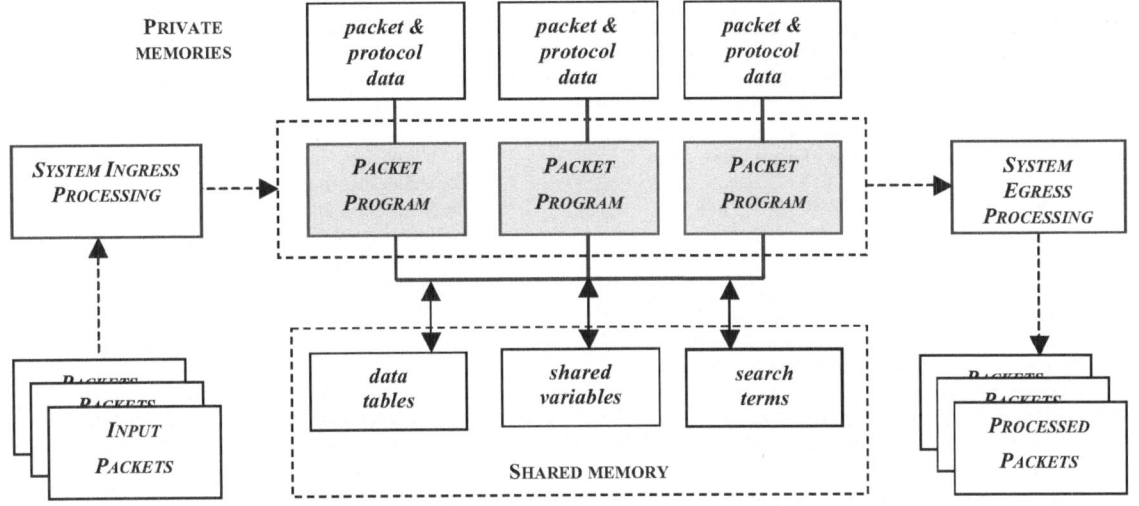

Figure 2.   Parallel model for packet processing. Copyright CloudShield Technologies, 2010.

Commercial developers using such specialized processors usually provide a separate toolchain to translate a text file of regex rules (in several popu   lar formats) into a binary image of a graph or state machine. Vendors typically provide calls to an API or library to allow high-level language dialects to load the binary i mages on a specialized regex processor, run them against a packet's contents and obtain the match results. CloudS hield's approach differs by providing regex (or string) rule specifications   and search operations in the form of high-level language constructs that appear in the application source code, rather than separately. Before examining the specific language constructs used in this way, we review our overall approach to parallelism.

IV.   A PARALLEL PACKET PROCESSING MODEL

The model's principal characteristics are as follows:
- Using coarse-grained, packet-level parallelism
- Hiding machine-specific characteristics
- Offloading program orchestration and pre-   calculation tasks to the host system
- Providing shared and private memory

Our model offers the developer an intuitive view of parallel packet processing at a coarse-grained level. Parallel tasks are copies of a small program that co   mpletely processes one packet at a time. Thus, we use single program, m ultiple data (SPM D) parallelism and free the developer from intricate task management and synchronization details.

The model requires the host system to play an active role in managing the execution of program copies, handling packet ingress and egress, and pre- calculating *layer offsets* (protocol header locations) that   are present in the packet (Fig. 2). Execution management involves preparing two things for a program copy prior to each execution:

- A copy of the packet as an array of unsigned bytes
- A collection of flags and integers (*the Packet Information Block*) that indicate whether protocol headers for certain network *layers* are present in the packet and, if they are, the offset at w   hich they reside

Calculating protocol offsets before the program runs:

- Lets users focus on application-specific concerns
- Facilitates using specialized hardware to do this

We describe processing and accessing this layer information in another paper [15].

The m odel partitions shared and private m   emory in a natural way:

- Global memory holds scalars and aggregates shared by all packet programs.
- Each program copy's private memory contains variables and aggregates i nvisible to other program copies.

Global memory contains three categories of data:

- C-style variables and a   ggregates shared among program copies (such as counters)
- Search terms – strings or regular expressions for driving searches (the focus of this discussion)
- Tables – various data in aggregate form

The model does not dictate   particular mechanisms for synchronizing access to global data.

347

A program ming language based on this m odel must provide packet-level parallelism, provide shared and private memory for program copies and offer data types that support classic network application operations on pay load search terms and table data. The following section sketches the packetC language we developed to meet these goals.

V. PACKETC LANGUAGE OVERVIEW

We developed packetC with the model and these goals:

- Use the C 99 variant of C for operators (arithm etic, logical and bitwise), conditional statements and syntax.
- Reduce runtime exceptions and performance uncertainties by removing pointers, address operators and dynamic memory allocation (and by using unsigned integer arithmetic that wraps, rather than over/underflows).
- Increase reliability via stronger typing rules and by disallowing implicit type conversions or promotions.
- Support the model's SPM D parallelism and its shared memory aggregates for table and search data.
- Hide m achine-specific r egister classes, caches, memory banks, etc.

Since another paper provides a more general language overview [3], this section provides only a language sketch, emphasizing features involve d with parallelism. The searchset construct central to the paper's focus is discussed in detail by the subsequent section.

- Packet program copies are expressed with a *packet main* program – this is the unit of parallel execution.
- Variables declared outside of either m ain or a function are deemed to be in the global (shared) memory; copies of all others are a ssigned to private memories.

The basic unit of packetC parallelism, a *packet module* or *packet main*, has the appearance of a C main function w ith accompanying type, variable and function declarations. Its structure is shown by the example code below.

```
packet module malwareDetector;
// GLOBAL SECTION
// type, database & searchset decls
// function declarations
int trojansFound = 0; //sharedCounter

void someUtilityFn(int i) {…}

void main {
// C-style blocks of decls & stmts
short myShortVar;
// body of program to be replicated
trojansFound++;
   …
}
```

Global declarations are visible from the point where they appear to the bottom of the module text. The extended

aggregate types, *databases* and *searchsets*, are always declared here and shared by all program copies.

Distinctive packetC data structures and types include:

- The pre-calculated protocol information is available to each packet main in a system -provided structure, the packet information block (PIB) [15].
- Shared session and protocol data for classic network application tables is kept in *database* aggregates and in individual *records*.
- String and regular expression search terms are stored in global aggregates of the extended *searchset* data type.

Having sketched packetC's approach to parallelism , memory management and protocol header analysis, we turn to this paper's principal interest – packetC support for searching packet payloads.

VI. SEARCHSETS

A packetC *searchset* is an aggregate data type that groups together either a set of strings or a set of regular expressions to be used in searches. The language defines **match** and **find** operators to search the packet or local variables for the presence of a searchset's elements. Since a realistic expe ctation is that these search terms may drive the loading of a special content inspection processor, the language does not specify how searchsets are represented in memory. Sim ilarly, the language specifies the semantics of **match** and **find** but not how an impl ementation must obtain that behavior.

A searchset declaration resem bles declaring a C -style, two-dimensional array of strings, as indicated below.

```
// declare a string searchset
searchset myset[5][3] = {"cat","dog","owl"};
```

The following searchset decla ration features distinguish them from C declarations.

- The leftm ost index indicates the num ber of elem ents (strings/regex) in the searchset.
- The rightmost index indicat es the maximum length of a searchset string or regex in characters.
- The presence of the **regex** keyword distinguishes a searchset with regex contents from one with strings (the two cannot be mixed).

```
// declare a regex searchset
regex searchset setA[3][14] =
    {".*?malware", ".*?from", ".*?mail"};
```

A. Null Termination Issues

Null term ination i mpacts searchsets by determ ining whether:

- Matching and finding operations treat searchset elements as having trailing null terminators.

- The memory space to be searched is, itself, null terminated (i.e., whether the search should terminate upon finding any null terminator in that space).

If the user does not want trailing null terminator s as part of any searchset string or want to stop searching on reaching a null term inator, no explicit null handling is needed. However, if the user does not want a traili ng null terminator for any searchset elem ent but *does* want the search terminated on encountering a nu ll terminator, then the user can add the pre-defined string literal constant, **NULL_STOP** as the *first* element of a string searchset definition or add **NULL_REGEX** to a regex searchset definition.

```
// where NULL_STOP is equivalent to "\x00"
const searchset  set[3][3] =
    { NULL_STOP, "cat", "dog"};
// where NULL_REGEX is ".*?\x00"
regex searchset  set[3][6] =
    { NULL_REGEX, ".*?cat", ".*?dog"};
```

Finally, if the user em ploys explicit null term inators in one or more searchset strings and wants the search to stop if it encounters a null terminator without matching any of those strings, then the user can add **NULL_STOP** as the *final* element of a string searchset definition or **NULL_REGEX** as the final element of a regex searchset definition (as shown below).

```
const searchset  set[3][4] =
    { "cat\x00", "dog\x00", NULL_STOP };
regex searchset  set[3][6] =
    { ".*?cat\x00", NULL_REGEX };
```

B. The MATCH Operator

Both **match** and **find** are packetC *built-in* methods that use C++-style method syntax, i.e., the operator keyword is separated from a searchset by a dot character ('.'), is followed by a parenthesized list of input parameters and delivers a structure result, (of type Search Result) as show n below.

```
// struct tags define a named type w/o typedef
struct SearchResult {
   int index;    // searchset elem matched
   int position;// search area where match ends
};
```

The **match** operator provides fixed-position matching for string-based searchsets but not regex-based ones; it determines whether contents starting at a given place match any of the searchset elements, as in the example below.

```
searchset pets[3][3] = {"cat", "dog", "owl" };
SearchResult ansStruct;
try {
   ansStruct = pets.match( pkt[64:66] );
}
catch ( ERR_SET_NOMATCH ) {…}
```

Even this simple-sounding scheme, however, has semantic complications when all the searchset element lengths do not equal the searched area's length. These rules apply w hen a searchset string, s, w ith length s_i is m atched against the contents of the k contiguous bytes that begin at the starting address of argument, a, with length a_k:

- When $s_i < a_k$ but m atches the first s_i bytes of the argument, the comparison is regarded as a match (searchset element "cat" matches argument "catapult").
- When $s_i > a_k$ the comparison is not a match.

However, a *near-match* results when $s_i > a_k$ but the first a_k bytes of s match the argum ent (i.e. , searchset element, "lightning" is a near-match for argument, "light"). Detecting and suppressing near-matches and, possibly, restarting matching actions afterward ar e implement ation-specific, because w e expect im plementations to utilize special regex or content inspection processors that lack a standard behavior for (or the ability t o) restart m atching. T his is esp ecially problematic w hen legitim ate m atches follow a near -match item in a searchset. C ompliant im plementations can suppress the near-match result through length analysis but may be unable to redo or restart the match process.

C. The FIND Operator

The **find** operator searches for each searchset elem ent, s, starting anywhere within the argument (usually the packet payload). Although matches occur regardless of a matching character sequence's distance from the argument's start, strings that occur close to the start w ill be found before those appearing farther away. W hen a searchset is declared without the **regex** keyword qualifier, attempts to find searchset string elements are made in the same order as their declaration: searching terminat es when a match is found. When a **regex** qualifier is used, the matching sequence and behavior depends on the characteristics of the regular expressions involved.

```
// 'mat' can be matched if 'mate' absent
searchset smart[2][4] = {"mate", "mat"};
// poor design, 'mate' is never matched
searchset dense[2][4] = {"mat", "mate"};
SearchResult ansStruct;
...
   try { // search the entire packet
      ansStruct = smart.find( pkt );
   }
   catch ( ERR_SET_ NOTFOUND ) {…}
```

VII. CURRENT HARDWARE IMPLEMENTATION

Our products (e.g., the CS-2000 [16]) are heterogeneous multiprocessors that use m ulti-core N PUs, FPG As and specialized processors to implement network applications.

- Microcode running on a dedicated subset of NPU *cores* works with FPGAs to control the packet pi peline, analyze packets and pre-locate protocol headers.
- Another group of cores, each running m ultiple *contexts,* hosts microcode that interprets copies of a packetC

349

program that has been comp iled into a virtual m achine byte-code.

- Specialty processors and FPGAs provide parallel processing for classic netw ork application functionality, such as large table look -up or payload inspection. This characteristic is critical for allowing packet programs to run within the time budgets dictated by network speeds of 1 Gbps and higher.

The packetC language does not specify any hardware aspect of how the searchset data type or the **match** and **find** operators are implemented. In practice, we use ternary content addressable memories (T-CAM s) and regex processors to implement searchset **match** and **find** operations for performance reasons, as detailed below. However, a compliant implementation need not use any particular vendor's chips nor use T -CAMS to im plement searchsets.

A. Associative Memory for the MATCH Operator

If a user employs the match operator with a string searchset, our compiler builds a packetC masked *database* [2] behind the scenes to represent the searchset in match operations. A packetC database is akin to an array of C-style structures in which every 'data' *struct* has a corresponding mask struct of the same type. The m ask-bits control whether the corresponding data bits are used in table look-up operations. In this case the compiler considers each searchset string's length, setting the appropr iate mask bits 'on' for defined characters and 'off' for nulls (Fig. 3).

CloudShield's CS 2000 [16] uses Netlogic NSE 5512 T -CAM chips to im plement packetC database constructs. packetC databases, like global scalars and arrays, are accessed via our 'Silicon D atabase' m odule, im plemented with a custom Xilinx Virtex-II Pro™ FPGA (Fig. 4).

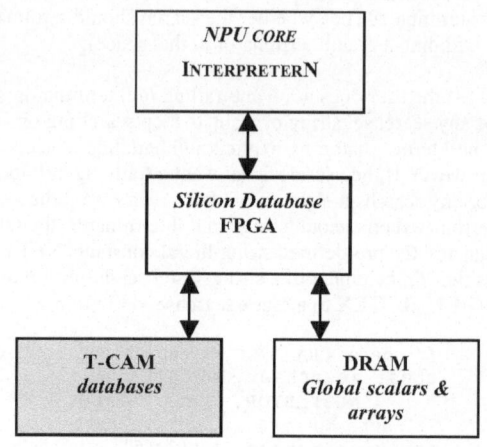

Figure 4. Using T-CAM for searchset **match** operations. Copyright CloudShield Technologies, 2010.

By using associative m emory to im plement the fixed - location searchset **match** operation, w e can com pare all a searchset's string elements to the **match** argument in a single parallel operation. The resulting performance effects are discussed in the experimental section below.

B. Regex Processor for the FIND Operator

We currently im plement **find** operations for both string and regex searchsets by downloading compiled rules for them to an IDT PAX.port 2500 content inspection eng ine [14]. The string searchsets are first preprocessed into simple regular expressions. Custom tools perform the preprocessing without packetC user interv ention and invoke the IDT PAX compiler to create the *pattern memory* contents that will be

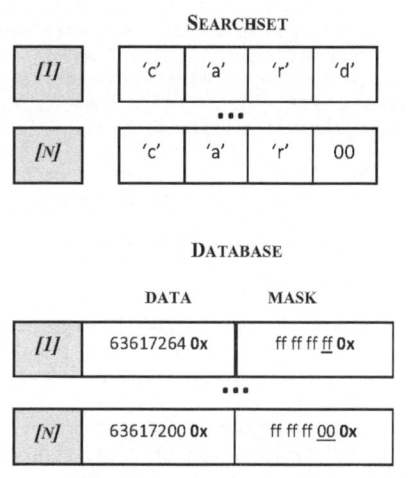

Figure 3. Representing a searchset with a database. Copyright CloudShield Technologies, 2010.

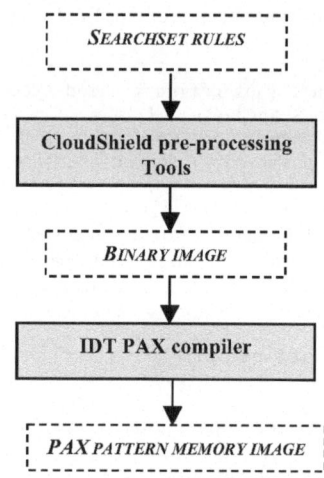

Figure 5. Simplified view of toolchain for compiling regex rules. Copyright CloudShield Technologies, 2010.

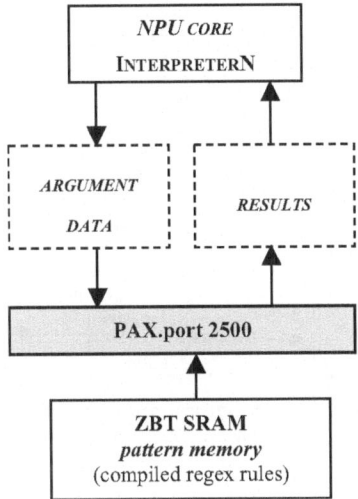

Figure 6.   Using PAX port 2500 for searchset **find** operations. Copyright CloudShield Technologies, 2010.

downloaded into PAX SRAM . A simplified view of this process is shown in Fig. 5.

At runtim e **find** arguments are sent to the PAX subsystem, which holds its compiled regular expression rules in its own IDT zero bus turnaround (ZBT) SRAM as the pattern mem ory (Fig. 6). The provisions for dynamically updating the pattern memory are beyond the scope of this paper and are not shown.

VIII.   PAYLOAD SEARCHING AND PERFORMANCE

Three considerations drive perform ance for packet payload searching: size, matching complexity and location.

- Size: Both the number of strings for which to search and the size of the packet can vary substantially and greatly impact search performance.
- Matching C omplexity: The performance of a regex processor may vary greatly in response to whether the regular expressions it is im plementing require significant *backtracking* or result in state explosion.
- Location: N aturally, m atching perform ance w ill vary according to whether matches are found near the start of small packets or at the end of large ones.

With this sense of fundamental causes for performance variation, the next section describes two simple experiments.

IX.   SEARCHSET PERFORMANCE EXPERIMENTS

This section presents two experim ents that dem onstrate realistic real-time performan ce when using packetC high - level searchset constructs. B oth experim ents used a Cloudshield PN41 Deep Pack et Processing M odule (DPPM) blade [17] to host their pac ketC application. Regex processing was provided by a pair of PAX port 2500

systems, each with a 2.5 Gig abit per second (Gbps) maximum throughput. We used an IXIA X16 traffic generator [18] with an LSM10G Ethernet processing blade to generate network traffic.

The testing procedures involved generating traffic up to the maximum rate of 10Gbps, us ing packet sizes of 300 or 700 bytes. W e sent the traffic to the DPPM , processed the packets with the packetC application and returned processed packets to the IXIA. If the PN41 and packetC programs cannot keep up, packets are dr opped. Examining statistics that the IXIA gathers determ ines application throughput and reveals dropped packets.

A.   Experiment 1: MATCH Operator for Strings

This experim ent involves searching 300 -byte packets for an exact match of a pattern (or one of a set of patterns) at a particular location in the packet. These patterns are defined as strings, and in this experiment they are all of the same length in order to avoid the semantic complications described in the next subsection. The application determ ines a m atch or no m atch result, along w ith the index and location of the matched pattern. W e tested packetC searchsets with as few as five patterns and as many as 30,000. A representative packetC source code example follows.

```
packet module searchset_match_test;
#include "cloudshield.ph"

searchset manyMatches[30005][10]=
#include "matches4.txt"
int Match[7], noMatch[7];
int manyMatchesIndex, manyMatchesPosition;

void main($PACKET pkt, $PIB pib, $SYS sys)
{
  SearchResult result;
  try {
    result = manyMatches.match (pkt[70:79]);
    Match[6]++;
    manyMatchesIndex    = result.index;
    manyMatchesPosition = result.position;
  }
  catch ( ERR_SET_NOMATCH ) {
    noMatch[6]++;
  }
  pib.action = FORWARD_PACKET;
}
```

The test application kept up with input transmission speed until input speed exceeded 8 -9Gbps. A slight difference was noted between match and non-match situations, w hich w e believe is due to taking slightly different execution paths through compiled code. The application performance shown in Fig. 7 had the following characteristics:

351

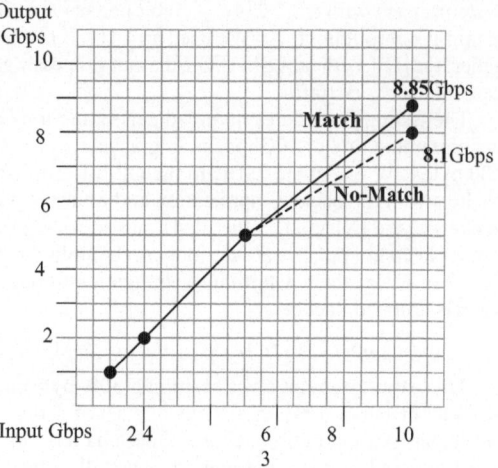

Figure 7. Experiment 1: matching fixed-location strings.

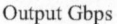
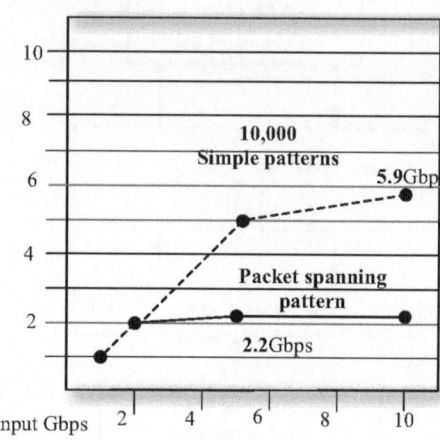

Figure 8. Experiment 2: finding strings and regex.

- The searchset had more than 30,000 entries.
- Searchset string elements were 10 characters long.
- Seachsets with an elemen t that matched packet contents topped out at 8.85 Gbps.
- Searchsets w ith no element that matched packet contents had a top speed of 8.1 Gbps.

Results running m ultiple tests w ith different searchset sizes or string lengths did not m aterially differ. This is expected, since the perform ance of the associative m emory chip used to implement matching operations should be impervious to those variations.

B. Experiment 2: FIND Operator with Strings and Regex

This experiment involves searching 700 -byte packets for the particular patterns defined in the searchset, which may be strings or regular expressions. The patterns may be located at any position in the packet. The application determines a match or no m atch result, as w ell as finds a m atched pattern's searchset index and packet location.

```
packet module searchSet_tests;
#include "cloudshield.ph"
regex searchset regSet1[3][77] = {
  ".*?[a-z]ztop",
  ".*?[b,B][e,E][a,A][t,T][l,L][e,E][s,S]",
".*?GET.*?HTTP.*?Host: www\\.ClShield\\.com"
  };
int Match[7], noMatch[7];
SearchResult result; // std result structure

void main($PACKET pkt, $PIB pib, $SYS sys)
{
  try {  // search the entire packet
    result = regSet1.find (pkt[0:end]);
    Match[1]++;
    regSet1Index = result.index;
    regSet1Position = result.position;
  }
  catch ( ERR_SET_NOTFOUND ) {
    noMatch[1]++;

  }
  pib.action = FORWARD_PACKET;
}
```

We tested different searchsets, i ncluding those with as few as five patterns and as many as 10,000. W e also used different kinds of pattern definitions, including simple strings, null -terminated strings , and regular expressions. A representative test application example is shown below.

In Fig. 8 w e report test results for applications w ith two different pattern situations.

- Simple patterns, which consisted of 10,000 regular-expressions with the following general form: ".*?pattern"*n //* where *n* is 1-5 digits
- 'Torture test' – the three regex shown in the code example above. The heart of this test is a complex regular expression that is meant to span much of the packet when it does find a match. This is the only one of the patterns that produces a match.

Since the system under test uses two PAX.port 2500 subsystems to implement the packetC searchset **find** operation, the observed results fall within expected behavior. The torture test's 2.2 G bps best speed (below a single subsystem's best) reflects having to ship all or almost all of every packet to one of the subsystems before a match is found. In con trast, the simple pattern case tops the two subsystems' cumulative capacity, since it often finds matches before shipping all of a packet's data to the PAX system.

X. SUMMARY

As a programming language, p acketC does not reflect a radical departure from existing languages. Instead, it combines familiar C features, stronger typing, coarse-grained parallelism and some novel data types to create an effective mechanism for programming high -speed network applications, particularly for d eep packet inspection needs. Similarly, CloudShield Tec hnology's network processing platforms combine familiar features, such as using multi-core

NPUs with more novel features, such as driving execution with micro-coded interpreters.

When we consider the packetC language and its hardware implementation as a unified whole, the following conclusions emerge. First, the features we have in common with other commercial systems for high-speed packet inspection include using:

- A C-based language dialect
- Multicore NPUs, accompanied by a general-purpose processor core
- Specialized regex processors

Distinctive features of our approach are:

- Embedding the declaration of search strings and regular expressions within a C dialect data type
- Disengaging developers from the regex toolchain
- Providing matching at both fixed and free payload locations and making it an integral part of the high-level language via operators expressed in C++-method-style syntax
- Handling fixed location string searching by automatically constructing packetC masked databases [19] in the background and then using T-CAM chips for high-speed matching

packetC is used in fielded applications developed by commercial, military and government users. Not surprisingly, performance characteristics of such systems is rarely published. Similarly, information about packetC's natural rivals, C dialects and interfaces from other Silicon Valley network systems vendors, is often veiled by non-disclosure agreements. In contrast, we want packetC to be non-proprietary and portable, not least to facilitate our on-going process of changing NPUs and specialized processors in our heterogeneous systems.

The 2-9 Gbps performance results reported above are within state-of-practice expectations; we present them to argue that payload inspection can be done at high speeds, driven solely by programs written in a high-level language and augmented with appropriate constructs. We plan to continue increasing our systems' speed with new components and to continue integrating network application domain needs with high-level programming language design.

ACKNOWLEDGMENTS

Peder Jungck, Dwight Mulcahy and Ralph Duncan co-authored the packetC language. Gary Oblock and Matt White contributed to compiler development. Andy Norton, Greg Triplett, Kai Chang, Mary Pham, Alfredo C horro-Rivas and Minh Nguyen provided valuable help.

REFERENCES

[1] Network Processor Design, Vol. 3: Issues and Practices," M. Franklin, P. Crowley, H. Hadimioglu, P. Onufryk, eds., Morgan Kaufmann Publishers, San Francisco, California, 2005.

[2] J. Friedl, "Mastering Regular Expressions," O'Reilly Media, Inc., Sebastopol, California, USA, 2nd edition, 2002.

[3] R. Duncan and P. Jungck. packetC language for high performance packet processing. In Proceedings of the 11th IEEE Intl. Conf. High Performance Computing and Communications, (Seoul, South Korea), pp. 450-457, June 25-27, 2009.

[4] J. Hopcroft, R. Motwani and J. Ullman, "Introduction to Automata Theory, Languages and Computation," Addison-Wesley, 3rd edition, 2006.

[5] R. Boyer and S. Moore, A fast string searching algorithm. Communications of the ACM 20(10), 262-272, October, 1977.

[6] R. Cole, Tight bounds on the complexity of the Boyer-Moore string matching algorithm. In *Proceedings of the 2nd ACM-SIAM Symposium on Discrete Algorithms*, San Francisco, California, USA, SIAM,1991.

[7] A. Aho and M. Corasick, Efficient string matching: An aid to bibliographic search. Communications of the ACM, 18(6), 333-340, June, 1975.

[8] Wikipedia, "Aho-Corasick algorithm." Retrieved on April 2, 2010 from http://en.wikipedia.org/wiki/Aho-Corasick.

[9] D. Passeto, F. Patrini and V. Agarwal, Tools for very fast regular expression maching. Computer, 43(3), 50-58, March, 2010.

[10] Netlogic Microsystems, Inc., "Products: NETL7™ Knowledge-based Processor Family." Retrieved on April 2, 2010 from http://www.netlogicmicro.com/Products/Layer7/Layer7.htm.

[11] Cavium Networks, Inc. "Products: NITROX® DPI Processors." Retrieved on April 2, 2010 from http://www.caviumnetworks.com/processor_NITROX-DPI.html.

[12] LSI Corporation. "Tarari Content Processors." Retrieved on April 5, 2010 from http://www.lsi.com/networking_home/networking_products/tarari_content_processors/.

[13] LSI Corporation. "Tarari T10 Technology: Content Processors." Technology brief retrieved on April 5, 2010 as http://www.lsi.com/DistributionSystem/AssetDocument/LSI-PB_2pg_T10_032509HR.pdf.

[14] H.J. Chao and B. Liu. "High Performance Switches and Routers." John Wiley and Sons, Hoboken, New Jersey, 2007, pp. 562-564.

[15] R. Duncan, P. Jungck and K. Ross. A paradigm for processing network protocols in parallel. Proceedings of the 10th Intl. Conf. on Algorithms and Architectures for Parallel Processing, (Busan, South Korea), pp. 52-67, May 21-23, 2010.

[16] CloudShield Technologies. CS-2000 Technical Specifications. Product datasheet available from CloudShield Technologies, 212 Gibraltar Dr., Sunnyvale, CA, USA 94089, 2006.

[17] International Business Machine Corporation. IBM BladeCenter PN41. Product datasheet available from IBM Systems and Technology Group, Route 100, Somers, New York, USA 10589, 2008.

[18] IXIA. Optixia®X16. Retrieved on 9/16/2010 from http://www.ixiacom.com/products/display?skey=ch_optixia_x16.

[19] R. Duncan, P. Jungck and K. Ross. packetC language and parallel processing of masked databases. Proceedings of the 39th Intl. Conf. on Parallel Processing, (San Diego), pp. 472-481, Sept. 13-16, 2010.

R. Duncan, P. Jungck, K. Ross, and S. Tillman. "Packet content matching with packetC searchSets." *Proceedings of the 16th Intl. Conf. on Parallel and Distributed Systems* (Shanghai, China), December 8–10, 2010, pp. 180–188. Reprinted with permission from the IEEE.

References for Run-time Aggregate Selection with Strong Typing

by Ralph Duncan, Peder Jungck, Kenneth Ross and Dwight Mulcahy

Abstract

Network packet processing often involves having the results of a database match or packet content search select the next program operation. Our packetC[1] language provides specialized agg regate data ty pes, *databases*[2] f or m asked matching an d *searchsets*[3] f or pack et pay load search terms. It is common to c hain operations on these types, so that th e resu lt of on e operation selects th e specific aggregate to use for the next operation. pack etC offers a *reference* data type to support this kind of chaining. A packetC reference provides an abstract way to refer to one of th e extended data ty pe aggregates in source code. At run time the reference construct's value will indicate a particu lar aggregate of the relevant type. T hus, this co nstruct is a classic *reference* in th e co mputer science sense of a mechanism f or in direct v ariable access. Unlik e a C++ ref erence ou r con struct m ust be assignable to support ch aining that is driv en by runtime resu lts. Unlik e a C- style pointer our reference must have strong typing, since runtime recovery f rom an illeg al ref erence v alue (indicating a nonexistent or in appropriate agg regate) is not practical in this unforgiving, high-speed domain. The paper illustrates practical applications and sh ows th at co mpressed co de f rom using references does not cause performance penalties.

Categories and Subject Descriptors D.3.3 [**Programming Languages**]: L anguage Co nstructs and Features – data types and structures

General Terms L anguages.

Keywords prog ramming languages; parallel processing, packetC, references, network processing

1. Introduction

Network applications of ten u se th e resu lts of matching packet characteristics against a datab ase or of f inding strings in th e pack et *payload* to select the next table on which to operate . For exam ple, w hen a pack et fragment matches an element in an array of virus signatures, the array index can driv e whether to m atch th e packet's origins against a database of government-sponsored hackers, versus one co ntaining freelance h ackers. pack etC[1], a C dialect for pack et proces sing, prov ides *reference* ty pes f or tw o specialized data types. A reference variable provides a way to determine at run-time which particular aggregate to u se.

Users can em ploy array s of reference variables to conditionally chain aggregate operations. When a construct containing a reference variable is e xecuted, the effect is as if the selected aggregate had been hard-coded at that location.

The reference co nstruct in volves reference variables, as well as **ref** and **deref** operators. A reference variable:

- Indicates a pack etC *database* or *searchset* without being synonymous with that aggregate.
- Has an implementation-specific v alue th at can not be directly manipulated by a user.
- Is restricted to a specific base type at declaration.
- Is only assigned a v alue by a **ref** operator applied to an aggregate of the right type as its operand.
- Behaves as if it h ad been rep laced in the source code by the aggregate value produced by applying the **deref** operator to the reference.

```
// Example database decls & reference variable
struct stype { short dest; short src;};
database stype malwareFlows[500];
database stype virusFlows[500];
// declare a reference var limited to
// databases with 'stype' base type
reference db : stype refDB = ref(virusFlows);
```

A **deref** operator's result can ap pear any where th at th e name of th e dereferenced ag gregate could ap pear (see e x-ample below). By dereferencing such a variable, developers can m ake an agg regate operation co ntingent on a result without produ cing co de th at enumerates all the possible dereferenced values. The following example uses types and variables from the code example above.

```
// deref entire DB element or individual fields
stype structVar;
structVar    = deref( refDB )[0];
structVar.dest = deref( refDB )[1].dest;
```

The paper is org anized as f ollows. First , we co mpare packetC references to C pointers, C++ references and rela-tional datab ase *foreign keys* . W e sk etch ou r parallel pr o-gramming model and pack etC language. Next we describe reference declaration s and operators. Experiments th en show that using references does not harm performance.

355

Table 1. Comparing C pointers, C++ and Java references and packetC references. Copyright CloudShield Technologies, 2011.

Construct/ Attribute	C pointer/Java reference	C++ reference	packetC reference
New valu e can be as-signed (*reseatable*).	Yes No		Yes
Can be assigned NULL value.	Yes No		No
Can be referenced as itself in source code.	Yes No		Yes
Must be assigned at declaration.	No	Yes Yes	

2. Related Language Constructs

Significant attributes of reference constructs include:

- Reseatability (value changeable after declaration)
- Strong typing protects against illegal values
- Values hidden to protect against illegal values.
- Nullability (reference can take a **null** value).

To show where packetC references fit into the spectrum of similar constructs, we compare them to their nearest analogs: C *pointers*, Java references, C++ *references* (Table 1) and to the database concept of a *foreign key*.

A C *pointer* holds a m emory address in the f orm of a numeric value. Despite som e implementation v ariability, users can depend on a poin ter holding the v alue of an ad-dress (or *null* value) and being am enable to *pointer arith-metic* operations [4]. Java ref erences share reseatability and nullability attribu tes but their values are g enerally n ot directly accessible to users (e.g., for arithmetic).

A packetC reference is not constrained to be an a ddress; it simply designates one of a f inite set of aggregates, all of which share a co mmon type signature and are v isible from the reference variable's scope. The user cannot assume particular m emory characteris tics for a ref erence v ariable in a given implementation (e.g., size or layout).

A C++ *reference* [5] is a more restricted construct than a C pointer or a pack etC reference. It m ust be declared with a non-null value that cannot be chang ed afterward. Subse-quently, source code cannot refer to the reference identifier as an entity in itself, since a ny occurrence of the identifier indicates the referenced object, instead.

In relational datab ases a *foreign key* specifies a co nnec-tion – and associated constraints – between two tab les [6]. The key identifies co lumns in th e *referencing* tab le th at refer to co lumns in th e *referenced* (i.e., th e f oreign) table (Fig. 1). The referencing columns must be *primary* or *can-didate keys* of the referenced tab le (i.e., th ey must be n on-null key values that uniquely select a sin gle row in a table). In addition, the value(s) in one row of the referencing co l-umns must occur in j ust on e row of th e referenced tab le. Thus, a row of the referencing table maps unambiguously to a single row of the referenced table.

packetC references can also be used to link certain kinds of agg regates tog ether or, m ore precisely , lin k opera tions on th em. T his requires organizing ref erence v alues in an array, as shown in Fig. 1. For example, match operations

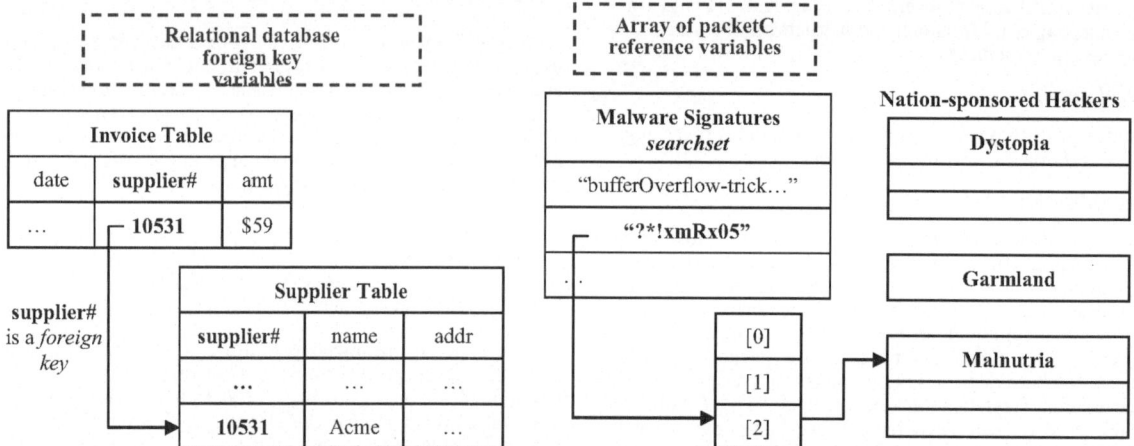

Figure 1. Table linkage with a relational database foreign key and via packetC references. Copyright CloudShield Technologies, 2011.

on packetC databases or searchsets return the index of the matching element if a m atch is f ound. B y arrang ing the array of references and the elements (rows) of a database or searchset a ppropriately, a u ser can m ake the match result select w hich agg regate to use in a su bsequent o peration (Fig. 1 and see section 7). T hese operations unfold as part of a broad er scheme for processing network pack ets in pa- rallel, a scheme that the next section sketches.

3. Parallel Processing Model

packetC reflects a parallel packet processing model (Fig. 2) with the following key attributes:

- Coarse-grained parallelism
- Machine characteristic hiding
- Host system executive responsibilities
- Shared and private memory division

The develo per expr esses parallelism at a coarse-grained level w ith a sm all prog ram (a pack etC *packet ma in*) that processes one packet at a time in end-to-end fashion. Thus, the model uses single program multiple data (SPMD) paral- lelism. This frees the developer from fine-grain mechanics, like synchronizing tasks.

Machine characteristics are h idden w hen possible, n ot only to facilitate customers porting their code but so that we can rep lace su bsystems w ith dif ferent chips or replace hardware with software im plementations without rendering existing prog rams obsolete. Hence, pack etC does not re- flect register classes, caches, memory banks, etc.

The model requires that the host system manage execu- tion of program copies, handle packet ingress and egress, and pre-calculate *layer offsets* of protocol headers present in the packet. Those offsets are stored in a system provided *packet information block* (PIB), described in [7].

The model partitions memory into:

- *Global* m emory w ith scalars and agg regates sh ared by all packet programs.
- A priv ate m emory f or each prog ram co py f or va- riables that are not visible to other program copies.

4. packetC Language Overview

Another paper g ives an overview of packetC as a language [1], so th is section prov ides only a sh ort sk etch. W e d e- signed the language to meet these goals:

- Use the C99 v ariant of C for familiar operators, con- ditional statements and overall syntax.
- Reduce ru ntime exception s and performance uncer- tainties by rem oving poin ters, ad dress o perators and dynamic memory allocation -- and by using unsigned integer arithmetic to avoid overflows and underflows.
- Increase reliab ility by stron ger ty ping ru les and by disallowing implicit type conversions or promotions.
- Support our processing model's SPMD parallelism.

Distinctive packetC data type extensions appear below:

- Descriptors: *structs* that 'float' to a packet location to overlay a packet protocol header [7].
- Databases: structure aggregates divided into 'data' and 'mask' halves for *wildcarded* m atching against packet contents [2].
- Searchsets: aggregates of strin gs or regu lar expre s- sions to match against packet contents [3].
- References: provide a classic reference capability for databases and searchsets. Unlike C poin ters or C++ references, th ese ref erences m ust b e assig nable (to chain on th e basis of r untime resu lts) and be pr o- tected by strong typing, since trying to access a non- existent aggregate creates an exception that cannot be handled in this time intensive application domain.

The next section describes reference constructs in detail.

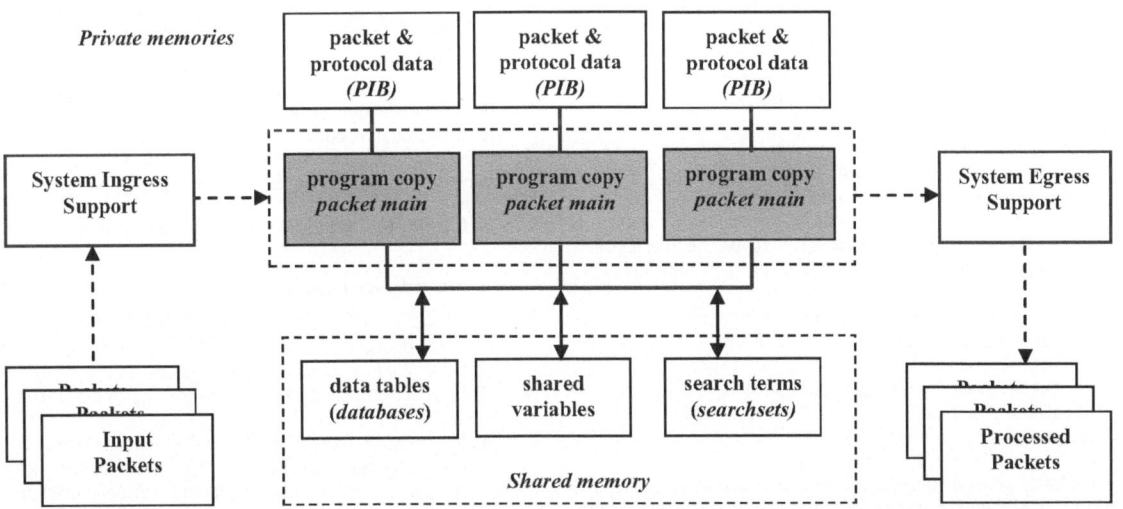

Figure 2. Parallel packet processing model and language features (in italics). Copyright CloudShield Technologies, 2011.   357

5. packetC References and Rationales

5.1 Motivation for Reseatability (Assignability)

Our m otivation f or a reference construct springs from network applications' need to selectively perform matching operations on the basis of a prelim inary m arch or search's results. Thus, a *reseatable* reference construct is required, so that the reference's value may be set at run-time in response to another operation's results, rather than be set only at declaration time, like C++ references.

5.2 Motivation for Strong Typing

packetC emphasizes reliab ility, sin ce real -time n etwork applications cannot tolerate high-overhead error-handling. No matter how the identi ty of a datab ase or searchset is represented in a ref erence v ariable v alue, some form of strong typing is required in assigning values to a reference variable because an illeg al value would cause unpredicta-ble behavior at runtime and packet processing applications lack the time bu dget f or elab orate exception h andling. Thus, reference v ariables are restricted to accessing data-bases (by structure base type) and searchse ts (by the two possible searchset ty pes). The n ext section describes these semantics in detail.

6. packetC References as Language Construct

6.1 Reference Variable Declarations

packetC *databases*[2] resem ble arrays of stru ctures; each array elem ent is a stru cture, su bdivided into nested *data* and *mask* stru ctures of a co mmon ty pe. Database ele-ments often contain selected packet attributes that charac-terize *flows*, related pack ets th at constitute a network dialogue. Databases allow matching a current packet to a flow in the datab ase by u sing m ask parts to select which data parts (which packet attributes) are used in the match.

Because databases have a st ructure base ty pe, packetC reference variables to databases are also declared in terms of a base ty pe and can only reference a database with that base type. T o ensure that a reference always has a legal value at run-time, the declaration m ust set th e ref erence variable to a legal, n on-null value. (Note: a *typedef* is n ot needed to establish a packetC type name).

```
struct stype { short dest; short src;};
database stype malwareFlows[500];
database stype virusFlows  [300];

// declare reference var of 'stype' base type
reference db : stype refDB = ref(virusFlows);
...
// 'reseat' reference to DB of 'stype'
refDB = ref(malwareFlows); // legal

// ERROR: try to reseat to DB of another type
database tuple5Type currentFlows[4000];
refDB = ref(currentFlows); // ERROR
```

packetC *searchsets*[3] contain either an ordered set of strings or of regular expressions for specifying patterns to be found in a packet's contents. Because these two forms have different restrictions on what methods can be applied to them, a searchset's elements cannot mix strings and regular expressions. T hus, ref erence v ariables f or sea r-chsets are declared in terms of in dicating searchsets f or strings or for regular expressions. The co de example be-low shows the two declaration forms.

```
searchset sSet[3][3] = {"dog","cat","bat"};
reference set: string refStr = ref(sSet);
//
searchset regSet[2][7] ={".*?from",".*?mail"};
reference set: regex refReg = ref(regSet);
```

6.2 The ref and deref Operators

The **ref** operato r h as already been sh own in declar ation examples. It takes a single operator, which must be either

- The n ame of a datab ase w ith th e sam e structure base type as the reference variable's base type.
- The name of a searchset with a string or regular ex-pression type that matches the **string** or **regex** key-word in the reference variable declaration.

The **deref** operato r takes a ref erence v ariable operand and produces the referent at that point in the source code. It is not as if all the aggregate's values were present at that code location bu t, r ather, it is as if the referent's current name had been hard-coded there.

```
// (types from 6.1) deref a database; same as
// structVar.dest = virusFlows[2].dest
structVar.dest = deref( refDB )[2].dest;

// reference a string searchset for match
// method with array slice operand; same as
// result = sSet.match(pkt[64:66]);
result = deref(refStr).match(pkt[64:66]);

// reference a regex searchset for find method
// with packet array slice as operand, same as
// result = regSet.find(pkt[0:end]);
result = deref(regSet).find(pkt[0:end]);
```

A pack etC deref erence produces an *lvalue* th at in di-cates an aggregate object. Thus, it acts as a su bstitute for the lvalue at that source code location. This property can lead to unusual code forms (much as pointer dereferencing does in C); h owever, it provides capabilities for compact, generic programming, as experiments show below.

7. Current   packetC Implementation

7.1 Ha rdware Implementation Overview

CloudShield Technologies' products [8] use multi-core network processin g u nits (NPUs), field-programmable gate array s (FP GAs) and oth er specialized processors . Our overall approach has the following characteristics.

- Microcode executing on a ded icated su bset of NP U *cores* works with FP GAs to co ntrol th e pack et pip e-line, analyze packets and locate protocol headers.

- An ensemble of NPUs, each running multiple *contexts,* executes SP MD co pies of packetC p rograms.

- A custom FP GA m anages sh ared m emory f or scalars and arrays, and m anages ac cess to tern ary co ntent-addressable memory (TCAM).

- TCAM chips and regu lar ex pression proces sors i mplement operations on packetC's *database* and *searchset* types.

7.2 So ftware Implementation -- Interpreting

Our packetC compilation tool-chain generates proprietary *bytecodes* that combine RISC-style arithmetic with high-level instructions. These include complex instructions for database and searchset operations, such as the one below.

```
// if a record matches a database
// element, return row that matched
rownum = myDB.match( myRecord );

// The corresponding bytecode
Database_match(maskKind, myRecord.data,
     myRecord.mask, returnInfoDirective)
```

Dozens of copies of a m icro-coded in terpreter ru n on the NPUs and interpret user prog rams translated in to the bytecode form. W hen necessary, these in terpreters pu sh data to specialized processors. T his is the case for operations on both data types used with references, databases and searchsets. T o prov ide i nsight in these mechanics before presenting the experiments, we sketch the hardware implementation for these operations below.

7.3 Implementation of Database Operations

CloudShield's C S 2000 [8] u ses Netlog ic NSE 5512 TCAM chips to im plement packetC datab ase o perations. Communications to effect those operations flow between

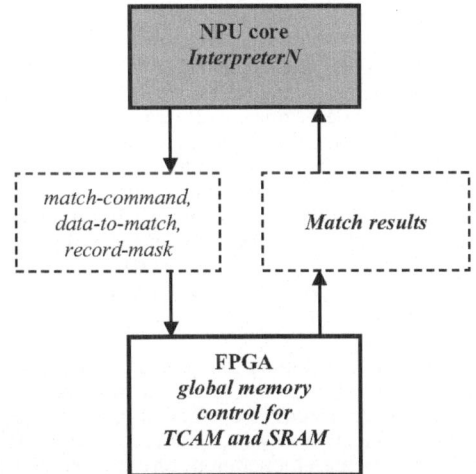

Figure 3. Com munications f or a d atabase m atch b etween an interpreter an d th e FP GA m anaging g lobal m emory an d TCAMs. . Copyright CloudShield Technologies, 2011.

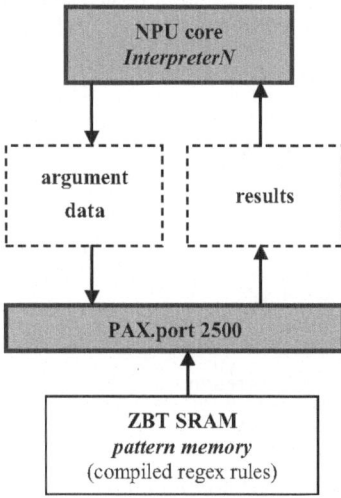

Figure 4. Using P AX por t 2500 for searchset **find** opera-tions. . Copyright CloudShield Technologies, 2011.

the interpreters and TCAM chips, mediated by a 'Silicon Database' module, implemented with a custom Xilinx Virtex-II Pro™ FPGA (Fig. 3).

7.4 Implementation of Searchset FIND Operations

We currently implement **find** operations for searchsets by downloading compiled rules that describe th em to an IDT PAX.port 2500 con tent in spection en gine [9]. String searchsets are f irst preprocessed in to sim ple regu lar e x-pressions by custom tools w ithout packetC user interven-tion and invoke the IDT P AX co mpiler to create th e *pattern memory* contents th at w ill be downloaded into PAX SRAM.

At runtime **find** arguments are sent to the PAX subsys-tem, which holds its co mpiled regular e xpression ru les in a specialized IDT zero bu s tu rnaround (Z BT) SR AM as *pattern memory* (Fig. 4). The provisions for dynamically updating the pattern memory are bey ond the scope of this paper and are not shown in the figure.

8. Ref erence Performance: Chained Operations

This section examines the reference construct's impact on source co de size and perf ormance. T he experiment co n-sists of coding a representative chained operation scenario with and without using packet references. The experiment used a Clou dShield P N41 [10] 10 Gigabit Ethernet blade hosting the pack etC ap plication. T he DP PM blad e co n-tains an In tel Corporation® IXP 2800 NPU an d cu stom Xilinx, Inc.® Virtex® 5 FPGAs. Netlogic, Inc.® NSE 5512 TCAM chips implement the databases. W e u sed an IXIA® XM12 traf fic g enerator [1 1] to g enerate network traffic at a maximum of 10 gigabits per second (Gbps) and approximately 14 million packets per second (pps).

Network packet *flows* are a related sequence of packets that form a coherent communication from a source to a destination across a n etwork. The experim ental application defines a packetC *database*, with each of the four database rows geared to matching one of the following kinds of network traffic: HTTP, VoIP, email, DNS. Based on which of the four database cases a pack et m atches, th e prog ram searches the packet payload for matches with strings in one of four possible searchsets.

The datab ase declaration and f low matching is conducted in terms of a structure with packet protocol information, as shown below.

```
struct ipv4Tuple {
    int      scrAddr;
    int      destAddr;
    short    srcPort;
    short    destPort;
    byte     protocol;
};
database ipv4Tuple flowTable[4] = {...};
try { matchRow = flowTable.match( flow ); }
catch ( ERR_DB_NOMATCH ) {...exit; }
```

The searchset declarations for each kind of network traffic we are handling follow.

```
searchset httpVerbs[2][4] = {"GET", "POST"};
searchset sipVerbs[2][6] = {"INVITE","BYE"};
searchset badGuys[5][20] = {"acapone",
              "jdillinger",  "pbfloyd",
              "bonnie",      "clyde" };
searchset sites[4][20] = {"yahoo.com",
              "google.com", "purepeople.com",
              "cnn.com"}; // DNS
```

8.1 Version 1: Without references

The v ersion without references m ust explicitly co de each possible searchset operation th at co uld o ccur, u sing the relevant identifier for each one. Since only one of the sear chsets could be used after a given database match, the code for th e possible searchset operation s m ust be stru ctured conditionally, e.g., by using a switch statement as we did to implement this version.

```
try { matchedRow = flowTable.match(flow); }
catch ( ERR_DB_NOMATCH ) {...}

try { // do the desired chained operation
  switch (matchedRow) {
  case 0:
    result=httpVerbs.find(pkt[0:end]);
    break;
  case 1:
    result = sipVerbs.find(pkt[0:end]);
    break;
  case 2:
    result = badGuys.find(pkt[0:end]);
    break;
  case 3:
    result = sites.find(pkt[0:end]);
    break;
  default:
    exit;
}
catch ( ERR_SET_NOTFOUND ) {...}
```

8.2 Version 2: Using references

To exploit the reference construct in this situation, we need an array of references in which the:

- Index v alues co rrespond to the database rows (records) to be matched during the initial operation.
- Array element values correspond to the searchsets to be used for the next operation.

The relevant array declaration is shown below.

```
reference set:string refSet[4] =
       {ref(httpVerbs), ref(sipVerbs),
        ref(badGuys),    ref(sites)};
```

We can now rep lace coding **find** operations for each of the possible datab ase **match** resu lts (i.e., f or each possible searchset name) with a single searchset **find**, abstracting out the individual searchset n ames and rep lacing th em w ith a solitary variable holding the reference array's index values. Using th e **deref** operato r on an elem ent of th at reference array at ru ntime ef fectively d elivers th e referenced aggregate as the searchset upon which the **find** method will operate (shown below).

```
try {
    matchedRow = flowTable.match(flow);
    result = deref(refSet[matchedRow]).find
             (pkt[0:end]);
catch (...) {...}
```

8.3 Results: Source Code Reduction and Performance

As expected, for a chained operation where the target oper ation involves *n* alternatives (i.e., su bsequent operations on alternative databases or searchsets), u sing a ref erence co nstruct can shrink the code from *n* constructs that reflect the alternatives (e.g., **try/catch** pairs, **switch** cases, etc.) to a single construct.

Our experiments suggest that, f or th is ap plication d o- main and h ardware, u sing ref erence constructs does not cause m eaningful perf ormance dif ferences. Fig 5 shows that, w hen m easuring th roughput in g igabits per secon d (gbps), the application's throughput for packet sizes 300 and 1000 bytes do not vary for hundredths of a gbps. Only at a packet size of 2000 by tes is there a dis cernable differ ence, with the using-references version achieving 6.15 gbps and the without-references ve rsion r unning a t 6 .14 gb ps. This small variation could be an artif act of experiment me chanics.

We were concerned that the overhead of moving packet data to the regex chip f or the sear chset **find** operation was dwarfing all oth er effects. T o check th is, we coded a ver sion of th e ap plication in which the second operation was another datab ase **match** operation, on e th at involved four alternative databases. The results in Fig. 5.c. show no mea ningful performance difference caused by re ferences being used or not.

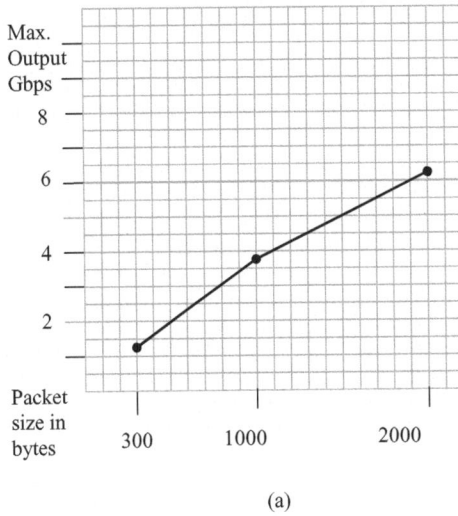

Gbps = Gigabits per second

Database op#1->database op#2		
Packet size in bytes	Throughput with references (Gbps)	Throughput without references (Gbps)
300	0.582	0.582
1000	1.9	1.9
2000	3.9	3.9

(b)

Database op-> searchset op		
Packet size in bytes	Throughput with references (Gbps)	Throughput without references (Gbps)
300	1.16	1.16
1000	3.88	3.88
2000	6.15	6.14

(c)

(a)

Figure 5. Performance with and without references. (a) Throughput sensitivity to packet size (database result drives searchset operation). (b) Comparison for database result drives searchset operation. (c) Comparison for database result drives a second database operation. Copyright CloudShield Technologies, 2011.

In th ese tested ap plications the version without references will req uire a co mparison and j umps to execu te the **switch** statement control flow. Even though we are currently treating the details of how we encode reference values as proprietary, w e can state th at a deref erencing operation typically involves 2-3 instructions to shift or m ask off irrelevant parts of the encoded data. A ny differences in application versions' execution time that are due to differences in which set of several 'ordinary' instructions are execu ted will be dwarfed by the time spent to move data to either the TCAM or regex subsystems. T hus, for the planned use of packetC reference constructs with databases and searchsets, there does not appear to be performance penalties.

9. Summary

In much the same way th at a sin gle v ariable can a bstract many individual literal values from sou rce co de, a single, reseatable ref erence co nstruct – in th e broad , co mputer science sense of 'reference' – can ab stract many individual variables from source code, rep lacing th e ap pearance of many identifiers with a single construct.

Our practical context for this kind of abstracting specific variables ou t of the source co de is to co mpress the coding for operation s on speci alized agg regates as part of high-speed network packet processing. In this context the benefits of the packetC reference construct are:

- To remove redundant code patterns that dif fer on ly by specific aggregate names (see sw itch statem ent in 8.1)

- To facilitate chainin g operatio ns on th ese aggregates in cases where th e resu lt of one operation selects th e sp e-

cific aggregate to use in the next operation. T his use al so in volves organizing references v alues in array s (see Sections 2 and 8.2).

- To prevent a reference variable or array elem ent from hold an illeg al value at run-time in an env ironment where graceful recovery from exceptions is rare.

We believe the experim ents sh ow it is possible to g et these benef its w ithout a discernable performance penalty. As long as the ref erence enco ding and decodin g schem es are straigh tforward, th is seem s to be a likely outcome. Such encoding schemes can be as simple as using integer or string values to uniquely identify a particular aggregate.

In ou r case, th e by tecodes for performing datab ase and searchset operations make it relatively easy to store, decode and u se su ch a desig nator. Specif ic bytecodes are not shown in the text ab ove because CloudShield co ntinues to treat the bytecodes as proprietar y details f or bu siness reasons unrelated to the packetC reference construct.

In conclusion, a reseatable, type-safe reference construct is u seful in a h igh-speed, pack et-processing env ironment, especially f or chaining operations co mmon to th e ap plication domain. It is possibl e to implement such a construct in ways with no discernable performance penalty, at least f or this specific environment.

Acknowledgments

Peder J ungck, Dw ight Mulcahy and Ralp h Duncan are the co-authors of th e pack etC language. Andy No rton, Greg

Triplett, Kai Chang, Mary Pham, Alfredo Chorro-Rivas and Minh Nguyen provided valuable help in many areas.

References

[1] R. Duncan and P . Jungck. packetC language for high performance packet processing. In Proceedings of the 11th IEEE Intl. Conf. High Performance Co mputing and Co mmunications, (Seoul, S outh Ko-rea), pp. 450-457, June 25-27, 2009.

[2] R. Duncan, P. Ju ngck an d K. Ross. packetC language and parallel processing of masked databases. Proceedings of the 39th Intl. Conf. on Parallel Processing, (San Diego), pp. 472-481, September 13-16, 2010.

[3] R. Duncan, P. Jung ck, K . Ro ss and S . T illman. P acket Content matching w ith packe tC S earchsets. Proc eedings of t he 16th In tl. Conf. o n P arallel and D istributed S ystems, (Shanghai, China), pp. 180-188, December 8-10, 2010.

[4] ISO/IEC 9899:1999. Standard for the C pr ogramming l anguage. May 2005 version. ('C99'), especially section 6.3.2.3.

[5] ISO/IEC ISO/IEC 14882:2003. (corrected version of the 1998 C++ standard).

[6] W ikipedia. Article on "Foreign key," Retrieved on January 22, 2011 from http://en.wikipedia.org/wiki/Foreign_key.

[7] R. Duncan, P. Ju ngck an d K. Ross. A paradigm for processing net-work protocols i n p arallel. In Proc eedings of the 10th Intl. Conf. on Algorithms and A rchitectures for Parallel Processing, (Busan, South Korea), pp. 52-67, May 21-23, 2010.

[8] CloudShield Technologies. CS-2000 Technical Specifications. Prod-uct datasheet available from CloudShield Technologies, 212 Gibral-tar Dr., Sunnyvale, CA, USA 94089, 2006.

[9] H.J. Chao and B. L iu. "High Performance Switches and Routers." John Wiley and Sons, Hoboken, New Jersey, 2007, pp. 562-564.

[10] International Business Machines Corporation. IBM Blade Center PN41. Product datasheet available from IBM Systems and Technol-ogy Group, Route 100, Somers, New York, USA 10589, 2008.

[11] IXIA. XM12 High Performance Chassis. Retrieved from http://www.ixia.com/products/chassis/display?skey=ch_optixia _xm12 on January 24, 2011.

Ixia is a tr ademark of I xia in the U nited States and/or other countries. NETL7 is a trademark of NetLogic Microsystems, Inc. in the United States and/or other countries. Xilinx Virtex-II Pro is a trademark of Xilinx Inc. in the United States and/or other countries.

R. Duncan, P. Jungck, K. Ross, and D. Mulcahy. "References for run-time aggregate selection with strong typing." 2011. Printed by permission.

REPRINT 7

■ ■ ■

Portable Bit Fields in packetC

by Ralph Duncan, Peder Jungck and Dwight Mulcahy

Abstract

Network packets place some *protocol* data in *bit fields* that are smaller than typical processor operand sizes. C language *structures* can represent such protocols but the uncertain layout and endian-specific nature of C's bit fields cause problems. Research has ranged from alternative bit field constructs, through specialized bit registers to using analytic techniques to identify programs' implicit *subword* usage. This paper describes the packetC language's two-fold approach to handling protocols in a portable way. The language addresses bit field layout and operation uncertainties as language design matters that can be overcome with a *container*-oriented approach and una mbiguous layout rules. It tackles the problems of endianness and of packet bit field processing by two means. On the language design level packetC imposes big endian byte allocation order for structure and packet array storage. Second, the language is built around a packet processing model that involves triggering a parallel copy of a program after the host system assembles the entire packet in a byte array, locates standard protocols within that packet and saves protocol location information. By providing both portable protocol representation and protocol *layer offset* calculation, packetC frees engineering resources to pursue other packet processing tasks.

Categories and Subject Descriptors D.3 .3 [**Programming Languages**]: Language Constructs and Features – data types and structures

General Terms Algorithms, Languages.

Keywords bit fields; byte allocation order; network processing; programming languages; structures

1. Introduction

Structure *bit fields*, such as those found in the C language. [1], are useful for many system programming tasks. They allow the programmer to manipulate individual bits or bit collections smaller than integer operands, facilitating high-level language control of entities like system status words or special-purpose registers.

Research supported by US Air Force contract FA 7037-04-C-0011.

This is relevant to computer network applications that process packets, because packets contain standard *protocols*, such as TCP/IP or IPv4, that provide routing, service and standards data. Such protocols and their component fields are naturally mapped to C-like *structures*. To minimize communications overhead, protocols represent information in as few bits as feasible. Thus, they often contain fields with fewer than 8 bits, as a fragment of the IPv4 (Internet Protocol version 4) header in Figure 1. shows.

However, there are significant difficulties in using C-style bit fields for network packet processing. (Throughout the paper we use C99, as opposed to *standard C* [2] or other variants, as synonymous with the C language).

- C rules that define bit fields allow compiler implementers a great deal of leeway with container size, padding and boundaries: a C structure that matches a packet protocol with one C compiler may fail to match it with another.

- C bit field structure declarations match the *byte-allocation order* of the target processor. Thus, an application written to run on a big-endian processor must be recoded to run on a little-endian machine [3].

4 bits	4 bits	8 bits
version	header length	type of service
16 bits		
total length		
16 bits		
identification		
3bits	13 bits	
flags	fragment offset	
8 bits		8 bits
time to live		protocol

Figure 1. IPv4 Protocol (first 90 bits).

packetC [4] is a C-like language developed by CloudShield Technologies for reliable, embedded network programming, particularly f or *deep p acket inspection*. Becau se th e lan guage is b oth designed f or p acket p rocessing an d intended to be platform-independent, p roviding p ortable b it field p rogramming is important for the language. packetC's approach to these problems can be summarized as:

- Center all b it field o rganization o n *containers* (unsigned integers) with explicit sizes an d require implementations to a d-here to unambiguous rules f or pa dding, stra ddling a nd boundaries.

- Require users to define structures in big-endian byte allocation order (including those with bit fields) and require compliant compilers to make an algorithmic correction to access bit fields for programs running on little-endian processors.

- Require that the host system pre-scan the packet, locating standard protocols and storing their packet offsets in a special, user-accessible data structure. Thus, responsibility for recognizing protocol bit fields shifts from the user to the runtime support system.

The f ollowing se ctions discuss these areas, first presenting C99 practice, then contrasting it with the packetC approach.

2. C's Bit Field Layout Uncertainties

The b it f ield im plementation freedom af forded b y C leads to a variety of uncertainties, as illustrated b y th e ex ample b elow (all quoted remarks below refer to section 6 .7.2.1, clause 1 0 of th e C99 Specification):

```
struct structTag {
        unsigned int nonbitfield;
        unsigned char first:  4;
        unsigned int second:  2;
        unsigned int third:  4;
} myStruct;
```

- *Handling 'Straddles'* – The entire field named *third* cannot fit in a b yte allocated for fields, *first* and *second*. Do es the com-piler let it 'straddle' bytes, with 2 bits in the byte allocated for the first two fields an d the remaining b its in a trailin g, conti-guous byte? Possibly, but perhaps not, since the C99 Specifi-cation d eclares th at strad dle b ehavior is implementation-defined. "If insufficient space remains, whether a bit-field that does not fit is p ut into the next unit or overlaps adjacent units is implementation-defined."

- *Container size* – If packing and straddling is not an issue, does the compiler reliably place a bit field within a container of the user-specified size? We cannot be sure, since the Spec. sa ys an implementation can use "any addressable storage unit large enough" to accommodate the bit field.

- *Bit field layout* – Does the compiler allocate the topmost fields in the declaration to the lea st significant b ytes of the co rres-ponding portion of the structure? How is the containing unit aligned? These matters, too, are implementation-defined: "the order of allo cation of b its-fields w ithin a u nit is implementa-tion-defined. The alignment of the addressable storage unit is undefined."

These matters are critical for packet applications, because they process protocols. For example, if an application copies the con-tiguous bytes of a packet that comprise a protocol into a structure, it is desirable to know that the compiler will organize the structure in a p redictable way that matches the protocol layout. Mo reover, it is desirable to be able to move th e ap plication to n ew targ et processors or c ompilers without re coding to re flect new bit field implementation peculiarities. P roviding predictable an d in tuitive layouts is th e key to th e packetC ap proach d escribed in the next section.

3. packetC's Container-based Bit Field Layout

packetC d esign g oals for p roviding b it fields emphasized provid-ing language users with a clear, unambiguous way to specify:

- The size o f th e storag e u nit th at holds related bits.

- Bit field p adding (esp. for n etwork protocol-specific padding, as oppose d to pa dding ne eded to align structure fields for memory references).

- Packing behavior w ithout unc ertainties a bout stra ddling mul-tiple storage units.

The resultin g packetC ru les p roduce the following syntax, us-ing th e stru cture f rom th e p revious ex ample (alp habetic sup er-scripts map to the bulleted points that follow):

```
struct structTag {
        int nonbitfield;
        bits short {ᵃ
                first:  4;ᵇ
                second: 2;
                third:  4;
                pad:    6;ᶜ
        } optionalContainerName;ᵈ
} myStruct;
```

a) Bit fields are explicitly grouped inside *containers*, which have one of packetC's 4 unsized integer types: **byte**, **short**, **int** and **long**.

b) Since a bit field is always part of a container with a type, indi-vidual b it f ields d eclare o nly th eir n ame and size but not a type.

c) Pad fields are always declared explicitly and, given packetC's emphasis on embedded system runtime re liability, a group of bit fields, including pad fields, must always sum to the size of their container. P ad fields ca nnot be accessed for test or se t operations.

d) The optional container name can be used to access an d mani-pulate the bit field collection as a whole.

This a pproach re moves lay out siz e, stra ddling a nd boundary uncertainties by guaranteeing th at the storage u nit size is th e one specified by the u ser, b y p recluding strad dling an d b y en suring that ev ery b it in the co ntainer h as b een ex plicitly d efined b y th e user.

Other packetC language rules for bit fields follow:

- A bit field width expression must be > zero and <= maximum number o f b its in th e asso ciated in teger storage type.

- PacketC bit fields are unsigned.

- If all of the bit-fields in a collection cannot be packed into the specified type of container, it is a fatal error.

- The sa me ru les g overn th e alig nment of an integer structure field, whether it is being used to store a b it-field collection or not.

- Unnamed bit fields are not allowed.

packetC ru les also clarify h ow b it fields act in o perations, as the next section describes.

4.   Bit Field Operation Semantics in packetC

In order to have portable bit fields, users must have predictable bit field behavior in o perations, as w ell as p redictable d ata lay outs. The p acketC u ser can test an d se t b it fields, u sing o perators for assignment, equality, inequality and the relational operators. As it was with data layout, the bit field container is the locus of operations. Our d esign goals were to produce the same logical results as C but to be more explicit about the mechanics through which those results are reached.

When an n-bit packetC bit field acts as an operand it behaves as if it occupied the least significant n bits of an integer the size of its container, with any other bits set to zero. T hus, it acts as th e sole b it f ield in a tem porary co ntainer. p acketC d iffers sig nifi- cantly from C in that there are no type promotions and no implicit type conversions (other than ascribing types to literals). The con- sequences of these combined rules follow.

- A bit field used as an operand takes the type of its container.
- The type of a b it field (container) u sed in a b inary o peration must match the type of the other operand,
- A type cast on a bit field changes the size o f its co ntainer, not the width of the b it field: it is still an n-bit field but occupies the least significant bits of a differently sized container.
- When a b it field is u sed in binary operations all the bits in its temporary co ntainer are u sed (w hich cau ses results to match those of C).

Defining bit field semantics in this way makes some otherwise obscure m echanics clea r. Fo r ex ample, consider when bit fields of different sizes are compared below.

```
struct s1 {
        bits short {
            a04:4;
            a12:12;
        } con1;
} sa;
sa.con1.a12   =   0xabc;
sa.con1.a04   =   0xd;
if ( sa.con1.a04  >  sa.con1.a12 ) {…}
// expression above evaluates to 'false'
```

If only th e 4 b its o f bit field $a04$ w ere us ed, the c onditional expression would be true, since 0xd > 0xc. However, the compar-

ison effectively takes place in a 16-bit container, so bit field $a12$'s high bits are also used.

packetC explicitly states how bit field assignments are made:

- An assignment expression result h as the type of the LHS con- tainer, even if the LHS bitfield cannot store all of that result.
- When bit fields ap pear on both sides of an assignment opera- tor, given a L HS bitfield, lbf with length $L1$ and a right-hand- side bit field, rbf with length $L2$:
  - If ($L1 <= L2$) lbf gets the least significant $L1$ bits of rbf.
  - If ($L1 > L2$) lbf bits 0:$L2$-1 = rbf and lbf bits $L2$:$L1$-1 = 0.

These ru les m ake operations on b it field clea rer than they are in C, at th e lik ely co st o f ex plicit ty pe-casts to g et operands to binary operations in containers of the same size. Thus, packet C language ru les prevent some of the layout uncertainties that bede- vil C im plementations an d they say more p recisely how b it field contents are to be compared and assigned. How ever, these ru les cannot prevent similar problems with endian-specific byte alloca- tion order, which is discussed next.

5.   Byte Allocation Order in C

Recall that p acket p rotocol in formation arrives in b yte-by-byte fashion in big-endian o rder. T hus, a stru cture h olding p rotocol information will p resent th e d ata in an in tuitive w ay if its field organization mirrors the order in w hich the in formation arrived. Recalling th e IP v4 p rotocol fragment shown in the introduction; an ap plication ex pects to en counter a b yte w ith th e *version* a nd *header length* information before the two bytes with *type of ser- vice* data. Two programming lang uage m atters are esp ecially relevant for this: field allocation and byte allocation order.

Field allocation order is the order in which a structure's de- clared fields are mapped to consecutive memory addresses. Both C and packetC map the first structure fields declared to the lowest byte ad dress an d th e last d eclared to th e h ighest byte address. This m atches th e ex pected o rder o f network protocol contents. Thus, field allo cation o rder i s n ot a problem but byte allocation order is.

C stru ctures d o n ot ex hibit th e sa me byte allocation order when the same code is compiled and run on big-endian and little- endian processors. C u ser operations on structure fields that cor- respond t o w hole i nteger v alues, l ike **int** or **short**, do not s how effects due to host processor endianness. However, operations on values, like bit fields, that can be sub-elements of integer storage units or can straddle such units do exhibit endian-specific charac- teristics.

To see why th is is so, co nsider th e following simplified case. Suppose we try to construct a 4 byte packet sequence by setting a 32-bit integer value, as shown below.

```
int bytes4 = 0xabcdef12, *p = &bytes4;
```

C compilers for b oth big and little en dian processors treat the leftmost portions of the litera l as th e m ost si gnificant b it v alues and p lace th em in m emory acco rdingly. Observe what happens when this value is mapped to a C stru cture with the following bit fields:

```
typedef struct sTag {
        unsigned int first : 8;
        unsigned int second: 24;
} sType;
sType myStruct, *pStruct = *((sType*)p);
```

gcc compilers on big and little-endian processors running linux (v 3.3.3 on a Sparc64 and v. 3.4.5 on an i686 platform respectively) both pack the two bit fields into a single 32-bit int. However, the programs on the two processors output different values for them. (The C program output below shows the most significant half-byte value to the left of the least significant half):

```
Big Endian                  Little Endian
first = 0xab;               first   = 0x12;
second = 0xcdef12           second  = 0xabcdef
```

The two processors store the byte sequences as shown below, where the lowest numbered byte addresses appear before higher numbered ones when read from left to right. The big-endian list is shown with big-endian *bit allocation order* (the most significant half of a byte appears to the left of the least significant one), while the little-endian list shows the least significant byte to the left.

```
// Big Endian:          a b | c d | e f | 1 2

// Little Endian:       2 1 | f e | d c | b a
```

For this reason, when C network applications use bit fields, they often employ *ifdef* constructs to define both big-endian and little-endian structure forms of a protocol header. Alternatively, some developers use macros to deliver big and little-endian results, although this this solution can be unwieldy, as shown by [5].

Clearly, it is preferable to code one version of an application, rather than two, so packetC chooses one endianness that best matches its overall processing approach, then uses relatively minor compiler adjustments to compensate.

6. packetC Processing Model and Byte Allocation Order

Several distinctive aspects of CloudShield Technologies' model of packet processing shaped the packetC approach to byte allocation order and bit field access. In this model parallelism is at the packet level: multiple copies of a program run in parallel asynchronously. Each program thread or context is triggered when the underlying system has prepared a packet in the form of an unsigned byte array, has located any standard protocols inside the packet and has prepared a Packet Information Block (PIB). The PIB contains detailed information about the presence of various layer protocols, where they are located in the packet, and what their contents are (Figure 2).

On CloudShield products [11] these functions are performed by dedicated hardware and firmware components, though packetC can be implemented on any system, including an ordinary desktop computer, that performs those functions. This approach affects packetC byte allocation design in two ways.

First, since the packet contents appear in network order, packetC structures and unions are required to be in packed, big-endian order to match the packet's organization and facilitate rapidly reading or writing protocol information between the packet array and user structures.

For example, packetC includes a distinctive form of structure, termed a *descriptor* that can be dynamically overlain on the packet array in a way that aligns it with a protocol present in that particular packet. As shown below, the descriptor is a structure with an additional location clause that specifies where it begins within the packet array.

```
descriptor ipv4Descr {
    bits byte  {
        version : 4;
        headerLength: 4;
    }
    short typeOfService;
    ...
} ipv4Header at pib.L4_offset;
```

Thus, the packet array, descriptors and structures share the same big-endian organization.

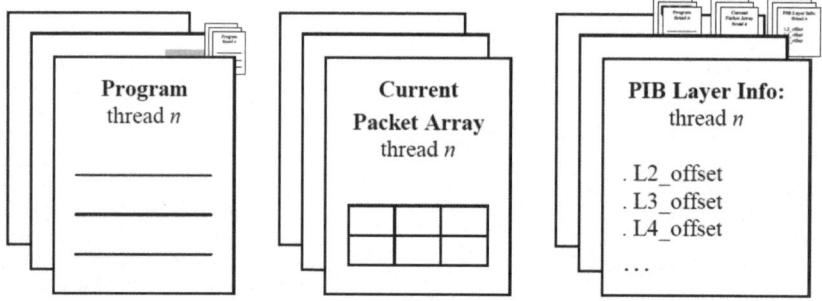

Figure 2. Packet information produced for packetC processing model.

In ad dition, since th e p rotocols have already been located within the packet, the primary requirement for arbitrary bit-length information is for bit fields in standard protocols to be as predictably organized and located in structures and unions as they are in the packet.

7. Managing packetC Byte Order Mechanics

If th e targ et p rocessor uses little-endian o rganization, a p acketC compiler is o bligated to b yte sw ap fields that are entire integers and to ad just co de f or testin g o r settin g a bit field accordingly. This frees the u ser from n eeding to co de se parate b ig an d little-endian solu tions. In p ractice, th e d ifferences in co de sequences that a p acketC compiler needs to produce for big and little-endian situations are minor for bit field access.

For ex ample, to p roduce th e v alue o f an y g iven packetC bit field, let th e to tal width in bits of its p redecessor fields within its container b e *fore* and the to tal width o f sub sequent fields b e *aft*. Both values are known at compile-time; one, neither or both can be zero. One approach is to produce the desired value by a pair of shifts o n a co py o f th e container value, using slightly different computations for big and little-endian scenarios.

```
// big endian
value = (container << fore) >> (aft + fore)
// little endian
value = (container << aft) >>   (aft + fore)
```

Consider this packetC structure with a 2-byte container:

```
struct  sType {
      bits  short {
            first: 3;
            second:8;
            third: 5;
      } aCon;
} aStruct;
```

Figure 3 sho ws how b it field v alues are easily isolated on big and little-en dian machines using a slig htly different pair of shifts. The figure depicts the three fields' bits using boldface, italics or underlining, respectively as in the assignments below:

```
aStruct.first = 3;
aStruct.second = 0xf6;
aStruct.third  = 0x19;
```

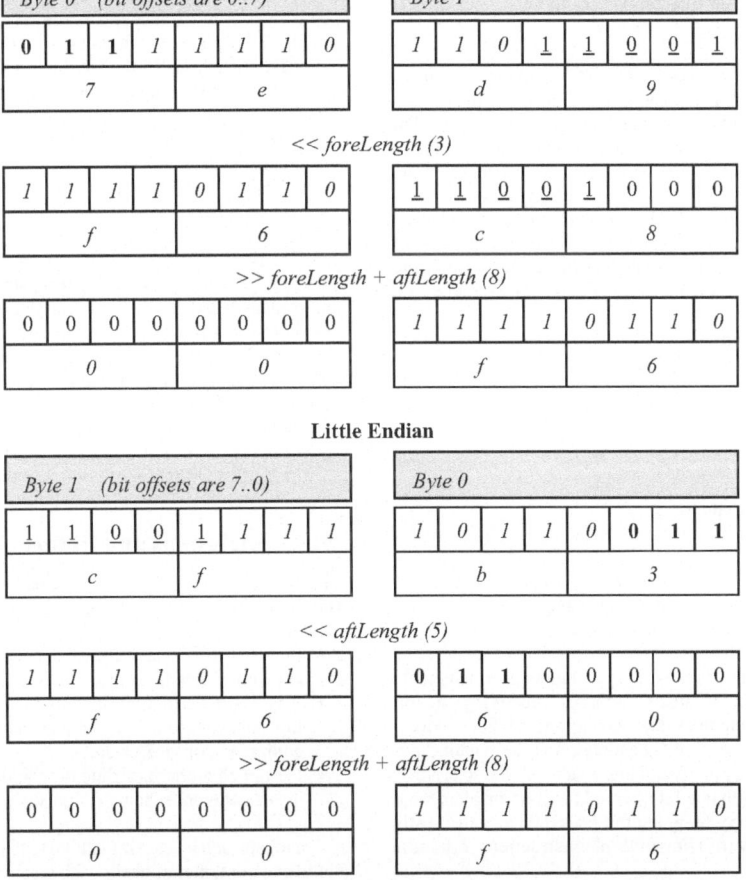

Figure 3. Shift code to isolate bit fields on big and little-endian platforms.

367

The example shows that the algorithmic adjustment needed to access big-endian bit fields on a little-endian machine is trivial. In practice the need to pipe scalars through byte swapping routines, such as *htonl*, is a more likely source of compiler complication for targeting a packetC compiler to a little-endian platform.

In sum, the packetC approach to bit fields is to define an unambiguous approach to container layouts, to impose a big-endian byte allocation order that matches a 'packet-centric' orientation and to require packetC compilers to manage differences on behalf of little endian processors. The next section reviews other approaches to managing bit fields for packet processing.

8. Related Research

Recent research includes efforts to explicitly define bit fields in various C dialects or in new languages, as well as research into recognizing implicit bit field use.

J. Wagner and R. Leupers described an enhanced C dialect and compiler for the Infineon NP [6]. This scheme maps C arrays with the register qualifier to a special register file, that supports variable bit-width operands and alignments. Through *intrinsics* (or *compiler-known functions*) and bit pointers, the user triggers special instructions on these registers, specifying bit offsets and widths. This replaces the usual C bit field scheme with an equivalent system for operating on the contiguous bit subsets of integer operands.

L. George and M. Blume discuss the NOVA language for the IXP network processor in [7]. The NOVA *layout* construct describes a given bit field in two forms: *packed* and *unpacked*. The packed form, despite some syntactic differences, approximates a C bit field description, although an *overlay* construct provides additional functionality to define alternative organizations for a given bit range within a layout. The unpacked form accords a word of storage or a nested unpacked form to each field. NOVA provides pack and unpack operations to mange the two forms. Two related layout examples from the paper are shown below

```
layout ipv6_address =
    { a1:32, a2:32, a3:32, a4:32 };

layout ipv6_header =
    version:            4,
    priority:           4,
    flow_label:        24,
    payload_length:    16,
    next_header:        8,
    hop_limit:          8,
    src_address:       ipv6_address,
    dst_address:       ipv6_address
};
```

A. Inoue, et al. define Valen-C [8], a language intended to support hardware design. Valen-C requires specifying the bit width of operands (and the mantissa and exponent sizes of floating point numbers). The Valen-C compiler uses a machine description to ascertain data path width and machine characteristics. The compiler guarantees that *n*-bit operands will be implemented with adequate precision, by mapping the operands to sufficiently large memory units or by utilizing multiple instructions to handle subsets of the operands.

R. Gupta, E. Mehofer and Y. Zhao detail an analytic approach to identifying *bit sections* (*subwords*) used as operands in programs [9]. First, local analysis identifies the implicit bit field assignments effected by C bit operations (e.g., bitwise AND, OR, NOT). Their graph representation replaces these operations with the equivalent explicit assignments to bit fields. Then, more global analysis of control flow interjects *split nodes* at the latest point that individual bit sections are needed and *combine nodes* at the earliest point that individual bit sections can be collapsed into a single operand. The resulting representation can be used for optimized code generation with appropriate instruction sets.

The PL8 language and its antecedent, pl.8, exhibit a concern with unambiguous bit field layouts, as W. Gellerich, et al, demonstate in [10]. As shown in the code sample below, prefix numbers indicate the nesting level of fields, a BIT type is available, and parenthesized values indicate a field's length.

```
DCL 1  ExampleRecord
       2  LongWord BIT (64)
      .2  BitLayout
           3 Flag1      BIT (1)
           3 Flag2      BIT (1)
           3 *          BIT (30)
           3 RegWord    BIT (32);
```

The dot syntax prefix indicates that the associated field (and its constituents at a deeper nesting level) redefines the preceding field. Thus, the redefined field, *LongWord*, serves to unambiguously specify collected field lengths, somewhat like a packetC container. PL8 is intended as a language for developing firmware for IBM RISC architectures, particularly IO management and error recovery. Thus, precise bit field layout is important to the language developers because they must match OS structures, such as IO status descriptors.. It is not clear how PL8 handles byte allocation order.

The packetC language fits into this spectrum of research in at least two ways: by exploring data structures that match network processing needs and by making high-level language constructs exploit specialized network processing hardware. packetC's concern for fine-tuning bit fields as a language construct seems most closely shared by the PL8 and NOVA approaches. Our scheme also reflects hardware support for the application domain, as do the Infineon NP and IXP NP/NOVA efforts described above. As the conclusions below suggest, the packetC language has its own distinctive combination of goals and tentative solutions.

9. Conclusions and Future Research

Three aspects of C-style bit fields and structures were primary concerns for packetC's designers:

- Precise bit field layouts are needed to predictably match packet protocol header layouts,
- It is desirable to avoid having to recode structures when moving packetC source code from a big-endian host to a little-endian one or vice versa.
- Design choices regarding bit fields and structures should fit into a coherent scheme for packet processing.

packetC achieves bit field layout precision by combining an intuitive container concept with a set of unambiguous rules. Advantages of this approach include closeness to existing C syntax and a clea r p icture o f h ow bit field o perations and assignments work.

Basic choices for managing b yte allo cation o rder in clude i m- posing b ig o r little -endian o rder, req uiring th e u ser to reco de when moving from one t ype of hos t t o t he ot her or hi ding t he differences behind an interface. Ch oosing b ig-endian o rder as a standard is a n atural p ath for packetC, b ecause a p acket arrives and fills up a buffer in big-endian order. If packed structures are mapped to the buffer, then they are in b ig-endian o rder. A s the packet goes, so goes everything else.

The most distinctive aspect of packetC bit fields is how they fit into an overall scheme for packet processing. packetC is designed to support a distinctive model for packet processing in general and deep packet inspection in particular. Although it should be possi- ble for packetC compilers to targ et a v ariety o f platforms, th e initial target is CloudShield products that are designed to support this processing model [11].

First, as sketched earlier, th e m odel p resumes th at, b efore an instance of the u ser p rogram is ex ecuted, the sy stem h as alrea dy examined the p acket, lo cated the p rotocols an d stored their loca- tions for the user. Thus, the packetC emphasis on bit fields is not primarily to he lp users find protocols: that has already been done by specialize d h ardware an d f irmware. Ha ving b it f ield layouts that match protocol layout in the stored packet array is m ainly to facilitate rapid protocol read ing, w riting an d m odification. In such a scheme finding p rotocols is m ore th e p reamble th an th e main text.

Second, t he m odel a ssumes t hat de ep pa cket i nspection w ill involve ap plying a h ost o f specialize d f unctions to th e p acket payload, as well as to the protocols – searching for patterns, com- paring character sequences, storin g an d se arching p ortions o f packets. Fo r these functions it is desirable to h ave absolute con- trol on the layout of a variety of data structures, including C-style structures with bit fields.

We have implemented a first p rototype p acketC co mpiler ta r- geted to our current multiprocessor product. Our likely research directions in the n ear future include im proving the quality of our emitted c ode (e specially f or unusua l lang uage constructs), fine- tuning new language features and developing compilers for other targets.

Acknowledgments

Peder Jun gck's vision of packet processing drove both Cloud- Shield Technologies' product development and the existence of a packetC lang uage. He, Dwight Mulcahy and Ralph Duncan are the co-authors o f th e p acketC language. P rofessors Rajiv G upta and Rain er L eupers p rovided h elpful citations and papers. The errors in the paper are solely the author's.

References

[1] ISO/IEC 9899: 1999. S tandard f or the C pr ogramming language. May 2005 version. ('C99').

[2] ANSI X3.159-1989. Programming language C. ('Std. C').

[3] D. Cohen, On ho ly w ars and a pl ea f or pe ace. U SC/ISI I EN 137. April 1, 1980. A vailable at http://www.ietf.org/rfc/ien/ien137.txt. retrieved November 5, 2008.

[4] CloudShield Technologies. "packetC Programming Language Speci- fication. Rev. 1.128, October 10, 2008.

[5] B. Gerst, Cleanup bitfield endianess mess. November 3, 2002 post- ing in L inux-kernel ar chives, r etrieved No vember 6, 2008 as http://www.ussg.iu.edu/hypermail/linux/kernel/0211.0/0927.html,.

[6] J. Wagner and R. Leupers: C compiler design for a ne twork proces- sor. IEEE Trans. On CAD, 20(11): 1-7, 2001.

[7] L. George and M. Blume. T aming the I XP ne twork pr ocessor. In *Proceedings of the ACM SI GPLAN '03 Conference on Program- ming Language Design and Implementation*, San Diego, California, USA, ACM, pp. 26-37, June 2003.

[8] A. Inoue, H. To miyama, E.F. Nurprasetyo and H. Yasuura. A pro- gramming language for processor based embedded systems. In *Proc. 5th Asia Pacific Conferen ce on Hardware Description Languages*, Seoul, Korea, pp. 89-94, July 8-10, 1998.

[9] R. Gupta,, E. Me hofer and Y . Zhang. A Representation for bit se c- tion based analysis and optimization. In *Proceedings of the Interna- tional Confer ence on Com piler Cons truction*, L NCS 2304, Grenoble, France, Springer Verlog, pp. 62-77, April 2002.

[10] W. Gellerich, T. H endel, R. L and, H. L ehmann, M. Mue ller, P . H. Oden and H . P enner: T he G NU 64 -bit P L8 Co mpiler: to ward an open standard environment for firmware development, IBM Journal of Research and Development, 48(3/4), 2004.

[11] CloudShield Technologies. CS-2000 Technical Specifications. Prod- uct datasheet available from CloudShield Technologies, 212 Gibral- tar Dr., Sunnyvale, CA, USA 94089, 2006.

■ ■ ■

packet Field and Bitfield Allocation Order

by Ralph Duncan

Abstract

C and C-based lan guages give implementations s ubstantial freedom in choosi ng sc hemes f or bit and by te allocation . The ensu ing variability ca n m ake it diff icult to port pr o- grams th at dep end on particu lar stru cture and bit -field layouts. W ith these proble ms in mind, pack etC prescribes that i mplementations use bi g endian b yte allocatio n order and little endia n bit al location order. T his pap er revie ws the related issu es of st ructure field, by te a nd bit allocation order and describes an algorith mic ap proach f or co mpen- sating when the i mplementation e xecutes o n a processor that uses little endian byte allocation order.

Categories and S ubject De scriptors D.3.3 **[Program- ming Languages**]: L anguage Constructs and Feature s – data types and structures

General Terms La nguages.

Keywords p rogramming languages; packetC, endianness, allocation order, bit-fields, network processing

1. Introdu ction

There are m any un certainties with C bitf ield i mplementa- tion, including

- Alignment.
- Packing behavior.
- Container types.
- Straddling.
- Endianness.

The problems are si gnificant enough to have spurred at- tempts to create se parate bitfield ABIs; see Richard Ho ga- boom, "A generic API bit manipulation in C," http://www.embedded.com/1999/9907/9907feat2.htm.

The problem of bit endianness within a collection of bit- fields is usually handled in one of three ways:

- Using s hifting and masking operations th at re flect endianness.
- Using #if def state ments to co mpile di fferent f ield declaration order for big and little-endian scenarios.

- Defining a co llection of macros to produ ce the d e- sired bit patterns.

Linux seems to have been e specially bed eviled b y bi t- field endianness problems. For further reading, see:

- "Linux: New firewall stack in development" for an example of this kind of problem , http://kerneltrap.org/node/7462.
- For an example of handling the problem with many macros, see http://www.ussg.iu.edu/hypermail/linux/kernel/021 1.0/0927.html.

2. Field Declaration Order

It is desirable to declare structures or descriptors in a way that naturally map to diagrams of well-known network pro- tocols' layouts. Thus, packetC maps structure or descriptor fields to memory by mapping from first-to-last field de- clared to the lowest-to-highest address. A packetC bitfield *container* (not an individual bitfield) behaves as a field for this purpose. Thus, if field Fj is declared before field Fk, it will reside at a lower-numbered address.

Rationale: t he pri mary use o f ou r str uctures/descriptors will be to describe fields in various network protocols (e.g., TCP, I Pv4 h eaders). T hese f ields are tra nsmitted a nd stored in n etwork order (big-endian order). Diagra ms of these headers and protocols typically show low to high byte addresses ru nning from le ft t o right and top to bottom . It will be in tuitive to make our source co de protoc ols match these la youts. T he example belo w sh ows how bytes 13 -16 of a TCP header are defined in packetC.

bits	*0..3*	*4..7*	*8..15*	*16-31*
bytes 13-16	data offset	rsvd	Flags	window

Figure 1. Fragment of a TCP header (bytes 13-16). Copyright Cloud- Shield Technologies, 2011.

```
struct myTCPfragment {
        bits short {
                dataOffset      : 4;
                reserved        : 4;
                flags           : 8;
        }
        short window;
}
```

The header struct declarations in packetC source code match the way people ordinarily represent and think about well-known headers, etc. Thus, our key rule is

As structure or descriptor fields are encountered in the source code from top to bottom, they are mapped from LSB to MSB.

A packetC implementation assigns the short containing the three bit fields to a lower address than the short containing the 'window' field, since the bit fields were declared earlier in the source code.

3. Byte Allocation Order within a Field

3.1 Within a Field Other than a Bitfield Container

The network protocols in a packet are stored in *network order* (most significant numerical part in lowest-numbered address).

- User arithmetic or logical operations on a field will be endian convention independent when they operate on entire variables of type **short** or **int**.

- User operations on byte-level components of a **short** or **int** (e.g., by equating a byte array with an int via a union) will necessarily reflect the host machine's endian conventions.

3.2 Within a Bitfield Container

Bitfield collections (*containers*) that are stored in multiple bytes cannot simply have their bytes swapped, too, because that would disconnect bits that need to be stored contiguously for the shift and masking instructions that isolate individual fields. Consider the example that follows and recall that little-endian depictions usually:

Big Endian

	Byte 0								Byte 1							
	1	0	1	1	1	1	1	0	1	1	0	1	1	0	0	1
Bit offset	0	1	2	3	4	5	6	7	0	1	2	3	4	5	6	7
Hex value	b				e				d				9			

Little Endian

	Byte 1								Byte 0							
	1	1	0	0	1	1	1	1	1	0	1	1	0	1	0	1
Bit offset	7	6	5	4	3	2	1	0	7	6	5	4	3	2	1	0
Hex value	c				f				b				5			

Little Endian (after byte-swap)

	Byte 1								Byte 0							
	1	0	1	1	0	1	0	1	1	1	0	0	1	1	1	1
Bit offset	7	6	5	4	3	2	1	0	7	6	5	4	3	2	1	0
Hex value	b				5				c				f			

Figure 2. Bitfields, endianness and byte-swapping. Copyright CloudShield Technologies, 2011.

- Show high-to-low numbered bytes from left to right,
- Show high-to-low numbered bits from left to right,
- Display hexadecimal values for 4-bit values without regard for bit order (i.e., if bits 7:4 are 1010, 'a' is shown, not 5).

In the subsequent example figures (e.g., Figure 2), the bitfield declarations are co   ded with co lors a nd f ont attributes to match storage bits to individual bitfields.

```
struct s {
  bits short {
          first  :3; // bold & italics
          second :8; // italics
          third  :5; // bold
    } con; // container name
  }
  s.con.first = 5;   s.con.second = 0xf6;
  s.con.third = 0x19;

// C displays the hex values shown in Fig. 2.
// from left to right when displaying an
// equivalent struct.
```

Note that after a by te-swap on a little -Endian machine, the bits for th e bit field, second, (sh own as green values) will no longer be contiguous. Thus, the shift logic that can be used to isolate individual fields on a big-endian machine will not deliver the correct results when used with this bit pattern.

Instead of applying byte swapping to fields that are bit-field co ntainers, it is   more useful to treat all bit fields, whether multi-byte or n ot, with a strate gy t hat ad dresses differences i n bit -order on big a nd little -endian machines. This strategy is described in the next section.

4. Bit Allocation Order Within a Bitfield

4.1 Ov   erview

First, the bit endianness problem for bitfields does not arise from pac ket bit tran smission/reception order. Alth   ough network b yte order is big -endian, the prescribed bit ar rival order at the physical layer can be little endian, i.e., th e least significant bits ca n have a lower wire address (arrive first). For exa mple, this is t   he ca se with Et hernet protoco ls. However, h ardware (e.g ., NIC s) co nverts this to th e bit endianness expected b y t he system CP U(s). (For   more details see the article below).

"Byte and Bit Order Dissection" by K. He, http://www.linuxjournal.com/article/6788, especiall y t he portion starting at section "Endianness of Network Proto-cols."

However, we do have a problem at the bitfield storage level. Big-endian and little-endian platforms will store the individual bits in a different order. The following problems with accessing bitfields can be identified:

- Compiler delivering the correct value for field selec-tion syntax.
- User obtaining correct results from explicit shifting or masking operations.
- User understanding displays for entire bitfield collec-tion (e.g., the containing storage unit).

Big Endian

	Byte 0								Byte 1							
	1	*0*	*1*	*1*	*1*	*1*	*1*	*0*	*1*	*1*	*0*	**1**	**1**	**0**	**0**	**1**
Bit offset	0	1	2	3	4	5	6	7	0	1	2	3	4	5	6	7
Hex value	*b*				*e*				*d*				*9*			

 **13 bits**

	Byte 0								Byte 1							
	0	0	0	0	0	0	0	0	0	0	0	0	0	*1*	*0*	*1*
Bit offset	0	1	2	3	4	5	6	7	0	1	2	3	4	5	6	7
Hex value	*0*				*0*				*0*				*5*			

Figure 3. Big endian result of >> 13 operation. Copyright CloudShield Technologies, 2011.

373

4.2 Th e Problem – an Example

The example recasts the packetC example from section 3.2 into C.

```
struct {
    unsigned short first    :3;
    unsigned short second   :8;
    unsigned short third    :5;
} s;
s.first = 5; s.second = 0xf6;
s.third = 0x19;
```

A gcc compiler will pack this into a **short** on 32-bit big-endian machines (S un, HP , A IX) a nd 32 -bit little -Endian machines (X86, DEC Alpha).

On a bi g-endian machine, this str ucture is stored in a way that w ould m atch n etwork order protocols. A u ser who eq uates th e structure to **short** and displa ys it i n hex-adecimal would see the value '0xbed9.' As shown in Fig-ure 3 , th e user (and t he co mpiler) can obtain th e value of the first field with an intuitive operation, using a C ">> 13" operation.

However, obs erve in Figu re 4 what h appens when th e user tries to get the first field via '>> 13" on a little-endian machine.

A li ttle-endian h ost will rep ort th e pre -shifted v alue as 0xcfb5 and th e value after s hifting as 0x 6 (the th ree most significant bits o f the third field). No te, however, that the

construct "s.first" yields the same results with a gcc compi-ler on big -endian and li ttle-endian machines. T he co mpi-ler's emitted code reflects whether it is on a big or little-endian machine but the user a ssumptions above do not take that into account.

4.3 So lution 1 – Alternative Declaration Order

One approach is to selectively declare reversed bitfield or-der on big vs. little-endian platforms. Consider a simplified example from the Linux kernel (taken from http://www.linuxjournal.com/article/6788).

```
          struct iphdr {
#ifdef (__LITTLE_ENDIAN_BITFIELD)
    __u8              ihl:4;
                      version:4;
#else
    __u8              version:4;
                      ihl:4;
#endif
```

Declaring bitf ields i n th e oppos ite or der f or a litt le-endian machine lets source code use the same shifting code with either endianness, since the reversed declaration order compensates for the reverse bit ordering on the two types of machines. T his solution a llows users t o directly obtai n bit field values with shifting and masking code.

Little Endian

	Byte 1								Byte 0							
	1	1	0	0	1	*1*	*1*	*1*	*1*	*0*	*1*	*1*	*0*	*1*	*0*	*1*
Bit offset	7	6	5	4	3	2	1	0	7	6	5	4	3	2	1	0
Hex value	*c*				*f*				*b*				*5*			

 **13 bits**

	Byte 1								Byte 0							
	0	0	0	0	0	0	0	0	0	0	0	0	0	1	1	0
Bit offset	7	6	5	4	3	2	1	0	7	6	5	4	3	2	1	0
Hex value	*0*				*0*				*0*				*6*			

Figure 4. Little endian result of >> 13 operation. Copyright CloudShield Technologies, 2011.

Big Endian

Byte 0									Byte 1							
1	*0*	*1*	*1*	*1*	*1*	*1*	*0*		*1*	*1*	*0*	**1**	**1**	**0**	**0**	**1**
Bit offset 0	1	2	3	4	5	6	7		0	1	2	3	4	5	6	7
Hex value *b*				*e*					*d*				*9*			

alen (3 bits)

Byte 0									Byte 1							
1	*1*	*1*	*1*	*0*	*1*	*1*	*0*		**1**	**1**	**0**	**0**	**1**	0	0	0
Bit offset 0	1	2	3	4	5	6	7		0	1	2	3	4	5	6	7
Hex value *f*				*6*					*c*				*8*			

alen + clen = 5+3 = 8 bits

Byte 0									Byte 1							
0	0	0	0	0	0	0	0		*1*	*1*	*1*	*1*	*0*	*1*	*1*	*0*
Bit offset 0	1	2	3	4	5	6	7		0	1	2	3	4	5	6	7
Hex value *0*				*0*					*f*				*6*			

Figure 5. Big endian behavior with the shifting algorithm. Copyright CloudShield Technologies, 2011.

4.4 So lution 2 – Macro Definitions

A set of macros is sometimes used to provide portable bit-field definitions. The following example of this approach shows how unwieldy it can be:

http://www.ussg.iu.edu/hypermail/linux/kernel/0211.0/092 7.html.

4.5 So lution 3 – Alternative Algorithms

The th ird altern ative is to co mmit to a si ngle b yte/bit all o-cation order sche me and req uire co mpliant co mpilers to compensate on machines with a different underlying repre-sentation sc hemes. For operands t hat inv olve an i ntegral number of bytes compensation take s the form of s wapping bytes. Ho wever, to work with bit fields t hat cross b yte boundaries co mpensation req uires t he co mpiler to u se a different al gorithm (i.e. e mit different co de seq uences) to isolate the bitfield value.

Consider the following al gorithmic approach. A ny bit-field, *b*, within a pac ketC bitf ield co ntainer can be d e-scribed by a tuple (*alen, blen, clen*), where:

- *alen* is the length in bits of all bitfields in the con-tainer declared before *b*.
- *blen* is the length in bits of bitfield *b*.
- *clen* is th e length of all bit fields in t he co ntainer de-clared after *b*.

Thus, the compiler could use the following source code to obtain the value of *b* for big and little endian machines.

```
unsigned short us = *(unsigned short *) &s;
// where 's' is the struct or descriptor.
#ifdef (__BIG_ENDIAN_BITFIELD)
        us <<= alen;
#else
        us <<= clen;
#endif
us >>= alen + clen;
```

For a big endia n machine Figure 5 s hows h ow the va-riant left bitwise shift yields the correct behavior to get the *second* field's value in our section 4.2 example (where *alen* = 3 and *clen* = 5.

375

Little Endian

	Byte 1								Byte 0							
	1	**1**	**0**	**0**	**1**	*1*	*1*	*1*	*1*	*0*	*1*	*1*	*0*	*1*	*0*	*1*
Bit offset	7	6	5	4	3	2	1	0	7	6	5	4	3	2	1	0
Hex value	*c*				*f*				*b*				*5*			

← *clen (5 bits)*

	Byte 1								Byte 0							
	1	*1*	*1*	*1*	*0*	*1*	*1*	*0*	*1*	*0*	*1*	0	0	0	0	0
Bit offset	7	6	5	4	3	2	1	0	7	6	5	4	3	2	1	0
Hex value	*f*				*6*				*a*				*0*			

→ **alen+clen = 5+3 = 8 bits**

	Byte 1								Byte 0							
	0	0	0	0	0	0	0	0	*1*	*1*	*1*	*1*	*0*	*1*	*1*	*0*
Bit offset	7	6	5	4	3	2	1	0	7	6	5	4	3	2	1	0
Hex value	*0*				*0*				*f*				*6*			

Figure 6. Little endian behavior with the shifting algorithm. Copyright CloudShield Technologies, 2011.

Figure 6 shows the shifting algorithm applied to isolating the same middle bitfield on a little endian platform.

5. Conclusion

Ultimately, the packetC language designers converged on requiring a compliant implementation to represent the packet array (and, therefore, packetC *descriptors* and *structures*) with big endian byte allocation order and little endian bit allocation order.

Thus, we gravitated to the third solution (section 4.5):

- Vendors and users supply only a single definition of network protocols (which uses big endian byte allocation order and little endian bit allocation order).

- User code is not required to contain platform-specific code that isolates individual bitfields.
- Compliant packetC compilers are responsible for emitting platform-specific code that manipulates field and bitfield contents on the basis of host machine attributes, when the user references them.

We believe this is the simplest, most intuitive solution. Subsequently, CloudShield has used this approach in delivering packetC compilers and an extensive set of network protocol definitions, expressed in packetC.

R. Duncan. "packetC field and bitfield allocation order." 2010. Printed by permission.

Managing Heterogeneous Architectures for High-speed Packet Processing

by Ralph Duncan, Peder Jungck and Kenneth Ross

Abstract

The centrality of n etworked co mmunications to ef fective military action is a truism of this age. A gainst th is back - ground heterogeneous parallel architectures h ave been su c- cessfully ap plied to cyber dom ains as diverse as *exascale* computing, m ultimedia applications and network processing. High-speed co mmunications are a natural match f or su ch architectures, sin ce th ey exh ibit a high de- gree of parallelism and are amenable to m ultiple k inds of specialized processin g. This pap er rep orts ou r novel ap- proach to developing communications applications for hete- rogeneous processors. Key aspects of the approach include extending h igh-level lang uages w ith domain-specific data types and operato rs, encapsulating th e extension s w ithin a virtual machine and implementing th e operato rs w ith sp e- cialized processors. Expressing the v irtual machine in mi- crocode prov ides an ef fective w ay to orchestrate communications with the disparate kinds of processors used - and to rep lace them with new kinds of processors. Bene- fits include speed to meet real-time demands, portable high- level language code and an extensible virtual machine.

Categories and Subject Descriptors C .3 [Special-Purpose and A pplication-Based Sy stems] microproces- sor/microcomputer applications

Keywords h eterogeneous architectures, parallel processing, packetC, network processing

1. Introduction

The cen trality of n etworked co mmunications to successful military action is a perv asive tenet in current military think- ing [1]. Virtu ally every asp ect of m ilitary operation s is affected, f rom expected areas lik e Command, Co ntrol, Communications, Computers, Intelligence, Surveillance and Reconnaissance (C4I SR) to relatively n ew ap plications, such as real-time transmission of complex medical data.

Two aspects of m ilitary co mmunications in general en- courage using parallel processing:

- Requirements for speed, sin ce timely knowledge can make the difference between success or failure
- Requirements to m ove ev er-more m assive am ounts of data

In addition, network packet processing's specific charac- teristics make it amenable to:

- Parallel processin g, because n etwork *packets* offer opportunities f or con current proces sing at several granularities
- Heterogeneous p rocessing, because pack et processing in volves operation s, su ch as m asked matching or searchin g f or strin gs, which are ef fec- tively implemented by specialized processors.

The last decad e h as seen the successful exploitation of heterogeneous processin g in a v ariety of areas, including network processin g, m ultimedia ap plications and *exascale* computing. Against th at broad back ground o ur particu lar approach f or applying h eterogeneous co mputing to pack et processing has several distinctive features:

- The granularity of parallelism that is exploited
- The manner in which a prog ramming language is ex- tended with application domain-specific constructs
- The m echanism thr ough w hich heter ogeneous p ro- cessors are in tegrated in to th e ov erall architecture and controlled.

The pap er is org anized as f ollows. First , we review re- cent h eterogeneous architectu re and th eir ap plication. Second, we summarize CloudShield's overall approach to parallelism and prog ramming for packet processing. W e then discuss in detail ou r ap proach to utilizing heterogene- ous architectures and analy ze the ensu ing im pacts on opt i- mization and ap plication develo pment. W e co nclude w ith summary remarks on heterogeneous computing's use in packet processing and military communications.

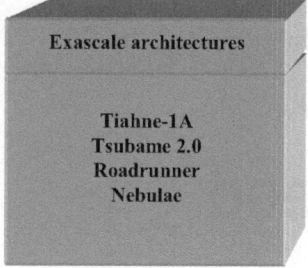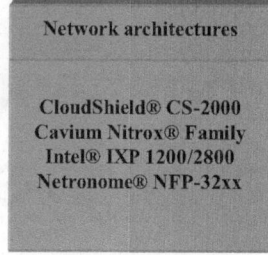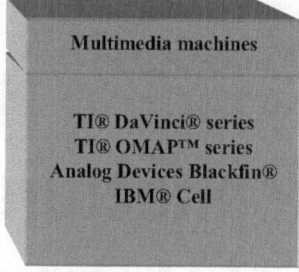

Figure 1. Example heterogeneous computer architectures. Copyright CloudShield Technologies, 2011.

2. Recent Heterogeneous Architecture Overview

In th e past decad e h eterogeneous architectures h ave en-joyed su ccessful ap plication to a wide range of technical areas. This section sketches representative developments in *exascale* co mputing, m ultimedia m achines and network processing (Fig. 1). Our motivation is to provide the reader with a sense of h ow w idely h eterogeneous processing has been ap plied and h ow diverse h eterogeneous architecture designs are.

As plans for *petascale* computing (capable of a *petaflop* or 10^{15} floating point operations per second) have evolved into plans for exascale computing (capable of 10^{18} floating point operations per second), th e most su ccessful designs have i nvolved usi ng t ens o r hund reds o f t housands o f processing n odes. In creasingly, each n ode is a multicore processor, usually combining one or more RISC processors with SIMD- oriented processor s, su ch as graphics processing units (GPUs).

As exam ples, co nsider three of the fastest four super-computers listed in the 36th TOP500 list (November 2010) of the world's fastest supercomputers, as measured by LIN-PACK benchmark performance [2].

- The m achine rank ed f astest is th e T iahne-1A at the National Supercomputing Center in T ianjin (Ch ina). This architecture consists of Intel® Xeon® X5670 6-core processors, Nvidia® Tesla™ M2050 GPUs and Galaxy FT-1000 8-core processors [2, 3].
- The th ird-ranked m achine is Nebulae (a Dawning TC3600 Blade System) at the National Supercomput-ing Centre in Sh enzhen (China), which is co mposed of Intel® Xeon® X5 650 6-core processors and Nvi-dia® Tesla™ C2050 GPUs [2].
- The f ourth f astest T OP500 m achine is the Tsu-bame 2.0 at th e T okyo In stitute of Technology (Ja-pan). It consists of Intel® Xeon® X56nn (Westmere-EP) 6-core processors and Nvidia® T esla™ M2050 GPUs [2].

Multimedia arch itectures usually combine g eneral com-puting functionality for control with specialized capabilities for v ideo, im age or audio pr ocessing. T hus, they often combine RISC or m icrocontroller processors w ith dig ital signal processors (DSP s) or oth er specialized processors

that are typically well-suited to SIMD-style execution. Ex-ample architectures include:

- Texas Instruments' (TI) DaVinci® lin e, w hich in -cludes combinations of ARM Holdings' RISC pro-cessors, TI® DSP s and on-chip periph erals (e.g ., controllers, encoders/decoders, converters) [4]
- Analog Devices' B lackfin® architecture, in w hich a 10-stage, 16 and 32 -bit in struction pipelin e f eeds a RISC m icrocontroller co re, a DSP unit and peri-pherals with specialized instructions [5]
- International Business Machines' Cell architecture, where a chip co ntains a 64 -bit P ower Architecture core and eight dual-issue, statically scheduled SIMD-style coprocessors [6].

Network processing arch itectures usually offer a RISC-style core f or co ntrol f unctions and n etwork processin g units (NP Us) f or specialized pack et processing, such as managing packet header information. T he v arious m odels of th e In tel® IXP n etworking m ulticores (IXP 1200/2400/2800[7]) embody this approach.

Network processor archite ctures m ay also use specia-lized processors f or encryption, strin g and regu lar expres-sion searching, m asked m atching or som e co mbination of operations. T he Netron ome® Netw ork Flow Proces-sor(NFP) [8] and Caviu m Nitrox ® P rocessor [9] produ ct lines furnish examples.

The current CloudShield® architecture, (e.g . the CS-2000 [10]), is a heterogeneous network processing architec-ture *par excellence*. This architecture builds on the kind of heterogeneous network multicore described above. T hus it has the following kinds of processors:

- RISC control processor (from networking multicore)
- NPUs (from networking multicore)
- FPGAs for in gress/egress processing and data man-agement
- Ternary co ntent ad dressable m emory (T CAM) chips (e.g., associative memory processors)
- *Regex* processors f or f inding character seq uences defined by strings or regular expressions

How we orchestrate this processor ensemble and provide mechanisms for prog ramming it in h igh-level, portab le fa-shion is the focus of the subsequent sections.

3. Parallel Processing Model

Our approach to h eterogeneous processin g is tig htly in te-grated with our general intention to presen t application d e-velopers with an intuitive view of parallel packet processing and a m achine-independent ap proach to prog ramming. T o support those goals, our approach has these features:

- Use coarse-grained parallelism at the packet level
- Hide m achine specif ics with pack etC [1 1], a hig h-level programming language
- Express domain needs with data type extensions
- Hide processor choices behind a virtual machine.

Developers express parallelism at a coarse-grained level with a sm all prog ram (a pack etC *packet ma in*) that processes one packet at a time in end-to-end fashion. Thus, the model uses single program multiple data (SPMD) paral-lelism. Coarse- grain parallelis m frees th e develo per f rom fine-grain mechanics, like synchronizing low-level tasks.

Our parallel packet processing model is shown in Fig. 2. As packets enter the system ingress processing finds packet headers and prep ares a packet array and packet information block (P IB) f or each pack et. T he system allocates each packet to a *context* (a copy of th e ap plication prog ram) which processes it from start to finish.

As an application executes, it may utilize data structures with domain-specific data ty pes. As described below, some of these structures reside in a *global* memory that is used by all program copies.

If a pack et is f orwarded by a program copy, rather th an dropped, it is s ent to an eg ress processor for post-processing and routing.

This model is im plemented by co mbining specialized hardware with a domain-specific programming language.

4. Programming Language Approach

The packetC lang uage [11] lets u sers develo p parallel n et-working applications by

- Writing a single short program – rather than a collec-tion of lower-level tasks
- Expressing pack et processin g functionality in term s of extended data types and operators that exh ibit fa-miliar high-level language look-and-feel

To support those goals, packetC uses the C99 variant of C for f amiliar operato rs, co nditional statem ents and ov erall syntax. The lang uage rem oves co nstructs likely to cause security or reliab ility problem s, su ch as address operators, pointers and dy namic allocation. pack etC adds the follow-ing data type extensions:

- Descriptors: *structs* th at autom atically 'float' to a packet location to ov erlay a pack et protoco l header [12].
- Databases: structure aggregates divided into 'data' and 'mask' halves for *wildcarded* m atching against packet contents [13].
- Searchsets: aggregates of strin gs or regu lar expre s-sions to m atch against pack et co ntents via C++-style *methods* [14].
- References: provide a classic, co mputer science re f-erence capability for chaining together successive da-tabases and searchsets operation s that are contingent on a previous operation's result.

These data types and operations on them can be im ple-mented by g eneral-purpose or specialized processors. Therefore, org anizing and encapsu lating the specifics of how th e ty pes are im plemented st rongly i nfluences ho w portable packetC applications are and h ow readily packetC implementers can chang e im plementation processors in a heterogeneous env ironment. T he n ext section sh ows how we use a virtual machine to isolate processor specifics.

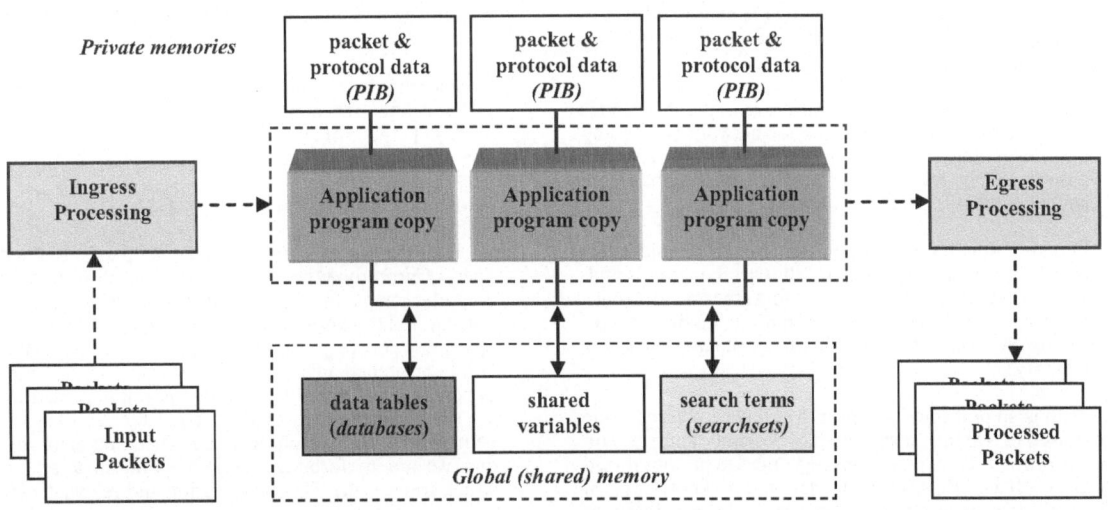

Figure 2. Parallel packet processing model and language features (in italics). Copyright CloudShield Technologies, 2011.

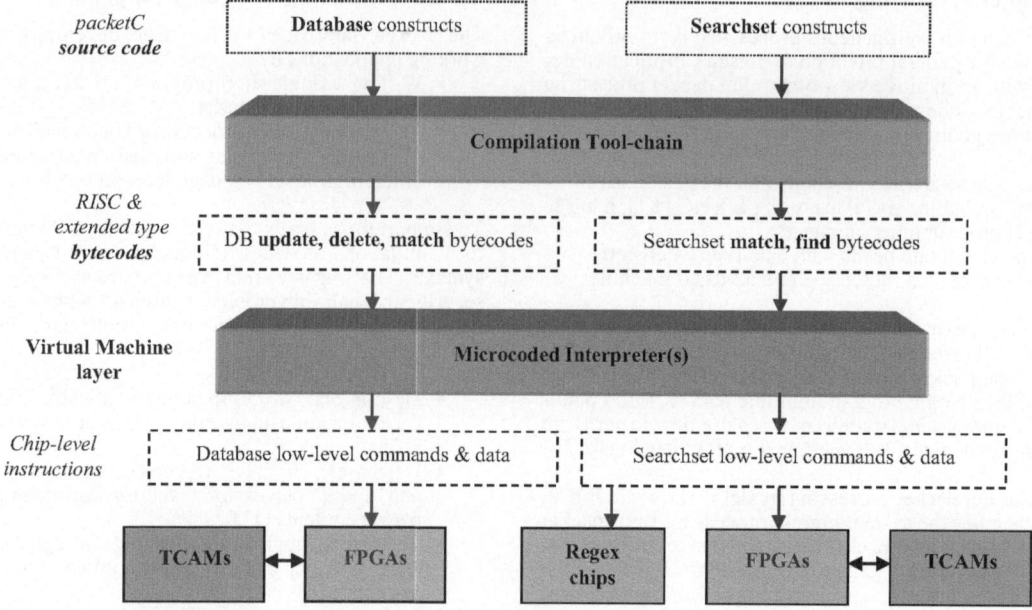

Figure 3. Using interpreted virtual machine instructions to hide and isolate machine control for heterogeneous processors. Copyright CloudShield Technologies, 2011.

5. Interpreting a Virtual Machine

Fig. 3 sh ows h ow h igh-level packet co nstructs are translated, first, by a co mpiler tool-chain into *virtual ma chine bytecodes*, then by in terpreters in to chip -specific co mmands for a v ariety of processors. The essential aspects of this approach are:

- Isolating dom ain-specific action s in h igh-level constructs (e.g., packet *tuple* matching is expressed as a pplying a m atch operato r method to an array of augmented, C-style structures).

- Translating these operations into high-level bytecodes that describe a v irtual machine for network processing (e.g., matching a packet tuple is translated into a dat abase m atch by tecode th at does n ot presu ppose h ow packet databases are implemented).

- Encapsulating hardware specifics in microcoded interpreters – running in parallel – that send operands and data to specialized processors and g ather results (e.g., sends co mmands to a T CAM to m atch a bit pattern against th e current contents of co ntent-addressable memory).

In th is ap proach develo pers m anipulate sou rce code composed of extende d stru cture ty pes and of array s of strings or regu lar expressio ns. Ex pertise in optimized coded of NP Us, T CAMs, et al., as well as knowledge of what processor types are in the system, is required only of the in terpreter im plementers. A pplication develo pers are presumed to be experts in networking matters, rather than

expert in machine details of a c hanging ensemble of sp ecialty processors.

6. Ex ample: Heterogeneity and Operations

Our current im plementation of packetC *searchsets* sho ws how extended data ty pes in a high-level lang uage can be mapped at run-time to heterogeneous processors.

Consider a searchset that contains a set of strings. The **match** operator compares the contents of a user-specified location against th e set, returning th e f irst to m atch as shown below.

```
searchset pets[3][3] = {"cat", "dog", "owl" };
SearchResult ansStruct;
try {  // match vs. a 3-byte slice of packet
  ansStruct = pets.match( pkt[64:66] );
}
catch ( ERR_SET_NOMATCH ) {…}
```

How the match is implemented is opaque to the developer. Currently, when a searchset **match** is presen t, our compiler maps the associated searchset's contents to a portion of TCAM (associative memory). At run-time, the operand value (e.g., packet slice, v ariable co ntents, etc.) will be m atched against all the relevant TCAM elements in parallel. A s Fig. 4 sh ows, this is implemented by having the pertinent copy of the interpreter send the value to be m atched, the searchset being u sed and an in dication that we are performing a m atch operation to an FP GA, which triggers the TCAM operation and relays the results.

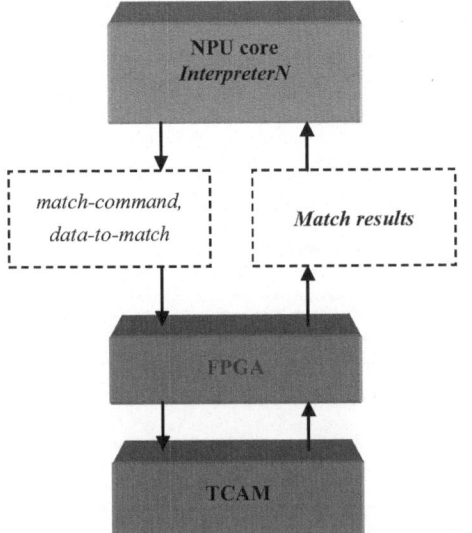

Figure 4. Interpreter performing a packetC searchset **match** operation via a TCAM chip (associative memory processor). Copyright CloudShield Technologies, 2011.

Now consider the same searchset in the context of a **find** operator, which searches anywhere within a specified location for any members of the searchset.

```
try    // search the entire packet
    { ansStruct = pets.find( pkt ); }
catch ( ERR_SET_NOTFOUND ) {…}
```

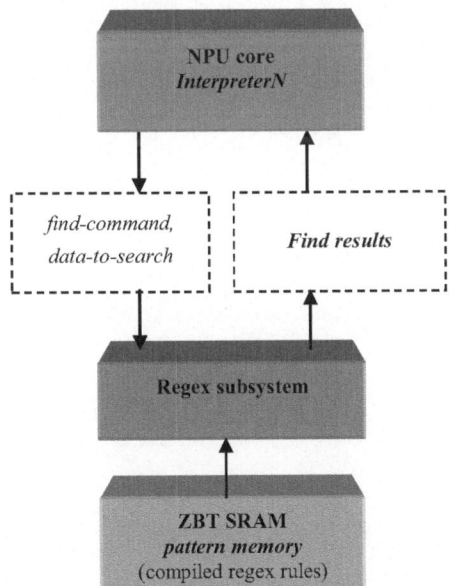

Figure 5. Interpreter performing a searchset **find** operation via a regex system. Copyright CloudShield Technologies, 2011.

In this case, too, the packetC developer is not concerned with whether a special processor is used to implement the **find** command or with its identity. Our current implementation uses another vendor's regex subsystem. Searchset contents are precompiled into a set of regex rules and loaded into a specialized pattern memory. As Fig. 5 shows, at run-time the interpreter ships the bits within which to search down (typically, a portion of a packet payload) to the subsystem, which returns the index of the first searchset element to be found (if any), as well as information about its relative location within the search space.

These examples underscore how processor heterogeneity is used in this scheme: the interpreter will typically execute arithmetic and conditional logic on whatever kind of NPU or RISC processor is its host. Complex, domain-specific operations, however, will often be expressed as high-level operators for packetC extended data types and be executed on special processors. This has significant implications for system architecture, program optimization and long-term system extensibility.

7. Impacts on Optimization and Control

As this system software architecture departs from classic practices, it focuses organizational efforts in new areas.

First, the principal optimization concern shifts from instruction selection and register allocation to

- Selecting the best kind of processor or system on a chip (SOC) to implement higher-level operations.
- Speeding communications with specialized subsystems by minimizing the amount of data to be moved and judiciously choosing the communications medium.

Second, optimizations in this application domain and architectural environment involve a mix of domain-specific skills and traditional concerns. For example, experiments with searchsets [14] show that performance is highly sensitive to

- The complexity of the involved regular expressions and the finite state machine that results
- The number of regular expressions
- The size of the memory to be searched (typically all or some portion of the packet payload).

8. Benefits

Distinctive aspects of this approach confer several benefits: portability, usability, reliability and extensibility.

The packetC high-level language promotes user application portability by omitting machine-specific features, such as register classes, cache details, FIFOs, etc. To accommodate new hosts, vendors rewrite portions of the interpreter, rather than require users to recode applications.

packetC also increases language and tool-chain usability by expressing domain-specific processing in terms of high-level operations on extended-type variants of familiar C data types, such as structures and arrays.

381

This architectural approach provides significant reliability through the use of dozens of concurrent copies of the micro-coded interpreter. The loss of an underlying *micro-engine* in the current implementation would diminish overall throughput while retaining a decisive majority of the available compute power.

The hallmark of this system is extensibility. The domain-specific actions most amenable to special processing are coded in a machine-independent way and the invocation of any special processors is hidden inside a virtual machine interpreter. Thus, swapping one specialized processor out for another, a hardware solution out for an algorithmic one, or a specialized processor out for a general-purpose one can all be realized without application recoding and often without making tool-chain changes outside the interpreter.

9. Summary

The discussion above summarizes an overall architecture that supports using heterogeneous processors for packet processing. This summary considers the principal aspects of the architecture as they relate to heterogeneous processing. First, we examine individual components' impacts and, then, assess the impact of the architecture as a whole.

Expressing packet operations in terms of high-level language data types and operators focuses attention on abstraction, rather than on machine-specific implementation. This is critical for making a heterogeneous system changeable.

The approach expresses packet-processing, as well as familiar arithmetic and control flow operations, with machine-independent *bytecodes*. This significantly reduces the tool-chain's dependence on particular hardware, which effectively delays introducing most processor-specific knowledge into the tool-chain prior to the interpreter.

Using micro-coded interpreters concentrates machine-specific coding expertise where it will do the most good for orchestrating communications with specialized subsystems. Interpreters can effectively use machine features like register classes to perform 'ordinary' instructions on the host, and use host caches, FIFOs and channels to optimize communications with specialized subsystems, like TCAMs.

From top to bottom this architectural approach facilitates using (and changing) heterogeneous processors by

- Encapsulating relevant operations in language operators that are readily mapped to specialized processors
- Hiding operation implementations inside a virtual machine, where they can be easily changed
- Using micro-coded interpreters to effectively get data in and out of different processors and subsystems.

Acknowledgments

Peder Jungck, Dwight Mulcahy and Ralph Duncan are the co-authors of the packetC language. Jim Frandeen contributed valuable technical information.

References

[1] D.S. Alberts, J.J. Garstka and F.P. Stein. "Network Centric Warfare: Developing and Leveraging Information Superiority." 2nd Edition, CCRP Publication Series, Washington, D.C., 2000.

[2] TOP500 Project. TOP500 List, 36th edition, Nov. 2010. Retrieved from http://www.top500.org/lists/2010/11 on March 30, 2010.

[3] Nvidia. NVIDIA Tesla GPUs Power World's Fastest Supercomputer. October 28, 2010. Retrieved on March 30, 2011 from http://pressroom.nvidia.com/easyir/customrel.do?easyirid=A0D622C E9F579F09&version=live&prid=678988&releasejsp=release_157

[4] Wikipedia. "Texas Instruments DaVinci," Retrieved March 29, 2011 from http://en.wikipedia.org/wiki/Texas_Instruments_DaVinci.

[5] Analog Devices. Blackfin Processor Architecture Overview. Retrieved March 29, 2011 from http://www.analog.com/en/embedded-processing-dsp/Blackfin/processors/Blackfin_architecture/fca.html

[6] International Business Machines Corporation. The Cell Architecture: Innovation Matters. Retrieved on March 29, 2011 from http://domino.research.ibm.com/comm/research.nsf/pages/r.arch.inn ovation.html.

[7] E. K. Johnson and A. R. Kunze. "IXP 2400/2800 Programming: The Complete Microengine Coding Guide." Intel Press, Hillsboro, Oregon, 2003.

[8] Netronome Systems, Inc. Network Flow Processors. Retrieved March 31, 2011 from http://www.netronome.com/pages/network-flow-processors.

[9] Cavium Networks, Inc. Products: Nitrox® DPI L7 Content Processor Family. Retrieved March 31, 2011 from http://www.caviumnetworks.com/processor_NITROX-DPI.html.

[10] CloudShield Technologies. CS-2000 Technical Specifications. Product datasheet available from CloudShield Technologies, 212 Gibraltar Dr., Sunnyvale, CA, USA 94089, 2006.

[11] R. Duncan and P. Jungck. packetC language for high performance packet processing. In Proceedings of the 11th IEEE Intl. Conf. High Performance Computing and Communications, (Seoul, South Korea), pp. 450-457, June 25-27, 2009.

[12] R. Duncan, P. Jungck and K. Ross. A paradigm for processing network protocols in parallel. In Proceedings of the 10th Intl. Conf. on Algorithms and Architectures for Paralel Processing, (Busan, South Korea), pp. 52-67, May 21-23, 2010.

[13] R. Duncan, P. Jungck and K. Ross. packetC language and parallel processing of masked databases. Proceedings of the 39th Intl. Conf. on Parallel Processing, (San Diego), pp. 472-481, September 13-16, 2010.

[14] R. Duncan, P. Jungck, K. Ross and S. Tillman. Packet Content matching with packetC Searchsets. Proceedings of the 16th Intl. Conf. on Parallel and Distributed Systems, (Shanghai, China), pp. 180-188, December 8-10, 2010.

■ ■ ■

Reference Tables

This appendix contains tables that provide valuable information for developers working with packetC. These tables include information concerning:

- Keywords
- ASCII table
- Bits and bytes review
- The TCP/IP and OSI model network stack
- Internet and Ethernet header formats

Keywords

The keywords listed within the Reference Tables below are all reserved words within packetC and shall not be redefined by a developer.

Unit Keywords

```
packet
library
shared
module
main
```

Declaration Keywords

```
entry       union       string
extern      bits        reference
byte        pad         descriptor
short       enum        record
int         typedef     database
long        buffer      db
void        const       searchset
struct      regex       set
```

Pragma Keywords

```
pragma
control
datatype
export
regex1
```

Expression Keywords

```
sizeof
offset
packet_offset
end
```

Method Keywords

```
match
find
delete
insert
replicate
requeue
```

Statement Keywords

at	return	lock
if	continue	unlock
else	switch	alert
while	case	log
do	default	ref
exit	break	deref
for	try	
goto	throw	
	catch	

packetC Pre-Defined Keywords

true	SearchResult	ERR_PKT_DELETE
false	NULL_STOP	ERR_PKT_NOREPLICATE
pib	NULL_REGEX	ERR_SET_NOMATCH
pkt	ERR_DB_FULL	ERR_SET_NOPERFORM
sys	ERR_DB_READ	ERR_SET_NOTFOUND
$PACKET	ERR_DB_NOMATCH	ERR_PKT_NOTREQUEUED
$SYS	ERR_LAST_DEFINED	
$PIB	ERR_PKT_INSERT	

ASCII Table with Decimal to Hexadecimal Conversion

Characters may appear differently in hex editors and packet analysis systems for characters outside of the printable standard alphanumeric sequences.

	0	1	2	3	4	5	6	7	8	9	A	B	C	D	E	F
0	NUL 0	⌐ 1	⌐ 2	L 3	⌐ 4	| 5	— 6	7	BS 8	TAB 9	LF 10	VT 11	FF 12	CR 13	14	15
1	+ 16	◄ 17	↕ 18	‼ 19	¶ 20	⊥ 21	T 22	┤ 23	↑ 24	⊢ 25	→ 26	← 27	28	29	· 30	31
2	32	! 33	" 34	# 35	$ 36	% 37	& 38	' 39	(40	) 41	* 42	+ 43	, 44	- 45	. 46	/ 47
3	0 48	1 49	2 50	3 51	4 52	5 53	6 54	7 55	8 56	9 57	: 58	; 59	< 60	= 61	> 62	? 63
4	@ 64	A 65	B 66	C 67	D 68	E 69	F 70	G 71	H 72	I 73	J 74	K 75	L 76	M 77	N 78	O 79
5	P 80	Q 81	R 82	S 83	T 84	U 85	V 86	W 87	X 88	Y 89	Z 90	[91	\ 92	] 93	^ 94	_ 95
6	` 96	a 97	b 98	c 99	d 100	e 101	f 102	g 103	h 104	i 105	j 106	k 107	l 108	m 109	n 110	o 111
7	p 112	q 113	r 114	s 115	t 116	u 117	v 118	w 119	x 120	y 121	z 122	{ 123	| 124	} 125	~ 126	127
8	€ 128	129	‚ 130	ƒ 131	„ 132	… 133	† 134	‡ 135	^ 136	‰ 137	Š 138	‹ 139	Œ 140	141	Ž 142	143
9	144	' 145	' 146	" 147	" 148	• 149	– 150	— 151	~ 152	™ 153	š 154	› 155	œ 156	157	ž 158	Ÿ 159
A	160	¡ 161	¢ 162	£ 163	¤ 164	¥ 165	¦ 166	§ 167	¨ 168	© 169	ª 170	« 171	¬ 172	- 173	® 174	¯ 175
B	° 176	± 177	² 178	³ 179	´ 180	µ 181	¶ 182	· 183	¸ 184	¹ 185	º 186	» 187	¼ 188	½ 189	¾ 190	¿ 191
C	À 192	Á 193	Â 194	Ã 195	Ä 196	Å 197	Æ 198	Ç 199	È 200	É 201	Ê 202	Ë 203	Ì 204	Í 205	Î 206	Ï 207
D	Ð 208	Ñ 209	Ò 210	Ó 211	Ô 212	Õ 213	Ö 214	× 215	Ø 216	Ù 217	Ú 218	Û 219	Ü 220	Ý 221	Þ 222	ß 223
E	à 224	á 225	â 226	ã 227	ä 228	å 229	æ 230	ç 231	è 232	é 233	ê 234	ë 235	ì 236	í 237	î 238	ï 239
F	ð 240	ñ 241	ò 242	ó 243	ô 244	õ 245	ö 246	÷ 247	ø 248	ù 249	ú 250	û 251	ü 252	ý 253	þ 254	ÿ 255

Bits and Bytes

The following section contains quick references regarding the sizes and values of packetC unsigned numbers. In the diagram, MSB is the most significant bit and LSB is the least significant bit in Big-Endian byte-allocation order systems such as packetC. Note that packetC also follows a Little-Endian bit-allocation order.

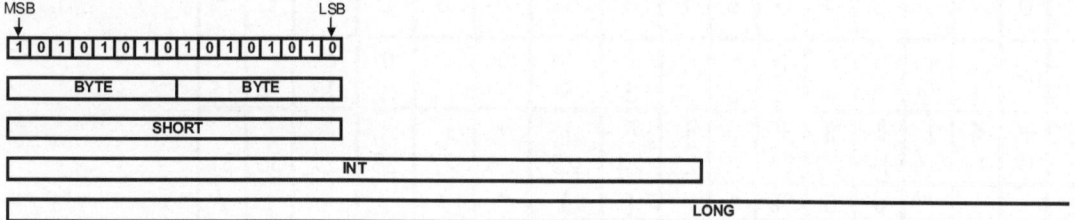

- 8 Bits per Byte

- 2 Bytes per Short

- 2 Shorts per Int

- 2 Ints per Long

- Byte = 8 Bits

- Short = 16 Bits

- Int = 32 Bits

- Long = 64 Bits

- Byte   Maximum Value 255

- Short   Maximum Value 65,535

- Int   Maximum Value 4,294,967,295

- Long   Maximum Value 18,446,744,073,709,551,615

TCP/IP and OSI Model Network Stack

The OSI model divides layers of the stack into strictly-separated roles and protocols. The TCP/IP model continues with the enveloping of protocols within one another but not necessarily defining their roles in such a strict manner with regard to transport and network layers versus application layers. In packetC, layers follow a physical construction model of representation. If a protocol follows a full Layer 3 IP Header, then that protocol is treated as a Layer 4 protocol whether or not it may be called that in the TCP/IP model. A simple reference view of this schema is shown below.

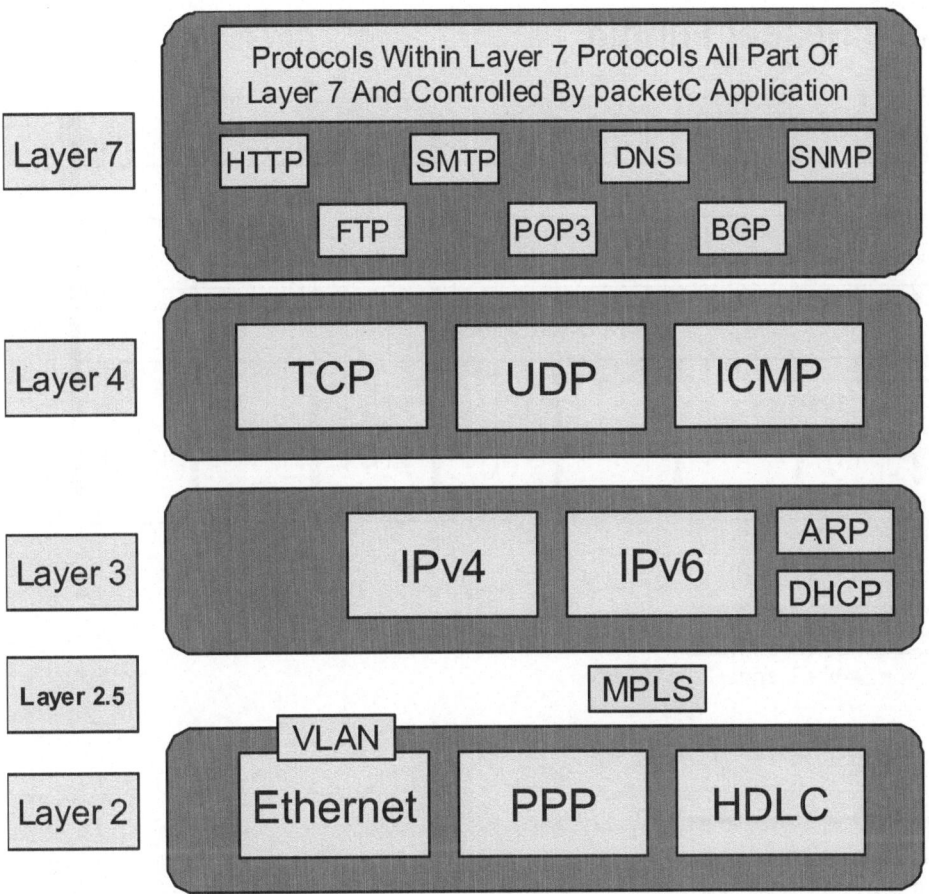

Header Formats

The following network protocols are provided for reference and have supporting descriptors defined in *protocols.ph* (see Chapter 25 for Standard Networking Descriptors). The following diagrams call out byte and bit positions matching the packetC big-endian byte order and little-endian bit order representation of packet fields when accessed directly or via descriptors.

Basic Ethernet II Header Format

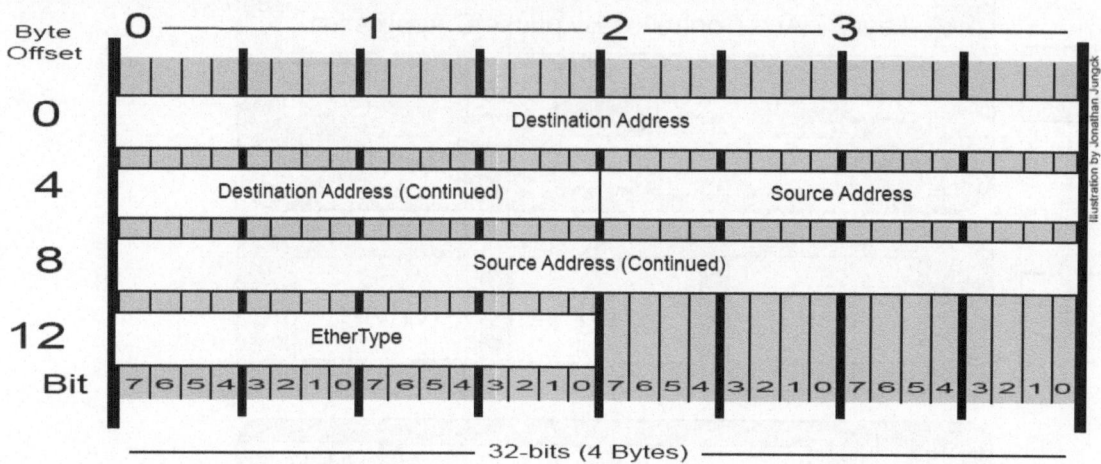

Destination & Source Address

48-bit Designator (Upper 24-bits Vendor)

00:0B:A9:xx:xx:xx - CloudShield Technologies, Inc.

Ethertype / Length

If Value <= 1500, then this is a length field
If Value > 1500, then this is EtherType

0800 - Internetworking Protocol (IP)
0806 - Address Resolution Protocol (ARP)
8035 - Reverse ARP
809B - AppleTalk
80F3 - AppleTalk ARP
8100 - 802.1Q (See Ethernet with VLAN)
8137 - NetWare IPX/SPX
C5C5 - CloudShield Proprietary EtherType
C5C6 - CloudShield Proprietary EtherType

Ethernet Header with VLAN Tag (802.1Q) Format

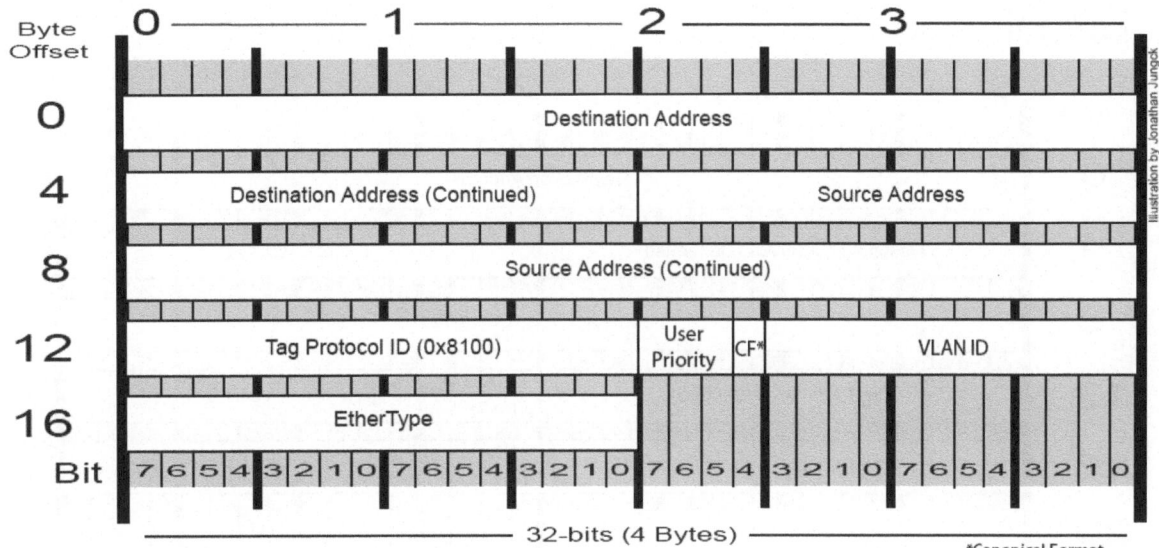

Destination & Source Address

48-bit Designator (Upper 24-bits Vendor)

00:0B:A9:xx:xx:xx - CloudShield Technologies, Inc.

Ethertype / Length

If Value <= 1500, then this is a length field
If Value > 1500, then this is EtherType

0800 - Internetworking Protocol (IP)
0806 - Address Resolution Protocol (ARP)
8035 - Reverse ARP
809B - AppleTalk
80F3 - AppleTalk ARP
8100 - 802.1Q (See Ethernet with VLAN)
8137 - NetWare IPX/SPX
C5C5 - CloudShield Proprietary EtherType
C5C6 - CloudShield Proprietary EtherType

Tag Protocol ID

8100 - 802.1Q Identifies VLAN Follows

User Priority (3 Bits)

0 - Best Effort
1 - Background
2 - Spare
3 - Excellent Effort
4 - Controlled Load
5 - Video
6 - Voice
7 - Network Control

Canonical Format Indicator (1 Bit)

0 - Canonical Format (Always 0 for Ethernet)
1 - Non-Canonical Format (Token Ring)

VLAN Identifier (12 Bits)

0x000 - No VLAN, Just 802.1p Priority
0x001 - Management VLAN ID
0x002 : 0xFFE - User VLAN Range (4093)
0xFFF - Reserved

Ethernet Header with Stacked VLAN Tags (802.1Q in Q) Format

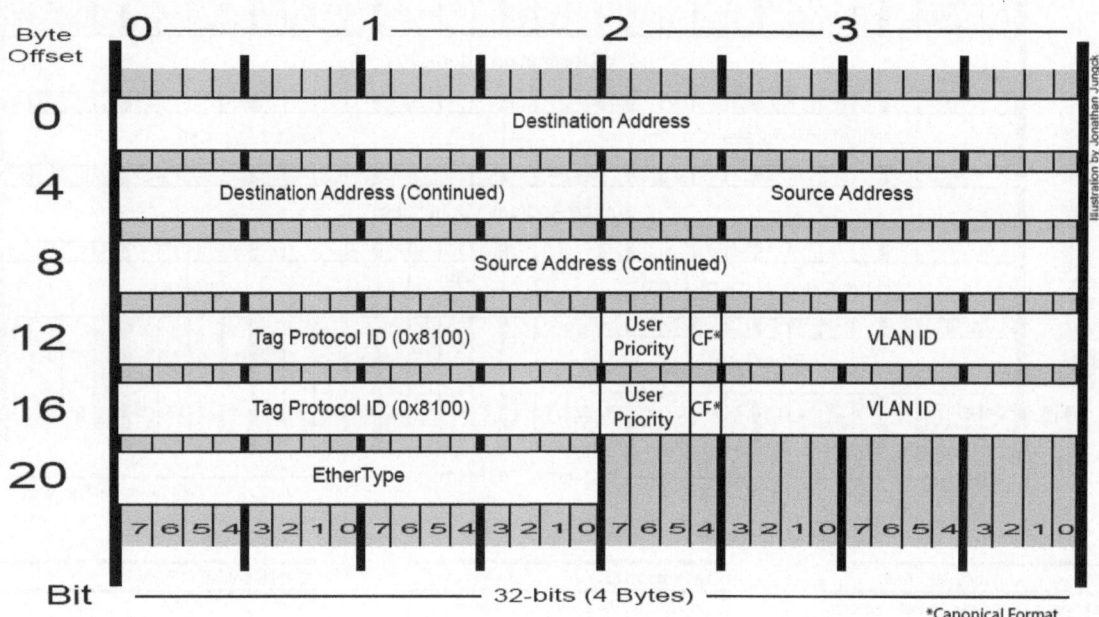

Destination & Source Address

48-bit Designator (Upper 24-bits Vendor)

00:0B:A9:xx:xx:xx - CloudShield Technologies, Inc.

Ethertype / Length

If Value <= 1500, then this is a length field
If Value > 1500, then this is EtherType

0800 - Internetworking Protocol (IP)
0806 - Address Resolution Protocol (ARP)
8035 - Reverse ARP
809B - AppleTalk
80F3 - AppleTalk ARP
8100 - 802.1Q (See Ethernet with VLAN)
8137 - NetWare IPX/SPX
C5C5 - CloudShield Proprietary EtherType
C5C6 - CloudShield Proprietary EtherType

Tag Protocol ID

8100 - 802.1Q Identifies VLAN Follows

User Priority (3 Bits)

0 - Best Effort
1 - Background
2 - Spare
3 - Excellent Effort
4 - Controlled Load
5 - Video
6 - Voice
7 - Network Control

Canonical Format Indicator (1 Bit)

0 - Canonical Format (Always 0 for Ethernet)
1 - Non-Canonical Format (Token Ring)

VLAN Identifier (12 Bits)

0x000 - No VLAN, Just 802.1p Priority
0x001 - Management VLAN ID
0x002 : 0xFFE - User VLAN Range (4093)
0xFFF - Reserved

IPv4 Header

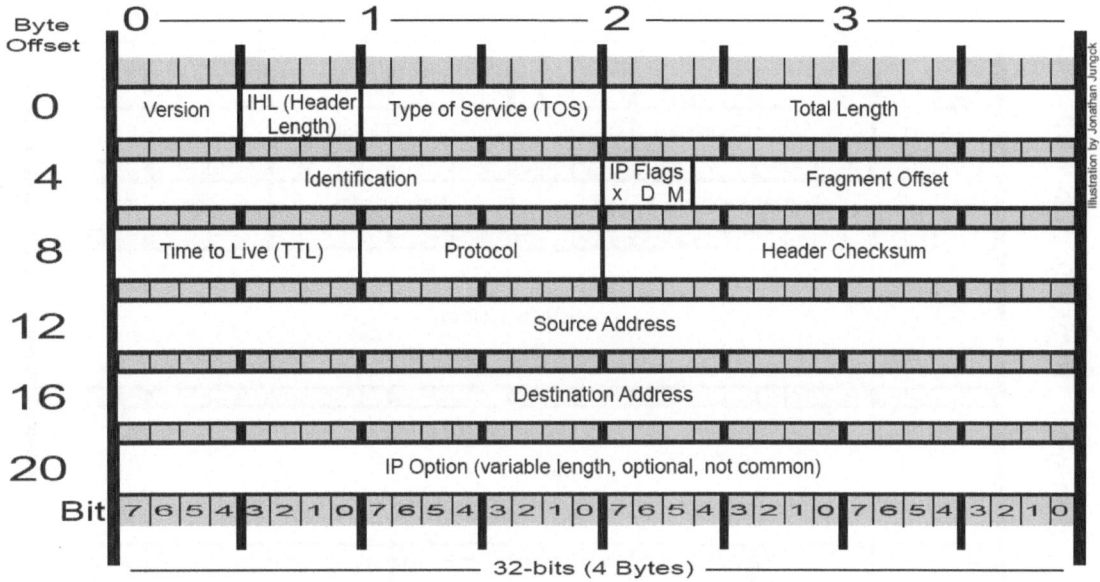

Version	Protocol	Fragment Offset	IP Flags
Version of IP Protocol. 4 and 6 are valid. This diagram represents version 4 structure only.	IP Protocol ID. Including (but not limited to): 1 ICMP 17 UDP 57 SKIP 2 IGMP 47 GRE 88 EIGRP 6 TCP 50 ESP 89 OSPF 9 IGRP 51 AH 115 L2TP	Fragment offset from start of IP datagram. Measured in 8 byte (2 words, 64 bits) increments. If IP datagram is fragmented, fragment size (Total Length) must be a multiple of 8 bytes.	x D M x 0x80 reserved (evil bit) D 0x40 Do Not Fragment M 0x20 More Fragments follow

Header Length	Total Length	Header Checksum	RFC 791
Number of 32-bit words in TCP header, minimum value of 5. Multiply by 4 to get byte count.	Total length of IP datagram, or IP fragment if fragmented. Measured in Bytes.	Checksum of entire IP header	Please refer to RFC 791 for the complete Internet Protocol (IP) Specification.

IPv6 Header

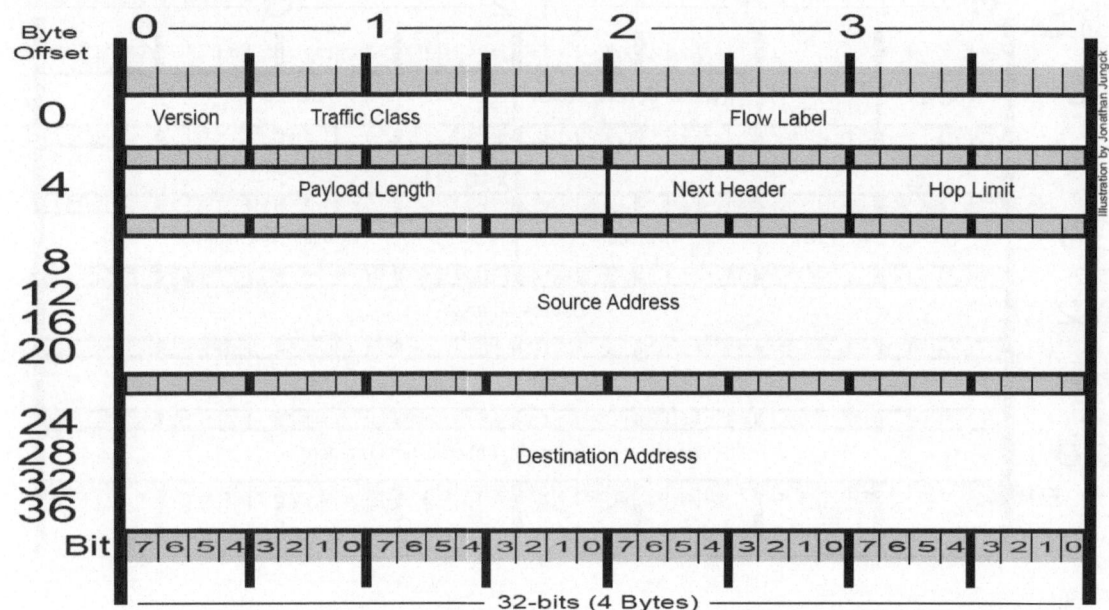

Version	Payload Length	Next Header	Hop Limit
Version of IP Protocol. 4 and 6 are valid. This diagram represents version 6 structure only.	16-bit unsigned integer. Length of the IPv6 payload, i.e., the rest of the packet following this IPv6 header, in octets. Any extension headers are considered part of the payload.	8-bit selector. Identifies the type of header immediately following the IPv6 header. Uses the same values as the IPv4 Protocol field.	8-bit unsigned integer. Decremented by 1 by each node that forwards the packet. The packet is discarded if Hop Limit is decremented to zero.

Traffic Class		Destination Address	RFC 2460
8 bit traffic class field.		128-bit address of the intended recipient of the packet (possibly not the ultimate recipient, if a Routing header is present).	Please refer to RFC 2460 for the complete Internet Protocol version 6 (IPv6) Specification.

Flow Label	Source Address		
20 bit flow label.	128-bit address of the originator of the packet.		

392

TCP Header

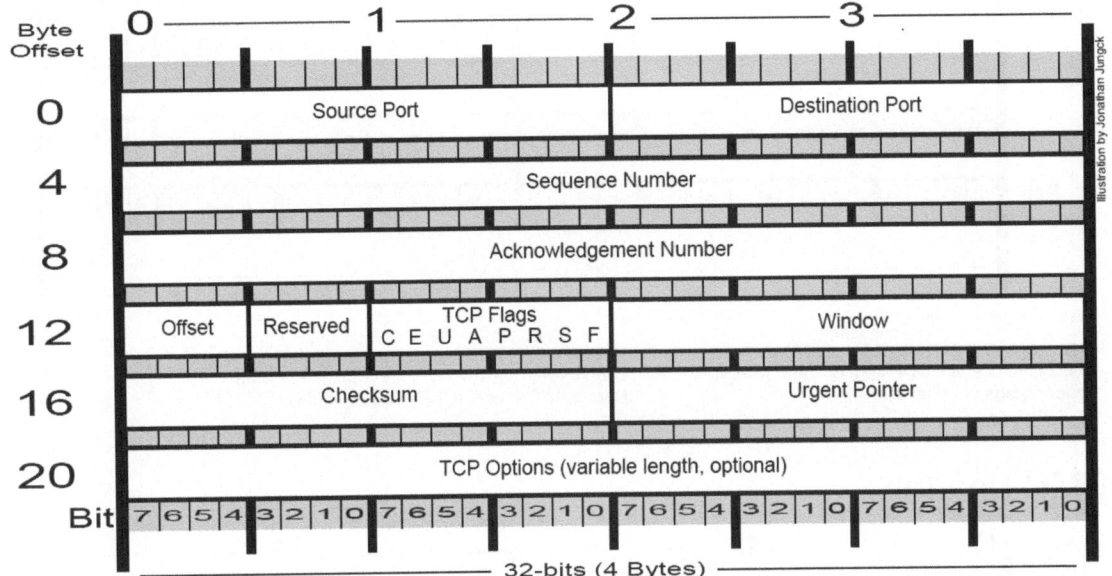

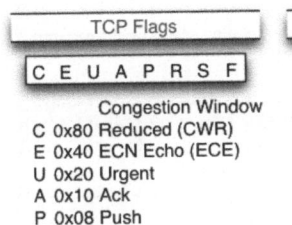

TCP Flags
C E U A P R S F
Congestion Window
C 0x80 Reduced (CWR)
E 0x40 ECN Echo (ECE)
U 0x20 Urgent
A 0x10 Ack
P 0x08 Push
R 0x04 Reset
S 0x02 Syn
F 0x01 Fin

Congestion Notification

ECN (Explicit Congestion Notification). See RFC 3168 for full details, valid states below.

Packet State	DSB	ECN bits
Syn	0 0	1 1
Syn-Ack	0 0	0 1
Ack	0 1	0 0
No Congestion	0 1	0 0
No Congestion	1 0	0 0
Congestion	1 1	0 0
Receiver Response	1 1	0 1
Sender Response	1 1	1 1

TCP Options

0 End of Options List
1 No Operation (NOP, Pad)
2 Maximum segment size
3 Window Scale
4 Selective ACK ok
8 Timestamp

Checksum

Checksum of entire TCP segment and pseudo header (parts of IP header)

Offset

Number of 32-bit words in TCP header, minimum value of 5. Multiply by 4 to get byte count.

RFC 793

Please refer to RFC 793 for the complete Transmission Control Protocol (TCP) Specification.

UDP Header

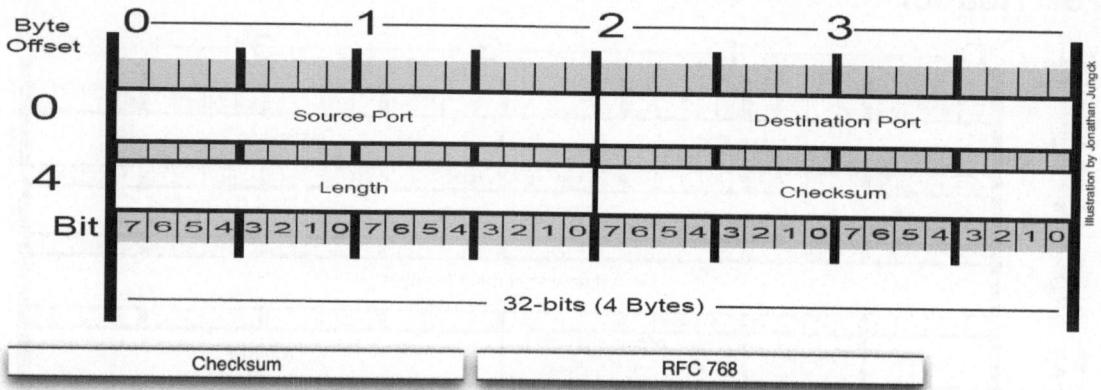

Checksum	RFC 768
Checksum of entire UDP segment and pseudo header (parts of IP header)	Please refer to RFC 768 for the complete User Datagram Protocol (UDP) Specification.

ICMP Header

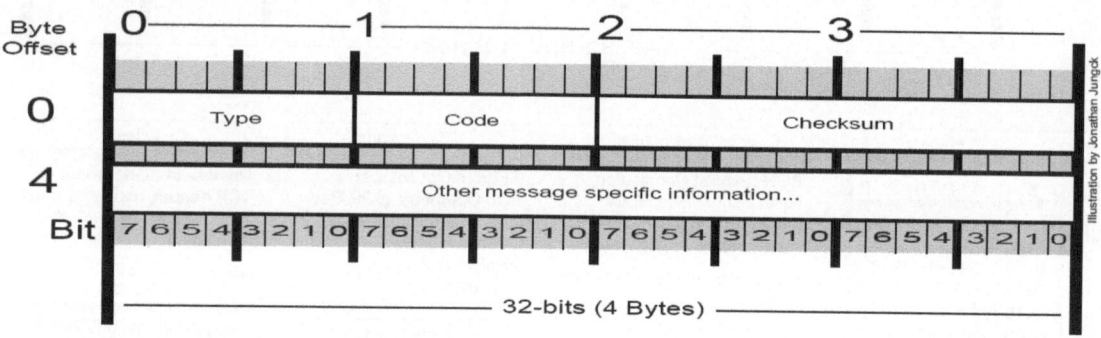

ICMP Message Types			Checksum

Type Code/Name	Type Code/Name	Type Code/Name	
0 Echo Reply	3 Destination Unreachable (continued)	11 Time Exceded	Checksum of ICMP header
3 Destination Unreachable	12 Host Unreachable for TOS	0 TTL Exceeded	
0 Net Unreachable	13 Communication Administratively Prohibited	1 Fragment Reassembly Time Exceeded	
1 Host Unreachable	4 Source Quench	12 Parameter Problem	**RFC 792**
2 Protocol Unreachable	5 Redirect	0 Pointer Problem	
3 Port Unreachable	0 Redirect Datagram for the Network	1 Missing a Required Operand	Please refer to RFC 792 for the Internet Control Message protocol (ICMP) specification.
4 Fragmentation required, and DF set	1 Redirect Datagram for the Host	2 Bad Length	
5 Source Route Failed	2 Redirect Datagram for the TOS & Network	13 Timestamp	
6 Destination Network Unknown	3 Redirect Datagram for the TOS & Host	14 Timestamp Reply	
7 Destination Host Unknown	8 Echo	15 Information Request	
8 Source Host Isolated	9 Router Advertisement	16 Information Reply	
9 Network Administratively Prohibited	10 Router Selection	17 Address Mask Request	
10 Host Administratively Prohibited		18 Address Mask Reply	
11 Network Unreachable for TOS		30 Traceroute	

APPENDIX B

■ ■ ■

Open Systems Vendors for packetC

This appendix contains a sampling of vendor information regarding systems designed and developed to support applications developed in packetC. The packetC language and tool-chain are currently supported on platforms employing CloudShield Packet Operating System (CPOS) or an emulation of this environment through the packetC Emulator (which operates on x86 Linux). As of the time of publication, the following is a list of shipping platforms and tools available for packetC application development and deployment:

Software

CloudShield Packet Works Integrated Development Environment (IDE) – Version 3.2 (see Figure B-4)

CloudShield CPOS (CloudShield Packet Operating System) Version 3.0.3 for CS-2000 (see Figure B-3)

CloudShield MC-CPOS (Multi-Chassis CloudShield Packet Operating System) Version 4.1 for BladeCenter

CloudShield MC-CPOS (Multi-Chassis CloudShield Packet Operating System) Version 5.0 for CS-4000

Hardware

CloudShield CS-2000 – 2U Platform – 1 or 2 DPPM Processors - Supports CPOS 2.x and 3.x Releases (see Figure B-1)

IBM BladeCenter H – 9U Platform – 1-14 CloudShield PN41 Processors – Supports MC-CPOS 4.x Releases

IBM BladeCenter HT – 12U Platform – 1-12 CloudShield PN41 Processors – Supports MC-CPOS 4.x Releases

CloudShield CS-4000 – 4U Platform – 1-3 DPPM or CPA Processors – Support MC-CPOS 5.x Releases (see Figure B-2)

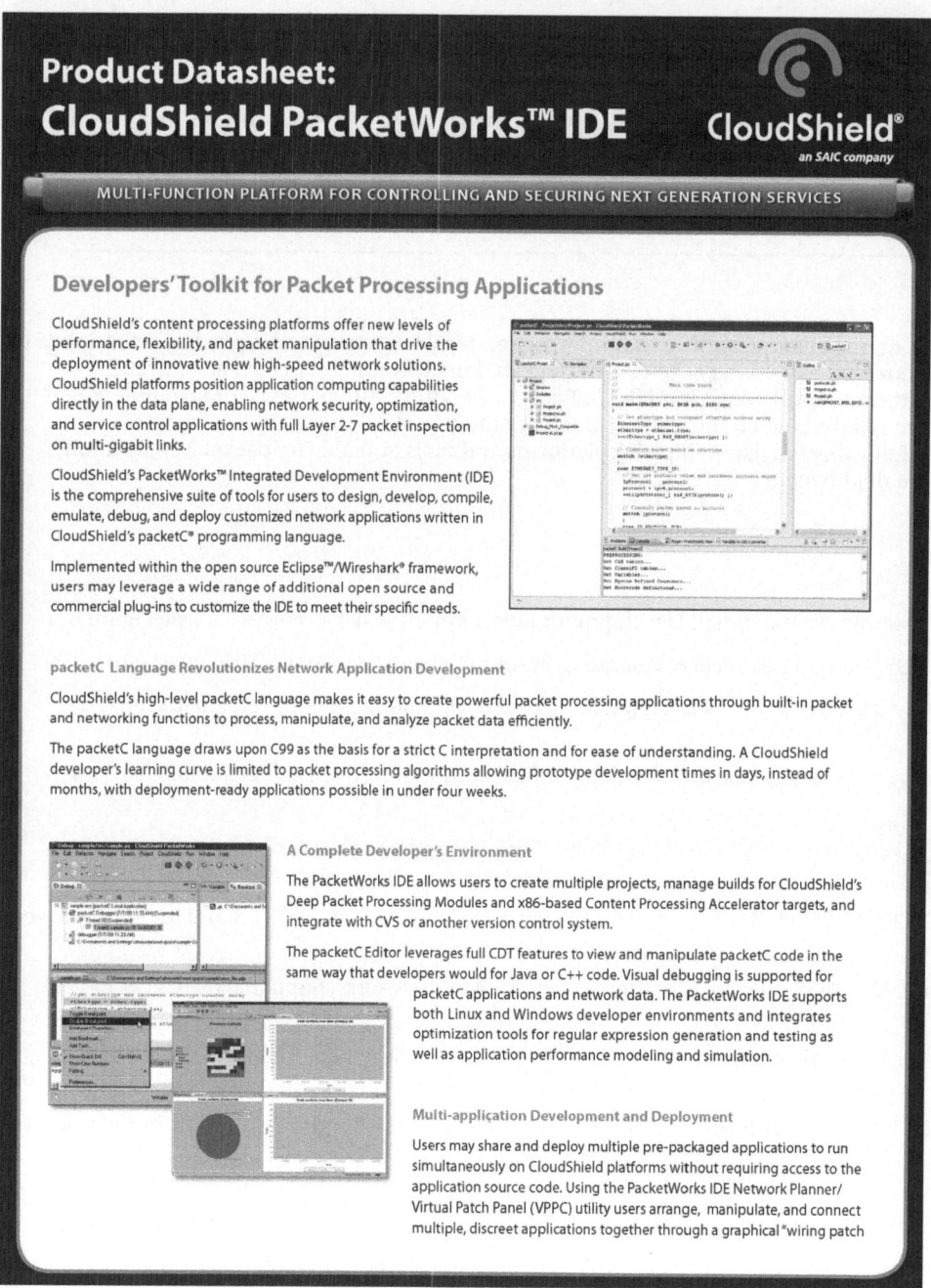

Figure B-1a. *CloudShield PacketWorks IDE data sheet*

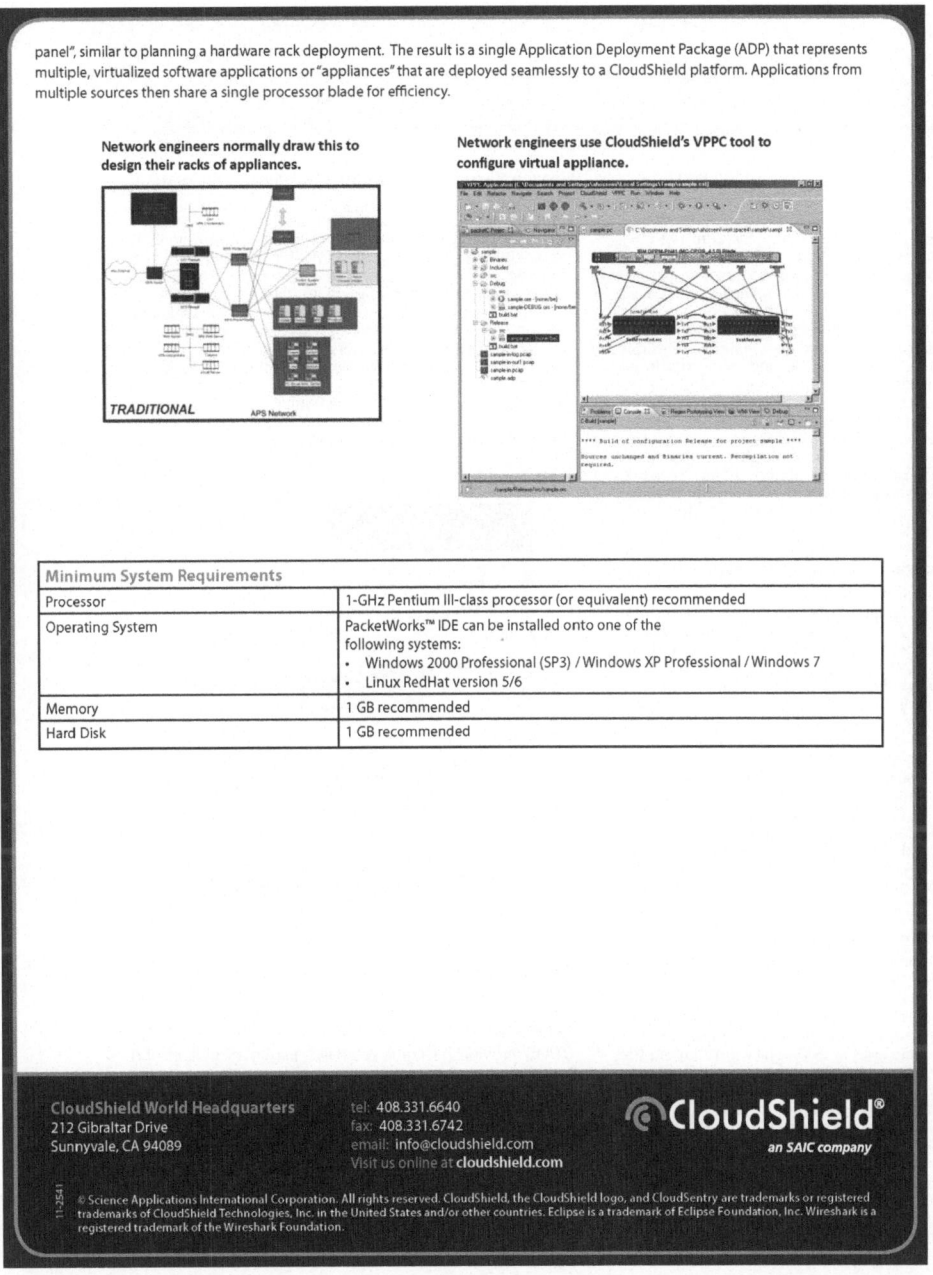

panel", similar to planning a hardware rack deployment. The result is a single Application Deployment Package (ADP) that represents multiple, virtualized software applications or "appliances" that are deployed seamlessly to a CloudShield platform. Applications from multiple sources then share a single processor blade for efficiency.

Network engineers normally draw this to design their racks of appliances.

TRADITIONAL   APS Network

Network engineers use CloudShield's VPPC tool to configure virtual appliance.

Minimum System Requirements	
Processor	1-GHz Pentium III-class processor (or equivalent) recommended
Operating System	PacketWorks™ IDE can be installed onto one of the following systems: • Windows 2000 Professional (SP3) / Windows XP Professional / Windows 7 • Linux RedHat version 5/6
Memory	1 GB recommended
Hard Disk	1 GB recommended

CloudShield World Headquarters
212 Gibraltar Drive
Sunnyvale, CA 94089

tel: 408.331.6640
fax: 408.331.6742
email: info@cloudshield.com
Visit us online at **cloudshield.com**

☁CloudShield®
an SAIC company

Figure B-1b. *CloudShield PacketWorks IDE data sheet*

CloudShield CPOS™

Revolutionary Open Network Operation System

CloudShield has invested more than 200 person-years to create the first open real-time network operating system called CloudShield Packet Operating System (CPOS). This revolutionary architecture delivers the most attractive economics, best performance, proven secure deployment and quickest programmability for DPI applications. CPOS enables the virtualization of multiple network appliances on a single CloudShield blade or platform resulting in the lowest DPI CAPEX and OPEX in the market. CPOS's layered architecture ensures that the underlying hardware architecture can evolve quickly to take advantage of the latest merchant silicon, achieving leading performance while ensuring existing applications will still run on the new platform generations. CPOS's proven secure architecture ensures that when deploying network applications additional vulnerabilities are not added to the network. Finally, CPOS's built in functionality enables applications to be quickly written or modified to respond to the latest security threat or customer requirement.

Application Virtualization – Delivers lowest costs

CPOS uniquely enables multiple stand-alone network applications to run simultaneously on a single CloudShield platform or blade. Now service providers can choose among the best-of-breed applications from CloudShield and other independent software vendors. Application virtualization solves the "appliance sprawl" problem common in so many network operating centers today. Multiple applications sharing a single blade minimize capital expenditures and lowers operating expenses by reducing power, cooling, rack space and management expenses. CPOS also enables the sharing of libraries and databases across multiple discreet applications delivering far more efficient system throughput. Finally, the virtual patch panel enables virtualized appliances to be graphically configured, deployed and reconfigured in real-time and without any packet loss or network downtime. CPOS virtualization delivers the lowest deployment and operating costs of any DPI platform.

Layered Architecture – Drives best performance

CPOS' architecture ensures a level of abstraction between the latest merchant networking integrated circuits and applications running on the CloudShield platform. Since CPOS's APIs are consistent from one version to the next, applications that were written for the first implementation of the CloudShield architecture in 2001 still run today on the 4th generation hardware platform. Meanwhile the system performance has improved many times by taking advantage of the latest high performance silicon. CPOS selects the most appropriate hardware resource to perform a particular application function resulting in the best overall performance while allowing the hardware architecture to freely evolve. Finally, CloudShield enables a higher performance system because functions which are handled on the control plane in most systems are handled in the data plane silicon database.

Proven Secure Architecture – Delivers peace of mind

The CPOS architecture enforces strict separation of the data, control and management planes within network infrastructures. This structure enables organizations to confidently deploy this platform for applications that manage traffic and secure their infrastructure without introducing new vulnerabilities to the network. CPOS' proven-secure architecture has been vetted and adopted by top service providers and by six technologically advanced governments worldwide, including several security organizations within the United States. In conjunction with CloudShield's hardware platform, CPOS provides peace of mind by enabling organizations to preserve revenue streams and ensure customer satisfaction and thereby protect their reputations.

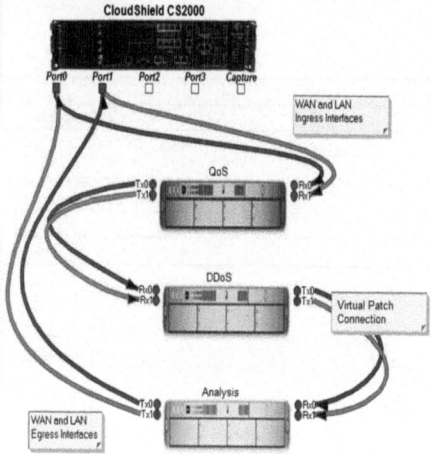

Figure 1: CloudShield's Virtual Patch Panel

Embedded Functionality – Reduces development costs

CPOS provides a comprehensive library of built-in and ready-to-run functions and APIs which reduce development costs and time to market. For example, functions like system back-up and restore or user set-up are built into CPOS. Software developers and system integrators don't have to code these common functions into applications thus saving development time and providing a consistent management interface. Additionally, since every application is deployed and managed the same way by service providers, roll-out and upgrade logistics are vastly simplified.

CloudShield Packet Operating System (CPOS)

Figure B-2a. *CloudShield Packet Operating System (CPOS) datasheet*

Operating System Overview

- CloudShield Packet Operating System (CPOS™): Three tiered architecture for secure management, control and execution.
- Data Plane
  - Execution on CloudShield DPPM, IBM PN41
  - Scalable and parallel packet processing
  - Open packetC execution virtual machine
  - Run to completion packet execution model
  - Native silicon database global memory support
  - Native POSIX REGEX Deep Packet Inspection (DPI)
  - Hardware LAN/WAN protocol support:
    - Ethernet (Nested VLAN, 802.1q, 802.1p)
    - SONET/SDH (PPP/HDLC)
    - MPLS (Up to 16 RFC, 3032 Labels)
    - IPv4, IPv6 Including Nested Headers
    - TCP, UDP, ICMP, SCTP
    - Full Checksum, CRC Inspect/Modify of Hardware Accelerated Listed Protocols
    - Additional Layer 2-7 protocols w/packetC
- Control Plane
  - Secure separation and performance protection
  - Hitless application package deployment
  - Automated Data Export and Log Management
  - System & Application Watchdog Support
  - Bypass Control Module Management (CS-2000)
- Management Plane
  - Device Element Management Interfaces
  - Mandatory Access Control with SE Linux Policies
  - Full System Backup and Restore Mechanisms
  - Web Based and CLI OS Application Updates
  - Redundant Management Plane Support (IBM PN41)

Mandatory Access Control

- Interfaces Enablement & Protection (COM, KVM, Ethernet)
- Services protection
  - Telnet, SSH, HTTP, HTTP-S, SNMP, SQL
  - Syslog, NTP, RADIUS
- Integrated network firewall
- Authorized hosts management
- User authentication (AAA)
  - Element level user management
  - Central authentication: RADIUS (RFC 2138, 2139)
- Per user privileges management (5 Domains)
  - System: Hardware, network, security
  - Software: Configuration, application API
- Separated log and report management
  - Reporting: Method per protocol & message severity
  - Host access control: Syslog, SNMP, SQL, JSON API

Device Element Management Interfaces

- Physical interfaces support: Ethernet, KVM, COM
- Command Line Interface (CLI)
  - Scriptable Command Line interface
  - JSON Web services application APIs
  - Telnet & SSH support over Ethernet
  - SSH Management & Key Regeneration
  - Console support over KVM and COM
  - COM support for Direct, Modem, Terminal Server
- Web-based Element Management Interface (WMI)
  - Traditional Internet Browser w/o Plug-Ins required
  - HTTP & HTTP-S Support Over Ethernet
  - HTTP-S Management & Keys Regeneration
- SNMP Element Management
  - SNMP v1, v2c, v3 GET/TRAP Interfaces
  - SNMP Security Management Including v3 VACM
  - MIBS/TRAPS: Chassis, Variable
  - Base RFCs: 1213, 1215, 1906, 1907, 2011, 2012, 2013, 2233, 2863
  - Extensions RFCs: 2558, 2665
  - System RFCs: 1659, 1697, 2790
  - Structure RFCs: 1155, 1157, 1905, 2570-2576, 2578-2580, 2786
- SQL reporting & monitoring interface
  - Native MySQL with ODBC driver support
  - System information & application reporting
- Syslog Log & Alert Support
  - System event reporting
- NTP synchronization server management

Security Accreditations & Certification

- Accepted for evaluation for Common Criteria EAL 4+
- Systems accredited In deployments to DCID 6/3 PL4

Network Virtualization Capabilities

- CPOS 3.x applications per blade: 31
- Shared library support: CPOS 3.1+
- Virtualization blade support: DPPM-500/510, 600, 800

Documentation & Training

- Web Management User Guide (150-1040): 186 pages
- Command Line Interface User Guide (150-1038) :150 pages
- Application Interface Guide (150-1039): 250 pages
  - Including SNMP & Web Services User Guides
- Traffic Control System User Guide (150-0304a): 24 pages
- Multi-App Supplemental Guide (150-0313): 74 pages
- Quick Start Guide (150-1043): 10 pages
- System Administrator Training Course (CS202): 2 days

+1 408-331-6640
sales@cloudshield.com
www.cloudshield.com

CloudShield®
212 Gibraltar Drive
Sunnyvale, CA 94089

© 2008 CloudShield Technologies, Inc. CloudShield, CPOS, packetC, RAVE are trademarks of CloudShield; other trademarks are property of their respective owners.

Figure B-2b. *Specifications for the Cloudshield Packet Operating System (CPOS)*

Product Datasheet:
CS-2000 Content Processing Platform

CloudShield®
an SAIC company

Multi-Function Systems for Controlling and Securing Next Generation Services

CS-2000 Content Processing Platform

The convergence of network infrastructures promises to reduce network acquisition and operating costs, but delivering advanced IP services with their expected revenue streams requires flexible control of traffic services and enforcement of finely tuned network policies. Additionally, securing converged infrastructures is significantly more complex than for service specific networks. CloudShield's adaptable, active network device, the CS-2000, enables network operators to deliver advanced services, enforce policies with precision, and tackle complex security challenges.

The CS-2000's modular chassis houses up to two Deep Packet Processing Modules (DPPMs) delivering up to 10 Gbps of full duplex, layers 2-7 content-processing capacity per system. There are three different DPPMs available, supporting three different network interface configurations, which enable operators to deploy service control and security solutions for GbE edge network, OC-48/STM-16 SONET/SDH interconnect, or 10 GbE data center and aggregation network installations.

Integrated service and security application software is provisioned onto the DPPMs and performs operations to fulfill each operator's unique requirements, and APIs on the CS-2000 ensure hands-free control from policy and subscriber management systems. Service providers can apply standard IT application practices to network service deployments, enabling them to adapt solutions to continually evolving services and security landscapes while protecting their networks, revenues, and their investment.

Incorporating Capabilities From Three Disciplines

Beyond advanced DPI, providing full-function service control and security solutions requires the functionality from three key network disciplines: service control, network security, and network transport. Inherent in the CS-2000 original design were capabilities from each of these disciplines, allowing the development of Integrated Content Control solutions that meet each service provider's unique requirements. Moreover, integrated solutions – instead of discrete appliances – reduce the number of network elements, the number of insertion points, and overall deployment costs.

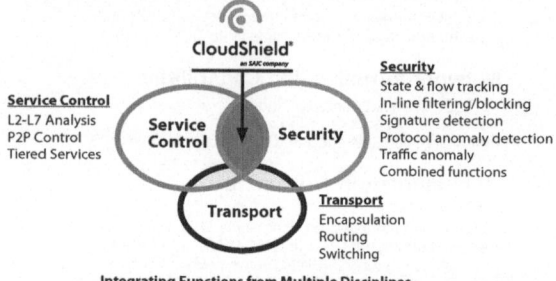

CloudShield®
an SAIC company

Service Control
L2-L7 Analysis
P2P Control
Tiered Services

Service Control

Security

Security
State & flow tracking
In-line filtering/blocking
Signature detection
Protocol anomaly detection
Traffic anomaly
Combined functions

Transport

Transport
Encapsulation
Routing
Switching

Integrating Functions from Multiple Disciplines

CloudShield Takes DPI To The Next Level

CloudShield's patented wire-speed deep packet inspection (DPI) capability delivers granular packet visibility, opening new levels of traffic classification and measurement. Enforcing policies for many advanced IP services where protocol transactions are text-based client/server exchanges found within the packet payloads, requires Layer-7 flow tracking and sometimes Layer-7 intervention. CloudShield's advanced DPI offers visibility and control of Layer-7 transactions, enabling the finest grained and most robust classification, measurement, security, and control of traffic and services from a single network device.

Features	Benefits
Flexible, multi-function operation	• Reduced device count and costs • Higher leverage network component investment
Scalable capacity	• Easily size systems for location and task-specific processing loads
Full Layer 7 processing & control	• Ensures control of today's and tomorrow's advanced IP services
In-line reliability (99.999%)	• Service control with service assurance
Robust solutions-software components with an integrated development environment	• Solutions can be tailored to operator-specific needs • Solutions can be fielded and updated quickly
LAN and WAN Interfaces supported	• One device for edge, aggregation, and interconnect location deployments

ENABLING COMPLETE NETWORK CONTROL

Figure B-3a. *Datasheet for the CS-2000*

CS-2000 Technical Specifications

Key Functional Specifications
- Up to 10 gigabits per second L2-7 inspection and analysis
- Detect and track up to 16 million simultaneous flows
- Secure, transparent network installation

System Management
- Web-based element management; SNMP v1, v2c, v3

User access:
- Telnet (CLI), SSH (CLI), and HTTP / HTTP-S (web)
- Ethernet (all), COM port (CLI), KVM (CLI)

Applications
- Cybersecurity, network optimization and control
- Ecosystem of software vendors, integrators

Deep Packet Processing Module Specifications

DPPM-510 – Gigabit Ethernet
- Gigabit Ethernet Network Interfaces full duplex):
  - Copper – 4 x 10/100/1000 Base-T Ethernet, RJ-45
  - or 4 x Optical / SFPs
    - SX: 850 nm, multi-mode
    - LX: 1310 nm, single-mode

DPPM-600 – Packet over SONET
- SONET / SDH Network Interfaces (full duplex)
  - 2 OC-48 / STM 16 POS
  - 8 x OC-12c / STM-4 & OC-3c / STM-1
- *Optics and SFPs*
  - SR-1: 1310 nm, single mode
  - IR-1: 1310 nm, single mode
  - LR-2: 1550 nm, single mode

DPPM-800 – 10 Gigabit Ethernet
- Two-Tiered Processing Architecture
  - 10 Gbps network and content processing capacity
- 1 x 10GBase optical XFPs bi-directional (full duplex)
  - SR: 850 nm, multi mode
  - IR: 1550 nm, single mode
  - LR: 1550 nm, single mode

Physical Specifications

Chassis
- Rack mounting: 2 RU universal EIA rack configuration
- Height: 3.44" (87.4 mm)
- Width: 19.0" (482.6 mm)
- Depth: 23.6" (600 mm)
- Weight (fully loaded): 25 lbs (11kg)

Product Safety
- CSA / UL 60950; December 1, 2000
- EN 60950; 300 386 V1.3.1:2001

Emissions
- FCC part 15.b Class A
- VCCI – A: April 2004
- ICES-003 Class A: November 22, 1997
- EN 300 386 V1.3.1: 2001
- En 55022:1998 Class A, Europe
- EN55204:1998, A1:2001, A2:2003
- CISPR 22 Class A

Regulatory Markings
- CE, FCC, ICES-003
- VCCI

Power requirements
DC power
- DC input power 500 watts (max)
- DC input voltage -40.5 to -72 VDC
- DC input current rating 6.25 amps (A) @ -48 VDC
AC power
- AC input power 500 watts (max)
- Universal AC power
- AC input current rating 2.5 amps RMS (A) @ 120V RMS

Environmental
- Operating temp: 50° to 95° F nominal (10° to 35° C)
- Operating temp: 50° to 113° F short-term (10° to 45° C)
- Non-operating temp: -4° to 149° F (-20° to 65° C)
- Operating humidity: 10 to 90% non-condensing
- Non-operating humidity: 5 to 95% non-condensing
- Operating altitude: 0 to 10,000 ft
- Non-operating altitude: 0 to 30,000 ft

All specifications subject to change at any time without notice.

Figure B-3b. *Specifications for the CS-2000*

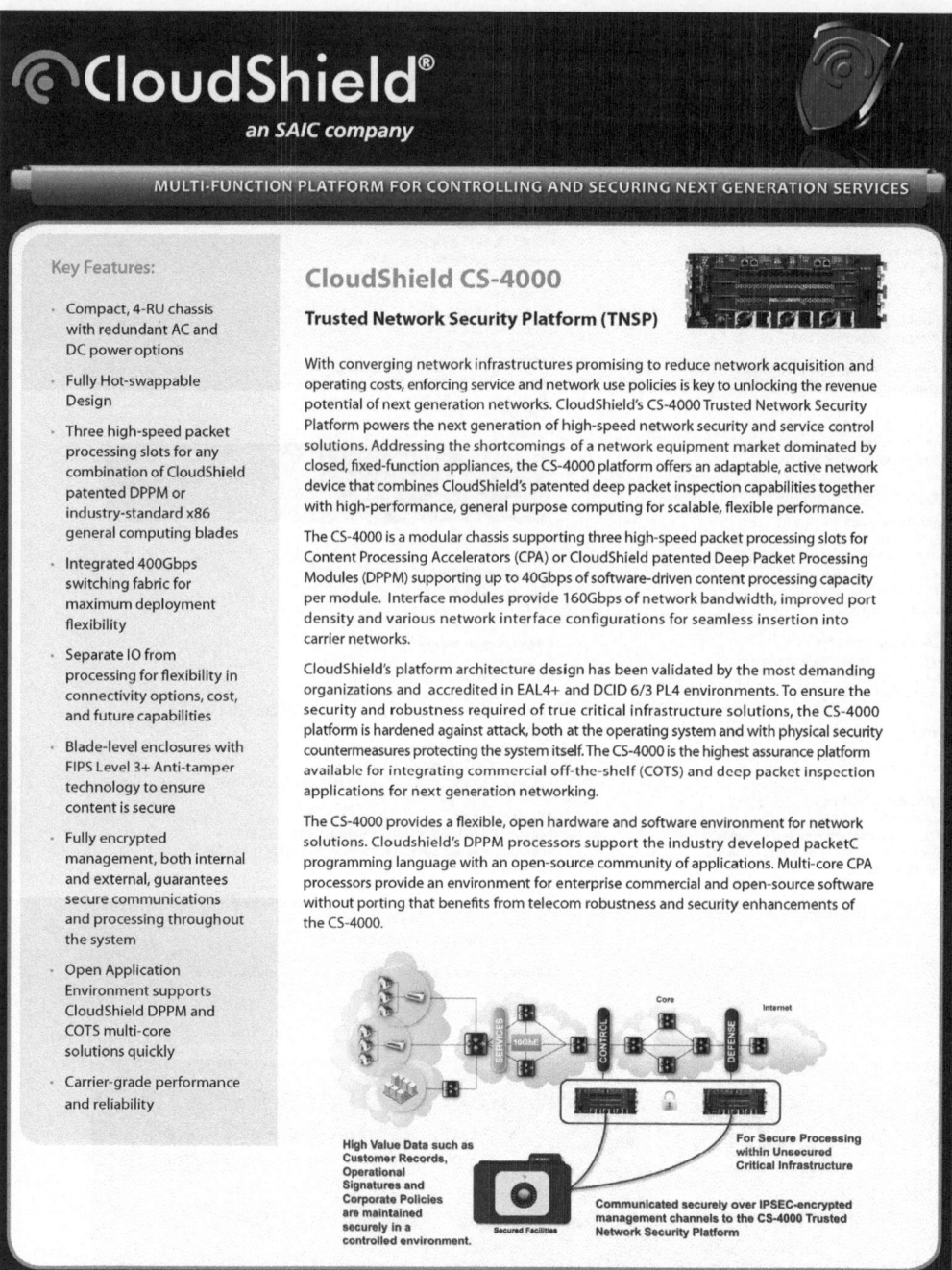

CloudShield® ®
an SAIC company

MULTI-FUNCTION PLATFORM FOR CONTROLLING AND SECURING NEXT GENERATION SERVICES

Key Features:

- Compact, 4-RU chassis with redundant AC and DC power options

- Fully Hot-swappable Design

- Three high-speed packet processing slots for any combination of CloudShield patented DPPM or industry-standard x86 general computing blades

- Integrated 400Gbps switching fabric for maximum deployment flexibility

- Separate IO from processing for flexibility in connectivity options, cost, and future capabilities

- Blade-level enclosures with FIPS Level 3+ Anti-tamper technology to ensure content is secure

- Fully encrypted management, both internal and external, guarantees secure communications and processing throughout the system

- Open Application Environment supports CloudShield DPPM and COTS multi-core solutions quickly

- Carrier-grade performance and reliability

CloudShield CS-4000

Trusted Network Security Platform (TNSP)

With converging network infrastructures promising to reduce network acquisition and operating costs, enforcing service and network use policies is key to unlocking the revenue potential of next generation networks. CloudShield's CS-4000 Trusted Network Security Platform powers the next generation of high-speed network security and service control solutions. Addressing the shortcomings of a network equipment market dominated by closed, fixed-function appliances, the CS-4000 platform offers an adaptable, active network device that combines CloudShield's patented deep packet inspection capabilities together with high-performance, general purpose computing for scalable, flexible performance.

The CS-4000 is a modular chassis supporting three high-speed packet processing slots for Content Processing Accelerators (CPA) or CloudShield patented Deep Packet Processing Modules (DPPM) supporting up to 40Gbps of software-driven content processing capacity per module. Interface modules provide 160Gbps of network bandwidth, improved port density and various network interface configurations for seamless insertion into carrier networks.

CloudShield's platform architecture design has been validated by the most demanding organizations and accredited in EAL4+ and DCID 6/3 PL4 environments. To ensure the security and robustness required of true critical infrastructure solutions, the CS-4000 platform is hardened against attack, both at the operating system and with physical security countermeasures protecting the system itself. The CS-4000 is the highest assurance platform available for integrating commercial off-the-shelf (COTS) and deep packet inspection applications for next generation networking.

The CS-4000 provides a flexible, open hardware and software environment for network solutions. Cloudshield's DPPM processors support the industry developed packetC programming language with an open-source community of applications. Multi-core CPA processors provide an environment for enterprise commercial and open-source software without porting that benefits from telecom robustness and security enhancements of the CS-4000.

High Value Data such as Customer Records, Operational Signatures and Corporate Policies are maintained securely in a controlled environment.

Secured Facilities

For Secure Processing within Unsecured Critical Infrastructure

Communicated securely over IPSEC-encrypted management channels to the CS-4000 Trusted Network Security Platform

Figure B-4a. *The CS-4000 datasheet*

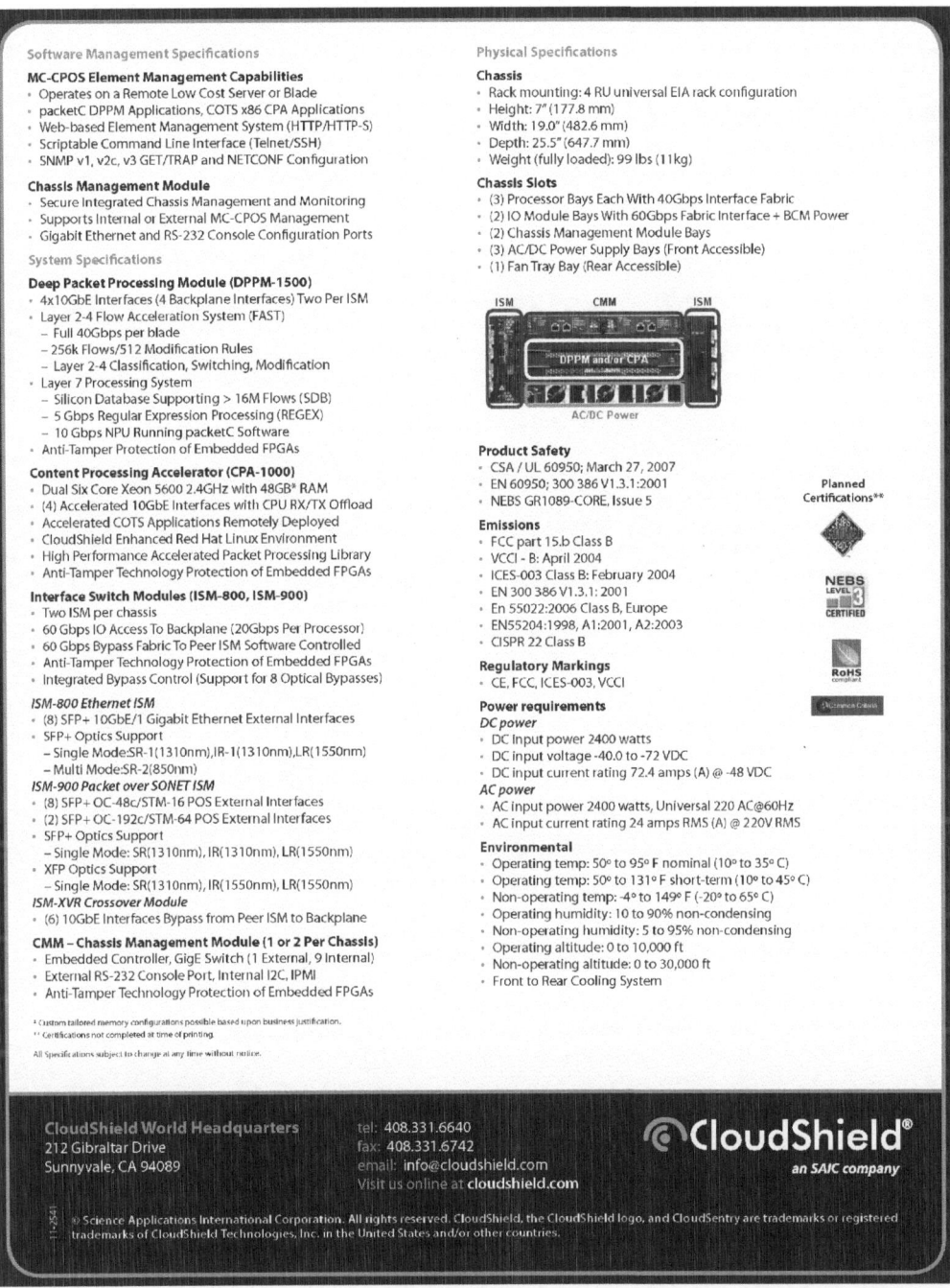

Software Management Specifications

MC-CPOS Element Management Capabilities
- Operates on a Remote Low Cost Server or Blade
- packetC DPPM Applications, COTS x86 CPA Applications
- Web-based Element Management System (HTTP/HTTP-S)
- Scriptable Command Line Interface (Telnet/SSH)
- SNMP v1, v2c, v3 GET/TRAP and NETCONF Configuration

Chassis Management Module
- Secure Integrated Chassis Management and Monitoring
- Supports Internal or External MC-CPOS Management
- Gigabit Ethernet and RS-232 Console Configuration Ports

System Specifications

Deep Packet Processing Module (DPPM-1500)
- 4x10GbE Interfaces (4 Backplane Interfaces) Two Per ISM
- Layer 2-4 Flow Acceleration System (FAST)
  - Full 40Gbps per blade
  - 256k Flows/512 Modification Rules
  - Layer 2-4 Classification, Switching, Modification
- Layer 7 Processing System
  - Silicon Database Supporting > 16M Flows (SDB)
  - 5 Gbps Regular Expression Processing (REGEX)
  - 10 Gbps NPU Running packetC Software
- Anti-Tamper Protection of Embedded FPGAs

Content Processing Accelerator (CPA-1000)
- Dual Six Core Xeon 5600 2.4GHz with 48GB* RAM
- (4) Accelerated 10GbE Interfaces with CPU RX/TX Offload
- Accelerated COTS Applications Remotely Deployed
- CloudShield Enhanced Red Hat Linux Environment
- High Performance Accelerated Packet Processing Library
- Anti-Tamper Technology Protection of Embedded FPGAs

Interface Switch Modules (ISM-800, ISM-900)
- Two ISM per chassis
- 60 Gbps IO Access To Backplane (20Gbps Per Processor)
- 60 Gbps Bypass Fabric To Peer ISM Software Controlled
- Anti-Tamper Technology Protection of Embedded FPGAs
- Integrated Bypass Control (Support for 8 Optical Bypasses)

ISM-800 Ethernet ISM
- (8) SFP+ 10GbE/1 Gigabit Ethernet External Interfaces
- SFP+ Optics Support
  - Single Mode:SR-1(1310nm),IR-1(1310nm),LR(1550nm)
  - Multi Mode:SR-2(850nm)

ISM-900 Packet over SONET ISM
- (8) SFP+ OC-48c/STM-16 POS External Interfaces
- (2) SFP+ OC-192c/STM-64 POS External Interfaces
- SFP+ Optics Support
  - Single Mode: SR(1310nm), IR(1310nm), LR(1550nm)
- XFP Optics Support
  - Single Mode: SR(1310nm), IR(1550nm), LR(1550nm)

ISM-XVR Crossover Module
- (6) 10GbE Interfaces Bypass from Peer ISM to Backplane

CMM – Chassis Management Module (1 or 2 Per Chassis)
- Embedded Controller, GigE Switch (1 External, 9 Internal)
- External RS-232 Console Port, Internal I2C, IPMI
- Anti-Tamper Technology Protection of Embedded FPGAs

* Custom tailored memory configurations possible based upon business justification.
** Certifications not completed at time of printing.

All Specifications subject to change at any time without notice.

Physical Specifications

Chassis
- Rack mounting: 4 RU universal EIA rack configuration
- Height: 7" (177.8 mm)
- Width: 19.0" (482.6 mm)
- Depth: 25.5" (647.7 mm)
- Weight (fully loaded): 99 lbs (11kg)

Chassis Slots
- (3) Processor Bays Each With 40Gbps Interface Fabric
- (2) IO Module Bays With 60Gbps Fabric Interface + BCM Power
- (2) Chassis Management Module Bays
- (3) AC/DC Power Supply Bays (Front Accessible)
- (1) Fan Tray Bay (Rear Accessible)

Product Safety
- CSA / UL 60950; March 27, 2007
- EN 60950; 300 386 V1.3.1:2001
- NEBS GR1089-CORE, Issue 5

Emissions
- FCC part 15.b Class B
- VCCI - B: April 2004
- ICES-003 Class B: February 2004
- EN 300 386 V1.3.1: 2001
- En 55022:2006 Class B, Europe
- EN55204:1998, A1:2001, A2:2003
- CISPR 22 Class B

Regulatory Markings
- CE, FCC, ICES-003, VCCI

Power requirements
DC power
- DC Input power 2400 watts
- DC input voltage -40.0 to -72 VDC
- DC input current rating 72.4 amps (A) @ -48 VDC
AC power
- AC input power 2400 watts, Universal 220 AC@60Hz
- AC input current rating 24 amps RMS (A) @ 220V RMS

Environmental
- Operating temp: 50° to 95° F nominal (10° to 35° C)
- Operating temp: 50° to 131° F short-term (10° to 45° C)
- Non-operating temp: -4° to 149° F (-20° to 65° C)
- Operating humidity: 10 to 90% non-condensing
- Non-operating humidity: 5 to 95% non-condensing
- Operating altitude: 0 to 10,000 ft
- Non-operating altitude: 0 to 30,000 ft
- Front to Rear Cooling System

Planned Certifications**

NEBS LEVEL 3 CERTIFIED

RoHS compliant

Figure B-4b. *Specifications for the CS-4000*

Reference

Further information can be found on CloudShield's website at www.cloudshield.com or at the packetC website at www.packetc.org.

Glossary

PacketC Language Terms

Aggregate Types
Structures and arrays.

Alignment
A requirement that objects of a particular type be located on storage boundaries with addresses that are particular multiples of a byte address.

Anonymous Type
A type without a name, e.g., created by "struct { int x; } s1;"

Argument
Expression in the comma-separated list bounded by the parentheses in a function call expression, or a sequence of preprocessing tokens in the comma-separated list bounded by the parentheses in a function-like macro invocation.

Associativity
The principle determining the order of processing operators in a statement when they are of the same precedence. Operators are processed based upon their precedence when parentheses are not present. Operators may be left-associative, right-associative or non-associative.

Bit
A unit of data storage in the execution environment large enough to hold an object that may have one of two possible values.

Byte
An addressable unit of data storage large enough to hold any member of the basic character set of the execution environment. A byte is composed of a contiguous sequence of bits, the number of which is implementation defined. The least significant bit is called the low-order bit; the most significant bit is called the high-order bit.

Character
A member of a set of elements used for the organization, control, or representation of data. Single-byte character: A bit representation that fits in a byte.

Compatible Types
A property of types that allows variables, array elements, and structure fields to be assigned to one another and otherwise exchange values.

Constraint
A restriction, either syntactic or semantic, by which the exposition of language elements is to be interpreted.

Control Plane
The physical hardware and associated software capabilities for displaying and managing system-level variable values and messages.

Data Plane
The physical hardware and associated software capabilities for examining, changing, replicating, and routing packets.

Endianness
The byte and bit ordering present in data types when stored in memory and accessed in packetC. Networks deliver data in big-endian mode, which means that the first bit received is the most important bit or the one that represents the largest value in a base 2 system. This applies both to bytes and bits, such that when inspecting memory containing a 16-bit variable, the first byte found in memory will contain the high order values with the first bit being the most significant for a big-endian system. In little-endian systems this is opposite and in some cases byte-level swapping may occur as well. In packetC, big-endian network byte order and little-endian bit order are always present. This matches network byte order and bit-level ordering found on Ethernet.

Forward Reference
The use of an entity before any declaration.

Instance
An individual, executable copy of a packet module or shared module. The packetC specification does not prescribe how parallel instances are to be implemented (e.g., as threads or processes).

L-value
An expression designating a location that can legitimately receive an assignment value. In packetC these include variables, array elements and structure fields. Context can determine whether an entity can serve as an l-value.

Nested Literal
A literal within curly braces that recursively represents nested structures with nested curly brace pairs and represents multidimensional array values by group values for lower (more rapidly varying) dimension elements within curly brace pairs that correspond to each element of a higher dimension. A key difference from C's compound literals is that nested literals are not preceded by a parenthesized type name.

Object
A region of data storage in the execution environment, the contents of which can represent values

Parameter
An object declared as part of a function declaration or definition that acquires a value on entry to the function, or an identifier from the comma-separated list bounded by the parentheses immediately following the macro name in a function-like macro definition

Proper Alignment
The practice of aligning data items to begin on byte addresses that are multiples of an item's size in bytes.

Scalar Types
Integer types and enumerated types.

Slice
A contiguous subset of an array, indicated by a range.

System-Defined Response
Error-handling behavior for specific conditions which each packetC implementation must describe.

Undefined Behavior
Behavior in response to an erroneous programming construct or usage for which the Language Specification imposes no requirement. The behavior may range from ignoring effects, through issuing diagnostics, to program termination.

Value
The precise meaning of the contents of an object when interpreted as having a specific type.

Networking Terms

ATM (Mode Asynchronous Transfer)
A wide area network technology for transmitting packets in small units called cells. Multiple connection-oriented sessions can leverage committed information rates to guarantee quality of service without packet inspection.

Backbone
The connective network acting as a conduit for traffic between multiple LAN or WAN networks. Often referred to as the core of the network as it operates at speeds that are orders of magnitude faster than the networks that it connects.

Bandwidth

The capacity in terms of bits per second that a network connection carries or processes in terms of a rate, such as gigabits per second.

Bandwidth on Demand

Describes the ability for network bandwidth, generally measured in a factor of megabits per second, to increase based upon a specific demand by the user. A demand may be very specific such as anytime a particular video is downloaded a users network performance peak may double for the period of the download. Alternatively, the demand may be a generic but specific transaction such as logging into a site and requesting increased bandwidth for a limited duration for a service charge.

Baud

Baud equals bits per second in most modern networks when a single bit is transmitted once per signal. Generically, baud refers to the unit of frequency for signals per second.

Binaries

A program or collection of instructions in a form readable by a processor. This is in contrast to source code, intended to be readable by a human which is later compiled into binaries.

Binary

Refers to a number system consisting entirely of ones and zeros where the possible states have only two possible values.

Bit

The smallest unit in data representation is a single binary digit, where the value contains but one element possible to reflect a state of one or zero.

Bits Per Second (bps)

The quantity of bits that will flow on a network link in a period of one second.

BOOTP

A network protocol in the TCP/IP that lets network nodes request configuration information such that code leverage to start execution can be retrieved from a server node. This "boot protocol" often allows computer systems without local persistent storage to connect to a network and retrieve information about the location of remote storage storing data that would have normally been placed on a local storage enabling the system to boot.

Bridge

A network device operating at the data link, or MAC layer, that forward or filters data on a link between two networks transparent to higher level OSI model protocols. A two-port Ethernet hub can be considered a modern simplistic bridge.

Broadband
A technique for data transmission allowing multiple signals to share the bandwidth of a single cable via frequency division multiplexing at high data rates. A generalized term for faster than PSTN dial-up networks that are wired such as DSL or Cable.

Broadband Network
A network that uses broadband principles for multiple carrier frequencies transmitted on a single cable not interfering with one another.

Bus
A LAN topology in which all the nodes are connected to a single cable. Early Ethernet networks using coaxial cables, or ThinNet, were the most common representation of a bus based network where all devices see all communications.

Byte
A unit of data consisting of eight bits. One of the earliest and best personal computer magazines.

Bytes Per Second
The quantity of bytes that will flow on a network link in a period of one second. Not to be represented by *bps* to avoid confusion with bits per second, which would cause values to be off by a factor of eight.

CloudShield
A secure layer of protection (shield) around the Internet (cloud) providing a superior adaptable defense system for the Internet. A Silicon Valley network equipment company and the inventor of packetC.

Cut-Through
An architectural method within network devices where received network data is pipelined to a set of elements for transmission while the contents are inspected to determine the actual destination within the device. Introduced in early Ethernet network switches, cut-through allowed the slow process of moving a packet from an input port to an output port to partially proceed while the output port was determined to reduce the latency of the packet switching through the device.

CSMA/CD
Carrier Sense Multiple Access with Collision Detection is the Ethernet media access method critical to shared transmission mediums. Bussed Ethernet and half-duplex Ethernet connections would use this to negotiate contention for the network amongst a group of equal systems on the network. When a device is ready to transmit it senses whether a carrier signal is available, and if so, begins its transmission. It then watches for collisions that would force it to back off for a delay period before retrying its transmission.

Data Link Layer
Layer 2 of the seven-layer OSI reference model for communication between computers on networks. This layer defines protocols for data packets and how they are transmitted to and from each network device. It is a medium-independent, link-level communications facility on top of the Physical layer, and it is divided into two sublayers: medium-access control (MAC) and logical-link control (LLC).

Denial of Service (DoS)
A method of attack or an unexpected condition under which a host on a network is overwhelmed such that it cannot process incoming requests causing its services to be denied to future requestors. A denial of service is a condition where a host has consumed its memory capacity or computing bandwidth.

Distributed Denial of Service (DDoS)
A method of attack where a host on a network has its incoming network bandwidth consumed by an overwhelming number of undesired packets. Furthermore, a distributed denial of service generally is sourced from by a large number of hosts on the network. A distributed denial of service is a condition where a host has consumed its network bandwidth.

Distributed Processing
Multiple computers in a network cooperatively processing data to improve reduce the time it takes to complete a data processing request.

Domain Name
One or more strings separated by a dot to form a unique name across internets used to convert the name to an IP address. A domain name is often something like cloudshield.com while pre-pending it with the name of a machine in the domain yields a host-name, such as www.cloudshield.com.

Domain Name System (DNS)
A layer 4 protocol operating on top of UDP and TCP generally on well-known port 53. Also, refers to domain name servers that act as a phone book for the Internet resolving user readable names to IP addresses.

Download
To transfer a data file from one network node to another. Often referring to a file transferred from a larger shared system to a smaller or personal system.

Ethernet

A network transport technology as well as a layer 2 data link protocol that identifies end stations using hardware addresses and is common among consumer and telecommunications equipment. Originally popularized due to a simple collision detection mechanism allowing low cost networking, the name has remained for higher speed networks that maintain layer 2 compatibility while transport technology migrated to point-to-point communications for multi-gigabit Ethernet standards.

File Transfer Protocol (FTP)

The Internet (TCP/IP) protocol and program used to transfer files between hosts.

Filtering

A process where a network device reads the contents of a packet and determines that it should be removed from the collection of packets traversing a network link.

Forwarding

The act of receiving packets on one interface and then subsequently transmitting them on another interface.

Framing

Dividing data for transmission into groups of bits, and adding a header and a check sequence to form a frame.

Full-Duplex

Simultaneous communications between two devices, where each device can transmit to its peer at the same time it is receiving data from that peer.

Gateway

A network device that connects two or more networks with different communication mediums, addressing schemes or network protocols. Often used synonymously with the term router in IP networks.

Gigabits Per Second (Gbps)

The quantity of bits calculated in billions that will flow on a network link in a period of one second.

Header

The beginning part of a data packet identifying information often used to determine where network devices should forward the packet or attributes of data integrity. In an IP network, this is often referred to as the TCP/IP header where the IP addresses and network ports are specified but not the contents of the TCP application header. The Ethernet, SONET or other transmission data prior to the IP protocol data is also considered part of the header. Early network usage policies would specify that devices could only look at the header, similar to the markings on the outside of a postal letter envelope, for privacy reasons.

Heartbeat

Sending a message across a network at a regular interval to elicit a response signaling that a device is healthy. Derived from the notion of checking an injured person for a pulse to determine whether they are alive.

Hertz (Hz)

A frequency unit of one cycle per second.

Host

A node on a network that can be used interactively either locally or remotely.

Host Table

A list of TCP/IP hosts on the network containing their name and IP addresses. Names are often fully qualified domain names.

IEEE

The Institute of Electrical and Electronic Engineers.

IEEE 802.3

The IEEE standard that defines the CSMA/CD media-access method and the physical and data link layer specifications of a local area network. This includes 10BASE2, 10BASE5 and 10BASE-T Ethernet implementations.

Internet

The collection of public networks that surrounds the earth. The Internet is based upon networking using Internet Protocols to define addressing of delivery of packets. The Internet grew out of research by the US Department of Defense to find a networking technology resilient to physical damage from nuclear attacks.

Internet Protocol (IP)

The addressing portion of the TCP/IP protocol suite where each host has a unique address on the network. Version 4 is the common variant of this connectionless protocol with host addresses consuming 32-bits while version 6 is in its infancy of adoption leveraging 128-bit host addressing.

IPX

Internetwork Packet eXchange. A Novell NetWare protocol similar to IP.

ISO

International Standards Organization. An organization that sets standard for computers and network communications.

Kilobits Per Second (Kbps)

The quantity of bits calculated in thousands that will flow on a network link in a period of one second.

Latency

The delay incurred by a network device between receiving a packet, processing the packet, and forwarding the packet.

Layer

A particular enveloping portion of a packet per the OSI model from the physical layer to application layer. (See OSI Layered Model)

Line Speed

The maximum rate at which data can be transmitted over a line by a device expressed in bps.

Load Balancing

Distributing network traffic among a collection of devices capable of performing equivalent processing such that each device shares an equal portion of the workload. Modern systems may not equally balance a load but rather utilize real-time device metrics or user information to determine how much to send to each device.

Local Area Network (LAN)

A communications network consisting of hosts or nodes that are generally considered local to one another in a geographic sense such as in a building or a logical sense, such as behind a common router.

Megabits Per Second (Mbps)

The quantity of bits calculated in millions that will flow on a network link in a period of one second.

MAC Address

In Ethernet, the MAC address is the hardware address of a device. MAC addresses consist of 6 bytes where generally the upper 3 bytes refer to a manufacturer of the equipment and the lower 3 bytes contain a serial number of the element. The first 12 bytes of a layer 2 Ethernet header start with the destination MAC address followed by the source MAC address.

MIB

Management Information Base. A database of network parameters used by SNMP to monitor and change network device settings. It provides a logical naming of all information resources on the network that are pertinent to the network's management.

Multicast

A networking technology where multiple hosts on a network segment can subscribe to a common feed of data and signal upstream routers to replicate messages to all interested hosts. Multicast networks use protocols such as IGMP to coordinate groups and require routers supporting replication of traffic, however, when used can save on backbone bandwidth for dissemination of network data such as IPTV video streams.

Name Server

Software operating on network hosts that resolves textual names into numeric IP addresses. Alternatively called a Domain Name Server (DNS) in TCP/IP networks.

NetBIOS/NetBEUI

Microsoft's networking protocols for its LAN Manager and Windows NT products.

Network

An interconnected system of computers that can communicate with each other.

Network Address

A unique location, generally a number or set of numbers, identifying a system on a network. Often defined at manufacturing time, however, these can be changed or additional addresses may be assigned. In an Ethernet network, this generally refers to the MAC address which is a 48-bit value represented textual in six hexadecimal values separated by colons. The first 24 bits in Ethernet Network Addresses refer to a manufacturer with the following being a unique serial number, e.g. 00:0B:A9:01:23:45.

Network Byte Order

The order in which bytes and bits are represented in data fields in network headers. Network byte order is big endian where the high order byte is first followed by descending importance bytes. In packetC, bit ordering follows a little endian approach. (See Endianness)

Network Management

The art and act of monitoring, tuning, and maintaining the operation of a network. Systems that perform these capabilities or aid in the diagnosis of problems or monitoring of performance are all acts of network management.

NIC

Network Interface Card.

Node

A device connected to the network. A node can be thought of as any device that has a "hardware address."

OSI

Open Systems Interconnection. A standard defined by ISO.

OSI Layered Model
A reference model developed by ISO specifies how a model to describe disparate networking technologies consisting of seven layers. From lowest to highest, they are: Physical, Data Link, Network, Transport, Session, Presentation and Application. Each layer performs a service for the layer above it. Pure OSI networks were rarely deployed; however, modern networks such as TCP/IP leverage this model for description. In TCP/IP, the Session Layer (5) and Presentation Layer (6) are presented as blended with the Application Layer (7) and often simply called Layer 7.

Packet
A series of bits transmitted across a network collected into a grouping identifying them as needing to be delivered together. The contents of which can be broken into numerous headers and payloads and provide endless hours of fun for packetC programmers to interrogate, redact and transform.

Physical Address
Address of a device locked to an interface uniquely identifying it. An Ethernet MAC Address is an example of a physical address.

Physical Layer
The first layer of the OSI model implementing the physical channel embodying the signaling on the transmission medium. This layer insulates the Data Link layer from medium-dependent physical characteristics.

Port
A numerical address of an application defined within the TCP header. Alternatively, a network connector on a device.

PPP
Point-to-Point Protocol. PPP provides router-to-router and host-to-network connections over both synchronous and asynchronous circuits. Often a data link network header on link based networks.

Protocol
Any documented method of communicating over a network often involving specified formats of data and conversation dynamics.

Quality of Service (QoS)
Represents a measurement of the delivery of voice, video, or data across a network with regard to business or technical expectations. This measurement often relates to bandwidth, packet loss, latency, or jitter can also be used to define a business commitment.

Repeater
A network device that repeats signals from one cable onto one or more other cables, while restoring signal timing and waveforms.

Request For Comment (RFC)

The proposed Internet standards issued by the IETF which define the protocols that operate the Internet as well as suggestions for how they are implemented. Each RFC has a unique number to identify it and a well defined format to make them appear consistent.

Ring

A network topology in which the nodes are connected in a closed loop. Originally popularized in early LAN's by Token Ring technology and still in use in metro networks, usually with a pair of rings operating in opposite directions, for high performance interconnectivity with a minimal number of links.

RMON

A SNMP-based standard consisting of ten different management groups for reporting detailed information about a network.

Routing

The functionality performed by a device acting as a gateway between multiple networks whereby the inspection of the addressing in packet headers determines the network pathway on which to steer the packet.

Route

The pathway that packet takes through a network as it moves from its originating source address to its destination.

Router

The device that performs routing. In IP networks, a router chooses the output port of a packet based upon its destination IP address in conjunction with routing tables that adjust due to network outages and saturation.

Server

A computer that provides resources shared on the network, such as files, or which performs services on behalf of hosts such as email storage and forwarding.

Session

A connection to a network service.

SLIP

Serial Line Internet Protocol. A protocol for running TCP/IP over dial-up and serial port lines.

SNA

Systems Network Architecture. A competitor to TCP/IP developed by IBM for mainframe communications.

SNMP

Simple Network Management Protocol. A TCP/IP host with SNMP provides an API to other system to collect network-related statistics. A common protocol to export data from a packetC system that is easily queried by both simple scripts and large network management systems.

Source Code

Software programs in the form written by a programmer that can be taken by a compiler or assembler to be transformed into a binary for use by a computer.

Spanning Tree

An algorithm used by bridges to create a logical topology that connects all network segments and ensures that only one path exists between any two stations.

Store and Forward

Technique for examining incoming packets whereby the whole packet is read before forwarding or filtering takes place. Store and forward is a method presumed by packetC to have occurred by the underlying operating system such that packetC applications can process the packet while it has been stored and decide whether it shall be forwarded.

Subnet

In IP networks, a network segment where the IP addresses of all devices share commonality and do not require a router to communicate.

Switch

In Ethernet networks, a switch inspects the destination MAC address to determine the physical port to transmit the packet. A switch was introduced to break up physical collision domains that impeded maximum utilization of bandwidth due to allowing only a single conversation at a time on an Ethernet network in a bus or hub configuration.

Telnet

An application that emulates a text terminal interface operating between hosts using TCP/IP. The contents are un-encrypted and easily inspected and modified by network devices. Data may be spread across several packets as it emulates actual character-based input.

Terminal Server

A network device translating serial connections into a network representation, such as over telnet. Devices often have an Ethernet interface presenting a means of access to terminals or terminal-like devices attached on serial interfaces. Often used for "lights-out" management of legacy equipment removing the need for a local operator configuring systems using a terminal connected to a console port.

TFTP

Trivial File Transfer Protocol. A TCP/IP protocol for sending files across the network with fewer security features than FTP.

Throughput
The quantity of data transmitted between two devices in a given amount of time, often measured in bits per second.

Topology
The arrangement and connectivity of the nodes on a network. Typical network topologies are ring, bus, star, and tree.

Transmission Control Protocol / Internet Protocol (TCP/IP)
TCP/IP is the fundamental layer 3 and layer 4 protocol on which the Internet is based. Though often referred to as a singular item, TCP and IP are distinct and may operate assembled in different manners in complex WAN deployments.

Transmission Control Protocol (TCP)
A layer 4 protocol designed to provide guaranteed delivery of packets including retransmissions.

Uniform Resource Locator (URL)
This is the full Internet address of a web page or other object which is used in conjunction with a name server, such as DNS, to resolve to a particular host and with the web server to find the specific page.

Virtual Local Area Network (VLAN)
Ethernet networking standard 802.1Q introduces the concept of a network segmentation technique and address in the Ethernet header to allow for networks sharing common addressing to reside on the same physical network and not collide. VLAN tags are 12-bit identifiers allowing up to 4096 unique network segments in a single Ethernet network and may be stacked to allow for even larger numbers.

Wide Area Network (WAN)
The opposite of a Local Area Network, a WAN is the network that covers a large geographical area or one which interconnects multiple smaller network segments. The Internet is an example of a large public Wide Area Network.

Index

Join packetC.org

CloudShield introduced the www.packetC.org website containing updates to documentation, system libraries, and a forum for communication within the development community. This open environment and forum for collaboration helps promote the growth of applications and innovation around packetC.

It is our intention, as a group of customers, partners and CloudShield individuals to promote packetC in the marketplace as the definitive standard for writing applications that live within the data plane of our most critical networks. As an open language with a visible community of support and a pathway to standards bodies and multi-vendor oversight, we believe that packetC is leading in this arena and will continue to do so. With available open platforms supporting packetC and a well-defined network language that can operate ubiquitously across platforms within the network, open source in the data plane can now grow and flourish. Prior to packetC, developing open source for the data plane of our networks either involved complex C-based systems littered with platform specifics or embedded development environments touting microcode or other difficult to program environments. At the same time, a plethora of vendor-specific scripting environments have emerged which provided simplicity but not flexibility for full-scale high-performance capabilities. With packetC, the standardization and simplification of data plane software development can now progress forward.

If you have not already joined packetC.org please do so now. This is your venue for questions, contribution, and dialog surrounding packetC solutions. If you are developing code that may be useful by others, www.packetC.org is the launching point to highlight and share contributions with the community.

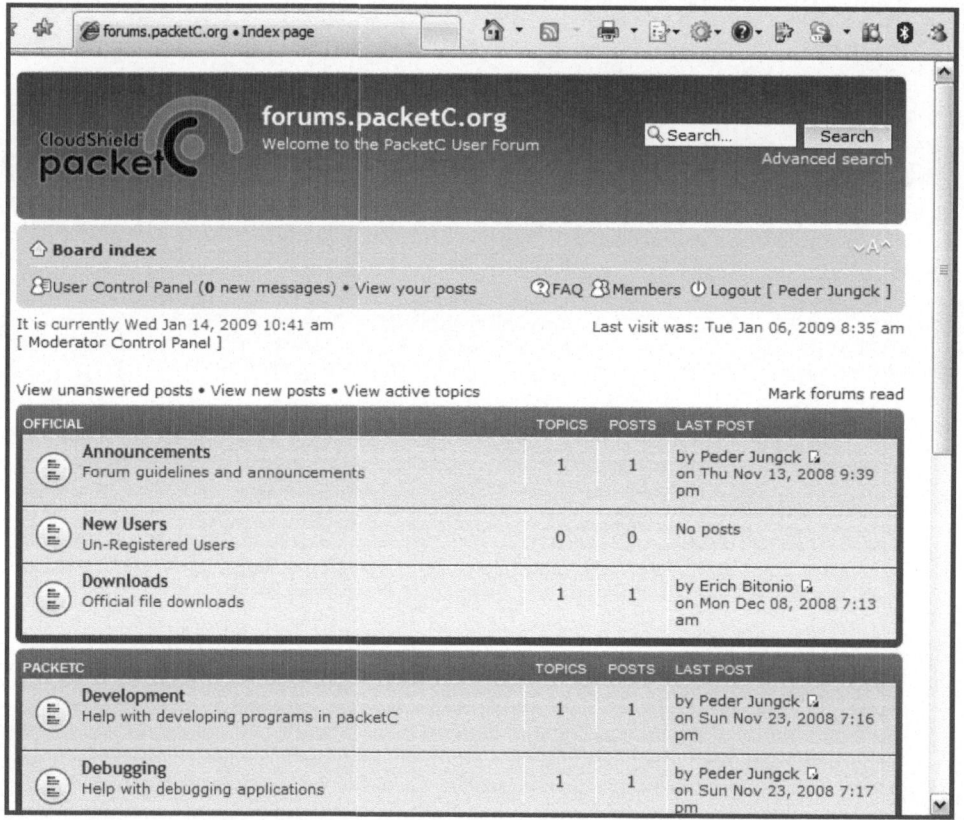

Furthermore, the most up-to-date documentation and releases of tools will be available on www.packetC.org first.